The Right Hand of Power

U. Alexis Johnson

with
Jef Olivarius McAllister

PRENTICE-HALL, Inc.
Englewood Cliffs, New Jersey 07632

To
Patricia Ann

E
840.8
$.J59$
$A37$
1984

Library of Congress Cataloging in Publication Data

Johnson, U. Alexis (Ural Alexis), (date)
The right hand of power.

Includes index.
1. Johnson, U. Alexis (Ural Alexis), (date)
2. Diplomats—United States—Biography. 3. Vietnamese
Conflict, 1961-1975—Diplomatic history.   4. Korean War,
1950-1953—Diplomatic history. I. McAllister, Jef.
II. Title.
E840.8.J59A37   1984   327.2'092.4 [B]   83-27067
ISBN 0-13-781139-X

2   3   4   5   6   7   8   9   10

Book design by Alice R. Mauro
Jacket design by Hal Siegel
Manufacturing buyer: Pat Mahoney
This book is available at a special discount
when ordered in bulk quantities. Contact Prentice-Hall, Inc.,
General Publishing Division, Special Sales,
Englewood Cliffs, N.J. 07632.
Prentice-Hall International, Inc., *London*
Prentice-Hall of Australia Pty. Limited, *Sydney*
Prentice-Hall Canada Inc., *Toronto*
Prentice-Hall of India Private Limited, *New Delhi*
Prentice-Hall of Japan, Inc., *Tokyo*
Prentice-Hall of Southeast Asia Pte. Ltd., *Singapore*
Whitehall Books Limited, *Wellington, New Zealand*
Editora Prentice-Hall do Brasil Ltda., *Rio de Janeiro*

ISBN 0-13-781139-X

·CONTENTS·

· PREFACE ·

I once wrote: "Nothing is more boring than the memoirs of worn-out diplomats."

While I was in the Foreign Service I had little patience with people who gave the impression of spending more time and effort writing long, carefully crafted memos that would read well in their "now it can be told" memoirs than in actually coming to grips with the problems at hand. So why have I ignored my own advice and succumbed to the lures of authorship?

It happens that my time in the Foreign Service spanned seven presidents and ten secretaries of state. It took me to many areas of crisis and often placed me at tables where crucial foreign-policy decisions were being made. Although I had preserved little in the way of personal papers during the long and lonely nights between coups in Saigon, it occurred to me that I would like to share with my grandchildren a little of the history and excitement I had witnessed. As I had just finished an "oral history" tape for the John F. Kennedy Library, this led me to begin talking to my grandchildren on tape.

I continued this intermittently after I left Saigon in 1965 until, by the time I retired in 1977, the tapes filled a file drawer. My son William, who is an electronics buff, consolidated them into larger reels that I agreed to deposit in the LBJ Library at Austin in exchange for the library's making available to me a copy of the transcription.

Mrs. Joan Kennedy of the library staff did a remarkable job of turning those tapes of varying quality and sometimes tortured syntax with many unfamiliar foreign names into hundreds of pages of smooth-reading transcript. With friends such as Leonard Marx urging me on, the idea of using the tapes as the basis for a book evolved. I was hooked when a friend from my Tokyo days, Leona Schecter, agreed to act as my literary agent, and she in turn introduced me to Jef McAllister, a young student of history with experience in writing and experience in Asia. Without quite realizing what he was getting into (neither did I), Jef agreed to be my collaborator, checking details and keeping a sharp eye out for inadvertent lapses into "bureaucratese." Then, when Dean Burton Sapin of the George Washington University School of International Affairs and Public Administration and Gaston Sigur, director of the Institute of Sino-Soviet Affairs at the University, arranged office quarters for me and made available Stephen Moss, a very capable graduate student of history, as a researcher, I knew that I could not back out. David Trask, the historian of the Department of State, promised whatever cooperation his office could give, as did William Price and Frank Machak of the Foreign Affairs Document and Reference Center. I am especially grateful to Jessie Williams of that center, who was patient and indefatigable in searching the files for matters in which I had been involved to check my recollections of dates, names, and places.

In addition to those who have helped Jef and me research, write, and rewrite this book, there are several people who have eased the path that we would both like to thank. Strobe Talbott originally raised the idea of our collaboration and has been generous many times before and since. Professor John Coogan reviewed several sections of the manuscript for accuracy and tightened up the prose. Nicholas Mills served capably as a research assistant in Oxford. Brian Doyle, Rags and Myree Muller, Brinley and Dorothy Lewis, and Ken, Sarah, and Lee Teslik looked after Jef during his stays in Wahington; Professor Margaret Gowing and Geraldine Cully allowed him the flexibility to work simultaneously on this book and on his thesis. His parents, Jack and Polly McAllister, and especially his wife, Ann Olivarius, offered ample encouragement and support even as the project expanded far beyond our initial expectations.

I have tried to tell my story as I experienced it, while respecting confidences that should be respected. In so doing, I have deliberately avoided footnotes and verbatim quotations from still-classified documents. I know that this may offend some of my academic friends. But this, after all, is not intended to be a definitive history. Rather, I hope that this personal narrative may eventually make its own small contribution to the conduct of our foreign affairs.

·CHAPTER ONE·

Trouble Ahead

AMERICAN FOREIGN POLICY IS IN TROUBLE. NO CATASTROPHE IS IM-
minent; we're not about to be conquered, or lose our allies or our
trade routes. But we do face problems, subtle and deep-rooted
and stubborn. The world around us is growing more complex in
ways we do not fully understand. The two-sided Soviet-American
conflict that has defined the basic equation of world politics since
1945 is being complicated by new variables—China, Western Europe and Japan—at the same time that developing countries, especially those with oil, are growing more assertive. More important, internally we are adrift. Our sense of what we want to
accomplish in international affairs has faded. The imagination and
will necessary for the United States to continue to prosper in a
rapidly changing world are not evident in its policy.

Consider the following: With 6 percent of the world's population, the United States consumes 28 percent of its energy and
25 percent of its raw materials. Yet the developing countries that
supply an increasing share of those resources are growing more
populous, relatively poorer, more frustrated, and better organized. Our "foreign aid"—a self-congratulatory misnomer for our
investment in the future of this small planet—is not keeping pace
with our capacity or with the developing countries' needs. Nor
do we have any consistent philosophy on how to work with developing countries in their efforts to move themselves into the
twentieth century.

Islamic countries control a critical portion of our oil, yet
we understand their cultures and politics poorly. The Iranian
revolution surprised us, but it is only one manifestation of a vast

movement sweeping through Islam's hundreds of millions, from Morocco to Malaysia, from Indonesia to India, that is not likely to benefit us.

Vietnam and Watergate made Americans both routinely mistrust their leaders and institutions and more suspicious of foreign commitments. The executive branch has a diminished ability to act; Congress has become so fractious that it cannot act at all. A passion for investigative journalism and freedom of information has made the media more powerful, prone to sensationalism, and answerable to no one but themselves and whets the appetite we seem to have to destroy our leaders. The speed and secrecy good diplomacy often requires, elusive enough in any democracy, are virtually impossible in present-day America.

As our interdependence with other countries increases, so does our need for quick, reliable, comprehensive intelligence. Yet we so overreacted to tales of wrongdoing in the intelligence community that, although it is making a slow recovery, it can no longer perform its vital function properly.

Because of Vietnam we have become allergic to helping those who face armed threats hostile to our interests. Unfortunately the Soviet Union has no such allergy. It continues to support subversion and open use of force—in Angola, Ethiopia, and Afghanistan—secure and correct in thinking that material, advisors and troops can be persuasive—and that we would not respond.

We are still not trained or organized to meet those indirect threats to our security that require limited use of some sort of force in response. If, for example, a Soviet-backed "liberation movement" threatened to take over Saudi Arabia, Iran, Egypt, or Indonesia, we should have no genuine option between denunciation and all-out war.

Whatever perspectives I may be able to bring to bear on these pressing problems are necessarily those of a career diplomat. Modest virtues, perhaps, but under-represented among those who have recently been setting the goals of American foreign policy. To explain what this book is all about, let me outline what I feel a professional diplomat's point of view might be able to contribute.

First, a trained diplomat should know how to operate in Washington and with foreign governments; this is vital to any progress in foreign affairs. But this skill is depressingly rare among academics and politicians—even presidents—eager to shift policies quickly and dramatically. It is one area, however, where I claim some competence. My experience has given me some background to get diverse elements within our sprawling government to agree on a common course and then to assure that it is actually followed. One compliment I especially cherish came from President Kennedy, no lover of the State Department, who is reported to have said that I was one of the few who could "get things done."

Actually there is no secret to operating effectively in Washington and foreign capitals. Like many Foreign Service Officers, I dealt with foreign governments both friendly and hostile, American congressmen and various interest groups, senior military officers, international businessmen—the whole range of actors legitimately interested in influencing American foreign policy. Soon I came to understand that, above all, foreign policy is a *process*—long, complex, usually amoral, often tedious, and cantankerous—a seamless web woven of countless incremental decisions, minor negotiations, and reactions to events beyond one's control. Keeping those who need to know informed, listening seriously to their opinions, so that no one feels ignored, preserving their confidence, never lying, always trying to expand the areas of agreement—these are the essential ingredients. They require time, patience, and respect for opposing views that often seem like bothersome impediments to achieving your objectives. Actually they increase your chances of success, because they create a better atmosphere for having tomorrow's initiative accepted. The most important thing to keep in mind in managing this process of foreign policy is that your country's interests must be promoted, not just today, but tomorrow and next year, too.

The second contribution I hope the recollections of a Foreign Service Officer can make to debates on present policy is to try to give a long view. Americans seem to have a disturbingly short memory for history. Our present stance in world affairs was largely shaped by World War II and its immediate aftermath, but to many people, anything before 1945 seems as remote as the founding of Rome. More recent developments like the Korean War, the origins of our involvement in Vietnam, and the growth of our alliance system and military base network seem no less murky. This lack of historical sense is dangerous for us as a people. Where knowledge and understanding are absent, cynicism and distortion fill in. Because the government's credibility took a battering during the Vietnam War, it has become fashionable to assume not only stupidity but nefarious motives in every diplomatic initiative since World War II. These suspicions not only lack foundation but taint public understanding of our present problems. A healthy national consensus on foreign policy depends on an intelligent popular debate based on facts, not myths and slogans. I was present at a number of the crucial places and times in the past generation of American foreign policy. I can report what I saw, what others thought, and how those responsible for setting our course in the world perceived the choices open to them. This book also gives me the chance, and the responsibility, to identify where we went wrong, why, and how things might be done differently to avoid similar errors in the future.

The third ingredient of effective diplomacy which these memoirs will illustrate is a skepticism toward magic answers and prophecies of doom. It is another way of describing the foreign policy doctrine of "realism," which simply means basing your actions on an understanding of the true strengths and weaknesses of nations, including your own. A realistic foreign policy sets its goals based on a rational assessment of what is possible, not on inflated optimism or fear of failure. Effective diplomacy requires keeping these goals in mind, staying tough but flexible, persevering, and waiting for tactical openings. If goals are realistic, disappointments come less often. I believe that realism will be crucial to the next generation of American diplomacy. As the world gets more complicated and our relative power lessens, the dangers of miscalculation and self-delusion will increase. Unfortunately, I see little evidence that we are moving in the direction of realism.

This tendency has deep roots in our history and national character. Americans, I believe, are basically isolationists at heart. In George Washington's words, we have never liked "foreign entanglements." Yet for the past forty years we have led a complex global alliance, and for the past thirty years our nuclear weapons have made deft diplomacy essential to national survival. Even so, we still have not grown comfortable with the long, messy, ambiguous process of running a foreign policy. We keep wanting the world to be simpler than it is, cleaner, more malleable and reasonable. It is from this that our problems have arisen; we seek to make policy for a world that exists only in our imagination.

In my lifetime the danger of oversimplifying international affairs has come in several forms. One of the most pernicious is a tendency to put faith in magic formulas that pretend to guarantee total security. We have not stopped yearning for the "splendid isolation" we enjoyed during the century following the War of 1812, when the Atlantic Ocean insulated us from having to contend with European powers for survival. After World War I, the "war to end all wars," was fought for the magic formula of "making the world safe for democracy," Secretary of State Frank

Kellogg persuaded fifteen countries to sign a pact "outlawing war." Thus "protected," we retreated behind our big oceans and convinced ourselves that Hitler and Japanese militarism really did not concern us. After World War II our magic formula was overwhelming nuclear superiority. As long as we could hold the Soviet Union hostage with "massive retaliation," we and our allies were safe from communist threats both great and small. Our nuclear arsenal has deterred general war with the Soviet Union, of course, but it did not stop Mao from conquering China, prevent the Korean or Vietnamese wars, or inhibit Soviet brutality in Eastern Europe and adventurism in the Near East and Africa.

In the 1960s John Kennedy pledged us to "pay any price, bear any burden, meet any hardship, support any friend, oppose any foe to assure the survival and success of liberty." Thus the new magic formula became *counterinsurgency*. We would contain communism in developing countries with Green Berets and covert action, fighting fire with fire. But our two chief targets, Vietnam and Castro's Cuba, confounded our best efforts. So then the magic formula became human rights. Preach insistently enough, went the theory, and dictators will disappear, the world will be remade in our own image and everyone will be happy. Now the test is how vigorously the leaders of a country oppose the Soviet brand of communism.

Even when the magic formulas fail, as they must, we continue to oversimplify—but in the opposite direction. We fear and resent the world when it resists our efforts to reform it, so we conclude that we have no constructive foreign role to play and withdraw into "Fortress America." We convince ourselves that all involvements abroad are doomed, either because we are inept or our enemies are so much craftier than we are.

It was such a wave of defensive xenophobia that defeated the League of Nations after World War I failed to "make the world safe for democracy." In the McCarthy period, Mao's victory in China and the anxieties of a grim, prolonged face-off with the Soviet Union convinced many Americans that every setback for the United States must be the work of a diabolic international communist conspiracy via its agents in the State Department. Now, in Vietnam's aftermath, we are going through another withdrawal phase. Liberals in Congress have limited the President's power to use our military forces abroad, tethered the CIA, and linked our foreign assistance and trade policy to an unmanageable tangle of strictures and exhortations aimed at coercing more satisfactory behavior from foreign governments. Conservatives are arguing that the Soviet Union is gaining such military superiority that even with our allies' support we are doomed to defeat unless we divert massive additional resources to defense. There are those who strike deep, resonant chords in large sections of America when they oppose the Panama Canal Treaty, SALT and other realistic accommodations to a world that never stops changing.

In sum, then, our isolationist habits of mind cause our foreign policy to oscillate erratically, between promoting idealistic magic formulas and short-sighted fear of the outside world. Neither extreme is worthy of a great power. A truly effective foreign policy demands long-term goals, persistence, and tactical agility that can absorb temporary setbacks without panic.

It is here, finally, that I feel my own experience of forty-two years can be most pertinent. On the whole American foreign policy has been successful since World War II. We have strong, friendly, prosperous allies throughout the globe, including our former enemies Germany and Japan. We have kept the nuclear genie in its bottle, we defeated Communist aggression in Korea, and we have encouraged cultural exchange, scientific cooperation, trade and economic growth to unprecedented levels. Granted, the wisdom of our leaders and the skill of our diplomacy have contributed something to these accomplishments, but I think we must credit the bulk of our success to America's sheer heft—our clear predominance in every measure of national strength, economic, military and political.

Now other countries are catching up with us, not because we have failed but because they are succeeding. As our relative supremacy fades we must adjust to that new reality and realize that future successes in foreign affairs will depend increasingly on mature and informed judgments, and this new realism about what the United States can and cannot accomplish abroad will have to pass far beyond the corridors of the State Department. It will have to be adopted by Congress, the media and the public. When the United States was preeminent, our foreign policy could absorb public opinion's abrupt swings from idealistic internationalism to defiant isolationism, but to prosper now that other countries can compete with us on more equal terms will require that professionals, as well as the entire nation, shed isolationist habits of mind and accept the world for the difficult but not impossible place that it is.

Diplomacy is not an esoteric art that only the initiated can fathom. It is really a very straightforward business—promoting the interests of your country. It does *not* require perpetual belligerency toward other nations. Certainly there is no country with which our interests completely overlap, but by the same token, there is no country with which there is not some overlap. Diplomacy is not a simplistic series of choices between good guys and bad guys, friends and enemies, but a process of finding and maximizing overlapping areas of common interest among nations, all of whom are seeking to protect their own interests.

Now more than ever before, meeting critical national needs depends on international action and cooperation. Narcotics cannot be controlled any other way. Air traffic cannot be made safe any other way. Inflation cannot be beaten any other way. The world environment cannot be protected any other way. These problems are not just made *easier* by cooperation among nations; there is literally no other way to solve them. The quality of our domestic life will depend increasingly on the quality of our foreign policy.

Still, I am not by nature a teacher or reformer. This book is a memoir, not a political science essay. My general thoughts of foreign policy flow only from the specific experiences of my career, which was oriented toward "getting things done"; and there was always lots to do. In my time I've coped with floods, faced starving mobs in China, been imprisoned by the Japanese Army, argued with presidents, authorized covert intelligence operations, negotiated nuclear arms limitation, and dealt with kings, dictators, prime ministers, and generals all over the world. My primary purpose is to convey to you a little of the sense of adventure and excitement these experiences stirred in me. But, of course, my memories are necessarily informed by my attitudes and by the conclusions I drew from my experience. So, I hope you will forgive me if, from time to time, I pause to interpret some of the events I shall relate, and even go so far as to suggest how the lessons learned might be applied to our present difficulties.

CHAPTER TWO

Early Years

FALUN, KANSAS—A TOWN LIKE A THOUSAND OTHERS SCATTERED across the Great Plains at the turn of the century. In all directions, as far as a team of horses could pull a farmer's wagon in a day, lay the flat rich earth planted with wheat. Swedes had settled the land after the Civil War, had endured its loneliness and wildness through bitter winters and parching summers, hailstorms and locusts, and had tamed it in a generation. The homesteaders were a hardy and straightforward people who relied on their own sweat, their faith in God and each other. The town existed to provide them with the simplest sort of conduit to the outside world, through a "depot" on the railway, grain elevators for selling their wheat, a school and a bank, a grocery and a hardware store, and a Lutheran church. Electricity, plumbing, paved streets, and automobiles, all had yet to come.

Into the uncomplicated life of Falun I was born at home on October 17, 1908, where the only sterilizing facilities were a tub of water boiling on the coal-fed kitchen stove. My father, Carl, a quiet, steady man, was the cashier and only employee of the Falun State Bank, and thus held a central place in the community—settling disputes, writing wills, financing farmers between harvests and selling them hail insurance to give them some security. My mother, Ellen, was a woman with talent and ambition unusual for her circumstances. It was she, characteristically, who decided to name me, her first child, "Ural Alexis." Not wishing to be the mother of yet another Carl Johnson in a Swedish farm town, she had looked through geography books for an alternative and had liked the sound of the Ural Mountains, which were supposed to represent strength and vigor. Alexis was a family name. The combination was certainly unique and, many years later would intrigue a number of Soviet diplomats.

My father spent a good portion of his time in a horse and buggy, of which he was very proud, visiting farmers to see how they were faring and trying to interest them in new agricultural techniques. Though well-regarded in the community, we were of modest means. By modern standards our house was primitive. A cistern caught rainwater that we used for our weekly baths; our privy was in the backyard next to the stable. The well water on the property was so bad that it became one of my regular chores to carry several buckets a day from my Uncle Gus's house across the railroad track.

As a girl, my mother, daughter of a Swedish immigrant who became county sheriff, was determined to get a higher education. She taught herself the piano and worked her way to Bethany College of Music in Lindsborg, about ten miles south of Falun. It was a surprisingly good, small music school that had an Easter musical festival where some of the world's greatest artists performed.

To make sure I, too, would receive a good education, she insisted on teaching me at home for the first two grades. When at last she relented and sent me to the two-room school in Falun, she took pains to see that I was always well dressed in short pants and a shirt, a mildly embarrassing requirement since my two classmates were farm boys in conventional overalls.

My father also placed considerable emphasis on education. He brought Chautauqua speakers and performers to town and we often put them up. He also worked hard to establish a union school in Falun that would consolidate all the tiny grammar schools spread throughout the countryside into a bigger, better one, and to start a high school in Falun as well.

Being a child of parents whose vision encompassed wider horizons than Falun must have had its effect on me, if only to make me feel slightly detached from my surroundings. I have heard other Foreign Service Officers of my generation report similar childhood feelings—perhaps not the worst preparation for a life of reporting events in foreign cultures. But if I was a bit irregular by Falun standards, I was not very aware of it then. The same as other little boys, I liked to wander the countryside with my dog, fish the creek near our house, and wait for the glamorous three-car evening passenger train that went all the way to Pueblo, Colorado.

When I was about eight my father brought me in to help him at the bank, paying me a sum so nominal that I cannot now recall what it was. He had one of the first Burroughs manual adding machines to keep track of accounts, and for several years I had to stand on a stool to reach it. Gangs of robbers still occasionally attacked isolated rural banks in those days, and in the absence of any police closer than Salina, twenty miles away, our anti-theft system consisted of a handbell and a shotgun under the desk. To get out of town any robber would have to pass by the hardware and grocery stores, and the plan was that if my father rang the bell the storekeepers would come running with their shotguns for an ambush. I learned to shoot as a boy, not only to accompany my father hunting, but to prepare me for an active role in this procedure. Fortunately we were never called upon to implement it.

As far as I was concerned, Falun's life had two high points. The first was Saturday night, when everyone in the area who could make it came to town to shop and socialize. The women would sell their carefully accumulated eggs for vital "egg money," the men would exchange news and gossip, and the young teenage bucks would look around for opportunities to blow off steam and buy bootlegged cigarettes. Their search was usually in vain, since Kansas then prohibited both alcoholic beverages and cigarettes.

The other excitement came once a year, at Easter. At the Bethany College of Music where my mother had gone to school, 500 amateurs would assemble to sing Handel's "Messiah." Competition for places in the chorus was intense and inspired diligent practice throughout the year. My parents, who both had fine voices and could sing the "Messiah" from memory, always took part. One of the most moving experiences of my childhood was to hear this group, not only because they fervently loved the music, but because they were so obviously animated by a deeply felt religious faith.

During my childhood the vast changes that the twentieth century was bringing to America first began to filter into our isolated rural outpost. Starting almost imperceptibly, the pace of new technological developments accelerated until the momentum became irresistible. My Uncle Gus bought the first automobile, a Rambler, with a rear seat that could only be reached by climbing a set of stairs at the back. Driving the twenty miles of dirt road to Salina was an adventure that took the whole day for a round trip and always produced two or three flat tires.

My father bought the next car, a Chevrolet Baby Grand that I began to drive at age ten. I remember distinctly when my father took his mother, 70-year-old Grandmother Johnson, who lived in Salina, for her first ride in an automobile. After she got out she sternly informed us that she took a very dim view of rushing along at twenty miles per hour and couldn't see why anyone would want to go faster than a good horse could pull a buggy.

My father and Uncle Gus were also instrumental in bringing electricity to town. It took years of organizing and lobbying among the conservative farmers, but the day the first houses got power and a small street light was turned on was a great occasion of civic pride and celebration.

After the First World War, Dad was also the first in Falun to buy a radio, a great complicated monster that worked on batteries and was full of incomprehensible dials. He installed it in the bank to get market quotations, which could just barely be heard through the earphones from a station in Kansas City. At that point very few doubted that all these new gadgets were an unalloyed good, a way of easing toil, facilitating travel and expanding the horizons of our existence beyond the confines of a backwater farm town. More recently, as the disruptions new technology can cause have become more evident, many people have been reverting to Grandmother Johnson's point of view.

Some other major developments that were rippling through the country also managed to find their way to Falun. The First World War produced big political rifts. Since Falun was predominantly Swedish there was strong sympathy for Germany, particularly among the older people, and long, heated arguments raged in the town. My father supported America's entry into the war and, as the banker, sold war bonds; thus he became a focus of much controversy.

Much more traumatic for me was the national influenza epidemic of the winter of 1918–19. First my father got sick, then Mother, then my four-year-old sister R'Ella (also invented by mother as a short form of "our Ellen"), and finally me. We all developed high fevers alternating with chills, nausea, and cramps. Sick as my mother was, she would drag herself downstairs to the furnace several times a day to shake out the ashes and shovel in some coal to keep the edge off the bitter cold outside. She did not have enough energy to cook, and even if she had, none of us would have eaten. The privy was a long walk through the snow and we resorted to chamber pots. The doctor from Salina would come by at two or three o'clock in the morning, utterly exhausted, naming the friends who had died that day and those who were likely to die the next. There was really no treatment for the illness or the pneumonia that often followed. People were panicked and refused even to enter the house of a sick person. For me the worst time was when my father got so sick he became delirious and could not speak coherently, which to an 11-year-old was terrifying. Fortunately our family all survived, but we were exhausted and our health broken. My mother, who was bored with Falun anyway, convinced Dad to vacation in California to recuperate, a trip for which he somehow managed to scrape up the money. We returned after a few months, but Mother, not content at the prospect of settling permanently into small-town life, finally prevailed upon Dad to move to California for good. In the spring of 1923 Dad managed to sell the house and bank and we traded the slow, comfortable rhythms of the prairie for boomtown Los Angeles.

Not many Americans grow up in isolated farmtowns anymore, and to make comprehensible the kind of outlook I took away from a childhood in Kansas takes some doing in this citified age. Automobiles, radio, television and electric power have destroyed the isolation of the countryside. Nowadays the farm life of that earlier day tends to be idealized; people who work in office buildings imagine it as a slow-paced paradise, forgetting the long hours, the nagging ever-present fear of weather and pests, and the loneliness. For me, however, Falun did provide the kind of solid background that small towns were then supposed to.

I grew up possessing the sense of security that permits self-reliance. That security was derived partly from the love of my parents, and partly from a more general conviction that those who worked hard would always be rewarded. Though there might be bad harvests and flu epidemics, most people in Falun believed that those who were diligent seldom went hungry. Our austere life provided a framework of personal morality that was unsophisticated but resilient; and perhaps because nothing we did could get lost in the impersonality of a big city we grew up learning to rely on our neighbors in adversity and to help them when we could.

California

When we arrived in Los Angeles I started tenth grade at Manual Arts High School in the south of the city. I found the school overwhelming; it was a shock having to adjust from two classmates to two thousand, and I was very green in the rough ways of a big city. By the time that school year finished we had moved to Glendale, a middle-class suburb close to Hollywood where my father had become the assistant cashier of a new bank.

In the fall of 1924, when I switched to Glendale High, the strain of moving to Los Angeles finally caught up with me. I became so ill that I had to stay out of school for almost a year. I am inclined to think, now, that a large part of my sickness must have been psychosomatic, sparked by the wrench of leaving familiar surroundings in Falun. In any event, I made a complete recovery and, in the fall of 1925, reentered the brand-new Glendale Union High School for eleventh grade filled with enthusiasm.

The whole family switched to a different and much faster lifestyle in Glendale. My mother recommenced teaching the piano and became so popular that her lessons began at seven in the morning and continued until late in the evening. My father changed from his bank in Hollywood after a few years to a small independent bank in Glendale, where he was cashier. I took on a paper route, helped my father at the bank after school, ushered at the Los Angeles Philharmonic in the evenings and studied late into the night. While we continued to be a close and loving family, we were also now all involved in our separate activities—a definite consequence of moving to the city.

Glendale was a good school and I especially liked the courses in history, public speaking, composition and journalism. I was accepted by my classmates and became active in extracurricular activities. Luckily I was able to get by on little sleep, for in addition to my after-school jobs I debated, worked on the yearbook, edited the school paper, and in my senior year ran for president of the student body. I lost, but not by too much. The winner was popular, handsome, and adept at the political art of promoting himself very hard while giving an impression of utter nonchalance, which, I suppose, only goes to show that I never would have made much of a politician.

It had always been my parents' determination to send me to college, and my father had managed to put enough money away after moving to Glendale to send me to a private school. I applied and was accepted to Occidental College, a small, first-rate liberal arts school located in Los Angeles about ten miles from Glendale.

Since my father was a banker, I had spent a lot of time around businessmen, and in the boom years of the 1920s, when President Coolidge declared that "the business of America is business," their stock was high. I entered Occidental to major in economics and then proceed to accounting and law school.

Perhaps it's just as well that the Depression knocked the wind out of my ambitions for a life in big business, because the summer before I entered college I certainly demonstrated no particular flair for selling. Somehow or other I got roped into a scheme for hawking subscriptions door-to-door for a woman's magazine, the *Pictorial Review*, in San Diego. There was a team of us, living in the YMCA, and each day we would rise early in the morning, plot our routes, and hit the pavement, going all over the city extolling the virtues of this magazine to housewives. The inducement, in addition to a small commission, was that the most successful workers would win a scholarship of several hundred dollars to help with college.

I'm afraid I barely covered my expenses. I usually got along all right with my potential customers, but I just didn't seem able to close the sale. One of my colleagues was decidedly more productive. He went down to the huge naval base in San Diego and, with some vague but swift talking, gave the sailors the impression that the magazine was a kind of *Police Gazette*, the *Playboy* of that era. He signed them up in droves and received a scholarship. Happily he was out of town by the time the sailors received their first issue. He eventually enlisted his formidable persuasive talents in a higher cause, and became a missionary in the Philippines.

In September 1927 I started school at Occidental. The first class of the day, at 8 A.M., was French—dreaded, awful French. I always did my homework and was very earnest about trying to grasp the language, but I just could never get the hang of it. If my advancement in the Foreign Service had depended solely on my linguistic abilities, I am sure I would still be studying French.

After the stock market crash in 1929 our economics professors labored mightily to make sense of the Great Depression, but not surprisingly the field was in flux and their theories often contradicted each other. Economics has undergone a considerable change since my college days, becoming much more quantitative and computerized, but its verities remain the same. I have found that what I learned at Occidental has stood me in very good stead for a Foreign Service career. There are a lot of hard factual matters important in international affairs—foreign trade, banking laws, tariffs, international exchange and arbitrage—that one cannot easily pick up on the job but must learn through study.

My one extracurricular activity was debating. Henry Shimanouchi, my partner, was a Japanese citizen raised in Los Angeles whose father owned the city's largest Japanese language newspaper. We made a good team. Henry was an efficient researcher while I was pretty good at extemporizing, and we went to tournaments all over Southern California. In those days debating stressed adroitness on one's feet rather than the current vogue of having a box of file cards abounding in arcane references. We discussed many subjects, including capital punishment, independence for the Philippines, and the practice of intervening in Central American politics to protect Americans' investments there. It strikes me that most of them would be equally topical today.

The Depression altered my life, like so many others', abruptly. Dad's bank began to falter as people withdrew their savings and began to default on loan repayments. By 1931 the bank went broke and was bought out, taking with it Dad's investment and most of the savings he had built up over a lifetime. He finally got a job in the Los Angeles County Welfare Department assessing property values and investigating welfare candidates. He was extremely grateful for the job and was never the type to complain about anything, but the comedown obviously left him with a feeling of failure and inadequacy that was only too common. Mother continued to teach piano but her earnings were insufficient to support the family. Having no way to pay for school, I had to scrap my plans to study accounting and law.

Washington, D.C.

Then a professor of labor relations at Oxy suggested that I might like the Foreign Service. I had never considered a foreign career before because the possibility was so remote. During my senior year, however, I wrote to Washington for information on the Foreign Service and its entrance exam. And several months after graduation, in September 1931, I trekked to Washington in my trusty Model A, bound for the Foreign Service School at Georgetown University to take courses that would broaden my education and improve my chances of passing the Foreign Service exam.

At Georgetown I took diplomatic history and international law at the Foreign Service School and commercial and maritime law at the Law School. It was the first time I had "been East" and I worried a bit about how I would stack up against my classmates from Harvard and Yale and other famous Eastern schools, especially because I would have to work a fair amount during the school year to make ends meet.

Financially I squeezed by. I was a proficient typist, and at Georgetown I had a steady stream of papers to run through my battered Royal portable. One job turned out to be lucrative. The First Secretary of the Turkish Embassy was writing his doctoral thesis on Turkish finance, and I not only typed it but composed a chunk of it as well from the collection of pamphlets he had assembled. He was a fairly young man who maintained an opulent set of rooms at the Hay-Adams, an expensive hotel just across from the White House, where he kept a stunning mistress who was usually still in bed when I arrived for work. For my labors he earned his Ph.D. and I earned the truly fantastic sum of $200. Academically the year turned out productively as well. I was really pleased to discover that my basic grounding from Occidental had been sound.

The class that had the biggest effect on my thinking was a small seminar on nationality law taught by James Brown Scott, a courtly, vigorous, old man who for many years had been the State Department's chief lawyer. Nationality law, the set of regulations that determines one's citizenship, is a complex maze in which few lawyers or judges have much competence. During the first half of my career in the Foreign Service I had to make frequent decisions on nationality cases, and I found that Scott had taught it so well that my notes from his class were an infallible guide. Scott was the one who induced me to change my name; he thought that "U. Alexis" would ring more impressively in the halls of the State Department than the odd-sounding "Ural A." I have never regretted taking his advice.

The most significant event of this year in Washington was neither study nor work, however, but meeting Patricia Ann Tillman, the woman who became my wife. My landlady asked me one evening in October 1931, not long after my arrival, to drive to Union Station to pick up a girl returning from California. None too enthusiastically I agreed. During the ride back to the boarding house Pat and I somehow hit it off. We continued to see each other at meals and began spending more and more time together, talking about ourselves and the future. Like everyone else she was working around town at anything she could find to make ends meet; perhaps our biggest common trait was relative poverty. Pat's mother had died when she was young, and she had grown up mostly in California under the care of her grandmother, a remarkable woman in her nineties. Her father, Colonel Frederick Tillman, worked in the War Department, had remarried, and lived in Hyattsville on the outskirts of Washington. Having no money for movies or restaurants, we spent what time we could together in the Model A driving around Haines Point, then deserted, and in the parlor of the boarding house.

We decided to marry in the spring of 1932, but there was a serious obstacle. Because depression budget cuts had caused the State Department to pare drastically the number of openings in the Foreign Service, I had only a small hope of getting an appointment as a Foreign Service Officer. Until the Department got on its financial feet again I thought I should aim for an interim lower-ranking job as a Foreign Service Clerk, but clerks' appointments were closed to married men at that time.

We resolved this problem on March 21, 1932—the first day of spring, and the wedding anniversary of my parents—by secretly marrying in Baltimore. We did not even tell our parents or closest friends, though some of them began to guess as time progressed. In June 1932, I stopped school and began to look for work so I could support myself and the new wife with whom I could not yet live.

In 1932, Washington, like the rest of the country, was desperate. Former tycoons were selling apples on streetcorners. But Pat and I were luckier than many, even though our first few years together were mostly an unrelenting struggle to keep eating. My freshly minted college diploma meant nothing. Only because I was a fast typist could I get work. I got to the head of the male typist list at several temporary employment agencies, and so I got a series of one- and two-week jobs addressing envelopes. Pat, who had to move in with her father and stepmother in Hyattsville to save money, worked in the accounting section of a department store and at a nursing home. I moved out of my boarding house to one where I got free room and board in exchange for stoking the furnace and doing maintenance.

Though our financial worries were constant, I was more depressed by how persistently my career goal, the Foreign Service, seemed to be eluding me. First came the hurdle of the exam. The three-day written portion was given all over the country in September 1932, with a combination of essay and factual questions on geography, history, law, economics, general knowledge, and English expression. The final half-day was devoted to a modern language, in my case, French. I was amazed to discover a few months later that I had passed, with a weighted percentage score of 78, and was wanted for a follow-up interview. I had done very poorly on French (32!) but well in economics (84) and general knowledge (86), which were weighted heavily.

I went to the old State-War-Navy Building next to the White House on the appointed day, not optimistic about the outcome. I sat outside the interview room in a cavernous corridor and made some desultory effort at small talk with a few other equally nervous candidates. After several hours I was called in and ushered to a chair at the open end of a U-shaped table, facing three examiners. Two were assistant secretaries of state and the third, and chairman, was the venerable Joseph Green. They started with a few straightforward questions about my background and education, and then Joe Green, after a long and convoluted lead-in, asked me to explain why gold prices had dropped in Europe at the start of World War I when their normal reaction to political crises is to rise as people hoard the stuff. I swallowed hard and thought harder, but could offer no plausible explanation for this anomaly and said that with all due respect the facts he stated did not seem logical to me. Another interviewer tried restating the question from another angle, and when I said I couldn't answer that one either the third panelist tried another tack. We spent the whole time going round and round on 1914 gold prices in Europe. By the end of the interview I hadn't answered a single question except my name and education, for the simple but unsatisfying reason that I didn't know the answers. I was devastated by my failure, but I felt I had given it my best try. Then came the oral exam in French, which was predictably painful. The examiner seemed impressed with my effort if not my pronunciation, however, and out of pity bequeathed the minimum passing grade of 65. Then I returned to the waiting area, unhappy that I had blown my chance for the Foreign Service after coming so far, and pondered what new career I should seek.

I could not have been more surprised and elated when I was told to proceed to the Navy Department for a physical, which, according to other examinees, meant I had passed. I guess the panel must have been testing how I would react to stress rather than what I knew. I have never since been tempted to fake a reply to a question I could not really answer.

I was now, out of 7000 applicants, one of 15 potential new members of the Foreign Service of the United States. Unfortunately, budget constraints still prevented the Department from actually appointing me to a job, so I had nothing tangible to show for my success and no indication of when I might start work. As the freeze on new Foreign Service appointments continued over the next several years, I began to fear that once the Department did get money to hire new officers it would bypass the 1932 entrants to choose younger candidates who had passed the exam in subsequent years. I could only wait and see.

My problems were merely a microcosm of the breakdown of a whole system that was daily evident in Washington. I was addressing envelopes at the Ford Motor Company offices on Pennsylvania Avenue near the Capitol when the Bonus Army marched on Washington in 1932. The marchers, World War I veterans from all over the country, some accompanied by wives and children, wanted the government to help them survive the Depression by paying a promised bonus several years in advance. President Hoover worried that their demonstrations could get out of hand and that they might try to take over the city, though most of the demonstrators had no such intentions. Hoover ordered General MacArthur, then Army Chief of Staff, to disperse the demonstrators, and he did so with overwhelming force. Tear gas fired on the marchers wafted into the Ford building and forced us to evacuate, so I could not see what happened afterwards. But at the end of the day there were over 100 casualties. Thus politics became an important concern for the first time in my life; I could not escape it. Living in the District of Columbia prevented me from voting in the 1932 Presidential elections, but I was rooting for Roosevelt and was happy to see him elected. His inaugural address electrified the city and the country and gave us real hope—the first in a long time—that things could be changed for the better.

In March 1933, just as Roosevelt was inaugurated, one of my temporary jobs became permanent. Call Carl, a city-wide chain of 24-hour garages, needed an assistant office manager for the night shift at its headquarters, so they promoted me from occasional typist and gave me the magnificent salary of $60 a month. Later that year I even received a $10 raise because the National Recovery Administration, one of Roosevelt's first creations, had established minimum wages for various classes of jobs and, according to the NRA classification, my job was managerial and deserved a $70 salary. At the same time Pat got a good job as a keypunch operator at the Census Bureau. On the strength of this "New Deal" for the two of us, and because getting a Foreign Service Clerk's appointment no longer interested me, we decided to splurge on a church wedding, which we did on May 6, 1933, at the Foundry Methodist Church. It's no exaggeration to say that

Roosevelt made our marriage. We found a $25-a-month furnished apartment, and set ourselves up as a family. My parents had not met Pat and could not afford to travel East for the wedding, but they were very happy for us.

Even now that we were living together as a regular couple, normal life was elusive. Pat's job was during the day, and mine went from 10 P.M. to 8 A.M. except on stormy days when it was round the clock, so at best we had only two or three hours together daily. Then Pat discovered she was going to have a baby, so we knew we would have to save some money for the time that she could no longer work.

To save rent we moved to a cheaper apartment. I had to sell Genevive, my beloved Model A, for $25. Pat and I started trading our $1 a week streetcar pass to each other so we wouldn't have to buy two. As it turned out, our first child, Judith Ann, was born on January 29, 1934, in the middle of a raging blizzard, which naturally swamped Call Carl with frozen and stalled cars. Hustling between the office, hospital, and home stretched my endurance, but our delight and amazement at the healthy arrival of this new family member kept me going.

I kept working at Call Carl on the day shift all through 1934, with no news from the State Department. I was beginning to doubt I would ever work in the Foreign Service. All I could do was to keep abreast of international news through the newspapers. In July Call Carl raised me to $125 a month, and I started discussing with accounting firms whether they would hire me for daytime work while I went to accounting school at night.

I had just about given up on the Foreign Service and figured the only way I could stop marking time would be to shift seriously into a business career. Then, on September 17, 1935, we read in the evening paper that the State Department was about to make some appointments, and the next day Harold Jones, an Occidental classmate who was living in Washington, called me at work to report that he had seen my name on the list of new Foreign Service Officers in *The New York Times*. I called the State Department to confirm and then, elated, called Pat, who was then working in the accounting department of the Agricultural Adjustment Administration. We both took the rest of the day off to celebrate and went to dinner and a show downtown. On my princely new Foreign Service salary of $2500 a year I knew we could afford it. After so many years of waiting, it was time to start our life's work.

In early October I was summoned to the office of Dr. Stanley Hornbeck, the redoubtable Director of the Office of Far Eastern Affairs. He told me that the Department needed Japanese and Chinese language specialists. There was a special dearth of Japanese experts in the Foreign Service, he said, and with Japan fast becoming a first-class world power, the greatest chances for advancement would probably fall to those willing to undertake a course of specialization; two years in Tokyo exclusively for language study, then three more working in the Embassy to master the language, with an expectation of spending another five to seven years in Japan and its territories after that. Incentive was provided by way of an automatic promotion from the rank of "unclassified C" to "unclassified B," with a $250 raise, if one passed the exam at the end of the first year, and to "unclassified A" at the end of the second year.

I expressed some honest doubts to Hornbeck about whether, in view of the difficulties I had had with French, I could master Japanese. He told me to go across the hall to see Bill Turner, a Foreign Service Officer who had already gone through the course. Bill asked me to say "sayonara." I said "sayonara." He asked me to say "konnichiwa," and I said "konnichiwa." He immediately assured me on the basis of this exhaustive test that I was a natural. On this authority Dr. Hornbeck welcomed me into his employ as a Japanese language officer. My career in the Foreign Service began.

·CHAPTER THREE·

Apprenticeship

Japan

ON WEDNESDAY, OCTOBER 12, 1935, I WENT TO THE STATE Department to be sworn in. After some last-minute packing of our few possessions, and farewells, we boarded a train two days later for Los Angeles. As the first paycheck of my supposedly munificent salary had not yet arrived, I had to borrow money to buy some decent suits. Then, after a few very pleasant days with my parents we boarded the *S.S. President Coolidge* at San Pedro.

It was our first sea voyage and our first real taste of luxury. The deck games, bountiful meals, swimming, dancing, and generally pampered life seemed like a dream. On board were five Foreign Service colleagues, some going to study Japanese and others going to study Chinese in Peking. At Honolulu the American Consul at Yokohama, and his wife, boarded the ship to start briefing us on the mysterious East. He also hosted a cocktail party, thus introducing us to that venerable diplomatic institution. I wrote my parents, who were strict teetotalers: "In the future don't get excited when I mention cocktail parties, for they are inescapable. But it doesn't mean that one must drink—many don't. For example, last night I had tomato juice." Though Pat stuck with tomato juice through years of countless cocktail parties, I must confess that my standards have been less strict.

Conversations with fellow passengers gave me a sense of the complexities of the contemporary Asian scene. One informant was a General Cohen, a Russian Jew by birth and soldier of fortune by profession, with the rank of General in one of China's many armies. A powerfully built, swarthy man, vociferous in many languages, he passed most of his time wagering huge sums of money at poker and bridge. After our three-year-old Judith overcame her initial shyness at his hearty approach the two became fast friends. (They remembered each other seven years later when Cohen passed through Rio de Janiero on an evacuation ship from China.)

In the early dawn of November 15 we caught our first glimpse of Mount Fuji rising above the mists. Soon we were in Yokohama Bay, crowded with square-rigged Japanese fishing boats, "one lung" coastal freighters, and larger vessels heading in and out of the busy port. After the normal confusion of customs and immigration we set foot in the country and, guided by an Embassy officer who had met us, took taxis for the twenty-mile ride to Tokyo, a little shaken at driving on the left for the first time. There were few cars except taxis, but the streets overflowed with every other sort of vehicle imaginable: horse carts, rickshaws, three-wheeled motorcycles laden with truck-sized cargos, and a fantastic profusion of bicycles weaving through the confusion. Some bicyclists steered with one hand while balancing in the other a take-out meal stacked ten dishes high. It was *schichi-go-san,* the festival when the three-, five-, and seven-year-old children pay their respects at the local shrine; thousands, looking like dolls in their traditional costumes, were streaming along our route. We ended our taxi ride at the magnificent Imperial Hotel, Frank Lloyd Wright's masterpiece in downtown Tokyo that had survived the 1923 earthquake. That night an embassy officer gave us a tour of downtown Tokyo, which even then had a robust nightlife, both traditional and imported Western.

Our first order of business, however, was to find accommodations, since the Imperial was expensive and language study was to begin within a week. But finding more permanent quarters was not easy. While American colleagues tried to be helpful they could not spend much time spoon-feeding us neophytes, and the Embassy had nothing that remotely resembled present-day administrative sections, charged with the care, feeding, housing and handholding of all American personnel.

Administrative sections, however, have their drawbacks. There is nothing like doing for yourself to teach, quickly, what a foreign country is all about. Tokyo possessed very few Western-style houses, and we were not really prepared to do without central heating or flush toilets, especially with a small child. So chasing down rumors, tips and ads in the English-language newspaper, we went back and forth across Tokyo, struggling with taxi drivers over addresses and fares. All taxi fares were a matter of bargaining, and among us language students a spirited competition sprang up to see who could negotiate the lowest fare.

To assist us our principal tutor gave us a sheet of Japanese "first-aid sentences" written in roman letters—questions like "where is a green grocer?" which usually would inspire a flood of utterly unintelligible Japanese. We slowly discovered that whereas most Japanese had no comprehension whatever of spoken English, large numbers had some reading and writing knowledge. Ultimately I carried a pad and pencil, as if I were deaf, for questions and answers. In later years I often recommended this system to traveling Americans, who seem to have unfailing faith that if only they speak English loudly and forcefully enough the other party will have to understand.

Even had I been a native speaker, however, I'm sure that Tokyo's city plan would have frustrated me, even as it frustrates many out-of-town Japanese. To begin with, there are no street signs, for the simple reason that streets have no names. Except for a small central core, Tokyo is an agglomeration of hamlets that grew into villages, that, in turn, grew into towns that eventually combined to form the modern city. All this is reflected in present-day Tokyo's organization, which comprises some dozen large districts, which are divided into *machi* (towns), which in turn are divided into *chome* (hamlets). These *chome* are themselves often split into numbered subsections, and within them each building has a number corresponding not to location, but to the order in which it was built. Thus No. 15 could be blocks from No. 16. The only way to proceed to a new address is to home in on the ward, then on the machi, then on the chome, then on the chome number and at that point stop at the local police box—a small structure with a telephone accommodating two or three police—to get directions.

Fortuitously we stumbled on a European tenant who was leaving a small Western-style house with all its furnishings. With a loan from my future brother-in-law, Gerald Warner, also a language student, Pat and I rented the house, bought his furnishings and moved in promptly. We had two neighbors, a Brazilian family and an American husband and wife journalist team, all living in a compound built by a Japanese at the end of his garden.

Our little compound was a western island, but the surrounding sea was entirely Japanese. We were quickly caught up in its currents. With the aid of our foreign neighbors, our landlady, and our Chinese cook who spoke some English, we paid dues and were initiated into the local neighborhood association. The association maintained a fire brigade and employed a night watchman who made his rounds clacking two wooden sticks together and calling out his presence—a very comforting sound during the night. During the day our lane was filled with other sounds: the distinctive cries of the tofu (bean curd) and soba (noodle) vendors; the bells of the goldfish seller; the flute of the blind masseur; the gentle tinkling of bicycle bells. Only rarely did an automobile penetrate to disturb the active street life. At bedtime we could hear the *amado*, or outside wooden shutters, clattering shut; in the early morning we could hear them being slid open again. When an earth tremor broke the stillness of the night, we could hear it coming across town as a wave of shaking amado.

The police box, placed where our lane joined a larger street, politely kept track of everything, occasionally calling to ask how things were going, checking on strangers, escorting drunks safely home. Keeping secrets from one's neighbors or the police was virtually impossible. Now the increasingly totalitarian government was using this ancient community system to control the population.

Our little house not only came complete with furniture but also a superb Chinese cook named Chin, who, on a salary of $15 a month, introduced us to the higher realms of Oriental cuisine, generally prepared on a charcoal brazier in the backyard. I will always remember the evening we were entertaining a few guests when Chin served a very large lobster whose eyes had been replaced by brightly shining electric flashlight bulbs. Our first cocktail party was a staggering success. Knowing nothing about mixing drinks myself, I relied entirely on Chin's professions of expertise. In the event, he substituted gin for water in all the whiskey drinks, with spectacular results.

Our second child, Stephen, was born in December 1936. Fortunately, by then we were able to afford an amah to help care for him.

My job in Tokyo was to learn enough Japanese in two years to make myself useful, if not fluent, in the language. Our chief tutor, Naoe Naganuma, was one of Japan's first students of linguistics. He had written an eight-volume set of Japanese readers *(tokuhon)* designed to lead military and state department beginners to the highest forms of classical Japanese then still used, for example, in formal notes from the Foreign Ministry. He had several subordinates, and, in keeping with the "immersion method" that banned English language and roman letters from the first day, few of them could speak English.

Six FSO's and four military officers—including a young captain named Max Taylor, whose name will recur in this narrative—were studying Japanese. Instructors would teach us individually at our homes, one hour in the morning and another in the afternoon. In between we worked at memorizing the 2,500 Chinese characters and two separate syllabaries, each with 75 symbols, that were considered basic Japanese at that time. Our natural confusion was intensified both because the spoken Japanese bore little relation to the several written languages and because the spoken language differed vastly depending on the relative status of the speakers and whether they were men or women, children, military or civilian, and so on ad infinitum.

On the positive side, we discovered that Japanese (unlike Chinese) contains no sounds that an English speaker cannot readily pronounce. The grammar is very simple and pronouns are rare, but this very simplicity can make comprehension more difficult, since so much of the meaning must be derived from context and from the particular verb or noun form employed. It is a rare foreigner indeed who really "masters" Japanese, and I do not number myself among them. I should add, however, that today's Japanese has been considerably modified and is simpler than what we studied, and nowadays Japanese are very tolerant of foreigners who sin against the strictest standards of the language. In short, acquiring working knowledge of Japanese today is not as difficult as it was and is very rewarding.

In addition to language study, we read (in English) Japanese history, culture, law, government, geography, and, in general what is now called "area study" in preparation for an exam. None of this left much time for exercise or other activities, and the combination of this unaccustomed sedentary life and Chin's culinary skills led me to gain forty pounds in six months. I was so shocked by this, as well as by the cost of alterations to my clothes, that I succeeded in arresting further growth.

Our contact with the official life of the Embassy was minimal and generally confined to picking up our mail and paychecks. Periodically we were questioned on our progress by William Turner, the Second Secretary, assigned to watch over us. We would sometimes be invited to some big reception at the Embassy residence, but since we language students lived scattered around the city and normally did not see much of each other, on these occasions we tended to drift into corners to compare notes. Whenever we did, however, one of us would feel a stiff poke in the back from Mrs. Crocker, wife of Edward Crocker, Second Secretary and protocol officer, who would fiercely whisper " circulate, circulate!" Alas, the conversations of the other guests always seemed mundane compared with our own engrossing concern with the language, and soon we would be looking for another corner.

In those days before air-conditioning, official life in the capital came to a halt during the stifling summer, and everybody who could went to the cooler mountain resorts. Our Embassy staff went mostly to Karuizawa, about five hours by train northwest of Tokyo. About three hours beyond Karuizawa, near the coast of the Japan Sea, was the largely missionary resort of Lake Nojiri. Because it was less expensive and less "social" than Karuizawa, we and the Yunis rented houses at Nojiri for the summer. Getting to our houses required a hike of somewhat more than three miles from the nearest station, Kashiwabara, and hiring spindly-legged porters who, using "A-frames" on their backs, managed trunks, furniture and other large items with seemingly the greatest ease. We lived pretty much in the Japanese style, with no plumbing except that furnished by the nightsoil collector and a Japanese-style bath of which we all became real addicts.

In that bucolic setting I had no difficulty rising at dawn, studying until about three in the afternoon and then devoting the rest of the day to learning to sail, playing tennis, swimming, and hiking in the nearby mountains. Our wives became absorbed in the treasures of a little silk shop in Kashiwabara and I occasionally went there to cash a check at the little local bank. This was no crass "quick in quick out" commercial transaction. First I sat on the matted floor in the manager's office to have a cup of tea with him, and we would discuss the weather and the crops. Eventually I would broach the vulgar subject of cashing a check. At this he would call his assistant who, bowing deeply, would receive his instructions and return with the money on a tray that he would ceremoniously deposit in front of me. After another cup of tea and exchanges of mutual respect I would pick up the money and depart, satisfied to have stumbled through the conversation in a highly unorthodox mixture of Japanese and English.

I also learned the etiquette (or lack of it) of Japanese trains. Like most people, but perhaps to a higher degree, Japanese have two behavioral patterns—one for private and family circles and another in public. In the queues at stations or elsewhere it was every man for himself, elbows freely employed, and no special treatment for foreigners. But all Japanese have a soft spot for small children, and our very blond, blue-eyed little Judith in her starched dress proved to be a passport to any seat in the car.

We also discovered that hot weather customarily inspired Japanese men, particularly those well dressed, to remove all their outer clothing after finding themselves a train seat. Carefully, they would fold their pants, shirt and jacket and place them on the overhead rack, then make themselves comfortable in their long underwear with their legs tucked under them. Once a very senior and somewhat portly army general went through this ritual in the seat across from us after receiving a ceremonious send-off from his troops. When we approached the next station he donned his uniform coat—but not his pants—and thus suitably attired at window level, exchanged bows with the delegation that greeted him, presenting to his fellow passengers a very large posterior covered only by underpants. He repeated this ritual at several stations until he had evidently passed beyond the boundaries of his command.

My sister R'ella visited in 1936. We gave a little party for her when she first arrived, and when it broke up, fellow language student Gerald Warner told me: "I'm going to marry that girl." True to his word they were married in Karuizawa that summer.

We led a fairly isolated life. We had neither time nor money for travel besides our summer excursions, and our language comprehension did not promote easy discourse. More important, the government—now largely controlled by extreme militarists—had directed the extensive police network to discourage contacts between Japanese and Americans. Ostensibly a precaution against spies, this policy really had more to do with encouraging the *kokutai*, or national spirit, against foreign influence, especially British and American. Since both countries openly disapproved of Japanese ambitions to conquer China and Manchuria, the leadership sought to weaken traditional Japanese regard for the Anglo-Saxon nations.

Naturally, we did not wish to embarrass or endanger any Japanese by taking the initiative to meet them; but one Japanese powerful enough to overrule our quarantine proved to be a very exceptional lady, Countess Tomeko Watanabe, who made it her business to introduce us language students to Japanese life. Her mother had come with Japan's first mission to the United States and was Vassar's first Japanese graduate. Her father was Field Marshal Oyama, a great hero of the 1905 Russo-Japanese War, and she had spent several years in London with her husband, an important banker. Thus Tomeko was a true cosmopolitan. In addition, she was a Christian, quite unusual for a Japanese of her rank. Ignoring the frowns of the police, she held a Japanese tea for us in her beautiful home every other Wednesday, during which she insisted that nothing but Japanese be spoken. So great became our mutual affection that when our first son, Stephen, was born in Tokyo in December 1936, Tomeko became his god-mother, giving him the Japanese name of Akira after her own eldest son.

We quickly came to understand that the government's war-iness of Americans was only one symptom of Japan's complex internal and international problems in the 1930s. The simplistic effort during World War II to depict General Tojo as another Hitler or Mussolini obscured the fact that Japan's march to war flowed from deep currents of its history and from the difficulties it faced in marching from anti-western isolation to full-fledged great power status in a single generation and coping with the world economic collapse of the 1930s.

Japan had completely exorcised Western cultural influence between 1600 and 1650 because it decided that European mis-sionaries and traders, to whom it had been quite receptive pre-viously, might become the opening wedge of European colonialism. The Japanese banned Christianity, expelled or killed Western missionaries and traders, and declared any contact be-tween Japanese and foreigners a capital crime. In the following centuries, Japan's high culture flowered in isolation.

The presence in Japanese waters of Commodore Perry's warships in 1853 forced the Shōgun, Japan's supreme military warlord and de facto ruler, to open a crack in the wall. Perry's unintentional humiliation of the Shōgun had important internal repercussions. By demonstrating the Shōgun's weakness, it acted as a catalyst for the growing anti-Shōgun forces, and in 1868, an alliance of various lords succeeded in deposing the Shōgun and restoring an "imperial rule" that acted through a Cabinet gov-ernment. This Meiji restoration, as it is known, brought to power a group of court advisors determined to transform Japan into a modern industrialized country before Western imperialism—then on full rampage in China and Southeast Asia—could subjugate it. And the Emperor Meiji himself used his considerable influence on their behalf.

Within a generation Japan became a power to be reckoned with. The Japanese, curious, extremely adept learners, assiduously studied Western technology and institutions to determine which they should adapt. Warships, shipyards, steel mills, railways, telegraph lines, banks, post offices, military conscription—all the sinews of a modern industrial state—were acquired virtually overnight from the countries Japan considered most advanced in those fields.

Despite this abrupt jump into the modern age, however, the Japanese never lost their unity or sense of direction. They have an unusual capacity for selective absorption, a trait they had long before developed in their ancient encounters with China. Though Japan had adopted Chinese language, government, religion, law and even city planning (the ancient capital of Kyoto, designed on a Chinese model, was probably larger than any European city of its time), Japanese national identity was never submerged. (Importantly, one element of Chinese social structure the Japanese never accepted was putting soldiers at the bottom of the social scale.) However, the process of modernization required reshaping customs and institutions upon which the stability of Japanese society had been founded for centuries. For instance, modern military strength required a large mass army, which in turn required that the all-powerful samurai renounce their monopoly on military activity. A mass army also required some system of mass education. And preparing the Japanese people to take a place on the world stage meant intensifying their nationalism, achieved by reviving the animistic cult of Shinto, with its deep native roots, and by accenting the mythical divine status of the Emperor.

Intense nationalism wed to modern technology and warmaking techniques soon bore robust expansionist offspring. In 1894, just twenty-six years after the young Emperor Meiji was carried on a palanquin the 325 miles from the ancient capital of Kyoto to be put on the throne in Tokyo, a modern Japanese Army and Navy expelled the Chinese Army from Korea, captured Port Arthur and the Liaotung Peninsula in South Manchuria, and sank a Chinese fleet near the mouth of the Yalu River. Much to Japan's extreme indignation, combined pressure from France, Germany, and Russia forced the return of Port Arthur and the Liaotung Peninsula (which Russia occupied shortly thereafter), and Japan was only slightly mollified by being permitted to retain Formosa, the Pescadores and a large Chinese indemnity.

Just ten years later Japanese armies routed Russian forces in Manchuria and again captured Port Arthur. Then, in a spectacular naval battle—the first ever between modern steam-powered, steel-hulled ships—the Japanese completely destroyed a large Russian fleet in the Tsushima Straits in May 1905. The ensuing peace treaty, secured through the mediation of President Theodore Roosevelt, recognized Japan's predominance in Korea and gave it control over Port Arthur and the Liaotung Peninsula, as well as all the strategic and profitable railways of southern Manchuria.

Japan had learned fast from its Western models, including the United States, which had just seized the Philippines, Guam and Puerto Rico from Spain. Most of all, the Japanese learned that military adventures might pay handsome dividends, for the "first victory of yellow armies over white," as the Russo-Japanese war was widely billed at the time, had boosted Japan's reputation world-wide; and even mighty Great Britain hastened to sign a strengthened defense pact with the Japanese. In Japan, the prestige of the military soared.

But with modernization and victory came an upsurge of xenophobia, for it was almost universally said that European intervention in 1895 and President Roosevelt's influence in 1905 had deprived Japan unfairly of much greater spoils. It became a national article of faith that Japan's own "manifest destiny" was to dominate the Pacific and "return Asia," then in the clutches of Western imperialism, "to the Asiatics."

By the time I came to Japan, economic troubles at home had given fresh impetus to Japanese imperial urges. The country's population had grown from over 30 million in 1880 to nearly 80 million in 1930, straining the country's meager agricultural resources. In the 1920s the cost of living outpaced salary increases to factory workers; then, in the wake of the Great Depression, exports slumped drastically, choking off the supply of Western currencies needed to purchase raw materials and machines vital to Japan's development. Unemployment increased, and famine struck several northern provinces. Western cultural imports—including fashions, flashy consumer goods, Marxism, and individualism—did not blend easily with the country's authoritarian and conservative ethos. Left-wing parties and unions sprang up for the first time, the assembly became more fractious, and the country's armed forces, which dominated political life, grew profoundly disturbed.

These trends in Japan were exacerbated by the thrust—shared by every major country, including the United States—toward autarky, following the collapse of the world economic system in the 1930s. Now Japan became increasingly determined to expand, in one way or another, the available area of markets and raw materials under its control. Unfortunately, like Germany, Japan chose the tragic road of military conquest.

A radical group of young officers believed that annexing Manchuria, then Chinese territory, would provide an escape valve for Japan's overpopulation and unemployment, secure a rich supply of natural resources, bolster Japan's great power status, and establish a buffer zone against Russia. By invoking loyalty to the Emperor and adherence to *bushido,* the traditional way of the warrior, the radicals tapped a large reservoir of latent chauvinism.

There was opposition to this policy, of course, mostly from civilian politicians and industrialists who believed that purely economic expansion would serve Japan best. But the country had grown tired of politicians who were perpetually embroiled in corrupt scandals and unseemly public brawling; and industrialists, during a period of general privation, seemed parasitic and symbolized all that was offensive about the soft, corrupt materialism of the West. The radical officers' appeal to deep, almost mystical chords of virulent nationalism had a particularly Japanese flavor.

The highest-ranking officers were not immune to the radicals' ambitions but were less fanatic. Some also felt that Japan should hoard its energies for war with Russia, now under communist control, instead of bothering with Manchuria. But the army chiefs in Tokyo could not control their younger colleagues. In some ways discipline in the Japanese Army was surprisingly loose. Each officer was entitled to consider himself a personal agent of the Emperor and believed it his solemn duty to disobey orders he considered contrary to the Emperor's intentions. This principle was called *gekokujo,* or insubordination. The Emperor Hirohito himself, by nature a retiring man and by custom rigidly prohibited from injecting himself in government policy except in supreme crises, did nothing to help. Thus it was not hard for strange, sometimes contradictory ideas about what the Emperor wanted for the country to take root in the army, especially because the officer corps was almost entirely segregated from civilian life. Future officers were taken from their families at thirteen, given no formal intellectual training except for chauvinistic history and military tactics, and subjected to extremely hard physical and mental discipline that promoted zealotry rather than reflection. The army was a world apart, imbued with a fierce sense of mission.

The most single-minded clique of radical officers was concentrated in the Kwangtung Army, a semi-autonomous force in charge of the Kwangtung Peninsula and the Manchurian Railway.

Japan had controlled the railway in southern Manchuria since the 1905 war with Russia. Through an efficient administration run by businessmen and aggressive tactics, the railway had become very profitable. Millions of Chinese immigrants poured into Manchuria and made it prosperous, but the Kwangtung Army officers wanted more. They were convinced that Japan's welfare demanded their seizing the whole of Manchuria, even though their superiors in Tokyo were only lukewarm and the civilian government was opposed.

They wanted to move quickly before China's new leader, Chiang Kai-shek, had time to consolidate his hold over the country; so, on September 18, 1931, some Kwangtung colonels staged several "attacks" on the railway to provide a pretext for a lightning conquest of Manchuria. Their quick victory, though officially disapproved, was greeted with jubilation by many in Japan.

Senior officers who detested the Kwangtung colonels' insubordination were disturbed by the prospect of airing the army's dirty linen in a public court-martial. They were even more dismayed by the potential for general insurrection among the fanatic officers, should Tokyo administer the really stiff medicine needed to bring them to heel. In any case, the Manchurian victory had undoubtedly contributed to the nation's glory, making it difficult to criticize the ringleaders. So the Kwangtung colonels were not punished for starting a war without Tokyo's approval—a clear incentive for further adventurism by the lunatic fringe. Eventually, the entire civilian government became subject to blackmail by these young Turks. Having obtained the right to approve an active officer as the cabinet's war minister, the army obtained a veto over government policy by withdrawing the war minister, thus bringing down the cabinet—a potent political lever. (The Navy, which also had this power, threatened its use much less often, and generally was more restrained about foreign expansion). Thus all the forces that eventually led to Pearl Harbor could be seen working in the Manchurian Incident and its aftermath.

International reaction to Japan's annexation of Manchuria was uniformly hostile. Japan tried to gloss over its aggression by concocting a puppet state, Manchukuo, with the exiled last emperor of China, Pu Y'i, as its head, but no one was fooled. Meanwhile, foreign criticism was intensifying Japanese patriotic pride. Japan withdrew from the League of Nations when that body condemned the Japanese conquest. America's opposition aroused particular Japanese ire. Secretary of State Henry L. Stimson issued loud, pious denunciations of Japanese aggression, but Japan thought him hypocritical. Had not the United States achieved its own greatness by marching across North America? Was not this same "moral" country excluding Japanese immigrants solely on the insulting grounds of race? And because the United States did not back up Stimson's words with troops or economic sanctions, some Japanese combined their anger with contempt for American weakness.

The Manchurian conquest, instead of satiating the radical officers, emboldened them. In February 1932, fanatics assassinated the Finance Minister and the president of the giant Mitsui industrial conglomerate, both of whom had opposed Manchuria's annexation. On May 15, nine young officers stormed the official residence of Prime Minister Inukai, another opponent of annexation, and shot him. The assassins were widely regarded as selfless and bold, attacking corruption and dishonorable restraints on the armed forces imposed by weak-kneed politicians, and they received only token punishment on the basis of their "sincerity." Inukai's assassination brought down the last effective civilian government to rule Japan until after World War II.

When I arrived in 1935, I was at first only vaguely aware of these political strains and crosscurrents. That changed literally overnight. On February 25, 1936, I awoke to find the city blanketed with snow and our normally populous lane ominously silent. The live-in amah nervously professed total ignorance, but no other servants showed up for work. My journalist neighbor had gathered only that some kind of revolution had occurred during the night. Both our telephones were dead.

I set out for the Embassy. Since all public transport had stopped, I hiked the three miles in the powdery snow, being careful to avoid several clusters of armed soldiers standing guard in doorways along the route. Near the Embassy I could see troops thronging outside and inside the Prime Minister's official residence on the opposite hill.

In the Embassy officers were trying to piece together what had happened. We learned that young Army radicals had broken into darkened houses all over Tokyo the night before aiming to assassinate not only the Prime Minister (actually they killed his brother-in-law by mistake), but many other high-ranking officials. Afterward, they occupied the central district of Tokyo and issued a manifesto justifying the carnage as their loyal duty to the Emperor. They had hoped that higher-ranking radical officers would take advantage of the turmoil to seize power.

The Emperor was said to be furious, and in one of his few initiatives was reported to have ordered the rebellion suppressed forthwith. Tokyo was thrown into tense quiet for four days until government forces, which surrounded the 1500 rebel troops, finally persuaded them to surrender.

There was a powerful backlash among the people and in the government against the radicals' brash insubordination. The army not only courtmartialled the ringleaders but executed them. But even so, civilian leaders were cowed. The army group urging expansion into China moved to dominate Japan's foreign and domestic policy.

Military spending increased and the economy went on what one finance minister described as a "semi-wartime footing"—this in 1936, more than five years before Pearl Harbor. Kwangtung Army officers hatched even more ambitious plans. They successfully schemed to take control of several North China provinces adjacent to Manchuria, and had their eyes on the whole country. Though simple chauvinism was the mainspring of their aggression, they had real geopolitical worries as well. Not only was Soviet power growing, so was Mao Tse-tung's, and nothing struck more fear into Japanese hearts than the prospect of communist Russia allied with a communist China against Japan. To be sure, Chiang Kai-shek was still nominally in control of China, but Mao and Chiang put aside their bitter differences to conclude an anti-Japanese alliance in early 1937. Now the Kwangtung officers reasoned that, with support from Tokyo, the most effective buffer against a possible Chiang-Mao-Stalin pact aimed at driving Japan from Manchuria would be to seize even more Chinese territory.

On July 7, 1937, they found a pretext for action. Japanese troops stationed near the Marco Polo Bridge outside Peking were fired upon. It is still not clear if the shots came from expansion-minded Japanese hoping to provoke a wider war. In any event, the incident released underlying tensions as if they had been tightly coiled springs. Japanese retaliation escalated into a full-scale war, and Imperial troops attacked Shanghai.

We language officers were recalled from our summer stint at Lake Nojiri to encode and decode cables that flew especially furiously after President Franklin Roosevelt's call for a "quarantine" against Japanese aggression inflamed Japanese opinion. One measure of the depth of anti-American sentiment—and the armed forces' lack of discipline—was the deliberate sinking by cannon fire from the shore of the American gunboat *Panay* in the Yangtze River.

Still, most Japanese were genuinely aghast at the sinking of the *Panay*. For those of us living in Japan, that was clear, for the Foreign Minister called on Ambassador Grew to convey the government's apologies, and thousands of ordinary citizens came or wrote to the Embassy to express their regrets.

But to average Americans, Japan seemed nefarious in the extreme. Combined with stories of atrocity about the Japanese "rape of Nanking"—some reports estimated 300,000 civilian casualties—the *Panay* incident firmly etched an image of an irresponsible Japan in the American mind. Tensions between Japan and the United States seemed destined to rise, as Japan's drive to establish a "Greater East Asia Co-Prosperity Sphere" eventually rubbed up against America's Asian interest in the Philippines and the Western Pacific.

In this climate of rising turmoil and uncertainty I took my Japanese exams in December 1937. Four bachelors and four married men took the test; the married men received their highest grades in written work, the bachelors—no doubt well-versed in the niceties of "social" conversation—did best on the oral exam. My native linguistic abilities probably had not progressed too much since my days of college French, but I found the intricacies of Japanese fascinating and managed to pass the exam satisfactorily. Thus equipped, I was promoted to "Unclassified A" and detailed to my first Foreign Service post as Vice-Consul in Seoul, Korea.

Korea

The Seoul consulate was an old palace located in a beautiful three-acre compound near the city's center. My boss, Consul-General O. Gaylord Marsh, the only other American, lived in the lovely rambling Korean-style mansion inside the compound. Pat and I inherited a smaller guesthouse nearby, and there was an office building near the gate that faced the street where Britain and France—the only other Western countries represented in Seoul—also had their consulates. A small foreigners' club next door and a missionaries' club down the block, where Pat and I sometimes went to bowl, provided our only diversion. Though Marsh had an automobile, I did not, so I hired a ricksha runner. A consulate normally handles visas, trade promotion, and looking after Americans in trouble. I found that I liked my work because I enjoyed dealing directly with the practical problems of real people. Also it gave me a better chance to show what I could do than would semi-anonymous service in a big embassy.

Since Marsh did not speak Japanese, my job was to look after American interests with the Japanese Administration. That primarily meant helping the few remaining United States businesses around bureaucratic roadblocks erected to force them out of the country. It also involved a great deal of work trying to keep American missionaries out of jail, a tricky assignment because the Japanese military considered American Christian missionaries subversive to their ultimate goal of completely "Japanizing" Korea.

As I have mentioned, Japan began taking over Korea after its 1894-95 war with China. The pathetically corrupt and weak Korean government offered no resistance. Japan annexed the country formally in 1910 (the United States was the first formally to recognize this) and ruled it directly with Japanese Army officers (generally less enlightened than the Navy officers who ran Taiwan).

Tokyo's aim was to make Korea an integral part of Japan, politically, culturally, and economically, despite intense Korean hatred for their occupiers.The Japanese established schools rapidly throughout the country that taught only in Japanese, stressed Japanese nationalism, and made every effort to wipe out Korean history, culture, and language. Men were forced to cut off their traditional top knots to conform to Japanese custom. Japanese administrators decided that Koreans wasted too much time washing their traditional white garments and banned them. Korean rice production was increased to meet Japan's growing rice deficit, leaving Koreans to subsist on less desirable millet from Manchuria.

Though Japan also introduced hydroelectric plants, railroads, hospitals, telephones, factories, mines, a stable currency, and sanitation measures that dramatically improved public health, the Japanese were not adroit enough to follow the British example of giving a significant group of their colonial subjects a piece of the ensuing prosperity. Any time a Korean merchant managed to carve out a little profit for himself, the Japanese would take him over as they took over the best rice lands.

For a time, after the bloody "Independence Riots" in 1919, slightly more enlightened forces prevailed in Tokyo during the 1920s. Civilians were appointed to govern Korea, a Korean university was established, and the campaign against Korean culture was relaxed. But by the time I arrived in 1937, the militarists who had gained dominance in Tokyo had reversed this relatively benign policy. The Governor-General, General Minami, had been Minister of War during the 1931 Manchurian incident and later commanded the Kwangtung Army. Bull-headed and autocratic, he restarted the campaign against Korean language and culture, and despite much propaganda about "Asia for the Asiatics," Koreans became second class in their own country. In 1938 Minami introduced a particularly brutal and inane measure requiring Koreans to adopt Japanese names. To get a child into school, to register a marriage, or to have any dealings with the government, you needed a Japanese name. It was a tremendous assault on national pride, more so because Koreans' Confucian heritage imparted the sense that their names were their links to their ancestors and thus embodied their very souls. I never did understand why the Japanese, whose sense of tradition and formality is so highly developed, could not see how offensive they were to Koreans and how much just a little tact might have earned.

Though American missionaries generally did not seek trouble with the authorities for its own sake, Christian congregations tended to become centers of anti-Japanese sentiment among Koreans. American missionaries had arrived in the 1880s and by 1936 there were half a million active Korean Christians, more than in any Asian country except the Philippines. Missionaries established the country's first educational system and even after Japanese annexation, mission schools retained significant influence. Japan kept a suspicious eye on the Christian churches and their American leaders, correctly viewing them as obstacles to its stated goal of turning Koreans into Japanese. Not many sermons were missed by plainclothes police, and any pastor leading the congregation in "Onward Christian Soldiers" or preaching David and Goliath was certain to receive a summons to police headquarters.

Though the mission schools had unwillingly accepted the authorities' order that all instruction be in Japanese and that the curriculum stress Japanese nationalism which involved sending their pupils and teachers to Japanese-Shinto shrines on specified occasions to make a ceremonial bow demonstrating loyalty to the Emperor. However, General Minami wanted to bring the churches even more under his heel. Thus, in 1937 he ordered that Christian congregations repair to the state-Shinto shrines in a body—a clear attempt to equate Shinto spirits with Christ. Korean Christians, backed in most cases by their associated American missionaries, insisted that the government was forcing them to "worship" false gods in violation of their conscience as Christians and refused to do it. The Japanese administration claimed that these ceremonies were not religious but a secular sign of "obeisance" toward Japan's "national essence," and held that refusal to participate was proof of disloyalty and was punishable by law. A virtual reign of terror was instituted against resisting Christians, especially the pastors. So I had my hands full; on the one hand intervening with the Japanese authorities to keep various missionaries out of jail, and on the other, prevailing upon 700 missionaries to take it easy and recognize that they were voluntarily living under Japanese rule.

While trying to work out the problems that were continually arising over the missionaries, I would often call on Mr. Oda, in the foreign affairs section of the Governor-General's office. The only card I had to play was to appeal to Japan's widely proclaimed policy of religious freedom, intended to show the world how advanced it was. Mr. Oda was a cultured, well-educated gentleman who obviously did not relish having to defend some of General Minami's more outrageous actions; correspondingly, I often had difficulty defending a small but persistent group of missionaries who seemed to enjoy provoking Japanese officials. We both understood that there was a certain amount of ritual posturing in our respective positions and had a good working relationship.

Occasionally Oda would give parties welcoming important American visitors, to which I was usually invited. It was always in the same restaurant, with the same kisaeng girls (the Korean equivalent of geisha girls) for entertainment. Once Oda's guest of honor was a dour, straight-backed Methodist bishop from the United States who did not exactly warm to Oda's idea of a good time. When I came in, the last to arrive, the bishop and missionaries were sitting with their wives in frosty quiet, eyeing the kisaeng girls stiffly. The girls, who had known me from other similar evenings, were so relieved to see a familiar face that they jumped up and ran over to greet me. "Oh Johnson-san! Johnson-san!" This certainly established my reputation with the bishop and his cohorts. Luckily, Pat was along.

In fact, I seemed to have better luck with Oda and his kisaeng girls than with my boss, Consul-General Marsh. "Guatemala" Marsh, as he was called, was one of the few people I have ever known whom I thoroughly disliked. I found him a narrow-minded, enormously self-satisfied and dedicated martinette. Nothing I did, no matter how good, seemed to deter him from chewing me out frequently in rough, vulgar language. He forbade us to associate with the very able British Consul whom he disliked, and called Pat in to complain about her taste in hats. Shortly after my arrival I actually came to physical blows with him. He had gotten so livid at our Chinese cook for leaving a door ajar in the compound wall that he started beating the man around the head with his cane, and I intervened. Marsh said he would have me fired within the week. I was convinced that I had disgraced myself irreparably in my first post. Marsh's crankiness was evidently widely known, however, because the Supervising Consul-General from Tokyo "happened" to show up, asked some discreet questions, and I kept my job. But Marsh and I got along no better; he wouldn't even let me use his car to drive Pat to the hospital to give birth to our third child, William, in August 1938. Luckily, he soon left Seoul for a prolonged home leave, and I was left in charge.

I had received no training in consular work at all, so being left in command presented a certain challenge. When people wanting a visa, or a ship captain wanting a discharge or to hire a seaman came to see me, I would often say that I had to look after some other business for a few minutes and duck into an adjacent office, where I would consult the consular regulations. For advice on thornier problems I went to the old-time Korean employees who knew the work backwards and forwards. I never got overly worried about being so green. I figured that I would pick up whatever I needed to know as I went along, and that, in any event, I certainly could do no worse than Marsh.

Once when Marsh was absent the Japanese police arranged a demonstration outside the consulate. They rounded up five hundred or a thousand Koreans, equipped them with banners decrying the latest deviltry of Yankee imperialism, and had them parade outside the compound to vent "the aroused anger of the Korean people." The whole thing was so obviously staged that I could not take it seriously. I sauntered out to the gate facing the street, took out my handkerchief and started waving to the crowd. They waved back, started laughing, then we started laughing, and discipline disintegrated entirely, much to the Japanese organizers' distress.

Despite such occasional minor victories against the government's more blatant inanities, Korea was otherwise a grim and efficient police state. Even though we had grown accustomed to constant surveillance in Japan, the atmosphere in Korea was determinedly more oppressive. I always used to feel a physical sense of relief, like weight coming off my shoulders, whenever I left the country. Fifteen years later, Stalinist Czechoslovakia would hold no surprises for me.

Seoul was always full of stories about this teacher or that doctor being taken into custody for no reason and released, several years later, broken physically and mentally. Foreigners entering Korea from Japan were often subjected to 25 detailed interrogations during a 24-hour journey. As consular officers, of course, we were immune from imprisonment, but as Americans in a Japanese police state we were prime targets for their heavy net of suspicion. Whenever I left the compound, a policeman followed; sometimes additional agents from the Kempeitai (military police) joined in. I got to know one of my Kempeitai tails particularly well, and worked out a deal to make the best of a bad situation: We went riding together weekly on the Kempeitai's excellent imported horses. I got to ride, and he got to keep track of my whereabouts.

Washington did not request much political reporting from Korea, because it was not a self-governing country, and the basic dynamic of Japanese oppression/Korean resentment had few variables. Nevertheless, I followed the local scene and wrote some reports, primarily on economic subjects.

To get a better feel for the country, however, I decided to travel around it in 1938. I went with a college classmate, George McCune, who had been born in Korea, spoke the language fluently, and was here to see his missionary parents and consult the former legation's archives for his thesis in Korean history. We journeyed northward. To test out what we might overhear in the other language, one day he would speak only Korean with fellow passengers, and I would speak only Japanese the next. Our first major stop was Pyong-yang, now the capital of North Korea, then a pious missionary center. The main street was lined with clapboard Protestant churches, and it had a curiously midwestern air. Then we headed north of Mampojin near the headwaters of the Yalu River, and took a large, sampan-type boat powered by an airplane propeller down the rapids to where the Japanese were building the Suiho Dam. The river trip took two days, which we spent inside the cabin while Japanese guards sat on deck with machine guns scaring off bandits.

I had given a visa to the chief engineer of the Suiho Dam to study the Boulder Dam on the Colorado, so he received us very hospitably. Thinking that we might learn too much, however, the police swooped down after a few hours and said they were very sorry but we would have to spend the night in a remote mountain village. We went as directed. The next morning I chartered a bus to take us to the last remaining American gold mine in Korea at Unsan. Naturally the police came to board the bus. They were plainclothesmen, and I wasn't supposed to know that they were police, but I did and they knew that I did. I said I was sorry, but I just couldn't take any more passengers. That certainly put them at a loss; they couldn't force their way aboard without wrecking their "cover," and there was no other way to get to Unsan. After some minutes of this impasse, which I enjoyed hugely, I said I might reconsider if they would agree to share expenses. After a lot of palaver, they capitulated.

I learned a considerable amount from this trip, especially a good sense of geography and climate that came in very handy when I was in Washington during the Korean War. I must say that it never did cross my mind during the trip or any other time that Korea would ever gain independence from Japan. That was simply too preposterous. The Foundry Methodist Church in Washington where Pat and I were married did have a Korean gentleman we knew who continually predicted and lobbied for his country's independence, but I never could take him too seriously. His name was Syngman Rhee, and we again met when he became the first President of South Korea after World War II.

In February 1939, we returned to the United States for home leave as a family of five, not counting Kiyoko-san, the baby amah. After seeing my parents and touring around some of the southwestern National Parks, we took the train back to Washington, and then back to Korea.

North China

Almost immediately after our return, in June, I was detailed for temporary duty in Tientsin, China. After arranging for Pat and the children to spend the summer at a missionary resort, I took the Japanese train through Manchuria to Tientsin, one of our larger and more important consular posts. It was Peking's port city and a major manufacturing center of about 1,500,000 people, thirty miles up a small river from the Yellow Sea. There, a large American community was engaged in exporting dried eggs, wool for rugs, and hog bristles—then irreplaceable for paint brushes—as well as importing oil products, autos, and machinery.

In the organization of its government alone, Tientsin symbolized the havoc imperialism had brought to China. It was divided into concessions, British, French, Japanese, where each colonial power enjoyed complete sovereignty under its own laws and provided all municipal services. Even the local Chinese police looked like bobbies, French gendarmes, or Japanese police, depending on where they worked. There was also a native Chinese section and two "special areas" which had belonged to Italy and Germany before they lost World War I. The United States, not wishing to encumber its activities in China with colonial territory, argued the Open Door policy and operated from offices in the British concession. We did have extraterritorial privileges like the other colonial powers, and American citizens were subject only to American law.

Japan had conquered Tientsin from the Nationalist Chinese in 1937. The Kwangtung Army decided to exploit its control to put the screws to Japan's rival, Britain, which helped supply Chiang Kai-shek through the Burma Road, ran the China Customs Service, had large concessions in Shanghai, Tientsin, and Canton, and controlled Malaysia, India, Burma, Australia and New Zealand. Japan could not undo Britain's empire but it could grind its heel into Tientsin. Soon after it conquered the city, the Kwangtung Army imposed a strict land and water blockade around the British concession (and the adjacent French concession) on the pretext that the British were harboring Chinese terrorists. Barbed wire barriers were built, and people passing through were searched, detained, and otherwise harassed. Though the blockade's target was Britain, and Americans were supposedly entitled to complete freedom of movement, the Kwangtung Army had no great love for Americans and life became extremely difficult for our businessmen. Following accepted diplomatic procedure, the American Consulate-General in Tientsin had tried protesting Japanese mistreatment to the Japanese Consulate in Tientsin, which in turn was supposed to bring the army into line. In fact, however, the army paid even less attention to the Japanese consulate-general than it did to the government in Tokyo. Under the doctrine of "imperial command," the army listened only to its own commanders, who seldom cared about the niceties of international law. Since our consuls in Tientsin spoke Chinese, not Japanese, the department hoped that sending me there might be a more effective way to prod some cooperation from the Japanese authorities. I became something of a one-man fire brigade, answering calls from Americans in real or imagined distress at Japanese checkpoints, and generally trying to keep enough pressure on the Japanese so they would translate their announced policy of cooperation into fact.

My work took me all over the city and to all levels of the Japanese Army. Normally I would try to expedite stuck American goods by going to the checkpoint in question displaying a huge identity card emblazoned with my diplomatic rank in Japanese. The first problem was convincing Japanese sentries that I actually could speak Japanese. I could see them tense up as I approached, fearing a difficult confrontation with a "gaijin" (foreigner) who would undoubtedly make trouble. While the sentry menacingly pointed his bayonet in my direction, I would repeat simple phrases like "good morning," "the weather sure is hot," "what's your home town?", until it dawned on him that this foreigner could really speak his language.

Once the sentry discovered that we could communicate, he would direct me to his officer in charge where several minutes of bargaining would usually secure the release of the detained American or American goods. I would depart with fulsome apologies and expressions of regard ringing in my ears. Several hours later the whole irksome process would recur, often at the same checkpoint.

Finally I determined to see the Tientsin area commander, Lieutenant General Homma, to work out some more definitive solution. Homma, unusually tall for a Japanese, had a shock of white hair that gave him a very distinguished appearance. He was a gentleman compared to the extremely brutal officers around him. They routinely slapped common soldiers and spoke to each other in a curt, guttural army dialect that was unbelievably crude. For instance, when Homma's orderly announced that the general was ready to see me, he would stand at rigid attention and shout at the top of his lungs, even though I sat just a yard or two away. Homma, on the other hand, always spoke softly and treated his subordinates well; he even spoke passable English. When I described the harassments Americans were suffering from his troops, Homma promised to investigate this and invited me to return should I have any need to. When Homma was executed after World War II as a war criminal charged in effect with responsibility for the Bataan Death March, I was saddened. Homma's responsibility was only nominal. Some American generals thought the verdict too harsh, and I had difficulty believing that the only gentleman I ever knew in the Japanese Army could have been so deliberately callous.

Despite my pleasant conversation with Homma, I quickly discovered that the principle of *gekokujo,* or insubordination, not only permitted the Kwangtung Army to invade Manchuria and China without Tokyo's authorization, but also inspired lower-ranking officers to disobey Homma's orders freely if they didn't feel like obeying, and that was often.

Tientsin was almost perfectly flat, except for a small depression where the consulate was located. Those simple facts of geography conspired to produce one of the more trying experiences of my life—the Great North China Flood of 1939.

What became a flood started one Saturday in August as an innocent trickle slowly meandering down Race Course Road, the main thoroughfare in the British concession. Although from the edge of the British concession, a sheet of water stretched as far as we could see outside the city, severe flood warnings still didn't seem credible, since the river snaking through the center of town was maintaining its normal level. But when the waters started lapping around the Consulate, the three of us junior officers who weren't on vacation rounded up a few Chinese employees and started lugging our files, furniture, and equipment to "dry ground"—the consul-general's residence, built on foundations eight feet tall adjoining the office. We still hadn't been particularly worried when we began, but by nightfall, when the job was completed, the water had already risen to hip-level, and all electricity and pumped water had been cut off. I waded back to the hotel and collapsed, exhausted, asleep.

When I awoke the next morning, the new waterline made it abundantly clear that the survival of our little outpost required relocating the office once more, this time to the eight-story Leopold office building downtown.

First I had to get myself to the consulate. Boatmen had not yet arrived to ferry passengers around the city and the water, which now came up into the hotel lobby, was too deep to wade. Swimming was not exactly enticing either, since the water was rank from the vast tons of dried eggs, Tientsin's biggest export, which had dissolved in the flood and started fermenting in the summer sun, giving the water the black sheen of crankcase oil. My swimming "companions" would have been coffins and corpses in various stages of decay, liberated by the flood from their traditional Chinese shallow graves.

Luckily, several asphalt-coated wooden blocks that had previously paved a nearby street floated by. Grabbing a long-handled broom from the hotel, I clambered aboard and propelled myself three blocks to the office. On the way, I had to laugh. The reputed allures of diplomatic life—elegant meals with fine wines amidst brilliant company, huddling with foreign ministers at cocktail receptions to advance vital American interests—seemed all-too remote as I punted my way to the office on a hunk of pavement.

At the office, we rounded up as many coolies with boats as we could, loaded up everything, and after many hours of muscle, reinstalled the Consulate at the Leopold Building. Luckily, at that point the flood reached its apex of about eight feet at the consulate. But since the city was almost perfectly flat we knew we had several months before the water would drain away.

The flood forced us to switch our focus from diplomacy to simple survival. The stench from the rotten eggs intensified so much that it peeled paint off the walls. The hotel had ample supplies of French mineral water, but once daily my boatman and I had to row over to the Marine barracks for canned rations. We were much luckier than most, however. The flood covered several thousand square miles, and tens of thousands of destitute peasants started streaming into the city. The Japanese, undeterred by the misery around them, actually seized on it to make life even more miserable for the British, and everyone else suffered as a result. Quickly reestablishing their barbed wire barricades and checkpoints, the Japanese troops permitted thousands of desperate refugees into the British concession, but would not permit additional food shipments or allow the Chinese through the French concession to leave via the railway. Tension rose as starvation loomed.

In addition, Chinese guerillas took advantage of the chaos to infiltrate the city in boats, which made the Japanese soldiers nervous and dangerous. Once, on the way back from an unsatisfactory conversation with General Homma about the refugee problem, I saw a boat carrying four well-dressed Chinese men inadvertantly nudge one carrying two Japanese privates. The soldiers, rising without a word, stepped into the Chinese boat, threw each of its passengers into the water, and beat them with oars until they stayed down. On another occasion, when I was being rowed back to my hotel through the Japanese area at night, a flashlight was suddenly trained on us, a heavy blow knocked my boatman into the water, and some Japanese soldiers began shouting. I don't know if they were stealing, checking for guerillas, or had orders to commandeer whatever boats they could find. I shouted back at them in the most forceful Japanese I could muster (unfortunately, there is no real way to curse in Japanese), mentioning often and stridently that I was an American diplomat. My bravado worked; they helped my boatman climb in and we sculled away as fast as we could, shaken but alive.

As the food and refugee situation worsened, our Chinese employees had increasing difficulty caring for themselves and their families. After much argument I obtained the agreement of General Homma's headquarters to permit them to leave Tientsin via the railroad in the French concession, provided I would organize the exodus. On the appointed morning we assembled the evacuees, about seventy in all, including children. Giving each one an armband inscribed in Chinese and Japanese, I instructed them to stick as close to me as possible. Then we set off by boat for the railway station, which was located on high ground across the river from the French concession.

Perhaps 25,000 refugees were packed on the patch of dry land on the French end of the bridge that led to the railway station, and every day these wretched people had to watch helplessly as the trains left the station for safety. We had no choice but to pass through this starving, sick, desperate mob. Once they grasped that our column had permission to cross the bridge, they started a stampede to follow, those in the rear forcing those in the front onto the Japanese barbed wire barriers. The nervous Japanese guards, fearing a full-scale riot, started beating them back with bayonets and rifle butts, and everyone began shouting and screaming. I could not move in the crush, nor could my charges, whom I was frantically trying to keep together.

There was no hostility specifically directed at us, only a universal frenzy aimed at escaping toward the railroad station. But a starving Chinese mob can be a fearsome thing, and for a time I doubted that we would ever get out of that maddened crowd alive. We finally struggled to the barricade; then came the job of convincing the sergeant that General Homma's order meant what it said, and opening the barrier sufficiently to let my charges, but no one else, through. When we reassembled on the other side I was tremendously relieved to discover that none of us was lost.

In about ten days our vacationing officers were able to return from Chingwangtao, which relieved the strain on us considerably. But the city still faced two crucial problems: relocating the refugees and draining the floodwater. The water would not drain naturally until spring, so the only thing to do was to build a levee around the city and pump it out. Consul General Caldwell agreed to a British request that I take up the subject with General

Homma. I tried hard with Homma, but to no avail. He claimed that the matter was out of his hands. The British and French then resorted to building a dike around their two concessions. The pumps were still working six months later.

The rest of my memories of Tientsin are a blur. So much misery and privation surrounded us every day and our individual struggles to stay alive absorbed so much attention that our sensitivity to suffering became dulled. In September, Germany invaded Poland to start the Second World War in Europe, but to all of us in Tientsin—British, French, German, Italian, Chinese and American—it seemed very remote and almost inconsequential compared to our own problems. Morale in the Consulate, oddly enough, was extremely high, all of us working around the clock doing things that cried out for doing. In all my years in the Foreign Service I have always found the highest morale in the most beleaguered posts.

Nowadays the State Department would probably airlift supplies, arrange emergency care for refugees, and deploy Army units to help build bridges, levees, and restore water and electricity. But 1939 was a different time. No doubt the Department knew about the flood, but it assumed we would do our best and that would have to suffice. Nowadays jets and electronics permit the Department to respond much more comprehensively to natural disasters, and this is obviously genuine progress, but it was more challenging to be a Foreign Service Officer when we had more autonomy.

In November 1939 my temporary duty in Tientsin ended when Bill Yuni, a fellow Japanese language officer, came to replace me. I returned to Seoul and acted as head of the consulate during several long periods while Marsh was (providentially) absent. Finally, in July 1940, I was transferred to a new post—Mukden, Manchuria. But it took me several years to shake off the memory of the misery of Tientsin, and it still remains firmly etched in my mind as the most concentrated dose of human suffering I have seen.

Manchuria

My Japanese language skills were once again the reason for my transfer to Mukden—or "Hoten, Manchukuo" as its Japanese occupiers had renamed it—since our consulate needed someone to deal with the Kwangtung Army. Japan had taken control of Manchuria from China in the fall of 1931 because Manchuria, three times the size of Japan itself, had mineral resources, good farmland, efficient railways, and was considered an effective buffer against Russian expansion. Since most of the world had condemned the invasion, to prove itself civilized and win the allegiance of Manchuria's 45 million inhabitants, Japan set up an elaborate puppet government for the "independent" state of "Manchukuo." This was wasted effort, since, while Japan had established all the proper forms of Manchurian "self-government," it ran the country as such a rigid military police state that it failed completely to win support from the Chinese population.

Tokyo had also started an ambitious program to encourage Japanese farmers to emigrate to Manchuria, intending both to reduce overcrowding on the home islands and seed a belt of conquered territory near the Soviet border with loyal subjects. Despite huge subsidies and intensive propaganda, however, fewer than 40,000 farmers had settled in the region by the time I arrived in 1940. Industrial development had fared only slightly better, since the hostility of Japanese industrialists toward the Kwangtung Army officers discouraged the kind of investment the region really required. And in 1939, Japan's Manchurian difficulties became even more serious when a major border clash with the Soviet Union broke out.

Mukden was an important commercial center that sat at the junction of the main north-south and east-west railways. Occasionally we traveled to Changchun (then Hsingking), the political capital of "Manchukuo," to deal with Japanese administrators on behalf of the few remaining American business interests. But American business activity was minimal, confined to a few leftovers the Japanese did not bother seizing from the American oil companies. The American missionaries who were left acted with discretion and caused the consul few problems. Nor were there any floods to occupy our time. So Mukden was chiefly useful as a window on the economic, political, and military developments in Japan's "Greater East Asia Co-Prosperity Sphere."

Travel around the country was difficult, because train journeys required a special permit and few roads were passable to automobiles. Even so, Bill Langdon, the Consul-General, and I often left our offices in the Hongkong and Shanghai Bank Building on hunting expeditions in Bill's old Ford. We headed for the railroad tracks, where we went after pheasant and accurate counts of Japanese troop trains. We were amateurs, but even we could see that the Soviet-Japanese border conflict that had started in

1939 was still big, involving about ten Japanese divisions. The large number of white boxes carrying cremated remains back from the front indicated that the fighting was rough, though we could never learn any details. True to form, the Japanese police kept close watch on us, but we managed to scrape together reports that we hoped Washington would find useful by pooling information with our British and French colleagues and by talking to the many White Russians still living in Mukden. Also true to form, we never heard a word from Washington about our reports.

Mukden's diplomatic community was even smaller than Seoul's, but Pat had the compensation of a large old Chinese house built around two courtyards where lovebirds chattered away. Pat, who five years ago had been trading her streetcar pass with me to save money, now had seven servants on my $3,500 salary.

Sometimes when we wished a change of pace we could secure seats on the South Manchurian Railway, either south to Dairen, north to Harbin, or to Tientsin and Peking. Harbin was an interesting stop. Its large White Russian colony, though poor, was always happy to use the excuse of a visitor, especially an American consul, to stage a rousing all-night party. In those tense days when war already raged in Europe, one sensed an element of the "dance macabre" in these parties, given by a people who had no homeland, no allies, and no place to go. Few of them survived the war.

Japanese rule in Manchuria was typically heavy-handed. Had the Army been slightly more enlightened the local population might have acquiesced to colonial control, since Japan did bring considerable material benefits to its new territory. But the Japanese treated the Chinese with open contempt, and usually expropriated the property of any Chinese businessman showing even modest success. Thus, the Army's clumsy policies ensured that virtually no Chinese had a stake in seeing Japan remain in Manchuria.

More important than domestic affairs, however, was the international scene. Distressed over Japan's long war against China, the United States renounced its trade treaty with Japan in late 1939. Japan retaliated by seeking strong anti-American allies, formally joining Hitler's Germany and Mussolini's Italy as a member of the Axis in September 1940. In October Washington embargoed the shipment of steel scrap to Japan and concluded that war was likely enough to warrant evacuating all dependents in East Asia. Washington also urged the departure of all "non-essential" American citizens.

I took Pat and the children by train to Chingwangtao, a seaside resort across the border in North China, where the ship *Mariposa* was scheduled to pick up the evacuees. We arrived early in the afternoon and spent a pleasant day with Bill Langdon and his wife, Laura.

Someone had to open the Mukden office the next day, however, so I could not spend the night. Leaving Pat and the children at the hotel, I set off across country in a rickshaw to Chinwangtao junction where I would catch the 2 A.M. train to Mukden. I remember feeling very much alone and sorry for myself. Pat was going off to create an entirely new life for herself and the children with a very slim income. With the clouds of war rising around us, I did not know when, or if, I would see them again.

I abandoned our house in Mukden and moved in with Bill Langdon at the Standard Oil Compound. With all American dependents gone and United States-Japanese relations frosty, there was not much diplomacy to transact. We kept in touch with Washington mostly by letters sent via diplomatic pouch. Hardly a perfect system, since the time elapsed between sending Washington a message and receiving a reply could reach four months. Also, the train carrying the State Department's pouch courier passed through Mukden at 3 A.M. In winter the wind on the open platforms could reach −40° F. and the train would arrive so sheathed in ice that its doors could not open until workmen with steam hoses thawed them out. My only consolation was that my ever-present Japanese police "tail" had to share my misery.

Telegrams from Washington were extremely rare, nor did we send any except those containing military information. Telegrams not only taxed our extremely limited budget but, since they required laborious hand-coding, our patience and eyesight as well. First the message had to be reorganized into code groups of five letters each. Then each letter had to be transposed according to a code table that shifted with each letter, and the table themselves were shifted every fifty or so groups according to an indicator contained in the message. After an hour of this tedious activity one's eyes would start to dance, and it was easy to make a slip that would entirely derail the rest of the message. The process was reversed for incoming telegrams, with one added difficulty: transmission errors that completely disrupted the decoding system. The only remedy when this happened was to imagine every possible glitch and try each in turn. If the message remained garbled after several hours of this guesswork, one had to code another message asking for clarification, take it to the post office for transmission and hope for a reply from Washington within two or three days. It was not a system designed to encourage verbosity, repartee, or a fast exchange of views. Needless to say, cryptography in the present computer-age is completely different. Unfortunately, the modern ease of encoding and decoding tends to encourage prolixity and literary flourishes that all too often detract from the intended message.

Our situation in Mukden worsened dramatically in July 1941, when Japan moved into Indochina, the United States froze Japanese assets, and the Japanese then froze American assets. That not only cut off our money, but all steamer traffic between the United States and Japan, and thus our mail. We still heard occasionally from Washington via telegram, but to get family news we had to sit up until 1 A.M. struggling to make out the personal messages beamed to my little Zenith radio from the San Francisco shortwave station KGEI. Ken Krentz, who had replaced Bill Langdon, and I made preparations to ready the Consulate for war, which we felt was now inevitable.

The Japanese felt the same way. One night, a fanatic Japanese officer charged with sword unsheathed into the bedroom of the British Consul General ready to kill for the Emperor's greater glory. The Britisher, fluent in Japanese, coolly talked him out of it. I didn't have that much faith in my nocturnal linguistic abilities; from then on I slept with my gun under my pillow. We also arranged a cooperative radio-monitoring system with my British colleague, Vice Consul Dudley Cheke, to ensure we had twenty-four-hour coverage for a possible declaration of war.

War

About 4 A.M. on December 8, Dudley charged up our stairs shouting that the Japanese had bombed Pearl Harbor. The BBC flash had provided no other details, and at first I was sure that there had to be a mistake. I had toured the base on my return to Japan from home leave in 1939 and been thoroughly briefed on its "impregnable" defenses.

Nevertheless, it soon became clear that the long-awaited war had finally come. We had already moved most of our files to the house in anticipation of having a State Department courier take them away for safe keeping, so we immediately set the servants to work burning them in the basement furnace. Then we went to the Consulate, where we destroyed a few sensitive papers and codebooks. We were careful to save our "Gray Code," one that we assumed the Japanese had long since broken and that we used mostly to save telegraph charges. We expected the police to burst in at any second.

When at, about 10 A.M., no police had shown up, I figured it would do us no harm to take some initiative and drove to police headquarters where I asked to call on the Japanese Vice-Chief of Police (the Chinese "Chief" was a puppet). Our personal relations had always been good, and he received me immediately and courteously. He had heard about Pearl Harbor. I said we were closing our Consulate, and with elaborate Japanese politeness, he expressed surprise and dismay. With what I hope was equal politeness, I explained that this was customary, when two countries go to war.

Deciding to go for broke, I asked him for a travel permit on the noon train to the Soviet border. Since he had been given no instructions, he approved my plans but said they would require confirmation from the Kempeitai, or military police. Exultant, I rushed over to the Kempeitai, and the major in charge promptly approved and gave me the permits. I knew this was too good to last, so I rushed back to the Consulate to tell Ken Krentz that we should get started on the next step of getting to the station. Once out in the street, however, I spotted Ken's car surrounded by Manchurian police. Orders had obviously arrived from Tokyo.

The police stuck both of us on our living room sofa. Thirty or forty of them started ransacking the place. Occasionally they would point their guns at us menacingly and shout "codes." After a suitable delay we produced the useless Gray Code, to their evident delight.

Periodically the soldiers would run outside to inspect the chimney, from which vast quantities of smoke and partially-burned paper were pouring, and then return to puzzle over the peacefully smoldering living room fireplace. After an hour or so, they discovered our servants in the basement furiously feeding the furnace, and beat them heavily. But most of the papers were already destroyed.

At nightfall they finally agreed to put us in an upstairs bedroom. The sounds from downstairs were not comforting. The police had discovered and broken into our liquor cabinet and were growing ugly. We could hear the screams of our servants. Occasionally the police would come upstairs and pretend to rush us with bayonets.

By dawn our situation was looking desperate. I wrote a note to the Vice-Chief of Police who had treated me so politely the day before and gave it to one of the more sober policemen, hoping only faintly that he might deliver it. Perhaps he did, because later in the afternoon the Vice-Chief arrived with a few plainclothesmen to rescue us. They berated and beat the drunken police viciously. Later we had visits and apologies from the Chief of Police and even the Chief of Staff of the Japanese Army in Manchuria. With the drunken police removed, we settled down to a fairly moderate regime of house imprisonment.

Several days after our internment, the Consulate's one Japanese employee, Yamada-san, showing enormous courage, visited us. We discussed practical problems, such as paying off the office staff, and gave Yamada-san money for them. After he left, we found we had a little cash left over, which a good thing, since the police said they had no funds to support us and that we would have to pay for feeding ourselves and the servants they let stay with us. Several months later our funds ran out, so the police sold our unused beds to a White Russian bordello, which gave us a good price. Then we had to sell the beds we slept in for delivery after we left Mukden. Soon thereafter, we ran out of coal in the middle of the Manchurian winter and our guards would not replenish the supply. We were reduced to huddling under our blankets for warmth.

We asked repeatedly for permission to contact Washington, the International Red Cross, or the nearest Swiss Consulate (Switzerland was the "protecting power" authorized to look after American interests during the war). That was refused on the grounds neither we nor the Swiss had any legal status vis-à-vis "Manchokuo." This left us no way to communicate even our existence to Washington. Our worries deepened when we heard how decisively Japan was routing our Pacific forces. We saw pictures of the Pearl Harbor debacle and read about the sinking of the *Repulse* and *Prince of Wales* and about the Imperial Army's advance into Singapore and Corregidor. The police had confiscated our shortwave radio, but gave us a small one so we could hear the local Japanese broadcasts. We discovered that if we turned up the volume all the way late at night, put one ear next to the speaker and blocked off the other with a pillow, we could just barely hear American broadcasts from Manila. It was a very lonesome moment for us when the station announced the American evacuation of Manila and signed off with "The Star-Spangled Banner."

Recognizing that we might be in for a long siege, Ken Krentz and I established a daily routine to try to give some sort of order to our featureless days. We slept for so long, then read, then talked, then played records on the Japanese phonograph. In the evening we played three-handed poker with our third fellow internee, Franklin Lewis, a consular clerk of uncertain allegiance, whose mother was American and whose father was Japanese. But despite our schedule, we grew bored and restless. Though a steady diet of Japanese newspapers boosted my reading ability to its highest level ever, ultimately I could not sustain my concentration.

We protested vigorously about not being permitted any exercise. Finally the police allowed us to walk in our walled compound, then in the two-acre vacant lot we owned next door. Ken and I would walk round and round, until the two police guards who followed us would tire and stand in a corner while we continued. Next to our vacant lot was an empty walled lot belonging to the French Consulate across the street, and next to that was the British compound where Dudley Cheke and his colleagues were kept.

The French consul and his wife, both Alsatians, were thrown into jail after Pearl Harbor. Since they nominally represented the pro-German Vichy government and were thus Japanese allies, the police soon gave them limited freedom. Actually they were staunchly pro-Allies. When the Consul's wife, a feisty and brave woman, saw us walking in our vacant lot she slipped across the street into the French compound's vacant lot next door. I saw her do this, but initially we made no contact. Each time we went walking, thereafter, she did the same thing. Gradually we worked it out that Ken would lure the guards into one corner of our compound while the French Consul's wife and I walked along opposite sides of our common wall, keeping our heads low, and conversing across it. She and her husband had paid a White Russian to build them a cigar-box radio which picked up KGEI from San Francisco, so she was able to give us some news directly from home. We also learned that the French and British could read blackboards held up in each other's windows, so now we could make indirect contact with Dudley and his crew; and through the French Consulate's servants, we communicated with a small group of Maryknoll missionaries interned in the Foreign Club down the street. It was amazing how much we could do when we put our minds to it, even with police constantly at our elbows.

An odd feature of our captivity was that we talked with many more Japanese than we had before Pearl Harbor. The police had kept us heavily quarantined while we were still free to report to Washington, but once they had us interned it became the "in" thing for high-level officials visiting Mukden to come see the jailed American Consul and Vice-Consul. My "friend" the Japanese Vice-Chief of Police also called on me weekly to chat. We had some very odd conversations. He frequently complained that the new German consul, his supposed ally, was a boor, comparing his manners unfavorably to the courtesy I had always tried to show him even when our official relations were extremely strained before Pearl Harbor. He also said: "You know, Japan can never win this war. The American Navy is just too good." I would counter: "Well, I am surprised to hear you say that. The Japanese Navy seems to be doing rather well, after Pearl Harbor, sinking the *Prince of Wales* and the *Repulse,* then capturing the Philippines and Singapore." "No, no," he would argue, "we just won't be able to win. The whole thing is hopeless." This, from the Japanese police chief who was then arresting thousands of Chinese (and even Japanese) on suspicion of harboring "dangerous thoughts," while Japan was at the height of its victories.

The months dragged on, and still we heard nothing about an exchange of internees. Each time a high-level visitor called on us and asked, in typically polite Japanese fashion, if we needed anything, we always emphatically requested contact with our government. Finally, one day in April 1942, a Japanese Army truck pulled up carrying electrical equipment. "You've been complaining all this time about not being able to communicate," said the officer in charge, "so now we're going to record your voice and broadcast it over Hsingking Radio." Krentz and I saw our dilemma immediately. If we said we were unhappy, the Japanese wouldn't broadcast it; if we praised our captors, we would become their propaganda tools. They permitted Ken and me to confer, and we wrote a careful script that we read into the microphone. The truck departed and we heard nothing more.

When I eventually got home, Pat told me a remarkable story about this recording. By then she and the children had settled in Laguna Beach, California. Several times a neighbor had invited Pat to listen to the radio, but she had never taken up the offer. One evening in June, as she was walking down the beach, she was suddenly seized with a desire to listen to this neighbor's radio. Several other guests were there, and the host was fiddling with the dials. Pat barely caught the words "Hsingking Manchukuo," and said, "Oh, get that. My husband's there." The announcer continued: "This is Radio Manchukuo. You will now hear the Prisoner's Hour. The first voice will be that of U. Alexis Johnson, American Vice-Consul in Mukden." Amazed, Pat absorbed every word. It was her first indication that I was still alive. I had given her address in the recording, so scores of people from all over the country subsequently called and wrote to her. I've never been the superstitious type, but Pat's freakish good timing certainly seems more than a coincidence.

Before internment I could never understand why someone, having done his duty and been taken prisoner, just didn't relax and permit events to take their course. By late spring, however, escaping had switched from being a wildly romantic pipedream to a full-time obsession, something Ken and I pondered and discussed (out of Frank Lewis's earshot) day and night. Our schedule had become so routine that our guards ignored us during the night, so we figured we would have a good seven or eight hour lead. The French Consul had established covert contact with the Chinese Communist Eighth Route Army, whose main forces were several hundred miles away. We started planning to conceal ourselves under a load of hay in an oxcart and make our way to the Chinese lines. Had our captivity endured much longer, we might even have risked this crazy scheme. But in June 1942, we were told to prepare one suitcase for our repatriation to the United States.

The day before we left, the Vice-Chief of Police and the Chief of the Foreign Section treated Ken and me to dinner at one of the geisha houses downtown—an interesting commentary on Japanese manners. One would have thought from our lavish treatment that we and the police officers were the best of friends.

The Japanese believe that prolonged sexual abstinence decays the brain, and throughout our internment they offered, even urged, the services of various local ladies. Our refusals always mystified them. At the geisha house, the police chiefs had troubled themselves to find some White Russian "ladies of the evening" who, given their profession, were relatively good-looking. The Japanese were very disappointed when we declined their hospitality, but we all still had a good time. Our hosts drove us home and we parted with mutual expressions of hope that the tragedy that had overtaken our two countries might soon be resolved.

The next day Ken Krentz and I boarded a train carrying the British Consul and his colleagues, as well as American and

British consuls from Harbin. Frank Lewis, torn between his American and Japanese loyalties, confirmed our suspicions by choosing to stay in Mukden.

We traveled through Korea to Pusan and boarded the regular ferry for Shimonoseki in Japan. After the ship got under way, zigzagging sharply to elude American subs, we were permitted on deck to get some air. Several Japanese approached me. "Are you American?" they asked shyly. "Yes," I said, "a diplomat." They had read about the exchange in the newspapers. "You are going home?" "Yes, we hope so," I said, "on exchange." "We hope you have a very pleasant and safe voyage," they whispered with complete sincerity.

It was eerie to see Japan again now that it was sending forth armies to kill Americans. From Shimonoseki we traveled by heavily guarded train to Kobe where we joined several score of Allied missionaries, diplomats and businessmen from Southern Japan. After about ten days the Americans were taken to Yokohama, and then to the old passenger liner *Asama Maru*, where I was put in an unventilated steerage cabin with two rows of four-decker bunks. For the first time we saw our Foreign Service colleagues from Japan, including Ambassador Grew and his wife who were installed in a suite on an upper deck. (To the distress of other official families in Japan, Mrs. Grew had refused to leave when other dependents were evacuated in 1940.) We were forcefully reminded of how cruel Japanese could be when "Chief" Mayer, the vigorous and likable head of the Standard Vacuum Oil Company in Japan, was carried aboard on a stretcher broken in mind and body after months of "interrogation" by the Yokohama military police.

Finally we heard the plan for our voyage from our Tokyo colleagues, who had been kept informed by the Swiss who had handled the long, circuitous negotiations. The *Asama Maru* was to make stops in Hong Kong, Saigon and Singapore to pick up additional passengers and then cross the Indian Ocean to Lourenco Marques in Portuguese East Africa. At Singapore we would rendezvous with the Italian vessel, *Conte Verde*, carrying internees from China. Simultaneously, the Swedish vessel, *Gripsholm*, laden with Japanese repatriates, would leave New York bound for Lourenco Marques. There the three vessels would trade passengers. Then the *Gripsholm* would sail around Africa to Rio de Janeiro to discharge some South American passengers, heading finally for New York.

The ship cast off and the engines started throbbing. Finally we were going home!

Until we arrived at Lourenco Marques we kept a close watch on the sun and stars to ensure we stayed on course. Plots circulated constantly on how we might try to take over the ship if it turned back. The Japanese crew, which clearly included many trained police, was alert to our mood, making relations very tense. At one of our meals of fish and boiled potatoes, a Japanese steward in our mess threw a glass of water in an American woman's face. The men at the surrounding tables immediately stood up to go after him, but almost as immediately, knife-wielding Japanese "waiters" appeared at every door. We sat down.

We worried that an American sub might mistakenly torpedo us. The *Asama Maru* rode with full lights at night and had large red crosses painted bow and stern, but we thought an enormous Japanese flag painted at the center might prove too attractive to hungry submariners. Several months after our return to the United States, a submarine captain showed me a picture of the *Asama* taken through his periscope. He nearly sank the ship because it had strayed far off the announced course and the Rising Sun tempted him until he moved closer and saw the red crosses.

Arriving in Laurenco Marques after our long voyage was a great thrill. Dozens of Allied ships in the harbor sounded their horns, broke out flags and cheered us as we steamed by. (When we disembarked, we ruefully discovered that a German submarine was keeping the ships penned in, so that the "armada" was more a symbol of Allied weakness than might.) The *Gripsholm*, which had ferried the Japanese repatriates from the United States, was awaiting us in the adjacent berth. With a line of freight cars on the pier separating us, the Japanese marched from the bow of the *Gripsholm* to the bow of the *Asama* while we switched from stern to stern. Aboard the *Gripsholm* I was able to shout across the fantail to my old debate partner at Occidental, Henry Shimanouchi, then a Japanese diplomat being repatriated.

An enormous buffet lunch, with hams, turkeys, eggs, plus showers and fresh sheets—luxuries we had all but forgotten during internment and the rigors of the *Asama Maru*—brought home to us that we were in friendly hands once more. Even so, our euphoria was quickly displaced by a mood of subdued introspection. Recent war news from North Africa and Guadalcanal was even worse than we expected. We had to scour our memories to write reports that might help our superiors or the military, and the grim tragedy of a world at war was all around us.

The *Gripsholm* stopped briefly in Rio de Janiero, where we received overwhelming hospitality, then sailed for New York. We returned to an America at war. Blimps flew above New York harbor, and just outside it, in sight of the Statue of Liberty, we passed a torpedoed ship still burning as it sank. When we docked, I spent twelve hours helping the FBI and Army officers process the passengers. Finally, at 6 P.M., I was allowed to step onto American soil and rejoin my wife. As recorded by *Time* magazine:

> Notable was U. Alexis Johnson, United States Vice Consul at Mukden. He rushed off the boat, calling to reporters: "I don't want to talk to newspapermen. I want to talk to my wife. I haven't seen her in two years." He spied her in the crowd, walked up to her slowly, gravely. "Hello," he said. "Hello, How are you?" "Fine, How are you?" They didn't kiss; they didn't even shake hands. They just looked at each other for a long while, then walked off and got in a cab." UPI published a large photograph of us fervently embracing each other, so you can take your choice.

What had my seven years in the Foreign Service taught me about Japan, its national character and United States—Japanese relations? "Though the military extremists leading Japan have a deep hatred of all non-Japanese peoples and ideologies," I wrote when I returned in 1942, "they have not hesitated to adopt the foreign institutions and technologies best suited to increasing their military potential. The best available machinery and methods for the production of steel, aluminum, magnesium, machine tools, refined petroleum, synthetic gasoline, and all other essentials for modern war were purchased abroad wherever necessary." The Japanese themselves were disciplined, highly motivated, and inured through a Spartan living standard to hardships of protracted war. Soldiers were well-trained and were conditioned to consider death in battle the highest possible glory.

Ultimately, however, I was convinced that the United States and Japan would have to find a way to coexist. America was sure to remain a great Pacific power. Japan's extraordinary cultural and economic strengths guaranteed its continued prominence after it recovered from defeat and restructured its institutions to banish militarism. Obviously, eventual cooperation with a country now straining every fiber to destroy us would take time. Even so, I thought it inevitable.

I was convinced that the Japanese people tended to respect

and like Americans in a way that was considerably different from their attitudes toward other non-Japanese. I had been struck by the great effort that the military leaders had devoted to conditioning the country for the possibility of war with the United States. Their approach did not deny our material accomplishments, but stressed a view of Americans as so softened by our luxurious life that we could not make the sacrifices necessary to beat the Japanese with their indomitable *Yamato damashii* (Japanese spirit). Before the war I was not sure they were wrong, but they made a colossal historical misjudgment in their surprise attack on Pearl Harbor. Good as the plan of attack was, it saw only the "trees" of military damage while completely missing the "forest" of an America united in outrage to defeat Japan. Pearl Harbor was meant to create a situation in which America would be tempted to negotiate a peace favorable to Japan; it had precisely the opposite effect.

If the Japanese failed utterly to understand American psychology, our own understanding of the Japanese was no better. In my lifetime American attitudes toward Asia had been more stereotype than insight, and Japan was no exception. The most pernicious stereotype was the "yellow peril," an unembarrassed racism that was particularly strong in the West, where many Japanese and Chinese had immigrated. That racism had received government sanction with the 1924 Immigration Act that banned all Japanese immigration to the United States, a dreadful insult to Japanese national dignity. Mixed with our distrust of the Japanese was a large measure of contempt. We considered them clever but basically dumb copiers, good at mimicking but incapable of inventing. A story popular when I was a boy had Japan buying destroyer plans from Britain that the British had maliciously distorted to unbalance the ship. Sure enough, the Japanese were such thorough copiers that the completed ship flipped over. The story was a complete fiction, but it illustrates what Americans were thinking.

Pearl Harbor overnight transformed the Japanese from buck-toothed bumblers to evil incarnate. Japan's image in America had been growing progressively darker since its attack on Manchuria in 1931 and the rape of Nanking in 1937, especially because Americans—quite irrationally, in my view—had considered themselves special friends and protectors of China, a "sister republic" led by Chiang Kai-shek, a good Christian. But the treachery of the unprovoked attack on Hawaii had Americans flocking to the "shoot-all-the-yellow-bellied-bastards" school in droves. Loathing of the Japanese was entirely understandable in 1942, I believed, but was no basis for future relations. After victory had given wartime hysteria a chance to dissipate, I hoped that Americans would come to understand Japan's intrinsic importance in the Pacific and would learn to deal with this difficult and enigmatic people.

CHAPTER FOUR

Wartime
and Occupation

AFTER I IMPARTED MY MEAGER STOCK OF KNOWLEDGE ABOUT current Japanese operations in Manchuria to the Department and Army Intelligence debriefers in Washington, Pat and I left for California in mid-October 1942. There I visited my parents and began to get to know my children again. It is not easy being related to a Foreign Service Officer, especially in wartime. Judith was now eight, Stephen six, and William four, and except for a couple of letters early in 1941 and my "prisoner hour" broadcast in the spring of 1942, my family had heard nothing from me since they boarded the *Mariposa* at Chingwangtao two years earlier.

It was a great joy to be with my family, but being especially conscious of the war, I felt impatient to play my part in it. I gave speeches describing the nature of our Japanese enemy to local civic groups and nearby army bases, but this was hardly a full-time occupation. Finally I telegraphed the Department, which told me in reply: "Be patient." At the beginning of December, to my astonishment, I received orders transferring me and my family to our Embassy in Rio de Janeiro, Brazil.

Brazil

Though I was delighted to have my family with me after such a long separation, Rio seemed like a long way from the war. However, the Department wrote me that most of my fellow Japanese language students were going to South America—Dick Richardson to São Paulo, Brazil; my brother-in-law, Gerald Warner, to Buenos Aires, Argentina; and John Emmerson was already in

Lima. Many Japanese, especially impoverished farmers, had emigrated to South America before the war, and we were wanted to help discover if any might be trying to sabotage the war effort. I also suspect that Stanley Hornbeck, savvy bureaucratic operator that he was, welcomed this opportunity to keep his Far Eastern assets intact for deployment back to the area when the time came.

Because the German submarine campaign was then at its height, the only practical method of travel to Brazil was by air. The whole family finally received the necessary priorities for travel by Pan American to Rio, a very difficult thing in wartime. On Sunday, December 6, we woke the children at 2:30 A.M. so my parents could drive us to the Glendale airport where we boarded a fifteen-passenger DC-3. With three or four other passengers and great mounds of freight, we took off at dawn for Mexico City.

The cabin was unpressurized, the air full of turbulence, and most of the passengers (including Pat and the children) became thoroughly ill. The rest of the nine-day trip was, if anything, worse. We seldom had a good night's sleep because takeoff was usually before dawn. We sweltered in broiling lowlands, then found ourselves hopelessly ill-clad for refueling stops at snowy mountain airstrips. The worst leg of the journey was from Arequipa, Chile, over the Andes to La Paz, Bolivia. To survive the 18,000-foot altitude the passengers were supposed to suck oxygen from hoses provided at each seat. The children just could not get the knack of this and quickly became ill from altitude sickness and lost consciousness. The pilot reassured us that they would be all right, but we did not rest easy until they regained consciousness at the 13,000-foot La Paz airport. That night weather forced us down in Oruro, a Bolivian mining city where the only vacant room was in a bordello. The only food I could find to revive my exhausted family was a $2.50 can of asparagus soup that I heated over a wood fire I made in the bordello's courtyard and ladeled into them with a borrowed spoon. Air transport has come a long way since then, I often remind myself as I sip martinis at 35,000 feet.

After a glorious night of recuperation at the Copacabana Hotel in Rio, I reported to the Embassy and called on the Ambassador, Jefferson Caffery, who even then had become something of a legend in the Foreign Service. Painfully shy and forbidding, heartily disliked by most of his staff and other Americans in Brazil, he was nevertheless a superb diplomatic tactician. The Department had apparently neglected to tell him why I had been sent to join his staff. I said I had been told to look after the

Japanese. He harrumphed, said the Brazilians could do that adequately themselves, and directed me to his Economic Counselor,
Walter Donnelly, who needed an assistant. He said Donnelly had
gone through three in as many months.

Walter told me that he was swamped. Wartime had made
our Brazilian Embassy a miniature replica of Washington's bureaucratic chaos. The Board of Economic Warfare, the War Shipping Administration, the Rubber Development Corporation, the
Proclaimed List Office (which blacklisted firms doing business
with Germany), the FBI and a host of other agencies all had
representatives in Rio. Each pursued its particular objective vigorously, jealous of each other and of any attempt by "mere diplomats" in the State Department to regulate their activities.
Walter's job was to bring some order out of this confusion, riding
herd on everyone to ensure that American policy was coordinated
and consistent.

The Embassy's overall mission was to hasten victory, pure
and simple. Brazil had rubber, industrial diamonds, quartz crys-
tals, and other scarce materials essential to the war effort that we
labored to get to the U.S. in the time and quantities requested.
Brazil, on the other hand, desperately needed machinery, spare
parts, and other commodities from the United States. All too often,
after months of struggling to obtain things the Brazilians were
clamoring for, we would learn that five out of six ships in the
convoy had been sunk en route.

One request we received from Washington shortly after
my arrival was to obtain samples of "rare earth" and send them
by air with the highest priority. We had to consult a dictionary
to find out what rare earth was, and call in the Board of Economic
Warfare mineralogist from the jungle to secure it. More orders
followed. Not even the mining companies that supplied us could
figure out why we needed so much; as far as anyone knew, rare
earth's principal active ingredient, thorium, was mostly used in
making mantles in gasoline lanterns. I only learned of rare earth's
other uses after the atomic bomb was dropped.

Walter Donnelly had Ambassador Caffery's complete confidence. Neither had any mandate from Washington to supervise
the other agencies, but that did not deter them. In place of formal
authority they employed two tools whose potency in a bureaucracy I later came to appreciate: the force of their personalities,
and control over communications with Washington.

Only the Embassy had the diplomatic pouch and encrypted
messages. One of my jobs was to screen all the cable and pouch

traffic to keep Walter abreast, which the other agencies resented. My other duties were also largely internal, except for some miscellaneous tasks, such as assigning civilian air priorities on American aircraft, approving requests for the wonder drug penicillin (then new and scarce), and working with the Brazilian foreign office to allocate Brazil's tire production to other South American countries. It was a valuable experience, my first exposure to the "big time" and the art of running a large, diverse organization. I enjoyed the job, and evidently managed adequately because when the Department sought to transfer me to Manaus in the heart of the Amazon, it retreated in the face of Caffery's and Donnelly's cries of outrage.

While Walter and I struggled to keep the Embassy machinery well-oiled, Ambassador Caffery looked after a vital element in our war effort—relations with Brazil's dictator Gertulio Vargas. At the beginning of the war Vargas had seemed to be tilting toward the Axis; Caffery's job was to persuade him to concede what we needed from Brazil to fight the war. He succeeded brilliantly. The most vital concession was getting—and keeping—Vargas's permission to ferry aircraft and troops to North Africa via bases in Brazil. In 1940, when war looked imminent but America was still officially neutral, President Roosevelt and a few far-sighted people in the State and War Departments arranged for Pan American Airways, on secret contract with the War Department, to construct some fifty-five airfields from the United States through Panama, Colombia, Venezuela, the West Indies, Guyana, and Brazil. An airstrip blasted out of the rock on the British island of Ascension in mid-Atlantic completed the chain across the ocean. Before Pearl Harbor our Army used the bases (with Brazil's acquiescence) to supply fighters to the British in North Africa; after we entered the war, the supply line aided our own forces in North Africa and extended through Africa, the Near East, India, and over the Himalayas—"the Hump"—to China. It was a major artery, and keeping it open, well-stocked and unimpeded by Brazilian red tape was Caffery's main job. He succeeded so well that Vargas shed his pro-Nazi sympathies and eventually even contributed a Brazilian division to our forces in Europe.

Despite his accomplishments with Vargas, Caffery had few admirers in the Embassy. That bothered me. Young and full of "modern ideas," I thought the Ambassador could improve his reputation by holding a staff meeting for the key people in the Embassy and other agencies. His assistant, Elim O'Shaughnessy, and I obtained his reluctant consent. It was a complete shambles.

He knew hardly anyone in the group or what their functions were. He made himself and everyone else acutely uneasy and no one profited—except for me, because I learned this important and enduring lesson: that an ambassador's effectiveness is independent of popularity, and each one must do things in the way he feels most comfortable.

Caffery taught me another important lesson, brevity in dispatches. He would get page after page of instructions from Washington; after a two-hour meeting with Vargas, he would wire back: "I saw Vargas regarding your telegram number so-and-so; he said no; I told him he had to, etc., etc.; he said yes." And that was really the essence of everything Washington needed to know.

My family life improved enormously in Brazil. It was the first time we had lived outside a police state since 1935. The climate was pleasant, we had a beautiful house, many friends and colleagues, and a good American school for the children. I didn't have much time to enjoy it, but the family found Rio extremely congenial.

But the etiquette of entertainment baffled us at the start, despite the Brazilians' outgoing hospitality. Our first dinner invitation was for nine o'clock in the evening, a bit late for our taste, but we nevertheless accepted and showed up punctually. This threw our hosts's household into turmoil. Both the host and hostess were still dressing. They came downstairs in about twenty minutes and the first guests started trickling in at 9:45. We had cocktails, then dinner at eleven, and adjourned for cards at about one. Ignoring our manners, we left "early" and arrived home at 2:30. As I had to leave for work each day by seven, our social life tended to be curtailed.

Even so, we did try to enjoy "Carnival," the week of wild revelry before Lent for which the whole city, especially the poor, seemed to live from year to year. The vigor and abandon of the celebration was something entirely beyond our experience. With some friends we went to the big floor show at the well-known High Life nightclub (pronounced "Heegi Leefi"), but one night of trying to dance among packed sweaty bodies and being sprayed liberally with cheap perfume was enough for my Scandinavian temperament.

The most important change in our family was the birth of our last child, Jennifer, in May 1943. The doctor at the Maternidade Arnaldo de Moraes, where Pat was being cared for, permitted me into the delivery room so I was able to hold Pat's hand while Jennifer was born. Afterwards I walked along the Copacabana beach, in the cool salty air, just as the sun was rising. It was a profound moment. At that instant, all over the world, people were endeavoring to kill each other on a scale never before seen. Yet here a new life, to which I had contributed, was defying all that to assert itself and remind us of what is really valuable in human existence.

My original reason for going to Brazil—to keep tabs on the Japanese community—absorbed almost none of my time. The Japanese in Brazil, like Japanese in virtually every allied country, did not try to create difficulties for their adopted nation. Once the São Paulo police called, certain they had cracked an important Japanese spy ring and requested my help. I went to São Paulo and was taken to a cell that housed an inoffensive-looking and very scared Japanese teenager. Triumphantly the police produced the spy document he had been carrying—a complicated wiring diagram. Inspection proved it to be a *Popular Mechanics* magazine blueprint for a simple home radio. The "master spy" was in fact a harmless adolescent electronics buff. The police were crushed.

In May 1944, my father died. After Mother called with the shocking news—Dad was only 64, and everyone expected him to live at least another 20 years—I hitched rides in the holds of Air Corps bombers to Miami, and there a National Airlines ticket agent put me on a plane for Los Angeles though I lacked the necessary air priority. Dad's loss grieved me deeply. He had lived an upright, good life and was well-liked and respected. All through his life he had helped hundreds of people untangle estates and write wills, but oddly neglected to leave one for himself. I spent several days with my mother, settling his small but complicated financial affairs. Then the Department summoned me: I was to fly to Washington before returning to Brazil.

In Washington I learned that the Far Eastern Bureau wanted to assign me to a Civil Affairs Training School, or CATS, that the Army was running to prepare officers for governing occupied Japan. Unlike the Navy, whose officers had traveled the world and understood the rudiments of international affairs, the Army had developed no international expertise. It wanted some Foreign Service Officers familiar with Japan and the normal conduct of diplomacy assigned to the schools where its officers (and some naval officers, too) were being trained for military government in Japan after the war. I was the first FSO ever assigned to a military school, and it wasn't really clear whether I would be instructor or student, but I agreed to attend a six-month CATS course located on the campus of the University of Chicago. I flew back to Rio by military transport, assembled our belongings, and almost immediately returned by air with the family to the United States. We took a train from Miami to Chicago in time for me to report for classes on July 31, 1944, and Pat and the children continued on to set up housekeeping with my mother in Los Angeles, starting our third prolonged separation.

The school at Chicago had about seventy students, two-thirds from the Army, ranging in rank from second lieutenant to lieutenant colonel. Many of the younger officers were lawyers. They studied Japanese language, history, culture, and economics, but spent most of their time working out sample problems in military government that ranged from the minutest trivia (for example, where to establish public bathing facilities) to questions of the highest policy, such as whether to retain the Emperor. The final stage called for preparing detailed plans for occupying and administering specific portions of Japan. The objective of these exercises was to give the officers broad intellectual preparation for handling complex and unexpected problems in the field, rather than to supply a fixed set of answers.

From the beginning I decided to live with the students in the university's International House, and went through target practice, physical training, and daily classes with them. At first I was very careful not to volunteer opinions or corrections, since I wanted to avoid giving the impression that I was trying to show up the Army's military government instructors, none of whom had been to Japan (though several of the civilian professors had Japanese experience). My policy of caution paid off. Soon the officers accepted me as a comrade and bombarded me—in class and especially at meals and after-hours discussions—with questions about Japanese culture, local government, and the State Department's thinking on postwar Japan. Though I keenly felt my own inadequacies, I found I was able to correct many misconceptions. I also delivered lectures on Japanese occupation techniques, State Department organization, and Japanese foreign trade. Though I was more instructor than student, the information flow went two ways, since I received a good introduction in military organization and the way officers typically approached politico-military problems. I discovered that the older officers' attitudes toward Japan were less objective and more emotional than the younger officers'. They had little patience for my attempts to explore how the Japanese might react to various types of occupation policy; they believed you just pointed your gun and the "yellow-bellied bastards" would jump. In general, however, I was favorably impressed by the students' adeptness and good judgment.

For a first experiment in exchanging personnel between the State Department and the military, I felt that my CATS tour worked well. The traditional military contempt for "cookie-pushing striped pants diplomats" did not materialize; I was even able to inform the Department at the course's end that "many of the officers have declared that they would be badly disappointed if State Department officers were not available for consultation in occupied areas." Since the Army was clearly going to be running the post-war show in Japan, I profited as well. If I were sent to Japan as I expected, I would have an inside view of the Occupation's organization and personnel that could only boost my effectiveness.

From these humble beginnings, State-Defense exchange has grown to include a State Department Deputy Commandant and FSO students at the National War College and the three service war colleges. Military officers attend the Foreign Service Institute as students and faculty members, and diplomats and military rotate regularly in operating positions in State and Defense in Washington. All combined commands have an FSO on the staff as a political adviser. In later years I became directly involved in establishing and expanding some of these programs to further State-Pentagon cooperation. The fact that understanding the Occupation Army would be vital to my future as a Japanese specialist was driven home in October 1944, halfway through the CATS instruction, when the Department said it intended to send me to Manila as soon as our troops had liberated it from the Japanese as "a springboard for projecting you into Japanese or Japanese-occupied territory as rapidly as it is occupied by our forces." Until Japan was defeated, I would assist Consul General Paul Steintorf in opening the Philippines consulate and repatriating the approximately 7,000 American civilians interned there by the Japanese.

In late January I finished up at Chicago, journeyed to California where I delivered lectures on Japan and State Department organization to Army civil affairs classes at Stanford, and spent time with my family while awaiting the call to Manila. With a fresh promotion from Vice Consul to Consul, I joined Steintorf, Rody Hall, and Dick Richardson at Travis Air Force Base and clambered aboard a C-54 on March 14, 1945, for the three-day flight to Tacloban, Leyte, where Douglas MacArthur had recently waded ashore to make good his promise, "I shall return." A twenty-mile jeep ride through the Philippine countryside would bring us to MacArthur's general headquarters, then to Manila.

The Philippines

Manila's devastation was immense. Block after block was gutted, heaped with charred rubble, pocked with shell holes and littered with scarred trees. It is said that only Warsaw suffered worse destruction from the war. Little groups of fanatic Japanese were still sprinkled throughout the city, particularly in Intramuros, the old walled section. Gunfire was constant. One Japanese unit had holed itself up in the legislative building and resisted tenaciously until a massive point blank artillery barrage collapsed the entire building.

We were initially billeted in a former apartment. Half of it had burned down, the roof was gone, and 150 men slept on cots under the stars on the third floor. Undrinkable water sometimes flowed through the mains, but luckily all our food came from the Army—a single egg would have cost 50¢ on the cutthroat open market.

Our new consulate was eventually located in the old German building, which, apart from having all its windows and doors blown out, had miraculously escaped serious damage. But as it happened, my work kept me away from our office. I had been waiting in the chow line on my first day in the city when the officer in front of me, a Colonel Ginsburg, noticed that my uniform carried no insignia and deduced I was a civilian. He was in charge of repatriating all the civilians the Japanese had interned in concentration camps at the University of Santo Tomas, in Manila's northern section, and at Los Banos, about forty miles south. Represented among the 7,000 internees were scores of different nationalities. Few had passports or other papers, everyone wanted to go home, and the Army knew next to nothing about the fine points of international law on nationality. At his request I went the next morning to Santo Tomas to help with the repatriation work. Along with the Army Counterintelligence Corps (CIC), which was trying to weed out collaborators and spies possibly planted by the Japanese, I developed a system centered around a simple, one-page questionnaire filled out by each internee. After examining it and any documents the internee had managed to save, I made a decision on his nationality and where he should go. When I initialled the bottom of the questionnaire, it then constituted both a visa and a ticket on military transport to wherever in the world the person was going.

Deciding the nationality of the original Santo Tomas internees was not too complicated, but when people who had hidden themselves from the Japanese started flowing in from the hills, sorting out the nationalities of Philippine wives, children and other relatives grew much more involved. Often I just improvised and hoped for the best. But I never heard any complaints, which only shows how wartime can sometimes successfully bend rules that would otherwise have been considered inflexible.

The misery at Santo Tomas was appalling. The Japanese had packed thousands of people into a stockade under conditions that at best were brutal. Toward the end of the occupation, when the Japanese themselves were running out of food, prisoners starved. People were still dying when I was working there, and all the rest were emaciated and sick.

I tried to help the CIC officers to determine which Americans had cooperated with the Japanese, but we found casting the first stone very difficult. The prisoners had been subjected to years of privation and stress, and though we did detect various degrees of collaboration, who were we to judge? Sorting out villains, heroes, and those who had alternately been both was beyond our powers. On the whole, we concluded, the people had behaved exceedingly well.

The Army had been pouring men and materiel into the Philippines to prepare for invading Japan itself. By August vast numbers of troops were stationed on the islands awaiting the final push. Given the ferocious resistance the Japanese had shown on Tarawa, Iwo Jima, Okinawa, and other Pacific islands, the Chiefs of Staff estimated that one million American soldiers would die conquering the Japanese home islands. So it is easy to understand why we in the Philippines greeted the news of Hiroshima's atomic bombing with jubilation.

Surrender

The surrender itself, on August 15, 1945, was the transcendent event. That evening was probably the wildest in Manila's history. Everybody who had a gun fired it. Machine guns, rockets, artillery shells, flares, cannonballs—you name it, people were shooting it. At one point during the height of the celebration I literally crawled under my cot for protection from the hail of bullets.

The next morning I was summoned by General Sutherland, MacArthur's Chief of Staff. He knew I had served in Korea and asked me to meet with General John Hodge, commander of the XXIV Corps, which was slated to land in Korea. Hodge knew virtually nothing about the country and had no one on his staff who did, so we had a long talk about Korean politics and culture, all of which he absorbed avidly. When he showed me his orders and instructions I was shocked; no one in Washington had thought to consider Korea as separate from Japan itself, so Hodge's orders for Korea were identical to those for Japan. They stipulated that the Army should seek to maintain order by retaining and working through existing local officials—a logical policy for Japan, but impossible in Korea since the only officials were the despised Japanese occupiers and their puppets. Hodge appealed to Sutherland to get separate orders for Korea, but Sutherland and MacArthur were unwilling to go back to Washington at that point. Hodge and I discussed ways of softening this bureaucratic error, but the orders were so fundamentally wrong that we both knew the United States would start off in Korea on the wrong foot. When Hodge tried to carry out his orders in Korea, he ran into a buzz saw of Korean outrage at the slightest suggestion that any of the hated Japanese officials should be retained for even a single day.

The Japanese, of course, held many prisoners of war in Japan at the time of surrender, both military as well as some civilians of American and various other nationalities, all of whom had to be repatriated. The Army asked the State Department for a Foreign Service Officer who could travel around Japan at the time of surrender, making contact with the civilian prisoners and establishing repatriation procedures. The Department told Steintorf in Manila to choose between me and Dick Richardson, which he wasn't about to do. So Dick and I drew cards, and for one of the few times in my life I won a gamble. Steintorf sent my name to Washington, and I readied myself to be the first State Department representative in Japan.

On September 1—the day before Japan signed the articles of surrender on the *Missouri* in Tokyo Bay—I received an urgent summons to Tokyo from MacArthur's headquarters. At dawn on September 5 I once again saw the unmistakable, stirring sight of Mt. Fuji, and by 8 A.M. I was stepping onto Japanese soil at Atsugi airfield, twenty miles outside Yokohama.

After a reconaissance, I finally located a harassed Eighth Army motor officer in a corner of a hangar at the far end of the strip. He promptly conjured out of the confusion a "liberated" Plymouth sedan, remarkably decrepit but still running, with an American driver whose masterly chauffeuring skills had been learned at the controls of an amphibious tank. Thus equipped we set off for Yokohama.

At first we saw few signs that a vast American army was in the process of occupying the country. Small villages appeared unchanged. Farmers were working their fields as always, and the rice crop looked healthy. Only occasional American soldiers were visibly scattered among the Japanese police guarding intersections. We knew that times had changed, however, when Japanese children playing by the roadside flashed "V for Victory" signs and grinned as we drove by.

We approached Yokohama itself from the hills that overlook the city from the south. The vista was an awesome testimony to American airpower. A flat, rusty-brown waste stretched to the horizon. We drove through deserted silent streets where I had once seen swarming millions shove and shout. The few Japanese we saw were apathetic, dazed, and spiritless. We had actually passed through the city and were heading for Tokyo before I could get my bearings.

We turned around and headed back to the waterfront, which was visible in the distance. Most banks, government buildings, warehouses, and piers in that area were still standing. Best of all, from my point of view, so was the American Consulate.

Prepared for the worst, I had arrived complete with sleeping bag, mess kit, emergency rations, and all the other paraphernalia of a well-equipped soldier (except a rifle; my weapon was a typewriter). All of it was tossed into the closet of my private room at the formerly sumptuous New Grand Hotel, still standing, incongruously maintaining its standards of service as if the war had never happened. Black-tie waiters served excellent meals, miraculously concocted from standard Army rations, on meticulously laundered linen with full sets of china and silver. Out my window I had the thrilling sight of a vast American armada at anchor in Yokohama harbor—the same harbor from which I had sailed on the *Asama Maru* only three years before. Instead of a sleeping bag I enjoyed my first hot-water bath and genuine soft bed since leaving San Francisco six months before. This was invasion de luxe.

The first night I walked down to the railroad station to observe the arrival and processing of several hundred POWs of many nationalities. It was very moving. The American group had fashioned a flag from the parachutes that had dropped supplies and clothes to them since surrender, and those able to walk marched joyfully down the platform. The remainder were borne by stretcher to waiting ambulances for a short journey to hospital ships docked nearby. The prisoners were dressed in the clothes that had been dropped to them and their eyes shone with joy and relief, but their haggard, sunken faces and bowed shoulders betrayed the years of hardship and anguish they had endured. A few shabbily dressed Japanese looked on impassively. Those of us who had observed the savagery of cornered Japanese troops in the Philippines considered it a miracle that any substantial number of American prisoners still survived.

The next day I inspected the consulate, which had escaped our bombs and had been kept in surprisingly good condition by its Swiss caretaker. Then I rode an Army jeep to Tokyo before American troops occupied the city. Not more than a hundred buildings were still standing along the twenty-mile route from Yokohama to Tokyo. In Tokyo itself the destruction was even more complete than in Yokohama—blocks and blocks heaped with charred rubble, wrecked cars, and twisted girders. I walked around the old shopping district where a few partially damaged department stores were still limping along (their only merchandise comprised a few can openers, some vases, underwear, toothbrushes, maps, and some drugs); apparently no one could afford anything since I was the only browser. Perhaps 90 or 95 percent of the prewar population had died, been evacuated, or fled in the face of the incoming American troops that Japanese Army propaganda had said were going to rape and kill. An almost surrealistic "ghost city" atmosphere emanated from the desolate expanses. In front of the Emperor's palace, where we sat in the shade munching our K-rations, a few older people shuffled up and prostrated themselves before the palace. I knew we had really won the war when several Kempeitai agents—arrogance and brutality personified when the Japanese Empire was riding high—meekly offered to trade *sake* for some of our rations.

That night, having returned to Yokohama, I was sitting in my room in the New Grand typing dispatches to the Department when an MP came up and said: "Jap woman downstairs wants to see you." Scarcely any Japanese remained in the city and I couldn't imagine who would want to see me, but I went down. There stood Kiyoko Matsuzawa, our children's nurse in Tokyo and Seoul, carrying a small bag of apples. It was extraordinary to see her. She said that she had left Tokyo when the big fire bombing raids started. She had been living with her relatives in northern Honshu when she heard of the surrender. She had learned that I had arrived in Yokohama and, though food was extremely scarce, managed to get hold of this bag of apples. She had taken a twenty-four-hour train ride to the outskirts of Tokyo, and since the train service had stopped between Tokyo and Yokohama, she had walked the rest of the way to Yokohama. This must have been enormously frightening for a single Japanese woman—an act of enormous courage, by which I was deeply touched. She asked nothing of me then, nor has she since. It was simply a friendly gesture. But then she was a very unusual woman. Some time later, entirely through her own abilities, she obtained concessions in American PXs to sell Japanese souvenirs and later started a very successful women's magazine.

Because the Japanese railways were in relatively good condition and Japanese officials were cooperative, this procedure for the quick repatriation of Allied prisoners was devised: those imprisoned in southern Honshu were sent to the port of Waka-no-ura, and those held in Kyushu were sent to the port of Nagasaki, before American forces had time to occupy those cities. The prisoners were met by Army-Navy shore parties landed from the sea. Interned civilians with special nationality problems began to accumulate at the ports as well, and someone was needed to help the officers in charge to sort them out. So after several days in Yokohama looking after civilians who had been sent there and trying to find some building where they could wait comfortably while we handled their applications in an orderly way, I was given a plane and crew to take me to Osaka, Nagoya, and Nagasaki.

The Japanese in Yokohama and Tokyo, I had written on September 8, "showed absolutely no sign of hostility. When I walked around without arms every policeman saluted; a dozen people jumped to answer any question." They seemed psychologically devastated by defeat, now unanimously convinced that they should cooperate with Americans, and trying diligently to figure out what acting "correctly" toward their conquerers required. Even so, my crew was not too keen on being the first "liberators" the Japanese in the areas we were going to visit had seen.

Our first stop was Osaka. We flew over the center of town, and a bunch of men who we could see were American prisoners came out onto the roof of a large building and waved their shirts. We located a usable airfield with difficulty, buzzed it several times, and landed. A group of Japanese Air Force soldiers came running out; my crew drew their guns. I told them to stay calm. In fact, it was clear to me that the Japanese were more scared than we. Just as Japanese sentries had been nervous in Tientsin whenever I approached a checkpoint, these Air Force men were tense because they didn't know how to behave toward foreigners. When I spoke Japanese and made simple requests—a car to take us into town and guards to be posted on the plane—they were visibly relieved and obeyed with alacrity. I set off with my crew for the New Osaka Hotel, where the American prisoners had been waving their shirts.

We saw during the drive that B-29s had pounded Osaka as severely as Tokyo and Yokohama, but many more people appeared to be on the streets. One of the most striking changes I noticed from pre-war Japan was the total disappearance of the *kimono* for women. Wartime austerity had prompted the government to substitute *mompei,* repulsive bilious-green pantaloons previously worn only by peasant women working the fields. Though Japanese women, repeatedly indoctrinated with the belief that Americans would be savage and rapacious conquerers, usually fled in terror when they glimpsed our uniforms, I doubt that GIs could have encountered anything less likely to arouse unlawful desires than a woman wearing those dreadful *mompei* padding down the street on broken wooden clogs.

The POW group at the New Osaka Hotel was amazing. Never have I been prouder of Americans abroad. These fellows had all suffered maltreatment from the Japanese, many quite severely. When the Emperor announced surrender, the Japanese guards had simply opened the prison gates. Instead of going on a rampage of revenge, the POWs moved into the hotel in Osaka and organized themselves into a disciplined, well-behaved military post. Over the hotel entrance, guarded by a British POW wearing an American uniform and carrying a Japanese rifle, flew the Stars and Stripes. At the reception desk sat another former prisoner who assigned us rooms and, with a practiced air, summoned a bellboy to carry our musette bags. In the lobby sat more former prisoners chatting quietly and drinking cold beer served by Japanese waitresses, and on the mezzanine the soldiers had established a full-scale, professional military headquarters. There were direct telephone links with all the principal POW camps and Yokohama, a "liaison office" where local Japanese government officials could work, a motorpool with several Japanese vehicles, and clerks, files, and typists. It was the most impressive demonstration possible to the Japanese of the initiative and self-restraint of the American soldier.

After lunch a shiny old Buick sedan with a Japanese driver was produced to transport me and two of my plane crew to Waka-no-ura. The car's perverse habit of stalling whenever the engine got warm combined with bad roads to stretch the estimated two-hour journey to five hours. When we reached the city limits of Waka-no-ura, we were startled to discover two files of police drawn up on either side of the road. It was alarmingly unclear whether these policemen might have devised some novel way of continuing the war, but my indecision about what to do was settled when the engine stalled just as we drew abreast of the two columns. As we coasted to a stop in the pouring rain, a man who identified himself as the Chief of Police took off his cap and executed a formal Japanese bow. This honor guard had been waiting for us in the downpour for eight hours. The Chief, declining my invitation to ride in the Buick, preceded us, bareheaded, in a motorcycle sidecar all the way to the port.

Thousands of POWs were streaming into Waka-no-ura, where Army and Navy shore parties were handling them just as in Yokohama. Few civilians were among them, however, so my services were not needed. But I was able to arrange transport for five freight cars' worth of excess relief supplies to Osaka, where distressed civilian internees could use them. Much to the dismay of local officials, who had arranged for me to stay in the province's finest inn, I had to return to Osaka for a 9:00 A.M. appointment. They obligingly produced a special train that got me there in 90 minutes, allegedly a new record.

The next day, September 15, we flew over Hiroshima to Nagasaki, where a Navy task force was due to enter to start processing prisoners. Most of the flight was over the Inland Waterway, which I had known previously as a furiously busy and crowded commercial highway; now only a few small fishing boats were visible. As to the atomic destruction of Hiroshima and Nagasaki, it has already been thoroughly chronicled, but in fact it was so vast that it can probably never be adequately described. I shall only say of it that it eclipsed anything I could then, or can now, imagine.

All the airstrips near Nagasaki had been ruined, so we landed about fifty miles away at a strip near Omura and were driven to the city in a Japanese Navy car. We passed large numbers of demobilized soldiers trudging along the roads. Dispirited and almost shell-shocked by Japan's defeat, they walked singly, avoiding each other. None displayed any hostility toward what must have been, for many, the first sight of an American uniform; surrender for the Japanese was psychologically total, in a way that few Americans can understand. We had seen it with captured Japanese soldiers during the war: At first they believed they could never honorably return to Japan, that capture had spiritually killed them. But after some time had passed, many did a complete about-face, embracing their new life fervently and even to the extent of exhorting their former comrades, over loudspeakers, to desert.

We drove through central Nagasaki's desolation to the harbor, where some piers were still intact. Just after we arrived, a barge and several landing craft were disgorged from one of the ships just entering the harbor and came storming up for an assault landing on both sides of the pier where I was standing. The first fellow off the barge was Captain Charles Rend, commander of the task force's flagship *Wichita* and our Naval Attaché in Rio de Janeiro when I was there. He was astonished and somewhat crestfallen to encounter a striped-pants diplomat instead of hostile Japanese, but we were both glad to see each other. I spent the night in his quarters on the *Wichita*.

On the day I returned to Tokyo, General Sutherland, MacArthur's Chief of Staff, called me into his office to say that General MacArthur hoped that the State Department would soon open a consulate in Yokohama. I was very pleased, because one FSO-7 toting a portable typewriter was hardly adequate to the workload. I had visited the consulate building an hour before and its Swiss caretaker had told me that General Eichelberger, Commander of the Eighth Army, had also been there that morning and planned to move in that afternoon. I pointed out to General Sutherland that if we were going to open an office, the logical place for it (and as far as I knew, the only place for it) was our former consulate. General Sutherland told me he would take care of it and I gave him a message to transmit to Washington informing the State Department of MacArthur's request. Sure enough, when I walked over to the building half an hour later to talk to the Swiss caretaker, I found that General Eichelberger's Eighth Army MPs had already been replaced by the GHQ MPs who had strict instructions to let no one enter without an order from General Sutherland himself. Though I had turned General Eichelberger out of a nice residence, we later became fast friends.

John Emmerson and Max Bishop had followed General MacArthur's move up to Tokyo. I joined them on September 19.

The only State Department representatives in the country, and quite junior ones at that, we were powerless to influence the huge and energetic Army occupation establishment—which is how General MacArthur wanted to keep it. His title was Supreme Commander, Allied Powers (SCAP), and he intended to be exactly that. When Undersecretary of State Dean Acheson made a statement in Washington on September 19 that included the phrase that the "occupation force (in Japan) are the instruments of policy and not the determinants of policy," MacArthur and his sycophantic staff took it as a direct assault on their command prerogatives and quickly let me know their displeasure. It was probably no accident that Senators Wherry and Chandler immediately attacked Acheson as "blighting the name of" MacArthur.

Their suspicions grew even darker when a press leak from Washington revealed that George Atcheson was going to be appointed as MacArthur's political advisor. General Sutherland immediately called me in to see what I knew about the matter, and it soon became clear they were confusing George Atcheson, a career Foreign Service Officer who had long experience in China, with Dean Acheson. Sutherland was greatly relieved to have this straightened out and dashed into MacArthur's office next door with the good news.

I had managed to establish good working relations with virtually every Army officer I encountered of all ranks, including MacArthur's immediate entourage, but we were never consulted or even informed on any matter of policy. It was clear that MacArthur meant to exclude the State Department from all important decisions, no matter what our individual personal relations might be. I regretted this attitude because I thought that we could be helpful without undermining the power base of MacArthur and his group. As I wrote the Department:

> It is no easy task to shift a gigantic military machine shaped for an assault on hostile shores to the vastly different mission of peacefully occupying and directing the civil government of an entire nation. Obviously, much of the staff eminently suited for the former mission are unsuited to the latter. . . . In the crucially important initial decisions the Commander-in-Chief's apparent advisors are not the best men available to the United States.

I felt that the military rulers, because they did not understand Japan, often took the path of least resistance, and thereby perpetuated some of the imperial system's worst features. For instance, the Army obtained local labor by requisition from prefectural governments, which simply sent out police to round workers up. MacArthur also prevented Army military government officers—the ones we had so laboriously trained in Chicago and elsewhere—from having direct contact with Japanese officials, so they were reduced to sitting in headquarters and reading reports instead of actually helping administer local areas.

As I saw more of the country and examined the results of interviews my consulate later conducted with thousands of *nisei* (persons born in the United States of Japanese parents) who had spent the war in Japan, I also began to wish that the Army had been more aware of Japanese realities during the war itself. It became my subjective judgment that the country had been effectively defeated by our submarine and mine warfare before our saturation bombing raids did any significant damage to the Japanese home islands. Japan's jugular was its almost complete dependence on foreign raw materials and supplies. Once we severed it—which we had, by early 1945—Japan's defeat was inevitable. I do not know when this slow strangulation could have been translated into the complete surrender that the atomic bombs produced in August 1945, but all subsequent inquiries indicate that the most important reason for continued popular support for resistance was a widespread conviction that we intended to execute the Emperor and abolish the monarchy. Various Americans, including former Ambassador Grew, had argued that we should retain the Imperial Institution and tell the Japanese so. Had we done this, I believe Japan might have surrendered in the spring of 1945, before Soviet entry into the Pacific war, before our heaviest firebomb raids, and before the atomic bombing of two primarily civilian targets.

Seoul

I was promptly removed from the treacherous political currents of MacArthur's headquarters by a request from General Sutherland to rejoin General Hodge, Commander of the XXIV Corps, now liberating Korea, ostensibly to assist in repatriating civilians. On September 22 I hitched a ride as the only passenger on a C-46 ferrying drums of aviation fuel to Seoul.

That evening I joined General Hodge and his staff on the balcony of their headquarters, the former Japanese Government General Building, reviewing American troops playing retreat in the courtyard. As a Vice Consul eight years before, I had known-

that building as the center of a repressive occupation aimed at crushing every vestige of Korean culture and self-respect. I never dreamed the Korean people would surmount it. Yet here I was witnessing the birth of an independent Korea, with the United States as its midwife. I felt very moved. And in a larger sense, my understanding of what was immutable in international affairs was receiving a severe jolt. Here was proof that the accepted order could sometimes be stood on its head. Dr. Syngman Rhee—
—the Methodist minister and pro-independence Korean firebrand in Washington whom I had always dismissed as a hopeless idealist—was right, and I, the "realist" who had never imagined Korean independence, was completely wrong. It was a good lesson.

The old consulate building, where I had cut my teeth on diplomatic work under "Guatemala" Marsh's unpleasant tutelage, had been pretty well cleaned out, so I went to the old royal palace to borrow some pots and pans. There, to my delight, I found my old cook, who soon was performing marvels with C-rations. Before long Merle Benninghoff, the State Department's appointed political advisor to General Hodge, arrived and joined me at the consulate; more important, I invited General Hodge's military government officer to live with me and through him kept my finger on what was happening.

Hodge's orders to retain Japanese officials had finally been rescinded. Now he faced the job of trying to establish some sort of native government and administrative structure. Unfortunately, the many Korean exile groups that had been fighting for Korean independence resented American control and knew how to agitate for freedom better than how to run their country. I thought Hodge a conscientious, able soldier and a more astute administrator than he has been given credit for, but as I have said, his original orders were wrong-headed and we started off poorly. I felt for him. Ironically, Korea was the only place where the Army made use of the military government officers we had trained in Chicago and elsewhere—the ones who had been trained exclusively for service in Japan.

Yokohama

On October 8 I returned to Japan. The Department had decided to reopen the Yokohama consulate, and I was designated its number two and told to get it functioning before my new boss, Bill

Turner, arrived. I had no staff, secretary or office supplies and was reduced to typing my own dispatches on old stationery I found lying around the building.

A vital step toward getting the consulate running was becoming friends with the major who was chief of staff of the quartermaster battalion that ran the port of Yokohama. Because the consulate was a large, beautiful building modeled after the White House with several apartments for staff, I was able to satisfy his desire for better quarters than were assigned to most majors. In return he became a ready source of everything including diesel generators, groceries, sheets, labor, and transport. It turned out to be a very happy arrangement for both of us.

By mid-October I learned that Bill Turner's assignment had been cancelled, leaving me in charge for the time being. A few former Japanese staff showed up and I hired them, but I had received no American help and no sign that any would be forthcoming. After much legwork I located a Red Cross girl who wanted to stay in Japan and said she could type, so Katy Harrington became my secretary. By October 28 we had done enough scrubbing, scrounging, begging, and organizing to open officially.

Business ballooned quickly. We found ourselves doing all the consular work for Japan, Okinawa, and the former Japanese Pacific islands. One of our first jobs was deciding the citizenship of some 15,000 *nisei*. Most of them were youngsters sent by their parents to Japan for schooling who then had to serve in the Japanese Army when war broke out. We had to screen them very carefully, developing an elaborate mechanism to find out what they had done during the war and the duress to which they had been subjected. Each case was also an absorbing human problem that required careful investigation and all the fairness and good judgment we could muster. The Department gave me a green light to develop whatever criteria and procedures I thought best, which is the way I like to work. Though it was distasteful to have to sit in judgment on thousands of people—basically determining whether they could return to their families and start a new life in the United States or be stuck in occupied Japan—I think I set up procedures that were fair both to the individuals and to the United States.

The crucial question for each *nisei* was the amount of duress to which the Japanese authorities had subjected him to convince him to contribute to war against the United States. The 1941 Immigration Act, which governed our determinations, permitted those who had served in the Japanese Army to retain their-

American citizenship only if the duress was considerable. Several *nisei* who had lost their citizenship under the 1941 Act brought suit against the State Department with the aid of their families in the United States and the American Civil Liberties Union. The courts, particularly the federal district court in Honolulu, turned out to be extremely lenient and defined almost any amount of official pressure as "duress." We had to change our procedures accordingly, and several thousand *nisei* applications were still pending when I left Yokohama in 1949.

Other consular activities included issuing passports for American personnel in Japan, administering funds sent from the United States for American civilian repatriates, searching for missing Americans, helping European refugees emigrate to the United States, and issuing visas for Japanese who wished to travel to the United States.

One particularly resourceful visa applicant was a White Russian woman, officially stateless, who had remained in Japan during the war and now wanted to emigrate to the United States. Unfortunately, Japanese police records suggested that her moral career had been such that I had to refuse her application. She was, among many other things, a singer of sorts. In the mail I soon received a song she had composed, with many verses, whose refrain was "Let me go, Mr. Johnson; I will be good." She actually made a record of the song and even embroidered it onto a pillow. Although I felt enterprise should be rewarded, I still had to continue to refuse her.

Another major consulate activity was marriages. Our marriage mill expanded dramatically in 1947, when Congress passed a law permitting GIs to bring back foreign wives to the United States if they married by August 21. Though the law was aimed at Europe, it unleashed an unforeseen flood of weddings in Japan. In the month before the deadline we married 883 couples. They would start assembling outside our doors at 7:00 A.M., and by 9:30 the line would extend out to the street. Many, of course, were only for formalizing an established fact; one of our "blushing brides" went into labor saying the "I do's" and we had to call an ambulance to rush her to the hospital. Our final customer, at 11:55 P.M., August 21, was brought in on the arms of MPs who had arrested him for speeding as he hurried toward the consulate. After the ceremony they took him to the stockade. Not surprisingly, in the following months we were smothered with birth registrations.

As the work grew, I sent officers periodically to Okinawa and Kobe to save people the trouble of coming to Yokohama, and eventually opened full-time branch offices there. FSOs and experienced clerks were in extremely short supply because the State Department's responsibilities expanded significantly after the war, but the American community in Japan grew so quickly—in addition to military personnel, 30,000 dependents and 10,000 civilian employees by the end of 1947—that the personnel division in Washington tried to be especially accommodating to Yokohama. Harold Tewell, with whom I had worked in Rio, was Chief of Personnel, and as my needs grew, Harold sent me a series of fresh Foreign Service Officers. Most of them had served in the military and some were very fluent in Japanese. They were outstanding men and delightful to work with.

My basic policy was, as I reported to the Department, "to give people the kind of treatment in our office that they do not ordinarily receive in most Army offices; in general, it seems to be noted and appreciated." The key to running a good consulate, I believed, lay in instinctively wanting to say "yes" instead of "no" whenever possible. I tried to convey this spirit to the staff. I quoted "Scattergood Baines," a fictional Will Rogers-type character, in a memo to the consulate in early 1948:

> A shortcomin' of heaps of folks is they hain't got no idee jest what their work is. They get a job, mebbe like your'n. With alot of rules to it. Sure, they got to enforce the rules. But the chief aim of a job like your'n hain't compellin' people to obey rules. It's finding a way so as people won't notice the rules and git riled by 'em. Nobuddy ever gits mad at a law he didn't notice. Ye kin even git people to enj'y quinine if ye make it taste like vaniller ice cream. It's a knack.

I've never found a more pungent description of how I feel bureaucrats should approach their work.

Pat and the four children sailed to Yokohama on the first transport carrying dependents, the *General Meigs,* in May 1946. That finally ended our spate of protracted separations until I went to Saigon in 1964. It was wonderful to see them again; the children and I had almost become strangers to each other after my long absence.

The city itself began to resemble American suburbia because the influx of American personnel prompted the Army to throw up a profusion of pre-fabs and California-style stucco bungalows in the areas that bombing had wiped out. There were American-style theaters, supermarkets, and even drive-in soda-fountains, "one of which," I wrote, "is almost in front of the Yo-kohama main railroad station so that the waiting Japanese can stand and drool at the forbidden fruits of democracy."

I did not always think the Army particularly sensitive to the impression it created among Japanese, but the Occupation machinery was a juggernaut I was certainly in no position to influence. As I wrote a State Department colleague in March 1946: "The administrative organization out here is becoming fantastic. There are around 15,000 people doing a job that literally 150 could perform much more efficiently. I sit on the sidelines and have a lot of fun just watching. If they ran out of mimeograph paper, the whole administration would collapse tomorrow."

From the Occupation's outset GHQ issued rigid instructions forbidding "fraternization" between Americans and Japanese. This applied to all personnel, including dependents and civilians serving with the Occupation. The orders not only forbad Americans from entering Japanese homes and restaurants, but also prevented any Japanese from entering any Occupation facility or home, even on invitation. While this policy may have somewhat inhibited harassment of Japanese by Occupation forces, and very slightly stemmed the growth of the flourishing black market, it also prevented any meaningful contact between Americans and the few well-educated Japanese remaining in the cities. The result was two worlds living side by side with no real communication between them. The Japanese-speaking Foreign Service Officers assigned to Tokyo found ways of maintaining discreet contact with a few Japanese there. In Yokohama, however, American forces occupied almost every remaining building and home, so I had virtually no contact with Japanese except those visiting the office on business.

The Japanese were enormously relieved and grateful that our troops were not brutal or excessive, and that the basic aims of Occupation policy were relatively benign. But they understandably resented being classed as pariahs in their own country. As time passed, however, the good sense of people on both sides prevailed and relations became increasingly normal.

The United States maintained no embassy in Tokyo when I was consul in Yokohama because the American Occupation Army was in charge of Japan's government. But George Atcheson, whom I have mentioned, did run the State Department shop in Tokyo. As MacArthur would not tolerate anything called "political advisor," the office was called the Diplomatic Section of GHQ. George also sat as MacArthur's deputy on the Allied Council for Japan, of which the Soviets were a member. MacArthur, its chairman, never went near the Council (with whom he was supposed to consult). George's job was to make sure that the Council never did anything. He succeeded, though the Soviet representative and some others became increasingly shrill as it dawned on them that MacArthur was not going to have anything substantive to do with them.

George's executive secretary, Jack Service (later run out of the State Department by McCarthyite hysteria), caught jaundice and had to be relieved; then his replacement, a fellow language student and especially close friend of mine named Beppo Johanssen, died of a heart attack. I was the only other FSO who had experience with the Occupation setup, so George made me his Executive Officer in July 1946, while I was still consul in Yokohama. The Yokohama staff was good and our procedures were fairly settled, so I was able to commute to Tokyo each morning and let the consulate more or less run itself, returning to handle a few of the most urgent problems in the evening.

General MacArthur, or "The General," as he was universally known, had been very careful to freeze Atcheson out of virtually everything. Our office was strategically placed eight blocks distant from MacArthur's headquarters. All communications to or from Washington had to go through SCAP. Occasionally MacArthur's staff threw us a few crumbs, but we were rigorously excluded from all fundamental determinations of policy. MacArthur's autocratic style meant that people in the State Department who had devoted their lives to understanding Japan were eclipsed in power by untrained Army officers.

Had MacArthur been a typical Army officer, this could have spelled disaster for the Occupation, Japan, and the United States. But MacArthur was a sort of genius, whose virtues were as pronounced as his faults. Certainly he was vastly egocentric and surrounded himself with small-minded sycophants who were extremely hostile toward advice or inquiry from "outsiders," whom they defined as virtually anyone. Directives from Washington were always handled as if MacArthur stood outside (or, rather, above) the normal chain of command, and were obeyed only if helpful to the General's image. Subordinate officers outside MacArthur's immediate court were simply cast into the outer darkness, their achievements drowned out by MacArthur's inveterate publicity-hogging. Four-star General Robert Eichelberger, commander of MacArthur's Eighth Army and an extremely able officer, grew so frustrated that in talking to me he usually referred to his chief as "the man who walks on water" and "Sarah" (for the great actress Sarah Bernhardt). In the July 4, 1946 military parade in Tokyo, MacArthur even made Eichelberger march past him on foot while MacArthur grandly stood on the reviewing platform. Eichelberger was furious at being the first four-star American general ever ordered to do a "march past."

Yet MacArthur's imperial demeanor, his grandiloquence and aloofness, meshed well with the Japanese idea of a ruler. His unquestioned military ability and the enormous charm and persuasive powers he could turn on also won him support from many influential Americans and thus guaranteed him considerable freedom of action. Time and again I saw groups of Congressmen, newspaper publishers, businessmen—not unsophisticated people—arrive at MacArthur's residence seething with anger at this or that policy, and emerge after lunch (the only meal at which MacArthur entertained visitors) placated and even enthusiastic.

As Atcheson's Executive Officer I was only on the fringes of high policy, but as consul in Yokohama I suspect I got a better view of the Occupation's effects on the Japanese than did MacArthur's Tokyo entourage. The basic object of the Occupation, of course, was to remake Japanese society so that its tendencies toward militarism and imperialism would be forever crushed. The policies MacArthur adopted to accomplish that object reflected MacArthur's enigmatic, often self-contradictory genius. The General considered himself the embodiment and agent of a highly idealized version of American democracy. While most of his immediate lieutenants were ultra-conservative—Courtney Whitney, chief of the military government section, was a politically reactionary businessman with substantial holdings in the Philippines; Lawrence Bunker, his chief aide, later became president of the John Birch Society—MacArthur also imported a horde of liberal social experimenters in education, land reform, and welfare who sought to recast Japanese institutions to conform with their staunchly progressive theories. This dichotomy of approach often resulted in oddly contrasting policies.

Probably the soundest of the Occupation's policies was land reform, which ended centuries of impoverished tenancy and promoted a dramatic increase in agricultural productivity and farmers' incomes. Wolf Ladajinski was in charge and executed his plans carefully. Absentee landlords had to divest themselves of all holdings over two and a half acres; owner-farmers could keep up to seven and a half acres.

In other areas, state support was removed from the Shinto religion. The public school system was reorganized around local school boards; the curriculum was changed to promote critical questioning instead of rote obedience. The Diet was restructured to breathe life into the country's political party system; police administration was decentralized. Other countries seeking transformations of such magnitude and liberalism in this century have turned to Marxism; but in Japan its unlikely agent was the American Army.

Other reforms had less firm foundation. Attempts to break up the *zaibatsu,* Japan's industrial conglomerates, foundered because they impeded the country's economic recovery and failed to acknowledge that Japan had no ready class of small entrepreneurs to replace the giants. Some of the education reforms (for instance, changing the grade level at which children advanced from primary to secondary school) simply upset the Japanese without achieving anything. And the new Japanese Constitution demonstrated unbelievable political myopia for a person of MacArthur's stature and experience. (He failed to consult with Washington about its contents.) Its renunciation of war and armed forces in Article Nine was an understandable emotional reaction given the long war, but MacArthur should have allowed for the possibility that some self-defense forces for a vigorous modern country like Japan might someday serve his country's interests. The Soviet Union's bellicosity toward Japan made Article Nine seem obsolete as early as 1948, but it still exists, inhibiting Japan from shouldering its legitimate share of defense responsibilities. The starriest-eyed pacifist would not have dared insert so bold a provision into Japan's fundamental law, but MacArthur, one of America's greatest soldiers, did.

I relinquished my Tokyo duties in December 1946, and happily returned to full-time consular work in Yokohama, though I still remained close to Atcheson. In August 1947, MacArthur agreed to let George go to Washington to start work on a peace treaty with Japan. I went to Haneda airfield to see him off, and was a little disturbed to see him crawl into the converted bomb bay of an old B-17 instead of the C-54 used by the General. Colonels Larr and Russell, good friends of mine from MacArthur's staff, joined him there. The next day we heard that the plane had crashed and Atcheson, Larr and Russell had been killed. I am sure that George's death set back the conclusion of a Japanese peace treaty by several years, since he was beginning to obtain MacArthur's confidence and had high standing in Washington.

In 1945, when I was ordered to open the Yokohama consulate as its number two under Bill Turner, I had not been particularly pleased by the assignment. It turned out, however, that no job has ever done my career more good before or since. My work in Yokohama, combined with the repatriation activities I had directed in the Philippines and Japan at war's end, won me the Medal of Freedom in 1946 from General MacArthur. And in 1947 I was promoted to Consul General. By the time I returned to the United States in 1949, I had reached FSO-2, the highest rank but two. I often cite this example of unanticipated good fortune to young officers wondering if they should take an assignment that seem undesirable; my advice is always "take what comes and make the best of it."

Much as I liked Japan and admired the Japanese, I cannot say that I ever fell in love with the country. But this was not the case with many of my compatriots. Some Army officers would arrive in Tokyo exuberant members of the "shoot-all-the-yellow-bellied-bastards" school, but take them to a *geisha* house, expose them or their wives to flower arranging and *kabuki,* and overnight they would become pro-Japan zealots. Many Foreign Service Officers became permanently entranced with Japan's fascinating language and literature, its highly formal art and complex social relations.

To fall in love with your country of assignment is a common enough affliction in the Foreign Service, especially contagious in Japan, but for good or ill I never caught it. I spoke Japanese adequately, enjoyed the country and its customs, and liked its people, but I never felt any mystical communion with its national spirit or thought of it a second home. I do not think that this interfered with my effectiveness. The Japanese are extremely tight-knit and believe that "Japaneseness" can only be conferred by birth, never acquired. They feel patronized and uncomfortable when Americans and other foreigners try to ape them. By keeping my distance, I fit in naturally with Japanese custom, which promotes formality in human relationships. And along the way, I think I may have helped enhance the respect the Japanese had for the country I represented.

·CHAPTER FIVE·

Korea:
War and Peace

THE RELATIONSHIP BETWEEN FOREIGN SERVICE OFFICERS IN THE field and our headquarters in Washington is curious. Obviously there would be no Foreign Service without the State Department. FSOs generally find Washington assignments attractive because they provide an opportunity for sustained influence over the information and advice that the President and other senior officials require to make important foreign policy decisions. But the fundamentals of our work, and much of its excitement, come from representing the United States abroad. For me, and I think for most FSOs, "home" is really abroad. Washington may be the center of power, but work in the field is our raison d'etre.

So it was with some misgivings that I boarded the S.S. *President Wilson* in the fall of 1949, returning with my family to the United States to take up the new job the Department had assigned me, Deputy Director of the Office of Northeast Asian Affairs, which handled Korea and Japan. Since I had never done a tour of duty in Washington, it was appropriate for me to learn the ropes in Foggy Bottom. It was also appealing to contemplate leading a "normal life" with my family in the United States for the first time since 1935. But I was not enthusiastic about trading my position as consulate-general, where I had independence and local importance, for the relative anonymity and powerlessness of being a middle-level Washington cog. Moreover, General MacArthur ran Japan by studiously ignoring the State Department, and Korea presented no problems of special interest. When I got to Washington, my predecessor commiserated with me over my bad luck at getting such a sleepy backwater to preside over.

We arrived in a much bigger and busier Washington than we had known before the war, bought a house, and I prepared to settle down to my new job and an orderly nine-to-five life. During my first week back, however, Harold Tewell, the feisty Chief of Foreign Service Personnel who had been so resourceful at filling my requests for workers in Yokohama, asked me to serve on one of the 1949 Foreign Service Selection Boards. These boards were a recent innovation. Mandated by a 1946 act that reorganized the Foreign Service, they replaced a system in which the Director of Personnel had sole discretion in recommending promotions. These new boards, composed of FSOs, officials from other government departments, and distinguished private citizens— eight in total—reviewed the files on an entire class of FSOs and ranked them by deciles, based on their cumulative written performance records rather than one person's subjective whim. This system is still used and I do not know of any system in government or private business that is better designed to achieve objectivity. There were three boards, each of which evaluated several classes. After we passed our recommendations back to the Personnel Division, promotions were announced based on how many new officers of each class were needed.

I found the process to be fair and an extremely interesting overview of the whole Service. The efficiency reports written by each officer's boss were confidential, so they were usually trenchant and reliable; but the Service was small enough that we knew which ones had to be discounted for personal reasons. Especially useful were the reports of Foreign Service Inspectors, who visited each post every few years and rated the strengths and weaknesses of every officer there. Our biggest difficulty was determining the lowest ten percent, who could be dismissed; the Service didn't really have that many "losers," and among the lowest decile there might be many officers doing good jobs and very much worth keeping, though not worth promoting. The Selection Boards took several months to do their job, so only in February did I take up my real job as Deputy Director of Northeast Asian Affairs (NEA).

I was quickly caught up in a strenuous pace of work as we wrestled with problems of the Japanese peace treaty and dealing with President Rhee in Korea, and I often found myself at the office Saturdays and Sundays. To compensate for my frequent absences from home, I promised my boys in the summer of 1950 to take their Boy Scout troop on a weekend hiking trip in the Blue Ridge Mountains. On the morning of Saturday, June 24, we set out in my stationwagon and spent a very revitalizing day climbing the hills of the national park, far from Foggy Bottom, recharging our lungs with crisp mountain air and setting up our little campsite of pup tents. The next morning we climbed some more, and then, as we were heading back toward camp, a Forest Ranger rushed up the trail. "Is your name U. Alexis Johnson?" he asked. "The State Department's been trying to reach you all night."

We returned to the ranger station and established a very bad connection to the Department on the field telephone. An assistant to Dean Rusk, the Assistant Secretary of State for Far Eastern Affairs, came on the line, but there was so much static and commotion in his office that I couldn't make out what he was saying. So I called Pat, who said the Department had been phoning frantically to tell me I was supposed to attend a United Nations Security Council meeting in New York at 1:00 that afternoon. It was already 11:00 A.M. I knew the Security Council never met on a Sunday, and even if it did it could not involve me, so I was sure she had gotten the message mixed up. But something major was clearly afoot, and I figured I had better return to Washington quickly. The Rangers offered to fly me in a light plane they had nearby, but as none of the boys was old enough to drive, I had no choice but to take the car through the Sunday traffic all the way to Washington. I had no radio in the car so I couldn't find out what the commotion was about. After I dropped each of the boys off I went home, where I finally learned from Pat what was happening; North Korea had attacked South Korea.

I washed my face, changed my clothes, hurried to the office, and didn't return for three days. Niles Bond, the Korean Desk Officer who worked for me, had attended the Security Council meeting in my place, but I had plenty to do. My direct boss, John Allison, the Director of NEA, was in Japan with John Foster Dulles working on the Japanese peace treaty; Allison's boss, Deputy Assistant Secretary of State for Far Eastern Affairs Livie Merchant, was put in charge of all the non-Korean aspects of Far Eastern affairs. That left me to work with Assistant Secretary Rusk on Korea, and as Rusk became the Department's center of gravity on the war I became his man Friday and alter ego. When Allison left his job in February 1951 to assist Dulles full-time on the Japanese treaty, I replaced him as Director of NEA, and in November I was promoted to replace Livie Merchant as Deputy Assistant Secretary, Rusk's immediate subordinate in name as well as fact. Then Rusk left the Department the following month to become President of the Rockefeller Foundation; Allison replaced

him, and left me to handle the bulk of work on Korea, as did
Allison's replacement, Walter Robertson, when the Republicans
came to power in 1953. My titles changed, but my job remained
essentially the same—"chief executive officer" for Korea in the
State Department, running the day-to-day administration of our
policy.

I do not wish to overstate my role, which was not fundamental to the course our policy took. The Korean War received
the deepest attention of the President and Secretary of State—
first Truman and Acheson, then Eisenhower and Dulles—and of
the Secretaries of Defense and the Joint Chiefs of Staff as well.
It was they who set the basic lines of our policy; I was only a
construction foreman who designed windows and doors and put
in the bricks and mortar according to their master plan. But minus
the first twelve hours when I was hiking with the Boy Scouts, I
was the highest-ranking person in the Department to have sustained involvement with Korea through both the Truman and
Eisenhower Administrations from the beginning of the war in
June 1950 to the signing of the armistice in July 1953.

A great deal has already been written about the Korean
War. There are no major secrets left to reveal. For me to relate
a minutely detailed history of the war would duplicate what exists
elsewhere and would be inappropriate to a memoir of this sort.
Instead, I will say something about the intense official activity the
war generated in Washington. The subject deserves more than a
cursory glance, for the war was a major watershed in America's
postwar military and foreign affairs, and in its wake came many
developments that set the basic framework of our Far Eastern
policy for a generation.

Certainly the Korean War moved my career onto a different plane. Instead of wading listlessly in a bureaucratic backwater
as I had feared when I left Yokohama, I was working all-out on
the leading foreign policy problem of the United States, with
regular access to the senior officials of State and Defense and not
infrequently the President. Thus I received a "total immersion"
course in operating in Washington, and left Foggy Bottom in 1953
as an ambassador, a considerable speed-up of the normal promotion process.

Prelude to Invasion

The very fact that I was hiking with a bunch of Boy Scouts on
the day the Korean War started shows how little Washington

expected the attack. I mentioned in the last chapter how I had observed the first weeks of the American liberation of Korea in September 1945 and tried to help General Hodge settle the thorny problem of who would take control of administering the country from the hated Japanese. In the intervening five years Korea had had a rough go of it, once more the recipient of undesired attentions from countries far greater than itself.

The basic features of the postwar Korean political landscape had been set by the Allies during the war. At the Cairo conference in December 1943, Roosevelt, Stalin, Churchill and Chiang Kai-shek had agreed that "in due course Korea shall become free and independent," though the exact form this self-determination should take was not clear. At Potsdam, the United States, Britain, and Russia agreed that they and China should govern Korea as trustees, leading to independence when the country was sufficiently well-organized for self-government. All parties also agreed that Soviet troops should accept Japanese surrender in the north of Korea and American troops in the south (the exact dividing line, the 38th parallel, was suggested by an Army staff colonel just returned from the Far East named Dean Rusk).

The Soviets moved into the northern part of Korea in August 1945, just as Japan was surrendering. General Hodge did not arrive in the south for nearly another month—accurately reflecting how differently the two countries perceived Korea's strategic importance. The United States, preoccupied with Japan, considered Korea a territory of secondary significance. But Russia—which shares ten miles of border with Korea near Vladivostok, and had fought Japan periodically to dominate it since the 1890s—thought it vital. One look at a map reveals the following reason why: Thrusting out of the Asia mainland like a dagger aimed toward Japan, only 100 miles away, and sitting between Japan and China, Korea would provide an excellent springboard for projecting Russian power elsewhere in Asia. Conversely, the Kremlin reasoned, if Korea fell into anti-Soviet hands, the point of the dagger might be reversed. Unlike the United States, which, following Roosevelt's dictum, was content to take up postwar political questions postwar, the Soviet Union keenly perceived the need to acquire strategic real estate at war's end. Korea was high on the acquisition list.

With a relentlessness indicating considerable advance planning, Korea, north of the 38th parallel, was turned into a Soviet-model communist satellite. Under the watchful eye of a Soviet-advised "people's militia," the Communist Party took control of the government, nationalized industry, and confiscated and redistributed landlords' estates. "Reeducation," vast propaganda campaigns, repression of opposing groups, and other unhappy consequences of communist takeover that were manifested equally in Eastern Europe at the time became central features of life in the North.

In the South the American military authorities tried to let the Koreans work out their own political future, which a fantastic multiplicity of contending factions made exceedingly difficult. The official policy favoring eventual unification also made Hodge reluctant to unfetter political activity completely until the form of the future national government became more definite.

As the communists consolidated their control in the North, the possibility of unification seemed more remote. Nevertheless, the December 1945 Foreign Ministers' Conference in Moscow agreed that a joint Soviet-American commission should see to the creation of a unified Korean government under a five-year international trusteeship. This plan outraged Koreans both North and South, who were fed up with foreign involvement in their politics. Riots swept the country. Nor could the United States and the Soviet Union agree in this joint commission on which Korean political parties to consult on the formation of a provisional government; the Soviets wished to exclude all non-communists. The commission failed to achieve anything, and the stalemate between North and South, Washington and Moscow continued.

The dominant South Korean figure was the seventy-year-old Dr. Syngman Rhee, the feisty and mercurial emigré leader I had known slightly in Washington as a fellow member of Foundry Methodist Church. He returned to the South in October 1945, and quickly set to work organizing an ultranationalist party espousing instant complete independence and unification at all costs, including war. With scant regard for democratic niceties, his party strong-armed moderate opposition. American policy still favored a gradual process of independence that we hoped would leave room for some negotiated solution with the North on rejoining the country. This appeared increasingly dubious, however, as the violently anti-communist Rhee came to dominate the South and the communists continued to make the North into a rigid Soviet carbon copy. We decided to increase Korean political control in the South gradually. We faced the same dilemma in Germany and Berlin; either we permitted unification immediately—on Stalin's terms—or we let normal political and economic life in our zones revive, which would inevitably bind them closer to us and make reunification hopeless. But half a country non-communist was better than none—for the people concerned and for us. In December 1946 a legislative assembly to advise the military government was created as the first step on a road to building a stable South Korean government.

In September 1947 the United States turned over the unification problem to the United Nations. Perhaps, we thought, the UN could manage to unify the country. If not, which was more likely, a South Korean government brought to life under UN auspices would at least have more international legitimacy than American sponsorship could confer. In November, over Soviet objection, the UN General Assembly agreed to a plan whereby a UN Commission on the Unification and Rehabilitation of Korea (UNCURK) would conduct general elections throughout the country leading to the establishment of a national government, after which Soviet and American troops would withdraw from the country. The commission began to function in January 1948 but was completely excluded from North Korea. Nevertheless, in February it announced plans for May general elections. Due to continued Soviet resistance, these occurred only in the South. Syngman Rhee's party won a majority of the 198-seat assembly, and in August 1948 he became President of the new Republic of Korea (ROK), which brought the end of American military government. In September the communists responded by hastily conducting their own elections in the North, which led to the proclamation of the Democratic People's Republic. Both governments claimed jurisdiction over all Korea, but in December 1948 the UN declared the ROK the only legitimate government on the peninsula.

Soviet and American troops withdrew as the governments of their respective allies got under way. Some State Department officials, notably Dean Rusk, then Deputy Undersecretary, John Allison and Walt Butterworth, Assistant Secretary for Far Eastern Affairs, had argued that a token American force should be left in South Korea as a symbol of our commitment, but the Pentagon was feeling severe budget constraints, and Secretary of Defense Louis Johnson and the Army Chief of Staff, General Dwight Eisenhower, had wanted to redeploy the troops elsewhere. We did not leave South Korea completely in the lurch, however; total aid for 1950 was pegged at $220 million, and we left a small team of advisors to help develop the fledgling South Korean Army.

The Republic of Korea had much to surmount in its infancy. With about 70 percent of the peninsula's total population and less than half of its land area, the ROK was poor and agricultural, possessing much less industry than the North. Its economy, which had been totally intertwined with Japan's, needed a major overhaul, which the American military authorities had neither the expertise nor the power to administer, especially in the uncertain political climate. Land reform—meaning a redistribution of former Japanese holdings—began in 1948, but the Conservative interests dominating Rhee's government lobbied to gain control of the program. The government probably reflected popular sentiment accurately in placing the attainment of national strength before civil rights or liberal social policies, but it was corrupt in the Chiang Kai-shek mold and treated its opponents harshly. We used what leverage we had with the unpredictable Rhee to promote political moderation and economic reform, but he was not overly interested in our advice.

Meanwhile, North Korea rapidly developed a Soviet-model economy under the leadership of Kim Il-sung. Massive Soviet aid spurred industrial production and especially aided the growth of North Korean armed forces; more than 100 tanks, 250 aircraft and smaller weapons of all sorts were delivered to Kim's troops. (We did not equip ROK forces similarly because we feared Rhee would attack the North if he were strong enough.) Perhaps emboldened by its military and economic superiority, the North fomented a large campaign of terrorist riots, strikes, and other public disorders in the South—an action that consumed much of the Rhee government's time and money. By 1950, however, the embryo ROK Army had restored order and Kim recognized that *agents provocateurs* could never catalyze a collapse of the South. On June 25, 1950, well-equipped North Korean forces swept into the South in a carefully planned invasion.

There has been some talk recently, among journalists and historians, that Kim Il-sung masterminded the invasion more or less on his own, with the knowledge, but not the active connivance, of the Kremlin. Our own National Security Council and State Department assessments of where the Soviets might make trouble at that time did not rank Korea highly because it was close to our bases and far from Soviet ones, so I suppose it is at least arguable that the invasion was a bit of local adventurism by an overexuberant client. But I do not accept this theory. We will probably never have access to the Soviet archives that could settle the question, but it strains one's credulity to imagine that a Soviet-installed puppet would undertake to conquer a country whose government had just been established by the United Nations and was adjacent to American-occupied Japan, at a time of bitter East-West tension over Eastern Europe and Mao's victory in China, without complete advance approval from the Kremlin. George Kennan, who was just taking leave from the Department in 1950 after heading its Policy Planning Staff, says in his memoirs that he thought the invasion might reflect Soviet anger at our developing plans to base American troops in Japan permanently and to conclude a unilateral Japanese peace treaty. Perhaps. But whatever prompted Kim to order the attack, this is certain: At the time no responsible official in the United States or among our allies seriously questioned that the aggression was Soviet-inspired and aimed principally at testing our resolve.*

The United States Response

Fast footwork by Secretary of State Dean Acheson led to the convening of a UN Security Council meeting on Sunday, June 25 (the one I had to miss), which voted unanimously (due to the providential absence of Soviet delegate Jacob Malik, who was boycotting to protest the presence of Chinese Nationalist representatives) to condemn the "breach of the peace" caused by the North Korean invasion. The vote called for an immediate cease-fire and a withdrawal of North Korean troops to the 38th parallel. President Truman returned from his home in Independence, Missouri, and for the rest of the week held sessions with his chief advisors to determine how we should respond in case North Korea did not heed the Security Council. Militarily the ROK forces were routed. Surprise and superior Soviet-supplied armor gave the communists a significant advantage that they exploited fully, and it became obvious that only American intervention could prevent the invaders from pushing the ROK forces into the sea. General MacArthur, Commander in Chief of our forces in the Far East, confirmed after a hazardous front-line inspection that sending American troops was necessary to prevent the South Koreans' total defeat.

---

*Khrushchev's memoirs confirm our initial hunch. They indicate that, while Kim originated the idea of the invasion, it had Stalin and Mao's blessings. (*Khrushchev Remembers*, p. 368)

What President Truman, Secretary Acheson, Secretary of Defense Louis Johnson and the Joint Chiefs of Staff, chaired by General Omar Bradley, had to determine before shaping the American response was what this invasion meant in a larger strategic sense. Was it the start of World War III, or simply a test of how forcefully we were prepared to resist communist advances in areas far removed from our own shores and those of our Western European allies? They concluded that Korea was not likely to signal World War III. But they also believed strongly that the chances of a major conflict would vastly increase if we stood by and did nothing while communist aggression wiped out an independent country of which we were the acknowledged protector, and which was important to the security of Japan. Very much in the background of their deliberations were their vivid memories of how the Western democracies appeased Hitler before the war.

On Friday, June 30, the President ordered that an American Regimental Combat Team be sent from Japan as the first step in a large commitment of American ground troops. We also introduced a UN Security Council resolution calling for other members to give Korea whatever help it needed to repel the attack. It again passed unanimously, thanks to Malik's convenient boycott.

Two important features of the American involvement were clear from the outset. First, we were fighting a limited war for limited objectives. Washington did not think the Soviet Union wanted a general war, and we did not wish to make it one. For example, Truman ordered the United States 7th Fleet to the Taiwan Strait, not only to protect Taiwan from Chinese Communist invasion while we were occupied elsewhere, but also to prevent Chiang Kai-shek from taking advantage of the international chaos to attack the mainland, which could easily have provoked a huge conflagration. We also refused Chiang's "generous" offer of 30,000 troops, which were needed in Taiwan anyway and could only have turned Korea into a new battleground for the Chinese Civil War. A unified Korea had been an objective of UN policy since the November 1947 General Assembly resolution; if we succeeded in arms this objective might become realistically possible and something we would have to weigh. Our basic policy, however, was to drive the invaders out of South Korea without provoking a wider war and to beat them badly enough so they could not repeat their aggression.

Second, the measures Truman ordered met with nearly unanimous support, from the State Department, the Pentagon, legislators of both parties, public opinion, and our allies. The need to respond to this blatant aggression was clearly perceived, and the carefully conceived nature of our response was widely applauded. Even General MacArthur, whose proconsular ambitions later inspired him to machinate for a general anti-communist war in the Pacific, understood and approved of Washington's desire to win decisively a limited conflict. Having this phalanx of supporters was a great initial asset, even though our allies' military contributions were largely token.

My contributions in these beginning days were slight. When I reached the Department on Sunday, we received a cable from our Ambassador in Seoul, John Muccio, a career officer of great ability and good sense, which we interpreted as implying that he might stay in Seoul to the bitter end. I drafted a cable, approved by the Secretary, telling him not to be rash and above all not let himself or his staff be taken hostage by the North Koreans. Muccio quickly replied he had no such intention. I also worked on setting forth the practical and legal considerations governing our blockade of North Korea and with the JCS staff in drafting messages to the field to implement decisions that were pouring down from more senior levels.

India, and to a lesser extent Britain, kept trying to convince us to accept international mediation and a negotiated settlement to stop the fighting. Britain was still basking in the twilight of Empire and thought it had a thing or two to teach us about the Russians. India, newly independent, was proudly pursuing a course of "neutralism," which to us usually appeared naive if not malicious. Both countries wanted us to offer concessions in return for an end to the Korean fighting by softening our position on Taiwan to permit an outright forced trade of the island to the Chinese Communists, or at least permitting UN membership for Peking. We thought these concessions, or any attempt to negotiate while we were still losing the war, extremely dangerous. I spent much time in the first months of the war trying to persuade British and Indian Embassy officers to see the Korean conflict our way and in deflecting their peace initiatives at the UN.

Actually, diplomacy, by definition, had to be somewhat inactive in the opening days of the war. Besides working out the mechanics of accepting support from other allies and establishing the UN command under General MacArthur, the State Depart-

ment could do nothing to end the war until MacArthur constructed a platform of military accomplishment from which we
could bargain. His first troops sent to help the retreating ROK
forces were largely fresh draftees with little training and no combat experience. They took a tremendous pounding but managed
to hold a 50 by 80 mile rectangle around Pusan, in the southeast
tip of the country. On September 15, however, in a move
MacArthur himself rated a 5,000-to-one chance, and which at first
the Joint Chiefs of Staff unanimously opposed, the Far Eastern
Commander conducted a brilliant amphibious landing at Inchon,
near Seoul, halfway up the west coast. This bold stroke completely
surprised the North Koreans and allowed UN troops to cut off
the invading forces from supplies and reinforcements. After inflicting heavy casualties on the communist troops and virtually
eliminating their effectiveness in the South, MacArthur began to
move north.

The 38th Parallel:
To Cross or Not to Cross?

Considerable debate ensued within the government and among
the "16"—the group of countries contributing troops to the UN
effort—about whether MacArthur should cross the 38th parallel
in pursuit of the still-fighting North Korean forces. George Kennan and members of his Policy Planning Staff raised this issue in
the Department as early as July, while we were still reeling in
defeat. They believed the Russians would react strongly if it appeared we were seeking anything beyond reestablishing the status
quo ante June 25. They argued that an unfriendly army on the
Soviet border might provoke the Kremlin to unleash a wider war;
and as much as we did not want a wider war, we wanted one
even less in Korea, where geography conferred on the enemy
inherent superiority. The logic of this position convinced some in
the Department, and certainly no responsible official wanted to
risk war with the Soviet Union. But the dominant opinion, advanced by Rusk and Allison and shared by Acheson and Secretary
of Defense George Marshall (and me), was that MacArthur should
proceed beyond the 38th parallel—cautiously. The parallel had
no inherent political meaning. It had only arisen as a convenient
dividing line for accepting Japan's surrender and offered no natural military defenses should the communists try aggression again.
United Nations policy aimed at creating a "united, independent

and democratic" Korea; and with North Korean forces in disarray (although still fighting vigorously) we had a chance to attain that desirable goal.

We "move-north" advocates were not reckless adventurists. We were not blind to Soviet and Chinese fears about American troops on their borders; indeed, there was some talk of halting the UN advance well south of the Yalu—say at the "waist" of the country—and creating a demilitarized buffer zone in the remaining North Korean territory. In any case, we envisioned using only South Korean troops close to the border, if UN forces did succeed in fighting all the way north. No UN resolution prevented us from uniting the country by force, but none mandated that we do so either. We wanted to take as much North Korean territory and establish as strong a position as we could without provoking Soviet or Chinese intervention. If the communists objected strenuously enough to our advance to send in more troops, we felt our intelligence would pick up evidence of their intentions early enough for us to pull back to a strong defensive line well north of the 38th parallel. Even that pessimistic scenario would give the Republic of Korea more security than halting our advance at the 38th parallel, which would allow North Korean forces to regroup without interference and resume attack when they pleased.

Washington had to assess the likelihood of Soviet or Chinese intervention from the opinions of those closest to the scene, and here General MacArthur's views weighed heavily. MacArthur argued that the chance of further communist intervention was negligible, and that if it did come his troops could crush it. Some of his confidence no doubt stemmed from his very healthy ego, which had received a big injection of growth hormone at Inchon. Part of it, too, was no doubt his genuine belief that he was the man of destiny whose mission it was to bring peace to Korea as he had brought it to Japan. And part of it may have stemmed from a semi-conscious desire to command a larger war against communism in the Pacific.

In the capital the General was not only a darling of the Republican right and Chiang Kai-shek lobby, but commanded a sort of awe from otherwise hardheaded generals (and, it must be said, diplomats). And it is true that Washington was not disposed to worry excessively about the consequences of intervention in late September 1950. The Policy Planning Staff may still have had some qualms, but most senior officials considered unification—after the breathtaking reversal of fortunes that followed

Inchon—a feasible, tempting prize. So when MacArthur said that Russia and China would not intervene, most remaining worries in Washington were extinguished.

Most, but not all. That there were still some qualms about inadvertently provoking a wider war is reflected in the basic orders to MacArthur prepared by State and Defense and approved by the President on September 27, authorizing an advance north of the 38th parallel:

> . . . you will continue to make special efforts to determine whether there is a Chinese Communist or Soviet threat to the attainment of your objective, which will be reported to the Joint Chiefs of Staff as a matter of urgency. Your military objective is the destruction of the North Korean armed forces. In attaining this objective you are authorized to conduct military operations, including amphibious and airborne landings or ground operations north of the 38 degree parallel in Korea, provided that at the time of such operation there has been no entry into North Korea by major Soviet or Chinese Communist forces, no announcement of intended entry, nor a threat to counter our operations militarily in North Korea. Under no circumstances, however, will your forces cross the Manchurian or USSR borders of Korea and, as a matter of policy, no non-Korean ground forces will be used in the northeast provinces bordering the Soviet Union or in the area along the Manchurian border. Furthermore, support of your operations north or south of the 38 degree parallel will not include air or naval action against Manchuria or against USSR territory.
>
> . . . If the Soviet Union or the Chinese Communists should announce in advance their intention to reoccupy North Korea and give warning, either explicitly or implicitly, that their forces should not be attacked, you should refer the matter immediately to Washington.

MacArthur submitted a plan of operations for implementing these orders to Washington the next day. It provided for the use of ROK forces exclusively, once UN troops reached a line about fifty miles south of the Yalu, and repeated his assurances that there was no indication of Soviet or Communist Chinese military activity in Korea. On October 7 the UN passed a British-sponsored resolution implicitly endorsing our policy by explicitly calling for a "unified, independent and democratic Korea," borrowing a phrase from the November 1947 UN resolution. It called for creating stable conditions throughout the country, holding elections under UN auspices, and aiding the country's economic reconstructions. Nowhere did it request that these objectives be imposed solely through force of arms; indeed, the resolution called for UN forces to withdraw from the country as soon as possible, and discussions with our allies showed that many voted for it hoping that the General's troops would establish control at a line comfortably south of the Yalu, after which diplomacy could secure some political settlement for the whole country. The crucial goal all our allies desired for Korea was basic stability, which did not necessarily imply UN occupation of every last square mile. The distinction between essential security and complete conquest was subtle, however, and not altogether obvious from the wording of the resolution. Secretary Acheson has written that while Washington did not perceive it at the time, MacArthur took the October 7 vote as a UN mandate to subjugate the country by force, the opposite of what the majority of nations who voted for it intended. (Acheson, *Present at the Creation*, p. 454)

It is clear with hindsight that this crucial difference between the military and political objectives of the war was only dimly perceived by those responsible for conducting it, myself included. General MacArthur may have been particularly blind, but to some extent, so was everyone else in authority. MacArthur was never told, "You will go so far and no further, leaving the final solution to diplomacy," because we did not really formulate clearly enough what our essential political objective was. In Washington we figured that the proper place for our advance to halt would become manifest as we drew closer to the Yalu. With a general more attuned to the political nuance of limited war, more careful and more faithful to the spirit of his government's policy, this open-ended approach might have succeeded. With MacArthur it did not.

Before MacArthur actually crossed the 38th parallel in the first week of October, we received signals through India that Chou En-lai, the Communist Chinese Foreign Minister, was displeased and agitated about our intention to continue the advance. Some Chinese troops had previously moved into Manchuria, and on October 3 Chou told the Indian Ambassador in Peking that China would intervene if UN troops entered North Korea. We were inclined to write off most of this belligerency as bluff, but was any of it real?

I had agreed with the decision to cross the parallel but I was concerned that we take pains to make our advance as unprovocative as we could, just in case the bluster from Peking indicated a genuinely raw nerve. I wrote Dean Rusk on October 3 that while Chou's statement was largely "directed at forestalling decisive action on the resolution on Korea, I do not feel that we can assume it is entirely bluff." I pointed out that "We are not openly committed to the use of UN forces across the 38th and it may, therefore, be well worthwhile to explore the possibility of using entirely ROK forces for the subjugation of North Korea" with the aid of our air and naval support. "This would maintain the UN umbrella over the operation while reducing the grave risk of calling the Chinese bluff . . . This also has the added advantage of avoiding the great complexities of carrying out genuine UN occupation of North Korea."

But General MacArthur insisted that South Korean forces alone could not manage the job, and Rusk felt that Rhee's unaccompanied troops might worry the communists (and us) more than a disciplined UN force. So northward our soldiers went, facing comparatively light opposition. Whatever nagging fears we had about Chinese intervention faded as the stream of good military news rose and no Chinese troops appeared. In October 1950, in fact, more worrisome than Peking was General MacArthur himself. Without actually disobeying any order he kept giving a curious but distinct impression that Washington's directives somehow did not concern him.

Proconsul MacArthur

Our Far Eastern Commander-in-Chief had been embarrassing the Administration since July 31, when he flew to Taiwan without even notifying Washington. There he consulted with Chiang on the possible use of Chinese troops in Korea, and probably also discussed the advisability of Chiang's attacking the mainland to divert Chinese attention from Korea (though he never did fully report his conversation to Washington). He ordered three squadrons of jet fighters to Formosa without telling his superiors; and he let it be known afterwards via the world press that he and Chiang agreed on the role Taiwan should plan in the Far East, which implicitly criticized President Truman's policy of neutralizing Formosa to make sure Chiang did nothing rash to bring China into the war. The ambassadors representing the "16" reported that their governments found MacArthur's comments disturbing and wondered who was really in charge of United States policy.

Not wishing to assume malicious motives, Truman at first speculated that the General might simply have gotten out of touch with Washington's thinking during his twelve-year absence from the United States. In early August the President dispatched his Special Advisor, Averell Harriman, a very savvy and tough operator, to explain in depth Washington's thinking about Taiwan and the Korean War in general to MacArthur. Harriman reported his conversations with the General to the President in a memo which Truman includes in his memoirs:

> For reasons that are rather difficult to explain, I did not feel that we came to a full agreement on the way we believed things should be handled on Formosa and with the Generalissimo. He accepted the President's position and will act accordingly, but without full conviction. He has a strange idea that we should back anybody who will fight Communism, even though he could not give an argument why the Generalissimo's fighting Communists would be a contribution towards the effective dealing with the Communists in China . . .

Nevertheless, MacArthur did tell Harriman he "would, as a soldier, obey any orders he received from the President." This, Truman thought, would end MacArthur's career as self-appointed Secretary of State for Taiwan.

Not at all. On August 26, after the JCS had sent him another cable explaining the government's policy on Taiwan, MacArthur issued a typically grandiloquent statement to the Veterans of Foreign Wars that again, without directly opposing government policy on Taiwan, left no doubt that the General considered it inadequate. The President ordered that MacArthur withdraw the statement (which only served, of course, to focus more attention on it) and sent him some more materials restating and explaining our Taiwan policy.

But explanations were not what was needed. The General's repeated failure to follow his orders was not due to lack of comprehension. Either he was trying to make political hay for his colleagues on the Republican right, or he really did want to get China involved in a much bigger Far Eastern war. Our allies asked us in some very stormy meetings of the "16s" ambassadors what most people in Washington had been thinking. If the UN commander cannot be controlled in what he says, can he be controlled in what he does? This skepticism received eloquent reinforcement from reports of the bombing of Rashin, a railway junction only seventeen miles from the Soviet-North Korean border, by American planes on August 12. The State Department protested to the Pentagon that it violated MacArthur's standing orders to stay well clear of the border. Though some members of the Joint Chiefs shared this view, the soon-to-be-replaced Secretary of Defense Louis Johnson rallied behind MacArthur, which did nothing to reassure our allies.

MacArthur Swaggers, China Intervenes

Given this checkered record of political reliability, it is not surprising that President Truman wanted to make sure MacArthur fully understood and accepted his responsibilities and limits as UN commander as UN troops began moving into North Korea in October 1950. With the remarkable generosity of spirit that characterized the President's attitude toward MacArthur, Truman decided to fly halfway around the world to meet him at Wake Island, thus saving the General a long trip away from his headquarters while his troops were in combat. At Wake, MacArthur—apparently having a difficult time remembering who was President—did not even bother to wear a tie or button his collar, and as soon as the meeting was over, whisked back to Tokyo, declining the President's lunch invitation. The discussions themselves, however, entirely satisfied the President. MacArthur said he firmly believed that all fighting would end in Korea by Thanksgiving and that most of our soldiers would be out by Christmas. He also reiterated his belief that China was very unlikely to enter the war, and that if it did, "there would be the greatest slaughter." MacArthur apologized for the embarrassment his statements on Formosa had caused, and the President returned to the United States fully satisfied. As he said on arrival in San Francisco on October 17, "there is complete unity in the aims and conduct of our foreign policy."

It thus caused the greatest possible consternation in Washington when, on October 24, MacArthur ordered American commanders in Korea to "drive north forward with all speed and full utilization of their forces," blatantly disregarding his basic orders of September 27 which stated that "as a matter of policy, no non-Korean ground forces will be used in the northeast provinces bordering the Soviet Union or in the area along the Manchurian border." At a meeting with the JCS that I was attending with Dean Rusk that same day, the JCS indicated great reluctance even to query MacArthur on the matter. Any other general would have been relieved on the spot, but such was MacArthur's standing among the JCS that all they eventually did was nervously ask him to explain his reasons. MacArthur replied that lifting the restriction on American forces in the border region was entirely consistent with his orders and had been directed as a "military necessity."

On October 26 scattered reports of bitter fighting between our advancing forces and concentrations of well-equipped and well-trained Chinese troops in North Korea started to filter up the chain of command. They surprised us all, especially since the Chinese then seemed to vanish. What happened to them? No one knew. Washington was totally dependent on MacArthur for all its intelligence on Korea, since he had absolutely prohibited the CIA from working in his theater. This would soon prove to have been a grievous error.

MacArthur's troops were overextended, poorly coordinated, and unprepared for defense. The Eighth Army, in the west, communicated with the Tenth Corps in the east only through Tokyo and could not link up a continuous defensive line across the country. Perhaps MacArthur's awareness of his troops' vulnerability explains the violent swings in mood, from panic to smug confidence, that began to seize him and made interpreting his cables so difficult for us in Washington. First, on November 4, he counseled caution until intelligence reports were more complete; then on November 5 he ordered massive airstrikes on virtually every target of importance in North Korea, including the Korean ends of all bridges crossing the Yalu, which carried the risk of damaging Chinese territory as well. We knew our allies would strongly oppose any hasty moves that might provoke China into redoubling its involvement, so Washington quashed the airstrike orders. MacArthur replied with the "gravest protest" he could make, saying that Chinese "men and material in large force are pouring across bridges over the Yalu" and predicting disaster for his command unless the bombing proceeded. Given this surprising new information about the extent of China's intervention—previously unreported by MacArthur—the President authorized the raids within less than twenty-four hours. Thus there is no basis for the myth that the disaster which the American forces were about to suffer resulted from a Washington veto of MacArthur's plans for bombing the bridges.

On November 7 MacArthur backed away from his apocalyptic vision of an overwhelming horde of Chinese and reported that he had been right in originally predicting that China would not make a full-scale commitment to the war; but on the same day he also advocated lifting the restriction on pursuit of enemy planes over Manchuria. On November 9 he reported a plan for a new offensive to drive to the Yalu that he said would require about ten days to reach. In the same spirit, he rejected advice several days later from the JCS that he should dig in on easily defensible high ground and wait. MacArthur's offensive took place as the General planned, starting November 24, despite great worry in Washington that it might be premature and irrational. After our troops had moved into the mountains in the northwest, massive and well-coordinated Chinese attacks bore down on them from all directions. The General had walked into an ambush, and on November 28 he reported "an entirely new war."

Was the Chinese intervention prelude to general war? While denouncing the move as unprovoked aggression and a serious threat to world peace, we did not see it as a prelude to global conquest. We believed the Kremlin wanted to reverse the UN's success, driving us far back into South Korea and off the peninsula entirely if possible. The President and his top advisors quickly concluded that we had to resist the attack without allowing our countermeasures to escalate piecemeal into a full-scale Pacific war. Neither we nor our allies wanted such a war. We were not prepared for it, and while Western Europe was still especially vulnerable to Soviet pressure, overcommitment in the Pacific would have been a major strategic blunder.

MacArthur demurred. He argued that any deviation from what he still mistakenly interpreted to be our basic policy—clearing all North Korea of Communism by force at whatever cost—would be disastrous to the morale of South Korea and his troops. He said that the Communists' objective was the total destruction of his command; given China's obvious local superiority in troops and supply, the only way to save it was to attack China's warmaking potential on its own territory. Thus he recommended bombing targets in China, blockading its coast, accepting Chiang's offer of Taiwanese troops, and even using the nuclear bomb in North Korea. Without these extreme measures, MacArthur hinted darkly, total defeat and evacuation to Japan would be the only feasible course. Newspapers the world over carried stories emanating from Tokyo attempting to put the whole blame for China's intervention on Washington, and complaining that only Washington's defeatism prevented the ever-ready MacArthur from trouncing the enemy.

MacArthur was especially insistent about ending the ban on air operations over China and Russia, which allowed Communist aircraft to retreat over the border to escape attack from our fighters. He considered this "privileged sanctuary" wholly unjustified and wanted to attack the airfields from which these planes originated, as well as the aircraft themselves in "hot pursuit." To prevent some overeager American pilot from provoking China or Russia into greater retaliation, the President continued the ban. MacArthur made great political hay out of this "sanctuary," but never mentioned that our airfields had similar sanctuary in South Korea and Japan, which communist bombers never violated.

Neither did he ever explain how dispersing our limited air resources over a wider area would make them any more effective. The air power we did have was already stretched trying to interdict supply lines between China and the communist troops in Korea, without also taking on a major strategic bombing campaign against China. We had undisputed air superiority over Korea, and with only three main lines of supply, the enemy presented a textbook opportunity for air interdiction. But our Air Force had deteriorated so much after World War II that we had insufficient planes and crews to do the job. We in State had long discussions with General Hoyt Vandenberg, Air Force Chief of Staff, and we all agreed that entirely apart from the political complications of attacking China or having our aircraft shot down in Chinese territory, it was to our military benefit to abide by the tacit arrangement leaving sanctuaries for both sides. Using nuclear weapons would have had much graver political consequences, but because the military could never find an appropriate target in Korea, we did not have to consider their use any further.

By the first week of December the illogic and even panic in MacArthur's reports had reached a point where the President's advisors doubted the soundness of his judgment. General J. Lawton "Joe" Collins, Army Chief of Staff, went to Tokyo to provide a reliable eye for Washington, and the Joint Chiefs ordered MacArthur to pursue this obvious and prudent course: to effect an orderly withdrawal that would above all preserve his troops while inflicting maximum possible damage on the enemy. He was authorized to consolidate his forces into beachheads if necessary. All of MacArthur's plans for arresting defeat by widening the war were rejected; he had no choice but to obey orders as the Chinese overwhelmed his badly exposed positions. But he continued to predict imminent collapse and to recommend evacuating his troops to Japan unless he was given a free hand and reinforcements to attack China. For a period his gloomy view seemed as

if it might be right since 200,000 Chinese "volunteers," as Peking
called them, pushed us back deep into South Korea, almost to
where the North Koreans had driven us before Inchon. The
"slaughter" General MacArthur had predicted at Wake if China
were to enter the war had indeed occurred—to his own troops.

But defeat had not entirely corroded MacArthur's soldier's
instinct. On December 23, Eighth Army commander General
Walker, in charge of the western sector of UN forces, was killed
in a jeep crash and Major General Matthew B. Ridgway was sent
from Washington to take over for him two days later. Ridgway
was a soldier's soldier, fully familiar with Washington's thinking,
extremely conscientious, inspiring to his men, and absolutely determined to stop the rot of morale that the longest retreat in the
history of American arms had inflicted on them. No MacArthur
sycophant, he obtained virtually a free hand from the Far East
commander. Within a month his troops started north once more,
disproving MacArthur's claim that China's troops could not be
defeated unless their base of supply was attacked. Despite heavy
opposition they kept going, inflicting severe losses on the Chinese
"volunteers." As we began to redeem our humiliating defeat and
attain some bargaining power, thought of a truce regained the
attention of Washington and our allies.

What Sort of Peace?

In the UN, where confidence in General MacArthur and American leadership was understandably low, agitation continued for
a quick negotiated end to the fighting. In December 1950, while
we pressed for a resolution condemning Chinese entry into the
war, Britain, India and Canada were masterminding a resolution
directing the President of the General Assembly to determine
the principles China would consider acceptable in a settlement.
When China denounced this initiative in January 1951, the peace-
seekers tried another tack, proposing a resolution specifying five
principles on which they thought a lasting peace could be based.
To entice China, most of the principles were ones we were known
to disfavor. Nevertheless, the Administration endorsed the resolution, which passed on January 13, to avoid fragmenting our base
of support in the UN; and very ill-received in Congress that decision was. Luckily, China rebuffed this initiative too, as we had
hoped. In February the UN came around to our point of view
more closely and condemned China's intervention. As General
Ridgway's forces made continued progress, the center of gravity
in proposing peace formulas returned to Washington.

The United States government's conception of an acceptable peace settlement began to take shape in late January and early February 1951. The main difficulty in framing plans for a settlement was blending political and the military requirements so that we obtained the best possible military position from which to advance our political goals without going too far and provoking China or the Soviet Union into redoubled aggression. Again the issue came down to whether the UN forces should try to drive the enemy well north of the 38th parallel.

A February 11 memorandum by Dean Rusk that Secretary Acheson saw, entitled "Outline of Action Regarding Korea," gives a good summary of how the State Department envisioned a workable settlement. It is a good example of what Dean's fertile mind did best—conceiving every possible alternative policy and putting each in plain language until the most sensible ones were manifest. First Dean dismissed these three extreme approaches to ending the war:

A. To reinforce U.S. and U.N. forces sufficiently to unify all of Korea by force.

This alternative must be rejected for the following reasons: (1) the U.S. and the U.N. do not have the necessary additional force; (2) even if adequate forces were available, it should not be deployed to Korea; (3) the Moscow-Peiping axis can always reinforce enemy effort sufficiently to prevent a full U.N. success in Korea.

B. To withdraw promptly, either with or without a pretext.

This alternative must be rejected for the following reasons: (1) the world-wide political effect of a demonstration of U.S. irresolution would be disastrous; (2) a major aggression by communism would result in a clear communist victory; (3) the position of the West in Japan would be badly undermined; (4) the sacrifices made thus far to meet the Korean aggression would have come to naught; (5) an abandonment of our Korean allies would be unacceptable as a matter of national honor and morality; (6) great confusion, anger and disillusionment would result in the United States; (7) withdrawal from Korea would require additional action against China, the nature, extent and results of which cannot be clearly seen.

C. To resolve the Korean affair by bringing down the Peiping regime through action against China.

This alternative must be rejected for the following reasons: (1) a general war against China must be avoided in the face of the world threat posed by the Soviet Union; (2) there is no assurance of bringing down the Peiping regime without a major commitment of U.S. forces to the China mainland; (3) if we make a major commitment of U.S. forces to the China mainland, there is no assurance that we can avoid general war at a time and under conditions of great disadvantage to us; (4) the U.S. would be politically isolated in any such effort.

Dean also opposed accepting a military stalemate without a negotiated settlement formally ending the fighting.

So what should we do? Rusk concluded that the most desirable alternative would be to promote a cease-fire where both sides would return to the status quo prevailing before the war:

> Although the U.S. and the U.N. should maintain the policy of unifying an independent and democratic Korea, it must be recognized that, realistically, the lines established by the cease-fire would be frozen and would produce in fact a return to the status quo ante June 25, 1950. An agreed modus vivendi for Korea inevitably involves the risk of future violation by the communists. This risk is world-wide and will exist so long as there is a noncommunist Korea. We cannot commit large U.S. forces permanently to Korea because of this risk, nor, on the other hand, surrender Korea to communism because of it.

In accordance with this limited politico-military goal, Rusk believed that UN forces should "pause for a period of rest" at the 38th parallel to give negotiations a chance, proceeding beyond it only if enemy troops appeared to be regrouping for attack.

While Rusk was composing this paper, I was drafting a tentative plan for arranging the mechanics of a cease-fire that included a proposed statement by General MacArthur and provisions for a five-day temporary truce during which conditions for a permanent cease-fire could be discussed. It was my first crack at plotting out a Korean armistice—which soon was to occupy me full-time for two more years, a far cry from the five days I originally envisioned.

Now that State had determined the outlines of an acceptable settlement, we had to get concurrence from the "business end" of our Korean involvement—the Pentagon. On February 13 I attended what was just becoming a regular and important institution in the government, a joint meeting between the principal Korean actors from Defense and State. At this session the questions raised by Rusk's February 11 memo were discussed, especially whether to cross the 38th parallel. The Joint Chiefs agreed with our position that a cease-fire was not purely a military problem, but had to be part of a larger political solution; all agreed that advancing north of 38 was fraught with political dangers, and that a final arrangement that would leave us short of that line was unacceptable. Because we still had not retaken Seoul, let alone reached the parallel, JCS Chairman Bradley accurately represented the dominant sentiment when he said he "felt that a 'cease-fire' in itself would not be advantageous at this time and that we would probably have to defeat the present attack (the Chinese had just mounted a new offensive) and probably one more attack before the Chinese would be ready to consider an acceptable agreement." (JCS-State meeting, *Memorandum for the Record,* February 13, 1951) After this meeting we in State drafted a policy statement for the President's approval that opposed crossing the 38th parallel, but while this position had fairly broad support in both State and Defense, the JCS did not want to issue orders to MacArthur flatly prohibiting it until his troops had gotten close enough to make the question more than academic.

This particular JCS-State meeting illustrates very well the sane and constructive tenor that always characterized them. Cooperation between us and the Pentagon during the Korean War was deep and genuine. In virtually every intragovernmental debate, both sides worked harmoniously to select sensible policies from a tangle of intertwined political and military questions. During World War II, President Roosevelt had objected to any attempt to inject political factors into strategic decisions, and kept the State Department weak and isolated. But President Truman had an entirely different style of operation. He actively sought the State Department's advice on Korea—which being a limited war raised as many political questions as military—and his strong Secretary of State was only too happy to provide what Truman requested. Especially after General Marshall replaced Louis Johnson as Secretary of Defense in October 1950, soldiers and diplomats collaborated at all levels. I became the regular staff contact between the JCS and my superiors in State. I commented on draft instructions from the Pentagon to the Far Eastern Commander, brought to Rusk's attention any political problem on which the Chiefs wanted advice, made sure the Chiefs saw our plans for revitalizing Korean political life after hostilities ended (which the military government would have to administer), and in general kept the bureaucratic wheels lubricated. The "executive agent" for Korean matters on the Joint Chiefs was Joe Collins, Army Chief of Staff, and my equivalent in the Pentagon was one of his assistants, the very able Colonel Jack Matthews. Among us we were usually able to work things out before they could become issues between the "two sides of the river."

By mid-March General Ridgway's troops had gotten close enough to the 38th parallel so that it was very difficult to see how anything could prevent them from reaching it. Our UN allies had no major complaints about either the conduct of the fighting or our plan for ending the war through negotiations based on the status quo ante June 25. They supported any cease-fire formula that would leave South Korea with all of its former territory, but agreed that we had no alternative but to keep fighting until China and North Korea showed some willingness to bargain on that basis. Between State and Defense, as between the United States and the "16," harmony prevailed.

But once again General MacArthur threw a wrench into the works. Throughout February and March he had been arguing with the Joint Chiefs over the directives governing his operations, continuing to press for permission to attack China's war-making potential on its own soil, opposing any thought of stopping Ridgway at the 38th parallel, repeatedly failing to understand that his mission was to fight a limited war on behalf of the United Nations, by whose directives he was governed, and not to take on the whole communist world as an independent actor.

There was nothing improper in the General repeating his advice to his superiors, however unsound it may have been. What was entirely improper, bordering on disloyalty, were his blatant efforts to pressure the President into accepting his views by advancing them publicly, even though they contradicted the established policy it was his duty to execute. He gave frequent press interviews in which he criticized the government's intention to seek a settlement short of reconquering all Korea.

He also derailed a presidential initiative to put an early end to the war. Washington informed him on March 20 that Truman was preparing to issue a statement, carefully prepared by State and Defense and checked with all of the "16's" governments, that indicated a UN willingness to open the way to armistice negotiations with the communists. Three days later the General announced an armistice proposal of his own, obliging Washington to send out a circular telegram saying that MacArthur's proposal "was not authorized, expected, or representative of the views of this Govt." In effect, MacArthur's proposal threatened Communist China with attack on its own territory unless it moved to the bargaining table. It also invited the Chinese commander to negotiate with MacArthur directly, as if the war were something he could settle privately.

I was among the group that brought MacArthur's invitation to the Chinese commander (obtained off the press ticker, as he had not even sent the Pentagon a copy) to Secretary Acheson at 11:00 P.M., March 23. We discussed it for several hours during which Acheson talked to the President, Secretary Marshall and Omar Bradley. It was agreed that we had to let reporters and our justifiably confused allies know that MacArthur had spoken out of turn; but the damage was done, and the president's proposed armistice statement had to be shelved. President Truman later wrote that this incident convinced him that MacArthur had to be replaced.

Yet it took one more example of insubordination before the President acted. On April 5, House Republican leader Joseph Martin read a letter from the Far Eastern Commander into the Congressional Record. It raised again the old issue of using Chiang Kai-shek's troops to open a second front against Communist China, which MacArthur's letter endorsed. It also implicitly criticized Administration policy for its willingness to accept a settlement short of holding all Korea against all comers. "There is no substitute for victory," MacArthur wrote. The President secured advice from his civilian and military aides over the next few days, and by April 9 they concluded that MacArthur was incorrigible and recommended unanimously that he be relieved. Secretary of Defense Marshall, after reading through the General's file, concluded that he should have been fired two years previously.

Though I was aware through Rusk that MacArthur's days were numbered (and glad to hear it), I made only one small contribution to the deliberations. Rusk called me from Blair House during the last strategy session to ask me, as a "Japan hand," whether I thought it would be possible to let MacArthur continue as Supreme Commander in Japan while divesting him of responsibility for Korea. I recommended against this course, believing that his prestige in Japan would not survive the blow and that it would not satisfy MacArthur himself. Rusk returned to the Department about midnight with the formal orders replacing MacArthur, in all his commands, with General Ridgway. As a courtesy to MacArthur, these orders were supposed to be delivered personally by Frank Pace, Secretary of the Army, who was visiting General Ridgway in Korea. A snafu in transmitting the orders to Frank disrupted this plan, however, and to make sure the General did not learn of his dismissal from the wire services, the orders had to be transmitted through normal army channels directly to the Tokyo headquarters.

MacArthur's dismissal provoked the predictable chorus of outrage from the Republican right. Our allies, and virtually everyone I knew working on Korea in State and Defense, were more than relieved to be rid of this consistently unreliable and unpredictable figure, despite his unquestioned military genius. But those seeking to discredit the Truman Administration invited the General to make a memorable—if demagogic—speech to a Joint Session of Congress, and arranged Senate hearings on the reasons for MacArthur's dismissal. They blamed the Administration for "losing" China to communism and saw in the firing of MacArthur—who, in their view, had been relieved only because he opposed the President's shameful policy of "appeasement" through limiting the Korean War—as a sinister design.

It was those Senate hearings that gave me my greatest contact with Secretary Acheson, the Administration's "star witness." To many on the Republican right, Acheson personified evil, and was a suave, polished Yankee aristocrat who used his position of trust to advance the day of the Kremlin's world conquest. Such a charge was ludicrous, of course, and Acheson, who did not suffer fools gladly, did not take great pains to conceal the disdain and impatience with which he regarded these "primitives," as he privately dubbed them. But MacArthur had sufficient public standing that any misstep during these hearings could wound the Administration badly. So the Secretary prepared carefully. Because I had followed the ins and outs of MacArthur's record as Department liaison with the Joint Chiefs and knew the diplomatic developments on Korea completely, I was designated to cull all the materials the Secretary needed for his seven days of testimony. I had kept my own thorough records of the most important cables, memos and letters on Korea, and compiled the appropriate ones for Acheson to read. I also wrote summaries and lists of talking points, which he examined before going through a dry run of his next day's testimony with me and his legal advisor, Butch Fisher. He was an extremely satisfying man to work for. He could instantly weave a very eloquent presentation out of my rather pedestrian dates, facts and talking points. His mind quickly seized what was crucial and remembered it precisely. These dry run sessions usually lasted long into the night. While Fisher accompanied Acheson up to the Hill, I worked preparing materials for the next day's testimony. Acheson performed superbly at the hearings, and the pro-MacArthur forces were not really able to lay a glove on him. Unfortunately, the Secretary was so obviously able and intellectually superior to his Congressional questioners that they resented him. He was right, but he rubbed them the wrong way.

MacArthur's dismissal may have enraged conservatives in the United States, but it delighted our allies in Korea. Throughout the period of the General's increasingly public deviation from United States and UN policy, they had grown restive. Washington told them one thing and MacArthur another, and what MacArthur did unmistakably pointed to a war with China none of them had any interest in fighting. Their frustration and tension broke through in its most concentrated form at meetings of the ambassadors of the sixteen troop-contributing countries, conducted in Washington every few weeks. The ambassadors would come in with fire in their eyes; in truth it was very difficult to defend MacArthur's actions, though our job was to put the best possible face on them and preserve allied unity as much as we could. At this Dean Rusk was a master. As he talked, the whole atmosphere of the meeting would visibly relax. He had a great facility for soothing people, skirting difficult points, glossing over the prickliest nettles of substance with such skill and sophistication that no one really realized that he was sidestepping exactly what they were angriest about. Until, that is, they returned to their embassies to draft reports of the meeting for their foreign offices, at which point they would call me up as Dean's deputy and ask: "Now exactly what did Dean say about this?" After every meeting of the "16" I would be deluged with calls. After a while I became rather adept at the "honest but defusing" turn of phrase myself.

Armistice Talks

General Ridgway continued to make progress in Korea as the storm about MacArthur's dismissal passed through the capital. By late April his troops controlled a line slightly north of the 38th parallel. In May some extremely determined Chinese offensives pushed them back slightly south of it, but they advanced once more and in June dug themselves in along a strongly fortified line that crossed the country about twenty-five miles north of the parallel.

Much blood, both communist and UN, testified to our determination to defeat communist aggression in South Korea, whether from North Korean troops or Chinese; for our part we realized that clearing a country of communism that bordered on China and the Soviet Union was impracticable. Our allies were satisfied with what we had accomplished and saw no reason to press further. The new UN commander had no desire to stir up general war. Militarily and politically, the time was right to renew our quest for a truce.

In this instance, making peace was almost as taxing as making war. We had no diplomatic relations in China or North Korea, and feelers extended to them through the UN, Sweden and others were ignored. It took several weeks before we got a nibble. George Kennan, on leave from the Department to write on Soviet diplomatic history, saw Soviet UN Ambassador Jacob Malik privately at Acheson's request to make sure the Kremlin understood we genuinely sought armistice talks. After Malik consulted with Moscow, he relayed to Kennan that his government believed that peace was possible and that we should approach the combatants directly. He repeated this advice in a public radio broadcast June 23, and inquiries through our Moscow embassy confirmed that Soviet officials had approved these views, though they said they could not speak for China.

Staff work preparing for armistice negotiations had been going on in earnest since April, when the pace of our advance against China had slowed and the 38th parallel, the starting line on June 25, 1950, looked like it would roughly approximate the finishing line, too. Our work on the armistice had concentrated on two main questions. First, what were our goals? Second, how could we best obtain them?

Defining our goals required considerable negotiation between State and Defense, building on the accord reached on Rusk's memorandum of mid-February, and then our allies had to be consulted. By mid-May the National Security Council had set out what we wished to accomplish in Korea, which was a political, as distinct from a purely military, solution that would end hostilities, establish the authority of the ROK government in the area we controlled (up to the 38th parallel at minimum), provide for the staged withdrawal of non-Korean forces, and build up the ROK Army so it could deter or repel another North Korean attack. We would not give into Peking's request for UN membership or taking control of Taiwan to stop the Korean hostilities; truce talks should be restricted solely to Korean subjects. If the communists would not accept our minimum terms, we resolved to keep fighting, though not to the point of extending the war elsewhere or unifying Korea by force. Both State and Defense agreed that trying to push the communists substantially north of 38 would be difficult militarily and dangerous politically.

We floated these ideas past our UN allies, which took time and tact. No one was unusually obstreperous, but the sheer number of actors tended to ensure that any position agreed to was a lowest common denominator even before we approached the enemy, a recurrent structural problem that deeply distressed Dean Rusk, though not much could be done about it. Because American troops were bearing the brunt of the fighting by far— the rest of the "16" having sent only token forces—we possessed a kind of deciding vote when serious controversies arose. But we invoked it seldom. Our most consistently agreeable ally was Turkey, which never fussed over anything and thereby won my heart. The 5,000 soldiers they contributed had been extremely good fighters, too.

The most troublesome ally, predictably, was South Korea. Rhee interpreted any American willingness to stop short of the Yalu as a dastardly betrayal and vowed hysterically to continue fighting, without us if necessary. Rhee's army was too weak to gain victory without our help, but it was certainly adequate to unhinge any delicately balanced armistice if he were as rash as his words. He quieted slightly when we stated that we would remain in Korea until an acceptable settlement was reached, but we knew that Rhee, like a dormant volcano, could shatter the calm without warning.

We also had to decide upon the best mechanism for conducting negotiations. This presented almost as many complications as working out our goals for them. There was considerable pressure from the UN and some of our allies to let the UN form the group that would set up the armistice with the communists. In this approach we had no confidence. The body was vulnerable to pressure and overly eager to reach agreement, even if the communists demanded political concessions (such as abandoning Taiwan or allowing Communist China into the UN) that had no relevance to settling the Korean War. Another drawback of proceeding through the UN was that the allied forces in Korea were UN forces and thus the UN was one of the belligerents.

Alternative approaches to making peace also presented complications. We had no diplomatic relations with North Korea or China, and the Chinese government did not officially accept responsibility for its "volunteer" troops in Korea. To sidestep these political traps—to avoid getting discussions on a purely military armistice embroiled in extraneous complexities that could only prolong the fighting—we proposed that the armistice talks be conducted between representatives of the two military commanders, who would be restricted to discussing solely military matters. Malik's UN radio broadcast of June 23 appeared to indicate that the communists sought peace, so we had General Ridgway broadcast on June 30 a carefully worded statement (in whose drafting I was closely involved) that suggested both our awareness that the communists might now desire peace and our willingness to hold armistice talks with their military representatives if that were the case. The communist commanders responded favorably on July 2. That they accepted a military channel for these talks gave us hope that a cease-fire could come quickly, leaving the cumbersome political issues for diplomatic resolution later.

We assumed that the talks would lead to a simple end of hostilities along existing battle lines, not the 38th parallel, since our front line was north of the 38th by some twenty-five miles across most of the country. We considered establishing an effective international supervision group vital, including a demilitarized zone across the country that would separate the two armies. And because we knew the larger political question of unification would not be solved quickly, if ever, we wanted to fashion in the armistice arrangements something we could live with for a long time.

In the talks between State and Defense leading up to Ridgway's June 30 announcement, both departments agreed that UN forces should not stop hostilities in the absence of a formal, supervised arrangement with the other side. This meant that fighting would continue during the period of negotiations. A central question in our planning thus became: how vigorous should this fighting be? We in State—including Acheson and Rusk—believed that the UN forces had to maintain military pressure if we were going to achieve an armistice within a reasonable period. We advised the Chiefs that while they should not start any offensive solely to influence the negotiations, neither should they shy away, solely for political reasons, from any military operation they would normally conduct.

It was a delicate situation, because the military was naturally reluctant to ask men to do battle if a cease-fire was likely the next day. Unlike the Second World War, when President Roosevelt believed strongly that military operations should be executed without regard to political consequences and that diplomatic maneuverings should start only after complete victory, the Korean War mixed up political and military problems inseparably. It was hard for the Chiefs—and for us diplomats too—to adjust to this fundamentally new style of thinking. But during the armistice sessions especially, all of us in Washington who worked on Korea learned a basic principle of how war and diplomacy work when the opponents are evenly matched, a principle that European countries understood well from their own history. As von Clausewitz put it, "war is the continuation of politics by other means."

We originally proposed that negotiators meet on the Danish hospital ship *Jutlandia,* in the North Korean harbor of Wonsan, but the communists instead suggested a small town called Kaesong, then lying between the two armies. We accepted. By the time representatives of the two sides met there on July 10, however, the communists had encircled it and took advantage of this fact to harass our delegation. They refused to permit our press representatives to accompany our negotiators into Kaesong, though General Ridgway had the right under the procedural arrangements to send whomever he liked. Ridgway demanded the completely reciprocal treatment to which he was entitled and refused to negotiate until all his chosen representatives were permitted into the conference site. After several days of dickering, the communists acceded and permitted our reporters in Kaesong. It may have seemed an insignificant point, but small symbols can mean a lot in negotiating. Ridgway's firmness reestablished that Kaesong was not a communist-held city to which we were begging to come, but a neutral site over which both sides had equal jurisdiction.

General Ridgway was perfectly correct to insist that anyone he designated be permitted into Kaesong. Whether he would have been wiser in the long run to exclude the press is another question. He decided to allow direct coverage of the talks in Kaesong on July 9, without consulting Washington. (Reporters were permitted onto the conference site but not into the negotiating building itself.) Ridgway recognized that the communists might attempt to make distorted propaganda out of the talks and wanted our press on hand to see for itself. While I sympathized with his motives, I considered the idea on balance unsound. Negotiating a complex agreement under pressure between wary enemies is hard enough in private, let alone in a fishbowl. We soon saw that having several dozen reporters clustering at the doorways, demanding a statement immediately after every session, nosing around for leaks and tidbits, detracted from the businesslike atmosphere most conducive to progress, and made the communists wonder whether we were more interested in propaganda than results. But the press is a jealous beast that even the most fearless general is wise to placate, and once it received permission to cover Kaesong the decision could not be lightly rescinded.

Ridgway's chief negotiator, Admiral Charles Turner Joy, our naval commander in the Far East, settled down to work with his communist opposite numbers on July 14. They were a North Korean, representing Kim Il-sung, and a Chinese representing General Peng Te-huai, commander of the Chinese "volunteers." Our representatives quickly observed that China dominated the other side, treating North Korea as a somewhat irksome inferior. The first topic for bargaining was, of course, the agenda. The needless diversion created over the reporters had alerted us to the possibility that the communists were planning to string the talks along at the slowest pace consistent with keeping them alive, hoping that the military and political "correlation of forces," as communists like to call it, would shift in their favor. The protracted agenda dispute that ensued deepened these unpleasant suspicions, for the other side was attempting nothing less than to determine the outcome of the conference by building their objectives firmly into the wording of the agenda. They proposed two topics: withdrawing all foreign troops from Korea, and establishing the 38th parallel as the cease-fire line. We considered the former a political subject to be irrelevant until the immediate problem of an armistice had been settled and depressingly reminiscent of Soviet propaganda about American troops in Western Europe; as for the 38th parallel, we had no intention of retreating to it.

Miraculously the agenda wrangle ceased by the end of July, which we hoped might mean that the communists were preparing to get down to business. But what the enemy gave with one hand it took away with the other. On August 4, North Korean troops carrying machine guns and mortars marched into the neutral conference area, violating the July 14 agreement that permitted only lightly armed guard troops in the neutral zone. General Ridgway had no doubt that the communists deliberately concocted this offense to assert their superiority. A direct and conscientious soldier, Ridgway found these childish games infuriating while men whom he commanded were dying on the battlefield. Worried by indications that the enemy was preparing for a major offensive, he sent a cable to the JCS on August 7 overflowing with his frustration. He requested permission to drop the studied blandness of diplomatic utterance in order to talk turkey with the communists. "The language of diplomacy is inappropriate and ineffective," he cabled.

> The discussions are between soldiers. One-half of them are Communists who understand only what they want to understand; who consider courtesy as concession and concession as weakness; who are uninhibited in repudiating their own solemn obligations; who view such obligations solely as means for attaining their ends . . . I propose to direct the UNC delegation to govern its utterances accordingly and while remaining, as they have, scrupulously factual and properly temperate in word and deed, to employ such language and methods as these treacherous savages cannot fail to understand, and understanding, respect. (C-68437, 7 August 51)

He also suggested proposing that the conference be called off unless the communists agreed to a joint inspection team for the conference site or moved it.

The State Department shared Ridgway's fury at the enemy's tactics, but we also had enough experience of negotiating with communists to realize that every affront was deliberately calculated to put us off balance and make us lose patience. So we advised a more stoical response than the one that Ridgway proposed, persevering at least for a while until the communists gave less ambiguous evidence of bad faith. If the talks broke down we wanted to be sure the world would know it was the fault of the communists. The JCS agreed with us and, unlike MacArthur, Ridgway loyally obeyed orders.

In late August the communists manipulated their physical control of Kaesong for propaganda advantage again. They planted debris and bullet holes to "prove" that an American plane had strafed Kaesong, and used this fabrication to justify breaking off the talks. Ridgway denied the charge and countered with a proposal that the talks be transferred to a genuinely neutral site. On October 10, Peking radio agreed to move the talks to Panmunjom, not an entirely neutral location, but one that was much closer and more accessible to the American lines and thus an improvement over Kaesong. Unfortunately, two of our planes attacked Kaesong by mistake two days later. We promptly accepted responsibility and punished the pilots, which seemed to satisfy the communists. At Panmunjom the attempts to embarrass us through violating conference site neutrality ceased; communist propaganda made use of more vile fictions, especially one that charged us with using germ warfare in Korea. This was utterly false, but it had a considerable impact.

Progress toward the actual armistice was as fitful as the wrangling over the agenda and conference site neutrality. The agenda agreed in late August comprised five items: the first was the adoption of the agenda itself; second was "fixing a military demarcation line between both sides so as to establish a demilitarized zone"; third was "concrete arrangements for the realization of cease-fire and armistice," including the establishment of an inspectorate to monitor compliance with truce terms; fourth was "arrangements relating to prisoners of war"; and five was "recommendations to the governments of the countries concerned on both sides," which we hoped could contain in one package all the diversionary political issues the communists were sure to raise despite the talks' military terms of reference.

Item two, the exact line from which the forces of both sides would withdraw upon signing an armistice, dominated the first phase of the talks. The communists wanted the line to be the 38th parallel. We wanted the line to be the "general area of the battle line," which had important military and political advantages over the 38th parallel. General Ridgway, after having his negotiators reiterate our position frequently to no apparent effect, tired of the seemingly pointless debate and understandably proposed on August 11 that we restate our case on the demarcation line once more, after which we would suspend bargaining until the other side agreed not to press the 38th parallel. Washington, again, cautioned: "It will take time for Moscow and Peiping to amend their position," the JCS wired the UN commander. "Protracted and difficult negotiations have been standard in dealings with communists in post-war period." (JCS 98713, 11 August 51) In fact, the communists did appear to move much closer to our approach on August 20, but immediately afterwards they invented the fabrication about our planes strafing Kaesong and stopped talking until mid-October.

When talks resumed, both sides presented proposed cease-fire lines. The communist line was generally eight to twelve miles south of ours, but the proposals were responsive to each other and in Washington we saw no political reason why a line could not be found by mutual adjustment. As talks continued through November, the two sides focused on whether the armistice line should reflect the existing position of the forces, which the communists preferred, or should be adjusted to reflect the position of the forces when negotiations on other subjects finished and the armistice was signed. Both sides agreed to a compromise on November 27; the demarcation line would be based on the positions of the troops on November 27, provided the entire armistice was signed within thirty days. If the armistice took longer to complete, the line would be redrawn in accord with the line of contact whenever signing occurred. The compromise also established a demilitarized zone two kilometers wide on each side of the dividing line.

So far so good. But we had the rest of a controversial agenda to cover, and certain aspects of the way this first round had gone disturbed me somewhat. It seemed to me that there was a structural flaw, not crippling but serious, in our conduct of the talks: the fact that we had to conduct our negotiations through military channels. To be sure, the Joint Chiefs—especially its Chairman, Omar Bradley, and Army Chief of Staff Joe Collins—could not have cooperated more closely with us in State. They invited our comments on each of Ridgway's reports and on each set of instructions they sent to him. While the negotiators were active, this meant that a new report from the negotiating tent had to be analyzed and a new set of instructions prepared for the President's approval almost every day. The ceaseless conflict pundits commonly assume is being waged between Foggy Bottom and the Pentagon never arose during the Korean negotiations; we both needed each other and knew it.

The difficulty occurred in the field, where admirals and generals unpracticed in the arcane arts of high-pressure diplomacy were having to learn on the job. In fact, the Pentagon would have much preferred to leave the talking to trained diplomats. The military accepted the task only because the reasons for keeping the talks between soldiers were compelling, but it placed a heavy and unaccustomed strain on them. An example of this was Ridgway's oft-repeated requests to Washington for permission to issue ultimatums to the other side demanding immediate agreement if they wished to continue talking. Ridgway, Joy and their colleagues were excellent officers but had little experience in assessing the potential political ramifications of every small suggestion and change of nuance. They were not practiced in foiling propaganda ploys or keeping cool during deliberately offensive harangues about themselves and their country, a common communist tactic.

And aside from their lack of negotiating experience, the negotiating team had an additional burden in that their instructions came through military channels as orders, which tended to produce a certain rigidity in how they were implemented. A diplomat is paid to know when to disregard his instructions, but the military decidedly frown on "freewheeling" of this sort. It was difficult to inject much subtlety into our positions.

During the next phase of the talks, concerning how the armistice would be implemented and inspected for violations, the drawbacks of bargaining through military officers abated somewhat as our negotiators developed a better feel for their opponents and for the wider political considerations that governed their superiors' thinking in Washington. Everyone responsible agreed that we had to slog it out at Panmunjom, fighting to maintain our military position against communist encroachments until a workable armistice was reached. The alternatives—developed in staff studies ordered up by Secretary Acheson—were either a wider war, which neither we nor our allies wanted, or some sort of political solution uniting Korea under a friendly government, which was hopelessly optimistic. Yet though the bargaining seemed interminable, the Joint Chiefs had no desire to repeat MacArthur's march to the Yalu. So the Pentagon concluded we were no worse off in pure military terms by having the armistice talks, even though they were lengthy and frustrating.

Admiral Joy and General Ridgway felt deeply that the armistice had to include strict, comprehensive provisions to ensure that the other side did not use peace as an opportunity to ready another sneak attack. They envisioned having inspection teams free to travel throughout North and South Korea to watch for war preparations. They also wanted to freeze the numbers of troops presently in Korea (though permitting rotation on a one-for-one basis) so that more Chinese "volunteers" could not suddenly materialize to threaten or overwhelm the Republic of Korea (ROK), and to prohibit the rebuilding of North Korean airfields damaged in the fighting.

The nub of this problem was the demand for an effective inspection system. As I observed in a memo recording a State-JCS meeting on November 16, there was "great communist sensitivity to outside observation of conditions in their territories," an attitude that had caused the Soviet Union to reject international control of atomic energy and to control all travel in its territory stringently. When we floated our inspection proposals at Panmunjom the communists strongly objected and countered with demands that all foreign forces be withdrawn from the country, which they claimed would obviate the need for inspection.

General Ridgway believed the other side might break off discussions if we insisted upon proper monitoring, but recommended insisting upon it anyway. When this issue was discussed at a State-JCS meeting on November 26, from which both Collins and Bradley were absent, the remaining Chiefs sided with Ridgway. Without thorough inspection, they believed, the risk of sneak attack would be high.

The State Department took a slightly different tack. Chip Bohlen, a wise and experienced Foreign Service Soviet expert who was then Counselor of the Department, and I, agreed with Ridgway that the communists would not accede to thorough inspection behind their lines; but we doubted that would make much difference to the security of our troops. By fighting in Korea we had demonstrated that we would not permit it to be overrun. There was virtually no chance that we would let the ROK be conquered in the event of some future communist aggression, and the communists could see that as plainly as anyone else. "The real deterrent to a renewed Communist attack was the overall United States-UN strength," I said to the Chiefs. Regardless of how carefully or sloppily inspection provisions were drawn up, the communists would not risk attacking if the presence of UN and United States troops and a strengthened ROK army meant they would end up no better off. Secretary Acheson and President Truman endorsed this argument and set the Department to work firming up allied support for a joint statement of resolve to resist any renewed communist aggression in Korea. This "greater sanction" statement, as it was dubbed, clearly indicated that we might feel compelled to attack China itself if China, after an armistice, rekindled the war. Our allies agreed to issue it after the armistice was signed. The JCS agreed that this approach would deter Chinese aggression sufficiently to make inspection a secondary problem.

Their assent cleared the decks for settling most of this third agenda item. By the end of December both sides had agreed to freeze the number of troops in Korea and to establish a Mixed Armistice Commission, with representatives of both sides, to supervise the armistice generally. It would rely on reports from an inspectorate composed of personnel from non-combatant nations.

What remained for settlement as 1952 began, therefore, was Item Four, the prisoner of war question. Deceptively straightforward at first, it turned out to be fiendishly complex, presenting profound legal, practical and moral questions. Basically, the issue boiled down to whether we would return all the communist POWs we held—some of whom violently opposed being sent home because they hated their life under communism or expected punishment for not joining pro-communist groups in the POW camps—or hold out for an agreement permitting the communist POWs to go where they chose as part of the armistice settlement. This latter approach was bound to excite violent opposition from the communists, who would see in it a potential for massive humiliation should large numbers of their soldiers choose to avoid returning home. It would also complicate the task of getting our own prisoners back.

With that clear-sighted sense of higher moral duty that guided him throughout his Presidency, Truman held out for the right of communist prisoners to refuse to be sent home to a life they hated, and possibly to a firing squad. Had he taken the easy way out, I believe an armistice could have been signed well before the 1952 presidential election. In that campaign, popular dissatisfaction with the stagnation in Korea significantly contributed to the defeat of Truman's hand-picked successor, Adlai Stevenson, at the hands of General Eisenhower, who promised to "go to Korea" to end the war. I am sure that Truman knew that by delaying a decisive end to the war he could hurt the Democratic Party in November. But he did what he thought was right for the nation regardless of domestic political consequences. I still consider Truman's firm stand for voluntary repatriation of POWs one of the greatest acts of moral courage I have witnessed in any President.

By the end of 1951 Rusk had left the Department and I had been promoted to Deputy Assistant Secretary for Far Eastern Affairs. As my boss, Assistant Secretary Allison, was handling everything but Korea, I became the "point man" in the Department for Korea. At meetings with the President or the JCS, higher-ranking State officials were present (usually Deputy Undersecretary Doc Matthews, Paul Nitze from Policy Planning, and Chip Bohlen), but I was normally the sole representative of "FE," the Far Eastern Bureau, and thus had responsibility for drafting recommended courses of actions, reconciling differences between State and the Pentagon, and making sure that what the President and Secretary directed was implemented.

Rusk's tutelage had prepared me well for this role. Our working relations were extremely good; his charge to me was to make any decision, take any responsibility I felt comfortable with, referring to him or to higher-ups only what I could not confidently handle myself. That suited me perfectly. I was never shy about taking responsibility, so when I became Deputy Assistant Secretary I had already been initiated in performing the tasks that came with the rank; namely, arguing with the Chiefs, flagging important developments for the Secretary's and President's attention, and developing new strategies to employ at Panmunjom. My replacement as Director of Northeast Asian Affairs was Ken Young, I had been very favorably impressed with from the Defense Department's Office of International Security Affairs, who had a deft hand for writing memos, and later succeeded me as Ambassador to Thailand.

As a junior officer I had always—perhaps unconsciously—assumed that some great gap in innate ability must exist between me and the senior members of government. I found later that this was largely untrue. Acheson was a clear exception, of course, and there were others, but in general I found that the people directing our affairs were ordinary men, who possessed good ideas and bad, imagination and common sense, in about the same degree I did. Such influence as I was able to exert on our policy derived as much from my experience as from any special insight I might have. In the first place, there was my knowledge of the subject at hand—the "feel" I had developed for Korea from having served there, as well as from my detailed knowledge of the war and armistice negotiations. In the second place was my personal policy of originating the drafts of memos and telegrams whenever possible. I had learned that willingness to commit pen to paper confers real tactical advantage in a bureaucracy. It is best to settle differences in conversation if possible—and here an informal lunch or golf game is vastly superior to a formal meeting, when people feel compelled to act their roles—but if differences are stubborn, initiating a draft forces potential opponents to amend something that is already concrete. I had also discovered that paragraph for paragraph, a succinct telegram of instructions to General Ridgway or Ambassador Muccio stood a much greater chance of influencing the decisions of my seniors than the most beautifully crafted and thoughtfully reasoned "think piece" memo. People with responsibility for decision prefer to weigh specific options rather than worthy generalities.

At first, no one had expected the POW question to present much difficulty. Our objective had been to get all our POWs back. The other side refused to submit accurate lists of the captives it held (though we submitted such lists to them), but we estimated that they held about 6,000 UN troops and 28,000 South Koreans. Against this we had captured over 100,000 North Koreans and

Chinese, the number growing daily (to a maximum of about 171,000) as our troops cleaned up communist units left behind in South Korea after Ridgway's offensive started in December 1950. The Geneva Convention of 1949, which the Legal Section of the State Department had helped draft and our government strongly endorsed, provided for the automatic and immediate return of prisoners to their homelands at the end of hostilities. As we held more of their soldiers than they did of ours, a "one-for-one" exchange of POWs held military advantages for us because it would prevent the other side from gaining a surplus of trained soldiers.

However, Ridgway and the Joint Chiefs felt deeply that simple loyalty to our men, plus the morale of our fighting troops, dictated that our overriding concern should be securing the quick and safe return of our soldiers, even if that required us to return to our enemies—for likely reincorporation into their armies—all the POWs we held. Reiterating the soldiers' basic position, Ridgway cabled the JCS on October 27: "We feel we should agree to exchange in bulk, including all-for-all if it is found necessary in order to secure agreement on the early release of UN and ROK POWs or in order to prevent a breakdown of armistice negotiations." (CX-55993) The Chiefs concurred. As we began to look more deeply into the problem, however, some flaws in the soldiers' straightforward approach began to appear.

First, we had to sort out the problem of which Korea our Korean prisoners gave allegiance to. A neat way the communists had developed to reduce their POW burden was to "release" captured South Koreans at the front and then impress them into the North Korean Army, some of whom we then captured. A number of these people had willingly collaborated with the communists; others had not. Some were South Korean civilians who had been caught in the early days of the fighting and others were soldiers. Some communist soldiers had helped us after capture and would be endangered if sent home. We could not very well consign the whole undifferentiated mass to the communists. The Chinese prisoners presented similar knots. Some were loyal to Mao and the revolution, while others had been stuck into the Red Army only after fighting it unsuccessfully as soldiers in the Nationalist army of Chiang Kai-shek, to whom they still gave allegiance.

The Chiefs, prompted by State, agreed to separate the civilian South Koreans (who came to 37,000) for pre-armistice release, but balked at withholding other categories of prisoners from return to the communists for fear of jeopardizing UN POWs. They also opposed trying any communist POWs for atrocities and other war crimes, despite some well-documented cases, for fear of reprisals against our soldiers. The State Department agreed that raising the issue of war crimes was dangerous—international law gave us the right to try them, but in practice only a victor could afford to do so—but we in State did worry about the Pentagon's intention of returning all non-civilian POWs to enemy control whether they wanted to go or not.

The first and most influential doubter was Chip Bohlen, the Counselor. He had personally witnessed the anguish of Russian prisoners forcibly returned home from German prison camps at the end of World War II, many of whom committed suicide rather than reencounter Stalinism. Tens of thousands of those who were repatriated were subsequently killed, imprisoned, or sent to Siberia. Our fight in Korea was not only a war against local aggression with troops and guns, Chip recognized, but part of a world struggle against a whole system of oppression. We had a reputation for being committed to individual freedom. Handing back the prisoners we held wholesale—some of whom were desperate to avoid repatriation, others of whom might be executed for having helped us—was no way to champion human liberty or reassure people living in other vulnerable free world outposts (like West Berlin) about our stoutness as allies. If we agreed to repatriate unwilling prisoners, we would violate a principle we were fighting to protect. State Department memos embodying this reasoning circulated to the Pentagon.

Our senior soldiers recognized the force of these arguments, but quite understandably sought to protect the men they led. All the enemy POWs had been captured in arms against us, they pointed out, and we had no obligation to let them express their wishes, much less give the other side any pretext for retaining UN troops. This was also a perfectly reasonable position.

But Bohlen and the Department had support where it mattered—in the White House. Undersecretary James Webb reported after a meeting with Truman on October 29, 1951: "With respect to prisoners, (the President said) that the plan to exchange all for all is, in his opinion, not an equitable basis. He does not wish to send back those prisoners who surrendered and have cooperated with us because he believes they will be immediately done away with."

Truman's position hardened as discussions between State and Defense plumbed the problem more deeply. He complained to JCS Chairman Bradley that the military's approach to the prisoners manifested "some fuzzy thinking" and requested that any directives to our negotiators on repatriation be cleared with him. Whatever fuzz remained in our thinking the President decisively cleared away. By the beginning of December, Ridgway's orders reflected the President's "strong view that negotiators should vigorously maintain position of one for one basis of exchange," which would allow us to retain and release certain classes of prisoners who did not wish repatriation, while still being able to return as many of their captured soldiers as they returned of ours, up to the total number of UN POWs they held.

On January 2, 1952, we made our first proposal at Panmunjom incorporating voluntary repatriation. Those communist POWs who wished to go home would be exhanged, one for one, against UN POWs, interned foreign civilians, and South Koreans presently in North Korea, whether they had been impressed into the North Korean Army or not. Delegates of the International Red Cross would be permitted access to assure that all repatriation was voluntary, and prisoners who did not choose repatriation would be released. We were prepared to retreat from this position slightly, but the communists found it so outrageous that no compromise seemed possible. The prospect of communist POWs going where they liked after a war opened up too wide a rent in the Iron Curtain for them to accept. The Kremlin, as well as members of our own government, saw that it might be more difficult in the event of "hot" war elsewhere, in Europe, for instance, for the Soviets to guard against large-scale defections of soldiers and civilians from Eastern European satellites if we were known to offer an inviolable sanctuary to POWs.

The enemy delegates denounced voluntary repatriation and devoted attention instead to a particularly vitriolic propaganda campaign featuring accusations of germ warfare.

Several weeks went by with no progress. To see if we could devise some way out of this stubborn impasse, I was named to chair a State Department working group on January 22 to examine all possible methods to get communist agreement on voluntary repatriation. We developed no startlingly new alternatives, but in the ensuing discussions Secretary Acheson suggested the procedure of immediately screening and releasing the POWs whose lives would be endangered if sent home, afterwards agreeing to an all-for-all exchange of the remainder. That way the communists would not have to agree to the principle of voluntary repatriation but would have no choice but to accept it in fact. The entire question was thoroughly thrashed out at a February 1 State-Defense meeting, directed by Secretary Acheson and Secretary of Defense Robert Lovett and including other Pentagon officials, the Joint Chiefs, Doc Matthews, Chip Bohlen and me. Even the career military officers concurred in the meeting's conclusion—that despite the risks involved, the government had to insist upon voluntary repatriation and should develop plans for presenting the communists with the fait accompli of unilaterally releasing the prisoners who would resist return to their homeland.

This approach posed a question of fundamental national policy, so the President's decision was necessary. I drafted a memo for the President on February 4 outlining the joint State-Defense suggestion. "(Voluntary repatriation) is a question of the utmost gravity," I wrote:

> The decision involves basic principles underlying our entire action in Korea, the fate of some 3,000 Americans and 8,000 other United Nations and Republic of Korea men held as prisoners by the Communists, and the question of whether the hostilities in Korea can be terminated or are continued indefinitely with unpredictable consequences.

Before the President could decide, however, we faced a serious rearguard defection in the Pentagon. Secretary Lovett wondered whether we had exhausted our "Yankee ingenuity" in finding better solutions; Admiral Fechteler, Chief of Naval Operations, and General Vandenberg, Air Force Chief of Staff, said they now opposed voluntary repatriation. Several hectic days of meetings followed. The State Department received timely countervailing support from a group of senators who favored voluntary repatriation, and though the Pentagon could not be induced to support our plan, Secretary Lovett agreed not to oppose it when discussing the matter with the President. On February 8 the President restated his approval for the principle of voluntary repatriation, but, taking account of the Pentagon's uneasiness with State's fait accompli proposal, directed that we maintain our present negotiating position while exploring plans for implementing this principle that would "minimize the recognized jeopardy to prisoners of war held by the communists and lead to successful conclusion of an armistice."

Just at this point, some extremely disconcerting and embarrassing reports about conditions in the prison camps arrived in Washington to underscore both the importance and difficulty of a quick solution to the prisoner problem. Seventy-seven prisoners had died during riots between civilian internees and South

Korean guards in one of the compounds. Unrest in other compounds neared the ignition point. What was going on? The camp authorities did not seem to know, and Lovett and Acheson thought it would help both Ridgway and Washington if someone could explore the whole problem of POWs with him and investigate camp conditions on the spot. On February 11, Army Vice Chief of Staff General "Ed" Hull and I left for an eleven-day trip to Tokyo and Korea.

We met with Ridgway, Van Fleet, and other officers to discuss the fait accompli approach to voluntary repatriation, and I also visited some of the prison camps to talk to our men on the spot. It was distressingly evident from just a brief investigation that our prison camp personnel were facing a problem completely beyond their experience and competence. The incipient anarchy, the smell of mutiny in the air, frankly shocked me. I also had the benefit of reports from an extremely perceptive political officer in our Seoul embassy, Phil Manhard, who spoke Chinese and had been working in the camps holding Chinese POWs for six months. (Phil was captured by the North Vietnamese in Hue in 1968 and remained their prisoner for more than five years.)

The prisoners inside the compounds represented a dangerously volatile mixture of North and South Koreans both communist and anti-communist, genuine soldiers and impressed civilians, and Chinese both pro-Chiang and pro-Mao. Our inept administration unwittingly provided ideal conditions for igniting the situation. Simply warehousing such a large population of captives away from the front lines had proved difficult in a country as small as South Korea, prompting the choice of the small offshore island of Koje for most POWs. With attention focused on the fighting war, the overcrowded prison camps tended to receive second-rate facilities and officers. Rations in some camps were inadequate, barracks were crowded, and we had almost no officers who could speak the prisoners' languages or really follow what they were up to. As long as our guards were not endangered, camp commanders took no interest in POW internal discipline, leaving that to POW trusties appointed by lower-echelon commanders on the basis of the trusties' self-styled anti-communism. Trusties assumed almost complete control over internal administration and judicial powers, removed rivals by informing authorities of alleged communist plots, doled out food, clothing, fuel and access to medical treatment to reinforce their powers, and conducted "reorientation" programs emphasizing anti-communist indoctrination in which POWs were compelled by force to participate. "For POWs the war was not over," Manhard told me.

The camps drifted out of our control, with politically active prisoners dividing themselves up into pro-communist and anti-communist factions and using kangaroo courts, violence, torture, and murder to "win" the cooperation of the mass of politically inert waverers. Our administrators attempted to divide and separate the factions, but screening was not foolproof, and in any case, the result was the creation of several defiantly pro-communist compounds, in effect self-governing. Under these conditions it was not difficult for communist agents, who had let themselves be captured, to foment disruptions; and our poorly trained guards overreacted, responding to taunts and stones with bullets.

At Panmunjom the communists were already exploiting the obvious propaganda openings. While we claimed to champion the humanitarian principle of voluntary repatriation, what appeared to be desperately mistreated POWs were rioting and being shot en masse by American warders. Our allies' confidence was shaken. When I returned to Washington I stressed to the Joint Chiefs privately that I thought the camps were out of control and required overhaul, but it took several months and several more ugly incidents before anything substantial happened.

As for finding any techniques for getting the communists to accept voluntary repatriation, our trip to Korea produced none. Consultations focused instead on what the UN Command thought of the idea of screening and releasing the prisoners who would resist being sent home. Sentiment was mixed. Admiral Joy believed that the enemy would consider it an act of bad faith and exact corresponding reprisals against UN POWs, but many lower-ranking officers thought this fait accompli approach would work and that the Army could develop adequate procedures for screening the prisoners quickly and peacefully. General Ridgway concluded that if the communists dismissed voluntary repatriation at Panmunjom, we should screen the prisoners ourselves to determine who would forcibly resist going home, and then trade the remainder for UN POWs, all-for-all.

Hull and I presented Ridgway's views, which we endorsed, to President Truman at Blair House on February 25. Without delay or equivocation Truman agreed that Ridgway should proceed with planning for unilateral release. He recognized that this would be an irrevocable step. Once we separated out those who would fight return, we could never accede to returning the self-identified anti-communists. The President reiterated this view two days later at a meeting with Acheson, Lovett, several of the Joint Chiefs, and other officials from State and Defense (including me), and corresponding instructions were beamed to Ridgway.

Tactical planning in the government next focused on how best to sell this "final" United States position on voluntary repatriation to the communists, since before we proceeded to the extreme of unilateral screening we wanted to give bargaining every chance. By mid-March Secretary Acheson had conceived a scheme to present it as one element of this more appealing three-part package: We would accept the communists' demands which were still outstanding to permit rehabilitating North Korean airfields and on permitting Soviet participation in the ostensibly "neutral" armistice supervisory commission, if they acquiesced in our screening the POWs prior to the armistice. That would settle all the remaining big issues obstructing an end to the war.

Ridgway opposed this package deal. He did not want any Soviets on the commission, regardless of who else was a member. He suggested that any screening of POWs should be done *after* the armistice was signed, so that the communists could not make an issue out of results that displeased them. Agreement on repatriation, he believed, might still develop from pressing the enemy delegates on this issue alone. On March 22, Washington gave him a temporary green light to pursue in private explorations, and we agreed to postpone raising the three-part package and fait accompli scheme until the private talks had run their course.

But in Washington we worried that a significant delay might permit the enemy to outflank us by making us an offer we could not refuse such as agreeing not to request Soviet membership in the supervisory commission in return for our conceding to their position on the airfields. That would leave the POW issue isolated and vulnerable. Sentiment among the public and our allies might favor an armistice so intensely that holding a hard line on voluntary repatriation—a complex issue on which opinion was divided—would be impossible. If the talks were to deadlock, as well they might, it would be better from our standpoint to deadlock over three issues than voluntary repatriation alone.

The executive session talks at Panmunjom quickly focused on the number of POWs we thought might resist going home. At one of the meetings our negotiators presented a guesstimate to the other side—we had no way of knowing definitely until formal screening occurred—that approximately 16,000 of our 132,000 military prisoners would resist repatriation, leaving 116,000 who would return. That was not a very large number. Hints dropped by communist correspondents at Panmunjom, and other data, led us to believe that, as Ridgway put it, the "numbers and nationalities of the POWs to be returned rather than the principles involved appears to be the controlling issue."

On April 2 the communists suggested that the POW debate be deferred until both sides determined a round figure of prisoners to be exchanged. Ridgway at once proposed to Washington that all prisoners be screened immediately. Washington approved the same day, April 3. Over the next two weeks the screening took place. The results astounded us. Our procedures were actually designed to favor repatriation. Within the camps, we publicized a communist offer of amnesty to all POWs who chose repatriation, stressed that refusing to go home might open their relatives to reprisals, made clear that those refusing repatriation might have to stay on Koje long after others had gone home, and promised nothing about what eventually would become of them. Even so, the screening revealed that only 70,000 of our military prisoners could be repatriated without force. That was a stunning drop from the 116,000 we had estimated to the communists in executive session. The communists, angry and humiliated, denounced this news bitterly. With a number so big, the possibility of their accepting voluntary repatriation even through a face-saving compromise seemed remote.

We did not want the talks to break off, especially with so much attention and pressure trained on the POW issue. So we quickly advanced our three-part package, trading airfields and Soviet membership on the armistice commission for voluntary repatriation. We stressed that we were prepared to return the 70,000 POWs who had chosen repatriation in return for the 12,000 UN prisoners they held; to quell their suspicions about the objectivity of our screening, we offered to let the non-repatriates be rescreened by some international body such as the Red Cross after the armistice was signed. But it was no dice—the communists denounced all our proposals out of hand.

The strength of our position on POWs had always crucially depended on the support we received from the American public and from our allies. Now that the communists were really turning on the heat, protecting this base of support was vital. Instead, we shattered it, through sheer incompetence.

The prison camps erupted into violence once more, and in trying to suppress the disturbances, we killed some of the rioters. Twelve prisoners died during disturbances in March, and on May

7, pro-communist POWs, who had refused screening, captured General Francis Dodd, commandant of the Koje complex, when he entered Compound 76 to negotiate with them. They imposed two conditions on his release: that they be allowed to organize POWs throughout all the camps, and that Dodd's successor, Brigadier General Charles Colson, sign a statement binding the UN command not to "mistreat" prisoners or screen them "by force" in the future. Colson signed the humiliating statement on May 10 to secure Dodd's release.

General Ridgway was just leaving Tokyo for Europe to take over the command of NATO, and his successor, General Mark W. Clark, immediately repudiated Colson's agreement and demoted both Dodd and Colson. But the communists reaped a propaganda bonanza nonetheless. Our "official confession" gave credence to their oft-repeated charges that we and our pro-Taiwan trusties were intimidating loyal pro-communist POWs into refusing repatriation. Even those who dismissed the wilder communist accusations saw plainly that the camps were essentially lawless, which cast doubt on the integrity of our prisoner screening. As I wrote Deputy Undersecretary Matthews on May 22, referring to this vexing incident,

> the officer who was in charge of the screening upon which our present stand on POWs is based has been shown to be incompetent. In time suspicion will inevitably arise that if the pro-communist camps were out of control and were able with impunity to terrorize anti-communist prisoners in our midst, the same situation might well have existed in the anti-communist camps, and that therefore the results of the screening may well lack validity.

Those suspicions did arise. Even Britain, Australia and Canada asked whether the figure of 70,000 repatriates might not have come out much higher had the POWs not feared reprisals in the chaos of the compounds. In any event, it now seemed impossible that the communists would ever accept our package proposal.

Our image was further besmirched on June 10, when General Clark ordered troops to reestablish order in the camps, and in fierce fighting thirty-one unarmed prisoners (and one American guard) died. It was a necessary step, for after the prisons were resorted and moved to less crowded compounds the riots ceased, though the atmosphere remained tense. But it took several months of relative peace in the camps to restore the confidence of our allies and repair the propaganda damage, and we were never sure if the peace would shatter gain.

One ally particularly acerbic in its criticisms of our POW management was Canada, through its Ambassador in Washington Hume Wrong. He berated us constantly and, without actually knowing a great deal about life in the camps, was quite sure that a few decent troops and officers could right the mess in short order. Canada, of course, had contributed troops to the UN command, and after Wrong's lectures continued for a while, I had the idea of assigning a Canadian unit to guard one of the camps, a plan I presented privately to the Chiefs. They gladly agreed. The fury and rage this move generated in Wrong were really quite remarkable, something I have seldom seen in diplomacy. Though he based his argument on the assertion that in all Allied operations since World War II Canadian troops had been kept together, what really bothered him, I knew, was that Canada could no longer nitpick about the POWs. I was able to say that the troop rotations were a routine command decision taken in the field, but Wrong knew what we were up to and knew he had been outmaneuvered. We had some of the most vigorous conversations I have ever had with a friendly ambassador.

While the POW issue was boiling, the Panmunjom talks were moribund. The fighting war continued as a moving stalemate with the line of contact staying roughly static despite small advances and retreats, and to disrupt enemy preparations for what appeared to be a large offensive, the UN unleashed a stepped-up air campaign in late June, including attacks on power plants previously spared. Diplomatic efforts to end this sanguinary impasse moved from place to place: to Peking through the mediation of London and New Delhi, to Moscow, to the UN General Assembly in New York, and finally back to Panmunjom. For the United States government, the second half of 1952 was a diplomatic odyssey of much effort and small return. The communists probably wanted to see if we would hold fast on voluntary repatriation, but they may also have hoped that the Republicans, who were running on a platform of peace in Korea, would offer better terms than Truman.

The search for an armistice was not our only problem in Korea. When negotiations at Panmunjom began to founder in May after we announced the large number of POWs who would refuse repatriation, our attention was quickly diverted to an internal South Korean political crisis precipitated by the reckless behavior of President Rhee. While we were laboring especially hard to maintain world support for the justice of our cause in Korea, Rhee had unconcernedly undermined us by subverting

Korean democracy. Since February there had been rumors that he was contemplating becoming dictator; the police and his goon squads were cracking down on all imagined opponents—inevitably labelled "communist agents"—including members of the National Assembly who did not happen to belong to his party. Some very plain talking from Ambassador Muccio, General Van Fleet, and letters from President Truman temporarily kept Rhee in line, but he was crafty, and fanatically devoted to his own power and to subverting any armistice agreement that would not quickly impose ROK control over the whole peninsula. We were never sure what he might do next.

On May 24, Rhee declared martial law in certain areas and used this power—which only the National Assembly could terminate—to arrest Assembly members. Our embassy could see no military reason for the declaration and termed it a solely political maneuver. When our charge told Rhee that his actions gave the outside world the impression that constitutional government was threatened, he flew into a frenzy. He declared himself the representative of the people's will, accused us of intriguing for his downfall, said the arrested assemblymen (who had voted against constitutional amendments that would expand Rhee's power) were traitors, and made other ridiculous assertions.

Some overeager staff officers in the Pentagon thought this development offered a choice opportunity to rid ourselves of this obstreperous old man by having the UN command take over Korea's government on the grounds that the UN could not carry out its mission if the entire Korean civil and military administration was paralyzed. Had the government's hold on the country degenerated to the point where the UN front line had been seriously weakened by distracted ROK units, perhaps higher levels of the United States government would have contemplated military intervention seriously, and the Army did prepare contingency plans for it. But political pressure proved sufficient. Rhee backed down at the beginning of July, accepting some compromise constitutional amendments and relenting on the arrested assemblymen. Our allies recognized that we were not responsible for Rhee's megalomaniac tendencies, but coming after the MacArthur mess and the prison riots, this internal crisis further tainted their confidence in our competence and intensified their desire to be done with the whole business.

Meanwhile, our activity toward an armistice centered on reports we received through the British Foreign Office that Chou En-lai had spoken earnestly to Indian representatives in Peking, indicating a desire to settle the POW question promptly to clear the decks for a wider Far Eastern accord. Acheson, though dubious, agreed to pursue this further through India's Ambassador in Peking, Panikkar. Reports of secret talks between Panikkar and Chou dutifully appeared, holding out various potential avenues to an armistice. We replied to these proposals through Krishna Menon, Indian representative at the UN, but nothing happened. The New Delhi connection seemed to have dried up as suddenly as it had appeared. In time we had reason to doubt that Ambassador Panikkar had ever conversed with Chou or that Menon had passed on our messages.

We learned to distrust Indian diplomacy thoroughly during the Korean War. New Delhi aspired to bridge the gap between Washington and Peking and claimed in each capital to provide a reliable pipeline to the other. In fact it had the confidence of neither. On several occasions, Indian representatives at the UN cajoled Western delegations into accepting China-appeasing resolutions on the assurance that Peking would negotiate at Panmunjom seriously thereafter, only to have Peking contemptuously reject them. Why distinguished Indian diplomats continued to behave in this way I do not know; perhaps they yearned so badly to establish themselves as the great power they thought they deserved to be that they could not help blurring the line between fact and hope.

After the Panikkar fiasco, we considered whether a direct approach to the Kremlin, even to Stalin himself, might unstick the logjam in Korea. It had been Kennan's conversation with Malik a year before that cleared the way for the armistice talks to begin, and Soviet UN representatives were dropping some intriguing hints that their bosses wanted an armistice soon. The question was put to Kennan, who had just become our Ambassador to the Soviet Union. He was skeptical of solving Korea through Moscow "unless we could demonstrate to the Soviet Government by actions as well as words that alternative to prompt action by Soviet Government to bring about armistice would be one having serious disadvantages for the Kremlin." Since the Kremlin, then in the deepest freeze of the cold war, had done everything it could to insulate itself from possible American pressure, Kennan could see no way for us to exert enough muscle to induce cooperation. On his advice, the Department chose in late July not to pursue this route.

So what next? The UN General Assembly was coming up in October. We could not hope to avoid discussing Korea in that unwieldy body, but we wanted at least to deflate in advance the criticism of those who accused us of inflexibility. So in August and September, the State Department developed a new approach for Panmunjom. We suggested that the United States offer an immediate cease-fire that would incorporate all the armistice terms so far negotiated and provide for the return of all prisoners who agreed to repatriation. That would stop the fighting, get all our prisoners back, and leave only the non-repatriates for further discussion. If the communists rejected this new proposal, we would be in a justifiable position to break off the talks until the other side advanced some new proposal of their own.

But our military colleagues demurred. They agreed it was appropriate to underscore our seriousness on voluntary repatriation, but they thought our original package deal provided a perfectly adequate platform for the talks. Lovett, the Joint Chiefs, and Clark distrusted any solution that would not resolve all remaining problems in a formal armistice. They argued that if we took the initiative to make a new proposal, the communists would sense weakness. And if the fate of the non-repatriates *were* left to future discussion, the communists would surely try to trade voluntary repatriation for concessions from us on broader issues—such as Chinese UN membership and United States withdrawal from Formosa—at a general political conference, which could only be treacherous.

The President sided with the military. He wanted voluntary repatriation settled within the armistice, not at some dangerously open-ended political conference. "Unless we wipe the slate clean, an armistice will do no good," he said at a September 24 White House meeting that I attended. Consequently our negotiators recapitulated our final stand once more on September 28; and when the communists did not respond or offer anything constructive of their own, Admiral Joy's replacement, chief negotiator Lt. Gen. William K. Harrison, announced an indefinite recess on October 8.

The truce tent stood empty for the next six months, but the search for peace continued. The UN took up the Korean armistice two weeks later, on October 24. The UN is inherently a complicated and demanding environment for diplomacy, combining the most public sort of posturing with private and delicate horse-trading. It demands fast footwork from a wide variety of delegations, often hostile, in the suffocating atmosphere of a company town. And the Korean discussions in the UN were not made easier by the Eisenhower-Stevenson election that took place at the same time, effectively neutering Secretary Acheson as spokesman for the departing Democrats a month before the maneuverings at Turtle Bay ended.

We entered the special session on Korea sponsoring a resolution supported by twenty other countries calling on China and North Korea to accept an armistice incorporating voluntary repatriation. But some other countries—notably Britain, Canada, and India—were so eager to end the war before the adjustment pangs of a new American administration imposed an inevitable delay that they intrigued furiously, and somewhat dishonestly, for alternative resolutions that appeared to support voluntary repatriation while in fact undermining it. Just getting them to state their counterproposals without gloss or obfuscation was a challenge. But after many weeks of adroit cajoling, persuading, pressuring, and straight talking by Secretary Acheson—plus China's and Russia's unceremonious rejection of the compromise proposals—we unexpectedly obtained acceptable results.

The final resolution, which we were able to endorse, amended an original India-Canada-Britain resolution to provide for the creation of a neutral repatriation commission, and put a definite limit of three months on the amount of time the commission could hold prisoners if it could not reach agreement on what should happen to them. The General Assembly passed it on December 3, by fifty-four votes to five. Peking, however, rejected it, and new outbreaks of disobedience in a pro-communist camp followed. Unfortunately, the Army had not learned anything since May about non-lethal riot tactics, and in a maladept restoration of control by South Korean guards, eighty-five prisoners who had been hurling rocks and other impromptu weapons died. I wrote Deputy Undersecretary Matthews on December 29: "On the basis of conversations with our Allies, I am satisfied that although they are very restrained in their comments, the incident served to a degree to shake confidence in our handling of the POWs which had been slowly reestablished since the earlier Koje incidents." The answer, I said, had to lie in discussing with the JCS ways of "making available to the men on the spot techniques and resources which will enable them to handle (such) incidents . . . without inflicting major loss of life." An interdepartmental committee to examine this problem, on which I represented State, was set up. But in fact, the camps saw no further serious bloodshed.

The War Reexamined

Since the General Assembly was Acheson's Korean swansong; and nothing significant developed in the month before Eisenhower and Dulles took over, this may be an appropriate spot to review, from hindsight and riper judgment, the basic Korean policies of the Truman Administration.

Our initial decision to repel the North Korean invasion was right, morally and politically. We could not afford to let naked aggression snuff out a country both beholden to us and located in a strategically sensitive region. Whether, as some have suggested, we could have averted the invasion to begin with—either by not withdrawing the American Regimental Combat Team from South Korea in 1949, or by the quite opposite course of closing down our military bases in Japan and neutralizing that country to allay Soviet fears of American encirclement—is impossible to say in the absence of solid information on why the communists chose to invade South Korea. But if we had it to do over again, I would put my money on retaining American troops in the country. Indeed, that strategy has been successfully employed since the armistice was signed. We maintain a token American contingent in South Korea to signal our determination to do whatever it takes to keep the country free. Though our troops could not now repel a concerted communist attack, they stand as a "plate glass" barrier that the communists cannot break without serious consequences. Because of ROK contributions to their upkeep, it costs less to maintain the American unit in Korea than those on Okinawa or Hawaii. It is very cheap insurance.

Despite our difficulties with MacArthur, the mistake of marching to the Yalu, the subsequent stalemate at the 38th parallel and the tortuous and disappointing armistice talks, the Korean War was, worldwide, a political triumph for the United States. It shook us and our allies out of a complacency that had infected our strategic thinking since World War II. American military spending, which had declined to less than $10 billion, rose enormously as we took precautions to deter future Koreas elsewhere. The economy was mobilized to re-equip our expanding forces. NATO was transformed from a "piece of paper" into an effective military force. Differences between us and some of our allies on the proper treatment of Peking faded. And mutual security treaties were concluded with Japan, the Philippines, Australia and New Zealand in 1952 that provided a firm structure of alliances in the Pacific.

We have learned since that the Korean War strained the Sino-Soviet alliance, contributing to the open rift of the 1960s. In Korea itself, the communists invested nearly one million soldiers (losing probably 750,000 killed as opposed to 400,000 UN soldiers killed) and great quantities of war material. They finished behind where they started, with the North Korean economy devastated. Whoever planned the North Korean attack certainly won no medals from the Kremlin.

Our success in responding to the invasion with this comprehensive array of constructive and practical policies demonstrates, I think, that our government is structurally capable of mastering the complexities of modern diplomacy, including limited war. But there are always several essential conditions that are unfortunately quite rare in Washington. First, the President must know his own mind; when a crisis comes, he cannot waffle or importune the heavens for guidance. He must act, and act decisively. This Truman did. The Secretaries of State and Defense must share the President's general outlook while retaining enough independence of mind to point out weaknesses in his strategy. Second, by setting a conspicuous example of good relations, the two secretaries must impose cooperation between their departments. (This equation has been somewhat complicated by the emergence of the President's National Security Advisor as an independent force in foreign policy, but the same principle applies.) Absolutely frank interchange must take place at all levels between State and Defense.

The military machine has certain built-in attributes that tend to magnify small mistakes into big ones, such as an acute sense of amour propre, a tradition of unquestioning obedience, and a devotion to applying standard procedures regardless of changing circumstances. These qualities the State Department can effectively counterbalance if it hews closely to its best traditions of careful reporting and friendly but skeptical questioning of policies, both current and projected. Military officers are no less intelligent than Foreign Service Officers, but the system they inhabit does not encourage criticism. Our two greatest failures in Korea—MacArthur's march to the Yalu and the inept administration of POW camps—evidence the military out of control, deaf to suggestions from State or elsewhere. MacArthur was even deaf to ideas from his superiors, insulated from contrary viewpoints by his sycophantic and xenophobic staff.

MacArthur does not deserve all the blame for China's intervention. Any general sending UN or ROK forces north of Korea's waist would probably have provoked it, and MacArthur's orders—reflecting Washington's failure to distinguish clearly between its war aims and its political aims in Korea—certainly never explicitly said "stop 100 miles south of the Yalu." But they did direct him to proceed carefully and use only South Korean troops in the extreme northern reaches. Had he obeyed, China might not have attacked, and certainly we would have been better posed for repelling the attack that did come.

The Joint Chiefs were too gentle with MacArthur, observing the protective rules of the generals' fraternity instead of the harsh dictates of tight command. Although we in State thought so at the time, we were reluctant to interfere in a matter of internal military discipline. Looking back, it is obvious we should have, though as time went by, we did tend to speak our minds more freely. Ideally, MacArthur should have been replaced after his triumph at Inchon and before he strayed too far north in Korea. But no one could have foreseen that at the time. His judgment was only shown to be seriously and obviously flawed by his erratic behavior during the hasty UN retreat. He could have been replaced legitimately any time thereafter, but his reputation was so towering, especially among conservative Republicans, that the case against him had to be overwhelming. Relieving him one or two months earlier would not have made much difference.

The prison camp fiasco provides another illustration of how American foreign policy can profit if the military posts a few State Department lookouts. Phil Manhard, the Foreign Service political officer who interviewed Chinese POWs at length, understood the prisoners' state of mind, grievances and organization much better than any of the officers guarding them. But the military largely ignored his reports, because they came from outside the chain of command. Their deliberate self-blinkering ultimately jeopardized the armistice and cost many lives. After the crisis had occurred, I was able to make good use of Manhard's reports in private talks with the Chiefs. But frank exchanges earlier, at lower levels, would have served the country much better than after-the-fact cleanup by Washington.

On most other occasions, however, State and Defense worked productively and harmoniously together, and the Korean War left me with a conviction that cooperation between soldiers and diplomats is vital to effective foreign policy. It also gave me considerable practice in making that cooperation work, as well as some ideas about how to broaden and deepen it.

About the soundness of voluntary repatriation I have no doubts. President Truman was right to identify it as an issue on which compromise was impossible. We had men in our custody whom we thought, rightly or wrongly, could only be forcibly returned, and if returned, would probably be executed. Thus we believed that tens of thousands of lives might hang on our decision.

This raises a larger question about the emphasis American diplomacy should place on protecting the human rights of other peoples. When the Carter Administration announced its human rights policy to the world in 1977, I joined many other career diplomats in decrying it. But what I was criticizing was the way he was going about it, not the underlying principle. A good deal of the Carter policy seemed to consist of pious pronouncements about things that weren't really our business, to countries where we had very little political leverage to begin with. Consequently we offended a lot of people without accomplishing much. I approve of injecting human rights into diplomacy, but in the words of that old song, "It ain't what you do, it's the way how you do it." In Korea we had many more communist POWs than they had of ours. That gave us leverage. We were willing to prolong the armistice negotiations and keep fighting to get agreement on voluntary repatriation, which also gave us leverage. And ultimately the communists knew we could release or repatriate the prisoners as we chose, unilaterally, which was decisive. In this case we were not exhorting some third party to clean up its behavior, but acting ourselves, with conviction and resolve, using tools at our command.

The final and most difficult question about Truman's Korea policy is: Could we have obtained the armistice earlier, even without relenting on voluntary repatriation? Perhaps if we had fought harder, mounting a serious offensive instead of digging in at a static line, we could have pressured the communists into conceding on voluntary repatriation and signing promptly. When the armistice talks started, State advised the military not to avoid doing any fighting it would have done otherwise, and the JCS and the UN Command agreed. But Ridgway and the Chiefs believed that the line we then held provided good natural defenses and that, for purely military reasons, holding it and fortifying it was the best course, unless basic policy dictated that we try to take a much larger section of North Korea. They also thought the communists could meet any local offensive we could mount from the virtually limitless pool of Chinese troops; so a bloody assault on the communists' equally well-prepared line might well have been reversed. The other side did have something of an obsession about the 38th parallel. A renewed offensive might have in fact prolonged the war; it certainly would have upset our allies and world opinion, unless it brought a quick victory.

And it would have disturbed American public opinion too. Never far removed from our analysis of the purely military advantages and disadvantages of mounting an offensive to hasten the peace was a lively concern for the tolerance level of our own people. At the beginning, public support was nearly unanimous. Pyongyang was far from Peoria, but the injustice of North Korea's aggression was unambiguous and excited Americans' natural sympathy for the wronged. As the war dragged on, however, especially after China's entry and the hard bloody slogging required to reestablish ourselves at the 38th parallel where we began, public opinion grew increasingly skeptical and disaffected. Why did our boys have to die just to regain the status quo? Limited wars do not make good public relations; MacArthur's call for total victory, even at the cost of general war with China and Russia, struck a deep if illogical chord in a nation still imbued with the World War II belief that war should be prosecuted to the limit, with the objective of making the world safe for democracy. When the armistice negotiations bogged down over esoteric issues like the neutrality of the conference site, rehabilitation of airfields, voluntary repatriation and riots in the POW camps, we could sense the national eye beginning to glaze.

Our government's concern about public feeling suggests a deeper question: Can a democratically elected government ever be sufficiently single-minded and ruthless to succeed in the world arena? In Korea the communists did not have to worry about their public opinion the way we did about ours. That gave them an advantage at Panmunjom. Every month they could prolong the talks dampened American public enthusiasm for the war, consequently diminishing the government's base of support for tough bargaining positions. In retrospect, I think a harder fight by the UN would probably have secured a quicker armistice and possibly fewer casualties in the end, but the American people would have taken a very dim view of what would have been required. What should President Truman have done—what could he have done—if, for instance, his advisors had recommended a major offensive as the only way to get the communists to conclude an armistice, but he felt the country would oppose it? In reality the dilemma was never posed so baldly, but we all recognized there was a finite limit of sacrifice and frustration the public would tolerate in Korea before it said "enough"—a limit that might have been less than was needed in the country's long-term international interest.

There is no easy answer to this problem. Democracies must maintain the consent of the governed or they cease to be democracies, and it is at least arguable that any war the public does not want to fight is a war that should not be fought. Unfortunately, our chief enemies feel the constraints of public opinion less often and less severely than we do. That leaves them freer to pursue a definition of strategic gain even at high cost, and to take advantage of our government's reluctance to enter into any messy foreign entanglements unless the need is so glaring that it can sustain public support over the long haul. The Kremlin may find in Afghanistan a guerilla every bit as draining and intractable as the one we faced in Vietnam, but there will be no antiwar demonstrations at Moscow University. Nor, I would wager, will Washington aid the Afghan rebels significantly, while a government less worried about fragmenting domestic opinion might decide on that course if it served our global interest. If a democratically determined foreign policy is not to produce serious long-term setbacks, the electorate from which that policy flows must school itself more closely in international realities, then change the policy accordingly.

I have found that most Americans will agree on the course we should take if they are all provided the same set of facts on which to base their judgment. The problem is getting the facts to them. Since Korea the facts have become more complex, and consequently, important elements of our consensus have faded. A greatly improved knowledge of history, economics, and even political philosophy is now required of our people so that active citizenship can have a firm foundation. Yet our schools and media seem to be less and less effective in developing such a citizenry.

1953: Armistice Achieved

The coming of Dwight Eisenhower ended twenty years of Democratic rule in Washington. All that time in opposition had made the Republicans hungry for power, suspicious of the bureaucracy, and determined to replace the New and Fair Deals with a distinctive new policy of their own. Nowhere was this truer than in the State Department. The McCarthyite anti-communist hysteria that blamed the Foreign Service for all of Mao's and Stalin's conquests was at its height. Our new Secretary, John Foster Dulles, had been preparing for the job most of his adult life and, under a President whom he expected to be relatively compliant, intended to make sure the world knew that a new chief was taking a thorough broom to that haven of fuzzy thinkers and appeasers in Foggy Bottom.

The faces changed, the official rhetoric became more strident, the dark forces of McCarthyism were invited to do their purging from within instead of without and the country lost some exceptionally able and perceptive Foreign Service Officers. But, at least in my little niche, every policy of consequence was retained as before. Dulles endorsed voluntary repatriation; after some dalliance with the idea of conquering Korea up to its waist and holding off Chinese numerical superiority with atomic bombs, the Administration settled down to accepting the armistice line already agreed upon. Despite the violent criticisms Dulles and his conservative Republican colleagues had directed at the Truman Administration for its handling of Korea, the armistice terms he accepted were essentially identical to those Truman put forward in July 1952.

I do not believe that his Korean policy was unusual in this respect. Dulles talked about "rolling back" communism, "unleashing" Chiang Kai-shek, containing Kremlin adventurism with the "massive retaliation" capabilities of our nuclear arsenal. In fact, he followed the basic Truman-Acheson line on NATO, communist China, Southeast Asia, all the major problems of the day. In some ways, all his strong talk concealed something of a traditional Republican isolationist. Our conventional armed forces during these years suffered badly, making anything but nuclear war almost impossible by the time Kennedy took over. We talked an aggressive line, but—witness Dienbienphu in 1954, Hungary and Suez in 1956, the Taiwan Strait crisis of 1955 and 1958—we did considerably less when push came to shove.

I had first met Dulles during the Truman Administration. Acheson had appointed Dulles in the spring of 1950 to negotiate the Japanese peace treaty, and he requested my views on it. I stayed at his apartment in New York and discussed it with him during a long evening. He was a perceptive, probing questioner, and, on personal terms, very pleasant and engaging. We saw each other intermittently until the treaty was signed in September 1951, when I was part of the American delegation to the con-

ference in San Francisco for concluding the treaty. My contribution to the negotiations was limited, since my former boss, John
Allison, was working for Dulles full-time and kept him well supplied with FE's opinions. Insofar as we did consult, I tended to
disagree with him on a series of minor points. I, an orderly bureaucratic soul, wanted the treaty to sew up all possible problems
in Japanese-American relations arising out of the war, especially
American financial claims against Japan. Dulles, despite being an
outstanding international lawyer with a proclivity for fine print,
did not want the treaty cluttered up with a lot of provisions that
would make it harder to negotiate and ratify. But our disagreements were mild and in the line of duty, and I never felt that he
held them against me once he became Secretary.

My personal relations with him as Secretary were always
cordial, but he was not a man naturally given to intimate friendship. Nor did he have a feeling of stewardship for the Foreign
Service, a sense of responsibility for its collective well-being, that
might have prompted him to take an avuncular interest or pride
in the career officers he found around him. He was essentially a
loner, intellectually as well as personally. He wrote his own
speeches and most of his own cables. Though he relied on the
Department to provide him with facts and observations about
what was happening in the field, he had an obvious confidence,
even arrogance, in the power of his own reasoning that made
him impatient with advice from subordinates. He was brusque
not only with subordinates. Other foreign ministers and Cabinet
secretaries—everyone, perhaps, except the President—felt that
dialogue with him was seldom really mutual. Dulles listened only
until he heard what he wanted to hear. Since I am not prone to
theorize about foreign affairs, I never sought to offer Dulles general advice, and perhaps because I did not challenge him on what
he considered his home turf, I did not make him wary and uncomfortable the way a George Kennan or Chip Bohlen could.

Dulles never established a sympathetic or effective working relationship with most of the Department. Possibly because
he had never before managed a large organization, he did not
understand how useful it could be. The first speech he made to
the Department, playing to the McCarthyites by calling for
"positive loyalty" to the Administration, shocked and somewhat
insulted most of the career service. We were prepared then as
always to give full loyalty to our chiefs; we wondered how Dulles,
who had worked with us closely in the last Administration, could
harbor doubts about that; and we were disappointed that the anti-

communist obsession of the Republican campaign was not abating with the Republicans' assumption of responsibility. The first rule that a Secretary who wants an effective Department must follow is that to get loyalty you must give it. Dulles ignored this principle.

I think he did so quite deliberately. In a way Dulles considered himself, as an individual, rather than the Department of which he was chief, the custodian of America's role in the world. As Eisenhower, who liked to delegate as much as possible, gained confidence in Dulles, this single-handed dominance of foreign policy became more tenable. Dulles did have a prodigious appetite for work; where a Secretary with less capacity for detail and concentration might have had to rely more on his senior staff as the crises and cables mounted, Dulles chewed it all up himself.

The only work he avoided was administrative; personnel and budgets were weak tea after the champagne of high policy, and he tried sloughing it all off onto Donald Laurie, brought in from the presidency of Quaker Oats to fill the newly created post of Undersecretary for Administration. Unfortunately, Laurie knew nothing of Washington. Thus when the Republican House cut the Department's appropriation by one-quarter, he calmly accepted it, not knowing that this was a traditional game, enabling Representatives to make a show of how tough they were going to be with the Department, and that his next move should have been to appeal strongly to the Senate to reinstate the funds, which it always did. Laurie's naiveté resulted in a large reduction in staff and sapped already sagging morale. Ultimately he left and Dulles assumed more of the administrative burden himself, but his heart was never in it.

Contrary to popular belief, Dulles could relax; whenever we flew together in those days of eighteen-hour trans-Atlantic flights, he always took advantage of the relative peace to have some drinks and a good dinner and to unwind. Then he could be a delightful informal companion, a man entirely transformed from the dour, sobersided Presbyterian preacher he generally appeared. Four or five hours after we got to sleep, however, the curtain on my bunk would be shaken, then I would be shaken, and there would be the Secretary, all business again, padding around in his bathrobe and asking what I thought of something he had been jotting down on his famous yellow legal pad. I always felt it was a pity that Dulles could not project something of his more appealing private personality into that grim, austere public image he seemed to feel was incumbent upon the man leading the globe's fight against communism.

I always found Dulles weakest when he attempted to play domestic politics. The histrionics about rollback and liberation were calculated to play in Peoria, not Paris, and certainly not Peking. Dulles had seen how Acheson's public and Congressional esteem had so eroded that only Truman's fierce loyalty had kept him afloat. That fate above all he sought to avoid for himself. To preserve himself, he judged the morale and integrity of the Department a necessary sacrifice.

For the first two years of Dulles' stewardship the attacks of McCarthy and his colleagues—including Senators Knowland and Bridges, radio columnist Fulton Lewis Jr., and a gaggle of others whom Dean Acheson had christened "the primitives"— called for blood from the Foreign Service to avenge the triumphs of Mao and Stalin. Believing these charges had not to be disproved but appeased, Dulles left the Service to fend for itself. He brought in Scott McLeod as the chief of personnel security. A former FBI agent and aide to Senator Bridges, McLeod had a mind that I can only call dirty, much in the pattern of McCarthy himself. Not particularly bright, and completely ignorant of the way the Department worked, his ostensible task was to install a complete personnel security system. But his obsession was to hatchet as many FSOs as he could, and he was none too particular about the means he used. When the evidence generated was not sufficient to prove someone a security risk through the Department's strict internal procedures, he often leaked the material in order to obtain a senatorial smear. Others, who could not be charged with disloyalty but who were too "Democratic" for McLeod's taste, were simply not promoted, or were shunted to backwater posts, never knowing why. Dulles could have controlled McLeod, even fired him, but here his political survival instinct outweighed the Christian principles he professed. John Paton Davies and John Carter Vincent, two China hands of great loyalty and perception, were cleared of security charges after repeated examination, but to mollify the Republican right Dulles dismissed them on grounds of "bad judgment." The real reason was that they had accurately reported Chiang's weaknesses and Mao's strength in a way that disturbed the China lobby's self-delusions.

The Far Eastern Bureau suffered worst because the China Lobby had close ties to McCarthy and his minions. Jack Service, another China hand of great probity and experience, was speciously axed; and my best friend in the Foreign Service since Tokyo days, John Emmerson, ran afoul of the security net on trivial grounds. I testified at the loyalty hearings of Emmerson

and Service and stated as forcefully as I knew how my conviction
that both were excellent, entirely trustworthy servants of the
United States, but my voice was inconsequential. The only person
powerful enough in every sense—in Congress, with the people,
with the right-wing Republicans—to have banished this Mc-
Carthyite disease was President Eisenhower. Dulles could certainly have shielded the Department more effectively, but only
the President had enough clout to expose and humiliate these
witch-hunters before the whole nation. Choosing to appear above
the political fray, he remained silent. During the Presidential
campaign he had even omitted from a speech a favorable reference to General Marshall, his old boss and a great statesman,
to avoid upsetting the McCarthyites, who disliked Marshall. With
political courage, at least in this area, Eisenhower was not richly
endowed.

My own brush with McCarthyism was minor, even benign.
I occasionally saw McCarthy at receptions but always avoided him.
Once, however, my wife got unavoidably cornered into meeting
him. He asked if I were her husband, and when she said yes, he
told her: "You can be proud of him. We all think he's a fine
officer." Pat, who disliked him and what he stood for as much as
I did, came home with her estimation of me considerably diminished. What dreadful thing had I done to warrant the devil's
praise? she demanded. The only answer to that question that I
have ever been able to think of is that I did not serve in China
during or after the war. Any FSO who reported the Mao-Chiang
conflict accurately was made a scapegoat for the displeasing outcome. Had I been sent to China after being released from Japanese imprisonment in 1942—which at the time I desperately
desired—I am sure that I too would have run afoul of Mc-
Carthyism. On such small quirks of fate whole careers can depend.

For permitting McCarthyism to flourish, the United States
paid a heavy penalty. Bad enough was the loss of many of our
best FSOs, whose wisdom and experience had been acquired over
a lifetime of study and observation. Much worse was the insidious
dry rot it injected into the collective intelligence of those who
remained. Our country cannot survive in international affairs unless its representatives can speak the truth as they see it, challenging current policy if they think the facts demonstrate its
inadequacy. Compliant, unimaginative play-it-safers who blandly
avoid controversy to protect themselves against future charges of
"disloyalty" dull Washington's perceptions of the real world. They
cripple our capacity to act intelligently abroad and are genuine

threats to our national security. Yet for a time the McCarthy purges left the Service as a whole, and FE in particular, cautious about revealing unorthodox thoughts.

Interestingly, it was the very conservative Republican-appointed Assistant Secretary for Far Eastern Affairs, Walter Robertson, who most stubbornly stood off the McCarthyites and fought for the Foreign Service. During his tenure every ambassador in his area was a career officer, and even though, as his deputy, I often had vigorous differences with him, he fought for me to obtain my first ambassadorial appointment at what was then a very young age.

The greatest harm McCarthyism inflicted upon American foreign policy, however, went far beyond its wounding of the State Department, which, though extremely detrimental, was at least temporary. Far more pernicious and long-acting was the way it cynically played on people's ignorance to make Americans distrust their own government. In every international problem it saw the hand of communism, and every advance of communism was cast as our government's fault, by omission or commission. McCarthyism created a mythical picture of a naive democratic America beset by a diabolical international conspiracy masterminded by the Kremlin and encouraged by agents in high places in Washington. The State Department had handed over Eastern Europe to Stalin at Yalta, went the McCarthy litany. And look at the traitors who undercut Chiang Kai-shek. Look at the Red sympathizers who conspired in Washington to tie General MacArthur's hands in Korea, and finally got him fired.

Diplomacy was obviously something to which America could not entrust its fortunes, said McCarthyism. It is a game we never win, and therefore one we should not try to play. Indeed, we should not even try to think like diplomats; simple, implacable anti-communism would be enough. Thus, because it froze thought and attacked those—like Acheson, Service, Bohlen and Davies—who were doing the most profound thinking about the approach we should take against Soviet expansionism, McCarthyism actually hobbled us with crude and brittle policies.

At its core, the foreign policy bred by the McCarthy worldview was really isolationism updated to account for nuclear weapons and the cold war. The only McCarthy answer to any international problem—and the answer of all who supported him—was to possess such awesome military strength that no one would dare challenge us. Overwhelming nuclear superiority became a way of obviating diplomacy, not making it more productive. Our strength would permit us to do whatever we thought necessary more or less unilaterally. Such isolationism laced with unilateralism was—and is—a dangerous brew.

Dulles himself was a committed internationalist who privately viewed with contempt the isolationist sentiments McCarthy and his right-wing colleagues excited in public opinion. But he was politically calculating and recognized their strength, and his own instincts were not always incompatible with theirs. For the most part his policies were intransigently anti-communist. He assumed that we were so superior to our enemies—economically, politically, militarily, morally—that genuine compromise with them could only diminish us. I personally saw this outlook at work in the way Dulles handled relations with communist China, and it was also evident in his attitudes toward Eastern Europe and the Soviet Union. It was particularly troublesome in his behavior toward what is now called the Third World. He had a tendency to treat those who were not "friends" as enemies, which alienated many countries remote from the Soviet-American conflict.

The Eisenhower-Dulles "New Look" military doctrine also imposed a restricting straitjacket on our foreign policy that eventually proved counterproductive. It sapped conventional forces drastically in order to build up nuclear capability against the Soviet Union, leaving us with few effective military options save "massive retaliation." Max Taylor opposed the "New Look" so strongly that he quit as Army Chief of Staff to write a condemnatory book, *The Uncertain Trumpet.*

But Dulles did some constructive things that have stood the test of time. His handling of the Japanese peace treaty was masterly. His close relations with Adenauer brought Germany more firmly into the North Atlantic community, and he performed ably on renegotiating our first security treaty with Japan. His foreign policy must not be confused with that of the isolationist know-nothing wing of his party. It is easy to forget today that communism not only appeared more virulent then than it does now, but was in fact more aggressive and threatening than a more moderate generation of leaders in China and the Soviet Union have since made it.

Yet, because Eisenhower and Dulles did not try to discredit McCarthy and the new isolationists around him, the seeds of discord and distrust the senator so effectively sowed among the people took firm root. Even today we still yearn for panaceas, and blame the government when they do not appear. This is McCarthy's most dangerous and enduring legacy.

During his election campaign, President Reagan called for scrapping the SALT II Treaty (of which I negotiated 90 percent under Presidents Nixon and Ford), opposed the Panama Canal Treaty, said he welcomed an arms race with the Soviet Union, and declared that "The Soviet Union underlies all the unrest that is going on." He showed very little understanding of Japan or the Third World. His basic implication was that easy answers in foreign affairs exist whenever a President has guts enough to implement them. (He has even been quoted as saying he thought that General MacArthur should not have been restrained from taking the Korean War to China—this from a *Time* magazine article on Reagan two weeks before election). Perhaps candidate Reagan was right. Certainly I endorse his criticism of President Carter for vacillation and inadequate resolve, but I still sense in Reagan's world view a whisper of McCarthy and Dulles, of unilateralism and "new isolationism" made newer still. To be fair, what President Reagan has done in office does not exactly match his campaign rhetoric. His principal advisors in foreign affairs have wide international experience, and, like any President, he discovered quickly that many problems abroad are impervious to American influence. Even so, I must say it does not reassure me to know that someone can convince a majority of our people to elect him President of the United States as a result of public statements, and apparent convictions, that have roots in a brand of isolationism that has never served our country well.

Let us return to the ticklish problems of the Korean armistice, which we left dangling at the UN General Assembly in December 1952. The plan, soon rejected by China, was to resolve the problem of voluntary repatriation of prisoners by turning them over to a neutral nations' commission, which would have to release the nonrepatriates after 120 days if both sides could not come to any further agreement on what to do with them. During the Presidential campaign, Eisenhower had pledged he would "go to Korea" if elected to see the situation for himself and determine a fresh approach to the deadlocked armistice talks. This he did in early December 1952, later joining Dulles and the prospective Secretaries of Defense (Charles Wilson, President of General Motors) and Treasury (George Humphrey, of the Hannah Co.) and the Chief of Naval Operations, Arthur Radford, aboard the cruiser USS *Helena* for several days of consultations. When they took over on January 20, we who had been handling Korea in the Department were prepared for substantial departures from the Truman-Acheson line.

The Republicans came to Washington convinced that only redoubled American toughness could overcome communist intransigence at Panmunjom. The armistice talks, which had dragged on long enough under Truman, remained indefinitely recessed. The communists had rejected the UN General Assembly's December 3 voluntary repatriation formula, which represented the maximum compromise we considered consistent with the basic principle involved. Dulles and Eisenhower ruled out taking a softer line on Korea. Nor could they just wait for the communists to make the first move; ending the war was an important priority. So in their determination to devise some way to unstick the armistice process, they concluded that the use of additional force held the best prospect for increasing communist pliability. On February 11, for instance, the National Security Council (including the President, Dulles, and General Bradley) discussed a report from General Clark stating that the communists had infiltrated the demilitarized zone around Kaesong with abundant troops and material; Eisenhower thought we should even consider using tactical nuclear weapons there if the armistice talks continued to languish.

But cranking up the war had a serious drawback. Our allies absolutely refused to participate in any war widened by our side. If the United States wanted to fight the communists to the bargaining table, we would have to do it alone and break up the UN in the process. Eisenhower and Dulles did not want to pay this price. Thus the three main options the new Administration could choose—making big concessions at Panmunjom, standing still until the other side made a move, or heating up the fighting—all looked unattractive. What remained? The answer Dulles developed was to become characteristic of him. Without actually using force, he threatened belligerently to use it to make our opponents more pliable. This delighted the Republican right. Whether it also softened up the communists, I tend to doubt.

That a strident verbal line was to be Dulles's chief tactic became clear around mid-April. Talks at Panmunjom had resumed at the beginning of that month when Chou En-lai, wanting a means both of feeling out the new people in Washington and of scoring some propaganda points, offered an immediate exchange of sick and wounded POWs. He also proposed a solution to voluntary repatriation. After signing the armistice, the non-repatriates would be handed over to a neutral state while their future was settled. This new stance was essentially similar to one we had taken in July 1952—as well as to the UN resolution China had rejected only three months earlier. It appeared to be a substantial concession. Our shellshocked optimism began to rise once more.

Dulles then unveiled his "tough talking" strategy for scaring the communists into keeping the talks moving. At an April 8 National Security Council meeting, he proposed throwing out what had so far been negotiated unless the communists retreated to Korea's waist; he believed that the Free World's relative global strength, compared to the Kremlin's, could force the move. He also wanted to discard the armistice altogether unless it led to a political settlement unifying the country in some form acceptable to us. Amplifications of this view, not directly attributed to him but bearing his trademark, soon appeared in *Life* magazine, in a statement by Senator Taft, and in news reports of a background briefing given by a "Mr. X." It was clear to us in the Department, as I think it was clear to Dulles, that the communists would never give up at the truce tent what we had been unable to take from them on the battlefield; nor was unifying the country under a regime acceptable to us remotely possible, since China had intervened to prevent us from doing just that. What effect Dulles's carefully orchestrated flurry of leaks had on China is not clear. The negotiations gradually resumed their earlier pace.

The Department's immediate task was less to soften up the communists with verbal assaults than to get out instructions to General Clark for every session at Panmunjom that would accurately reflect the new Administration's policies. This proved exceedingly difficult. Once again the greater part of this responsibility fell to me. I obviously knew the background of what had gone on before, and there was really no one else to do it. The change of administrations had cleared away everyone else who had followed Korea (including Nitze, Bohlen, and Allison) except Deputy Undersecretary Matthews, and he had many other responsibilities. Walter Robertson, an extraordinarily affable but virulently anti-Mao Virginia banker who became the new Assistant Secretary for FE and my immediate boss, was not appointed until March 27, so he was not yet able to speak for the government when the talks resumed. Somehow I had to represent the views of the new Administration faithfully in working out Clark's instructions with the Chiefs. The only place I could turn for reliable guidance was to Dulles.

But Dulles, to my considerable surprise, could not speak for the government either. His relations with Eisenhower in this period were distant, even a little uncomfortable; and instead of the finely crafted plan for ending the war the Republicans had intimated they possessed, both the President and the Secretary were clearly groping their way. Dulles may have felt confident enough to make belligerent anti-communist noises, but the specifics of our negotiating position were another matter. Here, Dulles was reluctant to act without a clear idea of the President's desires, but he was equally reluctant to bother the President for clarifications of small points or to challenge his views with contrary information percolating up from the Department. So the telegrams for Clark that were routed to Dulles for clearance sat on his desk for days.

Clark and the Joint Chiefs understandably chafed at the wait, but a Deputy Assistant Secretary like me could only push the Secretary so far. Then I resorted to clearing the telegrams with the new Undersecretary, Walter Bedell Smith, an Army four-star General who had been Eisenhower's Chief of Staff during the war, and, under Truman, had directed the fledgling Central Intelligence Agency. Bedell was an old Washington hand who knew the tricks of keeping the paper moving in a big outfit like State, and, most of all, had the President's ear. When a telegram covering an issue of fundamental importance needed clearing, Bedell would get on the phone to "Ike," even if the President was taking a bath, argue with him if need be, and get a decision. The mutual trust and regard between the two were evident, and until Dulles found his sea legs with Eisenhower, Bedell kept the Department going on Korea.

The pace of negotiation at Panmunjom began to pick up. By April 12, both sides had signed an agreement to exchange sick and wounded prisoners based on the Chinese initiative, and on April 19 the first trade occurred. Talks on the rest of the armistice resumed April 25. We were happy to accept Chou's proposal for solving the POW question—turning the POWs over to the custody of a neutral state while their future was being negotiated—as a starting point for discussion, because it accorded with the gist of several plans we and the UN had already advanced. We suggested Switzerland as the neutral and a sixty-day limit on further negotiations about the prisoners' fate, after which the non-repatriates could be released. But the communists rejected Switzerland, proposed a six-month confinement for the non-repatriates during which the government to which they belonged could provide information to allay their apprehensions about returning, and said that the disposition of any POWs who still refused repatriation after the six months should be referred to the political conference provided for in the draft armistice. That really meant the non-repatriates would stay imprisoned indefinitely.

We jockeyed for weeks attempting to reconcile these differences. On May 7 the communists put forth a new proposal that came closer to our position but still left large loopholes. Instead of one neutral country taking charge of the POWs, it suggested a commission composed of five neutrals: Sweden, Switzerland, Poland, Czechoslovakia, and a fifth to be selected by those four. It still offered no time limit on the period the prisoners could be kept captive. Another problem from our standpoint was that India, the likely fifth country for the neutral commission, had hardly been reliable in supporting voluntary repatriation at the UN. We also worried about having Czech and Polish troops behind UN lines in the ROK guarding the POWs, because of the inherent potential for brutal intimidation of anti-communist POWs.

Our counterproposal was made on May 13, after the usual interdepartmental discussion in Washington. We thought that having troops provided by one neutral country would vastly simplify problems of command authority, obedience, and malicious harassment of prisoners for political reasons. Though we were not exactly enthusiastic about India (and South Korean President Rhee had an abiding distrust of everything Indian), it was at least acceptable to both sides. We therefore proposed that India alone provide forces to control the POWs, under direction from the five-member Neutral Nations Repatriation Commission (NNRC). Because Sweden and Switzerland were "real" neutrals, not under our thumb as Poland and Czechoslovakia were under the Kremlin's, we thought voluntary repatriation might be jeopardized if India wavered, so to safeguard that fundamental principle we proposed that the NNRC make decisions by unanimous vote. Also, because China seemed really opposed to voluntary repatriation only in regard to its own prisoners, Washington suggested on General Clark's advice that the Korean non-repatriates be released immediately on the signing of an armistice. That would obviate the possibility of Rhee-inspired disorder among the Korean POWs, and leave only the Chinese for future solution. We maintained our stand that non-repatriates should be released within a definite period if both sides could not agree promptly on their disposition.

Our stand threw the Panmunjom talks into an impasse that quickly escalated into a crisis. Our position came under attack from two friendly flanks. Most of the "16" did not support requiring unanimity in the NNRC or immediate release for Korean non-repatriates; they considered these positions eleventh-hour diversions unlikely to lead to any viable conclusion. It was difficult for us to back down, however, because of President Rhee's intransigent opposition to anything that brought the armistice closer. He had been counting on the communists to frustrate it indefinitely, and now that both sides were pressing toward completion he had to frustrate it himself. He repeatedly subjected Ambassador Briggs to what Briggs called Rhee's "victory or death act," saying his country would prefer national suicide to partition at the 38th parallel. On April 24 he threatened he would remove ROK troops from UN control and order them to attack North Korea if the armistice permitted Chinese troops to stay in North Korea. Since we had never expected that the armistice would mandate the withdrawal of Chinese forces, Rhee was really threatening to destroy everything we had negotiated.

Some energetic interdepartmental debate in Washington, starting on May 18, tried to recast our bargaining position to satisfy our allies, Rhee, and ourselves simultaneously. On that day I drafted a memorandum that Bedell Smith took to the President on the 19th, suggesting several changes in our proposals designed to strengthen our bargaining position. I had never been particularly enthusiastic about releasing the Korean non-repatriates earlier than the Chinese; I agreed with General Clark that it was fairer to the Korean prisoners themselves, but I thought it created entirely unnecessary last-minute problems for obtaining the armistice and saw no reason why we should placate Rhee on this minor issue when it would make him no more likely to endorse the armistice. Accordingly I recommended that "Korean non-repatriates be turned over to the custody of the commission in the same manner as Chinese." I also recommended accepting majority rule on the NNRC instead of insisting on unanimity. But I advised that we stand firm on having the right to release all non-repatriates if the post-armistice political conference could not agree on what to do with them within 120 days. This package of proposals, I knew, would regain the support of the "16" and had a reasonable chance of getting communist agreement.

Our larger problem was with Rhee. A mutual defense treaty with the ROK might or might not subdue him, but it had the disadvantage of tying us closer to Rhee. Nevertheless, State and Defense started assessing its pros and cons. In the meantime, the JCS authorized General Clark on May 22 to put forth a final position along the lines of the memo I drafted for Smith on May 18, and to step up the fighting and release all non-repatriate POWs unilaterally if the communists rejected it.

While State and Defense had been working through this final position, Secretary Dulles was traveling in Asia. Contrary to the precepts of Teddy Roosevelt, he was continuing his strategy of talking loudly to make the stick he was carrying look bigger. On May 22, he told Indian Prime Minister Nehru, for transmission to Peking, that we would bomb the communist sanctuaries north of the Yalu if they did not come to terms quickly. Dulles never mentioned this to me or anyone else I knew at the time; in later years he was inclined to think this initiative was decisive in inducing the communists to conclude the armistice, but I doubt that. My own feeling is that when the other side recognized the Eisenhower Administration was not going to capitulate on voluntary repatriation, it decided to settle. The war was still costing them lives and money, and once we demonstrated no further willingness to compromise, they decided to cut their losses.

Dulles's absence from Washington only accentuated the indecisiveness and administrative confusion that seemed, from my bureaucratic perspective, to distinguish this government most glaringly from its predecessor. The exact terms we should authorize Clark to offer in our final bargaining position were a matter of fundamental national importance; if the communists rejected them a costlier war might be necessary, and unless the justice of our position were self-evident, our UN allies might leave us to go it alone. The President was the only person who could commit the government and the country when the stakes were so high. But when I accompanied Bedell Smith to the White House during this period in late May (and other times before and after with Dulles), Truman's crisp decisiveness was quite absent.

In addition to the State delegation to the White House, Secretary Wilson would represent Defense and Army Chief of Staff Collins would usually attend for the JCS along with his aide Colonel Matthews. George Humphrey, Secretary of the Treasury, was also often there because Eisenhower valued his advice. Completely inconclusive discussions would ensue. Wilson's grasp of the issues was vague at best and he normally held forth with a series of inane non sequiturs that had nothing to do with the problem at hand. Secretary Humphrey would ask one question, and one question only: "How much will it cost?" Apparently he was convinced that the cheapest price always meant the best policy. Dulles or Smith, Bradley and I tried to focus on the thorny issues we needed to settle so that Clark would know what to do at Panmunjom, but the Chief Executive so disliked messy and complex problems that he speedily tired of discussion, whereupon he would stroll around the Oval Office swinging his putter, his attention elsewhere. No accounts of these meetings exist in State Department files because I found them too meandering and meaningless to record.

Whenever these sessions ended, I was told to get together with Collins or Matthews to draft a cable to reflect the "conclusion" reached. That put us in considerable anguish because we had no idea what it was. We would write what we considered the best approximation to what transpired, and then the fun would start. Dulles or Smith would suggest revisions to square with their recollection of events; then Matthews would call from the Pentagon to report that Wilson or one of the Chiefs disagreed and had changes of their own to offer; and after some negotiating on the phone I would finally go to Bedell Smith with what I thought should be our final position. He would take the bit in his teeth and see Ike privately, and that way we could get something out of the White House. Later, when Eisenhower began to rely on Dulles more exclusively in foreign affairs, he resorted less to strategy sessions with other advisors; but I must say I have always been surprised that a President with Eisenhower's experience of management had so little evident aptitude for actually running the government.

Clark presented our final position May 25, and the talks recessed for a week to give the other side time to react. On June 4 the communists submitted a counteroffer that accepted most of our conditions—most crucially the one prohibiting the NNRC from holding non-repatriates past a set period, specifically 180 days. "Barring unforeseen developments," cabled Robert Murphy, then Ambassador to Japan and Clark's State Department Advisor, "it appears that PW issue has been solved." Two years after we started, we knew that we were at last going to get peace in Korea.

On June 8, General Harrison and the Chinese chief delegate, General Nam Il, signed the POW agreement. The negotiators then moved article by article through the whole armistice to ready it for signing. Unfortunately for us, this final evidence that peace was imminent set Rhee into high gear. When General Clark saw Rhee the day before POW terms were signed, he reported that he had "never seen him more distracted, wrought up and emotional." Rhee swore he would do anything he saw fit if we signed an armistice, including attack North Korea. Already we had become so disturbed by his accelerating truculence that State and Defense discussed a range of contingency plans should Rhee seriously jeopardize the security of our forces—taking over the Korean government and declaring martial law, withdrawing our forces from Korea to leave Rhee stranded, or precluding the need for such drastic action by sweetening Rhee up with a security pact. In the event, Rhee did make serious trouble. In the early hours of June 18, on Rhee's orders, South Korean guards at POW camps all over the country freed 27,000 non-repatriate North Korean prisoners in a meticulously planned scheme aimed at derailing the armistice. The Chinese remained imprisoned, but all the North Koreans—over whom we had wrangled so long with the communists to get them to agree to voluntary repatriation—were gone, beyond the reach of our military police or the NNRC. Almost all of the 27,000 escaped without a trace.

Ambassador Briggs called me at home at 3 A.M. with the news, and I immediately called Secretary Dulles. But after the initial shock wore off, there was nothing we could do but disavow responsibility, formally report the breakout at Panmunjom, and wait to see if the communists would choose to renege on the armistice because of it. Both sides knew that the 27,000 would eventually have been released under the terms of the POW agreement and that Rhee's plot speeded up rather than hindered the arrangement. But we were acutely embarrassed nonetheless. Not only did this incident add another chapter to a sorry history of inept POW control by the UN Command, but it also signalled unmistakably to the communists and everyone else that Rhee ranged beyond our control. If he could defy us by sabotaging the POW agreement, couldn't he also subvert the entire armistice by provoking or attacking the communists on his own?

Eisenhower was furious. At a National Security Council meeting following the breakout the President said that we seemed to have acquired another enemy and that Rhee had "welched on his promise not to take unilateral action without consultation with the UN Command." But our range of responses was limited. Rhee was so popular in his own country that deposing him was unfeasible. Since the non-repatriates were going to be freed anyway, it was difficult to justify deserting the ROK on this point after three years of bitter fighting to sustain it. So Eisenhower settled for a steaming letter to Rhee, drafted with the aid of Dulles and others, that pointed to the sacrifice Americans and other UN soldiers had made for the benefit of South Korea and threatened serious, but unspecified, consequences if Rhee tried any more sneaky moves to prevent the armistice.

Would Rhee take this threat seriously? To satisfy ourselves, as well as the communists, we had to be relatively sure about Rhee's intentions before binding ourselves to preserving the peace of the armistice. The Department, the President, and Congressional opinion all agreed we should iron out our conflicts with Rhee before we signed at Panmunjom. To perform this sensitive task, my new boss, Assistant Secretary Walter Robertson, was designated. On June 22 he flew to Korea to confer with Rhee, accompanied by Joe Collins, Ken Young, and the Department's chief press spokesman, Carl McCardle. It was something of an inspired choice. In Robertson, Rhee met his match. Garrulous, earthy, charming as it was possible to be, Robertson could out-talk even Rhee; and his voice had a kind of soothing richness that could tame even this crochety monomaniac. After two weeks of virtually non-stop sessions we had Rhee roped as much as he could ever be. The main tangible concession Rhee wrested from us— perhaps this was his plan all along—was a draft mutual defense treaty, with a pledge from Senate leaders to consider its ratification kindly. We also promised about $300 million in economic assistance. In return, after repeated attempts to avoid committing himself, Rhee put in writing that the ROK would not obstruct the truce and dropped his opposition both to the voluntary repatriation procedures and to the political conference on Korea's future outlined in the armistice, two items he particularly disliked. I think he realized that we really *would* abandon his country entirely if he did not uphold the armistice to the letter.

With Rhee more or less under wraps we could press on at Panmunjom. On July 10, the first session since the prison outbreak, Nam Il insisted that the UN Command round up the 27,000 escapees and asked what guarantees we could offer to ensure that South Korea would comply with the armistice, given this violation. Harrison replied that we would do everything we could to make sure the ROK fulfilled the truce, and gave them to understand that we would uphold it even if the ROK did not. To the communists, who knew how much Rhee depended on us, this was sufficient. On July 19 staff work started on redrawing the armistice line to accord with the present battle line. We had arrived at the final stages.

Rhee attempted some desperate machinations to secure an American promise to attack North Korea if the political conference did not unify the country within ninety days, but that did not trip us up. On July 27, Harrison and Nam Il signed the completed armistice at Panmunjom, without speaking to each other. Twelve hours later the fighting stopped. Peace in Korea had been achieved.

The reality of the armistice has corresponded closely to the paper agreement. The demilitarized zone exists today where it was created thirty years ago. With the "plate glass" of American troops shielding the South, and with considerable improvement in ROK armed forces, the country has never since been attacked.

The repatriation procedures also worked. According to the final armistice terms, sixty days were provided following the signing for exchanging prisoners who wished repatriation. The Neutral Nations Repatriation Commission was then to take control of the remainder, transporting them to camps in the demilitarized zone guarded by Indian troops, with another ninety days set aside for explanations from representatives of the prisoners' own governments to try to allay their fears about repatriation. Complaints from UN or communist observers about the execution of this plan were to be resolved by the NNRC, chaired by Indian Army Lieutenant General K. S. Thimayya, with its verdicts enforced by the 3,000 Indian troops he commanded. An additional thirty days were allotted for a political conference to reconcile whatever disputes were outstanding. All non-repatriates who remained in NNRC custody at the end of this total of 180 days, by January 23, 1954, would be free to go.

Though we had had considerable fear at the outset about the Indians' political reliability and military competence, Thimayya did an absolutely first-class job on both fronts. He zigged and zagged through the procedural labyrinth the communist NNRC members tried to erect, preserving the appearance of neutrality without once conceding the central principle that every prisoner should have the right to choose his future. And order within the compounds was remarkably good; the mature and efficient hand-picked Indian troops transformed prisoners who were scared and rioting into relatively calm and disciplined units. It was a masterly job.

Despite determined work by communist agents within the non-repatriate compounds, 21,805 out of the last 22,604 (mostly Chinese) communist POWs who still remained in our hands refused repatriation under NNRC screening procedures. This essentially validated our original screening. Thus, out of the total of 171,000 communist prisoners we had held during the war (including Korean civilians whom the communists had forcibly impressed into their armies, 87,000 ultimately chose not to return to communism. Approximately three out of four Chinese POWs chose not to go home. Out of 6,000 UN prisoners, 23—22 Americans and one Briton—made the corresponding choice to defect to their captors, as did 335 out of the 28,000 South Koreans held by the communists. At the time we considered this large proportion of communist non-repatriates a great moral and propaganda victory for the West; and as I was to learn the following year in negotiations with Communist Chinese Ambassador Wang Ping-nan, the communists felt the sting of this victory acutely.

Although constructing the truce had taxed our patience, imagination, and resourcefulness to the utmost, its structure was sturdy. It did, and is still doing, the job for which it was intended.

·CHAPTER SIX·

Czechoslovakia

IN THE SPRING OF 1953 I WAS APPROACHING AN IMPORTANT, THOUGH still unknown, change in my career. At that time, Foreign Service Officers were prohibited by law from spending more than four years at a stretch in Washington, so I knew I would have to be elsewhere by November, the fourth anniversary of my return from Yokohama. By sheer good luck for me, the Korean War had pushed my career into an updraft. But I was young for the position I held in the Department hierarchy, so even though I had spent my years in Washington dealing with Presidents, Secretaries of State, and the Joint Chiefs of Staff, I expected to descend, in my next assignment, to the less heady realms normally open to FSO's of my age and experience—say, number two at a mid-sized embassy. Still, I was eager to return to the field and was entirely willing to accept whatever the Department offered.

I have spoken about how my immediate boss, Assistant Secretary Walter Robertson, was a thoroughly affable Southern gentleman capable of uncompromising obstinacy. Those qualities, at this point in my career, made all the difference, because he was kind enough to think I should be an Ambassador and intransigent enough to insist upon it despite the objection of many who thought I was entirely too young at forty-five. (Nowadays Ambassadors in their thirties are not unusual at small posts, but then fifty was considered to be the minimum age.) Dulles finally agreed, and in the summer I was offered the embassy in Amman, Jordan. Although I was honored at becoming an Ambassador, I had no difficulty in restraining my enthusiasm at the thought of Amman. Nevertheless, I accepted. But Robertson insisted that he had to have me right up to the end of my four-year tour, and the Amman post needed to be filled immediately. So some weeks later I was offered Prague, Czechoslovakia. That very much appealed to me as it would give me an opportunity to see how a communist system actually operated. It was also a chance to leave Asian affairs, which had dominated my life so completely since 1935, and familiarize myself with Europe. I promptly accepted, cleared my desk in "FE" on October 31, the last day of my four-year term, and started a series of briefings on my new post.

I was startled at my first briefing to learn that a seemingly insoluble case would fall into my lap immediately on my arrival, that of Jan Hvasta. Hvasta was a young naturalized American of Czech origin who had returned to Czechoslovakia after World War II and had worked as a clerk in the American Consulate in Bratislava. He had quit working in the consulate but stayed in Bratislava to attend university, and after the communists came to power in 1948 they arrested him on the usual fake charge of espionage. He was tried and sentenced to two years. When he appealed his sentence it was extended to ten years.

In early 1952, some Czechs escaped into West Germany and told the authorities that Hvasta was free. They had escaped with him from prison but had become separated during the night, and they did not know what had happened to him. When we asked, the Czech authorities denied all knowledge of him. Eighteen months later, on October 2, 1953, Hvasta simply showed up at the American Embassy, walked in, and asked for asylum and return to the United States. After his jailbreak he had found shelter from the authorities with a peasant family in the countryside, but finally became so desperate that he made his way to Prague and our embassy.

Local Czech employees—all required to report to the secret police—had seen Hvasta enter the embassy, so there was no chance of smuggling him into West Germany in an embassy car. My predecessor as Ambassador, George Wadsworth, had wisely decided that the only course was to brazen it out and ask the Czechs for an exit visa on the passport the embassy issued Hvasta. The Czech government reacted violently, as was to be expected, insisting that Hvasta was a convicted criminal whom we had to surrender at once. The Czech Foreign Office was able to cite American and international law and State Department regulations to bolster its case that our embassy should not give asylum to a convicted criminal. On our side was the fact that the original charges against him were clearly spurious and that he, and those who had sheltered him, would probably not survive long after the frustrated Czech police got custody of them. The United States, which Secretary of State Dulles had said was committed to a policy of "liberating the captive peoples of Europe," had no intention of contributing to a flagrant denial of liberty in Hvasta's case. Hvasta himself, who had been brutally tortured in prison, was quite clear about his chances if recaptured. If we tried to turn him back or the police succeeded in their surreptitious but obvious efforts to get at him in the embassy, he threatened to commit suicide by the time-honored Czech custom of defenestration—throwing himself into the courtyard from the room where we were guarding him in the highest and most remote part of the old palace that was our chancery.

There seemed to be no room for compromise with the Czech government, and unfortunately we had very little bargaining leverage. The United States had recently severed all commercial ties with Czechoslovakia as part of a long and ultimately successful campaign to secure the release of an American Associated Press correspondent, James Oatis, who had been imprisoned on false espionage charges. It came to be tacitly accepted by the two governments that the impasse on Hvasta would be left to the new ambassador to try to break—not a first assignment I welcomed.

While I pondered what course I should take on Hvasta, and my appointment was being processed, I took my first leave in several years. Leaving Patricia in Washington with the girls, I took the two boys, who were then sixteen and fourteen, out of school and set off with them by car to visit some of my relatives in Kansas and give them an opportunity to see where I had come from and to meet some of their cousins. I wanted to show them that the rest of the United States was something more than a long and boring train ride, and to refresh my own memories of the great Midwest.

The trip snatched me from the heady air of high policy in Washington and the prospect of being an Ambassador and reintroduced me to the earthy concerns of Kansas farmers and those who serve them. Many of those I met, while by no means uneducated, were vague as to what the Department of State or an Ambassador really did. But with Fulton Lewis spitting McCarthyite venom every evening on the six o'clock radio broadcast, they were all too ready to believe that at minimum the Department was a nest of homosexuals and communists. When I called at the Court House in Salina on the old County Judge, who had long been a friend of the family, he greeted me warmly. When it was established where I worked, however, he had difficulty understanding how a boy from such a good solid family could get mixed up with that gang in the State Department. It was a sobering experience.

We returned to Washington, packed, took our daughter Judy for her junior year at Western Maryland College, and went to New York to board the *S.S. America* for Le Havre. It was our first taste of the side benefits that come with the title "Ambassador": a pleasant suite, extremely attentive service from the crew, and nice touches such as fresh fruit and flowers in our rooms every day. I must say that none of us disliked it. We landed in France on the morning of December 22—my first time ever in Europe—and armed with a not too satisfactory roadmap, I aimed my 1949 Ford stationwagon toward Prague, spending the first night in Metz and the second in Nuremberg.

On the morning of December 24 we set out from Nuremburg for the Czech border, escorted by United States Army military police. We encountered a heavy snowstorm that made driving treacherous but emphasized the coziness of the neat little German towns we passed through, decked out as they were in their wreaths and other Christmas decorations. Occasionally we caught strains of Christmas music, and the mood was festive and friendly. We reached the border at one o'clock. Saying good-bye to our escort and the German Border Police, we drove down across a little bridge over untracked snow to the Czech checkpoint. A heavy steel barrier set in concrete was raised by grim Czech guards toting tommy guns and we drove in. The first barrier was closed behind us while another faced us in front, and on the left and right barbed wire stretched off into the snowy hills. While other guards with dogs kept watch, the embassy officer from Prague, who was accompanying us, and I walked down to the guard house. Both the Czech Border Police and customs officers were courteous if icy, but it was only after more than an hour of filling out forms that the second steel gate was lifted.

Making a sharp S-turn through overlapping concrete barriers set across the road, we then moved slowly about half a mile through a series of anti-tank barriers until we reached another barrier, this time of barbed wire. A plowed strip of land, dotted with high guard towers, stretched on both sides as far as we could see. We passed through, and about a mile farther we came to yet another steel fence and barrier that blocked the road. Again we were stopped by guards with tommy guns and dogs, but after showing our documents we were permitted to proceed into what for miles was literally a "no man's land," with no sign of life except for an occasional deserted farmhouse. This area of rolling hills was the former Sudetenland, whose ethnic German population Hitler used as pawns in the Munich agreement that led to the destruction of Czechoslovakia and Hitler's opening moves in World War II. After Germany's defeat the Sudeten Germans fled for protection to Germany, and between the Czech government's policy of keeping a substantial area near the border free of population and the reluctance of Czech farmers to occupy disputed farmland, it presented a dismal sight in the fast-falling darkness of Christmas Eve. The first town on our route, Pilsen, was even more depressing. Although a few people and an occasional cart were to be seen, the city was utterly dark, with no street lights or even lighted windows.

After passing through all of this my youngest daughter, to whom I had previously been trying to explain the phrase "Iron Curtain," turned to me and said: "Daddy, I understand." So did we all.

We arrived in Prague about six, after nightfall. The streets were unlit, most of the buildings were dark, and only a few people were scurrying along the sidewalks. It seemed the most joyless prospect I had ever seen. We regained something of our spirits when we reached the embassy residence, however, for the lights were blazing, the servants greeted us warmly, and an enormous, beautifully trimmed Christmas tree stood to remind us of a reason for joy that no amount of barbed wire could banish.

The embassy residence, an enormous fifty-eight-room baroque-style palace built in the late 1920s by a Czech Jewish family who later left the country to escape Hitler, represented a fantastic change from our tiny row house in Washington. The staff was with us for eggnog on Christmas morning in a large downstairs winter garden room, when our son Bill (who had already discovered nine hidden wall safes) found a button, which, he being sixteen, naturally pushed, that lowered a section of bronze and glass wall probably seventy feet long by twenty feet high to open the room directly onto the garden. The house had two concert grand pianos, an outdoor and an indoor swimming pool (the indoor pool we kept closed for economy), an enormous library of old books, and a kitchen with bread ovens, meat ovens, cookie ovens, walk-in cold storage and every other conceivable appliance. All the rooms were panelled in exquisitely carved wood and the furniture and paintings belonged in a museum. My shower had twenty-six nozzles, my bedroom had six cedar-lined closets hidden behind wall panels, and Pat had a cabinet in her marble and gold bathroom simply for keeping her dressing gown warm. The heating system consumed a ton of coal each day. Everything had been designed with complete disregard for cost, and it was reputed to be the most luxurious residence in the Foreign Service. The State Department had acquired it at no out-of-pocket cost from the pre-communist Czech government in exchange for some surplus army trucks and construction equipment. Prague, I thought, was a long way from Falun.

Despite the excitement of having my first embassy and the splendor of our accommodations, I was more than a little troubled that Christmas season. Not only was there the immediate problem of how to extract Hvasta safely from the country, but Czech-American relations generally were at a very low ebb. The Republic of Czechoslovakia had been born from the disintegration of the Austro-Hungarian Empire in the days immediately before the end of World War I. Its first President, Thomas Masaryk (called the "George Washington of Czechoslovakia"), had close ties with the United States and was friendly with President Wilson.

Under Masaryk's leadership the Czechs (whose historical ties were with Austria) succeeded in keeping the outnumbered and poorer Slovaks (whose ties were with Hungary) in an uneasy alliance that lasted until Hitler dismembered the country in 1938. Edouard Benes was then President, having replaced the aging Masaryk in 1935, and he led a government in exile during the war. At the end of the war Benes formed a coalition government, including Communist Party members, which accompanied the Soviet forces as they occupied most of Czechoslovakia, including Prague. American forces occupied a small area in Western Czechoslovakia up to Pilsen, but in accordance with previous arrangements, shortly withdrew, to the disappointment of many Czechs. Under the circumstances, it was not surprising that the Communist Party emerged with a plurality in the first postwar elections and formed a government in which they held the key posts. Benes continued to hope that they would respect the Czech democratic tradition, but this was not to be. In February 1948, just before an election in which they feared they would lose ground, the communists staged a coup seizing full control of the government, thus paving the way for the establishment of a communist dictatorship under Klement Gottwald. Shortly after the coup, Jan Masaryk (son of Thomas), the respected Foreign Minister in the coalition government and a key pro-Western figure, was apparently murdered by being thrown from a window in his apartment at the Foreign Office. A bitter and disappointed Beneš refused to sign a Soviet-style constitution, retired to his home in the country and died shortly thereafter. This ended the first postwar effort to work with communists in a democratic framework and disillusioned those who had hoped to find a constructive basis for relations with the Soviets in Europe. The Czech coup was the culminating factor in persuading Western Europe and the United States to conclude the North Atlantic Treaty.

In Czechoslovakia the Iron Curtain descended with a vengeance. In 1952, a Stalin-style purge saw the execution for treason of the first communist Prime Minister and Foreign Minister. The regime became abjectly subservient to Moscow, symbolized by the gigantic and hideous statue of Stalin that dominated the beautiful old city of Prague, the Soviet flag that always flew alongside the Czech flag, and the playing of the Soviet national anthem whenever Czechoslovakia's own anthem was played. At the diplomatic level, contrary to established practice, the Soviet Ambassador was given precedence over all others and treated as dean of the diplomatic corps. At official functions at Hradcany Palace, the Soviet Ambassador, dutifully followed by the satellite Ambassadors, even entered by the main entrance while all others were ushered through a side entrance.

A gulf of conflicting ideology was obviously at the core of strained United States-Czech relations, but in addition to Hvasta there were several stubborn practical issues that divided us as well. After the 1948 communist takeover the new government had nationalized more than $100 million worth of property owned by Americans, many of whom were naturalized citizens of Czech origin who had fled the country during Hitler's occupation or after the communist takeover. The Czech government, which had paid no compensation to its citizens within the country for nationalized property, had no enthusiasm for meeting the claims of those it regarded as Czechs living abroad, many of whom it considered traitors. The United States government, however, endeavored to protect the interests of all its citizens whether naturalized or not.

To complicate the picture, a tripartite commission composed of Britain, France and the United States was holding $22 million in Czech gold (at the existing price of $35 an ounce) that had been recovered from Germany at the end of the war. There was no question that Czechoslovakia owned the gold, but until we received a satisfactory settlement on our claims for nationalized property, we were going to exercise our veto in the tripartite commission on the subject of returning it. This did not please the Czechs in the least, but they had no choice except to acquiesce since the gold was in Brussels.

A third problem concerned a $17 million steel mill ordered by the pre-1948 non-communist Czech government that was not completed until after the coup. The new Communist Foreign Minister, Villam Siroky, convinced the Czech government to pay the $7 million balance due on the assumption that the United States government would permit its shipment to Czechoslovakia despite American qualms about the new regime. Siroky turned out to have guessed wrong, however, and we refused to permit its shipment or return their money. Quite understandably, this not only angered the Czech government but acutely embarrassed Siroky, who, by the time I arrived, had become Prime Minister.

I was determined to exploit my status as a new actor on the scene to break the impasse on Hvasta as quickly as possible. It was not a problem that time would help resolve, and if progress were to come on other aspects of our relations, a success with Hvasta would have to precede it. The Czechs seemed to feel the same way, which was encouraging. The Foreign Minister received me for my formal call to hand over copies of my credentials and formal remarks on December 28, the Monday following my arrival; and the President, Antonin Zapotocky, agreed to receive my credentials formally just three days later on New Year's eve. This was unprecedented, especially in Prague at that time, when a month's wait was more typical.

I was told that the Czechs were retaining some of the old color in the presentation of credentials, so I looked forward to the ceremony. On the morning of the appointed day, the Chief of Protocol came to my residence to escort me to the Palace in the President's armored limousine. Followed by senior members of my staff in other government cars, we drove to Hradcany Palace, a huge collection of buildings started under the Holy Roman Emperors, to which many monarchs of the Austro-Hungarian empire had added abundantly and grandiosely. It overlooks the charming baroque city of Prague from a hill rising from the banks of the Vltava.

For the hour that the ceremony required, an American flag flew over Hradcany. On the large square in front of the Palace gates a considerable crowd had gathered, including Patricia and other members of the embassy staff with families. Inside the main gate a military band and honor guard awaited my arrival. Dressed in a formal morning coat and guided by the Chief of Protocol, I met the commanding officer who escorted me as I trooped the line to inspect the honor guard. We returned to the center of the line, and facing the troops I shouted *nazdar*, a Czech word of greeting, to which they shouted back in unison *zdar*, and the band then played a somewhat ragged rendition of the *Star Spangled Banner*.

Followed by the senior members of my staff I entered the Palace and walked up the broad marble staircase into a reception hall dominated by a gigantic (and none too friendly) portrait of Stalin. Shortly, President Zapotocky entered, also dressed formally. We shook hands, and facing him I read my bland formal address before handing him my credentials from President Eisenhower. He replied with an equally bland address. Then accompanied by an interpreter, the two of us then went to a small adjoining room for a private talk.

After we settled down in our chairs, I dispensed with the usual pleasantries and immediately plunged into the Hvasta case, a highly unorthodox approach. I was pleased to see that the President was evidently prepared for this. Instead of rejecting discussion, which he easily could have done on the grounds that it was premature and improper to raise with him a matter which should initially be raised with the Foreign Minister, we had a substantive thirty-minute talk. In contrast with other Czech leaders, President Zapotocky had an air of sincerity and an attractively plain manner of speaking. Nevertheless, he quickly reasserted his government's unwillingness to compromise on Hvasta. I was equally unswerving, so we made no headway. But Zapotocky agreed that we should try to settle the problem quickly. Satisfied at this start, I returned to the hall to rejoin my staff and the other Czech officials, who had been growing restive at the unusual length of my closeting with the President.

That same day, after I returned to the embassy, I requested an urgent appointment with Foreign Minister Vaclav David, but he put it off until January 6. On that date we had almost an hour's conversation. I quickly found David very frustrating to work with. He was a mouse of a man, terrified that he would be purged and killed if he deviated even slightly from total orthodoxy as Moscow defined it. (I must say that I had a certain amount of sympathy for his fears because two of his recent predecessors as Foreign Minister, Vladimir Clementis and Jan Masaryk, had in fact been killed.) He did not want any unrehearsed conversation, during which the bugs planted in his office might transmit to the secret police some imperfection in articulating the current party line to the American Ambassador. Instead, he wished us to deliver our respective prepared statements and stop.

This was the beginning of an odd diplomatic dance. I wanted the Czechs to pardon Hvasta or commute the sentence so he could leave the country legally. The Czechs had argued that no government could commute the sentence of someone who was not in their custody. So I presented to David a formula that I thought could satisfy both parties. We would agree to return Hvasta to their "technical custody" if they would agree to commute his sentence to expulsion from the country and to grant us unbroken "consular access"—that is, the right to have an American Embassy official present with him at all times while they went through the legal formalities of commuting his sentence and until he left the country. I also wanted David to agree to completing this whole process within the twelve hours of one working day.

David responded to this formula with a very hard line. While he said the Czech government was prepared to consider this proposal and Hvasta's application for commuting his sentence, it would not be possible to "attach any conditions to his surrender" to the Czech authorities. I interpreted this statement as an ultimatum to turn Hvasta over at once and trust to the Czechs' good faith that nice things would happen. This, of course, I would not do. I felt David was trying to soften me up by being tough, and bluffing to test my resolve. There was still time to maneuver; I doubted the Czechs would try any overt action against the embassy or Hvasta just after I arrived. We redoubled our watch on Hvasta in his fourth-story room, but having explained my proposal to David, I waited for him to reply.

I did not wait long. On January 15 the Foreign Minister asked to see me. He said that the Czech government had expected me to transmit to Washington its request for Hvasta's immediate surrender and had accordingly "postponed other actions" (presumably seizing Hvasta by force) in the expectation that we would comply, as we should under international law. With this threatening introduction he went on to say that after making inquiries, he could say that pardon proceedings for Hvasta would take three days, "perhaps a little less, perhaps a little more," but I should be clear that "the pardon prerogatives of the Czech President could not be made the subject of bargaining." He would make no promises about consular access, and gave me five days to comply with his terms. If I did not, he said, the United States "would have to bear responsibility for any action the Czech government found necessary" to secure Hvasta's return. This was an extremely provocative and serious threat, implying that the Czechs would break into the embassy and seize Hvasta unless we complied by January 20.

Although I considered David's formula unsatisfactory I reported it to the Department and discussed it with Hvasta. To my surprise they were both less negative than I. Hvasta even indicated some willingness to accept it on condition that we told the Czechs that we would break diplomatic relations if they broke the commitment to pardon and release him within three days. The tension mounted until January 20, when I asked to see the Foreign Minister. I told him that three days for pardoning was too long, but in any event it was absolutely essential that we have consular access throughout the entire time Hvasta was in their custody. He received this even more dourly and silently than usual and the atmosphere was very strained as we parted. The following day he asked to see me urgently and suddenly cancelled the appointment just before I left for his office. He was clearly playing a game of nerves. I was concerned that the Czechs would not bluff twice and might be planning to raid the embassy and grab Hvasta, so I passed word that I knew would quickly reach the police, and that was that if they entered the embassy, they could expect to see me inside the gate and to have to use physical force to move me. We kept close watch on Hvasta. Strange men declaring themselves "lost" turned up inside our walled compound at night.

This state of high tension began to weigh more and more heavily upon us. For the first time in my career I had difficulty sleeping. Further talks with David would be fruitless, I decided; he lacked sufficient authority to make independent decisions. So I arranged to see Prime Minister Villam Siroky on January 29. Siroky was Slovak. Slovaks had lived under Hungarian rule for a thousand years until the formation of independent Czechoslovakia in 1918, and they tend to be more demonstrative and tougher than the Czechs. Siroky was a hard man, and among his other reasons for disliking the United States he resented that we had blocked the export of the steel mill after he had prevailed upon his government to pay for it in full. But he said what he thought, and I was able to deal with him. Our conversation on Hvasta was heated, but at least it was a dialogue.

He repeated the demands Foreign Minister David had previously made, and I repeated my formula emphasizing these two points: 1) not more than one working day for pardoning Hvasta and, 2) continuous consular access. He asked bluntly "Don't you trust us?," and I gave an equally blunt "No." This set the tone for a real give and take, and at the end of our session he agreed to my formula. He said that I should work out the details with the Foreign Minister. I was, of course, elated and rushed back to the embassy where I immediately phoned for an appointment with the Foreign Minister, sent a flash telegram to the Department, and drafted an aide memoir to be left with the Foreign Minister in order to obtain his written confirmation of the procedure.

The Foreign Minister saw me at 5 P.M. He made an oral statement that conformed to what the Prime Minister had told me and suggested that Hvasta be delivered to the Interior Ministry at ten o'clock the following morning. When I gave him my aide memoir summarizing the arrangement and requested a similar one from him, however, he exploded with rage, saying they would not put anything in writing. But he did agree to accept my note and said he would immediately get in touch with me after having it translated.

I waited up all night for some word, but none came. This created a real dilemma for me. Siroky and I had agreed to a solution, but if his Foreign Minister refused to commit himself in writing, should I go ahead anyway? Was Siroky lying and setting me up, or was David just being typically hypercautious? If it looked like I would have to forego an exchange of notes to break an impasse, should I risk it?

The Department said that they would approve my waiving an exchange of notes if I thought it necessary in order to avoid a breakdown in negotiations. This, however, still left the final decision to me. It was not standard procedure in Dulles's State Department to trust the word of communist Eastern European leaders, and if waiving the notes turned out to be wrong, and the Czechs double-crossed me by seizing Hvasta, it probably would mean both his life and the end of my career. At the same time, if my insistence on confirming the procedure in writing meant that this whole scheme fell through, the consequences would also be hard to foresee. I wrote the Foreign Minister asking for clarification, but received none. Finally, I decided to trust Siroky's word without exchanging notes.

I then sent word that I was prepared to deliver Hvasta to the Interior Ministry in accordance with my conversation with Siroky and David, and arranged to do so at 10 A.M., February 4.

Slightly before that hour, in keeping with plans that had been carefully drawn up, Hvasta was driven out of the embassy accompanied by Jack Iams, the First Secretary, and the prayers of us all. Nat King, the Embassy Counselor, followed in another car and returned to the embassy after seeing Iams and Hvasta walk safely into the Interior Ministry. I waited by the phone for word from Iams, and after much stomach-wrenching it came at one o'clock. The formalities had been completed without incident. The Czech authorities had made a few attempts to separate them, but nothing Iams could not handle. King then left the embassy to meet the two of them as they emerged from the Ministry. Jack and Nat drove to Germany, mindful that the Czechs still might try to seize or kill Hvasta on the open road. My fingernail biting continued until 4 P.M. that evening, when the German border post at Waidhaus called to say that Iams, King, and Hvasta were safely in Germany.

That night I had the first really good sleep since arriving in Prague. Hvasta was safely on his way home without my having to pay anything for his release, and instead of being disgraced, I received a laudatory telegram from Secretary Dulles. In fact, the whole incident had hinged upon my reading of Siroky's character—and perhaps his of mine. Such incidents, I think, strongly argue against the theory that modern communications have reduced ambassadors to mere messengers.

I felt even more satisfied with the outcome when some months later I related the story to the Yugoslav Ambassador, Vevojda, who had arrived in Prague shortly after relations between the two countries were restored in 1956. Vevojda and I had taken an immediate liking to each other and we talked very frankly about the Czechs, whom he had known intimately (and disliked) since his education at Charles University in Prague. After I described the Hvasta case, he recounted a very similar tale about a Yugoslav, imprisoned in Hungary at about the same time, who had likewise escaped from jail and found asylum in the Yugoslav Embassy in Budapest. Since there was then no Yugoslav Ambassador in Budapest, Vevojda, who was a section chief in the Yugoslav Foreign Office with the rank of Ambassador, was dispatched from Belgrade to settle the matter. He worked out orally an arrangement almost identical to the one I had negotiated for Hvasta, the only difference being that it did not work. When he walked into the Interior Ministry with his citizen, he was shoved through one door while the man he was escorting was shoved through another and hung that night.

The day after Hvasta's release the Foreign Office hit me with a twelve-page note requesting the prompt shipment of that steel mill we were refusing to export, a good example of what diplomats call linkage and others call horse-trading. Siroky had helped me, and he wanted something in return.

The mill was, of course, simply one part of a larger complex of problems. The Czechs wanted us to ship the steel mill or return their payment; but as long as Czech steel went into Soviet weapons we were going to keep the mill, and as long as Czechoslovakia refused to compensate Americans for property nationalized after the 1948 takeover, we were going to keep the money. On another front, the Czechs did not want to compensate Czech emigrés who happened to be American citizens for expropriated property, while we sought to protect the interests of our citizens equally, whether naturalized or not. And then again the Czechs wanted the $22 million in pre-war gold, held in Brussels by the American-French-British commission, that we planned to keep until we had a satisfactory settlement on our claims. Finally, the Czechs wanted us to restore Most Favored Nation trading status to them, and thus permit a resumption of trade, which we had stopped to secure the release of AP Correspondent Oatis.

All of these problems were interwoven, so we pretty much had to get agreement on everything to get agreement on anything. I looked toward some kind of lump sum settlement that would avoid questions of principle for both sides, yet be sufficient to satisfy the claimants in the United States. With the help of my staff, I opened an exchange with the Department to set realistic objectives for a comprehensive economic settlement and to devise negotiating tactics. It turned out to be a remarkably frustrating problem. Though I and my deputy chiefs of mission worked hard on it, we did not get far.

It took many years before we could devise a package deal that would satisfy the Czechs, but even more stubborn were the large American claimants. They have held out for 100 percent compensation for their claims, though the Czechs were prepared fairly early to offer the normal Eastern European figure of 40 percent, which we had accepted elsewhere. The small claimants, who no doubt need the money more than their well-insured big brothers, could not muster sufficient political clout in Congress to prevail, and so the problem remained unsolved.

The total claims were valued in 1958 at a total of $73 million. In that year we seized and sold the steel mill to Argentina (it being one of the few countries using the fifty-cycle electric

current for which it was designed) for $9 million and distributed
$8.5 million to the smaller claimants. When the gold was worth
$22 million at $35 an ounce that left a balance of some $42 million
in uncompensated claims even if we had kept the gold for ourselves. It was only when the price of gold increased some ten-
fold many years later that we could get what we wanted, and the
Czechs could still be left with a substantial sum in gold.

Of course, at the time I did not know we would face so
many obstacles, and I tried hard to inject some life into the economic negotiations. I hoped that my freshness on the scene and
the momentum from the Hvasta solution might get us somewhere.
Prime Minister Siroky was also eager for quick progress. He felt
personally injured by what he considered our iniquity in accepting
payment for the steel mill without permitting its shipment, especially after he had gone to such lengths to resolve the Hvasta
case. He vigorously attacked me on the subject at every opportunity, and, though unable to agree with him, I could understand
why he felt so deeply. He seldom saw me officially. The only time
we could talk was at diplomatic receptions, when I would maneuver him into a corner and we would go at it.

He debated ably and seemed to enjoy matching wits with
me, but this happened infrequently and no tangible progress in
reducing the differences between our governments ever resulted.
Even so, these verbal duels were a welcome relief from my contacts with other ministers, who would at most shake hands and
then scurry off as fast as possible to avoid any conversation. It
was also a pleasant change from my sterile, official sessions with
Foreign Minister David. When we did discuss substantive topics,
which was unusual, he would read a prepared propaganda harangue on Washington's latest perfidy. After I listened to what
he said I would start making comments. He would look through
his notebook to find some reply that seemed appropriate, but
after one or two fitful attempts at this sort of "dialogue" he would
become flustered and ask me to stop. He just wanted me to transmit his views to Washington and give him our reply in writing.

Many of our discussions, in fact, revolved around the petty
but deliberate obstructionism of the Czech "Diplomatic Service
Bureau," which, along with trying to control other aspects of our
own lives, had to approve the hiring and firing of all servants and
Czech employees of the embassy. I wanted to hire the cook who
was leaving the Chinese Embassy; they said no. They wanted me
to release a long-time and very valued embassy driver; I said no.
Appeals had to be lodged with the Foreign Minister, and some-

times he helped. I also complained to him occasionally about "bugs" we had found planted in the Embassy or the propensity of police trail cars to engage in dangerous tailgating. To these he would respond with real or imagined sins committed against Czech diplomats in the United States by the FBI. It was not a very stimulating relationship, and came to symbolize the generally unproductive existence I had to lead in Prague.

Indeed, my appointment as Ambassador, which I had seen as a considerable step up, had the anomalous result of actually decreasing the responsibility I was called upon to exercise. My new title carried an aura of respect and responsibility that no person with a normal ego could ignore, and I was at least normal in this regard. It was pleasant to have a big mansion in which to live and entertain, to receive the deference of one's colleagues and to be looked upon as an oracle on all manner of subjects. But after the Hvasta case there was frankly not much else to do but "show the flag." I believe I did this creditably, but it did not call for any great exercise of intelligence or talent. Neither of our countries was ready at the time for any significant improvement in relations.

In April 1954 Dulles sent a telegram asking me immediately to return to Washington to coordinate the American delegation to the Geneva talks on Korea and Indochina (which I discuss in the next chapter). That kept me away from Prague until the fall, and from 1955 through 1958 I spent more than half my time away from Prague conducting talks with Chinese Communist Ambassador Wang Ping-nan. My attention to Czech affairs dropped off commensurately—no great loss, given that Czech-American relations seemed petrified anyway. Yet a few interesting things did happen in Prague before I left permanently for Thailand in 1958, and these illustrate some essential aspects of American diplomacy and Eastern European life in the 1950s.

In 1952 the Czech government had demanded we cut our diplomatic representation in the country from seventy-five to fourteen and close our consulate in Bratislava. We, of course, reciprocated by requiring the Czechs to do the same and close their consulate in Chicago. In view of the freeze in United States-Czech relations, I felt that fourteen well-qualified Americans (including secretaries, military attachés, and consular officers as well as senior staff) could accomplish just about all that was needed. In fact the small numbers helped break the monotony, and the reduced staff had the kind of high morale I have always found in Foreign Service posts living and working hard under difficult conditions. Everyone had to be prepared to handle several jobs, and with no Marine guards, everyone from stenographers to senior military officers and the Deputy Chief of Mission had to take turns staying after hours and sleeping in the restricted code and file area of the Embassy. As the Embassy's Czech drivers were not permitted to leave the country, all male members of the staff had to take turns driving the big "six by six" Army truck to Nuremburg every few weeks to pick up commissary supplies. In the winter this could be a memorable experience for anyone not accustomed to handling a heavy truck on an icy, tree-lined, two-lane road. Fortunately we never had a serious accident.

Because the Czechs treated all diplomats from outside the Soviet bloc much the same—i.e., as some sort of infectious disease requiring constant observation and quarantine—all of us non-communist diplomats were really forced together whether we wanted to be or not. I took advantage of our large residence and our access to the movie circuit of the United States Army in Germany to show three films a week, one at the Chancery, another on Saturday afternoon at the residence for children, and a third on Sunday evening for adults. These were enjoyable, heavily attended, created much good will, and helped me establish personal relationships throughout the diplomatic community. The informal conversations that took place at these sessions helped us all in our constant efforts to dispel the miasma of rumor and false information in which we lived.

As time wore on, and the central economic issues between us did not appear any nearer solution, Siroky and David discussed them with me less. Instead they began to concentrate on complaining about alleged FBI harassment of Czech diplomats in the United States and the broadcasts of Radio Free Europe (RFE) and Voice of America (VOA), especially their personal attacks on the Czech leadership. Privately, I agreed that RFE and to a degree VOA were too strident to be effective, though obviously I did not let them know that. Secretary of State Dulles was still talking about "liberating the captive peoples of Eastern Europe" and "rolling back the communists," even though he realized perfectly that these were just slogans upon which we had no intention of acting. RFE and VOA amplified this rhetoric through bitter and provocative personal attacks, sometimes based on false tales and rumors, against Eastern European leaders. RFE, which was then largely funded through CIA, was particularly inflammatory. Emigrés from Iron Curtain countries had too large a voice in its programming, and their test of a broadcast's success seemed to be how mad it made the regimes. Columnist Drew Pearson's scheme of launching balloons from West Germany that drifted over Czechoslovakia dropping leaflets was also of very questionable utility. I never found that making people angry was in itself a productive national objective. The Czechs turned the balloon gimmick back on us by alleging that a passenger aircraft crashed after tangling with one.

I understood the purpose of our propaganda campaigns, but after I spent some time in Prague I came to believe them ineffective and, in the long run, self-defeating. As Ambassador I was supposed to improve relations with Czechoslovakia and solve local problems involving Americans, while elsewhere the United States government was loudly promoting the overthrow of the Czech leaders I had to deal with. Considerable mental gymnastics were required to reconcile these contradictory strains of American policy, especially in front of David and Siroky.

I had some strong exchanges with Washington about the radio broadcasts and leaflet balloons. I also leaned hard on the Radio Free Europe headquarters in Munich to cease its rumor-mongering and to mute its tone of unrelenting personal hostility. I believed that the United States hurt its own credibility in Eastern Europe by endorsing broadcasts that were often as tendentious and slanted as those from the communist-controlled stations in Eastern Europe. I thought RFE should broadcast straight, solid news and let it speak for itself—becoming, as I termed it, the *"New York Times* of the air" from Western Europe. Not only might this increase people's trust in what they heard and improve chances of encouraging constructive internal developments, I thought, but it could also accelerate some of the natural tendencies toward national assertiveness and independence from Soviet domination that already existed in Eastern Europe. Eventually, especially after the 1956 Hungarian uprising, Washington did begin to realize that Eastern European nationalistic tendencies would not be encouraged by crude propaganda, and the two stations adopted a much more reasonable and trustworthy tone.

Even though there was not much diplomacy to transact with the Foreign Office, I did try to get a feel for the country and its people to make my reporting to Washington more accurate and my occasional negotiating in Prague more astute. As a people, the Czechs seem to me somewhat less adventurous than most. I certainly found that to be the case in their relations with the

Soviet Union. In my political reporting I was always perfectly safe in predicting to Washington that nothing would ever happen in Prague until orders had gone out from the Kremlin.

Historically the Czechs have not been noted for taking excessive risks, having had to learn to accommodate themselves to a series of foreign rulers since the Thirty Years' War in the seventeenth century. I did not blame them for their adaptability, though I never really warmed to it; they were solid, civilized, bourgeois people who had learned through hard experience to survive by not taking unnecessary chances.

To their credit, the Czechs recognized their habit of caution and enjoyed making fun of it. Once I was visiting some movie studios in Prague—Czech films are well-regarded internationally, and the industry is quite large—where they showed us "rushes" of films soon to be released. Most of them were typical dreary Soviet-style propaganda—well-scrubbed, hard-eyed heroes breaking production records to usher in socialist nirvana, a love story between a woman and a soldier where duty and the Army win out, etc. But then, to my intense surprise, they showed *the Good Soldier Schweik*, the story of a fictional pre-World War I character drafted into the Austrian Army who somehow embodies the essence of Czech national character. By deliberate as well as inherent stupidity, he manages to foil the most determined attempts of Austrian officers to make him a soldier. Its modern message, under the circumstances, hardly seemed pro-Soviet. As the film started, the wife of its director leaned over to me and whispered: "You know, this is the way we Czechs really are."

A typically self-deprecating joke was popular after the Sputnik launching in 1957. A Czech teacher was directed to inform her pupils about this wonder of socialist science. In a few years, she said, they would be traveling to the moon, and later there would be travel to Mars and Venus. Then, in the back of the class, a little girl raised her hand and asked: "But, Teacher, when will we be able to travel to Vienna?" Prague was always full of jokes, most with this kind of sardonic edge. This story-telling had become a way for Czechs both to vent their frustration and to substitute laughter for more active self-defense.

It was interesting to observe how the ever-adaptive Czech leadership reacted to Khruschev's rule. Stalin, for all his ruthlessness and paranoia, was at least easy to understand. But I sensed that the Czech communist leadership felt deeply disturbed when Khrushchev started attacking Stalin and encouraging the satellite countries to be more independent. The Czech leaders certainly did not believe their own propaganda. They knew that their enlightened rule had not transformed Czechoslovakia into a workers' paradise and that brute force alone kept them in power. If Khrushchev's pressures for ruling less oppressively forced them to make compromises, they worried that one compromise would lead to another and that their days would be numbered. I think their analysis was right. In Hungary and Poland in 1956, and Czechoslovakia in 1968, small reform quickly bred desire for more, until popular demand for fundamental change grew so strong, even among the normally passive Czechs, that only Soviet troops could extinguish it. Siroky, Zapotocky, and company understood that keeping an oppressive dictatorship in power required continued oppression.

It did not take much sophistication to recognize that most Czechs were not happy with their leadership or system. Before World War II the country had close political, cultural, and economic ties to Western Europe. Nicknamed the "Switzerland of Central Europe," its economy was prosperous. After the communist takeover, however, Czech living standards fell, partly because Moscow wanted the Soviet Union to lead the bloc in everything and partly because of the inefficiencies inherent in overcentralized management. The contrast between Czechoslovakia and prosperous next-door West Germany became ever more glaring. The Soviet-dictated collectivized agriculture system had succeeded in turning Czechoslovakia from a significant food exporter to a major importer, for which it paid by robbing the country of much of its industrial production, thus lowering living standards further. The Iron Curtain and the reorienting of the economy to support the interests of the Soviet Union came as a bitter pill to the average Czech. On the other hand, although the Czechs clearly despised Russians and disliked their own regime, I had the impression that they did approve of some of its reforms, such as free health care and the nationalizing of large industries. They wanted neither Soviet-style communism nor the largely unbridled capitalism of former days, but some intermediate form of democratic socialism.

Memories of the British and French betrayal at Munich and the Nazi occupation were still very fresh. The regime tried to keep them that way to make the Soviet "liberators" seem more appealing, but physically the country had escaped the war relatively unscathed. I remember the Yugoslav Ambassador snorting at oft-repeated Czech references to Lidice, a small town near Prague that the Germans wiped out in retaliation for the assassination of German "Protector" Reinhard Heydrich by Czech parachutists from England. The story of Lidice became a one-note song constantly played by the government, to which Vevojda responded: "Every town in Yugoslavia was a Lidice." He was exaggerating, but I understood his point.

The most glaring and monotonous feature of Czechoslovakia for Western diplomats, not to mention the ordinary people, was the ubiquity of secret police. Our telephones were tapped, we found microphones in our offices and under our beds, we were followed everywhere, our servants were required to inform on us—all the normal trappings of a police state.

It was impossible for us to meet ordinary Czechs, for whom any contact with Americans was dangerous. But we discovered two things: ordinary American magazines, and above all the *Sears Catalogue*, were the best propaganda we had, and that the embassy trash bin and hotel bedroom waste basket were their most effective means of distribution. I arranged to receive each month hundreds of old magazines, with particular emphasis on those dealing with women's fashions, homemaking and automobiles, as well as large supplies of Sears' big catalogue. On Sunday when strollers had access to the embassy grounds they would find that we had discarded on top of the trash bin many of these publications. They would all disappear within minutes of our opening the gates. In traveling about the country we would also "accidentally" leave a few on restaurant tables or in hotel rooms. Nobody ever sought to return them to us.

Since we were deprived of substantive diplomatic work to do, I thought it was valuable for embassy officers including me to travel widely throughout the country, flying an American flag on the fender to let people know we were still there. These journeys not only kept us in touch with some of the realities of Czech life but also kept up our spirits, which could sag after too long in the inbred atmosphere of the Prague diplomatic community. I had learned some good lessons during my World War II internment in Manchuria about the value to morale of sparring with one's captors. We lost no opportunity to razz the Czech secret police, who followed us everywhere—into restaurants, stores, and even rest rooms. (They would smile but never talked to us; after all, they were supposed to be "secret.")

One of my favorite sports was trying to drive fast enough to shake our police tails. I bought ever faster cars until I ended up with a big, souped-up Oldsmobile that could do about 120 miles per hour. The police's locally made Tatra cars could only manage about 100 mph, and I would always slowly gain as we tore along country roads full of bends but mercifully bereft of traffic. But since they were less concerned about hitting pedestrians than I, they usually managed to catch up by driving through inhabited areas much faster than I ever dared.

The police worked especially hard on our servants, trying to create such deep apprehension among them that none would dare hold back a single detail about our activities lest someone else report it first. (Nevertheless, the servants had unmistakable ways of letting me know what was going on without directly saying so and I, of course, took care to protect them.) Those who did not cooperate sufficiently had their work cards withdrawn, and I knew some long-time embassy employees who were thus reduced to real poverty. It was a nasty system, but very effective over a short period because it made the servants loath to join with each other or with us against the police.

The police devoted great effort to forcing the removal of any diplomat in a non-communist embassy who spoke Czech. If such an employee had Czech relatives, no matter how distant, the relatives would be harassed, so we avoided assigning these individuals to Prague. If he or she were not of Czech ancestry, careful and elaborate traps were set to provide a pretext for expelling the person. In fact, they were always at work to lay traps that would provide a basis to blackmail a person into working for them.

We were, of course, alert to this danger and often discussed it among ourselves. Occasionally, there would be object lessons of what had happened to personnel in other Western embassies. Because of our small numbers and necessarily close association with each other, however, I was confident that I had the situation under control. To avoid being trapped in black market deals, which were very tempting because of the vast gap between the official and black market exchange rates, I kept careful track of how much American currency each staff member exchanged at the official rate at the embassy and compared it with what should normally be expected. Since all of housing was government-furnished and our food supplies were brought in from the Army commissary in Germany, our need for local currency was minimal. In this way we avoided any problems arising from the black market. However, it turned out that I was too complacent and had underestimated the secret police.

The three women who were secretaries in the embassy lived together in small separate apartments in a building on the same grounds as my residence and that of the Deputy Chief of Mission. Their life was, of course, not very exciting, and social contacts outside our own embassy were confined to a few women working in the other Western embassies. On one occasion one of the secretaries (whom I will call Jane Doe) asked to take routine leave in West Germany, traveling by rail since she did not have a car. The other two went down to the station and saw her off on a Thursday morning, expecting that she would be back in about ten days.

Late Sunday evening while I was at home I received a call from the Foreign Office saying that Miss Doe had been arrested for traveling on false documents in a frontier zone; she was now at the Foreign Office and would I come up so that she could be turned over to me. I could not have been more astonished. I called the other two secretaries and they confirmed that they had seen her off on the train for Germany on Thursday as planned. Needless to say, however, I sent an officer to the Foreign Office. He met and brought to my office an obviously distraught and exhausted Jane Doe. The Foreign Office representative had told him the same story, that she had been traveling in a frontier area of Slovakia distant from Prague on false documents. When the police had established her diplomatic status, they very properly brought her immediately to the Foreign Office to be released to me.

Jane then told me a long and painful story. Because she could not drive, she had taken advantage of a very attractive and cheap offer by the Czech Auto Club to take lessons. The teacher assigned to her was a young and attractive Czech who spoke good English and was a good teacher. During the course of the lessons he began to speak of his personal life, his despair that he and his wife were not compatible, and how refreshing he found it to be with Jane. She was very plain and not accustomed to much attention from males. They arranged to see each other more frequently under the guise of her driving lessons and eventually she fell in with a plan for their spending a weekend together while she pretended to take leave in Germany. After she boarded the train in Prague, he would meet her at the next station and together they would drive to a beautiful mountain resort in Slovakia. He assured her there would be no complications, as she would travel and register at the hotel under his wife's identity card.

The plan went as scheduled and they had an idyllic weekend in Slovakia. They started back late Saturday evening and quickly encountered a police road block. When the police began

to question them, it became apparent that, contrary to her iden-
tification, she could not speak Czech. They were both promptly
arrested and taken to a police station, where several plain clothes
officers were waiting. They initially took a very hard line, pointing
out the seriousness of her offense, the disgrace she would suffer,
and how I would probably fire her from her position. They then
turned sympathetic and said she could avoid all of this if she would
only give them a little harmless help, none of which would involve
her fellow American workers or reflect on her loyalty to the
United States. All they wanted was a little information on the
personal characteristics and habits of some of her acquaintances
among the secretaries in other embassies in Prague.

If she would agree to provide this, they would see that she
was placed on the proper train from Germany with the proper
stamps in her passport so that she could be met by her fellow
workers as though nothing had happened. Jane was well briefed
enough to know where this apparently small first step would lead.
She refused to become entrapped, even though she had reason
to believe that exposure of what she had already done might well
lead to her dismissal from the Foreign Service. They kept after
her all night. When she continued to refuse on Sunday, they drove
her back to Prague, pressing her the entire way. After entering
the Police Station, she never again saw her "driving instructor."

I was impressed by her story of courage and judgment
under the most stressful conditions, and in my report to the Department I strongly urged that although she must immediately
be removed from Prague she be retained in the Service. I am
glad to say that my recommendation was accepted.

Blackmail of this sort is as old as espionage itself, but the
Czechs tried some newer tricks as well. One day, for example,
the American and British air attachés were driving in the north
of the country along a main, well-traveled highway. As they approached an airfield that the road skirted, a military policeman
appeared and directed them down a side road. They thought
nothing of it because this happened fairly often when convoys
were moving or troops were engaged in maneuvers. This small
road went directly past the airfield, and as they came abreast of
it a large truck suddenly pulled in front of them and stopped,
effectively blocking their way. The driver refused to budge. When
they started to back out, another truck pulled in behind so they
were stuck. As they discussed what to do, they noticed three
tractors heading toward them from the far side of the airfield,
dragging three decrepit, obsolete military planes behind them.

The tractors kept coming, and deposited the planes right next to their car. Then they heard a deep rumble; across the field three tanks lumbered toward them, finally stopping next to the airplanes. The purpose of these comic-opera antics soon became clear. In less than an hour—and Prague was more than an hour's drive away—a procession of cars pulled up, out of which popped newsreel, television, and still photographers eager to record this "evidence" of imperialist "espionage." After they finished, representatives of the Defense and Foreign Ministries duly appeared to arrest the attachés. They were released quickly—even the Czech participants must have found this escapade a little ludicrous—and hastened to Prague to tell the British Ambassador and me what had happened. We quickly saw Foreign Minister David, protesting this blatant entrapment in the most vehement possible terms. He seemed not to know of the plot. His ignorance, coupled with our prompt objections, kept the attachés from being declared *persona non grata* and expelled, but we could not prevent the Czechs from showing their "proof" of Western malevolence in every newspaper, magazine, and theater in the country.

Czech efforts at electronic eavesdropping were a constant problem for us, especially when miniaturized electronics made small radio transmitters possible. A favorite place for bugs, especially when we were traveling, was under the bed. Once we found a whole nest of microphones and wires that the Czechs were installing in the attic above our offices. The embassy building had been penetrated by putting a matching door in the thick brick wall separating the attic from a former school, and each night, above the heads of our Americans on watch duty, the "buggers" would stealthily add to the network. We discovered it by tapping the wall in a routine check and finding a slightly hollow noise where the door had been cut. Washington wanted to raise a big fuss about it immediately, but I persuaded them to let me handle it.

When Foreign Minister David next called me in to lambast the United States for some alleged outrage the FBI had committed on Czech diplomats in the United States, I recounted in detail the story of the door and pulled one of the microphones out of my pocket. David was embarrassed and had trouble refuting my evidence; he probably had been kept ignorant of the bugging and our discovery of it. Enjoying my temporary advantage, I laid my protest on pretty thick. At the end of my lecture he said, "That sounds like a fairy tale." I replied: "I certainly agree." He said he would investigate, but, of course, we never heard anything.

In 1956, Khruschev instituted a thaw in Soviet-American cultural relations, and the Czech regime had to go along, albeit uncomfortably. When I learned that the *Porgy and Bess* company was going to visit Moscow in early 1956, I received Department approval to try to arrange a visit to Prague. Its excellent music and engaging story of black life on "catfish row" made it a natural for breaking the ice with the Czechs in cultural relations, and the fact that it was going to Moscow cut away all the ground for opposing it from under the Communist Party ideologues. The company's very able advance man and I were finally able to wring an approval out of the authorities.

The cast gave a superb performance, and following the first one I gave a reception to which I invited a large number of Czech officials, artists and theatre people, as well as my diplomatic colleagues. All our facilities were overtaxed, including the enormous kitchen, but I had never seen such gaiety in Prague, let alone among officials. The cast mixed in at the reception like the professionals they were—singing, dancing with the guests, giving little impromptu performances themselves. At six o'clock the next morning we swept out the last guest and collapsed. It had been unquestionably the most successful, and substantively most useful party we ever gave. We were sure that a door to the country's cultural world had been opened. Parties can be a very important part of diplomacy.

The company stayed from February 8 to February 20, giving twelve performances to enthusiastic standing-room-only crowds. They were the sensation of Prague offstage, too, because they went around town spreading good humor and good will. The man who played Crown was an awesome six foot four or so and very black. He created real excitement when he went out with his equally attractive black wife and two young children. As an American I could not have been more proud of the whole group.

On September 11, Charles Munch conducted the Boston Symphony Orchestra at Smetana Hall. The Czechs, of course, have a great musical tradition. Dvořák and Smetana were Czech, Mozart lived and worked in Prague for a time, and the Czech people probably have as much sophistication in producing and appreciating music as any people in Europe. But since 1939, and especially since the descent of the Iron Curtain in 1948, the Czechs had been cut off from developments in the West. The Boston Symphony was the first Western orchestra to visit since the Communist coup, and so its coming was a real event.

Pat and I entertained the conductor of the Prague Symphony and his wife that night in a box in Smetana Hall. Munch opened with a stirring performance of the Czech national anthem. Then, instead of following with the Soviet national anthem that had been obligatory since 1948 and to which all Czech audiences were accustomed, he turned to the "Star-Spangled Banner," which his great orchestra played with very special verve in that setting. It was a deeply emotional experience for everyone. After the last note there was absolute silence for perhaps ten seconds and then pandemonium broke loose. People clapped, shouted, whistled, and embraced each other. Our two guests turned to us with tears in their eyes, for a few moments unable even to speak. The closing number in the orchestra's performance was Ravel's stirring *Daphnis and Chloe* which had been banned in Czechoslovakia since 1948. This produced another emotional outburst from the audience.

Following the performance, we gave another well-attended reception at the residence, establishing more contacts with the Czech artistic world. Unfortunately, this never developed so far that any of them felt able to accept our invitation except as a part of a large group, and no one felt able to reciprocate. In another few weeks an American jazz band was returning from a tour in the Soviet Union through Czechoslovakia, and I made arrangements for them to play in Prague. But the Boston Symphony had been too much for the nervous leadership. They prevented the musicians from getting off the train and passed it through to Vienna. We had no more cultural exchanges.

One of the best aspects of Foreign Service work is its variety, and even Prague had its share of surprises. Perhaps the most unusual involved the courtship of Harold Connolly, an American hammer thrower, and Olga Fikitova, a discus thrower who, as the country's only gold medal winner in the 1956 Olympics, was something of a Czech national heroine. They had met at the Olympics, fell for each other quickly and decided to marry. She thought of defecting to the United States, but in addition to being a heroine, she was an advanced medical student at Charles University and had parents living in Prague. She decided to return and seek to accomplish their purpose legally. Harold followed her, and together they sought both the necessary government permission for her to marry a non-Czech and an exit permit after their marriage.

The first official response was to refuse permission and to require Connolly to leave the country when his temporary visa expired. But the lovers were not to be put off, and somehow he obtained another visa and returned to Prague. Then they enlisted the help of Emil Zatopek, the great national sports hero who had won long distance runs in both the 1948 and 1952 Olympics, and appealed directly to President Zapotocky. Although not a word of this appeared in any Czech paper, every person in Prague knew of Olga's and Harold's struggle through RFE, VOA and the highly efficient rumor mill. Would love triumph over state and party?

Connolly, of course, kept me well-informed, and through him I kept in touch with Zatopek who was influential and very sympathetic to them. I tried to assist discreetly without making the matter a political controversy between the two governments, which we all agreed would be counter-productive.

Although small items on Harold and Olga had appeared in the American press and I had kept the Department generally informed, I doubt that Dulles had followed it at all. But when he was questioned about it at a press conference, he declared that it was the policy of the United States Government to "favor romance." Zapotocky was on the spot. If dour cold warrior John Foster Dulles was in favor of romance, could Zapotocky be any less so? Permission for the marriage was granted, and there ensued the most pleasant day we spent in Prague.

Three ceremonies were involved, all centering on the picturesque Old Town Square. The first was at the Town Hall for the legal formalities, the second was at the Protestant church for Olga, and the last was at the Catholic church for Harold. Harold asked Patricia to fill the role of the groom's mother, a tradition in Czech weddings, and I loaned him my official limousine and driver. We also offered to give the reception at the Residence for everyone they wished to invite.

Early on the morning of the wedding small crowds gathered in front of both the Chancery and the Residence, obviously in a festive mood and hoping to get a glimpse of the bride and groom. When Patricia drove with Harold to Old Town Square, the crowd there was overflowing into all the side streets, so my driver had great difficulty inching the car up to the Town Hall where Olga and her parents were already waiting. After the party emerged from the Town Hall to proceed to the first church, the throng had become so great and enthusiastic that even the police had to abandon their official posture of this being a "non-event" and help clear a path. By the time they left the Catholic church to drive back to the Residence, the crowd's enthusiasm became almost unmanageable. People rocked the car and climbed all over it. But Harold, Olga, Pat, and company managed to extricate themselves, and return for the reception. In addition to her parents and classmates and teachers at Charles, Olga had invited various Czech athletes, including Zapotek. I was only sorry Dulles could not be present, for he would have enjoyed it. Crowds gathered in front of the Residence, but nobody attempted to crash the party, and groups remained in front of the Chancery all day. The whole city was obviously wringing all the vicarious pleasure it could from the knowledge that romance had triumphed.

Government concern over this public attitude was so great that schoolteachers were instructed to inform their classes that Olga had been "blinded by American gold."

By the fall of 1957 it was clear that my talks in Geneva with Chinese Communist Ambassador Wang Ping-nan were frozen on dead center, and nothing was happening in Prague that required me to stay. Four years in a single post was longer than normal, and I began to receive soundings from my old boss Walter Robertson, still head of the Far Eastern Bureau, about becoming Ambassador to Thailand. I wrote him that I was very interested, but I knew that ambassadorial appointments usually move slowly through the Department and the White House. Though Walter usually got his way, I was not surprised to receive no further news.

In October, Thai Prime Minister Pibun was deposed in a bloodless coup by General Sarit, and I learned in a letter from the Department's Thai desk officer that Sarit disliked our present Ambassador. In the absence of some formal notification from the Department, however, I could not assume I would be the replacement or make preparations to go. On Christmas Eve, four years to the day after arriving in Prague, I received formal orders requesting my immediate arrival in Bangkok. I set the staff to work packing the same evening, and on Christmas Day had them prepare invitations to a reception on December 29. The normal routine for a departing Ambassador in Prague was a gruelling three-month round of farewell dinners and parties. My colleagues could hardly believe it when I told them at the end of the reception that we were leaving, thanked them all, and went around the room shaking hands. Then Pat and I got into our car, already packed, and drove off for Germany.

We arrived in Washington New Year's Day and I started briefings on my new post the day after. Many agencies in Washington had something to contribute—Defense, the Joint Chiefs, Treasury, Agriculture, CIA—and I had additional briefings on Thailand's neighbors and regional developments. My new job was clearly going to be much more active and challenging than my post in Prague.

The Senate was interested in Thailand, and I had to pay calls on the key members of the Foreign Relations Committee and prepare myself for confirmation hearings. They turned out to be uneventful. After them, but before I was confirmed, Pat and I drove quickly to Los Angeles via Omaha, where our daughter was expecting our first grandchild, the arrangement being that the Department would call me as soon as I had been confirmed so I could take my oath of office and depart immediately for Bangkok. Word reached me the evening we arrived in Los Angeles, and though the hour was late I routed out a notary public. She was apparently so impressed at giving the oath of an Ambassador that she did it for free. The next morning, leaving Pat to travel by ship, I took off for Bangkok.

Falun: dressed for church, with my friend Boo.

Johnson family house in Falun. On the front steps, my mother and father.

Tientsin. The Consulate Boat during the flood
of 1939.

Mukden, Manchuria. May 1942, with Japanese-Manchukuoan Guards. Seated
in the middle is Kenneth Krentz. Franklin Lewis is at the far right.

Consul General at Yokohama, 1946. *Left to right:* Stephen, Patricia, Jennifer, me, Judith, and William.

The Korean War. Surveying the DMZ with Lt. Col. Dewitt Cook.

Conferring with John Foster Dulles and Assistant Secretary Walter S. Robinson prior to the start of the repatriation negotiations with China. At this time I was still Ambassador to Czechoslovakia.

1962. As Deputy Undersecretary I host a lunch in Washington for astronauts John Glenn and Gherman Titov. *Left to right:* Ambassador Dobrynin, Col. Glenn, Mrs. Dobrynin, Mrs. Glenn, General Kamanin, Mrs. Titov, Major Titov, Pat, and me.

The Vietnam War: General Vang Pao and I make a helicopter tour of the Plaine des Jarres in Laos.

The Vietnam War: Inspecting a Special Forces camp in the Vietnam highlands.

The Vietnam War: A late-night session aboard Air Force One. *Left to right:* Vice President Humphrey, Dean Rusk, John Gardner, me, Max Taylor, Walt Rostow, and LBJ. The President was reporting to Humphrey on his just-concluded meeting with Thieu and Ky.

The Washington Special Actions Group, meeting on the situation in Southeast Asia. Henry Kissinger and CIA Director Richard Helms are at the ends of the table. On the left are Admiral Thomas Moorer, Chairman of the JCS; me; and Deputy Assistant Secretary William Sullivan. On the right (in full profile), Deputy Secretary Kenneth Rush.

· CHAPTER SEVEN ·

The 1954 Geneva Conference

<hr>

As I INDICATED EARLIER, DURING THE YEARS WHEN I HELD THE post of Ambassador to Czechoslovakia, I was simultaneously occupied in some other, quite unrelated, diplomatic activities. So, before picking up the chronological thread of my narrative in Thailand, I will now go back to some of these other involvements.

In March 1954, when I was settling in at Prague after having resolved the Hvasta case, I received a personal telegram from Secretary Dulles asking me to return to Washington by the first available plane. It was decided at the Four-Power Foreign Ministers' Conference (Britain, France, the Soviet Union, and the United States) meeting in Berlin from January 25 to February 18 to hold two major international conferences in Geneva, starting April 26. They were to cover the most pressing Asian problems of the day: Korea and Indochina. Dulles wanted me to coordinate the work of the American delegation. It was back to the center of the Washington maelstrom, but of course I agreed.

At that time Douglas MacArthur II, a nephew of the General, was serving as Counselor of the Department and in that role usually coordinated the international conferences attended by the Secretary. The decision was made that someone more familiar with the current intricacies of Asian developments should be assigned to Geneva. For the Korean portion of the conference, at least, I was a logical choice. I had followed Panmunjom from start to finish, knew Dulles, Bedell, Smith, and the diplomats of the "16," and could therefore hit the ground running. Nothing important was expected to arise from the bargaining, anyway, as neither side was likely to make significant concessions after three years of near-constant negotiation.

But Indochina was another matter. That phase of the Geneva Conference was expected to be a major international event, with the Soviet Union and China trying to parlay an imminent victory by Vietminh guerrillas under Ho Chi Minh over French colonial forces into a significant gain for communism in Asia. Though I knew comparatively little about Indochina, I discovered when I returned to Washington that this did not automatically disqualify me, since none of my State Department colleagues seemed to have any clear notion of what we could hope to get out of the conference, and I did not hear of anyone competing for my job.

My role as Delegation Coordinator for both phases of the Geneva Conference was similar to that of a military chief of staff. During the preparations in Washington I made sure the necessary position papers were drawn up, that Dulles and Smith were well briefed, and that the mechanics of our large delegation (sometimes exceeding sixty members) were functioning by the time bargaining began. In Geneva I kept the paper flowing, made sure that my superiors in Geneva and Washington were kept informed of significant developments and made necessary decisions in a timely fashion, ensured their decisions were carried out, and kept in constant touch with other delegations. It was a hectic and demanding job to make everything run with order and discipline. In practice this meant I was normally the first in the office in the morning and the last to leave at night, with the few hours in between frequently punctuated by flash messages from Seoul, Saigon, Moscow, Paris, and Washington marked NIACT—"night action." I was very grateful that Secretary Dulles had chosen for our delegation to have both rooms and offices at the unprepossessing Hotel du Rhone downtown, unlike most other delegations, which housed their senior members in handsomed leased villas on the outskirts of Geneva far from where they worked.

Paragraph 60 of the Korean Armistice Agreement signed July 27, 1953, had called for an international conference to settle the unresolved issues of withdrawal of foreign troops and an overall political settlement to the conflict. Both sides had known that such a conference, if it materialized, was unlikely to be productive. Neither side was going to give up at the bargaining table what it retained on the field. Our prickly "ally" Syngman Rhee had no interest in turning the affairs of his country over to outsiders, and the only negotiated settlement he would accept involved his government spreading its control throughout the whole of his divided country. But Rhee knew the only way he could achieve his ambition was via the efforts of UN soldiers, as his army could not take on communist China. And since no UN government desired more fighting in Korea, Rhee's only alternative was to play within the framework of international bargaining the Armistice Agreement had established, carping loudly at every opportunity to make sure we did not concede anything he considered vital, and hoping that events would break his way and force the UN into renewed fighting. Our intelligence estimates in the fall of 1953 rated unilateral action by South Korea quite possible. We felt Rhee doubted our ability to prevent his troops from causing incidents or to disassociate ourselves from them once the communists had retaliated. It was not a good climate for productive talks.

Nevertheless, we went ahead with preparations for the political conference as required by the Armistice Agreement. On September 15, Arthur Dean, Secretary Dulles' former law partner in New York, was appointed to represent the UN at talks with the communists in Panmunjom to settle the arrangements for the full-scale political conference. These sessions at Panmunjom turned out to be acrimonious and completely fruitless. The North Korean and Communist Chinese delegates bore down hard on Dean. An experienced advocate, perhaps he missed the presence of a judge to ensure some progress and basic fair play. After two months and forty-nine unproductive meetings, his patience snapped. At the fiftieth meeting on December 12, 1953, after listening to six hours of particularly rude and vituperative harangue from China's chief delegate Huang Hua (Harvard-educated, whom the world was later to know as China's suave and smiling first UN Ambassador), Dean walked out, saying he would not return until Hua at least withdrew his repeated charges of American "perfidy." Huang, startled, called out (using English for the first time) "come back!" as Dean disappeared out the door, but to no avail. Washington had not authorized the break. It was one of those moments when an individual takes history in his own hands. It took the Four Power Foreign Ministers' conference in Berlin to resuscitate the Korean political conference.

The closer we got to the start of negotiations at Geneva on April 29, the more obstreperous Rhee became. He steadfastly refused even to send a representative. Only the severest arm-twisting by Ambassador Briggs secured his consent to participate, six days before. Rhee sent his reliable, but not unduly bright, Foreign Minister Pyun. As Pyun saw no reason to make concessions merely to satisfy the other delegations on "his" side, maintaining a common front throughout the conference required lots of fast footwork from every American delegate. One participant compared his labors to "herding a bunch of rabbits through a hole in a fence."

My first job in Geneva was to satisfy Dulles' stringent and convoluted seating requirements. This was China's first major international conference, but we did not want to give its government any added status. Dulles refused to sit at a table with Chou En-lai, which meant auditorium-type seating was required. He also refused to sit near any communist delegation and wanted the South Koreans in front of us so we could keep a stern eye on them at moments when they might be tempted to strike off on their own. These requests meant that the well-established alphabetic seating system for diplomatic conferences (in French or English) would have to be modified, a view that my Soviet counterpart, Vice Foreign Minister Kuznetsov, did not share. His mission was to establish the full equality and prestige of China. For this he wanted a large round table. After many hours of wrangling with him and between our staffs, I managed to secure Dulles' wishes—two hours before the conference opened.

During the recess at the first session on Korea, an incident occurred which plagued our relations with Peking for many years. As Dulles walked into the lounge at the Palais des Nations, Chou En-lai, already there, started across the room to shake hands with a broad smile and his usual air of urbane familiarity. I was standing close to Dulles, who did not see Chou until he was very close. Taking a quick look at the press photographers poised to record the symbolic reconciliation, Dulles quickly turned his back on Chou, ignoring the outstretched arm. I always felt this deliberate rudeness was contrary to Dulles' natural instincts, but he was acutely aware of the political repercussions that a photograph splashed across the front pages would cause among congressional hardliners. It was this same sensitivity to domestic politics that had led Dulles to insist on the unusual seating. Chou never forgot the incident and often recounted it to visitors, adopting an air of injured innocence to good effect.

No one expected any real progress to come from the Korean conference. Both sides had already negotiated everything negotiable and had no basis for finding agreement. So the conference became, first and foremost, a public relations exercise. Speeches were designed for home consumption and propaganda. All our "rabbits," even Foreign Minister Pyun, proved more or less amenable to speaking their pieces and moving toward a rapid conclusion. The intricacies do not warrant relating, except for the final session on June 15.

With some difficulty, our delegation had worked out with the South Koreans and the "16" a scenario of set speeches after which we would adjourn the Korean phase indefinitely and issue a public communiqué to which all the governments on our side would subscribe. The choreography was precise and we were alert for any signs of deviation. At the end of a statement by Chou En-lai, during which we heard nothing remarkable or new, Belgium's Foreign Minister Paul Henri Spaak rose to his feet, saying he was pleased to note this important change in China's position and requesting further clarification. This was definitely not part of our scenario. We were baffled by Spaak's behavior. Chou, equally baffled, responded to what he thought Spaak had said and Spaak then countered, but both were talking past each other. We hurried over to Spaak to figure out what the problem was. Fortunately, Lt. Col. Robert Ekvall, our chief Chinese interpreter, intercepted us. He had by chance been listening to the French translation of Chou's speech, the one which Spaak had heard, and he reported that the interpreter had added a few words of explanation at one point to be helpful. Spaak had taken this as a last-minute Chinese initiative. Neither we nor Chou had heard the erroneous French interpretation. We explained all this to Spaak, reestablished some semblance of order, and concluded the conference according to our carefully plotted scenario.

While the Korean phase of the conference was going on, world attention was focused on Indochina. There, in the spring, a large force of Vietminh had encircled a French base at Dienbienphu, a small town near the Lao border in northwest Vietnam, in the culmination of eight years of war. The French had considered the surrounding territory impassable to heavy weapons, but the Vietminh had managed to bring in a large quantity of artillery from China and were giving the French a tremendous pounding. As their strength deteriorated, the French desperately sought American assistance, particularly in resupplying their besieged troops and in bombing the besiegers. There was even talk of using atomic weapons. But Eisenhower, with Congressional backing, refused. Dienbienphu fell to the Vietminh on May 7, the day before the scheduled start of the Indochina phase at Geneva.

Flush with victory, the communists expected to secure France's prompt departure from all Vietnam and international

recognition of their legitimacy as the country's government. Secretary Dulles had very different ideas. A Vietminh victory was
bad enough, but guaranteeing the communists the fruits of their
aggression in an international agreement signed by the United
States was unthinkable. Unfortunately, we had no means to undo
the Vietminh victory. Our allies were unwilling to engage in collective military action and Eisenhower would not do it alone.

Walter Lippmann described our dilemma well in a column
on April 29:

> Congress has deprived Dulles of the power to negotiate. He can
> make no concessions to the Vietminh or Red China. Leading
> Republican senators have no terms of peace except unconditional
> surrender of the enemy and no terms for entering the war except
> a collective action in which nobody is now willing to engage.

How did we come to be France's ally in Indochina in the first
place? Why did what happened at Dienbienphu concern us
enough to lead us even to consider going to war over it? To answer
these questions adequately requires a brief account of Vietnamese
history.

The ancient history of Vietnam depicts its people as alternately victors and vanquished in a long struggle to control the
whole of Indochina—present-day Vietnam, Cambodia, and Laos.
For over a thousand years, China dominated the region, spreading
its language, religions, and legal and economic systems throughout
its vassal states. These cultural legacies, as well as an abiding
distrust of China, remained in Vietnam even after the Vietnamese
homeland in the north gained a precarious independence from
Peking in 939 A.D.

Vietnamese expansion southward followed in later centuries. Venturing out from what today is North Vietnam, their an-
cestral home, the Vietnamese gradually supplanted the Khmer
(Cambodian) and Cham Empires of the south. By the eighteenth
century the Vietnamese had reached the Gulf of Siam and the
peak of their control over the various Southern ethnic groups.

That control, however, was tenuous at best. Seldom did a
single government rule over the whole country, and groups of
Vietnamese contending for national dominance subjected the
country to prolonged periods of civil war. By 1620 these rivalries
had resulted in the division of Vietnam into two separate states.
The southerners built two massive defense walls not far from the
17th parallel, which became the modern border between North
and South Vietnam, and for over a century the two sides refused

even to establish diplomatic relations or permit trade. The result was the development of two distinct groups, northern and southern, with distinguishable character differences. The differences were later accentuated by French colonial rule, and remained a strong factor in the modern country's complex political equation.

The melange of cultural patterns that French colonialism deposited in Vietnam were also significant. French troops gradually conquered Vietnam between 1850 and 1890, often citing the necessity of protecting French missionaries and their Vietnamese converts from persecution by Vietnamese emperors, who had observed how often the flag had followed the cross elsewhere in Asia. In an era of expanding colonialism, France was primarily interested in getting its share of the glories and profit of empire. Following Caesar's old maxim of "divide and conquer," the French accentuated the differences among the three major regions of Vietnam. Tonkin, the northern region, became a kind of French protectorate. Annam, in the center, retained Vietnamese kings, though French "advisors" administered the area through the indigenous governmental structure. Cochinchina, in the south, became an undisguised colony directly administered along traditional French lines. The French restricted communication among the three regions, both to calm ethnic rivalries and prevent the growth of nationwide collaboration against French rule. Travel, communication, and trade with the outside world (except France) was also discouraged. To send a cable from Saigon to Bangkok, a distance of only 450 miles, it was first transmitted to Paris, then to London, then to Singapore, and finally to Bangkok. Why, reasoned the French, should they bother to establish a direct link between the two capitals? The whole colonial mentality focused on France, on enriching it and/or transplanting its institutions to Vietnam rather than strengthening the indigenous culture and economy for the sake of the Vietnamese.

The particularly virulent strain of nineteenth century colonialism France transplanted to Vietnam gave the country its first rudiments of industrial infrastructure but also dissolved many institutions in which the stability of Vietnamese society had been rooted for centuries. Rubber plantations and large rice farms, with absentee landlords and sharecropping tenants, supplanted the traditional social organization that had revolved around small farms and villages. French colonial enterprises prospered, but the vast bulk of Vietnamese did not.

Of the peoples in the three regions into which French-ruled Vietnam was divided, the Tonkinese in the north were considered the most aggressive and energetic; the French used them to help run Laos and Cambodia. It was in the Tonkinese capital of Hanoi that the French established their only Vietnamese university. The Annamites in the center were considered less energetic than the Tonkinese, and the Cochinchinese were reputed the most placid of all. My experience in Saigon in 1964-65 confirmed these rough stereotypes, especially when the most effective civilian government to be established in several years fell in June 1965 because its Chief of State, a Cochinchinese, could not tolerate its Prime Minister, a Tonkinese.

In addition to these ethnic Vietnamese, who were all lowlanders, there were numerous distinct groups who knew no national boundaries and, who, with their slash and burn agriculture, roamed through the interior mountainous areas of Vietnam, Laos, Thailand, Burma, and southern China. In Vietnam, these peoples were collectively called Montagnards by the French. Being nomadic and accustomed to intertribal feuds, they were vigorous and tenacious fighters, especially when facing the feared lowlanders.

Many of them were recruited into the French forces used to suppress the Vietnamese, which only increased the already virulent national animosities between these peoples. In any Montagnard village there would almost always be a few men wearing loincloths and tattered French army jackets bearing corporal or sergeant's stripes.

The system of government France imposed sapped local autonomy and institutions. The Paris-appointed governors guarded the prerogatives of French rule jealously. In keeping with French colonial policy elsewhere, they appointed very few Vietnamese to positions of real responsibility. To govern the 30 million Indochinese they imported an enormous bureaucracy, three times as large as the British required to govern 400 million Indians. The traditional source of political authority in Vietnam, the village chief, became vestigial as the French system absorbed his functions. Inhabitants were untutored in government at any level, much less self-government at the national level.

The educational system, imported from France in its entirety, also worked to dissolve traditional Vietnamese society and national feeling. Vietnamese children studying in Hanoi or Saigon used the same textbooks as Parisian children. Since missionaries had official sanction, religious orders ran many schools, and Roman Catholicism, a total stranger to traditional Vietnamese Buddhism-Confucianism, became common among the educated.

No study of Vietnamese history and culture was permitted, which separated the best-educated from their own national identity. In fact, a Vietnamese friend once told me that he was sixteen before he realized that his ancestors were not from Gaul. Higher education in political science, history, and other "dangerous" subjects that might encourage anti-French activism was frowned upon, so the best minds tended toward medicine, a politically safe field. As a result, many post-independence politicians were physicians. And since the young Vietnamese who went to study in France were both anti-colonial and politically immature, the French Communist Party found them malleable listeners and avid converts.

Initial Vietnamese efforts to throw off the French aimed at reestablishing traditional society under the Emperor's rule. Several bitter revolts erupted in the 1880s and 1890s. But after superior French weapons and organization crushed them, Vietnamese nationalists decided it was necessary to learn from their conquerors in order to overthrow them. The French vigorously sought out these pro-independence Vietnamese so they had to resort to conspiratorial tactics and underground organization. Unable to work out their differences openly, nationalist groups each pursued separate visions of free Vietnam. They could not unite around a common program and leadership despite their shared hatred of French rule.

The one pro-independence group that did manage to meld itself into a disciplined, effective instrument of power under French occupation was the Vietnamese Communist Party, led by Ho Chi Minh. Ho, born in 1890, left Vietnam as a cabin boy in 1911 and after several years at sea made his way to Paris, where he built up contacts with the Vietnamese community and eventually became their unofficial leader. In 1919 he drafted a program for Vietnamese liberation for the Versailles Peace Conference, then meeting in Paris, which many hoped would restructure the international order in the wake of the war, but it was ignored. Disillusioned, he turned to the thoughts of Lenin and by 1920 had become a dedicated communist. He studied in Moscow in 1923, attended the Fifth Congress of the Communist International, and then, as a Comintern agent, journeyed to Canton, China, to organize a Vietnamese communist party.

In 1930, the newly formed party fomented a rebellion among the peasants of several famine-struck provinces in northern Annam. French administrators were driven out and replaced by local peasant soviets. The French regrouped, however, and retook the area in 1931 at the cost of 10,000 Vietnamese lives. Still, the rebellion was a kind of victory for Ho. It established the communists as the best-known anti-French party and demonstrated the value of organizing peasants—an approach that other nationalist parties, oriented toward urban intellectuals, could not readily manage. The Communist Party had other advantages, too. Its leaders had been well trained in the arts of underground conspiracy, so important to survival under French rule, and the French-controlled economy provided a model of exploitation that fitted well into the doctrine of Marx and Lenin. Ho, himself, as a leader, combined intelligence, pragmatism, and ruthlessness. In sum, the Communist Party grew into the most formidable anti-French force in Vietnam between the two world wars.

Following France's defeat by Nazi Germany in 1940 the French in Indo-China turned to Vichy. Trying to salvage what they could, they did not resist the Japanese advance into the area and for the most part cooperated with the Japanese occupation. This gave the Vietnamese communists and other nationalists their long-awaited opportunity. The communists formed a League for Vietnamese Independence (known as Vietminh) in 1941, which wisely included some token non-communist members. The Vietminh provided the Chinese Nationalists with useful intelligence for the remainder of the war. (Ho Chi Minh, which means "Ho who seeks after intelligence," is a name which Ho, previously known as Nguyen Ai Quoc, acquired during this period and thereafter retained.) The Vietminh also fought the Japanese and the collaborationist French.

In August 1945, Japan was defeated. Within a week the Vietminh controlled Hanoi, and by September 2, when Ho Chi Minh proclaimed the creation of a "Democratic Republic of Vietnam," most of Tonkin was at least nominally under communist-Vietminh control. Bao Dai, last of the hereditary Vietnamese emperors, resigned in deference to the Vietminh. At the time no other group in Vietnam was capable of challenging Vietminh authority.

Ho probably hoped that France's postwar weakness and Allied gratitude for whatever services the Vietminh had rendered against Japan would by default leave them in control of Indochina. Franklin Roosevelt, in fact, had considerable contempt for France's colonial record, and through 1943 and 1944 strongly promoted a postwar trusteeship for Indochina under UN supervision that would bring the area to eventual independence. FDR's scheme, however, encountered strong resistance on several fronts. France's new leader, Charles DeGaulle, was determined to prevent the United States from slicing off a large and profitable chunk of France's overseas possessions, which included not only Indochina, but islands in the Pacific and Indian Oceans, Madagascar, Djibouti, Equitorial Africa, Tunisia, Algeria, and Morocco. Also, Winston Churchill violently opposed any scheme to reduce France's authority in Indochina for fear that Britain's extensive empire would be FDR's next target. And, with the Soviet Union in the process of swallowing Eastern Europe and already starting to menace Western Europe, Washington had to do its utmost to ensure that France was strong and vital. The major thrust of American postwar policy was promoting Europe's integrity and unity. Since DeGaulle was threatening dire consequences if Indochina was wrested from French control, and Britain and Holland (which were planning to reoccupy their former possessions) strenuously supported him, Washington felt it had no choice but to acquiesce in French reoccupation of Vietnam.

When Chiang Kai-shek's Nationalist Chinese regime, on which FDR had been counting to become Asia's postwar policeman, began to falter badly because of corruption and Communist advances, FDR began to worry about Indochina disintegrating in Chiang's wake. Shortly before his death in April 1945, Roosevelt reluctantly chose the stability of colonialism over the risks of independence and endorsed France's return to Indochina.

Britain, knowing nothing of French Indochina, reluctantly agreed to accept the surrender of the Japanese forces in the southern part of Vietnam in mid-September 1945. The British Commander refused to recognize the Vietminh and rapidly returned effective control to France. In the north, the Chinese Nationalist armies that were deployed to disarm the Japanese recognized French authority in February 1946. For several months an uneasy peace was maintained as the Vietminh and French jockeyed for position in the North. But tensions crackled into open war in November 1946 when a French bombardment of Haiphong killed several thousand civilians. There was no outside force in a position to mediate. French troops moved to reconquer the country, and hostilities escalated.

Some have argued that if FDR and Truman had prevented France from seeking to retake Vietnam in 1945 (although it is not clear exactly how they would have stopped France) and thus confirmed Vietminh control of the country, Ho would have become the first communist leader to establish friendly relations with the United States, a sort of Asian Tito. I disagree. He did get good marks from Office of Strategic Services (OSS) agents and United States Army officers who worked with him during the war (as did some communist leaders elsewhere in Asia and Europe), and he did write President Truman several times in 1945 pleading for American understanding and support. But Ho had been a member of the Comintern since 1921, and his historical and ideological links with the Soviet Union were too strong to be severed lightly. In any event, not even Tito had invented Titoism by 1945; Soviet control of world communism was then all but total. Speculating about the "what ifs" of history is always tempting, especially when, as with Vietnam, the actual history turns out badly. But given Hanoi's unswerving devotion to Moscow and its unrelieved forty-year record of brutality to those under its control, I am not impressed by theories about what the United States should have done in Vietnam that hinge upon Ho Chi Minh's inherent moderation and reasonableness.

The French troops found quick victory to be more elusive than they expected. France's debts and deaths mounted and began to submerge the confident predictions of its generals. Not surprisingly, France turned to the United States for assistance on the basis of Ho's unquestioned communist ties. At first the State Department refused. The new "autonomous" government established by the French under the pliant Emperor Bao Dai in June 1949 to undercut Vietminh nationalist appeal was obviously a French puppet, and though Washington was wary of the Vietminh it was also wary of aiding naked French colonialism.

The Truman Administration's attitude fundamentally changed when Mao Tse-tung's armies swept through China in 1949. That event shocked America, conjuring up visions of a red wave swamping all Asia. When China and the Soviets recognized Ho's government in January 1950, Washington was already swimming in recriminations over "who lost China." The last thing the Truman Administration needed was another communist victory in Asia. In the American view, the Vietminh's ties with China and the Soviet Union obscured whatever merits their case otherwise might have had. Washington increasingly saw Ho, not as an indigenous nationalist leader who happened to be communist, but as an agent of a hostile and aggressive international communist movement, posing as nationalist, to further the Kremlin's grand design. In May 1950 the United States announced its first grant to aid French forces in Vietnam, an amount of $10 million. Further, North Korea's blitzkrieg into the South in June 1950, both confirmed Washington's darkest suspicions about Soviet motives and prompted the Truman Administration to boost military spending and foreign military assistance dramatically. Vietnam was now viewed as a battleground against communist imperialism, not just a struggle between France and the Vietminh. The conflict in Indochina had taken on an international dimension that was to dominate it for twenty-five years.

While continuing to urge France to adopt a more forthcoming policy on real independence for Indochina, American support for French forces in Vietnam increased until, by 1954, it was estimated that the United States was footing about eighty percent of the bill. Even so, France could not win, especially because its equivocal position on independence prevented it from enlisting the real support of non-communist nationalists. The Vietminh waged a costly war of attrition that killed or wounded nearly 100,000 men in the polygot French forces (French Foreign Legionnaires, Montagnards, Vietnamese, etc.), and exhausted the country's resolve.

Domestic pressure on the French government to withdraw from Indochina mounted severely in early 1954, but opposition from powerful colonial hard-liners precluded abandoning the country. Seeking an escape from this impasse, the government of Premier Laniel preferred an international resolution to direct negotiations with the Vietminh because it figured it could get better terms that way. Ho Chi Minh, like France, had needed outside help to fight effectively and now depended on Russia and China; if those countries could be induced to moderate Vietminh demands, France might secure a graceful exit. And the presence of Americans at the conference table could only strengthen its hand. Conversely, the Vietminh could only lose by letting the Soviets, Chinese, and Americans try to influence the settlement in Vietnam for their own purposes. But still they came to Geneva. Ho could not, or would not, act independently of Peking and Moscow.

For several months before Geneva, Dulles tried to build a consensus for armed intervention in Indochina, should the communists approach victory over France. This was important for signalling the communists to exhibit restraint. Congressional leaders gave Dulles approval early in 1954 to develop a basis for collective action in Indochina. He made a speech on the subject at the end of March that Eisenhower endorsed promptly at a press conference. The President also wrote to Prime Minister Churchill in early April urging support for a coalition to "check Communist expansion in South Asia" that would include the

United States, the United Kingdom, France, the Indochinese states of Vietnam, Cambodia and Laos, and Australia, New Zealand, Thailand, and the Philippines. Dulles immediately visited London to work out something tangible. In two days of talks he thought he had obtained British assent to constructing some mechanism for collective action before the start of the Geneva Conference. He then journeyed to Paris and extracted some concessions from Prime Minister Laniel and Foreign Minister Bidault that they had previously resisted. They agreed, he thought, to full independence for the Indochina states, and to participate in studying an "internationalized" security arrangement for Indochina. Previously they had insisted on direct ad hoc support by the United States in order to prevent dilution of their role. Laniel and Bidault also seemed to favor French ratification of the European Defense Community, a proposal to integrate Western European armed forces, including Germany's, under a supranational command. (We strongly endorsed EDC and the Soviets bitterly opposed it.) But in all of this Dulles was destined to be sorely disappointed.

Shortly after his return from Europe, Dulles proposed a meeting of the ambassadors of Britain, France, Australia, New Zealand, the Philippines, and the Indochinese states to make specific plans for a collective defense in Indochina. He was shocked when the British Ambassador replied on April 18 that he had been instructed not to attend the meeting because his government considered it premature. A crucial component of the consensus Dulles thought he had achieved on Indochina had come unstuck. The following week Foreign Secretary Anthony Eden put a final nail in the coffin, declaring that Britain was not committed to any intervention whatever in Indochina and would consider it a mistake. In the absence of allied solidarity Eisenhower felt obligated to refuse desperate French requests for bombing to stave off defeat at Dienbienphu. Eden did say Britain would be willing to join some collective organization for defending Southeast Asia once France had reached a settlement with the Vietminh, but only on the condition that the arrangement not cover Indochina. Our impression was that Britain was only interested in getting help in Malaya, for which it still had defense responsibilities. Acrimony persisted between Dulles and Eden throughout the conference. In one conversation between them, at which I was present, Dulles heatedly threatened that the United States "would go it alone" in Southeast Asia with "those willing to fight," like Rhee and Chiang Kai-shek.

All of this meant we entered the Indochina phase of the Geneva Conference without any clear idea of how it would conclude. We did not consider ourselves a central participant, as we had no direct responsibility for the fighting. France, which did, was in even greater turmoil. Its National Assembly was in recess and its Cabinet was paralyzed and likely to fall because of Dienbienphu. Extremely wary of creating any precedent that might embolden Algeria and other French colonies, the country's leaders could not face up to the reality of their defeat. Britain, too, was frightened and its government was weak. Our entire alliance structure was thus under severe strain.

Distance seemed the best policy for our delegation. To underscore the fact that we did not consider ourselves a central participant who would be bound by the conference results— which we expected would ratify the Vietminh gains in some way— Dulles departed Geneva on May 3, leaving Undersecretary Bedell Smith in command of our delegation.

This produced some positive effects. Though he could be as rough as a top sergeant with his subordinates, Smith could become a paragon of gentility and diplomacy when he so desired. At heart he had more sympathy for Britain's cold feet than Dulles, and he also had adequate rapport with Eden. Bedell was rough-hewn, having risen through every rank in the Army from private to four-star general, and he admired the refined aristocrat in Eden. Sometimes he got angry. For example, he cabled Dulles on May 29, after Eden had double-crossed him, that the British Foreign Secretary was "without moral or intellectual honesty," but generally they got along; and without going beyond his instructions, he managed to reestablish a dialogue between us and Eden. In fact, Smith's only real drawback as chief of our delegation was that he was suffering from a stomach disorder and drank a good deal to deaden the pain.

Only two formal plenary sessions on Indochina were held, one on the first day and one on the last. At the first meeting, on May 8, it was agreed that the chair would rotate between the USSR and Britain, and that subsequent meetings would be closed, with a limited attendance from each delegation. The communist side had three delegations—China, the USSR and Ho Chi Minh's Democratic Republic of Vietnam—and the Allied side had six, the United States, the UK, France, and the three pro-Western Indochinese states of Cambodia, Laos, and Vietnam. At first the communists made a strong play to invite the Vietminh front in Cambodia as a "participating state," but the Cambodian government and Foreign Minister Bidault turned this aside with deeply felt statements.

Even the restricted sessions were held only once or twice a week. More than at most conferences, the real business was carried on at lunches, dinners, and informal meetings at all levels. When Dulles or Smith were heading our delegation, they naturally led these discussions, though sometimes I participated and was always kept informed. When I headed the delegation from June 20 to July 17, I conducted them. The main substantive accomplishment at Geneva—establishing detailed ceasefire agreements for Vietnam, Cambodia, and Laos—was actually conducted outside the conference entirely, by relatively junior French and Vietminh military officers.

May and the first part of June were devoted to largely futile sparring between France and the communists. The victory at Dienbienphu was good propaganda for the communists, and so was the inability of the West to find a concerted position and stick to it. The longer our discomfort could be prolonged the better for them. Many strident harangues were loosed by Foreign Minister Molotov, head of the Soviet delegation, especially after his visit to Moscow in early June. These were probably intended to hasten the fall of Laniel's fairly hard-line government by scaring the French about the costs of remaining in Indochina. The French delegation, despite the trauma of Dienbienphu, countered with an unrealistic discussion of a "leopard spot" cease-fire arrangement that would give the Vietminh some isolated enclaves and let France retain most of the Tonkin Delta, including Hanoi, Haiphong and all of the South. The Vietminh would not even respond to these proposals, confining themselves, in the words of a June 7 telegram from Smith to Dulles, to "political polemics and rather truculent references to their victories and to their growing military strength."

While this was going on, Dulles and Smith continued to try to fashion some sort of Western collective security arrangement for Southeast Asia. We also worked hard to set up effective supervisory arrangements for whatever cease-fire terms were worked out. Our experience with the Korean armistice watchdog body, where the communist members had repeatedly hamstrung effective inspection with their veto, made us lobby hard for a genuinely neutral body able to decide by majority vote. In the absence of clear thinking in Paris on how to end the war satisfactorily, however, the central discussions limped along inconclusively. France was fortunate to have as its permanent representative to the conference Jean Chauvel, the Ambassador to Switzerland, who had remarkable skill at giving the appearance of cohesion to French policy.

We fully expected that any solution to which France and the Vietminh could agree would not be to our liking. Any recognition of Vietminh gains was contrary to our interest, but France could not avoid it. So our consistent approach, in the words of Undersecretary Smith on June 7, was to

> play the role of helpful friend . . . standing firm on the separate status of Laos and Cambodia but not opposing or obstructing any reasonable military compromise the French may be able to get, recognizing at the same time that it will be one that we don't like, and probably will not be able to publicly associate ourselves with.

Dulles asked Smith to come home in mid-June, having decided that the talks were not moving in a direction we liked and that the presence of Smith put pressure on France to make quicker progress than was wise. Eden left Geneva at the same time, telling the French that he would return. Smith said I would remain United States representative indefinitely. France did not like this, because it wanted public American endorsement at the highest level for whatever settlement could be reached with the Vietminh. But Dulles would not relent. He thought the only way to make Britain, France, and other countries focus on the need for establishing collective security arrangements in Southeast Asia was to direct attention away from the diplomatic dancing at Geneva. My instructions were to continue to take part in the meetings of the delegations, but in no way, expressed or implied, to commit the United States to anything.

That might have been all right except that on June 12 the government of Prime Minister Laniel fell, to be replaced on June 18 by one led by Pierre Mendes-France as both Prime Minister and Foreign Minister. He entered office with a dramatic pledge to resign unless he could settle the Indochina conference in a month, specifically by July 20. Suddenly Geneva became a very lively forum.

Mendes-France was supposed to be "softer" on Indochina than Laniel, and after his election the Vietminh saw all of Vietnam coming within their grasp and did not want to be put off. Their maximum concession was a "decent interval" for withdrawing French forces and some sort of rigged elections as a means of saving French face. In the meantime they wanted to occupy the whole country down to the 12th or 13th parallel, just north of Saigon. Mendes-France gave up the unrealistic and impractical "leopard spot" concept and began to bargain over the location of the armistice line. He wanted the 19th parallel, just south of Hanoi, and at least a two-year interval until elections. Because of Washington's unwillingness to back Paris unconditionally, the French played their cards very close to their chest. It was impossible for the American delegation to learn all of the many things that went on outside our formal restricted seasons. Even so, Chauvel kept me informed about the secret military talks between the French and Vietminh military officers.

Our government was very concerned that Mendes-France might have thrown away his bargaining power by announcing his own deadline for settlement. We also worried that he might capitulate on the European Defense Community in return for whatever help Moscow might give in moderating the Vietminh's final terms at Geneva.

Though there was never any hard evidence that Mendes-France had made an overt deal with the Soviet Union—to obtain a face-saving formula in Indochina in return for defeating the EDC in the National Assembly—I have always felt there must have been some sort of an understanding. During the conference there was certainly ample evidence that Russia moderated Vietminh demands on many occasions. During the restricted sessions I sat directly across the square open conference table from Pham Van Dong, Ho's Foreign Minister. Dong normally sat with his legs crossed, gently swinging a foot. As discussion got more heated and the differences between his position and that of the French became more pointed, his foot would swing in a wider and wider arc. On several occasions when his foot was really working, Molotov called a recess so that he could confer with Dong and Chou En-lai outside the room. When the session resumed, Dong would invariably take a position somewhat less extreme than his previous one and his foot would resume a gentle sway. I think the Soviet strategy was to urge the Vietminh to accept a delay in its conquest of the country—to take "two bites," armistice and elections, instead of "one bite"—confident that France would thereupon defeat EDC. And defeat it the National Assembly did, shortly after the Vietnamese cease-fire and while Mendes-France was still Prime Minister.

My position as head of the delegation during Mendes-France's thirty-day countdown was not always enviable. Ambassador Chauvel, whom Mendes-France wisely maintained, was an able operator, and the form of the cease-fire and its supervisory arrangements began to take shape. The main issues boiled down quickly to where the cease-fire line would be drawn and how long the interval between the cease-fire and elections for unifying the country would be, six months or two years. The future of Laos and Cambodia was also important. I grew perturbed at the increasing difficulty of following my instructions to commit the United States to nothing. In various ways I repeatedly pointed out to Washington that the middle ground I was directed to occupy between observer and participant simply did not exist. At the conference table and in private I was innundated with requests for the American view on various terms proposed for the final agreement. Even silence sometimes appeared to give assent. With the help of Phil Bonsal, my chief deputy, I was able to walk this tightrope to Washington's satisfaction, but the delegations at Geneva were not so pleased. Would we support, silently acquiesce, or even seek to overturn the final settlement that was taking shape? Such questions were not for me to decide, and despite discomfort, I followed instructions.

One debate in which I could take an active part was over international supervision, for whatever the final settlement, we wanted the oversight to have teeth. I freely cited our unhappy experience in Korea, where the Czech and Polish members of the Neutral Nations Supervisory Commission had frustrated entirely the conscientious efforts of the Swiss and Swedish members to carry out their responsibilities under the armistice agreement. I strongly advocated a United Nations body or, failing that, a group drawn from the "Colombo" powers—India, Pakistan, Burma, Indonesia, and Ceylon. My regular sparring partner was Vasily Kuznetsov, then a Soviet Vice Foreign Minister. Extremely personable in a delegation not noted for personality, he had an excellent command of English, having studied engineering at MIT and later worked at U.S. Steel and Ford. He valiantly but unsuccessfully tried to sell me on the neutral virtues of Poland. He would never accept my contention that a non-communist state could be truly neutral in a matter involving a communist state, and insisted that they have "their neutrals" if we had "ours." He was the first Soviet with whom I felt I could establish some communication, and I enjoyed debating with him.

Kuznetsov's boss, Molotov, was also in a relatively affable mood during most of the conference. Perhaps this was due to Stalin's death, perhaps to the smell of communist victory in the air, but all members of our delegation noticed how old "Iron

Pants" seemed much calmer and more confident than usual. He was a good host, giving excellent dinners at the Soviet villa and ready at all times with quick repartee laced with political barbs. One incident I remember particularly well was typical of his behavior during the conference. One of Dulles' favorite themes in his public speeches was the superiority of "free world diversity" to "communist conformity." At one session early in the Korean phase of the conference when Dulles was still there, he and Chou had both spoken and taken tough positions. As I was walking with Dulles to the lounge during the recess, Molotov fell into step with us, a mischievous twinkle in his eye. He said: "Mr. Secretary, you must have enjoyed today's session." Dulles sensed a trap but could only ask Molotov why he thought so. "Because there was enough diversity in the speeches to please someone even as fond of it as you!" Molotov replied. I do not recall that Dulles was able to make any rejoinder.

Molotov's repartee had enormous assistance from his remarkable interpreter, Oleg Troyanovsky. Born in Japan when his father was Ambassador there, Oleg came to Washington when his father was transferred there as the first Soviet representative to the United States in 1933. There he attended Sidwell Friends School and perfected American speech and mannerisms. His open, smiling face always stood out among his dour colleagues, and he had the gift of interpreting in both directions so perfectly, even mimicking tone of voice, that one was hardly conscious of his presence. Oleg became his country's Ambassador to Japan when I held the same position for the United States in the mid-1960s, and subsequently represented his country at the UN.

During the holding pattern I was ordered to maintain in late June and early July, Geneva was busy, but the most significant developments came from elsewhere. A five-nation military committee that had met in Washington in early June reported its findings about the possibility of intervention in Indochina. Its extraordinarily gloomy report threw considerable cold water on Dulles's hope that a consensus for intervention would firm up as the communists remained intransigent at Geneva. The military panel said that Chinese communist intervention was likely if we made major deployments to assist France. If China did intervene, they recommended that nuclear weapons be used immediately and the whole country blockaded. Even in these circumstances, Allied land forces would be insufficient to restrain Peking's massed manpower; thus plans should be made to establish a final defense line in the Kra Isthmus of southern Thailand.

Despite this grim assessment, Churchill and Eisenhower were able to establish a common approach on Indochina which held out the threat of joint military intervention should the Vietminh press for too much. They met in Washington following Mendes-France's election and issued a statement at the end of their talks, on June 28, which declared that the United States and Britain would work with other countries to form a collective defense organization for Southeast Asia (this ultimately became SEATO) no matter what happened at Geneva, and that if the communist demands at Geneva were so extreme as to prevent an "acceptable agreement," the "international situation would be seriously aggravated." Privately, they communicated to Mendes-France that both countries would be willing to "respect" a cease-fire arranged at Geneva if seven points were met. The most important accepted partition of Vietnam on the condition that no other aspects of the agreement would "lead to communist control" of the southern half. Other conditions included effective international supervision and withdrawal of all Vietminh forces from Laos and Cambodia. The French welcomed this initiative as putting the cease-fire within their grasp, but immediately started trying to water down the conditions, which they knew the communists would resist.

In early July, Molotov, Chou En-lai, and Eden returned to Geneva in response to Mendes-France's deadline. France and Britain ardently sought the return of Dulles or Smith to secure visible American endorsement of the settlement shaping up at Geneva, but Dulles refused. On July 10 the Secretary cabled a message that I delivered to Eden and Chauvel. Though the United States wanted to preserve a united front among Paris, London, and Washington, the Secretary said, "we are very doubtful as to whether there is a united front in relation to Indochina, and we do not believe that the mere fact that the high representatives of the three nations physically reappear together at Geneva will serve as a substitute for a clear agreement on a joint position which includes agreement as to what will happen if that position is not accepted by the Communists." France, meanwhile, was hedging on the seven points we deemed essential, including an armistice line too far south, hasty elections, improper supervision and allowing communist forces to remain in Northern Laos. Thus "an armistice might be concluded on terms substantially less favorable than those we could respect." France had every right to make whatever peace it felt was in its own national interest. "However, my government equally has the duty not to endorse a solution which would seem to us to impair seriously certain principles which the US believes must, as far as it is concerned, be kept unimpaired, if our own struggle against Communism is to be successfully pursued." It would be highly corrosive to US-French bonds, Dulles warned, if we had to "disassociate ourselves from the settlement at a moment and under circumstances which might be unnecessarily dramatic."

But Mendes-France would not be put off. He sent back a most eloquent plea that a high-level American presence was essential to strengthen his hand against the communists. If Dulles were present, he promised that France would not accept anything that the United States could not, thus giving us effective veto power. He stoutly affirmed that France would not retreat from the Eisenhower-Churchill seven points, but that no matter how good the settlement was on paper, it would be worthless unless the United States stood ready to guarantee it against further aggression.

Eisenhower was sensitive to the value of sending a high-level representative to bolster French resolve at Geneva. He said he was going to ask Dulles to fly to Paris to confer with Mendes-France and Eden, and if they could find common ground, then Dulles would have Bedell Smith return to Geneva. Unless Dulles or Smith were there, the President said, "the stories from Geneva will be entirely colored by Red propaganda and also by propaganda of our allies, particularly the French, who will then blame us for everything that goes wrong."

Mendes was delighted with this decision and invited me to fly to Paris with him for the conference with Dulles. Shortly before I had to catch the plane, that ubiquitous international meddler, Krishna Menon, insisted on seeing me (as he was to do at many other inconvenient moments in the future). He maintained that North Vietnam would quickly become a neutral "more or less like India" once a settlement was reached, so it would be in our interest to urge France to offer generous and liberal terms. His advice was not compelling.

After dinner at the Hotel Matignon on July 13, Eden and Mendes-France sat with Dulles for a four-hour talk, at which I and a few others were present. After Mendes described the current state of bargaining with the Vietminh on the location of the armistice line and other matters, Dulles explained in full his refusal to have high-level American representatives in Geneva. The time for military intervention had passed, he said bluntly, so if he did go to Geneva and faced an unacceptable settlement, he would have no choice but to disassociate the United States from it in a way that could only harm United States-French relations. America recognized France's difficulties and its right to make its own decisions, but "the United States Government cannot be associated with a settlement which would be portrayed in the US as a second Yalta."

Mendes-France said that if no agreement were reached by July 20, France would have to send conscript reinforcements, but these could not arrive until September. In the meantime the remaining French troops in Indochina could well be crushed. Eden suggested that we obtain the best settlement possible and then make it clear that if the communists broke it, everyone would take action. In the course of another meeting the next morning, Mendes proposed that an American guarantee against further aggression would be the best way to proceed to a workable Geneva settlement. Dulles agreed. The resulting United States position, which cleared the way for the settlement reached at Geneva the following week, was a complicated one, but it served the dual purpose of supporting France at Geneva while withholding unconditional endorsement of France's position. At my prompting, Dulles explained this in a conversation with Mendes and Eden at the United States Embassy on July 14.

In view of the controversy and misinformation that has surrounded discussion of the Geneva Accords ever since they were signed, Dulles's explanation of our stance as we entered the final stage at Geneva bears repeating. We could not join in any agreement guaranteeing the communists the fruits of their aggression, Dulles said, but we did recognize as a fact that people sometimes became the victims of that aggression when we were not prepared to go to war to counter it. It would be compatible with this principle to declare unilaterally that in accordance with the UN Charter we would not seek to disrupt by force any agreement reached at Geneva and would seek to induce others to behave similarly. We could also agree to respond to further communist aggression there with force, contingent of course upon Congressional approval. So while the United States could not itself join in the Geneva accords, it could commit itself to maintaining them against further communist encroachments. The only agreement Dulles was willing to guarantee in this fashion was one following the seven points Eisenhower and Churchill had settled in late June. That meant that the non-communists would get at least the southern portion of Vietnam, and that no other provisions in the agreements would lead to eventual communist takeover of the non-communist portion.

Dulles still insisted that he would not go to Geneva. He did agree, however, that Bedell Smith would attend for the few remaining days if his health permitted. That satisfied Eden and Mendes. Before leaving, Eden and Dulles also stressed to the French Premier the importance of granting full independence to Vietnam, Cambodia, and Laos. Otherwise there would be no hope of building a nationalist but non-communist alternative to the Vietminh. Mendes-France did not demur, but clearly had in mind the difficulty of mollifying the powerful pro-colonial forces in French politics.

Mendes-France and I returned immediately to Geneva on his plane, and Bedell Smith arrived the evening of July 17, leaving only three days before Mendes-France's deadline. Smith was obviously in considerable pain and consequently more irascible than usual. His instructions were to "assist, where desired, in arriving at a just settlement," but not to go beyond this role. In particular our delegation was to avoid participating in the negotiations to such an extent that the communists could contend we were responsible for the result and honor-bound to maintain it. Neither were we to give France the impression that we would send troops to Indochina should no settlement be reached. Our approach, therefore, was to try to keep track of the frantic comings and goings among the various delegations, but take no initiatives of our own.

On July 18, Molotov suddenly called for a restricted session to review "where we stood." He had recently become extremely intransigent. We thought perhaps the Soviets had been displeased by Mendes-France's unexpected toughness and wanted to bring down his government by demanding extra concessions France could not meet, or by insisting that we sign and fully guarantee the settlement reached. Since Molotov knew we would refuse to sign, he could maneuver the onus for bringing down Mendes-France onto us. But nothing notable occurred at the session and we never did find out the reason for it.

On July 20, the military armistice agreements for Vietnam and Laos were signed at 3:30 in the afternoon, but midnight came and went without an agreement on Cambodia. At about two in the morning the reason for the delay became clear. Nong Kimny, the head of the Cambodian delegation, called on us at the Hotel du Rhone with several members of his delegation. Bedell Smith, in considerable pain, received them in bed with Phil Bonsal and me also present. Unlike the Laotian delegation, they were holding out for the right to join a defensive alliance against further communist aggression. Almost in tears, the Cambodians said that Molotov and Chou En-lai were putting tremendous pressure on them to capitulate; so were Eden and Mendes-France, who were eager to conclude the conference. What should they do? We told them to stick to what they thought best for their country. So advised they went out into the night, and at six in the morning word came that they had won their point. I gained a great deal of admiration for the Cambodians' tenacity. When Cambodian leader Prince Sihanouk later routinely denounced the Southeast Asia Treaty Organization (SEATO), the irony of this incident never failed to strike me.

So, only fifteen hours after Mendes-France's deadline, at 3 P.M. July 21, the final plenary session of the Geneva Conference on Indochina was held. The main features of the final settlement included: establishment of a military demarcation line between the Vietminh North and the pro-Western South at the 17th parallel (which became the border between the two countries); a majority-vote International Control Commission comprising India, Canada, and Poland (better than what we had in Korea, but still problematic); and nationwide elections under ICC supervision to reunify Vietnam under one government in July 1956. The 17th parallel was a good line for us because it meant the Vietminh would give up about one-quarter of the territory it presently controlled.

The agreements giving force to these provisions were in fact an exceedingly complex array of documents, because not all nine governments present subscribed to all the provisions. The primary documents were the military cease-fire agreements separately drawn up for Vietnam, Laos, and Cambodia that were signed on behalf of the French and Vietminh commanders there. There were also unilateral declarations by Cambodia and Laos on holding elections and the future military status of their countries, as well as a unilateral French declaration recognizing the independence of its three former colonies and agreeing to withdraw French forces.

There was also an unsigned "Final Declaration" of the conference, which took note of these other agreements and unilateral statements. At the final plenary meeting, most delegations made oral statements concurring in it, but the United States did not. In accordance with the seven points settled by Eisenhower and

Churchill and the arrangement Dulles worked out with Eden and Mendes-France in Paris, Undersecretary Smith declared only that the United States "would refrain from the threat or the use of force to disturb the agreements." He in no way endorsed them. An extremely important part of Smith's formal statement, much misunderstood and overlooked in later years, concerned the elections called for in the agreements, which the ICC was supposed to supervise. Since we believed ICC supervision would be inadequate, Smith reiterated our post-Korea policy that "in the case of nations now divided against their will, we shall continue to seek to achieve unity through free elections, supervised by the *United Nations* to ensure they are conducted fairly" (emphasis mine).

The South Vietnamese Foreign Minister rejected the entire package of agreements in so far as they concerned Vietnam, specifically including the paragraph on elections. Smith's statement took note of that protest:

> With respect to the statement made by the representative of the State of Vietnam, the United States reiterates its traditional position that peoples are entitled to determine their own future and that it will not join in an arrangement which would hinder this. Nothing in its declaration just made is intended to or does indicate any departure from this traditional position.

Thus there is no foundation whatever to the charge, heard frequently during the Vietnam War, that the United States and South Vietnam "violated the Geneva Agreements" by refusing to hold elections in 1956 under ICC auspices. We purposely signed no agreement at Geneva; we called for UN, not ICC supervision; and our consistent policy throughout the conference was to reject any terms that would lead to eventual communist control of the whole of Vietnam.

After the final plenary, an exhausted Mendes-France invited a few of us to dinner. During the meal I asked him whether France was not moving toward a crisis in Algeria similar to what it had suffered in Indochina. He agreed that it was. When I asked whether he planned to do anything about it, he said it was much too early. The situation in Algeria would have to get much worse, he was sure, before he or anyone else could address it. That assessment, of course, turned out to be exactly right; the Fourth Republic had to collapse and give way to dominance by General DeGaulle before the French government could face up to losing Algeria.

Bedell Smith returned to Washington the following morning. After a few days of tidying up and saying goodbye to my Chinese counterpart (more about that in the next chapter), I returned to Prague ready for a good rest. When I arrived I received from Dulles a warm letter of commendation for my work at Geneva.

By the end of the conference, I doubt if many on either side honestly felt that South Vietnam would survive very long. The country was poor, weak, ravaged by war, and suffering from a long history of incompetent government. The Vietminh had acquiesced in a negotiated settlement only because China and the Soviet Union had pressured them into it. They never for a moment contemplated foregoing that "second bite," though I think they were relying on South Vietnamese internal disintegration to feed them the second bite as much as on their own ability to rig the inadequately supervised elections.

But we were all in for a surprise. During the Geneva Conference, the French puppet Emperor Bao Dai (who soon after resigned) appointed Ngo Dinh Diem Prime Minister of the country. An ascetic Catholic mandarin in a country of relaxed Buddhists, Diem turned out to be a nationalist zealot of considerable political skill. Thanks to him and to American aid, South Vietnam not only survived but began to gain strength. SEATO also contributed to Saigon's unexpected vitality. The Manila Pact, which established the organization, pledged its members (Britain, France, Thailand, Pakistan, Australia, New Zealand, and the United States) to aid each other if attacked. Though the Geneva agreements prevented Vietnam and Laos from joining any military alliance, we were able to extend SEATO's coverage to them by allowing them to request its help without their having to join.

I shall leave the story of Vietnam here, for the time being, but I shall have occasion to return to it again in the course of this book.

CHAPTER EIGHT

First Negotiations with the People's Republic of China

If the most powerful country and the most populous country in the world could not have a normal diplomatic relationship, they would have to invent a substitute.

Kenneth T. Young

IN THIS CHAPTER I SHALL DESCRIBE MY PART IN THAT SUBSTITUTE— the talks I conducted with The People's Republic of China (PRC) Ambassador Wang Ping-nan (now spelled Bingnan) from 1955 to 1958. These talks were the only substantive contact between the United States and communist China during those years, and produced the sole written agreement between the two governments from 1949, the year of Mao's victory in China, to 1972, when President Nixon travelled to Peking. Their beginning was bathed in the kleig lights of world publicity and aroused widespread hopes that the two countries would soon progress to virtually normal relations. For the first time in my career I was at the center of a national and international news story.

The talks' accomplishments, though significant, were considerably more modest than had been hoped. In retrospect I can see that the two countries were just too far apart and too deeply wary of each other to permit major progress. Neither side would make the concessions considered by the other prerequisite to healthy relations. At the time, however, I tried every trick I could muster to generate closer ties, for they sometimes seemed tantalizingly close. Indeed, the story of these negotiations raises some intriguing questions about how history might have been different had Wang Ping-nan and I been more successful. If China and the United States had been friendlier in the 1950s, would we have been so fearful of the advance of communism in Southeast Asia? Would we have become involved in the Vietnam War? Would the split between China and the Soviet Union have occurred earlier and more decisively?

When representatives of two governments sit down to hammer out mutually agreeable concessions, as I did with Ambassador Wang, they are only the most publicly exposed points of a vast, intricate and ever-shifting network of interactions that constitute the basic relations between two countries. That network sets the limits on the amount of common ground any negotiators, no matter how able, can find. The whole network can be pictured as having two layers. The first, relatively fast-changing and highly sensitive to shifts in official policy, concerns relations between governments. The second layer, more durable and more resistant to short-term intervention, concerns the fundamental realities of international power.

Managing relations between governments is the usual business of diplomacy. But such short-term relations must basically flow in the channels plowed by the fundamental realities of the respective international positions of states. These more enduring forces normally move so glacially that most diplomatic business treats them as givens. Currently, for example, the United States is allied with Japan, and the principal threat to Western Europe's security is the Soviet Union. Of course, today's axiom is often tomorrow's heresy. Japan and the United States were bitter enemies a generation ago. The sun has now decidedly set on the once invincible British Empire. These long-term shifts in international alignment are adjustments to changes in the relative strength— military, economic, social, ideological—of individual countries. But sometimes tiny, well-managed improvements in short-term relations can develop a momentum of their own that eventually transforms the fundamental realities.

Diplomacy cannot pull rabbits out of hats; it cannot conjure up friendship between nations whose interests are largely opposed. But at its most exciting and creative, diplomacy can link hard bargaining between two negotiators with shifting the course of the deepest currents governing the relations between their countries, surmounting conventional wisdom and established policies to produce cooperation where no one had previously perceived the possibility. That is the sort of accomplishment Stalin and Hitler sprang on an astonished world with the Nazi-Soviet pact of 1939, or on a more positive note, that the Truman Administration managed with the Marshall Plan. That was the sort of diplomatic league WangPing-nan and I were thrust into when we were delegated to hold the first substantive talks on improving United States-Chinese relations since their total collapse following Mao's victory in 1949.

The Chinese communists had, in fact, won the respect of many American diplomats and military officers who had observed them during the war against Japan, not only for their competence in warfare and government but for their professed desire for friendly relations with the United States. Some believed that Mao and his lieutenants were Chinese first and communists second; that the United States would do well to cast off the decaying albatross of Chiang Kai-shek and align itself with the force in China that seemed to have history on its side. Why then didn't the United States back Mao instead of Chiang?

The answer is complicated—partly because of Chiang's public relations and popular support in the United States, especially among conservatives; partly because Mao seemed so intertwined with the Kremlin that it was difficult to imagine him as our ally when Stalin was becoming our enemy. Partly, too, it was because many involved with our China policy in the crucial period after the war, particularly influential figures in the Congress, indulged in copious wishful thinking about Chiang's capabilities. This became coupled with a sense of popular outrage at the betrayal by the communists of our romantic notions about China. Even without these factors, however, I believe that the United States and a communist China would still have ended up on opposite sides of the fence—out of imperatives inherent in the Chinese revolution. China had finally regained control over its own destiny. All remnants of the degrading colonial era had to be banished so that the new China could regain the pride and strength of the old. The United States had been an important supporter of the colonial powers, and now was pre-eminent among them. Thus, it was natural that America should become the chief target of China's new masters.

The events immediately following Mao's victory tend to confirm this view. Diplomatic contact between the People's Republic and the United States quickly sputtered to a halt because Peking, not Washington, wanted it that way. The normal procedure, if you plan to recognize a new government that has seized power in a country where you already have diplomatic representatives, is to keep them in place. The new government accords them informal status for a period of de facto relations, eventually culminating in formal diplomatic relations. We followed this practice as the communist forces took over the country. When the communists occupied Nanking, our Ambassador, J. Leighton Stuart (formerly a missionary in China) stayed in the city while the Soviet Ambassador actually went south to Canton with the Nationalists. An Information Circular from the department to prepare our posts abroad for the possibility that Taiwan might fall to the communists was deliberately leaked to the press by General MacArthur's headquarters as a means of attacking the administration in Washington. But the communist authorities went out of their way to demean our representatives, arresting our consuls, occupying our buildings, summoning Ambassador Stuart to People's Court for mistreating his servants, and refusing to deliver telegrams addressed to the American Embassy. I would not say that the United States necessarily would have recognized the communist government, at least immediately, but we had not precluded that possibility until the Chinese, following the anti-foreign imperatives of the revolution, left us no choice. In any event, the massive Chinese attack on, and humiliation of, our forces in Korea in November 1950, followed by more than two years of vicious fighting and vituperative armistice negotiations, left feelings high on both sides. After the armistice, chilling stories from American prisoners about mistreatment by their captors, and the refusal of most of the Chinese prisoners we held to return to China, exacerbated the bitterness felt on both sides. Furthermore, in 1950 Mao had signed a thirty-year military alliance with the Soviet Union.

To this was added the mistreatment suffered by the few Americans who had remained in China. American missionaries, business people, and scholars with long records in China were arrested and jailed on trumped-up or nonexistent charges as the new regime tried to exorcise all foreign influence. At least 155

American citizens were detained between 1949 and 1955. Many were held under conditions of extreme filth and hardship and subjected to physical and mental torture until "confessions" were extracted, which were then used to give credence to anti-American propaganda, especially to vicious claims that we had used germ warfare in Korea. American diplomacy has always placed much stress on assuring the safety of our citizens abroad and we considered these jailings highly offensive.

Taiwan's importance as an ally was seen in a new light as we developed means to contain what appeared to be the dangerously aggressive appetite of world communism. The United States Seventh Fleet was dispatched to the Taiwan Strait at the start of the Korean War to protect the nationalists from communist takeover (and to restrain any ambitions Chiang Kai-shek may have had to attack the mainland, which could have provoked a wider Pacific war). American military aid to the Nationalists, which had deliberately been allowed to lapse after Chiang withdrew to Taiwan, was renewed after the outbreak of war in Korea. In general, the People's Republic of China (PRC) took a very deliberate and hard line. The United States countered it by signing a defensive alliance with South Korea, increasing support to Taiwan and, after the Republicans came to power in 1953, "unleashing" Chiang Kai-shek. (He was in fact again "leashed" against an attack on the mainland by the Mutual Security Treaty of December 2, 1954.)

The Chinese communists shifted to a more conciliatory approach in 1954. Having consolidated power internally, the Chinese leaders wished to achieve recognition for their country as a great power on the world stage, the final symbolic victory over their colonial past. To achieve this status China principally needed the recognition of the United States, which had effectively blocked Communist Chinese membership in the United Nations and kept it isolated in world councils. To reduce American hostility—or failing that, to win world support in the face of continued American hostility—Peking had to shed something of its aggressive image and appear statesmanlike. The Soviet Union, serving as Peking's diplomatic broker, pressed for Chinese inclusion in the UN and other forums where it would have equal status with the United States, but for a while Secretary Dulles successfully deflected this pressure. The necessary basis was finally found in the Geneva Conference on Korea and Indochina. France's rapidly deteriorating position in Indochina made an international conference seem the best hope for containing the Vietminh, and China had an obvious interest in the future of both Korea and Indochina. Especially since American and Chinese representatives had been meeting at Panmunjom despite both countries' continuing policy of not recognizing the other officially, we had no real basis for blocking a Chinese delegation to Geneva. Thus, the Chinese communists came to their first major international conference, not taking any great pains to conceal their satisfaction at having won a degree of equality with the Soviet Union, the United States, Britain, and France, or their expectation of soon becoming a UN member and an important actor on the world stage.

The start of the Korean conference on April 26, 1954, at the Palais de Nations in Geneva was where the embarrassing incident when Secretary of State Dulles publicly refused to shake Chinese Foreign Minister Chou En-lai's outstretched hand. Since press photographers were present, Chou's move was not without malice aforethought; indeed, Dulles' refusal was motivated by the thought of the headlines and photos that would be splashed across the front page of every American paper. It is difficult nowadays, after a decade of increasing warmth between Washington and Peking, to make the depth of mutual mistrust and enmity that guided our dealings with China in the 1950s come alive for someone who was not there to witness it. That unnatural gesture of Secretary Dulles distills the bitterness as well as any one thing can.

Afterwards American and Chinese delegates carefully avoided any contact outside the formal negotiating sessions, following the strange but well-understood conventions established at Panmunjom. But twenty stormy years of revolutionary politics had taught the very able Chou En-lai nothing if not tenacity and tactical flexibility. He wanted the United States to acknowledge publicly China's reemergence as a great nation, and he had a bargaining chip he knew we wanted badly enough that we would relent on our social quarantine tactics to get it. The release of some seventy-six Americans, forty-one civilian and the rest military, still held against their will in China was Chou's only lever against us, and he used it effectively.

Britain still maintained diplomatic relations with Peking and had charge of looking after American interests in China. We therefore asked the British chargé in Peking, who was attending the Geneva Conference, Humphrey Trevelyan, to pursue the question of our prisoners. The Chinese finally told the British that they would refuse to discuss the prisoners with anyone but a high-level American because they saw no reason to use intermediaries when American representatives were close at hand.

It was hard to gainsay the Chinese proposal. Informal preparatory talks were conducted with them via the British, but in response to a public hint from Chinese delegate Huang Hua on May 27 that China would be willing to hold direct talks on the prisoners, Washington still maintained that these discussions would be unwise and that it was not willing to trade significant diplomatic concessions for the American prisoners. It was difficult to stick to this position, however; American public opinion did not want the prisoners' fate to hang on diplomatic niceties, and our allies thought the chances for peace in the Pacific would be improved if China and the United States stopped treating each other like disease carriers.

In May 1954 our delegation in Geneva received authorization from Secretary of State Dulles, then back in Washington, to pursue the question of our prisoners directly with the Chinese. I was designated to conduct the talks. I believe Dulles chose me for several reasons: as Coordinator of the United States Delegation I had a diplomatic rank that was high but not too high; I knew the history of our negotiations at Panmunjom intimately; and I had shown my ability to deal with a communist regime on a knotty prisoner issue in my negotiations with the Czechs over Jan Hvasta. This last factor was especially important, I think, because under his fierce anti-communist exterior Dulles was interested in exploring possible avenues toward lessening tensions with the Chinese as well as obtaining the release of imprisoned Americans, and my record was such that he thought I could do that without raising the hackles of the powerful American "China Lobby." The Chinese then designated Wang Ping-nan, the Secretary-General of their delegation and my approximate counterpart, to meet with me.

Through the British we established June 5 as the date for the meeting, and selected the location. I deliberately chose a sitting room in the UN Building with several sofas but no table, hoping to make the atmosphere as easy and informal as I could contrive, and when Wang Ping-nan and his aides arrived I made a point of shaking his hand and made some light conversation before moving to business. This first meeting, in which the State Department press release described me as "accompanying" Humphrey Trevelyan, went on for half an hour and had none of the tension or acrimony of Panmunjom. We arranged to meet again and agreed that no stenographic transcript of our discussions would be taken. The Chinese agreement to this was a good sign; if every word is on the record (which might be leaked), there is less room for the kind of free-wheeling exploratory discussion that might actually lead to progress.

It was up to Wang to arrange the location of the second meeting. He must have been somewhat uncomfortable with the casualness of negotiating from sofas, because this time he had a large table set up so he and his aides could sit on one side and we could sit on the other. This apparent regression toward the stiffness of Panmunjom did not encourage me, but the meeting did produce arrangements for sending mail to our prisoners, and Wang accepted a list of people we believed were in Chinese custody about whom we wanted information.

We met three more times during the course of the Geneva Conference. My job was to ask for the return of the American prisoners; as a bargaining lever, and as a way of trying to maintain face and insisting upon China's equality with the United States in all ways, Wang countered by alleging that the United States was preventing many Chinese residing in the United States from returning to China. His point had some validity. During the Korean War our government had issued orders on the basis of legislation going back to 1918 barring the exit of certain Chinese who had been educated in the United States in technical fields like rocketry, nuclear energy, and weapons design whose talents might have been used against United Nations forces in Korea had they been permitted to return to China. Some had even had access to classified information and worked on sensitive projects. In total 175 of these orders had been issued, though the number in effect at any one time was always substantially smaller. Those restrained by the orders were, however, free to work, travel, and conduct their lives normally within the United States, unlike the Americans imprisoned in China. The United States Government had actually paid the fares for a much larger number of Chinese students (767) who chose to return to the mainland after 1949, as part of an $8 million program to help almost 4000 Chinese students who were cut off from financial support after Mao's victory.

American treatment of Chinese living in our territory since 1949 was clearly not symmetrical with China's treatment of Americans in its territory. But Wang picked out the single issue of the few Chinese technicians prevented from leaving the United States and harped on it, trying to establish that the Chinese and American positions had equal legitimacy, which I strongly countered.

We came to no agreement, but at our final meeting during the course of the Geneva Conference we agreed that contact should be continued through the Chinese and American Consuls in Geneva. Neither Ambassador Wang nor I had any reason to believe that we would ever face each other across a table again. Over the next year eleven meetings occurred between the consuls primarily to exchange messages, but there were no results. In the meantime I had returned to Prague where I was quite isolated from developments in Chinese-American relations.

Perhaps to test our depth of commitment to getting the prisoners back and to prod Washington into more aggressive courtship, China announced in November 1954 that it had sentenced thirteen more Americans, eleven airmen and two civilians. We reacted probably as Chou En-lai hoped: angrily, protesting via Geneva, the British in Peking, and the United Nations, which then dispatched Secretary-General Dag Hammarskjold to confer with Chou. Hammarskjold returned saying that the Chinese wanted contact with the West to continue and might take a more positive attitude toward releasing the Americans if other aspects of Chinese relations with the United States were to improve.

In fact, Chinese-American relations were going through a period of accelerating tension over Taiwan. Some of it was no doubt contrived by the Chinese to induce us to negotiate; the rest stemmed from the communist leadership's determination to restore to the "Middle Kingdom" the integrity of its borders, which seemed more feasible now that Korea was no longer a distraction. In early 1955 the Senate approved ratification of a mutual defense treaty with Taiwan that formally committed us to defending the island from attack. Immediately following, nationalist and communist forces started shelling each other across the narrow waters that separated some nationalist-held islands from the mainland, and the communists seized another of these small islands. Preparations for further hostilities advanced on both sides. Peking rejected an invitation from the UN to participate in discussions on a cease-fire in the Taiwan area. Washington came under pressure from allies and neutrals, especially in Asia, to establish some sort of dialogue with Peking that would derail the momentum toward possible war. The Soviet Union capitalized on these widespread worries by proposing an international summit to deal with Taiwan, with Peking, naturally, as a major participant but excluding Chiang Kai-shek's government. Soured by its experience of the Indochina Conference in Geneva, Washington took a dim view of another large-scale summit.

Since Dulles now faced two unpleasant alternatives—a possible war over Taiwan or substantive negotiations with Peking in one form or another that would confer upon it the added international legitimacy he sought to deny it—his response was to stall, waiting to see what would develop without closing off any options. He poured cold water on the Soviet summit proposals and said he believed Chinese-American negotiations unwise "for the time being." He doubted that Peking would actually try to conquer Taiwan at this point, but he left open the possibility of negotiations in case war looked imminent or international pressure on Washington to ease tensions became too severe. And in the meantime Washington gave Peking some subdued, but accommodating signals. The cases of the Chinese technicians still denied permission to leave the country were methodically reviewed, and by April 1955 more than half had been told they were free to go.

In Chou En-lai, Dulles had a formidable opponent, and in late April Chou showed again his mastery of the diplomatic medium. After several months of deliberately cranking up tensions over Taiwan, China electrified world opinion with a series of expansive and affable-sounding statements at a major conference of thirty non-aligned nations in Bandung, Indonesia. Among other conciliatory gestures he said that China did not want war over Taiwan and wished to negotiate with the United States to see if tensions could be lessened. Foreign ministries the world over exhorted Washington to accept. Chou had seized the initiative.

Several months of intricate multi-party diplomatic dancing ensued. Neutral countries, especially India, attempted to mediate between Peking and Washington, and messages were passed through the British chargé in Peking. Before committing the United States Dulles wanted some indication that China wanted the talks to be serious and productive, and that we would not be setting ourselves up as the centerpiece of some new Chinese propaganda offensive. A hopeful sign came May 30 when four American airmen imprisoned in China were released. What finally clinched Dulles's decision to negotiate was the upcoming four-power summit between Britain, France, the United States, and the USSR; pressure to include China could be deflected if the United States and China were seen to be moving toward direct bilateral talks. On July 11, one week before the opening of the summit, the United States proposed through the British a resumption of ambassadorial-level talks with China. During the summit, where the Taiwan crisis was a major topic despite its absence from the formal agenda, the finishing touches were put on the arrangements.

At the beginning of July, Secretary Dulles had sent me a telegram saying he was contemplating renewing talks with China and asking me if I would again serve as United States representative. I was somewhat startled, having not been party to any of this backstage maneuvering, but replied that, of course, I would be happy to do so. Dulles was a person who kept his own counsel and he did not say why he had again selected me for this sensitive job of talking to the Chinese communists, despite my relative ignorance of China. Mostly, I think, it was the easiest choice for him. I had done it before and served satisfactorily. In the delicate process of firming up these talks, my reselection was not provocative to China. Also, I know that the Taiwan lobby, McCarthyites and the right wing of the Republican Party were never far from Dulles's calculations on Far Eastern policy. I had not been "corrupted" in their eyes (as many China-expert Foreign Service Officers had been so unfairly) by wartime contact with the Chinese communists.

Dulles returned to Washington from Geneva on July 23, and sent an urgent cable for me to return to the United States and to tell no one why I was leaving. Keeping my staff, and even Pat, entirely in the dark, I left for Washington immediately. At Manchester, England, we stopped to refuel and I bought a newspaper. The major story, liberally splashed with headlines, announced that the United States and China were going to resume talks and that I had been selected as the American representative.

In Washington Dulles greeted me with the news that it now appeared that the Chinese were not really very serious about wanting the talks, since at the last minute they had raised a point on the spelling of their capital, insisting that our spelling of "Peiping" was entirely unacceptable to them. However, this monumental crisis had been averted when both sides accepted the British proposal that each side could use its preferred spelling.

I pointed out to Dulles (who had kept the whole thing so secret that no one knowing the Chinese language had been informed) that this apparently trivial matter had not really been a pretext on the communist side. I explained to him that in Chinese "Peking" meant "northern capital" and "Peiping" only meant "northern plain." When the nationalists had moved their capital from Peking, they changed its name to "Peiping," for it was no longer their capital, and christened their new capital "Nanking" or "southern capital." Thus for the communists to acquiesce in the use of the nationalist term "Peiping" would be to deny their own legitimacy. He expressed surprise that nobody had ever ex plained this to him and said he would immediately explain it to Eisenhower.

Dulles also told me that the Chinese had again selected Wang Ping-nan to represent them and described the difficult negotiations that had been conducted via the British to work out the final arrangements. The agenda for the talks had been the thorniest problem, and an impasse had developed that we finally broke by suggesting a simple two-point agenda in which China concurred: "The repatriation of civilians who desire to return to their respective countries" and "certain other practical matters now at issue between both sides." Peking had also acquiesced in the disclaimer at the end of our announcement saying that these talks did not imply American recognition of the communist Chinese regime.

In reply to my question of how long he envisioned the talks continuing, Dulles said, "I will be happy if you are sitting there three months from now." That remark spoke volumes to me—it meant that he did not want me to walk out in a fit of anger as Arthur Dean had done on Huang Hua at Panmunjom in 1953, and that though he did not expect much substance to take place, he did approve of the *idea* of the talks. Later during the talks, when the Department would send me an instruction for a particularly stiff presentation to Wang, Dulles would often add in one way or another that he hoped I could find a way to do it that would not lead Peking to break off contact.

In our private session I also asked Dulles's authority to carry out, at my own discretion, informal and private social contacts with Ambassador Wang in order to probe his intentions and establish closer relations in a friendly atmosphere. Dulles approved on condition that I "not get caught."

I also suggested that it would improve my credibility with the Chinese and underscore our seriousness if I saw President Eisenhower before I left for Geneva. Dulles replied that I really needn't bother, which I took to mean that he was basically handling the matter and considered the President somewhat superfluous. On reconsidering, however, he agreed that it would boost my weight with the Chinese and the next day we went to the White House together. Dulles showed my instructions to the President, who took a very cursory glance at them. It was clear that he was not deeply involved and that the center of gravity in foreign affairs, at least on this subject, lay quite heavily with Dulles. I was careful, however, to get the President's endorsement of my program of discreet private contacts with Wang in Dulles's presence and to have this included in my formal instructions. And Dulles had asked me to mention to the President something I had told Dulles the day before, that the anti-communists in Czechoslovakia had interpreted a comment the President had made at his last press conference as evidence that the United States was retreating from the Administration's, and especially Dulles's, well-known policy of "liberating" Eastern Europe. Anti-regime Czechs (90 percent of the population) had let me know that they were concerned at this apparent shift in our policy. I do not know whether the President had made this remark to deliberately undercut Dulles, which he occasionally did to make sure Dulles remembered who was boss, or had simply made one of his verbal gaffes. In any event, Dulles certainly did want me to convey this implicit criticism directly to the President, which I did. The President said that I should make it clear to the Czech people that he was "by no means disinterested in their fate." As a result of this exchange, a paragraph to this effect was included in my instructions along with the injunction to return to my post at Prague "from time to time."

My instructions also authorized me to say that if the United States nationals held in China were released, it would facilitate our "voluntarily adopting a less restrictive policy" on Americans traveling to China. In connection with my instructions to seek a renunciation of the use of force by Peking "to achieve its ambitions," I was authorized to emphasize that our arrangements with Taiwan were purely defensive—in other words, we would not in any way support an attack by the government on Taiwan against the mainland. At the same time I was enjoined not to accept any discussion of the rights of the Republic of China.

I had only two days in Washington before hurrying to Geneva for the start of the talks on August 1, but even two days was enough to get a sense of how much excitement and optimism the announcement of United States-Chinese negotiations had sparked. In a July 26 press conference, Dulles pointed to a series of conciliatory gestures from Peking in recent months and said that if the subjects China raised at the talks "directly involve the United States and communist China we will be disposed to discuss them with a view of arriving at a peaceful settlement." President Eisenhower also issued a hopeful endorsement, and some senators were taking it for granted that a meeting between Chou and Dulles was imminent. Foreign opinion was even more enthusiastic. Chou's statements from Peking were unusually accommodating. A kind of euphoria seemed to surround the subject.

Exhausted from my hectic consultations and the long journey, I arrived in Geneva late in the evening of July 31, struggling to get my thoughts in order for the next day. I was determined to get as much rest as I could, for I knew I needed to have all my wits with me when I renewed my conversations with Wang.

A little after two in the morning, the telephone in my room woke me up. Krishna Menon, the Indian Foreign Minister, was on the line. He said he had just arrived in Geneva and wanted to see me most urgently. Could he come right over? No fan of Menon's, I put him off until eight in the morning at my office in the hotel. As usual, he was completely self-absorbed. He insisted on keeping me in the conversation much longer than was necessary or considerate, seeking to impress me with his theories on how to deal with the Chinese, his efforts to get the American prisoners out of China, and his great "wisdom" in foreign affairs generally. I only succeeded in getting rid of him by telling him that I had fifteen minutes to get to the Palais des Nations to make my call on Adrian Pell who, as head of the United Nations European Headquarters, would be the host of our talks. Menon was the vainest man I ever met. He also struck me as one of the most untrustworthy, to the point of being truly sinister. (The gossip among our security officers was that even veteran New York prostitutes refused to have anything to do with him because he treated them so brutally.)

Face to Face

Through our staffs Wang and I had established the choreography for opening the talks. We had chosen a modest room in the Palais des Nations in which stood a large, highly polished table. Crystal water pitchers and glasses sat atop it. I and my staff arrived early for our first meeting at 4 P.M. When Wang came in with his aides I again made a point of shaking his hand warmly and exchanging pleasantries. The Chinese had already attempted to put us slightly on the defensive. The night before Peking had announced the release of eleven American airmen captured during the Korean War (for which Krishna Menon had tried to take credit in his talk with me), and Wang had told the press quite boldly that this move was intended to influence the talks. Wang tried to keep the initiative in his opening statement by mentioning the release of the fliers and expressing his expectation that the talks would not bog down in discussing the return of nationals but would move quickly to the removal of American forces from Taiwan, the start of full diplomatic relations between China and the United States, the end of the American trade embargo, and virtually every other significant objective in Peking's foreign policy. Not wanting to negotiate on his terms or let him divert attention away from "the return of nationals of both sides to their respective countries," the first item on the agenda to which China had assented, I made sure that Wang agreed to discuss the return of nationals first.

Wang also said he wanted reporters to be present or fully briefed on each session. I countered by saying that the United States intended these discussions to be serious, not a propaganda mill. I suggested that all discussions be private, with no official stenographic record, and that we not reveal the substance of negotiations without agreeing to the release or giving reasonable advance notice. After some discussion Wang assented. We then agreed to split the rental of our conference room—$1.15 per month! The whole meeting lasted only forty-five minutes, but it had cleared away the procedural underbrush so that we could proceed next time to the first item on our agenda.

As I have said, the United States places unusual stress on protecting the security of its citizens abroad and considered the release of our remaining forty-one nationals a fundamental objective of the talks and a prerequisite to progress on any other subjects China wished to raise. But we had to feel our way gingerly. Initially my assistant for the talks was a very able Foreign Service China language expert, Ralph Clough. He was followed by Douglas Forman, David Osborn, and finally Edwin W. Martin, all very able Chinese experts. Despite the background we all brought to Geneva, we felt we were entering a void where past experience had limited value. We had no idea whether China was really committed to this new policy of coexistence it had abruptly adopted after six years of violent anti-Americanism. We had no real sense of how Peking wanted to resolve the prisoner issue. Nor did we know if it had any sympathy with Secretary Dulles's proposals for "renunciation of force" over Taiwan, the item highest on our list of "other practical matters" to be taken up after the prisoner issue was settled. China and the United States were facing each other across a chasm of ignorance and hostility.

Discussions on the return of the civilians started August 2, at our second meeting, which lasted about an hour. I began. I assured Wang that the United States Government was imposing no restraint on the departure of any Chinese who wished to go to communist China, since all the technicians previously under

order to stay in the country had been told they were now free
to leave. I also handed him a list of the forty-one American civilians we knew were being detained in his country and requested
that they be released immediately.

Wang's response showed that the traditional concern for
keeping face in Chinese diplomacy had only been accentuated
by Peking's present drive for international recognition. He represented China's case for the return of its civilians as if it were
equivalent in all respects to our case against China for jailing and
mistreating Americans. He proposed that each side report on the
status of the other's citizens residing in its territory (including a
list from us giving the name and address of every Chinese in the
United States); that we "revoke" all prohibitions on the departure
of Chinese (though he did not present any evidence at this meeting or any subsequent one to contradict my statement that all
Chinese in the United States were free to leave at any time); and
that each side designate a third country to look after the interests
of its citizens in the other's territory. Finally, he proposed India
as the PRC's representative in the United States.

These proposals, though couched in the arid technicalities
of international law on diplomatic representation, were actually
a blunt and aggressive challenge. Wang implied that we were
forcibly restraining Chinese from leaving our territory, when that
was demonstrably false. By requesting a name list of Chinese
aliens in the United States, who numbered about 117,000, and
by proposing that the Indian Embassy look after their interests
for Peking, he was trying to destroy the standing of the Government of the Republic of China which at the time we recognized
as the only government entitled to represent the interests of
Chinese nationals in the United States.

I replied by saying that we recognized the Republic of
China (on Taiwan) as the only government empowered to act on
behalf of Chinese in American territory and that we could not
provide the name list in any event, since the talks' terms of reference specifically limited our discussions to "nationals who desire
to return." Since we were not restraining any Chinese from leaving the United States, there was no evidence that any of the
Chinese staying in the United States desired to return.

At the third meeting, after repeating my call upon the
Peking authorities to let all Americans in China leave immediately
and without preconditions, I took up Wang's suggestion that a
third party be designated to look after each country's citizens in
the other's territory. I thought the idea had potential, provided

the third party's powers were strictly limited to investigating the cases of civilians who genuinely desired to leave. But I said the United States would firmly reject any arrangement permitting the Indian Embassy to interview Chinese living in the United States solely at the request of the Peking authorities, without some indication from the individual that he or she actually desired to go to mainland China. A system like this could easily have degenerated into a messy and time-consuming fishing expedition that would not only have given Peking tacit jurisdiction over Chinese living in the United States but would have subjected those Chinese to harassment and intimidation. And at the fourth meeting, I presented a detailed plan whereby the Indian Embassy in the United States and the office of the British chargé in Peking could assist nationals of the other country who felt they were being prevented from leaving.

Ambassador Wang replied by repeating all his proposals from the second meeting and insisting that we accept them. This was to become a familiar tactic. He even raised a new point— that all Chinese prisoners in American jails should be released immmediately and given a chance to go to communist China. This approach assumed that the status of Americans in China, held on trumped-up political charges of espionage, many without any pretense of a trial or other judicial proceeding, was symmetrical with the imprisonment of Chinese in the United States for common crimes. I had no hesitation in dismissing the attempted analogy out of hand.

By this point both sides had stated their main arguments and given the other a chance to rebut them. The reporters swirling around the Palais des Nations, eager to chronicle each breakthrough in Chinese-American relations as it happened, began to sense at the same time we did that the release of the forty-one Americans was going to be a long and frustrating affair. The widespread euphoria that had greeted the announcement of the talks evaporated. The President, Secretary Dulles, and Chou En-lai still made optimistic noises, but the actual bargaining sessions were revealing that tangible achievement was going to require much time and labor.

As this disappointing realization spread, so did speculation that the talks would break off altogether. The fifth meeting had to be postponed twenty-four hours. The sixth, seventh, eighth, and ninth meetings, which took us through August 20, seemed to go nowhere, but I was not surprised that, having failed in his first objective of engineering a Dulles-Chou meeting, Wang was dragging his feet.

Wang continued to insist that we accept his initial position, and even added some more extreme demands. He proposed that Americans who were involved in "unfinished civil or criminal cases" be excluded from any repatriation agreement until their cases were settled, which of course would have given China the right to continue to detain all of them at will. Wang hinted that a number of Americans whose cases had been recently "reviewed" by the Chinese judicial authorities might be released if we would accede to their request for jurisdiction via the Indian Embassy over Chinese living in America.

But all this was unacceptable. We made it clear that we would firmly reject any deal trading the fate of our citizens for diplomatic recognition or other compromises. This was a hard, firm position in Washington with which I fully agreed, but I did not want to give China any room to misinterpret it as a bullying tactic for maneuvering them into breaking off the talks. So I told Wang I was not attempting to set an arbitrary deadline for the release of all the Americans or to dictate the procedures, "judicial" or otherwise, his government should follow in releasing them. But I wanted Peking to know that we could not accept any arrangement that left it free to hold the Americans indefinitely. This small attempt at conciliation produced no apparent results.

After the eleventh meeting State Department officials began publicly to express disappointment with the progress of the talks, and at the end of August we decreased the pace from three meetings a week to one.

By this point the actual mechanics of our negotiations had settled into a well-established pattern. Each of us would alternate giving an opening statement that would be delivered and translated paragraph by paragraph, usually from a prepared text. Then the other would respond in the same fashion, holding the floor until he was finished. There was no chance to ask questions as they arose during the opening statements. Then each of us would alternate holding the floor, talking as long as we liked, until both of us were finished. This alternation would often result in some fast repartee, straining the capabilities of our interpretors to handle it. When it seemed neither side had anything more to say, the one who had not opened the meeting would propose a time for the next one. Both Wang and I had aides who took notes and who would whisper or write notes giving us advice, but they never spoke at the meetings.

The atmosphere was business-like and, in its way, civil. We both presented our positions vigorously, and when things got tough, he would talk about my so-and-so's in Washington, and I would talk about his so-and-so's in Peking; but we both avoided giving any personal offense. The fact that Wang adopted the customary behavior of professional diplomats I considered a hopeful sign.

In every sense Wang was an opponent who stretched my own capabilities to the limit. He was a sharp debater, quick to pick up any chinks he saw in my arguments. I tried to do the same with him. He had been a long-time communist and confidant of Chou En-lai and showed a self-confidence in our free discussions, that contrasted with what I was going to experience with my Soviet colleague in the SALT negotiations twenty years later.

When later we settled into a routine of one meeting a week, Wang and I would often be on the same plane from Geneva (sometimes the only passengers) returning to our posts—I to Prague and he to Warsaw. Sometimes he was accompanied by his second wife, a very good-looking Chinese woman who had been a movie actress. On occasion we would be weathered in at Zurich and stay all night at the same hotel. Although we never discussed business without interpreters, his English and my knowledge of Chinese characters was sufficient for us to talk about such things as China's efforts to "romanize" the Chinese language or the experiences of both of us with the Japanese in China.

But though our personal contacts were pleasant, Wang's demeanor during the formal bargaining sessions accurately reflected the hostility dividing our two countries. He could ignore commitments previously made, advance specious arguments without the slightest hint of embarrassment, insist that I immediately give into all his demands to prove American good faith, leak inaccurate reports of our negotiations to the press despite his commitment to keep the talks private, and use the lives of American prisoners as a tool to pry concessions from me.

Bargaining, especially between communist and non-communist negotiators, often involves small games of nerves. One such game was Wang's insistence on having the last word at every meeting. He would say that he hoped I would think over his arguments carefully; I would say the same to him; but he would always continue the byplay until he had the last word. Since the conversations were private, this didn't make a lot of difference, but one day I just got my back up and decided that come hell or high water I was not going to let Wang always have this small satisfaction. The session started around 10 A.M., as usual, and at about one o'clock we finished our business and started our ritual closing dance. He put in what he thought would be the last word, and I topped it. He tried again. I said something else. Round and round we went for another two and a half hours before it became evident that my bladder capacity exceeded his and he had no choice but to let me have the last word so he could rush from the room. And after that I found that I never again had to fence him at the end of our meetings.

After the first meeting I drafted a brief telegram summarizing the discussions for Washington, in accordance with normal practice. I immediately received a message requesting more detail, and after a few sessions I found myself reporting virtually verbatim. This could amount to quite a few words after a four-hour meeting, and I often asked Washington whether it really wanted this mass of detail when so much of it was to me boring and repetitious. But I was told to keep it coming, that Secretary Dulles was reading every word trying to assess China's sincerity and looking for nuances that might indicate shift in Peking's position. This gave me the unsought reputation of having the longest telegrams in the Foreign Service. When the negotiations were fresh, I received instructions from the Secretary before every meeting; as they settled into a more established pattern, the hand of Herman Phleger, the Department's able legal advisor, become more apparent in what I received, although Dulles still personally approved every message. Walter Robertson, the Assistant Secretary for Far Eastern Affairs, was not given any real role. Dulles evidently felt that Robertson's deep hatred of the Chinese communists would taint his views.

A small ray of light entered my stalemated talks with Wang in mid-August. We wanted Peking to commit itself to releasing all captive Americans within a set period, but we did not want to aid China's drive for international standing in the process. If we could get some sort of written pledge from Wang on the prisoners, therefore, Washington wanted its form to be similar to the original announcement of the talks—two separate but parallel statements issued by the respective governments simultaneously. Wang was not too excited by this approach. At first he sought a normal diplomatic undertaking between his government and mine, since this in itself would confer legitimacy on Peking. But he ultimately conceded the point, and the next step was to devise language that would permit the parallel construction that Peking demanded in these two "separate" declarations, while encompassing the very different realities in the two countries.

Taking advantage of my authorization to have informal social contacts with Wang, I invited him to dinner at a small but excellent Genevois restaurant in order to work on prisoner return language to which we could both agree. He promptly accepted for August 22. Only the two of us were present, with our interpreters, and we conversed from 7:30 until midnight. I repeatedly expressed my unhappiness at his resistance to specific language about releasing the civilians, especially a date by which the process would be completed. I referred to the public statement Chou had made the day before our talks started which said that it "should be possible quickly to reach a settlement on the return of civilians. The number of American civilians in China is small and the question can be easily settled." Wang kept assuring me that a "very considerable" number would be released immediately after our two countries reached a formal agreement and that the number remaining for later release would "not be large." But he refused to give me any definite time period. I emphasized to him that the Chinese leaders were badly misreading American public opinion if they sought to gain an advantage from piecemeal releases, and that we were not going to go far on any other practical matters of interest to him until all of our citizens were allowed to return.

In our broader discussion I noted that in the period before the Korean War it was Peking that had precluded the establishment of formal diplomatic relations by its campaign of mistreating American official personnel. I said they had refused to recognize us, not the other way around. He did not attempt to refute my argument, saying only that in the early days they "had made some mistakes."

Wang countered by invoking a theme that would bedazzle many Americans in later years: China's hope to get American trade and technological and economic aid for the large development tasks they faced. I said that we, of course, looked forward to resuming economic relations, and spoke of the sentimental attachment most Americans had for China. All the more reason, therefore, for the two of us to clear away some of the underbrush that blocked friendly ties.

Wang invited me back to an excellent dinner at a Chinese restaurant the following week at which we covered much the same ground, without being able to settle anything.

In the subsequent months of our talks I looked for opportunities that would merit further private conversations and I presume he did the same, but as the negotiations developed no such opportunity presented itself. As a friendly gesture I invited him to a concert by the Boston Symphony when it visited Geneva, and he did the same for me when the Peking Opera came, but so as not to attract press attention, we did not sit together on either occasion.

The Agreed Announcement

At the August 31 session I tabled a draft text for a parallel but separate announcement covering the return of civilians. It called for both sides to take measures so that civilians could "promptly" exercise their right to return to their own country. The Chinese tabled their version at the next meeting, and we proceeded to the time-honored negotiating practice of reconciling the two texts word by word until both sides were satisfied. When the two languages involved are Chinese and English, this process can be extremely complex, because they are so dissimilar the exact translations often do not exist. Fine differences in shading can often turn an intended meaning on its head. Fortunately, interpreter Ekvall demonstrated once again his brilliance and versatility and we began to make some progress toward a joint text. The main semantic controversies centered on how quickly the civilians would be returned—we wanted a set period, then suggested "promptly" and agreed to a Chinese proposal for "expeditiously"—and whether the third parties chosen by each side to look after its nationals in the other's territory should be "authorized," "mandated," "entrusted," or "invited" to do so. The underlying source of this controversy was China's desire to empower India to initiate investigations on any Chinese living in the United States, whether or not those Chinese wanted to return to communist China. This might be a legitimate interpretation if the United States government "mandated" the Indian Embassy to look after the Chinese in United States territory, but not if India were only "invited" to look after them. We settled on "inviting," which implicitly rejected Peking's contention that all Chinese nationals living in the United States were its legitimate responsibility rather than Taiwan's.

At the September 6 meeting Ambassador Wang started with the surprise announcement that "reviews" had been completed on twelve Americans who would now be granted exit permits. In the next installment of our bargaining over the joint text on the return of nationals, however, he continued to claim Peking's right to initiate inquiries about the status of any Chinese in the United States. We thought that the release of the twelve might be intended to entice us to concede to China this right on the assumption that the remaining Americans would be freed in return. We were pleased at the encouraging sign, but "turning over" the 117,000 Chinese in the United States to Peking was unthinkable.

At the next meeting, on September 10, Wang finally agreed to a wording which allowed China to ask India to investigate the status of only those Chinese in the United States who had taken the initiative to contact the Indian Embassy in Washington first to say they felt themselves blocked from returning to mainland China. This cleared the way to settling the final text of the two statements that constituted the "Agreed Announcement." It was released to the press later that day.

In fact, this "Agreed Announcement" of September 10, 1955, was the only formal agreement reached between our two countries until President Nixon and Chou En-lai, then Prime Minister, signed the Shanghai Communiqué in 1972.

At the end of this meeting Ambassador Wang announced that ten more Americans were being freed, three who had been under house arrest and seven prisoners. It was a very hopeful sign, and now that we had a written agreement on the return of our nationals we hoped the remaining nineteen Americans would be home "expeditiously."

Other Practical Matters

The Geneva talks now entered their second phase, the consideration of "other practical matters." These negotiations were much more complex, and frustrating, than those on the return of citizens. The range of issues was almost infinitely broad, covering the whole of relations between China and the United States. Many were really fundamental, demanding major shifts in policy by one side or both as a prerequisite to reaching specific agreements. Despite hundreds of hours of meeting, we never got anywhere tangible. But the side benefits that Dulles hoped for when he gave me his injunction to keep talking were in large measure obtained. More American prisoners returned from China, tensions in the Taiwan Strait subsided, and Geneva became a safety valve and "post office" where both sides could pass messages, signals, and requests for information. Still, this was pretty small beer compared to the hopes the press furor had raised.

During the course of the talks, I sometimes felt that we might be able to forge some lasting links with China if we were to take slightly more flexible positions. By the time they ended, I came to the conclusion that there were no reasonable concessions we could make that would shift Peking's attitude away from diehard opposition to the United States and our Pacific foreign policy. Now, with hindsight, and with the knowledge of how the United States and China finally managed to normalize relations in the 1970s, I have moved to something of a compromise between my previous judgments.

I believe now that the amount of intransigence on both sides at Geneva, though considerable, was probably somewhat less than either side believed it to be. Not all the compromises between Peking and Washington that made normalization possible in the 1970s were politically feasible, in either capital, in the 1950s, and even the most astonishingly successful Johnson-Wang talks would not have resulted in full diplomatic normalization, at least not for many years. But had we concentrated at first on the easier issues instead of the most emotionally charged and difficult one—Taiwan—perhaps some small knots could have been tied. "A journey of a thousand miles," goes the Chinese proverb, "begins with a single step." In 1955 Wang Ping-nan and I could not have gone a thousand miles together, perhaps not even 100, but if we had tried to settle the easy issues first, we might have built up enough momentum to carry our two countries along for a brief but profitable trip. In any event, this did not happen.

After the September 10 Agreed Announcement we expected Peking to release the remaining nineteen Americans promptly. For several meetings I refused to move to the second item on the agenda, the discussion of "other practical matters," until China had complied with its own written commitment. But Wang took an entirely different tack. He igorned the prisoner issue altogether and pressed immediately for a meeting between Chou and Dulles and for the establishment of trade relations between the two countries.

On September 14, he leaked a detailed but biased account of his bargaining position to the press, contrary to our initial agreement on confidentiality. Peking also began to release propaganda stories alleging that the United States government was harassing and intimidating Chinese students who wished to return to communist China. It seemed to me that Peking, having agreed to release the Americans, was now trying to make us pay twice for the same thing—extracting political concessions from us before it would do what it had promised to do unconditionally. Though I was still inclined to begin simultaneous discussion of "other matters," Dulles had told me to stand firm on not discussing other matters until China had honored the Agreed Announcement.

Wang hinted broadly through the press that the talks might be broken off if I persisted in this approach, and I did not think he was necessarily bluffing. Having in mind Dulles's injunction to me to keep the talks going, I pressed for, and obtained, his agreement to proceed to "other practical matters," believing that the Chinese might release the prisoners more quickly if we could assure them that we were not going to hasten from Geneva as soon as the prisoners were safely home. On September 20, I agreed to move to the second agenda item, making it clear to Wang that I was free to raise complaints about China's implementation of the Agreed Announcement at any time.

The two main "practical matters" I raised differed from Wang's: the fate of 450 American soldiers missing in action since the Korean War, some of whom we believed the Chinese might be holding, but most of whom were probably dead; and a "mutual renunciation of force" over Taiwan. Wang refused to provide information on the military personnel in Korea, saying that the Military Armistice Commission (MAC) in Panmunjom was the proper forum for inquiry. In this he was technically correct, though there was nothing to forestall our raising it at Geneva. In fact, this issue of the 450 MIAs was a poor one and, as far as I was concerned, I raised it in Geneva only for the record. The way it was mishandled at Panmunjom had caused unnecessary and entirely unjustified anguish for the families of the men involved over many years. It began simply enough as a Korean armistice negotiating tactic; we took the position that in accordance with their responsibilities under the Geneva Convention, the communist side was obligated to account for all Allied personnel who fell into their hands, either as prisoners or deceased. Thus if a missing man had not been returned from POW camp or declared dead by the other side, we assumed he was still alive and being held prisoner. This was a reasonable enough negotiating ploy, but considering the nature of the terrain where much of the fighting was carried on and the casual attitude of the communists toward accounting even for their own casualties, we had little or no expectation that any of the 450 were in fact alive. It was cruel to mislead the families into thinking that they might be by raising the subject with Wang. In any case, doing so gave us no effective bargaining leverage.

"Two Chinas"

Securing Peking's agreement not to use force to solve its dispute over the status of Taiwan was the second and most important issue I raised in the second phase of the talks. It continued as an issue for twenty-five years, right down to the "normalization of relations" in 1980. Since 1954, the United States had pledged by mutual defense treaty to protect the Republic of China on Taiwan. It was completely unacceptable to us that Peking should ever seize it by force. Therefore we proposed a "mutual renunciation of force" under which Peking could continue to advance its position on Taiwan's legal status, but would agree not to go to war about it. Once communist China had demonstrated that it was willing to act peacefully over Taiwan—to "lay down the pistol" in Secretary Dulles's words—we could improve our relations in other ways, including UN membership, trade normalization, and a Dulles-Chou meeting.

The idea for mutual renunciation of force had originated with Secretary Dulles, who first advanced it at a press conference on January 18, 1955, as a significant move back from his "liberation" policy. Never enamored of negotiating with communists, and vehemently opposed to negotiating any agreement that would formally guarantee them the gains they had achieved by force, Dulles proposed renunciation of force as a general doctrine for dealing with communist countries. If we could agree to disagree on specific disputes—for example, Indochina or the division of Germany and Berlin—in an environment free of force or the threat of force, then we could wait for time to work out these problems without anyone having to fight. Dulles considered mutual renunciation of force particularly good for Taiwan because Washington and Peking would not have to conclude a formal written agreement to bring it about. We already subscribed to the principle in the UN Charter, and our treaty with Taiwan provided only for "defense." If Peking accepted the principle, it simply had to make a unilateral declaration to that effect.

But the Chinese took a diametrically opposed view. When I first proposed a "renunciation of the use of force for the achievement of national objectives" on September 20, Wang's response was generalized but highly negative. He denied that Peking had any intent of using force in international relations or that it wanted war with the United States. But he drew a sharp distinction between civil and international conflicts, and left no doubt that his superiors in Peking considered Taiwan a strictly internal matter in which the United States was an illegitimate intruder. He charged that we were actually the cause of unrest over Taiwan, because our "occupation" of the island prevented the Chinese people from "liberating" it. I detected in Wang a depth of feeling about Taiwan that was absent from his opinions on other matters.

On October 8, to make sure that China understood our Taiwan policy exactly, I made a detailed exposition of it and gave Wang copies of my statement. We were not proposing, I said, that either side abandon its views, its right to pursue its policies peacefully, or its right to defend itself. All we wanted was that Peking join us in renouncing the use of force both generally and particularly in the Taiwan area. In light of Wang's repeated demand for a foreign ministers' meeting, I argued that China should recognize that disputes could not be peacefully resolved at any level if discussions were conducted under an overhanging threat by one side to fight if it did not get what it wanted.

We then repeated the technique used during the talks on the Agreed Announcement of trying to reconcile written texts by both sides. The first Chinese draft, submitted October 27, quoted the UN Charter regarding the obligations of member nations to settle international disputes peacefully—a Chinese attempt to clothe itself in the UN mantle. It went on: "The PRC and the USA agreed that they should settle disputes between their two countries by peaceful means without resorting to the threat or the use of force"; but it also called for a foreign ministers' meeting to discuss a separate question of "relaxing and eliminating the tension in the Taiwan area." In essence, China was restating its demand for a Chou-Dulles conference while deliberately excluding Taiwan from the range of international disputes it promised to settle peacefully. To this we could not agree. Wang finally accused me of advocating what he called a "Two Chinas" doctrine, which he bitterly denounced. It was the first time I had heard the term.

To put pressure on us, the Chinese tried leaking detailed but slanted accounts of the talks, submitting conciliatory-sounding but ambiguous drafts that removed its call for a foreign ministers' conference, and other avenues. But they would not under any circumstances cede what they considered their absolute right to settle the "domestic" matter of Taiwan by whatever means they chose, including war if necessary. Wang and I devoted scores of meetings and hundreds of hours to finding some sort of modus vivendi on Taiwan. To no avail, because neither side was willing to concede what the other considered its minimum requirement.

Prisoners

Even while we discussed Taiwan we were deadlocking on another subject; namely, the return of the remaining American prisoners in China, which we thought had been settled by the September 10 Agreed Announcement. The text clearly stated that the PRC recognized that Americans "who desire to return to the United States are entitled to do so, and it has adopted and will further adopt appropriate measures so that they can expeditiously exercise their right to return." The text made no exceptions, and that is how the United States Government and the rest of the world construed the Announcement when it was issued. But to our intense anger and frustration, Wang almost immediately attempted to reinterpret it to justify his government's continued policy of dribbling the prisoners out sporadically as a combination carrot-and-stick to make us more amenable to China's position on Taiwan and other issues. The objective and presumably agreed standard the September 10 Announcement had provided for on the return of civilians was entirely disregarded.

Since Peking's main objective seemed to be a Chou-Dulles meeting, I wondered why it chose this hostile approach. At first Dulles felt, and I agreed, that Peking was angry at the press reaction to its release of the eleven American fliers at the time of the Agreed Announcement. Instead of the flood of friendly stories the Chinese expected, American papers featured reports of the gross mistreatment the crew had suffered in captivity. The resulting public indignation had been intense. At Dulles's suggestion I tried to counter this development with Wang by pointing out privately that such stories had to be expected, that the United States Government could do nothing to prevent them, and that, therefore, the best thing from everyone's standpoint, including China's public image, was to release all the prisoners immediately. Peking could not see it that way. As time went on and it became clear that we were not rushing toward a Chou-Dulles conference, the Chinese concluded that they could extract the most from us by dribbling out these bargaining chips piecemeal.

Before September ended, Wang had reverted to his old demand that the United States provide a list of all 117,000 Chinese in the United States, even though he had abandoned that position in the negotiations leading to the Agreed Announcement. Then he blandly asserted a distinction between "ordinary" Americans (comprising some forty-seven people who had defected to China—people who had never figured in our discussions) and the nineteen "criminal" Americans. The only responsibility Wang would accept for the "criminals" under the Agreed Announcement was to review their cases one by one. He said there could be no question of an expeditious return while they were still serving their sentences. I objected in the strongest possible terms, but it was clear that the negotiations were retrogressing.

As I continued during October and November 1955 to press for the immediate release of the remaining nineteen Americans according to the September 10 text, Peking angrily began to blame us for stalling the talks and mounted a large propaganda offensive claiming that our treatment of Chinese aliens in the United States violated the Agreed Announcement. Wang charged that we were forcing Chinese to obtain entry permits to Taiwan or apply for permanent residence in the United States, a deliberate misreading of our immigration regulations. In late October and early November five more Americans were released, coinciding with a Big Four Foreign Ministers' conference in Geneva. Then the releases stopped, and in December Wang began submitting names of Chinese in the United States whose departure, he alleged, we were obstructing. This was entirely a diversionary tactic; none of the allegations had any basis in fact.

He ultimately submitted fifty-five names. All of them were specifically informed of their right to return to communist China. Fifty-four preferred to stay in the United States. The fifty-fifth was a Chinese student named Liu Yung-ming who had had a mental breakdown while attending the University of Missouri and had been committed to a Missouri state mental hospital in May, 1949, with the approval of the Chinese Consul General in Chicago. There was no record of his having tried to return to China, and Liu's father, the only relative who had taken the trouble to correspond with the hospital, had requested that treatment be continued. Wang, however, asserted that Liu's wife wanted him back, so Liu was asked whether he wanted to return. He said yes, and was immediately put aboard a ship for communist China—only eleven days after our attention was drawn to the case. We put up notices in 35,000 post offices and advertised widely in newspapers and on radio and television, but the Indian Embassy in Washington received not a single complaint against the United States Government from Chinese claiming their return to China was being obstructed. And all the while hundreds of Chinese were freely departing the United States for communist China without reference to the Indian Embassy. By contrast, Americans jailed in China were not even being allowed to contact the British Charge's office, directly contradicting the provisions of our Agreement.

We knew that China had no real interest in Chinese in the United States sentenced to prison for common crimes; in fact Wang had never even mentioned Chinese common criminals in the United States during all the negotiations leading to the Agreed Announcement. But Washington and I decided to try to turn the tables on Peking by actually permitting all Chinese imprisoned in the United States, no matter what their crime, to return to China if they so desired. This involved elaborate but very quiet arrangements, including a census of prisoners in all state and federal prisons to determine how many Chinese prisoners there were. It turned out there were only thirty-four, all of whom were in state prisons for either murder or narcotics violations.

The State Department then approached every state governor concerned to secure their agreement to commuting the sentence (to expulsion from the United States) of any Chinese prisoner who wanted to go to communist China. The President agreed to do the same if any were subsequently found in federal penitentiaries. The plan also called for having an Indian government representative interview each of the thirty-four to determine who wanted to be released to mainland China; but to avoid a premature leak to the Chinese, we said nothing of this to the Indians at this stage.

By May 1956 we had the whole thing tied up, so I could present it at Geneva as a complete surprise to Wang. At our May 31 meeting I informed Wang that we would deport immediately any Chinese prisoner who desired to go to mainland China. I thought I really had him on the spot.

At the next meeting he rejected my proposal point by point, even though this put him in the ludicrous position of opposing a prisoner release he had previously been insisting upon with vehemence. He claimed we had already weeded out the Chinese prisoners who wished to return to mainland China, and so it would be no surprise when the Indian Embassy found that no one on our list wanted their sentences commuted to expulsion. Consequently his government would refuse India permission to participate. He went on to say that China wanted all the Chinese prisoners released unconditionally, after which they should be allowed to return to China if they wanted. I was quick to point out that the American prisoners in China had not been afforded any similar privilege, for which Wang had no direct reply.

It was clear that Wang feared a repeat of the humiliation of the Korean Armistice when three out of four Chinese Red Army POWs chose Taiwan over repatriation. He realized very well that if Chinese preferred American jails to life under communism, it would not exactly provide Peking with a propaganda victory.

The Chinese convicts were interviewed, nonetheless, by the American Red Cross instead of the Indian Embassy. By this time the normal parole process had reduced their number to twenty-four. Of these twenty-four, only one, who had served $2^1/2$ years of a seven-to-twenty year sentence for manslaughter, wanted to go to communist China. He was duly deported but changed his mind in Hong Kong. Two others desired to go to Taiwan, one of whom later backed out, and the other twenty-one chose to serve out their sentences. Wang never raised the subject again.

By the end of 1955 it seemed that the Johnson-Wang talks, which had started amidst such great expectations, were permanently deadlocked. Thirteen Americans remained imprisoned in China with no prospect of "expeditious" release. Peking was intransigent about renouncing force in the Taiwan area. And we were unwilling to accede to the battery of Chinese demands aimed at boosting Peking's status. Dulles was not inclined to grant China concessions under the best of circumstances, but until China changed its attitude on the prisoner issue and on the use of force against Taiwan, he would not even entertain the thought of relenting. It did not make sense to us to encourage trade relations, for instance, with a country that might quickly employ the benefits of that trade in a war with our allies on Taiwan. In retrospect, it is evident that the negotiations had entered a vicious circle. Peking refused to give up what it felt was its ace in the hole, our prisoners, so long as we adamantly refused concessions, concessions that in our view would be justified only after Peking had manifested its good faith by releasing the prisoners and renouncing force against Taiwan.

Journalists

The negotiations grew more stagnant as 1955 drew to a close, and both sides tried to revive them by applying public pressure through the press. But it was not until August 1956 that world press attention and some sense of public excitement returned to the talks, courtesy of the urbane Chou's diplomatic skill. Demonstrating a shrewd appreciation of the power of the American press, Peking unilaterally rescinded its entrance ban on American journalists and cabled invitations to fifteen important American media organizations for a month-long trip inside communist China. The journalists sensed a good story and, of course, wanted to accept. Secretary Dulles, however, did not wish to rescind the State Department's ban on the travel of Americans to China, either in general or, perhaps particularly, for journalists. He believed that permitting Americans to travel to China when thirteen civilians remained there as hostages would undermine our bargaining position in Geneva.

If Chou's objective in inviting the journalists was to divide and conquer by turning the American press against the State Department, no move could have been more deft. Editorial writers attacked the Department's position almost unanimously. Whether the government of a country dedicated to individual freedom should have the right to restrict travel by its citizens was a controversial proposition, both constitutionally and ethically, and sustained pressure was brought to bear on the Department for almost a year by media organizations. A few correspondents defied the legal ban and visited communist China anyway.

Finally Dulles decided to bend a little, rather than encourage domestic opposition to his entire policy of keeping China isolated. In August 1957, after working quietly with media representatives, the Department announced it would permit twenty-four news organizations to send correspondents to China for a trial period of six months and that this might be extended if the Chinese authorities permitted them to report freely. But the Department also stated that there would be no automatic reciprocity in the number of Chinese reporters wishing to visit the United States; they would be admitted only if they qualified under our applicable immigration laws, though Dulles implied that we would look favorably upon at least some of the applications.

Wang completely rejected this proposed arrangement when I raised it at our September 12, 1957, meeting. Peking objected to any scheme that denied what it would consider equal treatment for American and Chinese reporters. Wang said I was insulting China and obstructing a very straightforward chance for agreement. I pointed out that he had not mentioned reciprocal arrangements of any kind when China first invited the fifteen Americans in August, and that our immigration laws did not permit the State Department to grant entrance visas except after an individual review of each case.

Thus, when in August 1956, Peking proposed that American news correspondents visit China, we opposed; now a year later, when we acquiesced but added some reasonable conditions, Peking opposed. This was fairly characteristic of all our relations with them.

Next, Wang made a series of proposals on "mutual contacts," cultural exchange, and trade. Since he knew quite well that we would not accept them, they were presumably meant for propaganda rather than progress.

By this time he had also stopped proposing new formulations on renunciation of force, and prisoner releases had halted. Both Washington and I thought that the Chinese could well be building up to breaking off the talks. But then Wang stepped back and relaxed his attitude. Even so, the whole enterprise was stagnant, with only monthly meetings going into 1957.

By the end of 1957, Secretary Dulles concluded that the talks no longer justified keeping me in place. A new Ambassador to Thailand was needed, and Dulles apparently thought that after four strenuous years commuting between Prague and Geneva it was time to return me to Asia. On December 12, 1957, I announced my departure from the Johnson-Wang talks. It was their seventy-third session. I had pressed Dulles to select a replacement whose name I could give Wang at that meeting. He wished to downgrade the talks, though not terminate them, so designated my deputy, Ed Martin, as my replacement. Ed was in every way admirably suited for the task, but he was not an Ambassador.

Wang appeared upset at the prospect of losing his durable sparring partner. While expressing high regard for Ed Martin, he pointed to the undeniable fact of Ed's rank; the agreement establishing the talks had provided they would be at the Ambassadorial level. For reasons I never fully understood, Peking then seemed to attach more importance to continuing at Geneva than we did and resented Dulles's de facto downgrading of them. Only after almost a year, when Washington designated Ambassador Jacob Beam to resume the talks in September 1958 with Ambassador Wang Ping-nan in Warsaw, were the Chinese satisfied.

One of the most intriguing paradoxes of these talks, in fact, is that they continued at all. Despite a complete deadlock on matters of substance, despite the condemnations the two governments heaped on each other, despite the bitterness that increasingly seized Chinese-American relations outside of our contact at Geneva, we kept meeting—week after week, month after month, ultimately year after year. *The New York Times* commented on my part in the Geneva talks:

> For sheer endurance there has been no United States diplomatic performance comparable to Mr. Johnson's since Benjamin Franklin's efforts to get financial help from the French monarchy for the American Revolution.

I certainly was able to exceed Dulles's original wish to keep the talks going for three months, without deviating from the basically hard line I was instructed to take. The United States-PRC sessions continued with the same agenda for sixty-three more meetings over the next twelve years with the successive American and Chinese Ambassadors in Warsaw. They met in a room furnished by the Polish government in which the output of the "bugs" was obviously available to the Soviets, further inhibiting any meaningful exchange. The talks only ceased entirely with Henry Kissinger's trip to Peking in July 1971.

From our point of view there had been a few practical benefits. Of seventy-six American prisoners in China in August 1955, forty-one civilian and thirty-five military, all but thirteen had been returned by September 1957. (The last one did not make it home until after Nixon's 1972 visit to Peking.) Tension over the Taiwan Strait, including artillery bombardment and invasion threats, subsided when Wang and I started talking in 1955 and returned with a vengeance after we broke off, dying away again when the United States reestablished contact through Ambassador Beam. Other benefits from the talks were more diffuse, but no less valuable. Geneva (and later Warsaw) provided a window through which both sides could pass messages, detect changes in nuance quickly, and build up a reservoir of experience in dealing with each other that would be valuable when the fundamental political realities of our two countries, both internal and external, changed sufficiently to permit better relations. Neither country recognized the other formally, but since Western embassies in Peking were kept in strict isolation, the United States in fact had more real contact with the Chinese government during the period of the talks than any Western country having formal diplomatic relations with the PRC.

Is there anything the United States could have done differently that might have broken the logjam without seriously compromising American interests?

Second-guessing history is a notoriously hazardous occupation, and the Johnson-Wang talks are no exception. The Chinese were proud, stubborn, unpredictable, sometimes harsh opponents. They ignored written commitments when it suited them, as they did with the Agreed Announcement on prisoners. It is possible that no additional moderate concessions from us would have satisfied them in the absence of capitulation on the major issues of our accepting the principle of their right to use force against Taiwan and American diplomatic recognition of Peking as the sole government of all of China.

One thing is certain: If the talks were to have generated a major breakthrough, it had to come at the beginning, say in the first six months, when the spotlights and the pressure were on. The agreement on citizens, I think, basically satisfied both sides. It was reasonable for us to want our prisoners back, and quickly; China recognized our determination on this issue and agreed to make it the first agenda item. It was also reasonable to expect China to move cautiously on this issue at first. They were not sure Dulles had really overcome his long-standing aversion to negotiating with communists and wanted to make certain we were committed to discourse with them beyond regaining our prisoners. Nor were they likely without a formal, seemingly reciprocal, agreement to release all the Americans en masse; that would have been a humiliating tacit acknowledgement of wrongdoing. The six weeks of haggling leading to the September 10 Announcement, and our assent to permitting the Indian Embassy to look after Chinese who claimed our government was hindering their departure, saved Peking's face while giving us a piece of paper obliging China to release and return our citizens promptly. China's failure to carry through on that Agreement decisively reduced pressure on us to concede any of what the other side was seeking in the second stage of the talks on "other practical matters."

In fact, besides pledging peace over Taiwan, China could give us very little that we wanted. Probably there was no concession we could have made on Taiwan that would have obtained Peking's acceptance of a mutual renunciation of force. The Chinese communist leaders had spent virtually all their adult lives fighting. They had resisted the Japanese by force, wrested control of the country from Chiang Kai-shek by force, and consolidated their power internally by force. It would have been surprising had they been squeamish about using force to conquer Taiwan if they considered it possible to do so. From their perspective Taiwan was an integral part of their country, ruled by dangerous figures who were waiting for a chance to retake the mainland. They considered renunciation of force simply as Washington's way of putting a legal gloss on a policy of freezing the Taiwan status quo, which was already guaranteed by American armed forces.

In fact, it was not Peking but Washington that ultimately backed down, abrogating our mutual defense treaty and "de-recognizing" the Republic of China to permit full normalization of relations with Peking during the Carter Administration. Since then Peking has made no moves against Taiwan, but whether its forbearance will continue remains to be seen. The health of Peking's relations with Moscow are an important element in this equation.

If the United States had really wanted to thaw Sino-American relations during the Geneva talks, we would have had to put Taiwan on a back burner and take up other less thorny problems— relaxing the trade embargo, or permitting the exchange of journalists, and other cultural contacts. But to Secretary Dulles, unless Peking had made a prior commitment to standards of international behavior he could endorse, small agreements represented the first steps down a slippery slope at the bottom of which China would end up with added recognition and diplomatic clout without having been forced to take any steps to temper its fundamentally aggressive disposition.

More than most people Dulles was able to subordinate the innate human desire to reduce conflict with others to a long-term strategy that required writing off normal contact with half of humanity. That sustained toughness, completely principled but somewhat chilling, is what allowed him to refuse Chou En-lai's outstretched hand and spurred him to deflect any Chinese proposals made during the Johnson-Wang talks that would have enhanced Chinese power, prestige, or respectability as a condition for drawing our two countries closer together. He set out to play a defensive game, at which he was masterful. Only a startling degree of Chinese accommodation, or overwhelming domestic pressure, could have induced Dulles to reassess his basic perceptions and strategy. Neither condition prevailed in the mid-1950s.

After Wang left Warsaw in 1964, he went back to Peking as Secretary-General in the Foreign Office. Through Eastern European diplomats who had served in Peking, I learned that during the Cultural Revolution he and his wife had been sent to a "May 5 School;" that is, into the country, to live and work as peasants under the most primitive conditions. After the Cultural Revolution he reappeared as head of an organization for cultural relations with foreign countries. In the fall of 1979 the Chinese Embassy in Washington called me to say that he was coming to Washington and had asked if he could call on me. I invited him to lunch along with my first assistant in Geneva, Ralph Clough, and we had a most pleasant four-hour conversation on current events including Vietnam, Soviet expansionism, and the future of Taiwan. Wang said he had made a point of keeping track of me, just as I had of him.

Wang said that his wife had passed away; I inferred that she had probably died during their "May 5 School" experience. When he invited me to visit China with my wife, I warned him that I had taken vigorous public opposition to the way the Carter Administration had handled normalizing relations with Peking. I explained to him that I have always favored full diplomatic relations between our countries, but never understood why it had to be done on terms dictated by Peking. The concessions toward normalization came almost entirely from us. Chou En-lai got his talk with Henry Kissinger (instead of Dulles)—in Peking at that— and it was the President of the United States, Nixon, who paid the first tribute-bearing pilgrimage to the throne of the Middle Kingdom. Peking had obtained full recognition from the Carter Administration without agreeing to renounce force against Taiwan, and extracting from the United States the humiliation of descending to the transparent subterfuge of using a "private foundation" to act as a channel for government-to-government relations with Taiwan. In Geneva, Wang had always told me, "We can wait." Wait they did, and step by step a Republican Administration and then a Democratic one gave them everything they were waiting for. This sort of weakness, I thought, was not a good note on which to begin our formal ties with a people as proud and face-conscious as the Chinese. Wang's reaction to this explanation confirmed my view that kowtowing is not a good long-term strategy for dealing with China. He repeated his invitation to visit. "We know all this," he said. "But we respect you."

CHAPTER NINE

Thailand: War in Laos and SEATO

ASIAN CITIES HAVE RHYTHMS, SOUNDS, AND ATMOSPHERES LIKE NO others. Particularly distinctive are the smells. The aromas of spices, incense, gasoline, perspiration, muddy waterways, and hot cooking fat mix with the heavy vegetable scent of nearby tropical forests to form a single odor that is pungent and yet elusive. When I stepped groggily off the plane in Bangkok in February 1958, that familiar smell hit me and revived me. I had finally returned to Asia, and I was delighted to be back.

Washington had despatched me with haste because Thai-American relations had reached a dangerous impasse at a time when Thailand's importance as an ally in Southeast Asia was mounting. I had been told in Washington that my predecessor in Bangkok, Ambassador Max Bishop, had not been able to forge close links with Thailand's new leader, General Sarit, because he had been closely identified with Field Marshal Pibun, the "strongman" whom Sarit had deposed in a September 1957 bloodless coup.* Unfortunately, Max had also antagonized many other Thai and his colleagues on the SEATO Council, the governing body of the Southeast Asia Treaty Organization on which he represented the United States; they found him obstinate in refusing to consider points of view that diverged from his own. Nor had he endeared himself to the Thai press or royal household. He was credited with having forced Prime Minister Pibun into throwing

---

*From here on, I will follow the Thai practice of using only the individual's first name. Since there are many ways of transliterating Thai into Roman letters, I will use the spelling that is most common.

Kukrit Pramoj, the highly respected editor of Bangkok's largest paper and the king's close friend and supporter, into jail on charges of having slandered Max in his paper. In addition, the American community and press in Thailand, as well as the embassy staff, were sufficiently alienated from Max so that his isolation had been the subject of newspaper stories in the United States.

I felt badly about this because Max and I had been Japanese students in Tokyo together in 1935, and I knew that he had many capabilities. But from my briefings in Washington it was clear that I had my work cut out for me. One principal lesson I drew from Max's experience was to guard against becoming so identified with Sarit that American relations with Thailand became hostage to his personal political fortunes. As a first step in maintaining proper diplomatic distance before I left for Bangkok, I avoided calling on Sarit, who was at that time staying at Walter Reed Army Hospital in Washington for a liver operation. I sent him my best wishes, but I said I did not think it proper to call on him until I had presented my credentials to the king.

After I arrived at my new post, I must confess to having had recurrent pangs of disbelief that I really was Ambassador to Thailand. Presenting my credentials to King Bhumibol in the Great Throne Room of the Grand Palace seemed especially fantastic. Dressed in "white tie and tails" I entered one end of this enormous hall, lavishly adorned with exotic paintings and statues made of gold and precious stones, and headed toward the throne where the king awaited me surrounded by a beribboned crowd of courtiers. We exchanged our formal remarks; then I handed him my credentials from the President and retired from the room with my senior staff, being careful all the while not to commit the gross breach of protocol of turning our backs to the king. The Court of St. James in London, or even the Imperial Court at Tokyo, could not have given me a greater emotional thrill than the ornate Great Throne Room of the King of Siam, who to me as a boy had been an almost mythical figure. In a way, that ceremony symbolized fulfillment in my life's work. I had returned to Asia, having reached the upper rungs of the Foreign Service. I no longer had to prove to myself that I could make it. That is an immensely liberating realization. The only thing that mattered now was doing the job.

I quickly discovered that, unlike Czechoslovakia, Thailand was a country where, with hard work and some luck, an American Ambassador could achieve something significant. It offered scope for the skills I felt I had been developing for twenty years. The country's location, history, culture, and current leadership were conducive to the active embassy I intended to run.

In fact, it would have been difficult to run anything but an active embassy in Thailand. In contrast to the total of fourteen Americans on my staff in Prague, Bangkok boasted about 350 Americans and over a thousand Thai on the Mission staff. (The United States Mission comprised the embassy itself, the Joint United States Military Advisory Group (JUSMAG) headed by General Partridge, the United States Operations Mission (USOM), under Tom Naughten, which carried out all of our economic cooperation programs, and the United States Information Service (USIS), under Dick McCarthy, which handled our information, education and cultural exchange programs.) Within the embassy itself, there was a major economic section under Robert Cleveland and a large political section under John Guthrie, with subsections responsible for political-military affairs and for SEATO (since I was also the United States representative on the SEATO Council). The military attachés from the three services, and an agricultural attaché, all had staffs in the embassy; so did the special assistant for customs and narcotics control. There was also a program to develop Thai border police and paratroop units to resist Communist infiltration along the lengthy and vulnerable Thai border with Burma and Laos. On top of all this, there were several American engineering firms building major roads, and teams from a number of American universities advising the Thai government, which were also attached to USOM but were not directly part of the Mission staff.

A big outfit like this, if rudderless, tends to dissipate much of its energies, and between the changes in the Thai government following Sarit's coup and the switch of ambassadors, I knew my first task would be to reestablish morale and assure coherence and effectiveness of the program. I wanted to waste no time about it.

On the way in from the airport on my first day, I was told that the American and Thai communities were in suspense over whether I would renew the traditional July 4th open house at the embassy residence. Apparently Max had replaced it with an abbreviated, noontime wine-sipping affair to which only other ambassadors and senior Thai officials were invited. Without knowing exactly what minefields I was treading upon I said that word could be passed that my attitude on the question was "positive."

After a quick shower at the residence, I held a meeting of the senior Mission officers to convey my desire to get working quickly and to explain my basic working philosophy. I told them that I wanted a free and vigorous exchange of views up until a decision had been reached; after that, I wanted everyone to pull together to implement it. Next I invited each of them to sketch briefly what they considered to be the Mission's most urgent problems and attractive opportunities.

The next morning I started a series of detailed briefings, first from each of the section chiefs in the embassy and then from the chiefs of the Mission components. The day after I began visiting each embassy section and Mission component, meeting and receiving a briefing from the chiefs and senior members of their staffs, and then doing a "walk-through" where I made it a point to speak to every employee, Thai and American.

As soon as Patricia arrived by ship, we invited all Americans and their spouses to a reception at the embassy residence. Subsequently, we periodically invited all newcomers, from junior clerks to senior officers, to a reception at which I would briefly talk to them about their role in fulfilling the overall responsibilities of the Mission. I also paid calls on all the Thai cabinet ministers, seeking to impress upon them that I wanted to work with them toward common goals instead of telling them what to do. I also had a schedule of calls on the forty-odd other ambassadors stationed in Bangkok. On top of all this there was a great deal of social life, which to diplomats can be earnest hard work. Clearly, I was not going to lack for things to do.

Before I left Washington I had shopped around for a deputy, and on the recommendation of my good friend Marshall Green, then serving in the Bureau of Far Eastern Affairs (he was later Ambassador to Indonesia and Australia and Assistant Secretary of State for Far Eastern Affairs), I decided upon Leonard Unger, then a student at the National War College, whom I did not know. Len and I had a quick lunch to give us both a chance to size up each other; then he agreed to take the job as intuitively as I offered it. As time went on, I felt comfortable alloting to Len, who arrived in Bangkok shortly after me, an increasing role in the internal management of the Mission, as well as many other responsibilities. Len and his wife, Ann, formed a superb Foreign Service team. Len was to go on from Deputy Chief of Mission (DCM) in Bangkok to become Ambassador to Laos, Deputy Assistant Secretary of State for Far Eastern Affairs, back to Bangkok as Ambassador, and then to Taiwan as Ambassador to the Republic of China.

I also had enormous assistance from a superb and experienced Foreign Service personal secretary, Catherine Beller. She knew everybody and everything, made sure I was at the right place at the right time without fail, and in general, smoothed my existence.

The embassy chancery, or office building, was a barn of a structure with no redeeming grace. When I left Washington, I was told that there were firm plans to build a more suitable embassy, and *Life* magazine even published a picture of the plans which were attractive indeed, and would have harmonized nicely with the local scene. It still remains to be built.

The residence, sitting across the street from the chancery, could not have been further removed in tenor from the baroque opulence of our house in Prague. But to Bangkok it was ideally suited—a large, airy Thai structure, built in the early part of the century from solid teak, which stood on an eight-acre plot bounded on all sides by a canal and a magnificent stand of old trees. The Thai government rented it to us for the nominal sum of $200 a month. I resisted all efforts to replace it and my successors have done the same.

I embarked on a vigorous schedule of traveling through the countryside. Shortly after my arrival I had asked the staff to prepare an itinerary that would allow me both to observe at first hand what we were doing in Thailand and to meet local officials and ordinary people. I tried to get out of Bangkok at least one day each week, and by the end of my stint in Thailand I had visited more than sixty of the seventy-two *changwats*, or provinces. Normally I would fly with an embassy aircraft to some central point and then take whatever local transportation was available to the changwat capital. After a call on the governor, touring the countryside and visiting some local projects to which American assistance had contributed, I often would return to the governor's house and stay overnight. I found that most of the governors were capable civil servants who had risen through the ranks of the Ministry of the Interior's provincial administration service. Though some of them misused their office for personal profit, most had a good feel for the problems of their changwat, cared about the people and took interest in their jobs. Often we would discuss local problems long into the night.

Since most of the remote changwats were not accustomed to visitors from Bangkok, Thai or foreign, the presence of the American Ambassador always caused a commotion, especially when it came to figuring out what such a personage should be fed for dinner. The governor's usual solution to this thorny matter of protocol was to turn his kitchen over to the local domestic science teacher and her most advanced class. I invariably sat down to a seven- or eight-course banquet, artfully prepared and sufficient for at least three of me. As I finished the first course, I would usually see the little girls who had helped prepare the meal peeking around the kitchen doorway, giggling and curious about whether I would eat what they cooked. Unfortunately for my figure, I was never able to disappoint them.

In time I developed a reputation in the Thai government as the American who had seen more of Thailand than most Thai officials, and on that account became something of a minor celebrity. After seeing the advantage travel gave me, as well as the coverage it generated in the newspapers, Thai cabinet ministers began traveling to the countryside more often themselves. Though I found my journeys exhausting, they were too helpful to Thai-United States relations, and too valuable personally, to be curtailed.

The most impressive characteristic about all the Thai I met on my travels, even in the remotest villages, was their serene self-respect and dignity. Though they were interested in me as a stranger and as someone with a white face, and always received me with courtesy and friendliness, I never encountered that frantic curiosity and slightly degrading eagerness to please that I sometimes find elsewhere in Asia. I felt that the Thai looked at me person to person, not as brown person to white person, and they either liked or disliked me for what I was. Even when the children ran up to see me as the stranger in the village, they possessed a certain dignity and grace, and always smiled. I never served anyplace in the world where people smile more easily, or more spontaneously, or more from the heart.

The original Thai (which literally means "free") lived in southern China and were forced into Southeast Asia only in the thirteenth century, when Mongol invaders started encroaching on their lands. Through a complex series of migrations and wars, the Thai gradually pushed the Burmese to the west and the Khmer, or Cambodians, to the east and south. Over the centuries these wars left deep scars and animosities not dissimilar to those of the Balkans.

In the seventeenth century, Portugal, France, and Britain all tried to subject the Kingdom of Siam to various degrees of colonial control; and in the mid-1800s both Britain and France began eyeing the country as a candidate for direct colonial take-over. The wisdom and diplomatic agility of two Thai kings, Mongkut (whom Yul Brynner inaccurately but engagingly immortalized in the film *The King and I*) and his son Chulalongkorn, were partly responsible for preserving Siam's independence. But equally important was the desire of Britain, which held Burma and India, and France, which held Indochina, to keep Siam as a neutral buffer state between their two colonial zones. Thailand was, in fact, the only country in Southeast Asia never colonized.

Mongkut, Chulalongkorn, and their successors had the foresight to realize that protecting their kingdom's freedom against European invasion required modernizing and strengthening the country by adopting various aspects of Western government, finance, education, and military organization. The reforms came swiftly, especially when Chulalongkorn became king in 1873. Provincial administration was brought under central control. Slavery was abolished (although it had never been widespread or oppressive), and taxation was altered to relieve destitution among peasants and permit them to buy their own land. This last reform was crucial, because it relieved a huge potential source of peasant dissatisfaction that still plagues other Asian governments. For the most part Thai farmers not only won their own land, but about as much land as they can cultivate themselves.

Thus Siam entered the twentieth century with more control over its own affairs, and farther along the road to modernization, than any Asian country except Japan. In fact, once the country's neighbors managed to establish their own independence after World War II, they considered Thailand something of an outsider, a "misplaced European country" as one scholar put it.

But this is not to say that Thailand was without problems. Foreigners controlled most of the country's export industries, the growing class of Western-educated civil servants and army officers resented the royal family's monopoly on senior positions, and the king still ruled the country autocratically without benefit of broadly-based representative institutions. The monarchy had been crucial to Siam's modernization so far, but it proved unable to stay ahead of the forces of change it had unleashed. In 1932, after the

Depression reduced government revenues from foreign trade and forced the king to cut salaries and fire many government employees, a brilliant young French-educated lawyer named Pridi Panomyong led army officers in a bloodless coup that curtailed the monarch's powers and established various institutions of representative government. Several factions competed tempestuously to control the new system. Among these were Pridi and his followers, who were considered leftist. Then there were army officers and their allies among the large and frustrated royal family. And finally, there were the followers of Pibun Songgram, a man more militaristic and nationalistic than Pridi, who had gained prominence as commander of troops that crushed an anti-republican coup in October 1933. In January 1939, a period of relative peace among the various factions began as Pibun, who became Prime Minister, made Pridi Finance Minister and appointed army officers to other cabinet posts. The most important developments occurred in foreign relations, as the government accommodated itself to Japanese expansion in Southeast Asia. British Burma to the west, and French Indochina to the east collapsed under Japanese aggression at the start of World War II; Thailand had little choice but to accept the region's new colonial master and hope for the best. In 1942, Thailand even declared war on Britain and the United States, but the Thai Ambassador in Washington, Seni Pramoj, refused to deliver the declaration so the United States never formally considered itself at war with Thailand.

When the Allies defeated Japan in 1945, Seni Pramoj, the former Ambassador to Wasington, became Prime Minister, though Pridi held the real power. Territories that Pibun had annexed from Cambodia during the war with Japanese connivance were returned and Thailand sought to reestablish good relations with Britain, France, and especially the United States, which quickly became Thailand's most important great power ally.

Thailand faced many vexing problems arising from the war. Of course, it had all the difficulties of any developing country: a growing, largely agrarian population with little experience in representative government; poverty; industrial backwardness; inadequate roads, public health, education, power, and internal communication; and overdependence on one crop—rice—both internally and in foreign trade. But Thailand faced an additional problem: a China where communism was ascendent while the Thai government had not itself overcome the instability and weak leadership common to young democracies. Thai fears of communist takeover partly explain the remarkable rehabilitation of

Field Marshal Pibun, a hard-line anti-communist. In spite of his collaboration with the Japanese he returned to power in a 1947 coup that ousted the left-leaning Pridi and forced him into exile.

Pibun strengthened the armed forces, whose officers came to dominate the country's political life (and still do in considerable measure). But he also managed to win support from technocrats and civil servants and withstood several attempts to unseat him. Mao Tse-tung's victory in 1949 gave impetus to his anti-communist program, for now Thailand not only sat between communist guerilla movements in Malaysia and Indochina but faced an increase in revolutionary agitation in Thailand and a threat of direct invasion from Mao's armies. Quelling internal disturbance was not easy. Within the country's borders there were many non-Thai minority groups whom the government had often ignored or mistreated and who thus had no great stake in the present system. Many of these groups lived in remote but strategically important areas, like the sparsely settled north and northeast. And the Chinese, who lived mostly in the towns and cities, were rich, powerful, and well-organized. Among them, however, were some who for personal or ideological reasons were tempted to support Peking. Pibun built up troop strength in the border regions and attempted some economic reforms. In 1952, he instigated a sweeping anti-Chinese campaign, which also permitted him to silence many non-subversives who happened to be his political opponents.

As part of his anti-communist program, Pibun aligned Thailand closely with the United States. More than $60 million in American assistance, both military and civilian, flowed into Thailand under the Mutual Security Act between 1951 and 1955. After the Viet Minh victory at Dienbienphu spurred the formation of the Southeast Asia Treaty Organization (SEATO) as a vehicle for collective defense against communism in Southeast Asia, Thailand joined SEATO enthusiastically. It successfully agitated to make Bangkok the alliance's headquarters. The organization's first Secretary-General, Pote Sarasin, was Thai.

In 1956 Pibun reduced controls on the press, political parties, and dissent generally, permitting a vigorous opposition to him and his policies to take root. Communist propaganda and street violence increased. In February 1957 his party barely squeaked to victory in general elections, despite the aid of a campaign marked by such terror and vote fraud that the normally serene Thai were provoked into serious rioting. In October 1957, one of Pibun's deputies, General Sarit, capitalized on his superior's unpopularity and deposed him in a bloodless coup.

General Sarit was in fact in charge during my entire tenure in Bangkok. He had a superb political sense for the Thai system, but he was a genuine "character" with a very disordered personal life. He would normally have three or four women a day, not only for personal pleasure but as a very shrewd gambit in public relations. The story was commonly told that he used to pay the women to praise his amorous abilities; a reputation for extraordinary virility made him seem larger than life, and thus helped establish, among ordinary Thai, his right to rule.

General Sarit was also fond of drinking four or five "fifths" of Scotch each day, though I am aware of no Thai custom prescribing alcohol consumption as a rite of leadership. (In fact, in accordance with Buddhist doctrine, Thai are generally abstemious.) It was because his drinking had strained his health so badly that Sarit had had to go to Walter Reed Hospital in Washington for a liver shunt (by-pass) operation. He returned to Bangkok for several days in the spring of 1958, but then inexplicably departed for a long vacation in England.

During Sarit's absence Prime Minister Thanom, a pleasant and conscientious man whom everyone knew in those days to be Sarit's puppet, could not keep control over the increasingly fractious and noisy assembly. Most of its members were corrupt and brazenly traded their votes for money in a way that disgusted the Thai and disgraced democracy. So an old fixture in Thai politics, Luang Wichit, then Ambassador to Switzerland, visited Sarit in England and convinced him that Thailand's struggles against poverty and communism required strong, direct leadership that parliamentary democracy could not provide. Sarit was not averse to this theory. In October, 1958, he secretly returned to Bangkok and, taking care simultaneously to send an emissary to me (at my fiftieth birthday party) to explain what he was doing, organized a "revolution"—actually a glorified coup—that disbanded the assembly, arrested some communists and made Sarit Prime Minister.

About this revolution, which occurred six months after I became Ambassador, I was skeptical but not instantly critical. I approved of Sarit's arrest of communists and held no particular brief for the corrupt assembly; and although I was not particularly enthusiastic about the way he engineered these changes I felt he was in a much better position than any outsider to judge the necessity of the means he used. Sarit's cabinet was encouraging because it included few military officers and featured some extremely able and well-known technocrats in the important ministries.

My first order of business after Sarit's "revolution" was to ascertain his feelings about future United States-Thai relations. Despite the close Thai-American cooperation in SEATO and economic development, there was a noticeable strain of anti-Americanism in many politically conscious Thai. Of course, communist propaganda portrayed the United States in the most evil and lurid tones, but even among anti-communist leftists the United States was blamed for keeping the military in power and for having selfish designs on the Thai economy. Although he was a general, even Sarit had a reputation for sharing some of this anti-American sentiment. Some of it he had no doubt deliberately cultivated while maneuvering for support against Prime Minister Pibun.

I had already started trying to improve America's image in Thailand gently, so as not to offend Thai sensibilities. My travels around the country were partly aimed at bolstering America's reputation by letting the people see that I, an American, was human and involved, though by the time of Sarit's revolution this had not borne much fruit. I had also worked to repair the damage caused by the imprisoning of Kukrit Pramoj, the editor of the *Siam Rath*, for slandering my predecessor, but this too was a tricky business. Immediately after my arrival, Kukrit had gone after me as well, accusing me in his newspaper of *lèse majesté* because I had been photographed in a short-sleeved shirt shaking the hand of the King of Thailand. Actually, the king and I had both been attending a SEATO military exercise in the field, where because of the heat, informal dress was entirely acceptable, and, anyway, our meeting had been unplanned.

Within a few weeks I invited Kukrit to a private lunch and explained the incident. I turned on all my persuasive powers to convince him that I wanted to move beyond the nastiness that had previously separated him from the embassy. Soon the *Siam Rath*'s coverage of the United States became more balanced. But the central figure was obviously Sarit. If he wanted good relations with the United States, the bulk of the Thai establishment would follow.

Shortly after Sarit's October 1958, "revolution" the American Secretary of Defense, Charles Wilson, arrived in Bangkok on a long-scheduled Southeast Asian tour. The two of us called on Sarit, who was quite friendly and published pictures of our visit widely in the newspapers. I was pleased, but warned Washington against inferring too much. Sarit had not taken us into his confidence before carrying out his plans for the revolution, nor was he divulging future plans. I recommended that we not go overboard, and that we avoid giving the Thai the impression that we were hitching our wagon solely to Sarit's star.

Thailand, while I was there, was clearly not a functioning democracy. At first I was skeptical of Sarit's methods because I knew that military regimes can easily trap themselves in an escalating cycle of police repression and public dissent that culminates in blatant tyranny. But as time progressed my respect for Sarit's goals and methods grew, until I was compelled to reexamine the rather facile American assumption that representative democracy is the best form of government under every circumstance. Thailand's attempt at it, the Assembly, had been so corrupt and obstructionist that it discredited democracy's appeal; no one mourned its passing. Sarit's cabinet included the country's most able civilians, so many in fact that Sarit's officer colleagues on the Military Revolutionary Council felt frozen out of power and grumbled about replacing him.

Military expenditure actually dropped while I was in Thailand, as Sarit squeezed every last baht into the economic development of roads, schools, irrigation projects, rural health, and other genuinely needy areas. Bangkok had nothing resembling a police state atmosphere. Though Sarit clearly made final decisions, they were widely discussed beforehand. People seemed satisfied with political life, with the pace of economic development, and with Sarit himself. He had gained what I think is the first test of government, what our ancestors called "the consent of the governed."

And Sarit really did have the people's consent. When I first arrived, Bangkok's streets were so clogged with bicycle-rickshaws (called *samlors*) driven by tough, unruly fellows that venturing onto the streets was like entering a huge boxing ring, and getting across town required hours. This became a serious problem since the army and new industries needed to transport their goods by truck, so on a designated day Sarit ordered the pedicabs off the streets. Pedicab drivers were a notoriously rambunctious group, so few thought the plan would work. At precisely midnight they disappeared—forever. On one occasion, embassy Thai-speaking officers observed Sarit flying in by helicopter to settle a bitter water dispute over which two villages had fought for centuries. The embassy officers who were passing by asked some villagers whether they would continue the dispute if Sarit found against them. The farmers found the question incredible and said they would abide by Sarit's verdict whatever it was.

Part of Sarit's strength was his unerring sense of Thai character, which was normally gentle, Buddhist, and devoted to compromise. For instance, Bangkok had a serious problem with packs of stray dogs that roamed the streets carrying disease and occasionally attacking people. The simple and obvious solution, especially for a lifelong army officer, would have been to shoot them all. But Buddhists recoil from the violence of killing animals. So, after thinking for a while, Sarit had poisoned meat placed around the city. That got rid of the dogs while satisfying Buddhist ethics, because the dogs were technically responsible for the decision to consume the meat; no direct human killing was required.

As I began to reflect on Sarit's success as a leader, I concluded that the parliamentary form of government that Great Britain employs is probably the most difficult form of government to operate. It requires a sophisticated, generally prosperous and informed electorate, a responsible press, a responsive bureaucracy, military officers who can restrain their ambitions, and usually no more than three major political parties. It has never really worked well over an extended period outside of Britain and its former colonies. Yet the parliamentary form of government inherited from their former colonial masters has usually been the first type of representative government Third World countries employ when they achieve independence.

What I believe young countries need—and what the founders of our country had the wisdom and foresight to provide in our Constitution—is a strong executive, who can give the country stability and direction while staying reasonably responsive to the people. The presidential system has worked well in our country, but not in the Philippines or most of the South American countries where it has been tried. Military rule has thus far sufficed in Thailand, but it has often failed. Each country must provide for an effective executive in its own way, providing for orderly change in those occupying the leading positions, and otherwise modifying their institutions to keep pace with the growth of education and political sophistication in the population. That is why I judged Sarit by what people thought of his accomplishments— the "consent of the governed"—not by how faithfully he copied Western forms of democracy.

Another proof of Sarit's acumen as a leader and his sensitivity to what the people of Thailand wanted was his attitude toward the king and queen. The royalty had been anathema to most Thai politicians since 1934, when the king encouraged an unsuccessful anti-republican coup, then fled the country and abdicated. The more radical factions wanted to abolish the monarchy altogether, but Thai peasants revered their king. He was their protector, a living symbol of nationhood who embodied the mystic Brahmin concept of the holy "priest-king." The present king, Bhumibol, was an earnest, hard-working young man determined to be a good constitutional monarch. He was born in the United States in 1927 while his father, the abdicated king's half-brother, was studying medicine at Harvard. His mother was a graduate of the Nursing School of the University of California at Berkeley. Educated in Switzerland with his older brother, Crown Prince Ananda Mahidol, he spoke four European languages and had been widely exposed to Western ideas of modern kingship. Ananda Mahidol and Bhumibol returned to Thailand after World War II; Mahidol became king, but was found dead in his palace bedroom with a bullet through his head in 1946. Whether the death was suicide, murder, or accident remains a mystery, but rumors implicating a variety of politicians still circulate in Bangkok. Bhumibol, still grieving for the brother to whom he had been so close, became king at the age of nineteen.

General Pibun, dictator from 1948 until Sarit took over in 1958, disliked and envied the new king and kept him in the background. But Sarit recognized the king's value as a living symbol of Thailand and encouraged him to emerge from his seclusion. It was one of the smartest decisions Sarit ever made. Even though the king and his charming queen Sirikit held no real power, they had much influence and became great assets in promoting modernization and encouraging the loyalty of the Thai people to Thailand as a nation-state. They worked hard at their jobs and traveled throughout the country, focusing attention on economic development, listening to grievances, and letting rural people know Bangkok cared. Wherever I went in Thailand, even in the poorest hut in the remotest village, I never failed to see a picture of the king and queen proudly displayed.

Even the redoubtable Field Marshal Sarit (he assumed the title after becoming Prime Minister) displayed a kind of mystic reverence for the monarchy and even for the king himself. Once I saw him just after he had been summoned to an audience with the king; he was literally trembling at the prospect. And from my conversations with both the king and Sarit, I gathered that the king was perfectly capable of dressing down Sarit for some delinquency of government, usually involving corruption, and that Sarit took the king's reprimands seriously. My own sense of the situation was that the king should not appear to intervene in the running of the government too often lest his influence be diminished when really serious crises arose. He did not argue when I expressed this view to him.

As I came to know the king and queen, I developed great fondness and respect for them. The king had many surprising talents: he painted, composed music, and played a very creditable jazz clarinet and saxophone, even broadcasting a jazz program with his own orchestra each week over Thai radio from a studio in the palace. He was extremely open, direct, and friendly, with wide-ranging interests, including not only Thai politics, but farming, public health, religion, water-skiing, American culture and movies, and many other subjects. He established a school on the palace grounds for his own children that a number of children from various walks of life were also invited to attend.

I had two types of audiences with the king. The first was between the two of us, with only the king's trusted aide and confidant, General Suranarong, also in attendance. The second was when I escorted some senior American official to speak with the king. If the official's wife went along, Pat would accompany her and the queen would be present. It was, of course, not wise for me to be seen going to the palace too often for personal audiences lest other countries think the king played favorites, so we had two private channels, through General Suranarong or Phya Srivrsarn, President of the Privy Council, and a trusted officer from the embassy on my side.

No matter what the original motivation for my private meetings with the king, our conversation would usually range far afield. The irritating behavior of Cambodia's ruler, King Sihanouk, was a favorite topic; the king had never forgiven Sihanouk for having walked off with the gold-plated saxophone the king had loaned him during the period when Sihanouk had sought to bring pressure on the French to grant independence to Cambodia by removing himself to Bangkok. The king often cited this story as an example of the natural perfidy of Cambodians.

The king constantly expressed concern that American and Thai economic development programs did not sufficiently reach the people. He also worried about the danger posed by the continued activity of Pridi's many left-wing followers. And he asked repeatedly why the United States gave so much aid to neutralist India, compared to America's good friend Thailand.

He spoke softly but sat straight, never forgetting he was king. My audiences with him would normally start around 11:00 in the morning and often continued for three or four hours, until the king was reminded by his aide-de-camp that he absolutely had to proceed to his next engagement and, as required by protocol, took the initiative to terminate the audience, to the great relief of my growling stomach.

When I escorted American visitors to see the king, he always listened carefully to what they said and often questioned them closely. His basic friendliness to Americans did not inhibit him from freely expressing what he thought was wrong with us. I always warned my visitors not to expect the king simply to sit and listen to them without responding.

Queen Sirikit, also Western-educated and a regal beauty, worked as diligently as her husband. She took a special interest in promoting the Thai Red Cross and various relief projects. Pat led the embassy wives in supporting these activities.

I tried very hard to cooperate with the king and queen. When he wanted American films on reforestation to educate Thai officials, or sought American doctors to help cure a rare polio-like disease that was crippling children in Bangkok, I made sure to provide them. The king was scrupulously correct in fulfilling his duties and regularly saw ambassadors from other countries, but I do think my relationship with him was especially close and set an example that was not lost on other members of the Thai government.

The United States ran a large economic cooperation program in Thailand, and overseeing it was an important part of my job. I believe that cooperation with foreign governments to assist them in their own development efforts is an essential investment in the future of our planet. Having been born myself in a small town without indoor plumbing, electricity, or automobiles, I am optimistic about how much can be accomplished in one lifetime. Thai audiences were always amazed to hear that parts of the United States had been "underdeveloped" within living memory (some still are, of course) and took encouragement from it.

But many aspects of the current American cooperation program bothered me. The first was that we always proclaimed it "aid," which carries opprobrious connotations of superiority and inferiority. When I first arrived in Bangkok and called on the important cabinet ministers, each went through a formalistic set speech, not entirely sincere to my ears, expressing undying gratitude for the generosity of American "aid." This made me decidedly uncomfortable. I did not expect, nor did I feel that the United States deserved gratitude for our economic development programs. A secure, independent, prosperous Thailand was an object of *our* foreign policy; self-interest motivated our programs, not charity. It demeaned the Thai, and us, to demand gratitude for what was in reality a self-respecting, two-sided partnership from which both sides profited. I emphasized this conviction throughout my tour, both to the Thai, who found it refreshing, and to Washington, where it confronted too many self-satisfied aid dispensers (especially in Congress) to make much of a dent. This kind of smug paternalism still distorts our development programs.

I believed that American money and expertise should be applied as deftly as possible, meshing with Thailand's own plans and providing only what the Thai could not provide themselves. Although unschooled in economics and finance, Sarit gave high priority to economic development, appreciating the role it played in internal political stability and security. He brought the best Thai economic experts into his cabinet, and some of them were very good, indeed—sophisticated and honest, capable of dealing as equals with the United States Operation Mission's (USOM) competent director, Thomas Naughten, and other members of the embassy staff. Both personal and official relations were excellent and both sides enjoyed working with each other.

Normally, project initiatives would originate with Thai officials, and then Tom Naughten and his staff would work together with them to develop a proposal he felt both Bangkok and Washington could support. During the process Tom would discuss the proposal with me, and if it was sufficiently important it would be aired at a "Country Team" meeting where other Mission components like JUSMAG, USIS, and CIA could express their views and make suggestions.

Sarit particularly wanted to concentrate on economic development of the northeast, a poor, sparsely populated area bordering on Laos. Bangkok had traditionally neglected this area, only to discover that the communists were now attracting many supporters there. (We occasionally heard rumors that the Russians were directly supplying bands of rebels in the northeast, but we tended to discount them—until we found a crashed Russian helicopter sixty miles inside the Thai border.) We established a branch office of the USOM, our development funds agency, in the northeastern city of Korat. We also opened a major road, the Friendship Highway, to connect Bangkok with the northeast, and this was eventually extended to the banks of the Mekong opposite Vientiane in Laos. The road obviously had military implications, but we also saw it as the spine of a network of smaller roads that would eventually link villages in the northeast with the economy, culture, and political life of the rest of the country. An American construction firm was the principal contractor for the highway because the engineering work was very difficult, but we saw to it that they employed as many Thai subcontractors as possible so that the Thais could learn new skills that would stay with them. Congressman Otto Passman, a Democrat from Louisiana who made great political hay out of opposing foreign "aid", dubbed the Friendship Highway the "road from nowhere to nowhere." When he visited Thailand he refused my offer to drive him up to see the highway, saying disarmingly that if he did so he might have to change his mind.

The road was an immediate success. Hundreds of buses and trucks quickly started moving goods and people between the northeast and Bangkok, and with the extension to the Mekong it changed much of the face of the northeast. An entirely unexpected benefit was that within a few years of its opening, corn became the second largest export of Thailand. About the time the road was being completed, American agricultural experts were working with Thai experts on a particular variety of corn that came from Central America. In their experiments they happened to plant some in an area near the road. It did exceedingly well, and by the time the road opened, much of the land along the road had been bought by Thai, including a number of prominent Thai officials, and planted in corn, which found a ready market in Japan. Recalling how much of our own West was settled and developed by land speculators, including many in our government, I restrained any impulse to criticize those involved. Only the people who already possessed some money and clout had the capital to risk and the initiative to make the development a success.

From this and other roads we assisted in building or improving, I concluded that it is hard to make a mistake when building a road in a free-market underdeveloped country like Thailand. Just build the road and then jump out of the way; the development around it will take care of itself.

Another joint Thai-United States program for the northeast focused on its traditional lack of water, which hindered irrigation and stunted the growth of towns. We sent geologists to discover whether the area had suitable supplies underground. They came back with a positive answer, at least for some fairly extensive areas, and we helped with a large deep well-drilling scheme.

Thailand especially needed better internal transport. Many villages, not just those in the northeast, were remote from links with the rest of the country. Part of our effort to improve transportation was a program to assist the Thai in designing and building some 800 small concrete bridges to replace the fragile wooden structures that greatly constricted the already limited capacity of the graveled roads that formed the bulk of the country's road network. Pursuing our policy of developing native Thai competence and skills, we left the detailed design and construction to Thai contractors operating under the supervision of USOM engineers. Scores of contractors, most with no experience whatever, sprang up to take advantage of the opportunities and contracts were spread as widely as possible among the low bidders.

Elsewhere in the country we tried providing the "missing links" for all sorts of Thai development projects, including electricity generation, malaria control, irrigation, education, and others. Working through the Thai Ministry of Agriculture, for example, we helped distribute Rockefeller Foundation "miracle rice" and other high-yield seeds to farmers; established a seed testing center; assisted in a thousand farm demonstrations on protecting the new plants from pests and disease; imported improved varieties of pigs and cattle; demonstrated contour plowing at 200 locations; encouraged the creation of village cooperatives for selling crops and purchasing equipment; helped establish an agricultural extension service operating out of village community centers; promoted the digging of local fishponds to provide a source of cheap protein; and imported special varieties of fast-growing fish that could be raised in rice paddies.

We also supplied some missing links when a cholera epidemic hit Bangkok in May 1958. We obtained enough vaccine to inoculate 500,000 people and airlifted it to Thailand. I also requested the help of a Navy medical unit stationed in Taiwan and an Army doctor from Walter Reed Hospital, who brought with them special high-pressure needleless "guns" for mass inoculation. Cholera is a filth disease, of course, acquired from contact with the feces of infected persons; the British used to say that the best insurance against it was an income of £500 a year, and generally it was only Bangkok's poorest people, who used the canals for bathing and drinking, who were infected. The king and queen took great interest in the inoculation program and invited me to bring an American doctor with the special "gun" to the palace for a detailed briefing on its operation.

In two weeks of hard work, the American medics trained a large number of Thai doctors to use the "guns" and inoculated 20,000 Thai themselves. Washington responded well to requests for help in dramatic crises like this; enduring, complicated problems were harder for it to address.

Compared to most developing countries, Thailand managed its economy quite shrewdly. It maintained a healthy balance of payments and a foreign currency reserve that was actually increasing, the product of a conservative fiscal policy expertly applied. Thai currency remained at a steady twenty baht to the dollar without any serious black market trading. In Washington, beset by many countries' needs, it began to look like Thailand did not need either American money or technical advice as badly as less solvent countries. Bangkok's share tended to be the first place to squeeze whenever other countries required quick infusions of money. In Thai eyes, neutral countries which the Thai despised, like India and Cambodia, were "problems" for the United States and seemed to enjoy especially solicitous treatment compared to Thailand, a loyal ally that managed its finances responsibly.

The Thai resented what was to them, taking their friendship too lightly. Marshal Sarit often complained to me that Thailand would have gotten more money and concern from the United States if it had publicly courted the Soviet Union or overspent its budget recklessly. He had a point. I argued with the Department that we should not penalize Thailand because it ran its affairs competently, emphasizing that while its emergency needs were not great, the unusual soundness of its economy guaranteed our aid a correspondingly unusual impact.

It was a battle I never entirely won. American financial assistance to Thailand was relatively generous, running at about $35 million for non-military purposes each year while I was there, and reaching a cumulative ten-year total of over $200 million by 1960. (Military aid over the same period slightly exceeded $300 million.) American loans repayable in baht instead of dollars contributed another $65 million. But, especially for a free enterprise country, our aid bureaucracy required so many detailed advanced plans, forms, inspection trips, and studies that worthy projects were often tied up in storms of red tape and Thai officials, who were eager to get the money working, grew frustrated and justifiably impatient. They also looked skeptically at the American "Food for Peace" (PL 480) program, that supplied states like India, Indonesia, and Pakistan with large amounts of low-priced or gratis American surplus rice, and thereby undercut the world demand for Thailand's chief export. They also heard Congress periodically threaten to cut off funds to countries not doing our international bidding, making them wonder if our aid came with so many strings attached that it could choke their national sovereignty and self-respect.

I knew that only time and good behavior would convince the Thai that our aid was not a Trojan horse. But as I tried to advance Thailand's arguments for better treatment in Washington I also tried to ease Thai feelings about not getting a fair share of our development money compared to other countries. For example, in a speech delivered to the Royal Thai National Defense College on September 27, 1960, I pointed out that more than 70 percent of American assistance dispensed in the previous two years had gone to countries with which the United States had a defensive alliance, not to "neutrals" like Cambodia and India.

Another persistent problem with our economic development programs was Thai corruption. Civil service salaries were so low that government employees could only support their families by taking in a little on the side. To get goods cleared through customs, to register a license, to do almost anything with the government required payment of "tea money," never very large in individual cases, but cumulatively significant to bureaucrats' incomes. Of course, some of this money doubtless found its way into the pockets of senior officials as well.

I always advised American companies opening branches in Thailand to refuse payoff requests firmly from the outset, because otherwise they would be deluged, and in general, American economic programs were remarkably free of official "skimming." In fact, the Finance Minister, the Development Minister, and the Bank of Thailand chief particularly liked American projects because our rigidity about tea money permitted them to enforce clean behavior on their subordinates. But I also thought Americans' pious denunciations of Thai corruption—given our own history—was misplaced and somewhat self-righteous. Even the rich Thai who received big government contracts through political influence spent their receipts in Thailand—very unusual in a developing country—not on jewels or shopping trips abroad. Thai currency stayed hard and the money eventually made its way into other productive enterprises inside the country. The distinction between a legitimate tip and a bribe is one each country must draw for itself from its own traditions. With police on the take in every major American city, Mafia corruption rampant, and stories about corrupt congressmen (including, at that time, rumors about that most pious of all, Otto Passman), I did not think we could throw stones too vigorously at the Thai.

Despite corruption and Washington's tendency to give Thailand short shrift, I think that what our economic assistance tried to do, by and large, it accomplished. One could sense that progress was being made. In the long, awesomely complex process of forging a modern nation out of Thailand, I felt, and I think most Thais agreed, that the United States was genuinely helping. In the process we also maintained a valued ally.

American assistance to the Thai Armed Forces was an important aspect of Thai-American relations that kept Sarit and me busy. At that time communist China's shadow was looming menacingly from the north and North Vietnam was beginning to look outward aggressively after a period of internal retrenchment. Thailand was thus the key member of SEATO on the Southeast Asian mainland, for if China or North Vietnam penetrated fragile Laos, Thailand was next on the road south to Malaya, Singapore, and the Straits of Malacca, to say nothing of Indonesia, the biggest and richest country of the area.

Our Military Assistance Program was based on the same philosophy as our economic programs—that is, to help those who wanted to help themselves by supplying the missing elements essential to success. It was this philosophy that led President Truman to say, in 1947, when Greece and Turkey were threatened with communist takeover, "I believe it must be the policy of the United States to support free peoples who are resisting attempted subjugation by armed minorities or by outside pressures."

With the collapse of the French in Indochina in 1954, and the start of ominous broadcasts to Thailand from Peking in 1951, it was reasonable for Thailand to prepare against assault from without. Thailand recognized that collective security through SEATO had to be its fundamental strategy. Even in 1950, before SEATO's creation, Thailand was one of the first countries to contribute troops to the United Nations Forces in Korea (and, incidentally, to allied forces in Vietnam in 1965). Recognizing Thailand's importance as an ally in Southeast Asia, the United States established a Military Assistance Program in the country in 1950 to furnish military equipment that Thailand could not otherwise obtain—artillery, tanks, and aircraft—as well as training.

The Joint United States Military Advisory Group (JUSMAG) in Thailand was headed by an Army Brigadier General, and contained Army, Navy, and Air Force sections. The JUSMAG officers maintained excellent relations with their Thai counterparts, many of whom had received training in the United States and a few of whom were even West Point graduates. I took a strong interest in the military assistance program, receiving frequent briefings from the JUSMAG staff, and when I traveled up-country I always made it a point to call on the local commanders. A major part of our program, particularly in terms of cost, was supplying the Air Force. The Air Force was centered at the Bangkok airport (Don Muang), which was used by both civilian and military aircraft, including those of our own Air Force, and while traveling I sometimes used Thai aircraft or helicopters. I, therefore, had regular exposure to the progress of this program.

When I arrived in Bangkok an outstanding military issue was whether the United States should construct four airstrips in the north and northeast. The strips had originally been conceived as emergency fields for our medium-range B-47 strategic bombers. With the emergence of the longer-range B-52s this proposed function seemed less vital, but the Commander-in-Chief Pacific (CINCPAC), then Admiral Felix Stump, felt that the worsening political situation in the area made it wise to build them nonetheless. I agreed. We were successful in overcoming considerable resistance in Washington from the economy-minded, and the fields were completed during my tour. Subsequently, these strips became crucial to the operations of our own Air Force in Laos and North Vietnam during the Vietnam war.

Thailand was within CINCPAC's area of military responsibility, and CINCPAC was also obligated to provide military advice to me in my role as United States member of the SEATO Council. The two CINCPAC's during my tour, first Stump and then Don Felt, frequently came to Bangkok, and we maintained close contact. When they visited I would, of course, take them to call on the king and Prime Minister Sarit. Felix Stump was a hard-bitten old seadog of whom I became very fond, while Don Felt was a smoother personality. Both were excellent diplomats, though, and I always found their perceptions and advice shrewd and useful, as I did those of General Kuter, who commanded the Pacific Air Force.

The United States also undertook a modest naval project to dredge and improve the port facilities at the small Thai naval installation of Sattahip on the coast seventy-five miles southeast of Bangkok. This facility later became a key element permitting the rapid construction of the Uttapao airbase from which B-52s operated during the Vietnam war.

JUSMAG was separate from the Army, Navy, and Air Force military attaches, who were attached to the embassy proper. Each was responsible to the intelligence branches of their respective services. (This was later changed by Robert McNamara's creation of the Defense Intelligence Agency, DIA.) While they were each very able and competent, they frequently rubbed up against each other creating problems I was sometimes called upon to settle (like who was responsible for reporting to me on politically sensitive moves and transfers within the Armed Forces). But more harmful was the wide gulf that separated the attachés from JUSMAG. JUSMAG, charged with advising the Thai armed forces, believed it should punctilliously avoid giving any impression to the Thai that it was "spying" on them. JUSMAG officials thus refused even to talk with the attachés or pass them any information whatsoever. It was hard for the attachés, and me, to accept the proposition that in a friendly country like Thailand, whose military had such close relations with ours, the attaché function was somehow inimical to Thailand's interests. But I was never able to get the problem entirely resolved, and it still persists around the world in countries where we have both organizations. It has been my consistent experience as an ambassador that serious problems are much less common between the civilian and military elements of an American mission than between the various military elements themselves. Also these problems are less within a mission than they are in the jungle of the Pentagon. This does not stem from any lack of ability or intelligence among our military, but reflects the way things are organized (or perhaps not organized) in Washington.

Another element in our Military Assistance Program was very important to Thailand, though people evaluating the value of military aid to underdeveloped countries often overlook it. Military training programs taught many Thai skills essential to civilian economic development. Officers learned engineering, design, and construction, all of which very much apply outside the armed forces. Enlisted personnel studied the whole gamut of basic skills in electronics and mechanics, as well as discipline, hygiene, and public health. We often forget that our own first engineering school was West Point and that American Army officers played a vital role in building our first roads, railways, canals, dams, and other public works. They still contribute to many of these areas. It is much the same in any country with a trained military establishment.

If you asked a group of American ambassadors which audience they had the most difficulty pleasing, I am sure that many would not answer the State Department, or the Pentagon, or even their host governments. But very often they would point their fingers at the American business community. American business poeple are forever complaining that German, French, British, and Japanese firms win contracts because their embassies promote products more aggressively than do American embassies. They say the United States Government puts too many regulations and controls on doing business abroad and that it interferes with sound, profitable contracts in the name of politics.

Since I agree with some of these criticisms, when I arrived in Bangkok, I directed a number of changes to increase the effectiveness of the embassy's assistance to American trade and investment. To begin with, I assigned an economic officer as full-time liaison with the American business community. The commercial reading room was reorganized and restocked, trade lists were brought up to date, and I made a point of giving my first speech in Bangkok to the American Chamber of Commerce. I also saw to it that American business·people were invited to embassy functions so they could meet personnel from all levels of the mission as well as prominent Thai. After a while the business community decided that the embassy was serious about helping them, and relations between us improved.

In fact, not all, or even most, of the problems American companies faced in Bangkok were the embassy's doing. First of all, the Thai were leery of having foreigners control their economy and regulated outside investment strictly. Slowly, however, they liberalized the laws, so that considerably more investment was flowing from the United States by the time I left.

The sale of foreign products was less closely controlled than foreign investment, but here the companies seemed to create their own obstacles. The American firms represented in Bangkok were a heterogeneous lot, including Singer (which imported only from its British factory), the several big oil companies, TWA, Pan American, American President Lines, Bank of America, and various locally-based enterprises like Jim Thompson's Thai Silk Company. Many American companies had local agents with people from the home office visiting occasionally. Most of the American companies in Thailand did not impress me greatly. They just did not compete as hard as the Germans or Japanese. Their credit terms were not as generous, nor did they show as much enterprise, adaptability, and aggressiveness in trying to win contracts. Several Thai told me that they thought American manufacturers were simply not interested in selling to Thailand, and proof of that assertion appeared all too often. When the Thai national railway approached General Electric to buy some modern diesel electric locomotives, GE refused; adapting to Thailand's different gauge tracks wasn't worth the effort. A Japanese company got the order, and many more, subsequently.

This arrogance, which was by no means confined to Thailand, did not come from the local sales reps, who hustled just as hard as their non-American competitors, but from the home offices, where the vice presidents for exports, if they existed at all, were usually low-ranking executives. Unfortunately not much has changed.

King Bhumibol's irritation when Cambodia's exiled ruler, Prince Sihanouk, walked off with the king's favorite gold-plated saxophone was merely a trivial symptom of the deep animosity between the two countries that repeatedly discolored their working relations when I was in Bangkok. Along with my counterparts in Phnom Penh I found myself frequently trying to patch up nasty quarrels between Thailand and Cambodia. Clearly it was in our interest as well as theirs that two important non-communist countries in an unstable region be able at least to tolerate each other.

The Thai and the Cambodian (or Khmer) peoples had few racial or linguistic ties, and for a thousand years their political history had been one of unremitting hostility, as the Khmer were squeezed by Vietnamese from the north and east and by Thai from the north and west. In the fifteenth century the Khmer abandoned their stupendous complex of Angkor Wat and Angkor Thom when the Thai severely defeated them, and the area became lost even to Khmer memory until French archaeologists rediscovered it in the nineteenth century.

When the French established themselves in Indochina in the latter half of the nineteenth century they forced Thailand to cede its eastern provinces of Battambang and Siem Reap to Cambodia. During World War II, Japan forced the Vichy French to return them to Thailand, but at the end of the war Thailand had to cede them back to French Cambodia once more. The memory of these disputes was still painfully fresh in 1958. Even though the Thai had given refuge in the early 1950s to Cambodia's King Sihanouk no lasting ties of mutual regard were ever formed.

The Thai, in addition to disliking him and his people, had the most profound suspicion of Sihanouk's policy of "neutralism," which they were convinced would hand Cambodia over to the communists sooner or later. They lost no opportunity to criticize him publicly and privately and gave shelter to any Cambodians who opposed him. In turn Sihanouk raged at the iniquity of the Thais and charged that they were plotting with the CIA to overthrow him. Sarit's government did in fact do some plotting against Sihanouk, but the operations they hatched were amateurish and ineffective. Though the embassy would have been entirely discredited with Sarit had we appeared to support Sihanouk, we tried to discourage these gratuitously irritating Thai plots by emphasizing to Sarit how ham-handed they made the Thai appear.

Several times during my tour Thailand and Cambodia broke off diplomatic relations and then resumed them, once under the auspices of a UN Mission sent to recommend some way of improving the way the two countries got along. The American ambassadors in Phnom Penh, Carl Strom and then Bill Trimble, and I invested a lot of our time trying to maintain some kind of modus vivendi between the two governments without destroying our usefulness by appearing to defend one against the other. I was able to draw on the good relations I had established with some of the Cambodian leaders during the 1954 Indochina Conference in Geneva, but unfortunately these matchmaking efforts were repeatedly derailed. Even when Thailand and Cambodia did have diplomatic relations, Thailand sent very ineffective ambassadors to Phnom Penh, and the Cambodian ambassador in Bangkok was positively dedicated to doing all that he could to exacerbate tensions between the two countries. Insofar as the embassy could determine, he spent his entire day poring over Thai publications to find anything that could be interpreted as a slight or insult to Cambodia, especially to Sihanouk himself; these he would despatch by courier every few days to be placed directly on Sihanouk's desk. He usually succeeded in creating the explosion that was his apparent objective. Although I normally liked Cambodians, I found this ambassador to be nothing better than a low-grade agent provocateur.

SEATO, the Southeast Asia Treaty Organization, was a Dulles concept arising from the Vietminh victory at Dienbienphu and the uncertain outcome of the 1954 Geneva Conference on Indochina. The United States began to fear that communist expansion might soon swallow all of Southeast Asia. SEATO was in some ways modeled after NATO, but except for the common feature of having the United States as senior partner, the two alliances were fundamentally dissimilar. NATO, despite American preoponderance, was basically a joining of equals. Its Western European members had been major world powers themselves for centuries and had long experience in looking after their own interests. Their association with the United States for common defense took impetus from an obvious threat, the Soviet Red Army, and it grew naturally from the recent alliance to crush Nazi Germany. It had a working military command structure, committed American forces, access to American nuclear weapons, and the life and strength that comes from possessing a clear mission.

SEATO, from the start, was a more tentative and internally divided body. The United States, Thailand, Australia and New Zealand were its only enthusiastic members. The SEATO treaty bound the members of the organization, acting under constitutional processes, to defend any member under attack. In particular, it was designed to prevent the North Vietnamese from advancing beyond the lines that had been drawn in Vietnam, Laos, and Cambodia by the 1954 Geneva accords. Since the three states were forbidden under the terms of the Geneva accords from joining any defensive alliance, this was accomplished by a very adroit protocol to the SEATO treaty under which these three states were entitled to ask the protection of SEATO even though not signatories to the treaty. For the United States, Australia, and to a lesser extent New Zealand—all worried about falling dominoes—SEATO became the focus for collective military planning against the loss of Southeast Asia to the Soviet Union, China, North Vietnam, or their local agents.

SEATO's other members—Britain, France, Pakistan, and the Philippines—had their own reasons for joining. Britain had steadfastly opposed the idea of committing Western troops to Southeast Asia ever since Anthony Eden refused to join in Dulles's plan for collective action to rescue French troops at Dienbienphu in 1954. Having lost its empire and shrunk its armed forces into insignificance, Britain joined SEATO only to keep up the image of Allied unity. France's aims, on the other hand, were clearly obstructionist. Because it had colonized Vietnam, Laos, and Cambodia for nearly a century and still had pathetic dreams about maintaining its ascendency in those countries, it resented any growth in the stature of this new grouping that it did not dominate. Pakistan joined SEATO to win the United States as an ally against India; when Washington's relations with New Delhi did not cool immediately, Pakistan totally lost interest in SEATO except as a vehicle for increased economic and military assistance. The Philippines had its own mutual defense pact with the United States so it considered SEATO superfluous. Burma, India, Indonesia, Ceylon, and Malaya, all "non-aligned countries," had refused to join. So SEATO, which had no standing forces or established military command, was in many ways a rather ungainly paper tiger. It may have been a symbol of American commitment to anti-communism in Southeast Asia, but it required constant inputs of our zeal and money.

SEATO's weaknesses were most manifest during its infancy, from 1955 to 1957. Stalin died in 1953; afterwards Moscow and Peking softened their stance in Southeast Asia. Both countries, at least overtly, began to emphasize conciliation and the establishment of friendly relations with all countries in the region. The threat of direct Soviet or Chinese invasion appeared to recede, and North Vietnam was consumed with its own internal problems. In the balmier international climate the group of countries calling themselves the "non-aligned movement" became interested in staying clear of alliances with any big power, and at the famous 1955 Bandung conference of thirty "non-aligned" countries, Chinese Premier Chou En-lai managed to make China seem the champion of peace and Third World interests. Washington took the view that the conciliatory "spirit of Bandung" was primarily a tactical maneuver designed to win China support for membership in the UN and promote disunity among non-communist countries. But even so it was not a good time for SEATO. The organization's determined anti-communism and emphasis on military preparedness did not match the prevailing mood outside its member countries.

The fact that the communists still considered Southeast Asia a principal battleground of the Cold War soon became clear. But now the emphasis had switched from overt invasion, à la Korea, to internal subversion, for which it was necessary to develop indigenous communist guerillas. Thailand, Malaya, and the Philippines all had problems with communist rebels; and when I arrived in Bangkok, the most impressive communist advances were occuring in Thailand's next-door neighbor, Laos. This worried not only the Thai government, which turned to the United States for support, but the SEATO Council, on which I sat as United States representative. The Laotian situation grew increasingly troublesome, until it became the embassy's chief preoccupation and, by 1961, a major world crisis for President Kennedy.

A less likely venue for world crisis than Laos is scarcely imaginable. Its inhabitants at that time numbered barely two million, half of whom were Lao—a gentle people, living in the lowlands, who were closely related to the Thai and shared their particularly serene form of Buddhism—and the rest, a collection of mountain peoples. Laos's importance stemmed purely from its location; Burma and China lay to the north, Vietnam to the east, Cambodia to the south, and only the Mekong River separated Laos from Thailand on the west. Thus Laos was the ideal corridor for Chinese or North Vietnamese infiltration into South Vietnam, Cambodia, or Thailand. American policy held that its subjugation by communists would jeopardize the whole structure for the peaceful future of Indochina set forth in the Geneva accords. The communists would win a strategically significant piece of real estate and a resounding propaganda victory. They would get considerably closer to the Gulf of Siam, from which major sea lanes passing between Indonesia and the mainland could be interdicted. Thailand might then feel compelled to align itself with the ascendant power in the region. So history, in its curiously perverse way, had thrust this quiet backwater to the center of the Cold War.

Unfortunately for us, the politics of Laos were fiendishly complicated. Like Vietnam and Cambodia, Laos had been a French colony, and after World War II anti-colonialism was the dominant theme of its politics. The French forced their way back into the country and the newly formed Laotian government went into exile in 1946. By 1949, France was willing to grant Laos a small measure of autonomy; moderates decided to accept the offer, but the communist-dominated Pathet Lao and its political party, the Neo Lao Hak Xat (NLHX), built with Vietminh assistance, split off and joined Ho Chi Minh's struggle to rid all Indochina of French control by force. An added twist was that the Pathet Lao chief, Prince Souphanouvong, was the half-brother of the moderate leader who became Prime Minister in the new Laotian government, Prince Souvanna Phouma. Both of them had been trained as engineers at French schools in Indochina and at the University of Paris.

After the 1954 Geneva accords on Indochina, Souvanna Phouma attempted to bring his half-brother's Pathet Lao into a national government of reconciliation, but he did not succeed until 1957, when the "Bandung spirit" of cooperation was at its peak. Recalling the similar experiments in Czechoslovakia in 1948, however, Washington did not look favorably upon Souvanna's policy of incorporating the communists into the government and maintaining strict neutrality in the Cold War. Accordingly, our ambassador in Vientiane, Jeff Parsons, struggled to prevent the coalition government.

Early in 1958 Horace Smith had replaced Jeff Parsons as Ambassador to Laos. At that time there were two main pro-Western leaders: Phoui Sananikone, who stood for a policy of "pro-Western neutrality" that would curb communist influence in Laos while maintaining strict even-handedness in relations with the superpowers; and Phoumi Nosavan, a fervent anti-communist who wished to ally Laos firmly with the United States and stamp out the Pathet Lao. Phoumi had strong support from the CIA, the Pentagon (which was funding the Royal Lao Army), and from Marshal Sarit in Thailand, whom he called "uncle" as a sign of their unusually close relationship.

Thus when I went to Thailand at the beginning of 1958, not Vietnam, but Laos, was the primary source of concern to Washington, to SEATO, and not least, to Thailand. The two countries shared over 1000 miles of indefensible common border; Bangkok was Laos's only practical access to the sea; and the Lao and Thai had close racial, linguistic, and even family connections. The Thai inevitably became involved in Laos's internal difficulties. When combined with Washington's and SEATO's interest, this meant I ended up spending more of my tour in Thailand working on Laotian affairs, directly or indirectly, than on purely Thai matters. I necessarily maintained very close contact with our ambassadors in Laos, as well as with our ambassadors in Cambodia, first Carl Strom and then William Trimble, as well as with Elbridge Durbrow in Saigon. We eventually constituted ourselves as an informal coordinating group, periodically meeting together in one of our respective posts to exchange ideas and information in a way that was not possible just by telegram. (Later when I was Deputy Ambassador to Vietnam I revived this informal institution.)

My relations with our Ambassador in Laos, first Horace Smith and then Winthrop Brown, were obviously the closest; Bangkok became in effect the rear base for our embassy in Vientiane. In addition, what the Thai did or did not do during the frequent crises in Laos was often crucially important to what the Laotian government did in Vientiane.

The basic military threat to Thailand was two-pronged: the Vietnamese were moving into Laos from the east, assisted by their Pathet Lao allies, while Chinese military engineer teams were approaching from the north with a major road construction program that seemed to be directed toward the Thai border. There was real concern in Bangkok and Washington about the possibility of a coordinated Chinese-Vietminh thrust against Thailand. Even if an overt military invasion did not come, the presence of communist Chinese and Vietminh forces on the long and virtually indefensible Thai border would aid subversion in Thailand and make the Thai nervous. To make matters worse, the land on the Thai side of the border was thinly populated and its inhabitants were the most isolated, poverty-stricken, and neglected people in the country. The small towns that did exist there contained several tens of thousands of refugees from North Vietnam who had fled across Laos during the battles between the French and the Vietminh between 1945 and 1954. All in all, the border region was especially vulnerable to infiltration. To assure Thailand's security, therefore, it was important to prevent communist forces from directly occupying at least that section of Laos that bordered on Thailand.

It was understandable that Sarit, with strong support from his vigorous Foreign Minister Thanat Khoman, had little patience with United States policies or actions that did not rigidly promise to keep Laos out of communist or (to Sarit, equally dangerous and reprehensible) "neutralist" hands. While the United States had sympathy for Sarit's point of view, we could also see clearly that for Laos, "the perfect was the enemy of the good." We could not make the sizeable number of Laotian communists and neutralists simply disappear, so somehow they would have to be dealt with. Both Sarit and the United States wanted the most anti-communist Laotian government the traffic would bear; we disagreed (and Americans disagreed among themselves) in our assessments of what, in practical terms from day to day, the traffic would bear. We felt that Sarit's single-minded determination to insulate Thailand from communism made him overly partial to Phoumi and other reassuringly right-wing but impracticable solutions; Sarit and Foreign Minister Thanat felt that the United States naively failed to see that all communists were absolutely untrustworthy, and feared that our pressing global responsibilities would pressure us into accepting compromise solutions for Laos that put Thailand in jeopardy. Around this central axis Sarit and I debated Laotian policy for two years.

Unless I was escorting a visitor I saw Sarit without any of my supporting staff; he normally received me only with his confidant, Colonel Chalermchai, who also acted as interpreter. Although Sarit understood English quite well he was reluctant to try to speak it, and my Thai was very rudimentary. Depending on the subject, Foreign Minister Thanat Khoman might also be present, and he too acted as interpreter.

Sarit and I had an easy relationship, and he liked to engage in a little banter before we settled down to business. In mock seriousness I would question whether he was "staying on the wagon" as the doctors at Walter Reed had sternly warned him; he would inevitably protest that the liquid in the glass at his side was tea, and then kid me about the efforts that his Foreign Minister and I were making to play golf. The one who had requested the meeting would then open the serious conversation.

Both of us normally had a long list of items, and, depending on his mood and how much time he had, the discussion would cover a wide range of topics. At least once during a discussion he was sure to raise some treacherous thing Sihanouk had recently said or done, as well as his own intense dislike for any country espousing "neutralism" in its international alignment.

Because we did have some major differences over Laos, our sessions often became quite vigorous. But never did Sarit say something just to get rid of me so that he could proceed to do something else. This honesty was not always easy for him, especially when we asked him to abandon his Lao protégé, General Phoumi Nosovan, but he always stuck faithfully to whatever he promised.

On the other hand, he always refused to put his commitments in writing. This created considerable distress to the lawyers and punctilious-minded in both the State and Defense Departments, especially where United States expenditures were involved. My standard answer was that we could have things the way Sarit wants, or not have them at all. In the end Washington's answer was always the same: we would do it Sarit's way.

The Mission's most pressing concern during my tour was helping to keep Laos afloat. For the most part this involved trying to deal with an interminable succession of immediate crisis, but we did have longer-term programs as well. An important one in which Bangkok was involved concerned the Laotian mountain people. While the mountain people disliked the lowland Lao, they positively hated the Vietnamese. The Meo tribe (now called Hmung), in particular, showed themselves to be very courageous and adept at guerilla warfare against the Vietminh who, because they were strangers to Laos' rugged terrain, were largely confined to valley roads and trails. During my time in Bangkok, we obtained Sarit's approval to establish a training camp for the Meo. With a relatively small expenditure of resources and almost no cost in American lives, we began a very successful guerilla program. A Meo, General Vang Pao, turned out to be what many thought the most capable senior officer on "our side" in Southeast Asia. A visit to his headquarters and to his attractive people was always an inspiration. They were the last to succumb after the fall of Saigon and Vientiane in 1975, and tens of thousands eventually fled to Thailand when American funds ran out. (General Vang Pao himself made his way to the United States and became a very successful hog rancher in Montana.)

Another important long-term program arranged with Sarit involved training considerable numbers of the regular Lao armed forces at bases in Thailand. The program operated under severe handicaps—among which was the low level of Lao education. Also, as good Buddhists, the Laotians were averse to taking life of any kind. They did well enough with mortars and artillery, where they simply had to drop in the round or pull the lanyard without seeing what they were shooting at, but killing someone they could see was something else again. They were also terrified of the black-clothed Vietminh, who had no such compunctions. Simply a rumor that "black pajamas" had been sighted nearby was often sufficient to cause panic in a Lao unit. No doubt the training facilities that the Thai made available to the Laotian Army with our help were important in helping it become a more professional force, but no one could ever allege it could be a danger to anyone else.

Our long-term programs also encompassed SEATO, for the security of Laos and Thailand was obviously bound up on the health and vitality of all the non-communist countries in the region. It was in this area that SEATO—though much criticized—did make some positive contributions. To improve regional military preparedness, SEATO held joint field exercises in which all but the French and the Pakistanis usually participated. This gave the various armed forces practice in working together and let them test out communications and procedures, particularly in air and naval exercises.

In Bangkok, a SEATO Graduate School of Engineering was established, with excellent equipment and qualified professors from the United States, Great Britain, and France. This school met a real need, since trained technical personnel essential to development were in chronic short supply all over the region. It was open to qualified graduates in engineering from the whole area, not just SEATO members, and it gained great prestige and was eventually expanded into what is now the Asian Institute of Technology.

Among other SEATO-sponsored projects was a laboratory in Dacca, set up with multinational support, for advanced research on cholera. It still exists. In Thailand, a project for teaching basic technical skills at the high school level did much to upgrade and expand the Thai labor force. Programs in community development were started in the Philippines. SEATO also funded visits by lecturers to other member countries, thus encouraging cultural exchange between peoples who had been largely isolated from each other. In a small way that contributed to the growing sense of community feeling that resulted in the 1967 creation of the genuinely indigenous organization, ASEAN, the Association of Southeast Asian Nations, which has now become a significant political force in the area.

It would be misleading, however, to concentrate on describing the embassy's long-range programs for boosting Thai and Lao security. They were important and we devoted a lot of money and thought to them, but responding immediately to Laos's rapidly shifting, sometimes almost bizarre, politics demanded most of our energy.

The plot really started thickening in December 1959, when Phoumi, the hard-line anti-communist backed by the Pentagon, succeeded in ousting Phoui as Prime Minister and installing himself as Minister of Defense, with Kou Abhayas as Prime Minister. For a while it looked as if some progress was being made in keeping Laos's border with Thailand secure from infiltration. But over the longer haul, Phoumi proved unable to win over the country's other leaders, such as Phoui and Souvanna Phouma. He was also an inept administrator, and corruption began to exceed even the very liberal Lao standards.

In June 1960, an unknown Lao Army captain, Kong Le, mutinied and, with a small band of troops, executed a flawless coup, seizing Vientiane while Phoumi and his entire cabinet were visiting the king in the royal seat of Luang Prabang. Kong Le and his followers had grown distressed over Phoumi's rigid anti-communism, his government's corruption, and what they considered to be the excessive influence of foreigners (meaning Americans). They believed that the country could still be held together if its government was reconstituted to appeal to a wide spectrum, and so prevailed upon the king to ask that hardy perennial, Prince Souvanna Phouma, to return from exile in France and form a "neutralist" government.

Phoumi, though officially Deputy Prime Minister, refused to support the new government, and, with Sarit's support, started setting up a separate regime in the south. Our new ambassador in Vientiane, Winthrop Brown, recommended that we be responsive to Souvanna Phouma's request for our support. It was Win's view that, with his "neutralist" approach, Souvanna Phouma could come closer to achieving a non-communist consensus. But Win was not able to persuade Washington, where support for Phoumi was strong, especially in the Pentagon and CIA. Also Jeff Parsons, a former Ambassador to Laos, had returned to the Department as Assistant Secretary for Far Eastern Affairs, where his doubts about Souvanna Phouma could be effectively channeled. Though I recognized his weaknesses, I too was partial to Phoumi at the time. I hoped he would mature with experience and thus be able to draw together the non-communist elements in the country. So when Souvanna Phouma reopened negotiations with the Pathet Lao in September 1960, aiming toward a coalition government, Phoumi knew that this policy made many people in the United States government uneasy and worked in his home province to marshal forces for a countercoup.

Assistant Secretary Parsons traveled to Laos in October to persuade Souvanna to stop negotiating with the communists and start negotiating with Phoumi. After Souvanna held firm, Parsons and Brown came to Bangkok for several days to talk with the American ambassadors in the region. Brown persuaded Parsons to acquiesce in Souvanna's continuing negotiations with the Pathet Lao if Souvanna did not object to continued American aid to Phoumi's forces, which Phoumi had promised would only be used only against the Pathet Lao, not Kong Le or Souvanna. Souvanna agreed to this compromise.

Unfortunately, Phoumi did not keep his side of the bargain. Ambassador Brown suspected Phoumi of wanting to retake Vientiane from Kong Le. He was right, and by mid-December Phoumi's troops had surrounded Vientiane and heavily damaged it with indiscriminate artillery fire. We arranged for the evacuation of 400 embassy personnel from Vientiane on December 16.

Ambassador Brown's judgment that Phoumi was an ineffective leader proved to be correct, as Phoumi was unable to follow up his victory and Kong Le successfully retreated from Vientiane into the interior. Kong Le then requested and received substantial support from a Soviet airlift operating out of North Vietnam, but still called himself a "neutral"; at the same time, the government forces loyal to Souvanna Phouma stationed around the royal seat of Lunag Prabang refused to recognize Phoumi's authority and also called themselves "neutrals." So, in addition to all of the other contending forces, there were "their neutrals" (Kong Le and company) and "our neutrals" (the government troops). If at this point you are confused, all I can do is assure you that at the time we were too.

After Vientiane fell to Phoumi, Souvanna Phouma fled to Cambodia, and by the end of December 1960 it became clear that organized North Vietnamese forces were also entering the country to work with the Pathet Lao and Kong Le. Phoumi's position deteriorated rapidly. It seemed that our worst fears with respect to Laos—communist troops on the Thai border—might soon be realized.

Along with my staff, including my special assistant Bob Jantzen, I met with the Thai leadership almost continuously during this period—to exchange information, to try to calm their fears, to obtain their agreement to letting us use Thai airfields and other facilities in support of Phoumi's forces, and to persuade them to follow our rapidly shifting line in dealing with all the main actors. As I very much respected the Thai king's judgment and influence, I also kept in close touch with him through our private channels and by in-person visits.

The SEATO Council also started meeting almost daily. This required lots of preparation time for me and for my SEATO staff assistant, Jack Conroy, who had to prepare statements and make sure I was briefed to handle questions on overnight developments. Under instructions from their governments to avoid getting embroiled in Laos at all costs, the French and British representatives backpedalled as strenuously as possible from any movement toward SEATO military action to shore up the country, while the Thai naturally tried to prod the alliance into deploying troops. My position tended to be closer to that of the Thai. I felt SEATO had to show resolve if the Pathet Lao and North Vietnamese were going to be deterred, or beaten. But I too was wary of committing American forces hastily. Laos was not a good place for American troops. Moreover, there was no guarantee they would solve our problem, which was basically political, or banish the incompetence of the Lao leaders with whom we worked. At the same time the only thing that might frustrate communist plans for seizing Laos was a serious threat of SEATO (largely American) intervention. So I had to walk a tightrope: on the one hand, preventing Thailand or Laos from formally requesting SEATO military assistance, which would have split the alliance into two camps and eliminated any chance for collective action when time was riper; on the other, seeking some signs of commitment and toughness from France and Great Britain.

The Thai, particularly Foreign Minister Thanat Khoman, became increasingly frustrated, emotional, and vocal. Thanat was angry at what he felt was the sheer timidity of Britain and France, and he was disillusioned at the possibility of SEATO assistance even if Thailand itself were attacked. He started lobbying for a separate bilateral defense treaty with the United States that would pledge us to consider an attack on Thailand an attack on ourselves, similar to the formula employed in the NATO Treaty. The SEATO formula, which only provided for "consultation" in case of attack, was too ambiguous for Thanat, especially when he saw Britain and France drag their heels day after day. After long and spirited discussions on the subject, I went out on a long limb to reassure him. I took the position that Congress did not cede its power to declare war even under the NATO formula, and that if we made the decision to assist Thailand in case of a direct attack—which I thought we would—we could do so equally well under the SEATO formula. I pointed out that we had undertaken certain obligations toward Thailand under SEATO; if other members of the alliance chose not to carry out their obligations, this did not relieve us of our responsibility or ability to do so. This interpretation did not satisfy Thanat entirely, but it did relieve his worst anxieties for a while.

In February 1961, just after President Kennedy and his team had moved into their new offices and were still getting acquainted with their jobs, Laos came to a boil once more. Kong Le and the Pathet Lao, having already seized the strategic Plain of Jars (with significant help from the Soviet airlift), crashed through Phoumi's defenses and took a vital road junction on the Luang Prabang-Vientiane road. It looked as if Kong Le, the Pathet Lao and the North Vietnamese were ready for a broad advance that would install them on the banks of the Mekong opposite Thailand. Washington and SEATO again faced a wrenching choice between letting Laos slip away or rescuing the non-communist Laotians by a large and difficult military intervention. But this time the stakes were higher because the opportunities for any political compromise had faded.

The Joint Chiefs, still smarting from the frustrations of the Korean War, had no taste for a drawn-out struggle for limited political objectives in a remote Asian country with difficult terrain. They insisted that if the President were to send troops, he send lots—as many as 60,000—and permit them to range widely throughout Southeast Asia, including North Vietnam.

But the President also faced crises in Berlin and Cuba. A huge commitment to Laos was both strategically and politically unsound. So a negotiated solution leading to peace and a truly neutral Laos seemed the only realistic alternative. But the Pathet Lao, who currently had the upper hand and held reasonable prospects of complete victory eventually, had no incentive to bargain. We had to provide one. Washington sensed that Moscow, which faced its own crises in Berlin and Cuba, was counting on Laos falling into its hands easily and thus might push the Pathet Lao to the bargaining table if the alternative were American troops in Southeast Asia. So the President ordered a buildup of forces that signalled our readiness to intervene in Laos, while simultaneously calling for a cessation of the armed attacks supported by the North Vietnamese. On March 23, he said that "If these attacks do not stop, those who support a genuinely neutral Laos will have to consider their response." He went on to say that negotiations for a peaceful solution in Laos could not take place while military action was in progress and that "every American will want this country to honor its obligations" to Laos. He also said that the whole question would be taken up at the upcoming SEATO conference.

This was good news for me because I had been urging my old boss, Dean Rusk, now Secretary of State, to put Laos at the top of the agenda for the SEATO conference and for Dean himself to attend it, even though it meant a long trip to Bangkok. Dean's presence in itself would reassure the Thai and the Lao, I argued, and give pause to the North Vietnamese, who had recently announced the formation of a "National Liberation Front" to conquer South Vietnam. Also, while there was no real hope of turning around the essentially obstructionist attitudes of Britain and France, Rusk's attendance would put pressure on them to send their Foreign Ministers to the meeting, which would make sure they were personally acquainted with the hard realities of the situation. Given a chance, I thought, Dean might be able to encourage a more cooperative attitude on their part.

Dean did come to the conference, arriving in Bangkok March 26, as did British Foreign Minister Lord Hume and French Foreign Minister Couve de Meurville. As I was the United States SEATO Council representative and a long time friend of Dean's, I worked closely with him during the meeting and participated in most of his conversations with SEATO's other foreign ministers.

Though everyone in Bangkok recognized that the Laotian problem was very serious, Rusk had a near-impossible job in trying to get everyone to agree on a final communique that would show enough teeth to induce the communists to accept President Kennedy's idea of an international conference on Laos. France balked at committing to intervention. So did Britain, whose Prime Minister Macmillan, simultaneously meeting with President Kennedy in Florida on March 26, unenthusiastically agreed to intervene if absolutely necessary. SEATO's Asian members had no illusions about the constancy of their European allies and, taking their lead from France and Britain, tended to put short-term national interest ahead of the alliance. The only thing Rusk and the rest of the United States delegation could do was try to hold the alliance together while pushing it forward.

Rusk's presence in the new administration boosted Thai morale because of his well-known role in the Korean War. To reassure them further, he endorsed the position I had taken with Foreign Minister Thanat that the United States felt bound by its SEATO Treaty commitments regardless of other members' behavior. Rusk stated in a formal communication to Prime Minister Sarit that if Thailand were attacked as a result of its cooperation with us in Laos, we "would not condition our response" on obtaining the agreement of all the other members of SEATO. Later, when I returned to Washington, I was able to obtain agreement within the government to a somewhat broader position that was embodied in the "Rusk-Thanat Communique" of March 6, 1962. That communique stated that "The United States regards the preservation of the independence and integrity of Thailand as vital to the national interest of the United States and to world peace." The statement also publicly reaffirmed what I had been privately saying to Sarit and Thanat when I was Ambassador by stating the obligation of the United States to Thailand under SEATO "does not depend upon the prior agreement of all other parties to the Treaty, since this Treaty obligation is individual as well as collective." While temporarily mollifying Thanat, this did not fully satisfy him. Through the years he kept raising the subject of a bilateral mutual defense treaty. This would have been so obviously impossible to get through Congress that I finally became impatient at his insistence.

While reassuring the Thai about our military readiness, Rusk at the same time had to convince Lord Hume and Couve de Meurville that the United States was not rushing rashly toward war. He emphasized to them the crucial importance of SEATO unity in convincing the Soviets to bargain, and suggested that Washington, under the new President, understood that Laos was a subtle, complex problem that could not be solved solely through backing right-wing generals or even massive military force. He hoped that evidence of a new American sophistication would reassure our allies that we were not leading them blindly into a quagmire. I distinctly remember his telling Pote Sarasin, the SEATO Secretary General, that American policy was aimed at getting some sort of political solution, because even if SEATO put two million troops in Laos, the need for a political solution would remain.

At the end of the Conference, on March 29, Rusk believed he had made some progress. The final communique supported efforts to convene an all-parties conference on Laos, but also said: "If those efforts fail, however, and there continues to be an active military attempt to obtain control of Laos, members of SEATO are prepared, within the terms of the treaty, to take whatever action may be appropriate in the circumstances." It was encouraging to me that the new administration specifically approved this language, which I felt was stronger than anything we had thus far said. The first sign that Moscow was heeding our carefully orchestrated pressures for a Laotian conference came in early April. The Soviets, however, refused to agree to a ceasefire until the details of the talks were ironed out, hoping that stalling would help the Pathet Lao nibble further. There matters stood for some weeks. By the time they started moving again, I was back in Washington in a new job where Laos was only one concern of many.

After the debacle of the Bay of Pigs action against Cuba in April, the President had lost even more of his enthusiasm for military action, and by the end of that month he decided to support a British-Soviet call for an immediate cease fire in Laos and a twelve-nation conference to seek a negotiated settlement. To back this up and reassure the Thai, he obtained the agreement

of the Thai government to deploy a battalion of marines to Northeast Thailand. Fortunately they were able to fulfill their purpose
without having to enter combat.

Never in my Foreign Service career has the State Department saddled me with a job I considered dull or objectionable.
Each post has been stimulating in its own way. But Thailand was
something special. The work was absorbing, the Thai were friendly, my relationships throughout the government, especially with
the king and Marshal Sarit, were both effective and cordial, and
I had the feeling that I was respected and liked by the Thai. One
Thai editorial writer of the formerly hostile press was good enough
to comment when I left:

> Everywhere I have been in Thailand—in rural areas, in planta-
> tions, in rice-fields, even in outlying districts—I have found that
> Mr. Johnson is not only known by name to the people, but they
> also know him personally and intimately. He endeavored to meet
> and mix on intimate terms with them in their homes and in their
> daily life. No other foreign diplomat has been on such close and
> intimate terms with them as Mr. Johnson. My personal feeling is
> that he has set an excellent example of what cooperation based
> on friendship can be. (*Phim Thai*, "Between the Lines," April 6,
> 1961)

Several incidents, completely unconnected, some personal and
some highly official, I carry in my memory. These somehow distill
the depth of my involvement and satisfaction in Thailand.

The Thai Minister of Agriculture, Sawat Mahaphon, was an
exceptionally fine man and an able administrator. Because the
embassy was involved in so many programs to improve Thai agriculture, we often went together on excursions with our assistants
to see various projects and discuss future programs. In August,
1959, the two of us and Foreign Minister Thanat Khoman arranged a trip to Pucha Dung, a large mesa rising 4000 feet out
of a remote area of flat plains in the northeast. Thanat was especially interested in studying the practicality of establishing
some kind of tourist resort in the cool climate on the summit. We
were all intrigued and eager to see this curious mountain that
only a few had managed to visit via a long, tortuous trail up its
precipitous sides. I agreed to furnish a plane to the nearest airstrip
and then a helicopter that could land us on the summit, while
the Thai would furnish the food. I also agreed to take along a
USOM engineer who could make an educated guess about the
cost of building some kind of road to the top.

The heat and altitude forced the helicopter to abort its first effort to reach the top. After reducing the payload by unloading some of the passengers, the helicopter finally succeeded in getting all of us up by making two trips. Instead of the picnic baskets and sandwiches we expected the Thai to bring, we found a nicely tended camp with tents, tables, ice and cold drinks, china, silver and clean linen—all carried to the top by relays of porters!

A few days later the Agriculture Minister was dead. His second wife—who was also the sister of his number one wife— had murdered him. I heard a brief account when I arrived at work the morning after the murder, but I had to leave quickly for an early appointment with Sarit. I found Sarit really broken up. He had also been very fond of Sawat and told me that he had been up all night trying to learn the exact circumstances of the murder, for it was extremely unusual for Thai wives, whether first or second, to murder their husbands. As we reminisced about Sawat, Sarit said solemnly: "This just proves that you should never have two wives." Considering the prevalence of this practice in Thailand, Sarit's observation surprised me, but I thoroughly agreed and said so. Sarit continued: "We agree, but probably for quite different reasons. The moral as far as I am concerned is that if you are going to have more than one wife, you should have at least three. Triangles are dangerous."

Another episode that cemented the especially close attachment I feel for Thailand was the state visit of their majesties, King Bhumiphol and Queen Sirikit, to the United States in August 1960.

Many people think that, barring occasional calamities like the takeover of our embassy in Tehran in 1979 and the murder of scores of our embassy staff in Beirut in 1983, diplomats have a pretty cushy life, one reception after another, full of champagne and good meals and pleasant chitchat. Diplomatic life does require considerable social life, but to an active diplomat a reception is usually a workplace. Beneath the deceptive veneer of clinking glasses and fancy hors d'oeuvres lies a great deal of strenuous horse-trading guided by careful advance strategy. After the novelty wears off, parties become just another venue—even an exhausting one—for getting work done. And the ultimate form, perhaps, of diplomatic entertaining is the state visit.

When I was sent to Thailand in 1958, a part of my formal instructions directed me to inform the king that we hoped he and the queen would visit the United States soon. I extended the invitation at my first audience and he agreed that he would like to visit, but nothing specific evolved. Prince Dhani, President of the Privy Council, told me that the king would not want to go to Washington before 1960 at the earliest, so there seemed to be no rush.

In December 1958, the king's confidant and aide-de-camp, General Suranarong, called on me privately with the message that the king had decided with the government's endorsement to embark upon a series of visits outside the region and wanted the United States to be first. Could we arrange something, say a six-week tour with a varied program, for an official party of about thirty, within the next three months? I told him it would probably be entirely out of the question because our schedule of state visits is fixed from eighteen months to two years in advance, but said I would query Washington to see what they might arrange.

Washington was alarmed. President Eisenhower's schedule was entirely filled and they wanted me to stall the king as long as possible. I thought that we, having made the invitation, had to show some effort to honor it; the king kept pressing me for a date, and I knew that a state visit to Washington would be a real coup for America's reputation in Thailand. So I insisted to the Department that we set up the visit, but it kept procrastinating. It took a year of some rather pointed exchanges before they finally acquiesced—very grudgingly, it seemed to me—in issuing an invitation for August 1960.

After the date had been set the king asked whether we could arrange for him to spend some extra unofficial time with his family so they could all see and learn more about our country. The Department, continuing its foot-dragging, said that it could really do nothing to help. Luckily, Assistant Secretary of Commerce Henry Kearns visited Bangkok shortly thereafter, and knowing that he had a sizeable house in southern California I put the problem to him. He generously offered his house for however long the royal family wanted it and arrangements for the private portion of the tour, mostly prior to going to Washington, proceeded.

As their departure date approached the king and queen grew nervous. They were determined to win friends for their country in the United States and wanted to make absolutely certain not to commit the slightest error of protocol. The king peppered me with questions about proper behavior and dress. Should he wear a full military uniform? With ribbons? With a sash? Should he wear a full dress uniform or evening clothes to the White House dinner? Should he stand when the President stands? While on tour should he wear a hat, and if so what kind? Would people stand when he gave a toast? Should he give a major speech? I respected this earnest young man for his dedication to projecting a favorable impression of his country and to the best of my ability got answers to his specific questions from our protocol people in Washington. But mostly I stressed to him the same advice I give to Americans going abroad: relax and do what comes naturally. I knew that the king and queen were so basically kind and gracious that just "being themselves" would never fail them.

I was in Washington for a SEATO Council meeting when the king and queen left for the United States; I flew back to Honolulu to meet them at their first stop in American territory. It was a typically beautiful Honolulu evening and after the usual guard of honor and twenty-one-gun salute at the airport, the official welcoming committee (including the Governor, the Mayor, and the Commander-in-Chief Pacific, Admiral Felt) took leave of us and we proceeded in a convoy to the Royal Hawaiian Hotel, then standing in solitary splendor on Waikiki Beach. After the king and queen were installed in their suite, several members of their entourage and I went down to the lounge to have a drink and compare notes before our dinner. The king and queen were scheduled to rest and eat alone in their quarters. As those of us downstairs prepared to go into dinner one of the State Department security officers tapped me on the shoulder and said that the king and queen were on their way down. They showed up immediately behind him and joined us, saying that they wanted to chat. Two more places were set at the table and we spent a very relaxed and pleasant meal, afterwards taking a walk along the beach. This outgoing but dignified informality characterized their entire visit.

We flew from Honolulu to Los Angeles in the luxurious but propeller-driven CINCPAC plane, and spent a splendidly unhurried time getting to know each other better. The king and queen were both truly fun to be with. Ontario Airport, our intended destination, was not far from Henry Kearns's house where they were going to stay in southern California, but it was fogged in so we had to land at Los Angeles Airport, some fifty miles away. Patricia and my son Bill had come to meet us at Ontario as well as the security escort so they all had a wild ride across town behind the highway patrol escort to get to the other airport on time. Our plane held in the air until they arrived, however, so all was in order.

Their time in southern California before going to Washington was "unofficial and private" except for one day when the movie industry gave them a lunch and the Mayor of Los Angeles hosted a dinner. The Hollywood lunch was actually an occasion of some political sensitivity, for the recent block-buster musical *The King and I* had been banned in Thailand, and the king and queen had been concerned before and during the trip that this might cause hostility in the United States, particularly in the press and in Hollywood. I shared his worry and we had discussed the matter, but I had no idea how the king planned to handle it. The film was great entertainment and was not deliberately intended to offend Thai sensitivities, but the fact was that the king in *The King and I* was King Bhumibol's great-grandfather, Mongkut, a much revered and remarkable man who was far ahead of his time and country and was largely responsible for preserving Thailand's independence during the period of French and British imperialism in Southeast Asia. The Broadway musical comedy, and even more so the Yul Brynner film, caricatured Mongkut as a clever but half-naked potentate who sang comic patter and was fond of swooping up Gertrude Lawrence for spirited polkas in the Grand Palace's hallowed halls. In one scene Yul Brynner pats the head of a Buddhist image; in Thai eyes this is unbelievably crude sacrilege, the rough equivalent in Christian terms of spitting and trampling on the cross. The diaries of the English schoolmistress Anna Leonowens, on which Margaret Landon based her entertaining book from which the play and film are further romanticized, are derived more from Anna's very fertile imagination than from objective reporting.

I need not have had any concern about how the king would handle this delicate situation. When he stood to reply to the welcome he received at the movie colony lunch, the king said very simply: "Now this is just between the King and you about *The King and I.*" He said that he had seen the film and found it entertaining, but explained that it treats what the Thai consider matters of veneration in such a way that outrage and anti-American sentiment would undoubtedly have been aroused among the unsophisticated. Therefore, while Thailand was normally opposed to censorship, the decision had been made to protect Thai-American relations by not showing the film in Thailand. Everyone applauded the king's statement and the subject did not come up again during the visit.

In Washington the royal couple, of course, stayed at the Blair House (The President's Guest House) and there was the normal schedule of formal dinners by the President and Secretary of State Christian Herter, a reception by the king, a shopping trip for the queen, and so on. They charmed everyone who met them, and although the king as a constitutional monarch did not undertake any negotiations, the trip was a great success for relations between the two countries.

The centerpiece of their time in Washington was a white tie state dinner at the White House. We followed the usual practice under the Eisenhower's in that all of the guests stood for almost an hour in the East Room lined up in protocol order without so much as a glass of water while waiting for the President and First Lady to descend with their guests of honor. Then they passed around the line to shake hands and marched directly into dinner. After dinner it was a little more convivial for everyone.

When the king and queen left Washington for the remainder of their official visit—to New York, to Boston for a nostalgic return to the king's birthplace, and finally to Chicago—Pat and I left them and went by car to visit our daughter and grandchildren in Omaha, Nebraska, and then on to the High Sierras.

In the meantime, the king and queen completed their official trip and returned to southern California to be "regular tourists" with their children to the extent that their position and security permitted. From California they went to Europe for some more state visits, which by all accounts were also very successful. When they returned to Thailand, they gave a delightfully informal party for the ambassadors and their wives of the countries they had visited. The setting was outdoors at the site of an old palace up the river from Bangkok at the old capital of Ayuthia. A big dance floor had been set up and the king brought his own jazz band, the one he played with at the palace over Thai radio. They played until the wee hours, everyone had ample opportunity to dance with the queen, and the food was good. It was a very graceful and much appreciated gesture of thanks.

I look back with much satisfaction on my period in Thailand. The country was small enough and sufficiently at the malleable stage of its development that I could observe the results of what my staff and I were doing. Also, Washington gave me enough leeway and was sufficiently responsive to my recommendations for action in Washington that I could feel that I was having an impact on policy. When I left I felt that Thai-American relations were on a sound basis and that the misunderstandings of an earlier period had been overcome. This was particularly important since both countries were entering a difficult period in Southeast Asia which, as it turned out, demanded a great deal of cooperation, tolerance and mutual understanding between our two countries.

Additionally, my involvement with Laos and Vietnam, as well as service with my colleagues on the SEATO Council, extended the horizons of my work well beyond Thailand itself. Bangkok's position as an air transport hub with its large number of official and unofficial travelers between East and West kept me well exposed to what was going on elsewhere in the world. Thus when I was asked to take the Deputy Undersecretary job in the Department with its worldwide responsibilities I did not feel as ill-equipped as might otherwise have been the case. That job, then the most senior one open to a career Foreign Service Officer, was offered to me by my old friend and former boss Dean Rusk at the start of the Kennedy Administration, before Dean came out to the SEATO Conference. After the conference was over, I was able to leave Bangkok for Washington.

·CHAPTER TEN·

Deputy Undersecretary

I HAVE NEVER REGISTERED IN A POLITICAL PARTY. PARTLY BECAUSE my home base for most of my adult life has been the District of Columbia (though California was my legal residence), and partly because it is not my nature, either personally or as a Foreign Service Officer, to be partisan, I was never able to vote in a presidential election until after my retirement in 1977. Though in 1960 I followed the campaign closely, I was not committed to either Kennedy or Nixon. I had met Nixon only a few times when he was Eisenhower's Vice President, but he always made me uneasy. On the other hand I retained enough of my old midwestern Protestant prejudices to have some concern about electing a Catholic president. But Kennedy handled that issue so masterfully during the campaign that I was won over and took real pleasure in his victory. So I returned to Washington in 1961 with enthusiasm about having a chance to serve under President Kennedy and confident that his administration's foreign policy, under Dean Rusk's guidance, would be both sound and activist.

I arrived in Washington on Sunday, April 16. It was the height of the Bay of Pigs invasion. I obviously knew nothing more than what I was able to read in that Sunday morning's newspapers, but it was clear this was no time to bother Secretary Rusk. Instead, I paid a courtesy call on Under Secretary Chester Bowles at his house. I was astonished, with the way events were moving in Cuba, to find him relaxed and expansive. The President and the Secretary were obviously not seeking his counsel on the Bay of Pigs, and he was probably delighted not to have been involved. In the Department's hierarchy he was my nominal superior, but, as the senior career officer, I expected to be working with the Secretary, Under Secretary, and Under Secretary for Economic Affairs in a collegial way, with primary responsibility for coordinating the work of the geographical divisions and maintaining good relations with Defense, CIA, the White House, and other agencies with foreign policy interests. It became apparent that Bowles viewed my job somewhat differently, more as his immediate deputy or assistant (which, of course, the title seems to imply) instead of an almost-equal colleague. Even so, I found him a very attractive person and looked forward to working with him, even though he was a little voluble for my taste.

On Monday morning I saw Secretary Rusk briefly. I sensed quickly that Bowles had not been his choice for Under Secretary. They seemed to be operating independently of each other, with Bowles having little to do except deal with the White House on the selection of ambassadors. Indeed, it took only a few days on the seventh floor to realize that Bowles was estranged not only from Rusk but from the rest of the Department. Surprisingly, though he had been founder of the famous Benton and Bowles advertising agency, head of the Office of Price Administration during World War II, Governor of Connecticut, and Ambassador to India, he was a poor administrator. No one could get a clear decision out of him. He would call a group into his office to discuss a telegram of instructions he was drafting; after he delivered an hour's lecture—quite excellent, usually—about the broad aspects of the problem or something tangential, the group would depart no closer to resolving what should go in the telegram.

The assistant secretaries were frustrated, and Bowles's colleagues on various high-level interdepartmental committees, particularly those overseeing intelligence operations, complained quietly that he was not pulling his own weight. Because I knew the Department better than Bowles, had a good grasp of how it worked most effectively, and had re-established my close working relationship with Secretary Rusk, I found that subordinates began to look increasingly to me for decisions. Before long, McGeorge Bundy, the President's National Security Advisor, and others, began to make efforts to shift some of Bowles's interdepartmental committee assignments to me. I found this very difficult, for I liked Bowles, and my sense of discipline in an organization is that you give loyalty to your superiors. But the Department clearly needed an efficient channel to the Secretary and the President, and an operating officer abreast of what was happening at lower levels. This Bowles was not providing.

Bowles's ideas on ambassadorial appointments, which President Kennedy found attractive, ranged from brilliant to terrible. To their credit, Bowles and the Administration avoided political patronage appointments more than previous administrations I had observed and allotted career FSO's a healthy fraction of the available slots. Some of the non-career appointments—such as sending Harvard Professor Edward Reischauer, whom I had known in Japan from before the war, to Tokyo—were excellent. But James Gavin, former Chairman of the Joint Chiefs of Staff, worked out poorly in Paris. Either because of or, despite their common military backgrounds, he could not develop a good relationship with De Gaulle. George Kennan, the brilliant foreign affairs theoretician whom the Soviet Union declared persona non grata in 1954 when he was ambassador there, was made ambassador in Yugoslavia. Unfortunately he seemed to think that what Tito did, or what Congress did, was somehow aimed at him as an individual, and this colored some of his judgments. While George was a career FSO and an unusually subtle and profound thinker, I'm afraid he was an indifferent diplomat.

Another unconventional appointment was John Kenneth Galbraith, who went to India. He was undeniably bright, but vain beyond belief. He wrote his cables with great splash and style, and his tone generally conveyed considerable self-satisfaction. In November, 1961, he complained directly to the President about U-2 reconaissance flights over China (of which I was a strong proponent) because of the consequences to Indian public opinion if discovered. The protest included a strong personal attack on me. Mac Bundy told me not to worry because the President knew Ken and his foibles. But when China attacked India in June 1962—which U-2 flights might have helped us predict—I never saw a more abrupt turnaround. In came an urgent cable from Delhi requesting U-2 flights over China. In so far as I could tell, it never even occurred to Ken that he might have been wrong the first time. Though Galbraith was obviously closer personally to the President and his "Harvard mafia" than I was, they seemed well aware of his propensity for hyperbole and I never found that he upset my relations with them.

I was holding a meeting on my old subject of Czech claims a few days after I arrived in Washington when my secretary said that President Kennedy was calling. I was surprised, for a presidential call to someone other than the Secretary was an unusual event to my orderly bureaucratic mind, especially when that someone was me.

I picked up the phone, and that unmistakable voice asked me what was going on in the Dominican Republic! That floored me. Fresh from Bangkok and still immersed in the intricacies of Laos, I knew next to nothing about the Dominican Republic and told him so—promising, however, that I would find out and get back to him, which needless to say I did within the hour.

This call was an excellent introduction to Kennedy's style of leadership. I was certainly no expert on the Dominican Republic and the President must have known that. But he wanted to make sure I knew that he took personal interest in foreign affairs and expected fast, quality performance. I also saw as time progressed that his call manifested a customary impatience, and perhaps a certain ignorance about the ways of government departments and their chains of command. JFK was no respecter of titles. If he thought a country desk officer was the person he wanted to talk to, he would call and issue instructions of which four or five levels of higher-ranking officials would be unaware. That made problems for us, but President Kennedy did not seem to mind.

George McGhee, the Counselor of the Department, had already set up a regular Tuesday Luncheon Planning Group with McGeorge Bundy. These sessions gave me a chance to establish quickly a good working relationship with Mac, and, in turn, to obtain from him a feel for the President's views and desires. Mac had a brilliant and incisive mind and was able to translate the President's wishes into action very rapidly. Mac did not look on himself as an independent center of power nor did he seek personal publicity. He came close to that ideal of effectively serving the President while maintaining for himself a "passion for anonymity." It is regrettable that some of his successors did not follow the same rule.

Mac immediately told me that the President and the White House were looking to me to strengthen the Department's ability to deal with the Pentagon and the CIA in order to assure that foreign policy considerations were given their proper weight at the early stages of policy formulation. I said my desire was to assure that we did our best to serve the President as he wanted to be served, but I asked that he and his staff differentiate clearly between their views as individuals and those of the President. The former would be given consideration, while the latter would be considered instructions to be carried out without question.

Mac fully agreed and we operated on that basis throughout the time he was in the White House.

I also renewed my ties with Allen Dulles, Director of the CIA, whom I had known since the Korean War. In Bangkok I had considerable contact with the entire range of CIA activities and personnel in Southeast Asia, so we knew and respected each other. I served as State's representative on the interdepartmental committee that oversaw the intelligence community's reconaissance and covert political activities, so with Dulles and his successor, John McCone, I had ample contact.

Drawing on the ideas of George Newman, whom I kept on as the principal assistant in my office, and working with Lucius Battle, the Executive Secretary of the Department, I drew up a plan that the Secretary quickly approved for establishing within my office a Political-Military Section staffed by a few really specialized experts in all aspects of military affairs, including strategy and nuclear weapons. I was fortunate in obtaining Jeffrey Kitchen to head the section. Jeff had been personal assistant to Dean Acheson during the latter part of Dean's term as Secretary, and since then had steeped himself in politico-military affairs in various "think tanks" and government agencies. He in turn picked five people from within the Department, the Pentagon, and the CIA, each of whom thoroughly knew his respective field. (The fact that we could not locate a single Foreign Service Officer who was qualified for this section led me to lay emphasis later in seeking to develop such expertise within our own ranks.) Kitchen and his staff made a lean tight team who quickly won the respect of their Pentagon colleagues. Because they were part of my office, they also had clout with the bureaus in the Department, who all too often looked upon the Pentagon as a hostile force to be defended against. I was tremendously assisted in improving State-Defense relations by Paul Nitze, the Assistant Secretary of Defense for International Security Affairs (ISA), often called the Pentagon's "State Department." He was a good personal friend from the days when he had directed the Policy Planning Council in State under Acheson.

One of the major and lasting organizational changes I was able to institute in the Department, together with Luke Battle, was establishing the Operations Center. The concept originated in the fertile imagination of my assistant, George Newman. Previously, when a telegram arrived after the Department had closed up for the night, the watch officer in the communications section would try to reach one of the designated "duty officers" if the subject seemed sufficiently urgent. This was rather informal, when compared to the Pentagon's round-the-clock National Military Command Center or to the similar facility at the CIA. While one-third of the world is asleep, as Dean Rusk used to say, the other two-thirds is awake and "making mischief," and our antiquated communications procedures put us on the sidelines in dealing with it.

George persuaded me and Battle that the remedy was to establish an Operations Center manned twenty-four hours a day by responsible and informed officers. They would have communications links to the Pentagon, CIA, and White House, as well as the senior officers of the Department, receive all urgent communications from our posts overseas, and monitor news tickers. We encountered stiff opposition from some of the geographic bureaus, who feared encroachment on their turf. Secretary Rusk also seemed to be lukewarm, but told us to see what we could do. To mollify the bureaus we emphasized that the Op Center would be a centralized secretariat that would aid their work, not an independent source of power, and we established it under the aegis of the Executive Secretary. Within a year everyone wondered how they ever got along without it.

Since then its personnel, physical facilities, and communications equipment have grown and been refined. During any crisis, such as the 1973 Yom Kippur War, the evacuation of Saigon, or the seizure of our Teheran Embassy in 1979, the geographic bureau responsible will establish a task force in the Center with liaison personnel from the Pentagon, CIA, White House, and any other concerned agency. This becomes the nerve center for the operations of the entire government. The President, Secretary of State, Secretary of Defense, and other responsible officials can telephone to obtain the latest information on what is happening and what is being done. Nowadays, it seems like the invention of the wheel, its necessity and utility so obvious that everyone wonders why it was not done before.

The President and Rusk also had strong interest in improving the Department's scientific capabilities. Rusk's tenure at the Rockefeller Foundation had made him especially sensitive to the growing number of areas where science and foreign affairs overlapped. The peaceful uses of nuclear power, space vehicles, and satellite communications, the revolution in biology and its effects on food supplies, the problems of exporting sophisticated technology in electronics and other fields to potential enemies, and pollution of the seas and atmosphere all were complex international problems that no one country could solve unilaterally. All required the Department to display scientific competence. The President's Science Advisory Committee, on which I represented State, and the President's Science Advisor himself were also becoming increasingly importunate about our shortcomings in science. As a result the Department established in the spring of 1962 an Office of International Scientific Activities that was attached to my office. Our hope was to find an internationally distinguished scientist to head it, but none was ever willing to accept the position without obtaining some sort of guarantee that his views would be given precedence over those of everyone else in the Department. This no Secretary could tolerate. For a short time a less famous but very able scientist filled the job, but he found himself utterly at sea in the bureaucracy, and resigned when both of us recognized that it was just not working.

By default the office was left in the hands of its administrator, Herman Pollack, whose background was not in science. This worked out surprisingly well. He recruited the necessary experts, quickly became known in the scientific community, and most important, learned where to go in the Department and Washington for answers and results. He continued in the job up through most of the Nixon Administration.

I should also emphasize here George Ball's considerable role, first as Under Secretary for Economic Affairs and then Under Secretary replacing Bowles. He had great experience and competence in economic affairs and in our relations with Europe, and was highly respected in these fields. Our functions did not overlap much; his staff was fairly self-contained and he did not have my degree of interest in the Department's internal workings. Where we did overlap, we always had a very harmonious relationship. In fact Dean Rusk, George Ball, and I saw a great deal of each other, usually meeting over a drink before we went home in the evening.

My relations with Rusk were good, but, as was characteristic of him, not intimate. I was fortunate in that I was usually able to anticipate his views rather than having to wait for explicit instructions, which he was slow to give. We still followed the injunction he had given me during the Korean War: "Make the decisions you feel comfortable with, and I will back you up." My principal problem working with Dean was, as I sometimes gently complained to him, I did not know what he was doing. He played his cards very close to his chest. Unlike me, he refused to let his secretary monitor his phone conversations so that others could be informed of decisions made, information required, tasks assigned. He told me what he thought I needed to know, and only that. But his judgment was excellent; I cannot recall ever making a serious mistake because Dean had kept me in the dark.

Dean was also reticent about speaking up at interdepartmental meetings, especially when the President attended, surrounded by White House staff and others whom Dean regarded as hangers-on with no need to know. If he had advice to give, he would normally see the President before these meetings, perhaps with McNamara if a military matter was involved. Nor did he ever indulge in the temptation, very common among high officials, to report what the President told him privately. I think Dean modeled himself very much after his mentor, George Marshall, who was legendary in Washington for probity, competence, and a certain kind of remoteness.

I first met the President on April 22, the Saturday after I arrived in Washington, at a large National Security Council meeting he had called to discuss the disaster at the Bay of Pigs. All the senior officials of State, Defense, and CIA were present. In a masterly performance, the President described briefly what had gone wrong and emphasized that he took full responsibility for the disaster. He had made the decisions; he wanted no blame-shifting or recriminations. I certainly emerged from the meeting convinced that completely supporting the President in this was the only proper thing to do. At the time I was impressed, even a bit surprised, at how much self-confidence he manifested in the face of so embarrassing a reversal and how much courage it took for him to accept all the blame. In retrospect, I also see that he was a good politician, because his approach immediately quieted bureaucratic infighting that could have seriously divided and weakened the new Administration.

It was Bowles's failure to follow Kennedy's anti-backbiting order that sealed his fate in the new Administration. The following Monday, April 24, Bowles called me into his office and showed me, "in strictest confidence," a memorandum he had written opposing the Bay of Pigs. He soon disseminated this memo so widely that it became common gossip and eventually found its way into the newspapers. Bowles's appointment had been a concession to the Stevenson wing of the Democratic Party, and he and Kennedy had never been close. I noticed a distinct cooling between the two men following the Bay of Pigs leak. In a major shake-up of the Department in November, 1961, ratifying a decline in Bowles's authority that had taken place already, Bowles was removed as Under Secretary and replaced by George Ball, an international lawyer whose links to the Stevenson wing of the Democratic party were also good. George McGhee became Undersecretary for Political Affairs and Averell Harriman replaced Walter McConnaughy as Assistant Secretary for Far Eastern Affairs. Walt Rostow came over from Bundy's office to take George McGhee's place as Counselor.

But that gets ahead of our story. The week following the Bay of Pigs had me immersed in another foreign crisis equally messy and frustrating—Laos.

When we left the "Alice in Wonderland" world of Laotian politics in the previous chapter, the advance of Kong Le and the Pathet Lao in early 1961 toward the Mekong River and Thailand had been momentarily arrested. By April, Moscow had agreed to attend an international conference on the future of Laos that would lead toward some sort of neutralist government. The Soviets refused to agree to a cease fire until the details of the talks were ironed out, however, and no sign of interest in the conference came from the Pathet Lao. Onward they nibbled. Still, Moscow was not enthusiastic about provoking us into committing ground forces. If American troops stayed out, Khrushchev told the American Ambassador, Laos "will fall into our lap like a rotten apple." But when I arrived on April 17, it looked like someone was shaking the tree. Phoumi's grip was weakening further and there was talk of intervention according to SEATO Plan 5. The President was trying to force the conflict to the negotiating table by appearing ready to use force, and as a signal to the other side, our advisors to the Royal Laotian Army were ordered to wear their uniforms instead of civilian clothes. But we were quickly approaching the point where unless there was a genuine cease-fire, we would have to commit troops or decide to write Laos off.

On April 24, the Soviet Union finally joined with Britain (as co-chairmen of the 1954 Geneva Conference on Indochina) in issuing a public call for a cease-fire to go into effect on May 3. From the Pathet Lao there was no reply. The President had to face the possibility that the appearance of Soviet cooperation was only a sham. Ambassador Brown in Vientiane was requesting authority to employ A-26's against the Pathet Lao if the major remaining towns were threatened. On April 26 and 27 I attended meetings in the Cabinet Room with the President to work out our course of action. The President was under great pressure. The

Bay of Pigs was fresh in his mind and he was both wary of committing himself to an open-ended military adventure in Southeast Asia on the strength of half-baked advice, and aware that hesitation or the appearance of weakness would embolden the Soviets and Pathet Lao and open him to charges of having "lost Laos" and perhaps the rest of Southeast Asia, too.

The April 27 meeting was, to my mind at least, decisive. It started as a session of the NSC (with Bowles sitting in for Rusk, who was in Ankara, and Admiral Arleigh Burke representing JCS in the absence of its Chairman, General Lemnitzer), but it was later broadened by the President to include various Congressional leaders. The President said he was concerned that Vientiane itself would fall in the next twenty-four to forty-eight hours. If all the principal points in the country fell to the enemy there would be no point in having a conference with the Soviets, he said. Secretary McNamara and Admiral Burke presented the military alternative, SEATO Plan 5, but it was hardly encouraging. It envisioned landing 11,000 American troops in the major cities of the Mekong Valley in the first week, supplemented by 4,000 Thai soldiers and 2,000 Pakistani. Including the Laotians, our total input in thirty days would be 70,000 soldiers. The JCS said this was not enough. If the North Vietnamese or Chinese communists intervened, as well they might, the JCS estimated that they could put five soldiers in Laos for every one of ours. In this event the JCS thought we would have no alternative but to use nuclear weapons. Our strategic reserves were too low to permit a commitment of ground forces sufficient to do the job without nuclear support. A vivid image thus became fixed in the President's mind of a small band of beleaguered Americans stuck on the Vientiane airstrip while he contemplated resorting to nuclear war with China to rescue them.

The Joint Chiefs said they favored Plan 5 as the best way to deal with the communists' advance, but I thought Admiral Burkes's presentation of the risks involved did not take sufficient account of the formidable logistic obstacles the North Vietnamese and Chinese would have to face in deploying a major force down the Mekong. It was thus more pessimistic than the facts warranted. Burke said that we would either lose Southeast Asia without war or fight a "long, tough, hard war" that would eventually require nuclear weapons. The military was under-manned and had bad memories of Korea; perhaps the Joint Chiefs' way of avoiding another messy political war in Asia was to praise it with faint damns. After the military had finished its presentation, Acting Secretary Bowles also stressed the likelihood of Chinese intervention if we employed Plan 5.

The congressional leaders—Mansfield, Humphrey, Fulbright, Dirksen, Hickenlooper, Saltonstall, Russell, Bridges, Rayburn—faced with this gloomy assessment, opposed sending American troops to Laos. At the President's invitation, I then described the difficulties Thailand would face if Laos were overrun. I thought our best chance of avoiding war was to be seen as ready to use force. I was not advocating intervention, but I thought military signals would help. That was a tougher line than Bowles had taken, but I knew that Rusk agreed with me. Still, that did not make anyone enthusiastic about Plan 5. "I think the whole thing would be rather fruitless," said Mansfield. "When we got through we would have nothing to show for it," said Dirksen. "We should get our people out and write the country off," said Russell.

But if not Laos, then where would we draw the line? Some of the senators favored putting American troops in Vietnam and Thailand but letting Laos alone. The President thought deployments in Thailand might have merit as a signal of our resolve, but wanted to wait a few days to see what developed. In the meantime, he was still hoping for progress in Geneva, and asked the congressmen to guard against leaks, as our only effective card was communist uncertainty over whether we would fight. He did not commit himself either to intervene or not to at this meeting, but I felt the die had been cast against it.

In addition to the pessimism of the Joint Chiefs and the resistance of the congressional leaders, I believe another factor weighed heavily on President Kennedy to persuade him against Plan 5: the advice of General MacArthur. The President met with him in late April, just after MacArthur had returned from a visit to the Philippines, the same week as his meeting with the congressional leaders. Later, on July 20, he brought MacArthur back to Washington so that some others could hear what MacArthur had said. The Attorney General, a small group of senators and congressmen, and I were invited to a White House lunch at which the General held forth. He had obviously aged from when I had last seen him during the Korean War, but he was still in fine form. He spoke at length and with his usual eloquence against ever introducing any American troops in Southeast Asia under any circumstances. His argument was that they would be overwhelmed by the massed manpower of communist China. He felt we should draw our line elsewhere. Although I thought this view was not entirely rational—the number of troops that China could bring to bear in Southeast Asia being considerably limited by logistical difficulties—MacArthur's viewpoint appeared to make a deep impression on the President, somewhat less so on the congressional leaders. When sending American troops to Laos or Vietnam was later suggested, Kennedy often brought up General MacArthur's skepticism.

But our fears of late April were not realized. The Pathet Lao did stop before taking Vientiane. A cease-fire did go into effect, and on May 6, a fourteen-nation conference opened in Geneva to settle Laos, with feisty Averell Harriman, sometime Ambassador to Moscow and Governor of New York and now an Ambassador-at-Large, as the United States representative. We were not negotiating from strength, so Harriman's room to maneuver was limited. While he felt the Soviets wanted to avoid war in Laos, he was not so sure they had the capacity to restrain their more bellicose Chinese and North Vietnamese brethren. His best option seemed a political compromise that would put Souvanna Phouma, who had been in exile, at the head of a Laotian government that included the Pathet Lao and Phoumi. The President agreed.

There were many loose ends to tie up at Geneva to make sure the cease-fire held and the proposed government of national union was workable. Negotiations dragged on for months, and the other side kept up pressure by breaking the cease-fire. By late October 1961, the topic of contention was whether the International Control Commission (the body that would supervise the final agreement) would have automatic freedom to operate anywhere in Laos, or would have to obtain the approval of each of the three factions in the government every time it wanted to investigate something. Harriman felt we could not get any better than the latter alternative, but I, having unhappy memories of the way North Korea and North Vietnam had hamstrung their international supervisors, wanted us to hold out for inspection provisions with more teeth. With Undersecretary Bowles and Walter McConnaughy, Assistant Secretary for the Far East, I went to see the President in the evening of November 1 and, after a long talk, he asked me to come back early the next morning, when the two of us would talk with Averell in Geneva. We had a vigorous three-way exchange the next morning, with the President letting me do most of the talking. Averell declared his judgment that we could not get a better deal and that to hold out would tie down or break up the conference. I could not challenge his on-the-scene assessment, and the President told Averell to proceed.

Kennedy might also have thought that he had reached an understanding with Khrushchev on Laos at their Vienna summit meeting in July, so that perhaps it was not necessary to spell things out in too great detail. The President respected Averell's advice and wanted the agreement. Properly so, since we did not have much of an alternative. Also Kennedy was not given to looking very far ahead. If he had a weakness, it was his tendency to make today's decision today and let the future take care of itself. In this particular case, if the Laotian settlement ever had any hope of holding (which the politics of the region might well have excluded, whatever we got in Geneva), an ICC with teeth would have been essential. As it was, the Laos corridor from which the Viet Cong were supposed to withdraw under ICC supervision soon became a complex of pipelines and macadamed roads—an important part of the Ho Chi Minh Trail.

Despite the President's concession on the ICC, the conference dragged along inconclusively into the spring of 1962 while the Pathet Lao and North Vietnamese continued to push forward, improving their position on the ground and threatening the Lao government. When they captured the important communications hub of Nam Tha in May 1962, routing Phoumi's forces, and pushed toward the Thai border, the President deployed 5,000 American troops into northeast Thailand to demonstrate to the other side that he had not rejected military and to reassure the understandably nervous Thai. This halted the communist advance and enabled Souvanna Phouma to form something that resembled a government. It also induced the communists to settle at Geneva in June. Our troops remained in Thailand until the following December. This deployment, along with token participation from other SEATO countries, was the first time American troops were ever stationed in Southeast Asia. It should be recalled by those trying to assess what Kennedy's attitude might have been toward American ground troops in Vietnam.

The Geneva agreement provided for all foreign military personnel to withdraw within seventy-five days. We took ours out, though the North Vietnamese hardly made a pretence of it. We knew this was risky, but at least we wanted the onus of violating the agreement to be entirely on the other side. (We did, however, fund Phoumi's forces and Souvanna's government covertly to help them withstand the continuing North Vietnamese presence.) But in spite of everything, the agreement held—shakily. We concluded that the communists were willing for the time being to pursue Laos' conquest through the coalition government, as long as we kept troops in Thailand as a signal of our intention to fight if pressed, and did not press too hard to close the infiltration routes between Laos and South Vietnam.

Despite the relative calm, the country's politics continued to be labyrinthine. I toured Southeast Asia in December, 1962 and my informal report on Vientiane read:

> No one who has not experienced it can fully appreciate the incredible complex of factors and factions in the situation and the "Alice in Wonderland" atmosphere of what is essentially the village of Vientiane—three hundred personnel of the ICC sitting in camp waiting for something to do; Soviet planes and helicopters crowded on the airfield with those of Air America and the ICC helicopters; going from the door of an avowed rightist minister to that of an avowed Communist; plans for a police force with three chiefs, etc., etc. Our Country Team there is alert, has high morale, and seems to have as good a grasp of the situation as anyone could.
>
> While all the Laos talk glibly of plans and programs for integration of the armed forces, economic and political plans for the whole country, etc., it all seemed to have an air of unreality barring an unforseen and major conversion of Pathet Lao attitudes.

I noted, for example, that the new government budget showed revenues of $8 million and expenditures of $50 million. "The best we can hope for in the foreseeable future is a continuation of the present de facto situation with Souvanna Phouma continuing to hold a leaky but important umbrella over it. For such a situation to continue, it will be important that issues not be forced." The only thing worth forcing, to my mind, was effective operation of the ICC, especially in patrolling Laos's border with South Vietnam where the North Vietnamese were infiltrating. As far as the fantastic rivalries went between Phoumi, Souvanna, the Pathet Lao, Kong Le, and a new group of dissident Kong Le forces, I thought we should let time play itself out, but stand ready to supply Souvanna and Phoumi with means to resist if the Pathet Lao played dirty.

Part of our underlying hope was that Souvanna might eventually gravitate towards Phoumi on his own, transforming the balance in the internal political debate from Souvanna and the Pathet Lao versus Phoumi, as it had been, to Souvanna and Phoumi against the Pathet Lao. And this seemed to be occurring in December, when I wrote in my report: "Souvanna Phouma is now very outspoken on his primary difficulties with the Pathet Lao. Relations between him and the Phoumi group appear to be increasingly good."

We faced many more trials in Laos: assassinations of friendly figures by Pathet Lao, communist attempts to take over Kong Le's neutralist forces, even a wholesale attack on them by Pathet Lao and North Vietnamese troops when the takeover attempt failed. But we exerted pressure through Moscow and the temperature lowered once more. In any case, the arena of the communists' attentions was now shifting to South Vietnam. With Laos non-Western and their supply lines through it "overseen" by an impotent ICC they had all they needed for their offensive against South Vietnam. The interesting question is whether American forces could have been used in Laos then with sufficient effectiveness to have prevented the North Vietnamese from establishing the Ho Chi Minh Trail into South Vietnam, thus checking the escalation of the war into the south. We probably lacked the means to do this; certainly we lacked the will.

Besides Laos, the country that attracted the most concern in my first months in Washington was Cuba. Our failure at the Bay of Pigs had many consequences for the policies and machinery of the new Administration. The President was shocked and deeply disturbed by how inept the planning for the operation was, how it slipped through the senior echelons of the government, and how much the whole fiasco made him and the United States seem weak and indecisive. To conduct an inquiry into the affair he tapped my old friend from Japanese language school days, Max Taylor, Army Chief of Staff under Eisenhower. After leaving Washington he had written a book, *The Uncertain Trumpet*, to protest the Eisenhower cuts in conventional forces over which he had presided. It had been well received, notably by the Kennedy entourage. In 1961 Max was the Executive Director of Lincoln Center for the Performing Arts in New York. Literate, persuasive, an excellent linguist, Max was the very image of what a New Frontier general should be. When Kennedy asked him to be his Military Representative, a new office attached to the White House created for him, Max was somewhat skeptical. He did not wish to become a professional gadfly without administrative powers, and was reluctant to leave his nice set-up at Lincoln Center. But he knew his duty. Max and I were to share many causes together as we sought to revamp the bureaucracy in our different but overlapping spheres.

It greatly provoked President Kennedy and his brother, Robert, that the United States, the greatest military power in the world engaged in a global struggle against communism, could not keep its own doorstep free of Marxist revolutionaries. They considered Castro an affront and wanted him out even after the Bay of Pigs had shown how difficult that would be. A Special Group (Augmented) was established, on which I served, to oversee the activities of Edward Lansdale in mounting covert operations against Castro's regime that eventually, it was hoped, would lead to a popular insurrection against him. This campaign was known as Operation Mongoose; and I will return to it later.

The President, looking at Vietnam, Laos, and Thailand as well as Cuba, and hearing Premier Khrushchev's repeated endorsements of "Wars of National Liberation," believed we were facing a new kind of war throughout the world that we were not prepared to fight. Since World War II our emphasis had been on deterring the "big war," a major confrontation with the Soviet Union. For that we needed atomic weapons, missiles, large and highly-organized forces. The Soviets knew they could not win any such war, the President thought, so their strategy had shifted. Now they were trying to pick off developing countries one by one from within. With money, supplies, covert action, training, and political pressure, the Kremlin was helping small bands of communists in those countries use terrorism and guerilla warfare to destabilize governments whose links with their people were already inherently tenuous. ICBMs and big divisions could not fight this kind of war. Though we were not strangers to it—our Revolutionary War, Indian Wars, and conquest of the Philippines after 1898 had taught us about irregular war from both sides—a great deal had been forgotten in the drive for technological sophistication. The President wanted a major overhaul of organization, procedures, doctrine, and equipment throughout the government to make sure we could counter Kremlin-sponsored subversion of existing governments around the globe.

On January 18, 1962, the President established the Special Group (Counter-Insurgency) through National Security Action Memorandum (NSAM) 124. Max Taylor was Chairman; other members included Attorney General Bobby Kennedy, Deputy Secretary of Defense Ros Gilpatric, CIA Director Allen Dulles (and then John McCone), National Security Advisor McGeorge Bundy, United States Information Agency Director Ed Murrow, AID Administrator Fowler Hamilton, JCS Chairman Lyman Lemnitzer, and me. Our job was "to insure proper recognition throughout the United States government that subversive insurgency ('wars of liberation') is a major form of politico-military conflict equal in importance to conventional warfare." We were charged with reviewing all the government's resources for the internal defense of nations under attack from communist insurgents and making recommendations for strengthening such nations. We were also told to keep a special eye on Vietnam, Laos, and Thailand. This NSAM was the culmination of many discussions within the government, so it marked not the start of work on counter-insurgency, but its formalization.

In view of the importance the President attached to our work, we first met the same day. At the outset we established some useful ground rules: one meeting weekly for two hours, with no substitute members or rescheduling permitted. These rules insured that our sessions would be efficient, and decisions would not have to be postponed while superiors were consulted. There had already been considerable discussion about whether the Group should be an executive agency outside and above the existing departments, able to initiate actions throughout the government on its own authority, or a more usual sort of committee that would refer back our recommendations to our respective departments. Bobby Kennedy, the Defense Department, and to some extent the President never quite brought themselves to accept the fact that we were coordinating the departments instead of directing them. I always took the view that our decisions could have no meaning except insofar as we implemented them through our departments, which alone had the authority to allocate money and people to make them work. I do not believe the President always understood this. He typically wanted fast results and was inclined to feel that if he put somebody in charge of something, this person would be able to give directions that the departments would have to carry out. But creating jobs outside the chain of command expecting them to stand Washington on its head ignored the realities of power in the government, and the Congress, which hold the departments and their secretaries responsible for the way funds and personnel are allocated. This tension about the way the Special Group (CI) should run itself continued throughout its existence, though for the most part it was accepted that we acted on behalf of our departments.

None of us really liked the term "counter-insurgency," which sounded too negative. "Internal defense" would have been better to my mind, but General Taylor said the President had deliberately chosen counter-insurgency and counter-insurgency it remained. It was a vast, complex subject, whatever we called it. We worked very hard at thinking through what subversive insurgency really meant in the many different countries and cultures where it appeared, at devising programs to counter it, and at pushing these through the government. First we had extensive briefings on the political, economic, and military situations in Vietnam, Laos, Thailand, Iran, Indonesia, and other countries faced with internal defense problems, and these were supplemented with regular progress reports. From the experiences of these individual countries we tried to develop an appreciation of the nature of subversive insurgency generally. Revolutions were not always hostile to our interests, as our own history showed, and we did not want to adopt a blanket policy of opposing all change, even violent change, in developing countries. What we wished to combat was letting small groups of native communists confiscate the revolutionary process and convert it to their own ends.

After many months of debate and interdepartmental drafting, our views about what we were up against and how we should and should not combat it were embodied in a document chiefly written by State, with Charles Maechling a member of my politico-military staff taking the lead, entitled "United States Overseas Internal Defense Policy," better known as the "CI Bible." It pointed out that many factors contributed to the internal disorder that dedicated minority groups could prey upon to divert popular or group grievances into channels of their own. For one thing, the two superpowers, both wanting to avoid nuclear war, were intensifying other forms of competition. It was common for political groups in these countries to appeal for outside support, both ideological and practical, and communist ideology stressed the role of violent revolution. Developing countries were malleable, still recovering from the dislocations of World War II, still lacking established institutions and trained personnel, still facing great poverty, huge disparities in income distribution, migrations of rural peasants into cities, and a general revolution of rising expectations. Forty-three countries had become independent in the seventeen years since World War II; many of them had bitter colonial memories and a built-in dislike of the West. There was, the "CI Bible" stated, a "susceptibility of developing societies to dissidence and violence which can be exploited by the communists," and this "requires the development of indigenous capabilities to cope with the threat to internal security in each of its forms."

We believed that military measures alone were not the answer, that the United States had always to keep in mind that the *"ultimate and decisive target was the people."* As the "CI

Bible" continued: "The primary purpose of internal defense programs is to deal with and eliminate the *causes* of dissidence and
violence." And so our internal defense programs had to employ
every asset we could muster, from better information work abroad
to intensified economic development, to training local police in
non-violent crowd control. We also had to recognize that our
chances for success would be poor if the local government was
seriously inept or ill-motivated, because the problems and conflicts that encouraged insurgency could only really be indige-
nously redressed.

Neither the military nor the rest of the government was
used to defining its mission abroad as bringing economic and
political change to developing countries. With the "Bible" written, we thus had to spread the gospel. One of our first priorities
was to establish an extensive system of courses on internal defense.
Within a year, more than 50,000 people, mostly military, went
through such courses at the National War College, the various
Service colleges, and elsewhere. Our laws and traditions keep the
military out of politics, and they are trained to think that politics
stops when war starts. It was quite a change for the officers we
sent as military advisors to developing countries to think more
deeply about the root causes of the violence to which they were
supposed to design an effective response.

I took advantage of the counter-insurgency bandwagon to
establish an interdepartmental seminar for all senior personnel,
including ambassadors, being assigned to underdeveloped areas.
My interest was not only in counter-insurgency, narrowly defined,
but in the broader area of how the United States Government as
a whole could better bring to bear its human and material resources in cooperating with other countries in their efforts to
achieve development. To the degree that we could succeed in
aiding development, the conditions giving rise to insurgency
would be removed. The seminar was designed to bring together
senior American personnel before they went to their posts to give
them a common sense of the total mission and their role in it.
These people were often of extremely disparate backgrounds—
former journalists now in USIA, military officers from Military
Assistance and Advisory Groups (MAAG'S), economists for AID,
agronomist agriculture advisors. We could never have expected
an ambassador in the field to wave a wand over them as they
arrived and somehow convert them into a coordinated team with
a common approach. But a shared curriculum in Washington,
even if short, at least started imbuing a team approach. Eventually

this experimental five-week course grew into the Foreign Affairs Interdepartmental Seminar that continues to exist.

To promote further a unified approach in the field, we required the Country Teams in the countries concerned to develop a common Internal Defense Plan to orchestrate all Mission programs. These were sent to the Special Group (CI) for approval. Whenever we received an especially innovative approach, we would disseminate it to other Missions.

Because many of the countries we wanted to protect from communist takeover already facing sizeable guerrilla violence, the CI devoted considerable attention to examining and redesigning our programs for advising, supplying, and training paramilitary and military forces in developing countries. Armies in these countries were often politically powerful and resisted changes in organization or doctrine that would upset the promotion system or their privileges. They were often organized (on previous American advice) along traditional regimental and divisional lines that were obsolete when the military opponent was a guerrilla. As I told a National War College audience on June 11, 1962,

> Perhaps a well-trained policeman on the corner would be much more pertinent to the country's problem than an F-104. Perhaps a self-contained, lightly armed company of gendarmerie equipped with light air transport, perhaps bicycles, and efficient communications equipment, would be much more pertinent to a country's problem than a battalion equipped with a full complement of artillery, tanks, and trucks unable to move over non-existent roads.

But though in many cases our objective was to have our military advisory groups encourage the transformation of traditionally organized armies into small units armed with modern light equipment, this was often hard to accomplish because our own military felt comfortable only with traditional American-type organization: battalions, regiments, and divisions with their standard tables of organization and equipment. This was particularly true in Vietnam, where a different approach was badly needed at the time.

Somewhat more successfully, we encouraged the local military to take up substantial "civic action" projects, such as building schools and roads and improving sanitation and communications, to spur development and bind the military more closely to the population. These were particularly successful in Indonesia. We recast the courses that military officers from developing countries attended in the United States to reflect the special problems they faced in internal defense. We also encouraged the Pentagon to undertake research and development into new equipment for counterinsurgency. Village alarm systems, defoliants to reduce cover near roads for guerrillas, and better ground support aircraft were a few of the items studied. On a 1962 inspection trip to Vietnam, I discovered that the Army had no walkie-talkie capable of penetrating the jungle canopy beyond a mile, so I set the Signal Corps to work on it. It took an inordinate amount of time for these projects to grind through the Pentagon's labyrinthine procedures for research, development, authorization, and procurement. AID also faced the same problem in developing and buying devices pertinent to the needs of local police forces. So in both military and police research & development (R & D) we found ourselves turning to the CIA, not because the projects were inherently covert but because the CIA had the flexibility, both internal and legislative, and the imagination to do the job required.

Our own military forces were administered a stiff dose of CI medicine, too. President Kennedy was particularly enamored of our own Special Forces (Green Berets), and more were created. Their job was to train and lead local anti-insurgent paramilitary groups. On February 5, 1962, I visited their training center at Fort Bragg, North Carolina, with Max Taylor. I was certainly impressed by their spirit and demonstration of fitness and elan. But I also thought emphasis might profitably be placed on developing more sophisticated tactics for countering guerrillas. For example, if you had to protect your troops from fire coming from a village, how could you defend yourself without shooting civilians? How could you better distinguish enemy from friend?

Soon after their training was expanded to cover the special skills that a MAAG, faced with a sudden insurgency, might need in its advisors: psychological warfare, engineering, civic action, and public information. The CI also endorsed a policy of training Green Beret-like forces in the developing countries themselves and even of considering the use of these forces in third countries, should local forces or our Green Berets be inappropriate. The Montagnards in Vietnam were such a group.

Though the Green Berets were impressive, there was always a fundamental conceptual problem about how they should be used. The original purpose of their organization, equipment, and training was for them to act as guerrillas themselves and to form guerrilla units from within the local population behind enemy lines in a conventional conflict. The difficulty arose in trying to use guerrillas as defend against other guerrillas. It made sense on the surface, but did not turn out to be so easy in practice. The Green Berets also suffered from never being fully accepted by the army "regulars," and their separate command channels in Vietnam eventually created resentment and friction.

Other departments besides the Pentagon were also assigned important roles in internal defense. The Agency for International Development had charge of furnishing emergency economic assistance to areas under attack or threat, of coordinating civilian economic assistance and military civic action programs to maximize their usefulness, and its more usual function of providing technical assistance and funds for overall long-term economic development. In the ten years previous to 1962, 55,000 students from developing countries had come to the United States for training in fields from health to public administration under AID technical assistance programs, and these were stepped up. AID's basic task was to help develop the economic and social conditions that would promote orderly change in a country's government and institutions. AID officials often looked at their work as quite divorced from the shorter-term goals of American foreign policy, and resisted getting involved in the "dirty" business of internal defense.

I think this attitude was partly Chester Bowles's doing. He was chiefly responsible for changing the name of our foreign assistance programs to "AID," from the previous International Cooperation Administration (ICA), whereas I thought this change conveyed an unfortunate impression of superiority and largesse on our part. He also sold the concept that our assistance programs should be dictated solely by "clean" economic considerations, unsullied by politics, and Fowler Hamilton, the AID Administrator, bought this idea. Theoretically it was fine, but practically there are few things more political than giving away money. The Special Group (CI) insisted that in some countries AID's long-term objective would have to take second place to more urgent internal defense requirements. Only after some persuasion did AID accept this obvious truth.

The Special Group CI also approved an increase in USIA programs for internal defense. Most important was providing equipment and technical assistance to governments in public information and internal communication. As I had seen in Thailand, one of the most vexing problems these governments faced was simply communicating with the populace, especially peasants and those living in outlying areas. USIA helped distribute radio sets and advised on how to make government broadcasts interesting and trustworthy. I myself had seen in Thailand what a difference a few low-powered television transmitters and a receiving set in the village square had meant in the ability of the government to communicate with its citizens.

The CIA was directed to increase its assistance to intelligence and counterintelligence work in appropriate countries, to increase R & D in its area of expertise, and to look out specially for incipient insurgencies in its world-wide intelligence assessments. The Agency also continued its very successful projects to organize the Montagnards in Vietnam (later transferred to the Defense Department) and the hill tribes in Laos.

One of the most important and sensitive elements of internal defense efforts cost no money at all: getting the governments concerned to adopt them. We deliberately eschewed a narrowly military definition of the problems of insurgency; the "Bible" explicitly recognized that the fundamental problem was political and economic and could not be solved unless local governments took steps to redress popular grievances. But as I wrote in the July 1962 Foreign Service Journal ("Internal Defense and the Foreign Service," pp. 20–23):

> Here we leave the relatively safe confines of military and economic assistance and enter the delicate province of a country's internal affairs. To bring about some degree of social, economic and political justice, or at the very least to ameliorate the worst causes of discontent and redress the most flagrant inequities, will invariably require positive action by the local government. In some cases only radical reforms will obtain the necessary results. Yet the measures we advocate may strike at the very foundations . . . of the government's control.

There was no easy way around this problem, for many Third World elites were quite right in perceiving modernization as a threat to their continued power. The only way we could attempt to get around it within the limits of diplomacy was to identify potential insurgencies at the earliest possible moment and persuade the governments to adopt remedial measures while time was still on their side. The amount of influence an ambassador could exert on a government that was determined to parry, procrastinate, or subvert was small.

We ought also to recognize, I believed, that American advice might not always be worth taking. These countries did not offer simple problems or solutions, as both Thailand and Laos in their different ways had shown me, and Americans were not singularly privileged interpreters of the Third World. There is a very delicate balance between proper advice and overbearing interference, and I think I understood as well as any member of the Special Group that strong pressure from Washington and from themselves for succeeding in internal defense might push some ambassadors (and other Mission members) over the line. Because there could be no success whatever unless the local government had the will and capacity to help itself, however, the ambassador as persuader held a pivotal role in our counter-insurgency programs that could not be finessed.

In all the debate that led to issuance of the "Bible," I pressed very hard to make sure the ambassador was acknowledged to be responsible for all internal defense programs. Though Defense, CIA, USIA, and AID had important roles to play, proper direction and control over programs so complex and sensitive could only be provided by a single person, of necessity the ambassador. If he could not do the job, he should be replaced. The "Bible" did in fact give ambassadors this primary responsibility and I considered that an important accomplishment.

The CI Group and the Administration generally also wanted our people in developing countries to avoid taking an overly simplistic view of the "communist threat." We recognized that the United States had lost ground under Eisenhower and Dulles by acting as if those who were not our friends were our enemies, instead of allowing for more diversity. I told a National War College audience in June 1962:

> Representative democracy is usually *not* the goal [sought by developing countries]. Neither capitalist free enterprise nor socialism is the goal per se. But in most of these societies there is a practical rather than an ideological attraction to state management of the economy. State-instituted land reform and industrialization often seem the only practicable means to progress.

So I advised them to look deeper than the common practice among politicians in developing countries of attaching the label "socialist" to everything they admired. Why should that raise hackles when American politicians, diligently denouncing socialism, voted for Tennessee Valley Authority (TVA) and Social Security? We did not care about labels. What we did care about in the developing world, I told the Marines at Quantico in July, 1963, was "only that states not be the tool of our enemy. If they are maintaining their own independent existence and are determined to do so, we have a basis for working with them".

Another aspect of the Special Group (CI)'s work in which I became heavily involved was redirecting and expanding our programs to advise and equip the police forces in developing countries. Normally police are the most visible and important link between a government and its people. Professional and disciplined police can be a powerful and positive influence in winning for the government the "consent of the governed". An untrained and lawless police can cause the opposite effect. We have seen this amply demonstrated in our own country, and it is even more true in an underdeveloped society.

In April, 1962, I was made chairman of a government committee consisting of all the concerned agencies, including the CIA and FBI, to study our entire effort in this field. We examined, in the words of the NSAM that established us, the "training of foreign police forces of the newly emerging countries to insure that order can be maintained without excessive use of violence".

The problems police faced in developing countries were vast. They often lacked competent supervisors or literate rank and file and suffered from obsolete techniques, poor training, and inadequate equipment. The criminal justice systems of which they were the most visible part were often corrupt and violated individual rights, making the police themselves suspect. And our earlier police assistance programs, my committee discovered, had not come close to being able to cope with this complex of stubborn problems.

The committee reported on July 20, 1962. We advised expanding our foreign police assistance programs significantly, doubling within the first year (to about $25 million) and growing afterwards as necessary. The cost of equipping and maintaining the average policeman was one fifth that of the average soldier, yet the police were often more central to internal defense. Our report said the police were a "very important but neglected part of our intensified effort to help emerging nations counter subversion and insurgency."

The most important recommendation was for tighter and more vigorous management. The disarray of our present programs had prompted Defense to make a bid for taking over the tattered remnants from the administration of AID, but I and others strongly resisted that in what soon developed into a monumental bureaucratic struggle. We wanted the emphasis (and image abroad) of our police programs to be civilian, not military. But we also said that AID must significantly upgrade the quantity and quality of its public safety advisors, and that the police programs must be reorganized to give them greater clout within the Agency. Byron Engle, a sophisticated professional with long experience abroad, was brought into AID to direct the entire program, and our recommendations were carried out. A new Inter-American Police Academy, first created in Panama, was soon absorbed into a new International Police Academy in Washington, which had funds and personnel adequate to the task of professionalizing the many police forces it served. Within five years over 1500 officers from forty-three countries attended it.

During the anti-police, anti-military reactions of the 1960s and 70s in this country, stories were circulated to discredit this police program on the ground that we were teaching police how to torture, kill, and terrorize. Nothing could have been farther from the truth. The Americans associated with the program were trained and disciplined professionals, and every truly professional police officer knows that torture and terror are in the end counterproductive. If these practices occurred in any police forces with whom we had association, they were not inspired or condoned by any American. And to disband the police program because of these accusations would have been to disband our useful instrument for discouraging the practices the accusers spoke of, as well as one of our most important instruments for assisting in a country in orderly development. Yet in time, the program was disbanded and has not been active since.

I believe our police assistance programs have been beneficial to the people of the countries involved. Their objective has been to make the police more humane, more concerned with justice in its full sense, as well as more efficient. The objectives we stipulated for our police programs were not only to strengthen civil police and paramilitary forces to enforce the law with the minimum use of violence and to counter communist-inspired insurgency, but to "encourage the development of responsible and humane police and administration and judicial procedure to improve the character and image of civil police and paramilitary forces, and bind them more closely to the community". The rule of law, which alone could guarantee basic rights as well as the catching of insurgents, needed truly professional law enforcement. And, not incidentally, such law enforcement was far less expensive in every way than attempting massive build-ups of local military forces.

In October 1962 General Taylor left his job as the President's military troubleshooter and became JCS Chairman, which meant he also gave up his chair of the Special Group (CI). Considerable discussion ensued as to who should replace him. By this point we had done most of our ground-breaking work and it seemed an appropriate time to move the Special Group out of the White House into the State Department where, by normal bureaucratic function, it ought to have been. Dean Rusk, Mac Bundy, and I agreed about this, but Bobby Kennedy was very eager to assume the chair of the CI himself, for the Group was his only post in the government, other than the National Security Council, where he could reflect his interest in foreign affairs.

Unfortunately, under his prodding the CI had sometimes ranged pretty far afield from its original agreed charter to consider unrelated foreign and defense policy questions; and it was certainly not desirable to give Bobby a platform where he could become a shadow Secretary of State, especially given his hope to make the Special Group an executive rather than a coordinating body. Nor did the Pentagon or we in State feel that the Attorney General should properly chair this kind of committee. In order to keep Bobby a member while putting the Special Group more firmly within the established departments, it was agreed after discussion with the President to keep the Special Group under White House auspices with me as Chairman and Mike Forrestal replacing General Taylor as the White House representative. I was thus placed in the position of chairing a committee when I was junior in official rank to some of its other members, notably one who was a Cabinet Secretary.

My most delicate problem was keeping the Group to what I felt were its proper responsibilities while letting Bobby feel that he was participating in a meaningful way. The normal processes of the government were not, after all, working too badly, and even if they had not been working properly, the Special Group was certainly not a good place to try to do anything about it. Bobby, thoughtful and generous though he could be, was also ruthless when protecting what he thought were the President's interests; and though my personal relations with him were always good, I found him, as a member of the CI, something of an unguided missile. He tended to come to meetings unprepared, which was understandable, given his many other tasks, but he bore down unmercifully on subordinate officials to shake them up. His prosecutor's manner, especially with AID, undoubtedly accomplished a useful purpose, but I thought these shakings up sometimes degenerated into browbeating and that he sometimes forgot that junior officials had difficulty talking back to the Attorney General who was also the President's brother. On one occasion, an army colonel made a somewhat inept presentation on the development of walkie-talkies for the jungle. Bobby was so disgusted that he got up, slammed his chair into the table, stalked out of the room, and slammed the door, leaving behind a very shaken colonel.

I did not believe this was a proper way to treat the Special Group or the officer involved, and I felt I should have done a better job protecting him. I talked to Mac Bundy and the Secretary and asked to be relieved as Chairman. After some discussion it was agreed that Averell Harriman, then serving as Under Secretary for Political Affairs, would take my place. Harriman had faced down Stalin and had a reputation in the country and with the President, independent of his official rank, that led everyone to think that he would be able to handle Bobby better than I had. As it turned out, I do not think Averell was very much more effective in controlling Bobby, who was simply too strong-minded and vigilant on his brother's behalf. Despite these difficulties, it was my experience that Bobby's instincts were sound on the important issues.

Another involvement I had with the Attorney General that demonstrated his sound instincts coupled with an impatience about practicalities came over psychological warfare. An aspect of Kremlin success abroad that particularly galled the President and his brother was the apparent ease with which the Soviets could orchestrate demonstrations of young people around the world against the United States. During the Berlin crisis in 1961, when Khrushchev was threatening to evict the Western powers from the western sector of the city, "rent-a-mobs" protesting against the United States swept through many cities, particularly in Western Europe. Bobby was upset that we seemed unable to put our point of view across effectively in foreign countries, especially to labor and student groups who he thought should be attracted by the idealism and activism of the Administration. Accordingly he called the State Department, the CIA, and USIA to task. Max Taylor was given the job of seeing whether we might not do a better job of mobilizing public opinion abroad.

It was clear that Bobby did not think or know much about what we were already doing in this field, so on August 12, Taylor, Allen Dulles, Ed Murrow, and I met with him to discuss it. Murrow, Dulles, and I explained our existing programs and took the position that while there might be more we could do, we believed we had been about as effective as we could be using overt means. This evidently did not satisfy the Attorney General. First he pressed the appointment of a Presidential committee of private citizens to make recommendations for strengthening our activities in this area. Nothing came of this. Then on August 31, after a conversation between the two Kennedys and Secretary Rusk, I attended another meeting on this same subject with the same people, plus Arthur Goldberg, Secretary of Labor. Goldberg proposed the immediate formation of a "Psychological Warfare Board." I expressed considerable skepticism, but Bobby was all for it. Since the others did not oppose, I tried to steer the project in as constructive a direction as possible. Max suggested that C.D. Jackson, Eisenhower's psychological warfare chief who had become editor of *Fortune*, chair the board, and we agreed on some other members as well. I drafted the letter the President sent inviting them to serve, got them briefed about our present activities, and attended a meeting between them and the Attorney General. Alas, he was not impressed, so this approach fell through.

Finally, as often happens when political authority has a favorite project it cannot quite figure out how to implement, it was suggested that a Special Assistant be appointed to handle it. I thought that this was probably the best idea so far and supported it at a meeting with Bobby on September 11. I believed there would inevitably be conflicts with the Secretary if an important new foreign policy post were based in the White House, and creating another Under Secretary would take time and legislation, and would point worrisomely to a profusion of Under Secretaries. A Special Assistant to the Secretary seemed the best bet. This view was accepted. In October, several names were discussed for the Secretary's Special Assistant, including Douglas Cater and Clark Mollenhoff, but in the end nothing specific was done because no candidate both suitable and acceptable to the White House was found. This disappointed Bobby. I ended up taking charge of psychological warfare for a while, and when George Ball replaced Chet Bowles in November I happily transferred the function to him.

This story provides an object lesson on how to operate in Washington. I understood the frustration of the President and his brother during the Berlin crisis. If the Soviets could get out mobs to shout slogans, smash windows, and mount big demonstrations, why couldn't we do the same? From the start, however, I thought it was a bad idea to try to create a similar capability within our government machinery. It had not worked under Eisenhower, and I was not sure we would want to stage manage foreign demonstrations even if we could accomplish it. I also thought that whatever "psychological warfare" we conducted must flow directly from our broader foreign policy. They are not distinct spheres that can be bureaucratically separated.

With the pressure to retaliate against the Soviets so strong, I could not attack the idea head on, especially given its authors, but I thought it would fall of its own weight. I was not trying to sabotage Bobby's efforts, but I also knew that he was ignorant of how much had been wasted in this area already. I could not very well tell Bobby directly that his idea was stupid; I just let it speak for itself, and eventually it did.

Having a Marxist regime seventy miles from American soil worried President Kennedy and offended him. Castro provided a base of operations for expanding Soviet influence in Latin America and made the United States look impotent and rather foolish. His takeover also seemed a classic example of how a tiny core of dedicated Marxists could ride to power on a wave of popular resentment against an unpopular government, subverting and destroying the non-Marxist majority of revolutionaries after obtaining power. This was the counterinsurgency problem we faced world-wide. But the President felt personally humiliated by a communist Cuba, and toppling Castro became something of an obsession for him.

After General Taylor's review of the Bay of Pigs had been completed, Edward Lansdale was given an office in the Defense Department to act as "Coordinator of Cuban Affairs" with a wide mandate to "do something" about Cuba. Lansdale was famous as the director of those CIA operations in the Philippines that had helped Defense Secretary Ramon Magsaysay defeat communist insurgents in Luzon during the 1950s. The "something" he envisioned was mostly covert actions, using Cuban emigres in Florida and native anti-communists to keep the Castro regime off balance. These were supposed to mount in tempo and intensity until a popular insurrection toppled the government. This covert program was known as Operation Mongoose, and to oversee it a committee called the Special Group (Augmented) was created. It consisted of Taylor, CIA Director McCone, Deputy Defense Secretary Gilpatric, Bobby Kennedy, JCS Chairman Lemnitzer, and me.

It was a very secret operation. Lansdale's shop was put in the inner inner sanctum of the Pentagon and had complete carte blanche to use all the assets of the United States Government to bring Castro down. The Special Group (Augmented) never discussed assassinating Castro, and I never had any knowledge of any plan for doing so. (Though I fail to see a moral distinction between killing a sentry and killing his chief; both are abhorrent.) Rather, a huge CIA station in Miami under William Harvey was Lansdale's operational arm, and elaborate plans were developed for fomenting a full-scale rebellion (which, if successful, would have probably resulted in Castro's death).

Recognizing that internal circumstances in Cuba were not right for a quick overthrow, however, the Special Group (Augmented) agreed that the United States should first concentrate on acquiring hard data about possible targets, infiltrating the island with exile guerrilla teams, recruiting local agents, isolating Cuba economically and diplomatically, mounting covert actions that would disrupt the economy, and planning for decisive military intervention. But none of this was to get to the point of inspiring a revolt in Cuba that would require American military intervention to sustain it. We wanted to test the waters before jumping in with both feet. At the same time, we did not want anti-communist groups in Cuba to give up hope for liberation or provoke their counterparts in Florida into mounting irresponsible unilateral actions from our soil.

Lansdale directed this campaign of harassment. A submarine off the coast made broadcasts as if it were an indigenous guerrilla group. Agents were recruited. Locomotives and trucks were sabotaged with contaminated oil. Oil tankers were put out of commission. A substantial propaganda effort was made in Latin America with movies, comic books, broadcasts, and other media to discredit Castro's brand of communism. Even after a huge expenditure of time and money, however, the mass insurrection for which we hoped these covert operations would be the catalyst showed no signs of materializing. Lansdale was always gung-ho and Harvey even more so, but the CIA leadership and the Special Group (Augmented) recognized that we were able only to create the image of movement, not the real thing. Though conditions in the country were not good, few people actively opposed Castro. By March, 1962, even the President said he was skeptical that a revolt in Cuba would ever get to the point where United States troops would be required to help it, though he wanted contingency planning to continue.

By the middle of that year, Operation Mongoose fizzled out, and it was formally wrapped up after the Cuban Missile Crisis. The State Department then established its own Coordinator of

Cuban Affairs to regain the initiative from Defense and head off any attempts to establish a Coordinator in the White House.

The President and all of us on the Special Group (Augmented) were frustrated by our inability to turn Operation Mongoose into an effective enterprise. Bobby once said, "We are in a combat situation [with Castro] and we have complete command. There is no excuse for failure. There is no reason that the richest, most powerful nation in the world can't do this." But the covert tools of Mongoose were just not adequate to the task. We could have toppled Castro had the President been willing to order an all-out invasion of Cuba, but he did not want to use American force in such a crude and overweening way. Though he stood strongly behind Mongoose and encouraged Lansdale to use his ingenuity, when it came down to approving specific covert actions that had fairly high "noise" levels, he would often draw back. And rightly so, I thought. There were intense bureaucratic conflicts between Defense, CIA, and Lansdale—another example of the President putting someone "in charge" and expecting the government to heel, with indifferent results—but this did not seriously influence what was destined to be an unsuccessful outcome.

I never had moral qualms about Mongoose—I thought Castro was a real threat and that we should make as much trouble for him as we could. But I never thought much of the operation, either. It was the sort of thing we are never very good at. One of the projects Harvey's group dreamed up typifies to me how ludicrous "dirty tricks" can get and why we should not rely on them as an arm of policy except in extreme circumstances. Cuba's economy depended largely on sugar exports, and because we had closed off the American market the Soviet bloc countries were buying it up. Harvey's people developed an idea to inject a drug into a cargo ship full of sugar bound for Eastern Europe that would make people very, but not fatally, ill. This was supposed to frighten them off future purchases. Harvey's people actually managed to do it. The ship had sailed by the time the Special Group (Augmented) got wind of this, but luckily it had to put in to the Virgin Islands for repairs. We bought up the whole cargo and dumped it.

A major overt effort aimed at isolating the Castro regime involved attempting to cut off Western shipping to Cuba. This proved to be exceedingly difficult. Many countries, even those sympathetic to our objective, had no legal way to do it. Countries offering flags of convenience, like Lebanon and Panama, had virtually no control over "their" ships. We tried refusing American port and bunkering facilities to ships trading with Cuba, but this had many loopholes. If, for instance, one British vessel traded with Cuba, we could hardly take sanctions against all British vessels. So instead of keeping score by country, we tried going after companies that owned errant vessels by taking sanctions against all their vessels. Ship ownership is extremely difficult to trace, however, and even companies that had certified they would not trade with Cuba would endeavor to mislead us by using dummy firms. In the end the only practicable way to enforce sanctions was to do it vessel by vessel, which required lots of reconaissance, record-keeping and effort. And of course the whole system was completely ineffective against ships that did not want to use American ports. I was in the middle or this, trying to keep the ball rolling while sorting out interdepartmental conflicts and pacifying irate foreign embassies. But I was never very optimistic. It caused some embarrassment to Cuba and increased the cost to the Soviet Union of supporting Cuba, but I doubt that this balanced the tremendous effort expended.

More successful were our other economic warfare measures, especially prohibiting American exports (except medicine). The island needed American spare parts for many of its machines, so this measure hit fairly hard. The Cubans tried going to Canadian subsidiaries of American firms for the spares, because Canada still traded with Cuba. We would complain to the American parent company, which would take steps with its subsidiary, but the Canadian Government naturally took a dim view of our trying to exercise jurisdiction over Canadian commerce. Of all our political and economic measures, the export embargo probably hurt Castro the most. In fact, it is still in force. But all in all, though the Administration's desire to rid Cuba of Castro generated a lot of heat, it never came close to shaking his hold on the country.

Yet another Special Group took up my time as Deputy Under Secretary. This was the 54-12 Committee, later known as the 303 Committee, still later known as the 40 Committee, and finally just the "Special Group." The reason for these cryptic and changing titles was the extremely sensitive nature of our work, namely reviewing all plans for covert political action and reconaissance operations. "54-12" was the number of the National Security Council action that first established it in 1954 (a less formal predecessor group had been known as the 10/2 Committee). In 1961 a somewhat garbled account of our work and membership leaked in a book, so to preserve our cover we named ourself after a new NSAM, 303, that was issued to reconstitute the committee. It became the 40 Committee during the Nixon Administration.

Many accounts of American intelligence activities abroad have emerged through congressional inquiries and newspaper stories in the past few years. Some of the covert operations that we approved have been revealed, such as training Meo tribesmen and funding Thai units to fight in Laos, contributing to the political campaigns of non-communists in Italy and building the *Glomar Explorer* to recover a sunken Russian submarine and its weapons from the seabed three miles below. Many have not, including most of the more successful. It is true that during the Nixon Administration the President and CIA bypassed the Committee on sensitive topics, notably the campaigns to "destabilize" the regime of Chilean President Salvador Allende in 1973. I will later discuss the Nixon era, but I can say now that during my service on the Special Group during the Kennedy and Johnson Administrations, I never encountered any evidence to support charges that the CIA itself was freewheeling. All programs originated by CIA or proposed by other agencies were carefully staffed and considered by the Committee. No operations we approved came back to haunt us, many useful ones were undertaken, and I felt we served the President well.

In the Eisenhower Administration, oversight of the CIA was certainly less formal. With Allen Dulles having a good relationship with Eisenhower and a brother as Secretary of State, coordination was done in private phone calls rather than committees. Others in State were much less informed or involved. Below the top level, I think the State Department was often as responsible as the CIA for lack of coordination, because we did not always assert ourselves forcefully enough in Washington or through individual ambassadors in the field.

But at the beginning of the Kennedy Administration, the largely informal procedures for CIA coordination with State were systematized both within the two organizations and between them, as well as with the White House. In State, the Intelligence and Research Bureau was given the responsibility for assuring that all proposals were properly staffed within the Department.

I had known Allen Dulles and many of his subordinates for a long time and had little reluctance about fighting for the Department's interests in interdepartmental disputes. In general, I think relations between us were healthy and effective in this period and that State was able to exercise more influence over the Agency without generating unnecessary friction. I certainly never thought of my role as "controlling" the Agency, but rather as assuring that this valuable and important instrument, composed of Americans no less loyal or patriotic than others in the government, was utilized as effectively and intelligently as possible. It was a "tool" available for use by State as well as by the President and Defense, and I so regarded it.

Members of the Special Group organized under the Kennedy Administration included Mac Bundy, who was Chairman; the Deputy Secretary of Defense—first Ros Gilpatric and later Cy Vance; the CIA Director—first Dulles and then John McCone; and me. The Chairman of the Joint Chiefs was not included at that time unless the subject had military implications. Bobby Kennedy made a strong play to join, but the presence of the Attorney General on a foreign intelligence committee was not thought proper. He was put on the Special Group (Counter-Insurgency) as a sort of consolation prize.

I originally joined in June, 1961. Chet Bowles had been representing the Department but the other members had found him indecisive. After some maneuvering between Bundy and Rusk, I was invited to substitute at one meeting when Bowles was out of town and then he was not reinvited to subsequent meetings. He finally realized he was not wanted, but we never exchanged any words about it. I respected and liked Chet, but he was just not good in this sort of assignment.

The Special Group considered two sorts of proposals: covert action, like helping a friendly politician (sometimes without letting him know the source), building the *Glomar Explorer,* or training the Meo; and reconaissance over China, Cuba, and the Soviet Union to collect intelligence. Some of these flights aimed to stimulate the Soviets to activate their radars, enabling us to determine their location and characteristics, which was very important to the Strategic Air Command.

We met once weekly, or more often at call. Covert action proposals from CIA, State, Defense, or other agencies and reconaissance proposals from Defense, CIA, or State were submitted to members in advance. Each of us consulted with the relevant officials in his Department. In State, for instance, in addition to the Bureau of Intelligence and Research (INR) staff, I usually talked to the appropriate regional Assistant Secretary. If the subject was unusually sensitive, I discussed it with Rusk, but normally I was able to anticipate his views. Each Special Group member came fully prepared to discuss the subject in depth and to reach decisions. Deputies or briefcase-carriers were not permitted, and our discussions were frank and thorough. I would say we reached a firm decision in all but a very few cases. Mac Bundy consulted with the President to the degree he considered desirable, but he did not necessarily tell us whether he had, or if he had, what the President's views had been. The objective was to put an insulating barrier of "plausible deniability" between us and the President and protect his freedom of action. When the proposed operation carried very high risks or carried moderately high risks but had divided the Special Group, the President would meet with Bundy, Rusk, McNamara, the CIA Director, and me to make sure he had all the facts clearly in front of him.

My position on the Special Group was not always enviable. The CIA and Defense Department, both being action agencies, often proposed schemes carrying risks I thought would be excessive if the operation were exposed. My attitude earned me the good-humored sobriquet of "Dr. No," even though my stance was by no means always negative. I knew as well as anyone that unless we could find ways to support our friends, the field would be left to our adversaries, who had no qualms about supporting those who served their purposes. In fact I proposed many projects and strongly supported many others. And when I was the negative dissenting voice, I always resisted taking a parochial "State Department" position on the Special Group. I tried to put myself in the President's shoes, balancing as best I could the risks of the operation against its probable rewards to judge whether it was in the overall foreign policy interest of the United States. All "high risk" proposals were required to include a contingency plan for public handling in the event of exposure so as to avoid the confusion and delay like the one that followed the Soviet announcement of the shootdown of a U-2 during the Eisenhower Administration.

A widespread misconception has grown up about the work of the Special Group and the intelligence agencies in general. Again, I can only speak for the times I actually served on the committee, and I recognize that there are important exceptions, like the Chilean "Track Two" ordered by President Nixon and Henry Kissinger, when we were kept deliberately ignorant of an important CIA covert action program (which in fact the CIA itself opposed). But to stress "dirty tricks" skews out of recognition the work we did. Our covert actions were covert because it was politically necessary for them to be secret, but that did not necessarily make them "dirty." When we funded Radio Free Europe, the

Asia Foundation, or non-communist publications in Italy, this was important and useful work. Radio Free Europe (RFE) has been a vital and worthwhile source of news for millions of people in Eastern Europe. The Asia Foundation has supported a wide variety of projects in education, rural development, and cultural exchange in Asia with a flexibility and inventiveness impossible in AID. When the Soviets were pouring millions into Italy to help the communists win elections, making sure the non-communists could compete—and these were not the ultra-right wing, but moderate and liberal parties—was justified. In the early 1960s the Soviets lavishly financed communist youth groups and orchestrated a campaign to have them take over national and international student oreganizations and conferences. Our own voluntary student organizations were helpless without outside funds, which could only be funneled through covert channels. In the twenty years between 1947 and 1968 the Soviets undoubtedly spent hundreds of millions of dollars on eight "World Peace Conferences" and two "World Youth Festivals." In the face of this massive Soviet investment, our own and other friendly youth organizations would have been helpless without some assistance from the United States Government. The fact that the Soviets now seem largely to have dropped these brain-washing circuses is an indication that our investment in groups desiring to counter them was not in vain. We have no mechanism that does for our government what the British Council does for Britain; namely, fund cultural projects in foreign countries without government strings attached. We could have used such funds for RFE or the Asia Foundation. A partial step toward this was initiated at the end of the Johnson Administration and completed during the Nixon Administration with the establishment of a Board of International Broadcasting that channels funds to, and oversees, Radio Free Europe and Radio Liberty. However, such organizations as the Asia Foundation have to live hand to mouth from the crumbs of contracts from government agencies.

It seems that Americans get much more incensed by this sort of operation than people of other countries. When we had to surface CIA funding of the Asia Foundation and RFE and cut them off as a result, our friends abroad were not particularly surprised. They had assumed we were doing it all along. Even Prince Sihanouk kept the Asia Foundation in Cambodia. He said he thought it was doing good work. I think we on the Special Group could have been more aggressive in persuading the Congress to fund some of these programs overtly, saving them from the appearance of sinister involvement when actually there was none. But my basic point is that our work involved little or nothing that most people would find reprehensible. When the government did try "dirty tricks" in Mongoose or elsewhere (a very small proportion of its activities), it did not do very well.

Let me give another example of the sort of work the Special Group approved. In Laos, after Harriman reached agreement with the Soviets in Geneva in June 1962 on a plan for Laos to continue an independent existence under a neutralist government led by Souvanna Phouma, all foreign forces were supposed to depart. We pulled out our advisors to the Royal Loatian Army and all other American military personnel. The Viet Minh withdrew exactly seven soldiers, asserting ludicrously that seven was the total. Phoumi and Phouma needed backing against the Pathet Lao and their Viet Minh allies, but preserving the facade of Phouma's strict neutrality was also essential. So instead of channeling our support through Defense, we sent it through CIA.

Some would argue that we had no business being there anyway, that Laos would have been much better left alone. I would agree that CIA and Defense went overboard in supporting Phoumi against Souvanna Phouma in 1958–59. Our eyes were bigger than our stomach, ignoring Hanoi's ability to counteract through the Pathet Lao whatever Phoumi gained. After spending millions of dollars helping to oust Souvanna Phouma we had to return to his neutralism as the best workable alternative. We made serious errors in tactics. But if we had left Laos entirely to its own devices in the 1950s and 1960s, the North Vietnamese and Pathet Lao would have picked it off in a few years, whereas it finally fell only after the fall of Saigon. I do not know any place in the world where we received greater return on a smaller investment, both in material and personnel, than the support we gave non-communist elements in Laos through the CIA. Although the few Americans directly involved came from military backgrounds, the flexibility permitted by CIA funding and the small overhead this required produced large returns. Also the CIA's ability to recruit, train, and maintain personnel in Laos over long periods (in contrast to the rapid rotation typical of the military) meant that they knew the language and country thoroughly and could establish the all-important sympathetic personal relationships that gave each American maximum effectiveness.

The Special Group's responsibilities for reconaissance introduced me to the esoteric and then highly secret world of "Oxcart," the ultra-high-performance successor to the U-2, and intelligence-gathering satellites. "Oxcart," now known as the SR-71 in the Air Force, originated out of the very productive combined imaginations of the National Reconaissance Office, CIA, and Kelly Johnson of Lockheed Aircraft. The U-2 had demonstrated the vital importance of high-level reconaissance when, in the 1950s, it penetrated the secrecy surrounding the Soviets' deployment of intercontinental ballistic missiles. Clearly there was nothing more important than preserving the physical security of the United States, and when the Soviets developed the capability of shooting down U-2's, a substitute had to be developed. While satellites held out much promise, they were still unproven, so the Oxcart's production was continued, if only to provide a temporary substitute for the U-2. As part of my briefing on the subject I went to the "Skunk Works" airfield in a remote part of Nevada to see the Oxcart demonstrated. This big aircraft looked like something out of Buck Rogers, and the people testing it were impressive indeed. Eventually, the success of our photo reconaissance satellites, for which the technical genius of Ed Land (developer also of the Polaroid camera) must receive great credit, obviated the need to send Oxcart over the Soviet Union, but the plane performed very useful service over North Vietnam.

Although while I was impressed by these devices and the intelligence data they could produce, I also felt we were becoming unduly enamored of gadgets, to the detriment of our abilities in the hard, dangerous drudgery of old-time espionage. I thought that was very important for us to improve in this area and think so still. Counting tanks or missiles from the air and keeping track of communications are excellent for revealing what an enemy's capabilities are but very seldom disclose how, or if, he intends to use them. I often discussed this with McCone and other CIA officials and they agreed. But this gadget bias is deeply ingrained.

I also worked hard to get the CIA to shift more of its agents to deeper cover, even though that takes a long time to set up. I had some success, but not as much as I would have liked. Deep-cover intelligence is an area where real successes must forever remain unknown to the general public and only failures surface. Americans have trouble accepting this stern discipline. Our society produces very few people willing, in time of nominal peace, to submerge themselves into complete anonymity for years or a lifetime, yet this is what an effective agent must do. It is human to seek at least some recognition from one's family and friends. To forego it, the sense of self-regard that comes from helping one's country must be large. When our society labels those who enter this field as evil, and Congress and the press compete with each other to expose their "nefarious" activities, it is not strange that we can find few Americans or foreigners willing literally to put their lives at the mercy of sensation-seeking politicians and journalists.

My final intelligence-related task as Deputy Under Secretary was handling relations with the FBI. Traditionally, the Department and the Bureau had kept each other at arm's length, J. Edgar Hoover not having much confidence in an organization he suspected of being a sieve for secrets, and the Department not forgetting the rough treatment FSOs suffered at the FBI's hands during the McCarthy period. We had a fair amount of business to transact, however: setting up surveillance and protection of foreign diplomats, guarding against espionage against us by Eastern European diplomats, structuring our foreign police assistance programs, and establishing the International Police Academy.

On espionage cases, it was my feeling that Hoover was sometimes more interested in a splashy arrest than in extracting the maximum benefit for the broader interests of the United States. Another source of friction was the pressure Hoover put on FBI liaison officers stationed at embassies abroad to come up with exclusive political tidbits about foreign leaders, information he could take over to the President. I made a point of calling on Hoover soon after I arrived in Washington and tried to establish a personal relationship with him and his subordinates. While they could never be called ideal, over time I think relations between the Department and the FBI became more harmonious and effective.

My principal charge from Kennedy and Rusk was to make the foreign affairs bureaucracy more agile and effective. I took it seriously. I believe I had some success, or at least the President seemed to think so when he told Arthur Schlesinger that I was "one of the few people who could get things done" in the State Department.

Compared to my previous stint in Washington as Deputy Assistant Secretary in Far Eastern Affairs, when for several years I handled nothing but the Korean armistice, the range of subjects I encountered as Deputy Under Secretary was extremely broad. But my basic style of operation remained constant and still worked. I kept myself acquainted with the expertise the Department had acquired at many levels—a commodity greatly undervalued and underutilized by the White House and the rest of the government—and did not worry too much about rank if I found someone who knew what he was talking about. I made sure that problems flagged by lower levels reached the President, if necessary, but tried to take as much responsibility and as many decisions on my own as was warrented. I also worked hard to communicate all decisions quickly and clearly to lower levels.

I was not shy about pressing for policies I thought correct in the face of opposition from Defense, the JCS, CIA, or other departments, because I thought State was usually the right place in the government, below the President himself, to weigh the full range of military, social, economic, intelligence, and political factors in a given foreign affairs issue. Interestingly, I found that other departments would accept State asserting itself as long as they felt we were genuinely trying to look after the national interest and not a piece of bureaucratic turf. I found a great deal of truth in the old adage, "Power flows to those who use it."

Finally, though I never thought much of empire-building for its own sake and kept my own personal staff to a minimum, I also knew that the best way to assure enduring change in the government's behavior was to institutionalize it—in programs, money, and personnel built into the existing departmental structure rather than temporary task forces standing outside. My politico-military staff, the Operations Center, and the Science Office are examples I have already mentioned.

One of my first tasks in Washington was to prepare a letter for the President's signature asserting the primacy of the Ambassador in our overseas missions. My experience in Southeast Asia was that ambassadors did not always keep a tight hand on the activities of Country Team members who represented other Washington agencies, especially Defense and Intelligence. Some agency representatives did not consider themselves responsible to the Ambassador in any serious way, just to their bosses in Washington. This produced mistakes and distortions in the balance of our total effort. We could not afford to let our programs in foreign countries run away without a central figure to assess the whole and prune or encourage accordingly. That figure of necessity had to be the Ambassador. Truman and Eisenhower had written letters recognizing this coordinating function of ambassadors, authorizing them to wear a "Presidential hat" as well as a "State Department hat," but these were not Executive Orders and had no force of law. The Eisenhower letter was in many ways worse than useless because it specifically exempted intelligence activities from the Ambassador's authority. To make sure that all departments in Washington and abroad, and ambassadors themselves, understood the strong role our system required of ambassadors, I drafted a new letter for President Kennedy. The most difficult issue I faced in drawing it up was meeting the concerns of the CIA, which had a legitimate need to protect its sources and methods of intelligence collection from idle curiosity, particularly of inexperienced "political" ambassadors. There was also a question of how much to tell an Ambassador about operations targeted, in good intelligence fashion, against a third country from his country's territory. The CIA believed that while any political action programs legitimately concerned the Ambassador, covert intelligence collection—especially the identity of its local agents—was solely its own responsibility. The military intelligence services took a similar view. It was difficult to find language, even in the confidential supplement that was attached to the letter, satisfactorily covering these areas while still assuring ambassadors access to the information they needed to carry out their responsibilities. My experience is that an ambassador and a CIA chief who have experience, sophistication and mutual confidence can work things out satisfactorily, but is not possible to spell out such a relationship in a document of general application.

In the letter that was finally approved by President Kennedy the broad Eisenhower exemption for "intelligence" was dropped and the President made it clear to each ambassador that he "counted on him to oversee and coordinate all the activities of the United States Government" in his country of assignment and to supervise "all" operations of the United States Diplomatic Mission and supervise "the representatives of all other U.S. agencies which have programs or activities" in the country. A confidential supplement spelled out in more detail how this was to be applied so as to permit the CIA to maintain its responsibilities for protecting the identity of covert agents.

With minor revisions a similar letter was transmitted to ambassadors by Presidents Nixon and Carter and subsequently embodied in legislation, most recently in the Foreign Service Act of 1980.

Even in peacetime—perhaps especially in peacetime—military and foreign policy are completely intertwined. Potential foes must consider our military strength and readiness in figuring out what moves they can take, and our friends correspondingly must weigh that equation in determining their policies. Thus, the number, equipment, and disposition of our forces around the world are highly political matters. If anyone needs convincing, Korea, Laos, and Vietnam provide excellent examples, each quite different, of how total military victory—the "unconditional surrender" of the First and Second World Wars—has very little relevance to the limited wars that have predominated since then. Even in the absence of war, relations with allies have important military components. Where do we build foreign bases? To whom do we sell American weapons and high-technology goods that might be used in warmaking? For what sorts of wars do we need to develop doctrine and equipment? What are the local repercussions of our military aid and advice to foreign countries? All these questions involve broad political judgments. Close working relations between State and Defense at all levels seem an obvious necessity.

But many traditions in our national life frustrate this sort of cooperation. We spent the nineteenth century aloof from European politics and largely outside its wars. We were not used to manipulating a balance of power or maintaining a large standing army with a professionally trained officer class. Our foreign entanglements of this century have been presented to us as moral crusades, to "make the world safe for democracy" or "save civilization from Naziism." Huge conscript armies were raised virtually overnight and fought to win absolutely, not to achieve carefully defined political ends. We still think of soldiers and diplomats having roles that are separate, not complementary; one begins when the other is done. And we have seen, the need to limit our punch during the Korean War for broader political ends proved immensely frustrating to a people used to unconditional surrender. State and Defense worked effectively together during the Korean War, but the liaison turned out to be temporary and in a narrow area.

Subsequently, the Eisenhower-Dulles military doctrine focused so exclusively on our central confrontation with the Soviet Union that it sacrificed conventional readiness to nuclear readiness. Though Eisenhower called this military doctrine the "New Look," it actually widened the traditional separation between military and foreign policy. At the end of the 1950s we were actually musclebound, able to do little with our military forces except deter a major war with the Soviet Union. President Kennedy and the Special Group (Counter-Insurgency) discovered too well that our military tools did not correspond with our political needs.

What surprised me most when I started working in this no-man's-land between State and Defense was the superficiality of the wariness and distrust between military and Foreign Service Officers. Once they had some experience in collaborating, they worked very well together indeed. The channels of communication between Foggy Bottom and the Pentagon had been so paltry that mutual suspicion had inevitably arisen, but setting that right just took time and some new structures in the government.

A large part of operating effectively in the government has very little to do with formal organization charts. I found that one of the best devices for creating harmony between State and Defense was my telephone, because in a call to Deputy Secretary Ros Gilpatric (later Cy Vance) or the Assistant Secretary for International Security Affairs, first Paul Nitze and later John McNaughton, I could often smooth out problems that months of memo-writing would only have complicated. Paul Nitze claims that a Defense Department research effort costing hundreds of millions of dollars was started by a conversation we had at lunch one day. I told him that we needed to develop the technology for a "land blockade," so that North Vietnamese weapons and soldiers could be prevented from infiltrating the South. Paul put the Pentagon to work on this idea and it developed into the elaborate program of "people sniffers," microphones and other automatic devices that fed back data to a central computer in Thailand. Enemy movements were plotted accordingly. This land blockade system was dubbed "McNamara's Wall" and never worked as efficiently as had been predicted or hoped, but it does illustrate the importance of effective personal relationships in Washington.

I still think land blockade is a capability we badly need to develop. If we had worked on it steadily for ten years instead of making it a crash job, devoting five percent of the money and brain power invested in tactical nuclear weapons, I think we could have made it work. It might even have changed the story in Vietnam. I hope that in the aftermath of our defeat we shall not simply forget all the experience and lessons gained with "McNamara's Wall" and that a similar need in the future will not find us equally unprepared.

Over the longer run, however, improving cooperation between State and Defense also required forging some new formal links. My second week back from Bangkok I revived an extremely useful institution that had rusted into disuse since the Korean

War—regular meetings between the Joint Chiefs of Staff and high-ranking officers in State. We discussed so many important subjects and found the sessions so useful that I find it hard to imagine why this forum had ever lapsed. Its value came from letting both sides hear the other's point of view in depth, without pressure for instant decisions. The Chiefs are surprisingly isolated from what goes on elsewhere in Washington and appreciated the chance to be more involved. Though some participants, like Air Force Chief of Staff Curtis LeMay, tended to take stock military positions on most questions, most of us on both sides rapidly found ourselves trying to find the best course for the government as a whole from the range of political and military options open to us. I was normally the highest ranking person from State, regional Assistant Secretaries and others attending as needed. Whenever ambassadors to key countries were back in Washington for consultations I made a point of bringing them to our meetings so the Chiefs could get a better feel for certain political factors they might otherwise neglect. Our agendas included Cuba, Laos, the Congo, Soviet attempts to penetrate Morocco, the positioning of military bases and carrier task forces, efforts by the South Korean Government to bring American troops stationed there under its jurisdiction for certain offenses, defoliation in Vietnam, the 1962 Sino-Indian War, and the future of Guantanamo, among much else.

Paul Nitze and I saw eye to eye on the need to build respect and easy rapport between military and Foreign Service Officers, and we developed several programs to do this. First, we started exchanging mid-level Pentagon and State Department personnel. We took majors and colonels and put them in actual State Department jobs for two years in the geographic bureaus to learn our procedures and ethos. I always had a colonel on duty in the political-military section of my office. Conversely, we put an equal number of FSOs in Pentagon slots. One, for instance, became a Deputy Chief of Operations for the Air Force. The adjustment was trying for both sides, but that is exactly what was needed. By 1965 we were exchanging twenty officers from each side at a given time. A number of the alumni have gone on to very senior jobs in their respective departments, and the exchanges still continue. Their value has varied with the interest senior officers in State and the Pentagon have taken in them and the caliber of officers assigned.

Another program to improve State-Pentagon relations that Paul and I worked on was assigning State Department political advisors to all major military commands. Many commands—like CINPAC, the Strategic Air Command, the Military Airlift Command, or the new Rapid Deployment Force—make contingency plans and decisions with important political repercussions. There would be no point, for example, in making plans to support a force in the Middle East that absolutely depends on using our bases in the Azores or Spain, unless Portugal and Spain would grant landing rights when the time came. Nor would there be much purpose in making elaborate plans for SEATO involving forces from all the member governments if when the time came they were unlikely to act. I wanted to give the commander a senior FSO, not as a liaison from Washington but as a member of his staff responsible only to him, who could keep the command plugged into Washington's foreign policy machine and give personal advice on politically sensitive subjects. A few such political advisors existed under Eisenhower, but the program had never taken off because of military suspicion of State Department kibbitzing. The breakthrough came when Felix Stump, Commander-in-Chief, Pacific, reluctantly accepted John Steeves as a political advisor (POLAD) in 1957. Felix had a reputation for eating FSOs for breakfast and his command is one of the most visible in the Armed Forces. By the time I became Deputy Under Secretary he had moved Steeves into an adjacent office and never traveled without him. So when I pushed for more POLADs, they quickly became the "in" thing among commanders—so much so that we had to turn down many requests. By 1965 there were thirteen POLADs assigned to ten military commands. I am sorry to see that the number of officers has since been reduced to eight.

I also arranged for State Department people to be sent to the Army, Navy, and Air Force academies as full-time instructors and expanded the numbers going to the Service war colleges as students and instructors. I wanted to build mutual understanding and the habit of cooperation as early as possible. Unfortunately, these positions have also been reduced.

In June 1964, we achieved a really valuable link between Defense and State when ISA and the Defense Comptroller agreed to regular State participation in preparing the Pentagon's five-year Force Structure and Budget, which set long-range priorities for the whole armed forces. Their short-term plans and formulations of strategy were decided within the framework of this five-year plan. Rusk and McNamara had been holding annual discussions on what the Pentagon's priorities should be, but the Pentagon had a large staff constantly working on the subject and a chance for regular State input was invaluable. My politico-military staff consulted with Pentagon counterparts on a wide array of issues, including the introduction of Pershing missiles into Europe, the problem of Soviet overseas submarine bases, pre-positioning of military equipment overseas, expanding collaboration between us and our allies in anti-submarine warfare and so on.

I felt strongly about this long-term budget collaboration because it seemed to me a truism that the Pentagon no longer needed "war plans" but politico-military plans. Our forces were strung all over the world and could not be deployed in a political vacuum. Yet when I began to examine some of the contingency plans the Chiefs had drawn up for Laos, Berlin, and other trouble spots, I found them distressingly lacking in political awareness. Especially after the Cuban Missile Crisis, I became a strong proponent of joint State-Defense politico-military planning. The Chiefs tended to resist this, pretending that "pure" military plans were good enough and worrying (with some justification) about State's ability to contribute meaningfully and maintain security. Even so, I was able to convince them to have the European Bureau and my politico-military staff sit down and thrash out some contingency plans for Berlin, which Khrushchev was then threatening to sever from Western access. There were other plans drawn up for the Dominican Republic and elsewhere.

The value in contingency planning is not in having ready a cookbook that can be pulled out of a safe to describe in minute detail what should be done at every stage of an international crisis. Forward planning can never be that exact, but there are really difficult questions that are likely to stay constant no matter how the specifics evolve. It is important that the major participants are able to think through these. Developing adroit solutions to crises often requires penetrating questions and thoughtful answers, but the time for this sort of philosophical debate is not when seconds count. Contingency planning also ensures that everyone concerned is familiar with the subjects and personalities involved before pressures start to mount. Of course, to be useful, the plans must be continuously reviewed and revised as the personnel change and the situation abroad evolves.

Another development along these lines I strongly welcomed was the inclusion State Department officials in the "war games" that the Chiefs and Pentagon hierarchy played periodically. These games were typically an imaginary but realistic local war (say a Soviet invasion of Yugoslavia following the death of Tito) and usually involved two separate teams, one representing the United States and the other our opponents, with a control group as "umpire." The teams, which sometimes included Cabinet members but more usually comprised the Joint Chiefs and the regional Assistant Secretaries of State, were given the initial scenario and a description of the forces available and told to work out the next move. The two teams would give their decisions to separate groups of lower-ranking officers to staff and "implement," and after an appropriate number of hours or days would reassemble to see how developments had progressed (a report the control group presented). The game ended after a week or two of this, and all of the players then came together with the control group to hear criticism of the two teams' procedures and decisions. These exercises were always stimulating and useful. Like contingency planning, their main value was in forcing people to think hard.

The point of State-JCS meetings, POLADs, exchanges of officers, joint contingency planning, and budget formation was a very simple one: to make better policy. It did not always work, but I think it helped. Here are a few examples:

By the early 1960s Europe had largely recovered from the devastation of the Second World War and our NATO allies were seeking to regain some of the authority they had traditionally wielded in world affairs. Since nuclear weapons were something the superpowers obviously had and the allies lacked, and because doubt lingered about whether the United States would really "push the button" to repel a Soviet invasion of Europe, pressure began to mount in Europe for nuclear weapons of their own. Britain already had them, but we had no enthusiasm for further proliferation. We also thought our nuclear forces would continue to protect Europe successfully, so we began to develop ideas for deflecting the pressure for autonomous nuclear forces.

The Policy Planning Council under Gerard Smith and Henry Owen came up with the concept of what came to be called Multilateral Nuclear Force (MLF). The idea was to have NATO submarines manned by mixed crews drawn from member countries—Britain, France, West Germany, Holland, Italy, the United States, and so on—carrying nuclear missiles to which the United States would still retain the "key." An interdepartmental task force was set up under Gerard Smith to implement the concept. The Navy always opposed this plan, understandably dismayed at the prospect of trying to run a sub with such a diversity of nationalities and languages. My politico-military staff was skeptical, and I became so, too, for I could not see how the Europeans' desire for nuclear weapons of their own would be satisfied by sending their sailors to ride on a sub whose missiles were still controlled by Washington. My attitude came to be shared by Rusk and the President, and, as a compromise, the Navy was directed to examine the feasibility of the approach by running a mixed-nationality destroyer. That worked well enough, but it did not eliminate the other drawbacks of an inherently gimmicky idea.

MLF eventually fell of its own weight, but the problem of nuclear weapons for Europe continued to surface throughout my time in Washington. One episode I felt demonstrated inadequate politico-military cooperation occurred in December, 1962, at the Kennedy–Macmillan summit in Nassau. The Pentagon had been building a long-range airborne ballistic missile called Skybolt that would give added range and capabilities to our B-47s and B-52s. The British were very interested because it would permit them to keep alive their V-Bomber force. The negotiations on Skybolt had been between our respective military people and had largely bypassed State. At the summit, having arrived at a cost-benefit conclusion the Skybolt was unnecessary, Secretary McNamara informed the British without ceremony that we were cancelling the program immediately. Not surprisingly, the British were deeply upset to discover that their main nuclear delivery system for the future had been eliminated so casually. The resentment festered for many years.

Another politico-military issue with nuclear implications for Europe was the possibility of reducing our troops there significantly. To improve our balance of payments and reduce the heavy load we were bearing in NATO conventional defense, various people in Congress and the Pentagon, after the 1961 Berlin crisis, proposed bringing some American combat units home. Even though the government as a whole had not come to any decision, Pentagon planning for the reductions moved irrepressibly forward. I leaned hard to slow down the Pentagon juggernaut, for I thought any hasty or major withdrawal of troops would be a serious mistake. It was clear that any substantial withdrawal of our forces from Europe would require placing increased emphasis on the "nuclear option" in defending Europe. More important, if the Europeans got the sense that our commitment to their defense was wavering, we might set in motion a train of events leading to a "nationalist Europe" along the ideas of De Gaulle. We had learned in two world wars that we could not remain aloof from Europe's affairs nor divorce its defense from ours. Therefore, I felt we should be extremely cautious about doing anything that might jeopardize our leadership of NATO. Certainly our balance of payments difficulties were not sufficient reason. I stated this opinion often in 1962 and 1963.

Secretary McNamara fully understood this point of view, but he was eager to demonstrate his ability to cut defense spending and reduce our balance of payments deficit. Nevertheless, we managed to limit the troop reductions and concentrate them on non-combat support units. We also pressed the Europeans to increase their own ground forces and buy materiel from American suppliers.

The idea of pulling our troops home has surfaced regularly since then and is likely to continue as long as we have a major commitment to NATO and to Korea and Japan. I think we would be very shortsighted to pay heed to them. Because of the contributions we receive toward the support of our troops from the countries where they are stationed, less budget expenditure is usually required to keep troops abroad than in the United States. The savings are especially dramatic if one factors in the cost of the extra aircraft and ships that would be necessary to deploy home-based troops to a forward area during an emergency. Troops stationed abroad are more effective because they are familiar with the area where they may be called on for combat. And also we should bear in mind that sending troops abroad from the United States could fuel a crisis atmosphere at a time the objective would be to dampen it; troops already abroad do not have this drawback.

Another example of politico-military collaboration during this period concerned the Azores, a group of islands about 800 miles west of North Africa in the Atlantic and have been Portuguese possessions for hundreds of years. They were the site of a major American air base used for the KC-135 tanker aircraft required to refuel our SAC B-52s, and this base was vital as a stop-off point for aircraft and supplies bound for the Middle East. We used the base under an agreement drawn up in 1951 when Portugal joined NATO. We had automatic rights to use it in fulfillment of NATO obligations, but our non-NATO peacetime uses were subject to periodic renegotiation. The original agreement lapsed on December 31, 1962, so in June 1961 we opened talks by requesting a five-year extension of our current arrangements. If the agreement were not extended, its terms required us to evacuate the base within six months to a year.

These negotiations would probably have been routine except for another Portuguese colony, Angola, where an insurgent movement led by Holden Roberto was trying to throw off 400 years of Portuguese domination. Angola and Mozambique (another Portuguese colony) were the last two major European colonies in Africa and Portuguese administration was extremely backward. The Portuguese were attempting to put down the insurgency in Angola with brute force and needed American money and arms. They disingenuously claimed that Angola was administered as part of metropolitan Portugal and was thus not a "colony." But the Assistant Secretary of State for African Affairs, G. Mennen ("Soapy") Williams, wanted us to endorse Roberto openly, and it was obvious to everyone but the Portuguese that their time in Angola had ended. Nevertheless, before renegotiating the Azores agreement, Portugal insisted on discussing "other aspects of our bilateral relations;" namely, our lack of support for its aims in Angola.

I never agreed with Soapy Williams that we should "recognize" Roberto, since Portugal was a NATO ally and we had an important interest in the Azores that we could not sacrifice lightly. Rusk shared this view. At the same time, I wanted to make sure we avoided being on what was obviously the wrong side of history. I agreed strongly with our policy of not licensing the export of any military equipment to Portugal that might be used in Angola and I had no particular objection to our letting Roberto come to the United States to visit the United Nations or holding conversations with him.

The most ardent advocate for Portugal's position within the United States Government was naturally the Air Force, which valued its Azores bases. Air Force Chief of Staff Curtis LeMay and I had a vigorous exchange on this subject at a March 23, 1962, State-JCS meeting. LeMay said our Air Force was very friendly with Portuguese Air Force officers, and he could not understand why the State Department was being so stupid about Angola. The Portuguese had gambled on us winning World War II, LeMay said, and now we were turning our back on our NATO ally in its hour of need. The military equipment we were refusing to ship to Portugal—F-86 spares, parachutes, transport—were not intended for Angola anyway, just Portugal's NATO commitments. We needed the Azores. The State Department should get into the twentieth century and stop being inflammatory over Angola. LeMay concluded by wishing we *would* sell bombs to Portugal to help it put down the Angolan rebels.

I agreed that the Azores were important to American interests, but I thought LeMay was doing a disservice to our bargaining position by stressing to Portugal our dependence on the island. Instead, I thought we should emphasize how important it was to Portugal that we continue to use the Azores, lest they think they could push up our settling price by being stubborn. As far as Angola was concerned, I told LeMay that Portugal "cannot obtain American support unless they take some actions on their own to improve the situation there." We had offered advice and aid to Lisbon for its colonial problems, without response. Every NATO ally except France joined us in opposing Portugal's approach to Angola, and we had to make Lisbon "recognize the facts of the twentieth century." I predicted that within a year or two at most, Portugal would lose Angola under tragic circumstances, just as the Belgians had been evicted from the Congo.

The strategy I thought we should adopt in the Azores negotiations was "business as usual," to show no anxiety whatever about reaching an agreement. If we insisted on getting something down on paper, Lisbon could use that as a lever to extract concessions on Angola that we were not prepared to give. I felt that we should try to continue to use the bases under the terms of the old agreement gambling that Portugal would not expel us from the Azores for fear they would lose their only lever to influence our policy toward their African possessions. In fact, that is exactly what we did until after Portugal gave independence to Angola and Mozambique. We concluded a new agreement for our Azores air base with the new Portuguese Government most recently in 1979.

I found the Air Force similarly short-sighted about the political ramifications of its desire for bases at all costs when it pressed, in mid-1961, to increase its personnel and facilities at its communications station at Peshawar in Pakistan. It was clear to everyone observing Pakistani politics that its government was likely to eject the station altogether at an early date, and that asking to expand it would only hasten its departure. This is exactly what happened in 1967 after the fall of Ayub Khanh.

Besides Angola, another legacy of European colonialism that put me at loggerheads with the JCS was the conflict between the Netherlands and Indonesia over the future of West New Guinea, a desperately poor and primitive area, with no racial or cultural ties to Indonesia, where the Dutch were losing money just by holding on to the territory. However, missionaries working there had great influence in the Dutch cabinet, and in early 1962 the possibility began to emerge that Indonesia and Holland would fight over the province. Indonesia wanted the Dutch simply to vacate West New Guinea so it could seize the area. The Indonesian Army began skirmishing with Dutch border patrols and the conflict became very tense. We knew that if it came to a fight, it would be very difficult for the United States to abandon Holland, a NATO ally. But we also knew that supporting Holland in a manifestly colonial cause against an important developing country, no matter how weak Indonesia's case, would be very dangerous for our interests in the Third World generally. Holland pressured us to stop our military aid to Indonesia, but we did not.

The situation was complicated by the involvement of the Soviet Union. The Indonesian Communist Party was the largest in Southeast Asia and, at the time, the most effective political force in the country. Indonesian resentment against the Dutch, generally, and their position on West New Guinea, particularly, proved a powerful propaganda tool for the communists. Moscow supplied aid and equipment to the large Indonesian Army and had commensurate influence within it. By March, 1962, we had concluded that the Soviets desired to see an Indonesian-Dutch fight over West New Guinea, hoping that this would inflame anti-Western feeling in Indonesia and thus bolster the position of the Communist Party. We thought the only answer was a negotiated settlement, painful though this might be for The Netherlands. However, there were elements in The Netherlands, especially those interested in missionary work among the New Guinea natives, who were pushing for the use of force to resist the Indonesians. While they recognized that they did not have the capability of deploying the military force that would be necessary for a successful defense, they hoped that if the situation came to active hostilities, the United States would be unable to resist pressure to come to the aid of its Dutch ally against a crypto-communist Indonesia.

Probably with this in mind the Dutch undertook to transport some troops to West New Guinea in the spring of 1962, routing the ships via Pearl Harbor Naval Base for refueling. In order to disabuse the Dutch of any thought that we were going to become involved, we asked the Department of Defense to send instructions to Hawaii not to permit the Dutch troops ashore in Pearl Harbor. This disturbed General LeMay and some of the other Chiefs.

I strongly supported State's position in a State-JCS meeting on May 11. I pointed out that the Dutch were conducting a general campaign to get us more involved in the war, and that the Chiefs would permit it to succeed. The Dutch ships, I pointed out, could easily go from Panama to West New Guinea directly without stopping in Hawaii, and if they wanted to stop in Hawaii, there was no reason they had to call at our naval base instead of the commercial docking facilities available. In any event, our position was maintained.

The result was that both The Netherlands and Indonesia accepted our offer of good offices and on August 8, 1962, that incomparable negotiator, Ambassador Ellsworth Bunker, took delegations from both countries to a private house out in McLean, Virginia, and they did not emerge until they had arrived at a peaceful and orderly settlement. Today, Indonesian relations with the Netherlands are probably closer than with any other country.

In 1963, I and the head of my politico-military office, Jeff Kitchen, had an important series of exchanges with the Pentagon over the desirability of sending a carrier task force occasionally through the Indian Ocean. Especially given the way events in Laos and Vietnam were moving at the time, we thought that in the long run the United States might find it valuable to establish a permanent naval presence in the Indian Ocean. We thought we should prepare the nations of that region gradually. The best way to do that was by running some occasional voyages through the Indian Ocean en route from Atlantic to Pacific. I was surprised to discover resistance from the Navy. It considered the carrier task force its main contribution to nuclear deterrence and did not want that nuclear role downgraded vis-à-vis the Soviets (and thus perhaps lost to the Air Force) by using carriers for "conventional" missions like signalling our interest in the Indian Ocean. I believed strongly that the carrier was an extremely potent politico-military tool. Vastly more flexible than a land base, it could be moved at will to signal our resolve without committing us irreversibly to military intervention. I thought the Navy's role in nuclear defense was guaranteed by Polaris submarines, and that they and land-based missiles were inevitably making the carrier less useful as a nuclear weapons platform.

Eventually, the Navy adjusted to the idea that the carrier has great political importance and accepted an Indian Ocean cruise. The first one came in early 1964 when we moved a carrier task force from the Atlantic to the Pacific via the Indian Ocean. It made the Indians quite nervous, but as these voyages continued intermittently, their acceptability increased. It was my work in this area that earned me the nickname in the Pentagon of "Admiral Johnson."

We also thought it would be a good idea for the British, then in the process of granting independence to the Seychelles Islands in the Indian Ocean, to exempt the island of Diego Garcia so that we might establish a base there. In addition to its usefulness to the Navy, we also very much had in mind the importance to our lines of communication of a stepping stone in the Indian Ocean for long range transport aircraft that would not require the tolerance or agreement of another country. Jeff successfully negotiated this with Britain, and a United States base at this key point in the Indian Ocean was eventually constructed. Its value was dramatically demonstrated when in 1979 we deployed two carrier task forces to the Middle East.

Space

At one of Secretary Dulles's staff meetings in 1953 which I attended, I remember the indulgent smiles that greeted Len Meeker, then Assistant Legal Advisor, when he suggested that we should get to work formulating laws to govern the use of space. Everyone thought he had been staying up too late reading science fiction. Four years later, Sputnik more than confirmed the prescience of his suggestion. One of my first important jobs in the scientific field was to oversee the government's work in drawing up a comprehensive position on setting international law to govern the uses of outer space that would protect our interests.

Even before the Sputnik launch in October 1957, the United States had proposed the establishment of an international system for registering and verifying all objects sent into space. In August of that year a group of Western countries including the United States included a proposal for outer space inspection in an arms limitation package. But the Soviet Union rejected both ideas.

Starting in 1959, two separate chains of developments— one highly public and the other highly secret—began to affect our thinking on international regulation of the uses of space. The first was a desire in the United States and many other countries to make sure that rapidly expanding American and Soviet space programs did not open up a new arena for the arms race. The second was some remarkable advances in American technology that opened up the possibility that orbiting satellites could provide detailed information on Soviet missile and bomber development, replacing the now-vulnerable U-2 as the source of this vital information. Everyone recognized that satellites could be equipped to take pictures, but the sensitive questions were the quality of such pictures and the reliability with which they could be obtained. If one could photograph the Soviet Union, one could photograph any country, and other countries besides the USSR would be highly sensitive about the United States keeping an eye on them from space. So we had to be extremely careful about the way we handled this issue, which was daily becoming more urgent.

On May 26, 1962, I was appointed to head a task force to develop a coordinated national policy on the uses of space. Our objective was to permit maximum development of civilian satellites by NASA while protecting our military reconaissance programs against physical or political interference from the Soviets or others. At the UN there was considerable interest in limiting the uses of space to "peaceful" ones, and many well-meaning but uninformed proposals, including American, were circulating that we feared might interfere with our objectives in reconaissance and civilian programs.

Following some preliminary discussions among those of us who were knowledgeable of both our reconaissance programs and the disarmament discussions with the Soviets and others at the United Nations in New York and Geneva, the President issued an instruction on May 26, 1962, to State, Defense, NASA, CIA, and the Arms Control and Disarmament Agency (ACDA) to develop a coordinated national policy on the subject and report their recommendations to him by July 1. I was selected to head a task force on the subject. Defense designated Paul Nitze; the National Reconaissance Organization (NRO) selected Joseph Charyk, also Deputy Secretary of the Air Force; CIA picked Herbert (Pete) Scoville, Jr.; ACDA, Adrian Fisher; NASA, Robert Seamans, Jr.; and the White House, Carl Kaysen. I designated Raymond Garthoff of my staff to be my assistant for the purpose. Each had the special clearances required to permit us to treat the subject comprehensively.

We had our first meeting on June 1, and 32 days later, on July 2, Dean Rusk signed a memo to the President transmitting nineteen comprehensive recommendations affecting each of the Departments and agencies represented on the task force, all of which, except for two relatively less important details on handling the subject in the UN, were unanimously agreed. In addition to chairing the group, I had the job of making sure that no one in the Department or in our Mission to the UN did anything that would prejudice the American position. Secrecy was so tight that the possibility of many crossed wires below was great.

The basic problem at the UN was the beguiling phrase "peaceful uses." Was photographing another's territory from space "peaceful"? If not, at what point did it become "non-peaceful"—an astronaut's 3×5 Kodak snapshot showing clouds and a sketchy outline of land below? Photographs from NASA satellites to map weather patterns and natural resources? To state the problem is to demonstrate that no meaningful distinction between "peaceful" and "non-peaceful" is possible. While everyone accepted as fact that a country had a legitimate right to control the airspace above its territory, it was ludicrous to think of this domain continuing indefinitely into the heavens, any more than a country could prohibit photography of its territory from a ship on the high seas. We on the task force quickly realized that a major requirement of our policy had to be accustoming the world to the fact that in an era of manned and unmanned space travel, there was no way to hide what could be seen from space.

We proposed that the United States adopt the position that outer space be considered "free," like the high seas, for all peaceful purposes, and that any observation of Earth be considered peaceful. We also recommended that we gradually reveal our capability in satellite photography to other countries through appropriate and carefully timed releases of NASA photographs, first to high officials in other countries, and later, in consultation with them, to the public. We should point out the practical utility of these images for mapping, surveying natural resources, and predicting weather and crops. We also agreed to continue the tight security surrounding the capabilities of our military reconaissance satellites, first to avoid presenting the Soviet Union or anyone else with a direct challenge, and second, to avoid disclosing exactly what we could and could not detect from above. To impress our allies with the importance of military reconaissance to our joint security, however, we briefed a selected group of foreign leaders in August 1962, urging that they not do anything in the UN or elsewhere that could embarrass us or jeopardize these activities. We recognized and accepted that there would be gradual leakage about our satellite reconaissance, but hoped that this would induce others to acquiesce to the principle while enabling us to maintain secrecy about our exact capabilities.

At the United Nations, which discussed the subject sporadically, our careful preparation of public opinion and friendly governments paid off, especially when the Soviet delegation argued that all space reconaissance was "non-peaceful" and should thus be banned. This was an extreme position, and not many countries found it compelling. It puzzled us, however, that the Soviet delegation took this position when they were clearly developing their own reconaissance satellites. I assumed that their program, like ours, was so secret that their UN delegation, and probably their Foreign Office, did not know about it and could not coordinate their policy accordingly. One use of space that we and the Soviets joined the rest of the world in considering "non-peaceful" was deploying nuclear weapons in orbit. We all opposed it.

In January, 1967, a treaty on outer space was signed in Washington, London, and Moscow, embodying all the policies pertinent to our 1962 recommendations. Nuclear weapons were banned from space, but all reconaissance was permitted. It also called for UN registration of all space launches, a provision the Soviet Union and the United States still follow. A more important recognition for the principle of satellite reconaissance came in the May 1972 SALT I agreements between us and the Soviets, which permitted each country to use "national technical means at its disposal"—it was understood that this included satellites—to verify compliance by the other, and prohibited interfering with such means. One of our hopes in 1962 was that a wider use of satellite reconaissance would deflate the archaic concept of total secrecy that prevailed in the communist bloc, and I think it has had this effect. No country has ever raised a serious challenge to the potentially very ticklish principle of satellite reconaissance, and it is gratifying that the program we developed in 1962 has proved adequate over a long period.

Another one of my satellite-related activities was arranging for Japan to use an experimental American communications satellite and a Defense Department receiving station to broadcast the 1964 Olympics to the United States. Maeda, the President of the giant Japan Broadcasting Company, came to me with an introduction from the Foreign Minister to ask my assistance in arranging for satellite transmission. He had been trying to get the necessary approvals from Defense, whose receiving station on the west coast would have to be used, but without success. I thought satellite transmission would be good for our relations with Japan as well as a big boost for NASA and American technology. Thus I went to work on it. The satellite needed was SYNCOM III, an experimental device. NASA was worried it would not work consistently, but I managed to talk them into it. I also got approval from Defense to use its ground station to receive the transmission. NBC, which had bought the American right to televise the games, also had to agree on satellite transmission instead of the slower but surer traditional way of shipping the film by air. It all worked perfectly, and was a well-publicized success. It was fun to arrange; it did no one any harm; it earned some lasting gratitude from the Japanese; and it was just a matter of pressing the right people a little bit.

Sometimes my space and politico-military responsibilities overlapped. One such case was our policy toward South Africa. Its geographic position made it the only possible location for a tracking station that was vital for monitoring lunar and interplanetary probes. We already had a station for tracking ICBM tests located in the country. In June 1961, Washington weighed whether it wanted to pay the international political price for going ahead with the space tracking complex. Even moderates in Defense were convinced that we needed the stations urgently, and I, too, was persuaded. But Soapy Williams was strongly opposed. Though South Africa was in his bureau's area of responsibility, he treated it as a pariah to be attacked at every opportunity. President Kennedy had given him a mandate to repair relations with black Africa and he naturally recognized that any degree of cooperation with Pretoria was suspect and offensive in other African capitals. On the other hand, we needed this facility and the only place it could go was South Africa, so a purely vindictive attitude was unproductive. While I had no sympathy whatever for the internal policies of South Africa, there were certain issues on which we had no alternative but to find some degree of cooperation. I respected Williams and believed our government was well served by his being a strong exponent of black Africa's interests, but I thought it was important that we maintain a certain balance. South Africa also granted us landing rights, port and dock facilities, and other privileges that were important to the position of our Navy and Air Force in the South Atlantic and Indian Oceans, and which would become extremely important indeed if the Suez Canal were cut off. This tracking station issue was only the first of many occasions on which I found myself intervening or arbitrating on a small African problem contrary to the position of the African bureau.

The President, on reviewing the case, decided to seek South African permission to build the stations. But he also directed that we distance ourselves from Pretoria in other ways. South Africa approved a fifteen-year agreement governing the space tracking facility, but its quid pro quo was not long in coming. In September Pretoria requested our approval to purchase $100 million worth of F-104 fighters and C-130 transport aircraft, and our backing in its drive to become a member of the UN Outer Space Committee. Simultaneously it dragged its feet in renewing the agreement for the ICBM tracking station, which expired in December. Assistant Secretary Williams recommended that we reject both South African requests, but I argued we should approve the sale of the F-104s. Our general policy on South African arms purchases was to refuse those that could be used internally to quell civil disturbances and approve those that were intended to protect the country from external attack. This was an extremely difficult line to draw, of course, but it was adequate for deciding to approve the F-104s and disapprove the C-130s.

In March, 1963, following this policy, we offered to sell several conventionally-powered submarines to Pretoria, to give them some capability against the Soviet Navy. In June, however, Williams recommended a total arms embargo to South Africa. I opposed him. I argued that such a policy would equate South Africa with the Soviet Union and Communist China, that other suppliers would take up the slack, and that our present, more flexible policy was much more effective in applying leverage. While I tended to support a non-vindictive policy for South Africa more than some others in the Department during our internal wrangles, I had no hesitation in strongly criticizing apartheid and other repressive South African policies. In my conversations with the South African Ambassador, I said that in the long run it could only hurt South Africa's whites and our common international interests. I was not too surprised, however, to find my unsolicited advice producing no discernable effect.

In May 1961 President Kennedy made the first public announcement of our intention to undertake a program to land a man on the moon. While the NASA satellite communications programs, beginning with ECHO I in 1960, have unquestionably had much more direct impact on life on this planet than the Apollo moon program, from the time of its announcement until the first landings, the moon program excited and brought together our own people and the world in a way that is still unprecedented.

When Neil Armstrong took his "first step for mankind" in July, 1969, the whole world responded with a "We have done it," mankind has done something together. It was a rare and intoxicating moment in history, which unhappily faded all too fast. Yet I think that it has left some residue. It was also a high point for Americans. For the first time something other than war united us around a single goal, and it gave us a sense of confidence and elan that also faded all too soon. It needs to be recaptured.

It was my rare fortune, as the representative from State on the Space Council during the Kennedy, Johnson, and Nixon administrations, to have some small participation in this enterprise almost from the very beginning. The Council was chaired by the Vice President, and in the Kennedy Administration a great deal of the excitement derived from the personality of Lyndon Johnson. It was one of his few substantive responsibilities and he attacked it with a characteristic blitz of gusto and determination that was enthusiastically supported by the eloquent Jim Webb, Director of NASA. The other members were Bob McNamara and Glenn Seaborg, Chairman of the Atomic Energy Commission. Being very much an earthling, to whom talk of "going to the moon" seemed utterly fantastic, I listened with considerable skepticism to the briefings of such experts as Wernher von Braun. My mathematical training ended with high school algebra, so it was incomprehensible to me how even computers could solve the equations involved in intercepting the moon and then making a soft landing at a predesignated spot. But I took advantage of my good fortune to visit Cape Kennedy a number of times while the awesome facilities there were being constructed, and I also visited the Space Flight Center at Houston where the astronauts trained and which was to be the nerve center for controlling the flights. Eventually I would witness most of the important launches and come to be totally in awe of the whole operation. By the time when, in the Nixon Administration, we were briefed on the project to land man on Mars and bring him back in an expedition that would last several years, I was prepared to believe that it could have been done. However, the project was not pursued because as the costs would have been enormous, and the benefits not sufficiently greater than those obtainable from the unmanned vehicles that we ultimately landed on that planet.

In addition to space, the Council dealt with the project for constructing a Super Sonic Transport (SST), as, in addition to space, the first "A" in the NASA acronym stands for "aeronautic." The task force examining the feasibility of an SST was under the chairmanship of Najeeb Halaby, Administrator of the Federal Aviation Administration (FAA). Jeeb was an ardent supporter of an SST as, of course, was the Defense Department and the aircraft industry. The argument was that in addition to its obvious benefits for air travel, an SST would, like the Apollo program, confer much prestige of the United States, and Jeeb made strenuous efforts to persuade me that State should back this line of reasoning. I took the position, with which Dean Rusk fully concurred, that if the SST could be a commercial success like the 707 or DC-8, the prestige would follow; but if it was an economic white elephant, there would be no prestige for anyone.

Of course, it was never built. Boeing, which received the contract for its development, worked for several years on a swing wing design that turned out to be impractically heavy. Even when it shifted to a more conventional "V" wing design, the SST seemed less and less economically viable. One of the problems was the cost and difficulty of fabricating titanium, large quantities of which would be necessary in the air frame if the craft was going to have a "growth potential" beyond the severe strength limits imposed by aluminum.

When we finally shut down the SST project, I could recognize the economic wisdom, but in view of the time, money, and expertise that had already been invested in it, I felt that we might have continued some R&D to make sure that we did not miss a breakthrough that would make it practical. Of course, the British and French went ahead with their aluminum frame Concorde which, while technically practical, has turned out to be just the kind of economic "white elephant" we feared. I still have a notion that it may some day be possible to skip over the supersonic stage and jump directly to hypersonic speeds by flying at great altitudes where there is no resistance from the air. Theoretically, there should be great savings in fuel on journeys covering distances up to or approaching half the diameter of the earth—from New York to Sydney, for instance.

Atomic Energy

By the 1960s, spurred by the Eisenhower "Atoms for Peace" program and our confidence in the cheap abundant electricity that was expected to ensue, many countries were seeking the advantages of atomic power for themselves. Knotty foreign policy questions were generated as a result. Who would supply the fuel and the reactors, and who would process the waste products? What safeguards could be developed against diverting power reactors to making plutonium for weapons? How could agitation for membership in the nuclear weapons club be discouraged? As the person on the seventh floor with responsibility for both science and politico-military affairs, I was immersed in trying to bring some order to this field.

My main activities involved serving on the interdepartmental task force trying to settle on recommendations to the President as to whether the government or private industry should provide the large amount of capital required to build the plants that would be necessary to produce the increased amounts of fuel we were going to be required to supply to those buying American reactors. One difficulty in trying to interest private industry in investing the massive amounts required to build gaseous diffusion plants was that those with a knowledge of the highly classified research that was being carried on feared that cheaper centrifuge technology might well be ready for large scale production by the time gaseous plants could be completed.

We also tried to devise ways to assure buyers of American reactors that their supplies would not be subject to the shifting whims of American political life. To meet their legitimate concerns, some of us proposed that if groups of countries would form consortiums to build and operate fuel enrichment plants so that no country could obtain an exclusive advantage, we would sell them licenses to use some of our technology. In this we ran into an absolute buzz saw in the form of the Congressional Joint Committee on Atomic Energy, and particularly of some of its staff members, who dogged every step taken by the Atomic Energy Commission. The Committee staff was obsessed with safeguarding our supposed technological monopoly, even in gaseous diffusion. That monopoly had, of course, long since been broken by the Soviet Union and France, and China seemed to be in the process of doing so. And now others have leap-frogged our original gaseous diffusion technology in favor of developing the centrifuge technology for themselves. This is already happening in Japan, and with a German-Dutch-UK consortium.

The concerns of these countries over our reliability as a supplier of fuel were even at that time fed by the policy we adopted toward fuel for a small research reactor we had sold to South Africa in the 1950s. In 1961 the South Africans sought to buy from us the small amount of fuel required to resupply the reactor. The African Bureau of the Department felt strongly that we should punish Pretoria for its racial policies by refusing to sell them the fuel. However, this could have a cost as South Africa was a large producer of uranium ore being purchased by France for its own program. This led to a proposal that we would ship the fuel to South Africa if, in turn, France would agree to accept International Atomic Energy Agency (IAEA) controls on the ore it was buying from South Africa to assure that the product was not used in the French weapons program. Of course, both France and South Africa indignantly rejected this idea. In the end we accomplished nothing save incurring the hostility of both countries to our policies; and South Africa went ahead to develop its own capacity to produce fuel, anyway.

It is ironic that the United States, the first proponent of nuclear power, has since become so obsessed with its risks, real and imaginary, that it is virtually withdrawing from a field in which we had such a large technological and industrial lead. All sources of power, in fact any human activity, carry some risk, but properly handled, nuclear power probably the least of all. It is equally ironic that the Japanese, whom we used to scorn for their "nuclear allergy," are perhaps more vigorously than any other country developing nuclear power.

In the 1960s France decided to build its own nuclear weapons. For this they wanted American help—supplies of uranium, testing equipment, expertise— and France tried to procure these from us under arrangements comparable to those we had with Britain. In addition, to reach its nuclear weapons test site in the Pacific the French team had to pass through the Panama Canal; and to support them France wanted to fly food and supplies to them over American airspace.

But under the Non-Proliferation and Limited Test Ban Treaties, we were prevented from helping "non-nuclear countries" to test weapons. We permitted the French team to travel through the Panama Canal and allowed flights with food, but refused to supply testing equipment or permit French aircraft to transit the United States with any weapon components or testing equipment. This, of course, angered the French, but as their whole effort to achieve nuclear autonomy was part of a campaign to distance themselves from the United States, we were not unduly troubled. In fact, France managed to offend a good many countries with its testing program. It was not a signatory of the Non-Proliferation or Test Ban Treaties, and chose the South Pacific site in order to conduct atmospheric tests, which are cheaper and provide more information than those underground, but produce fallout. Australia, New Zealand, Chile, and Peru protested strongly, but DeGaulle, being DeGaulle, simply dismissed these objections.

Japan, too, presented some problems of atomic diplomacy. The Japanese ports of Sasebo and Yokosuka had large American naval bases, and we wanted our nuclear powered ships to be able to call there. But since the Japanese were then extremely sensitive about nuclear power, we wanted to introduce them gradually and receive full Japanese government approval in advance. In the summer of 1963 we asked Japanese permission to have a nuclear-powered submarine call in Sasebo. To certify that the vessel would not endanger health in Japan, Dr. Kankura Kaneshige from the Japanese AEC was sent to Washington in August so that the Japanese government could say that it had satisfied itself that the ship presented no danger.

Kaneshige was to call on Admiral Rickover, head of the Navy's nuclear-powered ship effort. Rickover, in his single-minded determination to make the Navy go nuclear, had developed a thick skin protecting a large ego. After their meeting Kaneshige returned to my office very shaken. He said that instead of discussing any of the questions he wanted to ask, Rickover had handed him the text of the "report" he should make to the Japanese government and people. The draft report said that Dr. Kaneshige "had the inestimable pleasure" of meeting Admiral Rickover, the "world's greatest authority" on nuclear ship propulsion, in his "simple and unadorned office." "Admiral Rickover assured Dr. Kaneshige, on his word of honor, that the submarines are safe." End of report. It took considerable "diplomacy" on my part to obtain from Rickover and his staff a little (but not much) more for Kaneshige to carry back with him.

Not all our weapons problems were nuclear. The State Department's Office of Munitions Control was responsible by law for licensing all exports of arms, ammunition, military equipment, and military technical data. This office reported to me. I was also involved in the licensing to Soviet bloc countries of items called "dual use" (e.g. computers), which, though sold for civilian applications, might be pressed into military service. The Commerce Department had responsibility for them but input from State, channeled first through the Economic Bureau, was usually required.

The Munitions Control Office referred potentially controversial license applications to the various agencies concerned, including Defense, AEC, ACDA, NASA, and the appropriate geographic bureau of State. Commerce did the same for dual use items. Of the tens of thousands of applications each year, the vast majority were handled routinely in accordance with established regulations and guidelines. When a request for military equipment or dual use items like light airplanes came from a politically sensitive country like South Africa or Portugal, however, the differences between and within departments could be intense. The same was true of requests for dual-use items from Soviet bloc countries, especially computers and communications equipment. These devices almost always had some military value despite an ostensibly civilian destination. And the controversies were further complicated by the Coordinating Committee (COCOM), composed of the NATO countries and Japan, which met in Paris to harmonize policies about exports to the communist bloc, so that one country did not provide what other countries refused to.

One of the great advantages of an in-house Department science office was its ability to provide an independent analysis of the technological significance of some of these dual use exports. As far as the Soviet bloc countries were concerned, the specific disagreements stemmed from a broader question: were we engaged in full-scale economic warfare with the Warsaw Pact, or were we simply trying to prevent the export of materials with actual warmaking potential? The government never resolved this question systematically, and we dealt with all too many requests case by case. I often found the Pentagon staff excessively conservative. Once Defense strenuously opposed the export of a new civilian telephone system to Bulgaria, arguing that any improvement in its communications would contribute to the warmaking potential of a Soviet bloc member. The Department of Commerce, of course, tended to favor the exports, and State usually sat somewhere in the middle. In many cases it was clear that if we denied the license, the equipment would simply be bought from another country.

When agreement eluded the staff level, the matter would usually be referred to me. If I decided to pursue it, I would go to the Secretary if the controversy was internal, to the Department or to the Deputy Secretary of Defense if interdepartmental. In rare cases involving fundamental policy, like licensing General Electric to enter into a contract with a French company to develop an advanced jet engine, I sometimes appealed to the White

House. My general inclination was to be liberal in approving export requests and I pushed in that direction. I did not feel we were wise to use exports as a stick to enforce compliance with our policies except in very serious circumstances.

Cuban Missile Crisis

As I write this, on the desk next to me sits a small silver calendar for October, 1962, with the days from the 16th to the 28th etched in bold figures. At the top are engraved the initials "UAJ-JFK". It was a momento President Kennedy gave to the fourteen members of the original Executive Committee of the National Security Council, or Excom, who met continually over those thirteen days to consider and execute the government's response to the Soviet introduction of medium and intermediate-range nuclear missiles into Cuba. We have never come closer to nuclear holocaust. That the Cuban Missile Crisis was successfully resolved is a tribute to the good judgment and steady nerves of President Kennedy. Our success also reflected a degree of cooperation among all his subordinates, military and civilian, that I think can fairly be called impressive. We thrashed out alternative courses of action, prepared contingency plans, put in motion complex and interrelated strings of military and diplomatic activity under conditions of excruciating tension, without thought of rank, department, or self. It was the finest example of complete politico-military cooperation and integration I have ever seen, and President Kennedy's calendar is a momento I treasure.

The story of the Missile Crisis naturally breaks down into four periods: intelligence gathering, prior to October 15, when the CIA and other parts of the intelligence community sifted information from refugees, sources close to Castro, and U-2 pictures to assemble conclusive evidence of ballistic missile site contruction; planning, from October 15 to the President's speech on October 22, when we weighed alternative courses and prepared for them; action, from the speech to October 28, when we put into effect our naval blockade around Cuba to interdict further Soviet nuclear weapons shipments and cajoled the UN, Organization of American States and governments around the world to support us; and resolution, after October 28, when Moscow announced it would withdraw the missiles. In return we pledged not to invade Cuba, and several months later, though not part of a strict quid pro quo, we removed some obsolete Jupiter medium range nuclear missiles from bases in Turkey and Italy.

Some have charged that the missiles should have been discovered earlier: that the intelligence community was lax in interpreting the increasing number of reports it was receiving about new types of missiles in Cuba, and that the State Department prevented earlier discovery of the missiles by rejecting requests for U-2 overflights. These assertions are wrong. As soon as the intelligence community got wind that something new having to do with missiles was going on in Cuba (by analyzing reports that by themselves were vague and inconsistent), additional U-2 flights were programmed. Unfortunately, weather conditions over the target area were cloudy for long periods, delaying flights already scheduled. Meanwhile, the Soviets were also building anti-aircraft missile sites on Cuba, and agents and refugees naturally had trouble distinguishing these from MRBM and IRBM construction.

We had to be cautious about approving U-2 overflights, given the potential presented by these anti-aircraft sites for shooting them down. CIA Director McCone argued for extensive U-2 overflights at a Special Group meeting on October 4, but because of concern about the anti-aircraft, others present (including me) asked for a report on all alternative methods of reconnaissance. We heard this on October 9, and then went on to approve the overflight that ultimately produced the first hard evidence of nuclear missile installation in Cuba. I can state categorically that there were no requests from anyone, rejected by the State Department or otherwise, that could have led to earlier discovery of the missiles.

No matter how comprehensive one tries to be, intelligence collection by its nature has an element of luck. I believe the intelligence community followed up its leads promptly and aggressively and that its performance both before and after October 15 cannot be faulted. Indeed, we are extremely fortunate it worked as efficiently as it did; had the information come a week or two later, the missiles might have been operational before we could have done anything about them.

Bad weather had delayed the overflight authorized on the 9th until the 14th. I first received word that our photo-reconnaissance interpreters had discovered MRBM sites in Cuba at a black tie dinner that Max Taylor was giving at his quarters in Fort McNair on October 15. Thereupon started an extended period of round the clock activity so intense that its details are a blur to all who participated. None of us kept a detailed account. At the President's request, however, soon after the crisis was over, I oversaw the preparation of a 200-page Top Secret chronicle of events by Frank Sieverts of the Department's public affairs staff that consolidated the recollections of all the participants and drew on the written notes of Paul Nitze, the only one to take notes. So though what I write here is not blow-by-blow, it is nevertheless based on the best existing record.

I was a member of the Excom from start to finish. I participated in all its deliberations and in the frequent long conferences in Under Secretary Ball's conference room that became our working center. While a great deal has been written about "hawks" and "doves"—those who wanted to take out the missile sites with a series of air strikes versus those who preferred less drastic measures, ranging from doing nothing to a naval blockade—I think it is safe to say that almost everyone changed his position at least once and sometimes several times up to October 22. My own initial preference was for the air strike. I thought it would be the quickest and most certain way of eliminating this threat to our national survival and would present a fait accompli to Havana and Moscow without giving them time or opportunity to do anything rash before the status quo was restored. However, as the number of anti-aircraft missile sites revealed by further reconnaissance increased and the number of sorties and bombs the Air Force estimated would be required to eliminate them mounted, it became clear to me that no such air strike would be "clean." I had lots of experience from the Korean War in inflated Air Force claims of probable effectiveness. In this case, many Cubans and Russians, civilian as well as military, would be killed as the anti-aircraft and missile sites were destroyed. And so I came around, along with most of the Excom, to favor a blockade (called a "quarantine" in the President's speech to make it more acceptable under international law) that would prevent further shipments of missile-related equipment to Cuba—including, we hoped, their nuclear warheads, which reconnaissance had not yet revealed to be present. That would give the Russians a chance to save face and signal the restraint and care we hoped they would exercise. Blockade was a decisive yet gradual step that preserved our options to the maximum extent possible.

Here I think Bobby Kennedy's good sense and moral character were perhaps decisive. He spoke with great feeling about how reprehensible it would seem if the United States launched an air attack without warning on our tiny island neighbor, a kind of Pearl Harbor with us playing Japan. He made his argument very powerfully and I believe it strongly influenced the Excom to move more or less as a group behind the "political track," as the blockade was called.

The President attended few of our meetings to make sure he did not inadvertently influence our deliberations. Nevertheless, when Excom consensus settled on blockade, the President, on Thursday, October 18, directed that military planning for it begin. But on Friday this decision came unstuck after Dean Acheson made a strong plea for the air strike. The President, careful not to arouse undue suspicion, had gone on a campaign trip to Chicago and the Excom continued debating through the day. Still convinced in my own mind that blockade was the right route, I immediately agreed with Paul Nitze's suggestion at the end of an afternoon meeting in George Ball's conference room (nicknamed "the thinktank") on Friday that we develop a specific plan for the blockade detailing exactly what to do and when to do it. We went to my office at 8:40 that evening and talked it over. We needed some centralizing concept to impose coherence on the detailed scenario we wished to draft, and decided upon the President's speech announcing to the world the missiles' presence and our blockade response. The President had tentatively set the speech for Monday night. I worked out all the diplomatic steps that needed to be taken before, during, and after the speech to make sure that support was obtained from the appropriate governments and organizations. Paul worked on the necessary military moves. Everything was coordinated to the President's speech, which we labeled "P hour." By midnight we had each worked out a comprehensive program and melded our two strands into one document. Like the rest of our work during the Missile Crisis, we were so careful about security that we did not even give it to our secretaries to type, doing our own work in longhand.

The next morning at the Excom we did not show anyone our scenario. But we did tell Ted Sorenson, the President's speechwriter, that we needed a draft of the Presidential speech announcing the blockade around which the scenario was designed. Ted said he could not write any speech as the Excom was still debating and the President has not made up his mind. We told him not to worry, that all we wanted was a draft. He asked against which country the speech should be directed, Cuba or the Soviet Union. In keeping with an Excom consensus reached in the President's presence on Thursday we told him the Soviet Union. When the full Excom assembled at 2:30 on Saturday afternoon at the White House after the President returned from his campaign trip, we were ready with the draft speech and scenario. This focused discussion considerably; now we had a planning job before us instead of a gabfest. The President had been moving towards the quarantine approach for several days, but I believe our written scenario helped firm up this conviction and the pro-blockade consensus that had dissipated since Thursday.

As I have said elsewhere, I have often observed that a telegram directing an ambassador to take a specific action is the best way of taking hold of the government, much more effective than the most thoughtfully crafted analytic paper. The role of the scenario Paul and I prepared for the Excom is analogous.

The scenario went through many revisions, even up to the time of the President's speech. What follows is the final version as it appeared at the time of the speech:

Quarantine
Action Contemplated

The objective of this action is immediately to stop a further buildup of an offensive capability in Cuba and ultimately to eliminate it. This initially involves a naval quarantine against offensive weapons within the framework of the OAS and the Rio Treaty. Such a quarantine might be expanded by subsequent steps to cover all types of goods and air transport. The action would be backed up by some form of surveillance of Cuba.

Elements in Course of Action

Time	Action	Action Responsibility
P Hour	Public statement by the President	Sorensen
	Steps Prior to P Hour	
P hour minus 24	1. Instructions to all military commands to go on DEFCON 3 as appropriate, effective at P hour.	DOD
P hour minus 24	2. CONAD AND SAC instructed to put forces on such air and ground alert on P hour as dictated by military readiness requirements. (No publicity.)	DOD

P hour minus 24	3. Instructions to CINCLANT to mobilize force for imposition of blockade and to protect U.S. shipping.	DOD
P hour minus 24	4. Instructions to CINCARIB to prepare for furnishing military riot control support to selected Latin American countries.	
P hour minus 24	5. Summon Congressional leaders to Washington.	W.H.
	6. Notification as follows to key NATO countries by U.S. Ambassadors at capitals:	
P hour minus 12	U.K.	EUR
P hour minus 4	France	EUR
P hour minus 2	Germany, Canada, Italy, Turkey	EUR
P hour minus 12	7. Special intelligence briefing through intelligence channels of U.K. and Canada.	CIA
P hour minus 8	8. Approach to Latin American countries by U.S. Ambassadors in capitals to warn them possibility internal civil disturbances in next 24 hours and to ask for appointment with chief of state for P hour minus 1.	ARA
P hour minus 6	9. Complete reinforcement of Guantanamo.	DOD
P hour minus 2	10. Notification to NAC.	EUR
P hour minus 2	11. Consultation with Congressional leaders.	W.H.
P hour minus 1/2	12. Inform remainder of allies, both in capitals and at organization headquarters where appropriate (SEATO, CENTO, ANZUS, China, Japan, Korea), and certain other non-Bloc countries.	
P hour minus 2	13. Approach to chiefs of state by U.S. Ambassadors in Latin American countries, informing them of substance of President's statement and seeking their prompt support for convoking "Organ of Consultation" and decision on Articles VI and VIII of Rio Treaty.	ARA

P hour	14. Military alerts declared in accordance with foregoing.	DOD
P hour	15. Evacuate dependents from Guantanamo.	DOD
P hour	16. Dobrynin informed, being given text of President's statement and transmittal message to Khrushchev which will also be delivered to Moscow as soon as possible thereafter.	Secretary
P hour	17. Take whatever action has been decided upon in reinforcing Europe.	DOD
P hour minus 1	18. All allied embassies in Washington given full briefings and hear President's statement.	
	Latin American Ambassadors	ARA
	All other Ambassadors	U
P hour	19. Ask for Security Council meeting for following morning.	USUN
P hour plus ½	20. Briefing of OAS Ambassadors.	ARA
P hour plus 1	21. Briefing of Neutral Ambassadors.	Secretary
P hour plus 14	22. OAS meeting, at which the Secretary would represent the U.S., followed as quickly as possible by an "Organ of Consultation" meeting.	ARA
P hour minus 14	23. Security Council meeting at which U.S. Representative would, pursuant to Article 54 of the Charter, inform the UN Security Council of the action being proposed to the OAS.	USUN
P hour plus	24. Following favorable OAS action, issuance of Presidential Proclamation on blockade with grace period of 24 hours.	(State (Justice (W.H.
	25. Imposition of blockade.	DOD
	(This becomes B day)	

In the two days preceding "P hour" the State Department, among other things: informed twenty-one embassies in Latin America (without giving them the substance) of the upcoming Presidential broadcast and instructed them to be prepared to talk with their governments; dispatched special briefing officers (one of whom was Dean Acheson) to London, Paris, Bonn; sent the text of the speech as it was being delivered to 129 embassies and consulates; organized a meeting of the Organization of American States; provided oral briefings to ninety-five foreign ambassadors and an unknown number of newsmen by top Department officials; requested an urgent UN Security Council meeting; and sent, in addition to the President's speech, personal letters we drafted for the President to Khrushchev, Macmillan, DeGaulle, Nehru, Adeneuer, Canadian Prime Minister Diefenbaker, Italian Prime Minister Fanfani, and West Berlin Mayor Brandt. If the Soviets did respond with force, we expected it would be someplace other than Cuba—perhaps, Berlin, or Turkey where our Jupiter missiles were based—because of our tactical advantage in the Caribbean, and we wanted our allies to be prepared. We also prepared a legal justification for the blockade.

Throughout the ordeal the President was serious but never panicked. As usual he was excellent at asking probing questions and guarding against overly precipitate consensus. Kennedy did not irrevocably commit himself to the quarantine until drafting the final versions of his Monday night speech. We needed to have the text late Sunday night, October 21, to prepare it for transmission to the appropriate embassies in time for them to inform their host governments. Only that deadline forced the President to tie up some of the detailed decisions that went into the speech. If a security leak had permitted the Russians to put us on the defensive or if the missiles had become operational earlier, the week the President took after October 15 to establish the government's course of action might have been fatally long. But nothing succeeds like success. During the Missile Crisis, Kennedy's fondness for government by seminar, natural restraint of character, and aversion to making decisions until necessary served the country very well.

There are four chief lessons I learned from those thirteen days in October about the way our government can best organize itself to handle this kind of vastly complex foreign policy crisis. First, as I later repeatedly emphasized to the Joint Chiefs, we have left behind forever the era of neat "war plans" composed by colonels in splendid and artificial isolation from political reality. The scenario Paul Nitze and I prepared demonstrated conclusively that political and military plans must meld intimately if they are to have any value to the President. I believe the Missile Crisis drove home that proposition to the then existing JCS, but subsequent Chiefs have usually had to undergo their own crises before being persuaded.

Second, when the consequences of mistake may be nuclear war and virtually unlimited destruction, the President will rightly demand unlimited control of the government, down to its minutest activities. The Chief of Naval Operations, Admiral Anderson, had some very heated exchanges with Secretary McNamara about how the Navy should conduct the blockade and its searches of ships bound for Cuba. Anderson said the Navy knew perfectly well how to search ships and should damn well be left to get on with its business. But the extreme political delicacy of the blockade made the President insist on controlling individual destroyers from the Cabinet Room of the White House. And he was absolutely right. Gone are the days when an ambassador or field commander can be dispatched to carry out a sensitive mission with broad guidance and lots of hope. The world is entirely too dangerous for that. Devastating war can start from a spiral of inadvertencies as well as malice aforethought.

A third lesson of the Missile Crisis is the absolute necessity of having the means to back up our words. We never bluffed (which is different from saying that we could not have failed). Khrushchev knew that we could attack Cuba at a moment's notice and were prepared to do so if missile construction continued. Furthermore, he knew we had a superiority of nuclear weapons: indeed, it was the inadequacies of Soviet ICBMs, in part, that provoked him to the audacious gamble of deploying shorter-range ones in Cuba. It was our unarguable military superiority, both tactical (in the Caribbean) and strategic (in nuclear weapons) that permitted President Kennedy to opt for the non-military solution of the blockade. He could not have gambled our national survival without knowing he had the aces. Our words, actions, and potential for further action communicated to Khrushchev that we meant absolutely what we said. Since the Missile Crisis the Soviets have expanded their conventional and nuclear capabilities relentlessly. I wonder if the Kremlin's present leaders, faced with an identical crisis, would back down as Khrushchev did.

The fourth conclusion is more technical than the others but raises important questions about the government's ability to continue governing when it faces the risk of nuclear war. Elaborate plans existed at the time of the Missile Crisis for relocating the government away from Washington if war seemed likely. Plans for the State Department, for example, involved breaking the senior leadership into two groups, one of which would go by helicopter to the Pentagon's hardened relocation site in Maryland and the other, also by helicopter, to another underground command post in the Virginia mountains. In case you missed the choppers, you were given driving instructions. At no time, of course, were you supposed to say a word about your impending disappearance to your family. I had difficulty imagining myself, or anyone else, driving into the Virginia countryside, leaving my family to probable destruction without so much as a good-bye. During the Missile Crisis it was clear that the President would not have considered leaving the White House, even though at some points we all believed nuclear war to be very possible. Evacuating the senior members of the government from Washington would have deeply alarmed the country and perhaps convinced the Soviets that we intended nuclear war, provoking them into a preemptive strike. We consequently reviewed these arrangements. Consideration was given to building a shelter half a mile under Washington connected to the White House, State Department, Pentagon and other important centers, but this presented obvious engineering and secrecy problems. Now, the plan is for the President to board a 747 equipped with a stupendous array of communications gear, from which he can direct Armageddon impervious to ground attack. Surely this would be as unattractive to a President now as the Virginia getaway was then, but there seems to be no satisfactory alternative. The terrifying speed with which a nuclear war could be fought makes the preservation of a functioning government essential.

The most difficult aspect to convey· of a Deputy Under Secretary's job is its endless bewildering variety. I was at the office at least ten hours a day six days a week, usually half a day on Sunday, with receptions and dinners in the evening every other day. As the chief liaison with Defense, the FBI, and the intelligence community, as the one who supposedly could "get things done," mine was a life of lighting and extinguishing many brushfires. Of course I had enduring concerns, like politico-military affairs and organizing the Department to get the best out of it. But I also had charge of hundreds of shorter-lived issues. Some turned out to be tempests in a teapot; others could easily have shattered the teapot and lots more besides. To give a picture of what I was doing in this period, let me describe just a few of the mini-crises that filled my days.

American diplomats in the Soviet Union, then and now, are subject to strict controls on their whereabouts. They are permitted to travel only a short distance from Moscow without Kremlin permission, and large areas of the country are closed off permanently. The regulations are intended to impede anything the Soviets would consider espionage. As a result of this treatment, the National Security Council in 1954 instituted a strictly reciprocal set of restrictions on travel by Eastern European diplomats in our country. In 1963, however, the FBI found some Hungarian military attachés traveling by car within sight of one of our ICBM silos in the midwest. At Pentagon urging, large areas of the United States were then closed off to all Eastern European official personnel regardless of whether their individual countries placed similar restrictions on American diplomats (which some did not). The State Department believed that these additional restrictions were useless. There was nothing a diplomat could discover driving a car that Soviet satellites could not see better. It made us look silly to be even more secretive about our territory than the Soviet Union, and it invited the Eastern European countries to retaliate with similarly harsh constraints on American travel. In early 1966 all of our Eastern European chiefs of mission petitioned the Department on their own initiative to seek a return to the pre-1963 system of reciprocity. We took up the cause, but foundered in the face of tough opposition from Defense and Justice. Only later did we finally go back to our former policy of strict reciprocity with each country.

Soviet travel of a different type caused difficulties later that year. The Department had a policy of refusing to issue visas to delegations of Soviet trade union officials for visits to the United States. George Meany, the fiercely anti-communist President of the AFL-CIO, had significant influence on this policy. Not without reason, he believed that Soviet trade union chiefs were merely cossetted lackeys of the Communist Party and should not be allowed to meet with American workers to extol the virtues of Soviet labor relations.

On June 8, 1966, I had a phone call from an angry Victor Reuther, head of the Autoworkers' Union. Reuther, who was more liberal than Meany, said that at the request of the Citizens Exchange Council in New York, a private group, his union had worked out an interesting program of tours and visits with congressmen, civil rights leaders, and others for a group of Soviet private citizens, some of whom were officials of their engineering union. He said he had had the approval of Averell Harriman, then Ambassador at Large, who was out of town. Now, a few days before they were due to arrive, the State Department had told him their visas had been refused because they were trade union officials, not shop workers. He would not have his union embarrassed like this, he insisted. These were tourists, not an official union delegation. He vehemently asked whether the State Department was running American foreign policy or George Meany? In what was hardly a coincidence, Senator Joseph Clark of Pennsylvania called me later that day to say that refusing the visas was "terrible" and that he hoped something could be done.

The Department had already suggested to the Citizens Exchange Council that they invite the Soviets to send a different group that would exclude union officials. Reuther thought that was unseemly and embarrassing, and I agreed. We worked out a compromise; we would ask the Soviets to enlarge the delegation to include some non-union people. This was done—not without protest from George Meany—and the expanded group came.

Other problems that took up my time in this period were with Canada, which wanted to draw lines across the mouths of its large bays (including Hudson's Bay) and make them territorial waters instead of international (a topic that resurfaced again in the 1970s), and with Japan. The Japanese had an extremely important and profitable industry fishing for king crab off the west coast of the United States on our continental shelf. The whole problem revolved around whether the king crab maintained contact with the continental shelf throughout its life cycle, in which case we had exclusive rights to harvest it under international law. If at any point in its life cycle the crab lost contact with the bottom, however, it was considered a pelagic resource of the high seas open to fishing by all. Marine scientists were never able to answer this question conclusively. In 1964 a bill was sponsored by Senator Bartlett from Alaska that would have wiped out the Japanese industry. I worked out a compromise with the Japanese Ambassador, Ryuji Takeuchi, that we would consider king crab a seabed resource but would license Japanese vessels to fish for them.

An altogether more important problem was whether to take steps towards a closer relationship between the United States and Peking. This was obviously a decision that only the President could make. President Kennedy was not willing to risk the political consequences of inflaming the Taiwan lobby until his second term. And later, with the Vietnam War accelerating, President Johnson did not even consider it a possibility.

After my many years of experience with Wang Ping-nan I did not believe there was any present hope for normalizing relations with Peking unless we were willing to abandon Taiwan. China's consistent position had been that the pressure of events would eventually force us to attenuate unilaterally our close ties

with Taiwan, so that they only need wait. (In this they turned
out to be quite right, as President Carter demonstrated when he
de-recognized Taiwan in order to recognize Peking in 1980. In
the early 1060s, however, I saw no possibility of that happening.
I thought smaller initiatives—for instance, withdrawing our ban
on grain sales to Peking, as Averell Harriman and others suggested
in the spring of 1962—would go nowhere unless we were prepared to make some really fundamental concessions on Taiwan.

Peking had rejected overtures from us very rudely at the
beginning of the Kennedy Administration, when we offered to
consider licensing shipments of food and medicine. My own basic
position was that we should show receptivity to any initiative
Peking made but not make any of our own, since there was no
evidence that Peking would be responsive if we did so, and their
own internal politics made the chances of accommodation very
slight. Nevertheless, I thought we would lose nothing by loosening
some of the Dulles era's more rigid restrictions on exchanges
between us and Peking. On March 15, 1962, for example, I met
a delegation from the American Friends Service Committee headed by its Executive Secretary Colin Bell, to discuss its programs
involving Communist China. They wanted to know how the Department would react if some distinguished American Quakers
like Hugh Borton, President of Haverford College, joined an international group of Quakers traveling to China. I said that my
experience was that if we approved Peking would automatically
reject, so we would not commit ourselves, but if Peking showed
any willingness to have them, which I doubted, we would be
willing to consider it. They also wanted to know if the eligibility
of American Foreign Service Officers to attend their international
seminars for diplomats would be affected if communist Chinese
diplomats also attended; I said no.

Kennedy Assassination

On November 22, 1963, I was having lunch with Howard Jones,
our Ambassador to Indonesia, on the eighth floor of the Department when a Secretariat officer tapped me on the shoulder to
whisper to me that the President had been shot and that George
Ball wanted to see me immediately. I rushed to his office, where
we listened in shock to the radio and then heard the announcement that the President was dead. With details of the shooting
nonexistent, we worried that it might be part of a larger plot to
paralyze the nation, perhaps perpetrated by a foreign govern-

ment. We set to work feverishly trying to insure that the transition of authority to President Johnson was completely orderly.

We sent word to Secretary Rusk, en route to Japan with other Cabinet secretaries for a meeting with their Japanese counterparts, to return at once. We sent messages to our embassies and consulates giving as much information about the shooting as we could confirm. Most important, we were in touch with the FBI, CIA, Joint Chiefs, and Secret Service to see if there was any evidence of a wider plot to disrupt the government or if the Soviets appeared to be making any military moves to take advantage of the tragedy. In a few hours, the Secret Service called me to have us search our passport files on a man called Lee Harvey Oswald. When they revealed that he had lived in the Soviet Union for a time and recently visited the Soviet Embassy in Mexico City, we really suspected a plot. I also got our records people to pull the files on President Roosevelt's funeral, the most recent equivalent ceremony, to check what the precedents were. We also performed one of the domestic responsibilities of the State Department—notifying all the state governors via telegram of who is the new President.

When Air Force One arrived carrying President Johnson and President Kennedy's body, George Ball was there to meet LBJ. Even if the Soviet Union had nothing to do with the assassination, we were both extremely concerned that any sign of discontinuity or hesitancy would invite Soviet adventurism, and George conveyed to the new President the suggestion that he move into the Oval Office immediately. LBJ had the good sense to resist that, which would have looked disrespectful to Mrs. Kennedy's grief and the slain President's memory. Instead he occupied an office across the street in the Executive Office Building. When Secretary Rusk arrived at Andrews Air Force Base at twenty-five minutes after midnight on November 23, George and I met him and briefed him on what we knew.

The Attorney General took charge of arranging his brother's funeral, and after his decision to invite foreign representatives I took charge of the immense amount of work this meant for the Department. Invitations were dispatched to all chiefs of state and heads of government. About fifty accepted, all of whom had to be met and looked after properly. Rusk, Ball, McGhee, and I shuttled from airport to airport greeting them as they arrived. The President was supposed to meet DeGaulle, but could not get away from ceremonies then going on at the Capitol, so I did it. The French Ambassador burst into tears when I told him President Johnson could not be at the airport. DeGaulle, however, was relaxed and gracious.

So that the foreign leaders and President Johnson could meet each other, a reception at the State Department was arranged following the funeral on November 25. The timing was very tight. We had to make sure everyone got a chance to speak and be photographed with the new President and that no one was kept waiting too long. We also had to make sure the President had thirty seconds to read the 3 x 5 card containing a thumbnail sketch of each visitor that we had prepared. The President stayed in a side room off the main eighth floor reception room. The basic approach was to allow five minutes for each visitor—one minute to usher out the last visitor and usher in the new one, each accompanied by the appropriate Assistant Secretary, during which the President could read his briefing card, and four minutes for conversation and a photograph. Then the visitor was ushered to the seventh floor to see the Secretary of State. With fifty visitors at five minutes each this meant over four hours for both the President and the Secretary. My jobs were to see that each Assistant Secretary had his charges in tow and was ready at the proper moment and to deal with the inevitable foul-ups. But using the Secret Service and our own Security Service, with their radios and our Operations Center communications, everything went reasonably smoothly. The only problem, predictably, was De-Gaulle, who swept in with a large entourage and expected to have an hour with LBJ while other world leaders cooled their heels. The President somehow managed to finish with him in fifteen minutes.

The more time you spend in Washington, the more you observe that personality, particularly the President's, leaves a distinct imprint on policy. That was especially obvious to me when President Johnson came to power. He was at once more personally dramatic and more orderly in his way of structuring the government than was Kennedy. While Kennedy often acted as his own Secretary of State, having great interest in and convictions about foreign affairs, Johnson entered the White House much less certain of himself and eager to demonstrate continuity with his slain predecessor by relying heavily on the subordinates JFK had chosen. As a result, Dean Rusk's significance in Washington increased. Dean had always shown great respect to Johnson when he was Vice President, an attitude Johnson had not universally encountered. Dean had seen LBJ regularly to brief him and solicit advice.

Possibly the fact that both came from poor rural backgrounds may have helped cement a personal relationship. Dean had even assigned an FSO full-time to the Vice President's staff to make sure LBJ could keep in touch with the Department quickly and easily. Thus when Johnson became President he already knew Rusk and the Department and was willing to lean on us for advice.

My own first contacts with Johnson had come when he was Vice President and had made a good will trip to Southeast Asia in May, 1961. To accompany the Vice President I sent my staff aide, Frank Meloy (who, as Ambassador to Lebanon in 1975, was murdered as he drove to arrange a cease-fire between the warring factions). On May 12, at the end of the visit to Saigon, LBJ had some questions about the communiqué to be issued. He had been told in Washington that our military communications system was a marvel and that all he needed to do to reach us during the journey was pick up the phone, an instrument of which he was powerfully fond. Very early in the morning I got a call from the Vice President asking my clearance on what he proposed to say in the communique. Unfortunately, it turned out to be stronger in support of Diem than the Administration's line at the time. The connection was dreadful and only once or twice was I able to hear his voice. Finally, what he said was repeated by a sergeant in Manila to a sergeant in Honolulu to a sergeant at the White House, who repeated it to me. This was obviously a very unsatisfactory method of conversation. I kept telling him to put the draft language on the State telex and I could have it on paper in front of me in thirty minutes, but he insisted on using the military phone. So we continued "talking" in fits and starts in this fashion for the entire day, which was through the night in Saigon. After we finally settled the wording late in the evening Washington time, Frank told me they got on a plane, still in black tie from the dinner they had attended the night before, and left for Manila. Frank was a pretty stout fellow, but he found working for the Vice President so exhausting that he had to go to bed for two weeks afterwards.

Frank's ability so impressed LBJ that he tried to persuade him to join his staff on Capitol Hill. But after that overwhelming trip Frank was not too eager to work for Johnson without prospect of escape. So I put Johnson off. But he was not an easy man to thwart. He continued to insist, and then he and Lady Bird had Frank to their house for a barbecue and really put the rush on him. With Frank's enthusiastic but discrete approval, I kept interposing myself between LBJ and him to say that I just could not release him. As it ended up, Frank stayed with me. And LBJ never let me forget it. For years afterwards he kept reminding me, "you're the man who wouldn't let me have Frank Meloy." But in fact LBJ never held this incident against me, and it may even have done our relationship some good.

A well-publicized event during the Vice President's trip was his chance meeting with a Pakistani camel driver in Karachi, to whom LBJ promised he would send a jeep, a symbol of the better life to be had through modernization. When the Vice President returned to Washington the task of somehow getting a jeep to the camel driver inevitably fell to me. I contracted our Office of Maritime Affairs which regularly dealt with the shipping industry. By chance, a shipping conference was meeting in New York that day, and after a few phone calls I found someone who would transport the jeep free of charge, provided there was no publicity of that fact. I was able to call the Vice President back the same day to report the arrangement, which naturally pleased him. This incident was minor but illustrates how knowing how to tap the store of expertise squirrled away in the Department can be useful in getting things done.

When I say that LBJ was personally dramatic in his style of governing, I mean that he had a kind of raw, overpowering actor's persona that he could make assume whatever shape he needed at the moment. When he wanted to be angry, he could be angrier than anyone I have ever known. When he wanted to be kind, he could be kinder; when he wanted to be crude, he could be appalling. His personality radiated energy and force. He dominated any group he was in, and this was not just because he was President. Unfortunately, he seemed to turn to wood whenever he had a television appearance or major speech to make, as if he felt that in public he had to "act Presidential." In private, he may have not always acted Presidential but he was without doubt the President.

I think a lot of people were as fooled by LBJ's proclivity for juggling many balls at once as by his kaleidoscopic personality. Many perceived him as impulsive and emotional. It is true that sometimes he did move more quickly than was wise, but more often he liked to give that impression when in fact he was moving very deliberately. He was willing to read, to study, to listen, and to hear opposing points of view thoroughly before deciding. And when he made up his mind, everyone understood his instructions. In that respect he was very satisfactory to work for. I think he diminished his own effectiveness by acting so hard at trying to seem a powerhouse, larger than life.

It is said that towards the end of his Presidency, the frustrations of Vietnam pushed LBJ to the brink of nervous collapse. I was in Tokyo after November 1966, but until then I never observed him at any time to be anything but stable. On the other hand, I did have many occasions to witness his mounting anger because of his inability to end the conflict quickly and satisfactorily. What the President perceived as disloyalty particularly infuriated him. During the well-known Vietnam hearings before the Senate Foreign Relations Committee in February, 1966, for instance, when Senator Fulbright put before the public eye a long series of dissenters to the President's policy, I received a barrage of Texas-sized ire. On February 11, after the anti-Administration testimony of George Kennan and James Gavin, LBJ called me for a half-hour stream of complaining and prodding. This was two days after we had returned from a summit with Thieu, Ky, and other South Vietnamese officials in Honolulu that we all thought had been very successful. "Isn't someone analyzing the opposition testimony?" he asked me angrily. By the next day he wanted a briefing on the SEATO Treaty, an account of "the shifting positions of the loyal opposition," and especially some examples of how Senator Fulbright had been contradicting himself. "The Soviet Ambassador was the author of a good many of the moves" that Fulbright and company were making, he told me; a parade of people, all of whom reported conversations with the Soviet Ambassador had been to see him arguing that Moscow could settle everything. "They think they are going to win this thing here in Washington. Alex, do you think we have our first team working on it?" He wanted me to send cables to Saigon setting a target date of June for a review of the social programs discussed at Honolulu, asked for the current aid figures to Saigon, and questioned the motives of columnists and television reporters who were criticizing his policy. "They are out to destroy Rusk, the Department, and our position. They are out to change the foreign policy of this country." It was a vintage LBJ performance.

I mostly listened, made sure the information he requested was sent to him, and offered support without becoming his partisan. Thus, when the President said he thought the Soviet Ambassador was orchestrating the dissent, I said nothing but did agree with his assertion that Moscow certainly knew what its Ambassador was doing. And as gently as possible I pointed out to him that George Kennan had never been to Southeast Asia and made no claim to being expert on Vietnam. I assumed that what the President really wanted to do was let off steam, and I did not interfere. In any event, I agreed with his Vietnam policy.

When Max Taylor and I returned from Saigon in the fall of 1965, we carried with us a conviction that our programs abroad involving more than one government department had grown so numerous and complex that some new administrative arrangement was necessary in Washington to insure we could respond to new problems quickly, imaginatively, and with the full weight of our resources. Max, who became a Special Consultant to the President, obtained from him a mandate to develop a plan for reorganizing the government so that it could manage interdepartmental programs abroad—and, in a broader sense, all aspects of our foreign policy—more effectively. Max and I worked closely together to develop this plan. Given his strong view that the State Department should "take charge", he found a stout ally in me.

What culminated from our efforts was NSAM 341, issued in March, 1966, which instituted some far-reaching changes in government structure. We had both been impressed by the value of the Mission Council, or Country Team, in obtaining the maximum aggregate effectiveness from the variety of agencies represented on it. A crucial element in its success, we recognized, was the primacy of the Ambassador, who pruned or encouraged Mission programs in pursuit of the best overall interests of the United States. In Washington, however, no one performed this central coordinating and directing function short of the President, whose time is obviously limited. That meant a lot of coordinating and directing simply did not happen.

Proceeding by analogy from the Ambassador's role within the Country Team, Max and I began to consider making the State Department the President's "Executive Agent" in providing overall guidance to our overseas activities. This had the great advantage, unlike an approach Kennedy might have entertained, of fixing the authority to settle interdepartmental disputes within an existing agency of the government with the resources of people and information to do the job.

I thought there would be mammoth resistance to this concept from other departments, jealous of giving any increased clout to a bureaucratic competitor. But the plan Max and I worked out was careful to protect other departments' prerogatives, and we found when discussing the idea around town that they were actually quite willing, and even desired to recognize State Department primacy in directing interagency activities abroad. I realized that making such a system work would require State to take "Presidential" views of issues rather than parochial self-interested ones, but Max and I thought State was up to the challenge and was really the only logical place to center this directing function short of the President.

President Johnson approved the NSAM embodying our recommendations and announced them to his Cabinet on March 4, 1966. Its central provision read:

> To assist the President in carrying out his responsibilities for the conduct of foreign affairs, he has assigned to the Secretary of State authority and responsibility to the full extent permitted by law for the overall direction, coordination and supervision of interdepartmental activities of the United States Government overseas."

To assist the Secretary in carrying out these new responsibilities, some new structures were established in the government. The first was the Senior Interdepartmental Group (SIG), including the Deputy Secretary of Defense, the AID Administrator, the CIA and USIA Directors, the JCS Chairman, The President's National Security Advisor, and the Under Secretary of State as "Executive Chairman". This novel title signified that he had authority not only to preside but decide, subject to the right of any member who strongly opposed his decision to appeal to the Secretary of State and the President. Because all SIG members had very high ranks within their agencies and were not permitted to send deputies unless sick or out of town—a valuable lesson drawn from the Special Group (Counter-Insurgency)—we expected that they would be able to commit their agencies solidly at SIG meetings and get results when they returned to their offices. Departments not represented on the SIG regularly were entitled to send representatives if business before it concerned them. To support the SIG, five Interdepartmental Regional Groups (IRGs), drawing on the same government agencies for members, were also established. Each had the appropriate Assistant Secretary of State as Executive Chairman. Both the SIG and the IRGS were given full-time staffs, and to further streamline the government a new way of organizing the Department itself was announced simultaneously. Instead of relatively junior "desk officers" in charge of individual countries reporting to their Assistant Secretaries through an Office Director in charge of a group of countries, we proposed to have relatively senior FSOs take on the new position of Country Director, eliminating the Office Director level eventually and giving the Ambassador someone of his approximate rank in Washington to whom he could turn.

We had no desire just to create six more Washington committees with NSAM 341. Between the SIG and the IRGs, with their regular senior membership and Executive Chairmen, we believed we had established a mechanism for settling major matters of policy quickly and decisively, leaving the Secretary of State and the President more time to concentrate on the really difficult questions. Since the White House had representatives on the SIG and all the IRGs, however, we felt the President would be able to keep abreast of what the Government was doing in foreign affairs in as much depth and detail as he wished. We also thought these committees would be particularly adept in crisis management. The members would already be used to working with each other and to making decisions as a group. While we expected SIG-IRG would act as an efficient filtering and decision-making apparatus, we also knew that would depend largely on how the participants used it; for while an Executive Chairman, like an Ambassador in the field, could tell the representative of another department not to do something, only that department itself could decide to commit people and money to something new.

When this plan was taking shape, Max had wanted to give State even more authority to act on the President's behalf. I convinced him that this would raise too much of a storm. I also knew that Dean Rusk would have great reservations about any system that took too much away from his Cabinet colleagues, for whose prerogatives he had great respect. Dean was never a tough infighter, never one to use his elbows or build bureaucratic monuments. Personally, I often would have been glad to see him act more assertively, but that was the way he was, and I knew that the SIG-IRG system had to reflect realistically his temperament or be stillborn. Max thought I should be the one to chair the Senior Interdepartmental Group, but it was clear that the rank of the other members required that the Under Secretary be the Executive Chairman, and thus George Ball took on the job with me as his Deputy. The new system did have some effect on my responsibilities, however; for the Special Group (Counter-Insurgency), on which I had sat since 1962 but which had become moribund, was now folded into the SIG.

In operation SIG-IRG never came up to our hopes. George went through the motions of using the SIG but it was not in his nature really to push it hard; and some of the Secretaries, particularly Secretary McNamara, did not hesitate to go directly to the President whenever the SIG made decisions they disliked, which undermined its authority. President Johnson understood and endorsed the system, but as far as he was concerned the people involved were more important than the committees they did or did not attend. Some of the Regional Groups worked well, and others did not, mostly depending on how adept their Executive Chairmen were at forging consensus. In any event, as I left Washington to become Ambassador to Japan in November, 1966, I did not have much chance to help make this new apparatus function, and Nixon destroyed it as soon as he became President.

CHAPTER ELEVEN

Deputy Ambassador Saigon, 1964-1965

AT THE CLOSE OF BUSINESS ON WEDNESDAY, JUNE 22, 1964, DEAN Rusk called me into his office for a brief chat over a scotch and soda. Henry Cabot Lodge was resigning as Ambassador in Saigon to run for the Republican Presidential nomination, and Rusk said that LBJ had settled on a replacement: General Maxwell D. Taylor, currently Chairman of the Joint Chiefs of Staff. Taylor was the nation's senior military officer, having also been JCS chairman under Eisenhower and Special Military Representative for JFK. He was also broadly cultured, urbane, and articulate. A logical choice, I thought, who would clearly signal LBJ's determination to make Vietnam work.

Much to my surprise, however, Dean also said the President wanted to know if I would serve as Taylor's number two. Max and I had been official and family friends since 1935, when we both studied Japanese in Tokyo. During the past few years we had worked together on President Kennedy's Counter-Insurgency Group and, after he became JCS Chairman, on the multitude of politico-military matters arising between the chiefs and state. I had come to respect Max highly as an officer whose wisdom and ability far transcended any conventional military mold. We worked well together. Dean said we would only be expected to remain in Saigon for about a year, and I could see the virtue of the President's desire to send a soldier-diplomat team. So before the ice cubes had time to melt, I agreed to serve in Saigon.

Dean promptly called the President, and both of them wanted to know what title I would consider appropriate for my new job, since I was now the Department's senior Foreign Service Officer with a permanent rank of Career Ambassador. I was going as Max's number two, so clearly I could not be called "Ambassador," but standard diplomatic titles made no provision for the two-man team LBJ was now inventing. Off the top of my head I suggested Deputy Ambassador, a title not to be found in any book on diplomacy. The President approved immediately and then asked if I could be on my way the next morning, in twelve hours. I replied that I had a wife, a car, a house, and a mortgage, and requested twenty-four hours more to settle my affairs. LBJ agreed that I could leave the day after, Friday morning, on a special KC-135 tanker aircraft that would fly directly to Saigon. Pat, as usual, would have to stay behind in Washington to pick up the pieces. Taylor would follow as soon as the Senate confirmed his nomination. And to my delight, the President and Secretary Rusk also approved the temporary assignment, pending his becoming Ambassador to Laos, of Bill Sullivan, an experienced officer for whom Max and I had great respect.

Pat was hardly thrilled to learn of my hasty exit from Washington, but LBJ was not a consummate politician for nothing. That night he spied her at an Indonesian Embassy reception, made a beeline across the room to her, and with his forceful charm told her how much he appreciated the sacrifice she was making. Then, in a voice clearly audible to the surrounding cluster of reporters and other onlookers, the President assured her that as compensation "she would eventually get the post she wanted most."

The subject had never come up between me and LBJ or even between me and Dean Rusk, but anyone who knew Pat knew that her heart's desire was to return to Tokyo as the wife of the Ambassador. Sure enough, LBJ remembered his promise to Pat and dispatched us to Japan in 1966. In the interim, however, he routinely denounced "those pinheads and youngsters over in State" for "wild speculations" that he was going to appoint me to Tokyo. I was luckier than many others in that LBJ did not change his mind just to prove news stories false.

So after some hurried packing, a brief call on the President, in which he told me to make Vietnam "work," and a gruelling twenty-five hour flight, I found myself deposited at Saigon's Tan Son Nhut airport at 9:00 Sunday morning, June 28, in the middle of the Vietnamese conflict I thought I had left in Geneva ten years before. I delivered an arrival statement for reporters that I still think accurately reflects the spirit Max and I brought to our Saigon duties: "Both General Taylor and I are approaching this assignment with a good deal of humility. We have no magic answers but we are determined to do our best." I also said that we had faith in the South Vietnamese people and "their ability to save their freedom and independence from those who would seek to destroy them." I feel that this best expressed our objective as we saw it.

Lodge, who was due to leave for the United States at 1 P.M. on the same plane that had brought me, met me at the airport. We had a hurried conversation as we drove to the embassy and then returned to the airport for Lodge's departure, where General Khanh, the current Prime Minister, gave Lodge full military honors and the two of them exchanged fulsome speeches in the broiling sun. Khanh liked Lodge and even presented him with a special hand-made ceremonial robe that looked rather incongruous on his 6'4" patrician frame.

Lodge had a reputation in the embassy for not immersing himself too deeply in the details of South Vietnam's intricate political situation; in fact, the only thing I can now recall of our brief conversation in the embassy limousine was a story he told about his first days in Saigon. He was visiting the Saigon Zoo, dressed in an immaculate white suit, and while he was inspecting the tigers' cage one of its inhabitants lifted a leg and soaked both suit and Ambassador. This allegedly delighted the Vietnamese present, who told Lodge he should interpret the incident as a good omen. I made a mental note to avoid the zoo.

As a taste of things to come, Lodge also told me that while he was packing that morning a delegation of Buddhist monks from Thich Tri Quang's group had come around to the residence bearing a gift. When Cabot opened it, there was a nicely framed picture of a monk burning himself to death in the middle of a street! It was later reported in the press that after a look of total shock, Cabot politely thanked the group and returned to packing.

After Lodge departed, I returned immediately to the embassy to meet the principals of the American effort in South Vietnam: General William Westmoreland, head of MACV (Military Advisory Command, Vietnam); Agency for International Development (AID) chief Jim Killen; USIA chief and mission spokesman Barry Zorthian; CIA Station Chief Peer de Silva; and Melvin Manfull, the embassy's Political Counselor. The first order of business was tightening the Mission's administrative structure. The Saigon Mission was then employing the country team approach, but the team met only occasionally. Of course, Max and I wanted to consult with the Mission's principals, but we thought the term "country team" carried too much implication of a Board of Directors deciding matters by a majority vote. Max and I had agreed in Washington that for good or ill, we wanted unambiguous responsibility for running the show. I made it clear to those present that we brought such a mandate from the President, and to distinguish our new, more hierarchical way of operating from a "country team," I rechristened the group a "Mission Council." Max formalized the new structure after his arrival July 7. The weekly meetings of the Council became an excellent forum for exchanging ideas, coordinating actions and issuing instructions. While debate was often vigorous, rancor was largely absent. We succeeded in getting several of the Vietnamese governments that held power during my tour in Saigon to set up a counterpart organization with which we could hold joint meetings, but the Vietnamese did not take readily to the rather stiff chain of command required.

During my first few days I toured American facilities in Saigon, met with Prime Minister Khanh, Foreign Minister Quat, and other government officials, and moved into the house vacated by Lodge, where Max and I set up housekeeping together pending the arrival of our wives. Mostly I devoted my time to briefings by MACV, CIA, the Political Section, and the Provincial Reporters. This last group consisted of young FSOs whom the embassy had deployed after I concluded during a 1962 inspection trip that it was too isolated from the countryside. Though the briefings were not gloomy, neither were they particularly encouraging. The extremely complex collection of domestic and international ingredients affecting South Vietnam's vitality had grown, if that is possible, even more intricate since I had last observed them in detail during the 1954 Geneva Conference.

As we have seen, most of the Geneva Accords were technical military disengagement agreements worked out by French and Vietminh officers. Each force was to regroup on opposite sides of a temporary dividing line, the 17th parallel, and permit free movement of civilians and ex-soldiers across it. France was to depart Vietnam entirely by October, leaving control of the southern part to Bao Dai and his newly appointed Prime Minister, Ngo Dinh Diem (whom the French had always strongly opposed). To save France the humiliation of immediately surrendering the whole country to the Vietminh, and to permit it to carry out an orderly withdrawal, Ho was persuaded to accept a "two-bite" formula for his country's future. The first step was the actual Geneva Accords themselves, which ended hostilities and set an armistice line at the 17th parallel. The second step was so-called elections to unite the country under a single government. The balloting was to be held in both North and South in July 1956 under the "supervision" of the International Control Commission, composed of Poland, India, and Canada. This commission was considerably better than the one arranged for Korea, in that no member had an automatic veto, but in practice, India's spinelessness, combined with the absence of real sanctions against North Vietnam's refusal to allow the Commission to travel freely, made it a paper tiger. Had the ICC been the election watchdog, non-communist votes would have been counted sporadically at best, and such "elections" would have been an egregious mockery. At the 1954 Geneva Conference the United States and South Vietnam had pointedly taken exception to ICC supervision, holding out instead for the UN to do it. When Diem refused to hold the 1956 elections, we fully supported him. In fact, the United States never did endorse the Geneva accords, saying only that it would not seek to overturn them by threat or use of force. We did, however, declare ourselves ready to protect South Vietnam, Laos, and Cambodia against further communist aggression. In SEATO we thought we had established a relatively effective mechanism for doing that, should it become necessary.

In 1954, as I have said, no one gave South Vietnam much chance of surviving infancy. Even the United States, which wanted a non-communist pro-American South Vietnam to prosper, gave a gloomy prognosis. Gangsters, militant religious sects, corrupt officials, and scheming politicians had taken firm root there during French rule and the disruption of the long war. The country had a one-year-old army and no civil service, political traditions, or much of a working economy. To make a country that would work, nation-building and social and economic development would have to occur simultaneously.

The south also had to absorb nearly a million northern Catholics who had flooded south after the Geneva Accords to escape Ho's rule. Some were educated professionals and military officers, others were Catholic peasants who united around their parish priests and moved south in groups. The differences between northerners and southerners were only exacerbated by Catholic-Buddhist tensions, especially because many northerners were vigorous, energetic anti-communists who gravitated toward leadership positions in South Vietnam. The country was a bewildering jungle of squabbling politicians whose shared hatred of French rule had made them tough and resilient, but had left them unschooled in the essential "three C's" of democratic government: communication, conciliation, and consensus. Individually these "intellectuals" could talk very eloquently and persuasively to American journalists and embassy political reporters about what was wrong with the incumbent government and what should be done to cure it, but they were completely incapable of working together on any coherent plan or policy. I remember that after the High National Council was formed in 1964, the only time its members managed to get down to real discussion was when Ambassador Taylor or I would invite them to our residence and catalyze the exchange of views. And as Prime Minister Phan Huy Quat once told me, not entirely in jest, "The critical mass for a Vietnamese political party is twenty. One more member and it splits."

Efforts to "broaden the base" of Diem's government, as urged by well-meaning foreigners, only led to paralysis because of the politicians' inability to work together. (Of course, this phenomenon is not entirely unknown in France itself.) Even individual politicians, with their French-Roman Catholic educations grafted on Vietnamese-Buddhist-Confucian roots, held world views bordering on the schizophrenic. Sometimes they reacted in a Vietnamese frame of reference, sometimes a French frame, more often an unwieldy melange of both. Over this volatile assemblage presided the ascetic Catholic-cum-Chinese Mandarin Ngo Dinh Diem. It is difficult to imagine a country with more strikes against it at the outset than South Vietnam.

President Diem had resisted the French. Although he came to power without a broad base of support, no one in South Vietnam could claim such a base. He did, however, possess several assets: a powerful, well-connected family; considerable intelligence and political acumen combined with implacable anti-communism; and American support—by 1956 United States aid had reached $250 million annually. But most important, the vast majority of his country's 16 million people clearly wanted to construct a viable non-communist alternative to Vietminh rule.

Diem passed his first big test when he trounced a collection of militant religious sects and powerful gangsters who had united to overthrow him in the spring of 1955. These gangsters, called the Binh Xuyen, were former river pirates who had succeeded in taking control of the Saigon police force in the turmoil following the disintegration of French control after World War II. The leader of the anti-Diem group would have been at home in the Chicago of Al Capone. Besides the police force, this mob controlled the Saigon port and the casinos, brothels, and opium dens of the area.

His power consolidated, Diem actually developed into a

much more effective leader than had been expected. He was a single-minded zealot determined that South Vietnam would survive as a non-communist state. With Wolf Ladajinsky, the architect of MacArthur's successful land reform program in Japan, as his personal adviser, Diem started an ambitious land reform program. He also organized an army and resettled the refugees. Rice output, rubber production, and school attendance had all soared by 1960. Passably free elections were held in 1959 for a National Assembly, though Diem acted more out of personal than national interest when he invalidated the victory of a respected non-communist who opposed him, Dr. Phan Quang Don. Diem was no Thomas Jefferson, but he was doing a creditable job in an inherently chaotic situation, one that compared reasonably well with that done by leaders in other developing countries.

In fact, the best and nearest contrast to Diem's rule was that of North Vietnam. Forced collectivization of farmland following the Geneva Accords threw the country into terror and near famine. Thousands of people were killed or imprisoned and rice production dropped. The pace of industrialization did not meet expectations, and Soviet and Chinese aid had to be increased. By 1957 even Ho recognized the chaos that had been spawned, and he reorganized the Communist Party leadership. Even so, Ho's ability as a government leader did not match his revolutionary skills. The relative strength in the south and the stumbling in the North had made Vietnam, by the early 1960s, a secondary issue for the United States Government, whose attention had been focused almost entirely on Laos as the danger point.

Ho and his colleagues in the north, however, had not forsaken their lifelong dream of one Vietnam under their rule. By 1959 Diem's growing authority and confidence had demonstrated that the south would not collapse spontaneously, nor was there any chance that Diem would voluntarily agree to his own destruction by the kind of elections envisioned by the Geneva Accords or through some form of coalition government. In fact, he was beginning to step up his campaign against all opponents of his regime, particularly southern remnants of the Vietminh.

Now that communist control was securely established in the north, Ho and his colleagues opted to overturn the South Vietnamese government by force.In 1959 communist cadres in the south, who had lain low since 1954, were ordered to organize peasants and discredit the government's authority through widespread terrorism. Several thousand southerners who had gone north in 1954 were dispatched southward to form the backbone of an armed insurgency. Military equipment started flowing from north to south over a network of supply lines passing through Laos known as the Ho Chi Minh trail. In December, 1960, Hanoi announced the formation of what was called a National Liberation Front.

To Diem's other headaches was now added a determined, well-organized guerrilla insurgency directed and supplied by a skilled adversary whose mentors included the Soviet Union and China. Even the largely worthless ICC recognized that North Vietnam was breaking the Geneva Accords by infiltrating into Vietnam and Laos. After the June 1962 Sino-Indian war, when India figured it had nothing to lose in its relations with China by telling the truth, India combined with Canada to issue (as two-thirds of the ICC) a "minority report" detailing Hanoi's repeated violations of the Accords. It was good to see the ICC performing its function at last, but of course sterner measures had been necessary in the meantime.

To crush the Vietcong, as the southern communists were called, Diem turned to his novice military forces. France had permitted no native army until just before the Geneva Accords, so Diem's officer corps was green. Even his senior officers had only been sergeants and sub-lieutenants in the French forces five years before. Though American advisors tried to reduce the deficit of military experience, they did not know much about Vietnam or guerrilla war. Diem also made enemies by arresting vocal opponents who were not communists. Because of these and other factors, Diem was unable to counter the increased infiltration from the north and communist strength continued to gain. By 1961, reports on President Kennedy's desk said that the Vietcong controlled considerable areas of the South Vietnamese countryside.

The Administration was spurred by recommendations Max Taylor and Walt Rostow made after an October 1961 inspection trip. I agreed with most of those recommendations, but Taylor had also wanted to deploy up to 8,000 United States combat forces as a signal of our firm intent to persevere, and to be ready if necessary to strike at North Vietnam itself, viewed as the source of aggression. I and others in the Administration thought this premature. "If there is a strong South Vietnamese effort, they may not be needed; if there is not such an effort, United States forces could not accomplish their mission in the midst of an apathetic or hostile population," I wrote in a November 11 memorandum to the President that laid out the joint views of Rusk and McNamara. Unlike next-door Laos, where we were pushing for a negotiated settlement under the neutralist Souvanna Phouma, I felt South Vietnam had the necessary political, economic, andmilitary elements to build itself up as a non-communist state and that we could not afford defeat there. I thus endorsed the Taylor-Rostow recommendation of increasing our military advisors to the South Vietnamese Army and supplying helicopters, light air transport, air reconaissance, naval patrol craft, and more civilian economic aid. President Kennedy agreed with these views. In return, we sought a commitment from Diem to broaden the political base of his government and overhaul its administration to make it more effective in fighting the war and promoting economic development in the countryside, where the Vietcong were still recruiting successfully. He acceded, grudgingly.

Military credits and weapons shipments accelerated ($207 million in 1963). Green Berets, President Kennedy's favorites, arrived to out-Giap Giap. Diem also undertook a strategic hamlet program, patterned after the British experience in Malaya and designed to create enclaves safe from Vietcong terrorism where people could live normal, productive lives. (These, however, were more numerous on paper than in fact.) Substantial programs in the economic, agricultural, medical, and educational fields were also undertaken. Under these programs, imports were held down so that there was no runaway inflation. Hospitals, rural health clinics, and inoculation programs were established throughout the country. The number of public primary schools and pupils tripled in the seven years from 1954 to 1961. A national radio system was installed covering both broadcasting and communications from village to district headquarters. A road construction program was undertaken. A rural credit program together with improved seed and methods of tillage greatly increased rice yields, and high grade swine were brought in to upgrade this important source of animal protein. In short, massive and successful civil programs were undertaken in the countryside. Yet it was never possible to obtain any American media coverage of them. Even when correspondents could be persuaded to do pieces on them, their editors threw the stories out in favor of more spectacular accounts of fighting, street demonstrations, immolations, and the like.

These efforts taken after October 1961 seemed to be working. While I was in Washington as Deputy Under Secretary, Sir Robert Thompson, the British architect of the successful anti-guerrilla campaign in Malaya who had become Diem's counter-insurgency advisor, reported to us that by April 1963 the Viet Cong were slowly but steadily losing and that South Vietnamese morale, not only at the government level, but among the peasants, was rising. Our own information confirmed his optimism. The number of Viet Cong armed attacks had dropped to half of what it had been a year before. Though Diem was far from being a true democrat, his authority seemed to be holding and his United States—financed reform program was gaining some momentum in the countryside. We thought time was on our side.

It wasn't. By November Diem had been deposed from power, with American encouragement, and had been murdered in the process. What caused the abrupt reversal? Basically, Diem had always been vulnerable because he lacked broad political support. No southern politician had had that in the chaos of 1954, and in the nine following years Diem did not manage to create it. That failure resulted from many factors, including his personal aloofness, the corruption of his family, his strict Catholicism in a Buddhist country, and his inability to enlist the politically active intelligentsia.

But the immediate set of events that toppled Diem was a series of violent street demonstrations organized by the Machiavellian Trich Tri Quang, leader of a faction of militant Buddhists from Hue, the ancient capital of Annam. In early May, inept government handling of a deliberately provocative demonstration Tri Quang organized in Hue led to the death of eight people (though some evidence suggests that Vietcong terrorists, not government troops, caused the deaths). In protest, Tri Quang then instigated a series of large and threatening anti-Diem demonstrations in Saigon. Several obscure monks loyal to Tri Quang, frail-looking bald-headed figures in flowing saffron robes, doused themselves with gasoline and burned themselves to death at times and places carefully selected by Tri Quang to guarantee maximum coverage in the American media. He also demonstrated surprising public relations sense in portraying his group to the American press corps as a persecuted religious organization instead of what it was: a potent political force seeking to establish and control a Vietnamese "Buddhist state." The American press bought Tri Quang's skillful pitch. The journalists found the Buddhists irresistibly colorful and began to slant their stories against Diem. American public opinion followed. Diem's sister-in-law, the infamous Madame Nhu, did Diem no good by publicly delighting in each time a monk "barbecued himself." Her husband, Diem's brother Nhu, also did not help by acting as Diem's mysterious *eminence grise.*

Catholics, particularly the northern villagers who had emigrated south in 1954, hated and feared Tri Quang, and mounted massive countermarches in Saigon. Diem's legendary grip appeared to be slipping. The smell of blood encouraged his many enemies to gang up against him. By summer, Saigon was boiling with coup rumors. Diem finally declared martial law in August, simultaneous with massive raids on Buddhist pagodas to crush Tri Quang's organization. Some calm returned to Saigon, and National Assembly elections were even held in late September. But by this time, President Kennedy and several of his advisors—including Under Secretary George Ball, Assistant Secretary Averell Harriman, State Department intelligence chief Roger Hilsman, and White House aide Michael Forrestal—had concluded that Diem was repressive, clumsy, and vulnerable. They started publicly distancing the United States from him, and those signals emboldened his highly alert opponents. Finally, without having any idea of who or what could follow Diem, Kennedy gave permission to Ambassador Lodge to signal various South Vietnamese generals that the United States would not oppose their seizing power. Shortly after 1:00 P.M., November 1, tanks and armored personnel carriers rumbled into the square opposite Gia Long Palace, Diem's residence. Twenty-four hours later, Diem and his brother Nhu were dead, and the business of reconstituting the government of South Vietnam had begun. Fortunately for her, Madame Nhu was abroad at the time and survived to shrilly denounce United States involvement in the coup.

I never held much of a brief for Diem, but neither was I enthusiastic about recommending his ouster, because I could see no one better equipped to lead the country. Consequently, I played no role in authorizing the coup. On Saturday, October 27, when I was playing golf with Undersecretary Ball at the Falls Road public course, Averell Harriman and Roger Hilsman interrupted our game, and they gave him a telegram to sign. George was Acting Secretary in Rusk's absence from Washington. I found it somewhat curious that they did not also show it to me, but there was no special reason I had to see it, so I kept out of their discussion. Ball signed the telegram, the two departed, and we continued our game. It turned out that this was the "green light" telegram authorizing Ambassador Lodge to signal that we would not oppose a coup against Diem. Looking back on it, I am relatively sure that Ball, Hilsman, and Harriman knew that I would oppose it and excluded me from their discussion on purpose.

When I arrived in Saigon in the aftermath of the Diem coup, I still had an uneasy feeling about his ouster. Just because Diem was flawed did not mean his successors would be any better. In addition, summarily ejecting one head of government inevitably lowers the psychological barriers to deposing the next one. During my fourteen months in Saigon there were six coups or attempted coups. Though we were never able to establish any cause and effect relationship, and Ambassador Taylor certainly never shirked his duty, it so happened that five of these coups occurred while he was away fighting the battle of Vietnam in Washington.

What Diem's detractors in Washington did not fully realize was that the unrest that culminated in his downfall stemmed as much from the political immaturity inherent in South Vietnam as from Diem's personal failings. The country was poor, politically undeveloped, ethnically and religiously splintered, and still recovering from a century of colonialism and fifteen years of continuous war. The government's reform programs—like land reform and strategic hamlets—had typically been underfinanced, overly ambitious, and clumsily administered. The government still had to convince its people that it could be an honest, efficient instrument that would bring a better life. These were the basic tasks facing Diem's successors and, by extension, facing the United States Mission as we tried to help. Making South Vietnam prosperous and peaceful was the key issue, not picking the ideal president.

I knew that success in helping South Vietnam face its basic tasks of nation-building would require our most sensitive perception and earnest effort. I tried never to lose sight of the larger goals even when things in Saigon got hectic. But during my stint as Deputy Ambassador, I found myself so nearly completely preoccupied with trying to keep the central government simply existing that there was hardly time for tackling the country's fundamental problems.

Presiding in South Vietnam when I arrived in June 1964 was General Nguyen Khanh, an army officer who, in January, had deposed "Big" Minh and Duong Van, the generals who had mounted the November coup against Diem. Khanh was attractive, flamboyant, and a beguiling speaker in both French and English. Ambassador Lodge had thought him South Vietnam's best bet for effective leadership among the crop of officers vying for the top job. On LBJ's orders, Max Taylor and Defense Secretary McNamara (who both then liked Khanh) had barnstormed the south with him in March. Frequent joint platform appearances, ending with the cheer "Vietnam muon nam!" (Vietnam a thousand years!) were intended to signal would-be coup plotters that Washington was tired of instability and intended to prosecute the war vigorously under Khanh's leadership. (LBJ, who had a real genius for pressing the flesh, had unbounded faith that Asian politicians could soar in popularity if they would only follow his example and "get out with the people;" thus the Taylor-McNamara-Khanh campaign. On LBJ's first trip to Southeast Asia, as Vice President in 1961, I vividly remember the story of him ordering the car to stop on the journey from the airport into Bangkok, climbing aboard a bus, and pushing through the crowded aisle with his typical overpowering heartiness to shake hands. The gentle and reserved Thai, who hadn't the remotest idea of who or what he was, were thoroughly bemused.)

Though Khanh was bright and beguiling, he was also mercurial and, as it turned out, utterly devoid of character. He seemed to delight in plots and trickery. No sooner would he launch one scheme for governmental reorganization than he would abruptly terminate it without so much as a prior hint to his closest associates. He was once described as a man who excelled in a juggling course but missed the last lesson; able to hurl multitudes of objects into the air but not able to get them back down.

With no firm direction from the top, the whole government seemed frozen. Diem's fall had resulted in widespread purges of provincial officials accused of being his toadies. Not only were the replacements inexperienced, but they refused to stick their necks out for the tough measures that wartime administration required until Khanh's new regime could demonstrate its staying power. Khanh managed to bring other military leaders to heel for a time, but the crazy-quilt civilian political scene constantly frustrated him. Trich Tri Quang's militant Buddhists quickly started to oppose him. Buddhists and Catholics competed raucously for Saigon's streets once more. Politicians felt cheated because Khanh did not go through with permitting political parties to function openly, as he had hinted. Though Khanh had outlined an extraordinarily ambitious rural reform and pacification program to McNamara and Taylor during their March visit, he devoted himself so utterly to political machinations that little happened in the countryside where it counted.

After one period of particularly furious plotting by General Khanh, there was even a coup attempt against him, on September 13, by other members of the Military Revolutionary Council, the generals' own political arm. The coup leaders failed to capture Khanh at the outset, and during the stalemate that ensued I made it clear to them, during a heated three-hour conversation in my office (Max was in Washington), that Khanh retained American support. General Phat, the leader of the coup, left my office and called it off.

By the fall of 1964, South Vietnam was clearly slipping. The level of Vietcong activity and North Vietnamese infiltration was rising. Khanh was producing no fundamental progress in the complex combination of nation-building and social reform that South Vietnam needed to survive. Pessimism was in the air, and some even charged the embassy with fomenting it. Father Quynh, the leader of the militant Catholic refugees from the north, paid a formal call on me October 14 to ask me bluntly whether my role in the Taylor-Johnson team was to encourage the Buddhists to stir up so much trouble that the United States would have a pretext to quit Vietnam altogether.

As a matter of fact, it is clear in retrospect that just a little less American effort to pick up the pieces during one of the coups could easily have induced enough turmoil to justify our washing our hands of the whole mess. But the direction of policy from Washington at that time was exactly opposite. President Johnson was determined not to lose Vietnam. He had stepped up covert actions against the north in February and directed the government to prepare contingency plans for bombing the north should infiltration cause the situation in the south to deteriorate. There was no question of our leaving, whether events in Saigon could justify it or not. Since 1949 the fate of Vietnam had been a matter of international significance to the United States as a test case of our resolve to resist international communism. Turmoil in Saigon was regrettable, but it could not and did not affect Washington's view of why South Vietnam's survival was vital to America's interests. LBJ was running where his predecessors had only walked, but the direction was the same.

The level of American commitment to the south got a big boost from the Southeast Asia Resolution of August 7, 1964. This kind of a resolution had long been under contemplation; Secretary Rusk said in his formal presentation to the Foreign Relations Committee that the attacks by North Vietnam on our naval vessels were only the immediate occasion for it. He pointed out that "these attacks were not an isolated event but were related directly to the aggressive posture of North Vietnam and to the policy that the United States had been pursuing in the free nations of Southeast Asia and particularly South Vietnam and Laos in defending themselves against communist aggression. . . ."

The resolution, which later came to be called the Tonkin Gulf Resolution, was sponsored in the Senate by Senator William

Fulbright, Chairman of the Foreign Relations Committee, and passed the Senate by a vote of 88 to 2 and the House by a vote of 416 to 0. Its language is certainly not ambiguous: " . . . the United States is prepared, as the President determines, to take all necessary steps, including the use of armed force, to assist any member or protocol state of the Southeast Asia Collective Defense Treaty requesting assistance in defense of its freedom." We in Saigon interpreted it to mean what it said. It seemed an overwhelming endorsement by the Congress of what we were seeking to do. No matter how tempting it might have been to us to leave Saigon's squabbling generals to their own devices, after Tonkin Gulf we were sure that not only the President, but the country as a whole, considered South Vietnam's preservation an important national goal. As professionals, we wanted to do the best job we could to help accomplish that end.

For the able and experienced members of the Congress who supported that resolution to say later that they had not understood what it meant is sophistry of the least appealing kind.

As far as the incident in the Tonkin Gulf was concerned, we in Saigon were only peripherally involved. The destroyers were a part of the Seventh Fleet that was directly under the command of the Commander in Chief, Pacific (CINCPAC) in Honolulu, who in turn reported directly through the JCS to the Secretary of Defense and the President. Thus, while we received information copies of most of the cable traffic, we were not direct participants and my account of the incident cannot be first-hand. But as to the much-disputed question of whether our destroyers had in fact been attacked by North Vietnamese gun boats, my own judgment, on the basis of the traffic I saw, is that while there might have been some questions concerning the facts of the second attack, there were none whatsoever about the first.

After the Tonkin Gulf Resolution the Mission began jointly to work out with Washington a two-pronged strategy. The first prong was to build greater internal political stability by encouraging Khanh to form a government that would be broadly based but cohesive enough to be effective. After the government had gotten on its feet, the United States would provide the second prong: a limited bombing campaign against the Ho Chi Minh Trail and selected targets in North Vietnam, a dramatic step that we hoped would boost sagging southern morale and deter the north from further escalation. General Khanh carried out his part of the bargain on September 26. He announced the formation of a High National Council whose seventeen members, if not particularly well-known, were carefully apportioned among the country's religious and ethnic groups. Its job was to draft a provisional constitution and appoint a Chief of State and a provisional assembly.

On October 24, having completed its draft constitution, the HNC appointed the aged but respected Phan Khac Suu as ceremonial Chief of State. He then appointed Tran Van Huong, the stubborn and honest Mayor of Saigon, to be Prime Minister. Khanh remained Commander-in-Chief of the Armed Forces. The rest of the Cabinet was not spectacular, but even so, a fairly encouraging civil government was in place just one year after Diem's ouster. Though we were still skeptical about General Khanh's future intentions, the modest progress so far was a good sign.

These developments allowed Max, in a late November trip to Washington, to obtain permission to start joint planning with the Vietnamese for bombing limited portions of southern North Vietnam and the Ho Chi Minh Trail, subject to one essential condition: continued stability in Saigon. Above all, no more military coups. Max made sure Prime Minister Huong, General Khanh, and other key figures understood the United States position when he returned to South Vietnam. His strict injunction against further rounds of "musical generals" won apparent universal expressions of understanding and support. Huong's government and the United States Mission started cooperating on developing a countryside pacification program and absorbing a horde of refugees that Mekong Delta floods had generated in early November.

Two weeks later, however, General Khanh and a few young Turk officers (who felt the High National Council was blocking their promotions in favor of older officers) dissolved the HNC, which had become the interim legislature for Huong's government. They arrested most of its members and flew them to detention in the highland town of Pleiku. Max and I only heard this distressing news when we called on a despondent Huong the next morning, December 20, to discuss another matter. The embassy strenuously tried to get hold of Khanh for details, but he was avoiding us. Instead, four of the young Turks, including Air Vice Marshal Nguyen Cao Ky and General Nguyen Van Thieu, called on Max and me at noon to explain their action. We deliberately gave them a frosty reception to underscore our deep disappointment. Ky said the demi-coup was aimed at "strengthening national unity by purging disruptive elements from the HNC," but

Max and I were not impressed. Not only had they broken all their assurances about preserving stability, we told them, but Washington would now have to reevaluate the long-term strategy of support we had so carefully worked out. Max asked them to reconsider what they had done.

The young Turks, of course, immediately reported back to Khanh and we arranged to talk with him the following day, December 21, at his command center in the old French military headquarters just outside the Saigon airport. Khanh dropped his customary cherubic facade and belligerently took the offensive in the conversation, accusing Max of insulting Khanh's colleagues. Max Taylor was not the kind of man inclined to retreat in the face of attack, so a very vigorous conversation ensued. During the course of this angry dialogue Max took advantage of an opening Khanh gave to say we had lost confidence in him and that the common cause would profit if he withdrew from public life in Vietnam. Understandably the meeting was terminated at that point.

We might have thought that to preserve his carefully cultivated image as the one Vietnamese who could deal with Americans, Khanh would have kept his blowup with Taylor secret. On the contrary; Khanh's mind was much too fertile for that. He decided to publicize the imbroglio to his fellow generals as an insult to the sovereign integrity of Vietnam. Having wrapped the flag around himself, Khanh let it be known that the sullied honor of Vietnam could only be assuaged by Ambassador Taylor's speedy recall. Rumors circulated widely as Christmas approached that Khanh would have Max declared persona non grata. That threat took nerve, but Khanh had become desperate to keep himself at the top. He even made a secret deal with the militant Buddhists to hold raucous anti-Huong and anti-American demonstrations to bolster his position.

Even the young Turks were aghast at Khanh's selfish maneuverings, especially his attack on Max. It was obvious that Washington had no intention of recalling him to please General Khanh. But it also seemed clear that if he did depart, the American effort would accompany him. Max and I kept our silence while the young Turks worked out their position. Very shortly I received a sounding asking whether I would meet a few of the young Turks to see, in good Vietnamese fashion, whether we could mediate between Khanh and Taylor. With Max's approval I arranged a meeting with them on neutral ground, in a private Vietnamese home. Admiral Cang and General Thieu showed up. I did not attempt to force the pace, so we talked around the subject and then agreed to meet again. At our second meeting they took the initiative to say that perhaps General Khanh had spoken a little hastily. I responded that I was sure Ambassador Taylor had meant no insult to Khanh or Vietnam, though they must understand how deeply it distressed Taylor to see his plans for Vietnam so blithely jeopardized and their assurances of no more coups so lightly disregarded. We agreed to pass on our exchange to our principals and agreed to meet once more. At our last meeting we agreed to recommend to our principals that the matter be considered closed and that Taylor and Khanh should seek a suitable opportunity to resume normal relations. In the meantime, Chief of State Suu and Prime Minister Huong reached a compromise with the military over the future authority of the High National Council which defused the young Turks' dissatisfaction. Suu then held a tea party January 14 at Gia Long Palace to mark the end of the crisis and reassemble all concerned. A composed Taylor and a smiling Khanh were photographed shaking hands.

Though this whole episode ended peacefully, the demi-coup had sapped the Suu-Huong experiment in civilian government of its prestige and authority. Khanh sealed its demise on January 27 when the Armed Forces Council dissolved Huong's government. After several weeks of jockeying, during which we had to discourage Khanh's grandiose scheme to make himself an all-powerful Chief of State, a la De Gaulle, the Armed Forces Council tapped Dr. Phan Huy Quat, a northerner, to head a new civilian government under the Armed Forces Council's general direction. We had known Quat well from the time he had been Khanh's foreign minister a year ago and respected his ability. We hoped that he might establish an effective government if given a chance. He took office on February 19.

But all this turmoil in Saigon since Diem's ouster had exasperated us in the United States Mission. The President and Congress had directed us urgently to build up the competence of the Saigon government so that the communist north would not conquer the whole country. We knew that succeeding depended on positive support of the South Vietnamese, which in turn required Saigon to institute land reform, spread government health and education services, and make the countryside secure from Vietcong terrorism. But these coups kept pulling the chair out from under us. A stable government, let alone a healthy country, was simply beyond our power to create. The central thrust of America's anti-communist policy for the 1960s—frustrating communist-inspired wars of national liberation—had ended up hinging upon a group of squabbling, second-rate generals.

Dean Rusk aptly termed our predicament the "tyranny of the weak." The United States had gotten itself into that most treacherous of political positions, having responsibility without authority. The Saigon government was our ally, not a satellite whose policies and leaders we could dictate. In the final analysis we had to work with whoever was in power. The only weapon we could brandish to coerce cooperation from the coup plotters was total American withdrawal, and that threat was simply not credible. Withdrawing support would jeopardize our own strategic goals, and the generals understood perfectly well that we could not forsake South Vietnam simply to punish them. This inevitably led to our shouldering more of the effort ourselves, which took the immediate pressure off Saigon, but also made it more dependent on the United States. And in the long run, having to shoulder more of the burden ourselves would lead logically and inexorably to the deployment of American troops. Even before American combat soldiers arrived, Max had compiled a flow chart of all the various programs we were seeking to have carried out by the Vietnamese government. It turned out to be sixty-eight—the chart was huge—and we never did figure out how to strengthen indigenous Vietnamese institutions without smothering them. All too often Washington's response to LBJ's urgings to "do something" was to come up with a new program for an already creaking government structure.

Yet despite our frustrations with Saigon's irresponsibility, we never seriously considered withdrawal, which would have compromised our own objectives in the south. In the first place, many people in the south, especially in leadership positions, had fled from the north in 1954 and knew first-hand how brutal Ho's rule could be. They wanted independence. As I have said, southerners in general distrusted the Tonkinese, regardless of ideology, and preferred to be ruled by their own. The Vietcong controlled their areas in the south so harshly—for example, taxing the peasants more heavily and conscripting boys at a younger age than Saigon—that their ideological appeal had dwindled.

Second, we had ample evidence that the south was willing to fight for itself: 23,000 South Vietnamese soldiers lost their lives between 1960 and 1964, and between 1965 and 1969, another 80,000 laid down their lives. Relative to size of population, these losses would correspond to more than one million American deaths. The army always had a problem with deserters, but they almost always returned home, because of family problems or dissatisfaction with military life, rather than defecting to the Vietcong. Neither did any middle-grade or senior civil or military officer ever switch to the Vietcong during those many years of fighting.

In fact, the pattern of defections ran very much in our favor and encouraged our determination to persist. About 135,000 identified Vietcong turned themselves into the government between 1963 and 1969 under an amnesty program known as Chieu Hoi (Open Arms). My purpose in citing these figures is not to reopen old wounds, but to show why we felt the South Vietnamese were willing to fight for themselves and were worth supporting.

During the various coup attempts the embassy was very busy, consulting with present leaders and their would-be replacements, monitoring troop movements, sometimes providing temporary refuge for the vulnerable. (Even Trich Tri Quang, staunchly anti-American, resorted to our protection. During one coup, he traded in his customary flowing saffron robes for a Catholic clergyman's cassock and showed up past midnight at the house of Jim Rosenthal, the political officer who had the duty of keeping in touch with him.) No period stretched us so thoroughly, however, as February 19–27, 1965, "the week that was," when two wild coups finally rid Vietnam of General Khanh. It was like living through a movie shown several times normal speed; I had to strain just to follow what the actors were saying and doing, let alone make sense of it all. To give a feeling for what Saigon was all about in the tumult following Diem's ouster, let me replay "the week that was" at a normal pace.

At 10 A.M. on Friday, February 19, a hot, steamy day, Max and I journeyed to Joint General Staff Headquarters at Tan Son Nhut airport for a meeting with Prime Minister Quat, who had taken office the day before, and his cabinet. General Khanh also attended. The atmosphere was calm and cordial. Everyone was looking forward to a period of stability and hard work. We discussed a joint organization for working together and adjourned at 12:15. Khanh told us he planned to spend the weekend at Vung Tao, a lovely seaside resort thirty miles south from Saigon. Max and I drove back to the embassy, where I met *Washington Post* correspondent Warren Una to take him to my house for lunch. We were just settling down to our soup when the embassy watch officer called to report a coup in progress. I thought I had heard some trucks and tanks rumble down my street (known as the "coup route"), but I had not paid any special attention, nor had my Marine guard on the second floor balcony said anything. Sure enough, I went to the window and saw some unusual troop movements. I went to use my phones but discovered that all were dead except my special military line. Something clearly was up; so much for our morning optimism. Warren and I broke off lunch. I assembled my driver and police guard and together we weaved through the tanks to MACV headquarters. By this time General Westmoreland had reached his office. I established communications with Max, who had gone to the embassy.

At MACV I learned that the coup leaders had tried to capture General Khanh as he left the meeting we had attended at Tan Son Nhut. As he prepared to take off for Vung Tau, tanks and trucks had driven across the runway. Khanh quickly grasped the danger and managed to take off from a taxi strip. Air Marshal Ky did the same, so two top figures had eluded the plotters' grasp. This latest round of musical generals turned out to be the brainchild of my old "friend" General Phat (the one whom I had dissuaded from finishing a coup in progress after three hours of tough talking in my office September 13) and a relative newcomer, a Colonel Pham Ngoc Thao. The latter had been press attaché for the Vietnamese Embassy in Washington and was well-known as an inveterate plotter. (After the war Hanoi told Stan Karnow that Thao had been their plant from the beginning.) After learning all I could at MACV, I hurried back through five blocks of tanks and trucks to the embassy where Max and I exchanged information. We managed to phone Prime Minister Quat, who professed complete surprise at the turn of events (on this his second day in office!). He said he did not know the motives of the coup leaders except that their moves so far seemed to be aimed at General Khanh. Khanh, who had arrived safely in Vung Tao, also expressed astonishment and said he was still trying to find out what was happening. The city remained peaceful as our political section staff phoned their usual contacts to try, with MACV and the CIA, to piece together the plot.

In the afternoon General Westmoreland came over to the embassy and the three of us discussed our next steps and the consequences of this coup. Max then went home to prepare for a dinner to which he had invited a number of officials of the new government. About 6:30, Westy heard from one of his officers at Tan Son Nhut that Air Marshal Ky, who had escaped to Bien Hoa Air Base, was now preparing a bombing attack on coup headquarters at Tan Son Nhut. Ky had warned the Americans there to evacuate by 7:00, when the raid was scheduled to begin. Sure enough, in about ten minutes, planes clearly loaded with bombs started circling over Saigon at low level, making turns above the embassy building to start their run on Tan Son Nhut. Embassy communicators, working furiously, patched us through to Ky at five minutes to seven. Westy and I argued as persuasively as we knew how that the bombing would cause carnage without ending the coup and make Ky, the Air Force, and South Vietnam look like fools and butchers, Ky listened calmly, and finally agreed to relent. With less than sixty seconds remaining, the planes turned away. Our temporary sense of relief was exceeded only by our fears that the coup was degenerating rapidly into chaos and that we needed a better way to exert influence than last-minute phone calls. Westy and I agreed to dispatch Ky's favorite American military advisor, Brigadier General Robert Rowland, to Bien Hoa post haste so he could stick with Ky. Major General Joe Moore, head of the air force section at MACV, went to his desk at Tan Son Nhut where the coup leaders were holed up. Both of them had previous coup experience and their reports to us through the night proved very useful.

In spite of the day's commotion Max and I decided to let the invitations for the 7:30 dinner stand and see who showed up. After we were sure that Ky had definitely called off his attack, I headed to Max's house. At about 7:30 Prime Minister Quat called to find out whether he could join the party and we of course told him he was welcome.

Quat, normally a quiet man, was even more subdued. This blow to his infant government obviously distressed him, but since he and his cabinet had not been arrested, he still hoped that the coup leaders had no grudge against him or civilian rule. During the course of our conversation Quat made clear that he had been unable to reach General Khanh or Marshal Ky all day, so we used American military communication channels to put him in touch with both officers for the first time from Max's study.

In the meantime, however, troops and tanks kept moving through the city and serious fighting loomed as a very real possibility. General Phat and Colonel Thao, the coup leaders, realized that victory was remote since Khanh and Ky were free and retained loyal forces, but still we worried they might try something rash to regain the initiative. Working through Westy and General Moore at Tan Son Nhut, we managed to persuade Phat and Thao to visit Ky at Bien Hoa under the safe conduct of an American officer, and they agreed to keep their respective troops from shooting during the night. After this temporary cease-fire was accomplished, the party broke up and I went home for what happily turned out to be an undisturbed night's sleep.

Early the next morning, February 20, we arranged to get Prime Minister Quat to Bien Hoa to confer with Ky and several other generals who had gathered there. By 10 A.M. the coup leaders realized that they could not topple Khanh or Ky and decided to decamp. When they headed for their escape auto parked outside General Staff headquarters at Tan Son Nhut, they discovered that even their sentries had deserted. So they darted back inside, donned civilian clothes and dark glasses, and disappeared in an unmarked car. (Thao emerged in May as planner of an abortive coup against Quat and subsequently was found dead.)

Congratulating myself that the coup had ended before Sunday, our usual day for coups, I headed out to the old and once exclusive French-built golf course near Tan Son Nhut. It may seem a bit odd that I should leave the political whirlpool for the links, but, being something of a golf addict, it takes more than a simple two-day coup to keep me off the fairways. So that Saturday I played eighteen holes, as usual accompanied by two police guards. One stayed close by me while the other went ahead to rake the sand traps (where I landed all too frequently) for grenades. We had to pause often for the down blast from helicopters passing just above our heads in their landing pattern. To make matters worse, there were numerous Chinese funerals in progress in two cemeteries next to the course. The noise from their vigorous horn-blowing and clashing cymbals were not conducive to a steady putting hand.

While I was slicing down the golf course, the Armed Forces Council, with Prime Minister Quat attending, was holding a long, stormy meeting at Bien Hoa. The generals were disgusted with Khanh. Since Diem's overthrow in November 1963, South Vietnamese soldiers had pointed guns at each other four times with Khanh as cause or target. Efficiency and combat morale, to say nothing of the country's overall struggle for survival against North Vietnam and the Vietcong, were suffering. On Sunday the 21st, the AFC voted to oust Khanh and sent a delegation to Chief of State Suu to inform him of their decision, thus signalling the AFC's continued commitment to civilian government.

Khanh was too wily to surrender without a fight. He started phoning colonels and other lower-ranking officers not on the AFC to round up troops. The AFC quickly countered by warning the officers that Khanh was through, but for good measure started rounding up its own troops. Khanh called us from Vung Tao saying that he was going to fight. Then the AFC called us to say that blood would flow unless Khanh capitulated. We sent two officers to Vung Tao who arrived at 1:00 A.M., just as Khanh's plane was preparing for takeoff. The first, Army Colonel Jasper Wilson, was the American advisor closest to Khanh and was best able to keep track of him and try to talk some reason into him. He hurried aboard and relayed word via the second officer that Khanh threatened heavy carnage by morning if the AFC did not reinstate him. Khanh, with Jasper in tow, then took off into the night, his destination unknown to us.

We heard that a column of tanks was moving on Bien Hoa, but not at whose behest. We also learned that more tanks were moving on Vung Tao, but again we did not know whether Khanh or the AFC were in command. In the meantime, Jasper Wilson spent a crazy night flying frantically around Vietnam in Khanh's C-47 as the general desperately tried to rally support. First Khanh flew to My Tho, fifty miles south of Saigon, where the forces even refused to refuel his plane; then to Nha Trang, 200 miles north. Again he was rebuffed without refuelling. His gas was now running low, but Khanh headed for Saigon. There the runways were blocked to prevent his landing, so with almost no fuel left he headed for a rough, unlit hilltop airstrip near Dalat, a mountain resort in the central highlands. He, with Jasper still along, finally touched down in the cool, pitch-dark stillness at 5 A.M. without enough fuel to restart the engines.

Later that day (Monday, February 22) Khanh started talking with the AFC by phone and radio. Argument continued through Tuesday, when Khanh, resilient to the last, made one more stab at a comeback, trying to round up troop support. On Wednesday he finally capitulated. He said his only condition was that he be allowed to leave the country in some dignity. The AFC, of course, was justifiably wary of a trick, especially since Khanh was still maneuvering quietly to conjure up support. On Thursday both sides agreed to a face-saving compromise that designated Khanh Ambassador-at-Large. So on Friday, exactly one week after my lunch with Warren Una, I attended a brief ceremony at Tan Son Nhut where General Tranh Van Minh took over from Khanh as Commander-in-Chief. Khanh, all smiles, received a formal farewell and full military honors. Then, ostentatiously clutching a plastic bag full of Vietnamese soil, he boarded a Pan Am clipper with his family and headed for Paris. There was not a wet eye in the crowd.

I next saw Khanh in 1966 at the Waldorf-Astoria in New York. I had returned to Washington as Deputy Undersecretary and Khanh, from what I heard, was running a restaurant in Paris.

He sent very private word through a retired United States Army officer he had known that he had established an important contact with the "other side," but would only discuss it with either Secretary McNamara or me. He was flying to New York in a few days to bring his daughter for medical treatment, and I agreed to meet him. I took a military plane to New York on July 17 and was met by State Department security agents who had arranged a "safe" suite in the Waldorf where I could have lunch with Khanh. Other agents brought him to the hotel. He was his old affable self. After several hours, however, it became evident that he could not match his enthusiastic generalities about peace feelers from the north with any specifics. I agreed to see him again on his next trip to New York, but there was nothing new. He never asked for another meeting and I have not seen him since.

In Saigon, universal relief prevailed at Khanh's exit. But his machinations had deprived the country of strong government for more than a year. In the meantime the Viet Cong had gained measurably and a pressure for doing more was building in Washington. It was Dean Rusk's "tyranny of the weak" taken to its logical conclusion. If Vietnam's survival is vital to our interests, and they cannot do it themselves, then we must do it for them. Although Max had returned in December 1964 with agreement that Washington would approve some bombing the north only if the Saigon government remained intact and in control, its complete instability over the next few months became an even more compelling argument to launch the bombing. If we meant business in Vietnam, we had to boost southern morale and convince the north to halt its infiltration of men and supplies. We could only use the tools available to us. Standing still could only lead to defeat. The killing of eight American advisers during a February 7 Vietcong attack on an airbase in Pleiku was the trigger that led LBJ to approve the start of regular bombing strikes against military targets and supply lines in the southernmost part of the north. "Operation Rolling Thunder" had begun.

We in Saigon had long been urging some bombing of supply routes in the north. We hoped bombing would raise morale in the south and, unlike committing ground forces, still leave us some political freedom of action. In fact, the raids did boost southern morale. As I said in a press conference April 2, "I feel there is a different psychology in the country. I am much more optimistic than I was prior to February 7. I think we have made some gains and that we are going to continue making them." We also had some secondary hope that bombing might restrict the flow of supplies from the north, but none of us who had observed the Korean War expected that bombing could do much against oxcart-and-bicycle supply lines. Our basic target was the will of Ho and his colleagues to continue. Bombing was a tool to force negotiations, not totally to destroy northern industry and transport.

We in the embassy had this one other hope for Operation Rolling Thunder: that it would quiet the growing push from Washington for the commitment of American ground forces. Regular North Vietnamese Army units had started crossing into the south in December 1964, before the start of American bombing, and we realized that for the north to send its regular troops as well as guerrillas marked a serious escalation that the South Vietnamese would be hard-pressed to contain singlehandedly. Even so, we thought American troops were not suited to a jungle guerrilla war. Sending GIs to Vietnam would also commit American prestige irretrievably to a country with serious internal flaws, and I did not feel enthusiastic about that. I could, however, understand how the push for American forces came about. As things were obviously not going well in South Vietnam I could well envision LBJ urging, in his own inimitable way, that somebody "do something." The one additional thing that was entirely under our control and could be done promptly was the deployment of American forces.

Ironically, it was the decision to start bombing that indirectly led to deploying the first American ground forces. It started innocently enough: the Air force, conducting its raids on the north from Danang, a base just south of the Demilitarized Zone from which maximum loads and a maximum number of sorties could be generated, was understandably worried because the base had no anti-aircraft protection. We considered their concern legitimate and approved the deployment of a Marine anti-aircraft battalion carrying HAWK missiles. As the battalion began setting up in the hills surrounding Danang, its lack of protection against Vietcong ground attacks was clear. True enough, there were insufficient Vietnamese forces in the area. We had no real choice but reluctantly to permit the Marines to send another battalion to guard the missiles that were protecting the base. This immediately generated a cable from the JCS for a plan to send an entire Marine Expeditionary Brigade of more than 5,000 men, carrying its own artillery, tanks, and fighter aircraft. Max and I were appalled and refused to approve this grandiose scheme. It went far beyond anything we envisioned or the military requirements could justify. That night Washington compromised by approving two Battalion Landing Teams, 60 percent of the force the JCS originally proposed. We replied that we reluctantly concurred on the condition that there would be no more and that these would be withdrawn as soon as Vietnamese replacements were available. The words were hardly out of our mouths when 3,500 Marines, who had been waiting off shore, stormed ashore in full battle dress at Danang—to be greeted by smiling Vietnamese girls offering flower leis.

Those Marines were the psychological wedge that advocates of American combat forces had been waiting for, and from then on the momentum of American troop commitments cascaded irresistibly into a massive military effort. Even before the Marines landed at Danang on March 16, Washington proposed additional deployments. Max sharply replied that he thought the JCS had agreed not to send more troops for the time being and that certainly we should wait to see how the Marines fared at Danang before jumping in with both feet. He drew on his long experience to inveigh against committing Americans to fight an Asian jungle war for which they were not armed, trained, or psychologically prepared.

Max journeyed to the United States in late March to plead his case in person, and returned April 5 with what he thought was a commitment for restraint on further troop deployments. I was pleased and relieved at the news; after visiting the Marines in the field April 16 with Prime Minister Quat, I told Washington that the trip had reinforced my conviction that we should be very cautious about introducing more GIs until we could see how the Marines worked out. But shortly thereafter we were inundated with plans for putting in more American troops. The Pentagon proposed introducing cadres of American troops into Vietnamese units, placing Army Civil Affairs officers trained for military government duty into the provinces, distributing American food through American channels to Vietnamese forces and their families, and other schemes all of which we rejected because it gave the appearance that we were completely dominating the situation. Our zealous President was obviously whipping Washington into a fury of activity as only he could do. The dike was springing more leaks than we "go-slowers" had fingers, however, and soon it was swept away altogether. At an April 18th conference in Honolulu, Secretary McNamara, JCS Chairman Wheeler, and CINCPAC commander Sharp obtained Max's reluctant consent to an increase in American troops to 82,000. By the end of June,

ington had jacked up the proposed end-of-the-year ceiling to
175,000.

Neither Max nor I had any enthusiasm for Americans fighting in Vietnam, but once our superiors made the decision we did
not continue to resist it. Certainly the war was not going well.
We knew that North Vietnam was stepping up infiltration. (During "the week that was," the South Vietnamese captured and
sank a large freighter bringing medicine, ammunition, and thousands of rifles from the north to the Vietcong—the first hard
evidence we had of infiltration by sea.) We in the Mission had no
good answers; if those in Washington thought they did, perhaps
they were right. At the time it was difficult to be sure that introducing American ground forces might not tip the balance in
our favor, particularly because most were headed for the thinly
populated areas where they could slug it out with regular North
Vietnamese Army units without having to worry about local inhabitants.

Military escalation was transforming our lives in Saigon.
Already we had sent our dependents home and had grown accustomed to guards tailing us in our houses, in shops, and even
on the golf course. The center of gravity was shifting towards
General Westmoreland and MACV as the American involvement
militarized. But even so, both the Vietnamese and we fully realized that the struggle and our response could not be solely
military. The economic, social, and administrative parts of our
programs must also be greatly increased. Like any other underdeveloped country, Vietnam had the problem of building its basic
administrative structure to reach from the central government
to the provinces, districts, villages, and hamlets. This required
experts and trained administrators able to translate national policy
into effective programs at the local level, and to report on local
developments. These persons were all too rare. To build such a
structure for the future required starting with education at the
primary level.

Everywhere we turned there was work to be done. The
economic structure required the development of transportation,
communications, power, industry, agriculture, and so on almost
ad infinitum. We equipped and helped staff a medical school and
built hospitals where none existed. We helped build a school of
public administration, improved and strengthened the civil police, and financed thousands of school rooms, printing presses,
radio stations, and communications equipment for isolated vil-

lages. We worked to cover the large gap between Vietnamese exports and imports, which together with able Vietnamese fiscal management prevented any serious inflation until late in the war. We built refugee camps, cared for tens of thousands of direct and indirect civilian victims of Viet Cong terrorism, and resettled them, in addition to the one million who fled the north in 1954. We helped rebuild roads, bridges, schools and homes destroyed by Viet Cong attacks.

These were by no means just paper programs. They involved hundreds of Americans living without their families, in many cases in isolated areas, vulnerable to Viet Cong assassination. Because their relations with the local Vietnamese were almost without exception friendly, however, they received protection from the Viet Cong and the number of assassinations was gratifyingly small. During the time I was in Saigon I never heard of a case in which an American who was betrayed to the Viet Cong by another Vietnamese.

In spite of the political turmoil in Saigon, progress was made. The number of students in government schools almost doubled to two million by the end of 1965 as compared with the 1.3 million in 1960. With assistance from Australia and the Republic of China, some 14 million school textbooks written in Vietnamese by Vietnamese educators had been produced by the end of 1966—a far cry from the previous dependence on French-language texts. Land reform continued with 600,000 acres distributed to 115,000 farmers between 1957 and 1965. A further 650,000 acres was distributed to 150,000 farmers in 1966 alone. The introduction of "miracle rice" from the Rockefeller experimental station in the Philippines further increased the productivity and income of farmers, and so on. We were proud of these programs and the Americans working on them. Our regret was that in spite of our best efforts, we could not make them better known.

A big embassy is a complex organism. Staffers come and go, programs are invented and discarded, ideas percolate, directives and queries rain down from Washington, arguments ricochet until they are finally resolved. I consider our people in Saigon among the finest group of Americans I have ever worked with. They had discipline, dedication, and zest for what they were doing. As a group we may have made mistakes, but even under pressure and hardship no one degenerated into cowardice or jealousy.

Of course, we were hardly immune to disagreement. Max and I tried to let the agency chiefs run their own shops as much as we could, but sometimes we had to intervene. Max had to spend considerable time in Washington, but when he returned we took care to see each other often and set common positions before important meetings to make sure no one saw daylight between us. To handle problems, all we had to do was to pop through the door that connected. our two offices. Of course, if we disagreed I bowed to his higher authority, but that seldom happened on any matter of real moment. Max was an excellent ambassador, intelligent, savvy, and forceful both in Saigon and Washington, with a deft touch for bureaucratic maneuvering and embassy management.

Vietnam was not a joyful place, but still my stint there was rewarding. The Japanese have a word, "genki," to describe how I felt. The word embodies that sense of vigor and zest that come from employing every bit of your energy and ability on an absorbing task. I have a reputation in the Foreign Service for driving myself; Marshall Green, a former Assistant Secretary of State for Far Eastern Affairs, says that my eyes really light up only when the problem at hand is so thorny that it's near insoluble. In that sense I suppose Vietnam was a perfect post for me. Each day was full. I saw an endless stream of journalists, businessmen, congressmen, ambassadors, and Washington officials, and faced endless problems. With no wives there was little social life, and what there was was all business.

Occasional attempts on my life made my job that much more stimulating. Once a loaf of bread containing a grenade was thrown at the embassy entrance just as I was being driven up to the door; it failed to explode. Another time I was taking my morning walk around the inside of the seven-foot masonry wall, topped with barbed wire, that surrounded the considerable gardens at my house in Saigon. On my last round I deviated from my usual route and instead cut diagonally across the lawn. Suddenly there was a heavy explosion the loud concussion of which shattered the wall I would have been walking along, destroyed much of the garage, and blew out all of the windows on that side of the house. I ran for shelter as the debris came showering down around my head and my Marine and police guards came running out with their guns drawn. Fortunately, I was unscathed. The Saigon police said afterwards that a loft next door was being used as a storage area for explosives for a war movie, which had "spontaneously" gone off. I never quite believed the coincidence, but I was so thankful to have escaped that I never pushed for a more thorough investigation.

The third time, however, was worse. It occurred on March 30, 1965, which started like any other Saigon day, hot and clear. Max was in Washington. I was at my fifth-floor desk by 8:00, dictating telegrams about the progress of the Quat government and preparing for meetings later that day with Westy. The British Ambassador and Robert Shaplen of *New Yorker* magazine were also due to call.

At 10:46, a man on a Lambretta motorscooter drove by the six Saigon police guards stationed outside the embassy and parked across the street. Then a Renault sedan slammed into the curb alongside the embassy (where parking or stopping was strictly prohibited) and the driver jumped out. When the guards (who I am ashamed to say we nicknamed "white mice") ordered him to move the car, he pulled out a gun and began shooting. So did the motorcyclist. The guards returned the fire. One guard was wounded, the Renault driver was killed, and the other gunman fled.

Our Consular Section, which handled passports, visas, and so on, was on the ground floor with a large window facing the street. When the car screeched to a halt just a few feet from the window and the shooting started, everyone dropped to the floor. Upstairs, most people, myself included, went to the nearest window to see what the commotion was all about. At that moment the 250 pounds of plastic explosive filling the back seat of the car exploded, hurling a storm of glass shards and metal window frames into the faces of those who had gone to see. Shielded by a concrete ledge just below the window, only three of the many visitors and employees in the Consular Section were killed, but many were wounded. A packed Chinese restaurant across the street collapsed and caught fire, and the bodies of many killed and wounded passers-by littered the street. The last thing that Peer deSilva, the CIA Station Chief, saw from his third floor window was the driver of the car lighting the fuse stuck in the explosive. Professional that he was, Peer recognized the fuse for what it was but did not react in time to shield himself and was blinded in both eyes. Happily, unlike some others, he recovered partial sight in one eye after some months of intensive treatment in the United States.

Once more I was lucky. When I heard the gunshots, I, too, wanted to see what was happening. A ledge obstructed the view from my office to the street, so I headed to Max's office where there was a narrow balcony. To get there I had to pass through a small connecting office where my secretary, Betty Brooks, sat.

Just as I was opening the door into her office, the blast shattered the window in my office and sent the frame flying across my desk to the opposite wall. The door which I had just opened was between me and a section of the window, and its whole back was shredded by glass shards. Had I been sitting at my desk, I certainly would have been seriously injured or killed, and had I moved forward one more step through the door I would have caught the glass from the window in Betty's office. For a moment I was stunned. They I saw that Betty, who sat well back in her office, was bleeding around the face and arms but was conscious and apparently all right. We were the only people on the top floor.

I had never liked our Saigon embassy building, an aging French structure located on a busy intersection near the port. It was a rabbit warren, poorly designed for office work and impossible to protect against attack. It had only one narrow staircase that spiraled around its one creaky elevator. There were no fire escapes or emergency exit routes to other buildings, and I had often worried about what we would do in case of fire. Getting money out of Washington to build a new embassy had been one of my pet projects since I arrived, but to no avail.

My first thought after the blast was that the supporting pillars had been blown away, as they had at a troop billet in Qui Nhon, and the whole embassy would collapse. Betty and I quickly got in a doorway for protection. When the building appeared to be standing intact, we quickly locked away our loose papers and waited to see if Vietcong would come charging up the stairs brandishing Kalashnikov submachine guns or if fire would cut us off from escape. Soon we smelled smoke and heard the flames crackle, but the fire appeared to come from the Chinese restaurant opposite us. I went down the stairway, checking each office to see that there were enough able-bodied to aid the injured. Then I went out to the street, down stairs already slippery with blood. Fire trucks, ambulances, and military police were beginning to arrive, summoned by General Westmoreland, who had seen the blast on his way to an 11:00 A.M. appointment with me. I directed the rescue workers to the worst-hit areas and returned inside to the communications section, where the operator was standing by his post. I got off a quick message to Washington on the one working military circuit saying we had been heavily hit but I was unhurt and would report further as soon as I could size up the situation.

Going back outside, I passed a stretcher sitting in the street with the remains of an embassy secretary, still clutching a ball-point pen, whose face had been entirely obliterated. Realizing I could do nothing further, I picked up a jeep and an armed MP and headed for MACV, where I sent another message reporting that some of the staff had been killed and that I could be reached through MACV. Westy was surprised and relieved to see me, and after I washed my superficial face cuts we drove to the little American hospital where ambulances and trucks were already unloading the dead and injured. In the emergency room surgeons were operating on several people. Blood was everywhere. I could not recognize any of the disfigured faces. In the upstairs wards I tried to console the less seriously wounded, saying the inane things one says at such a time. Prime Minister Quat arrived to offer his condolences, then Dean Rusk, who was attending a White House dinner, tracked me down by telephone at the hospital to offer whatever help we needed. I returned to MACV to meet with the uninjured members of the Mission Council and plot our next steps.

In total, twenty two people died from the blast and 190 were wounded. Two of the dead were Americans, three were local Vietnamese employees working in the consular section, and three were Saigon policemen who so bravely stood by their post. The rest of the dead were innocent Vietnamese pedestrians. All that remained of the bomb-carrying Renault was a three-foot crater in the pavement.

After attending to the wounded, the next order of business was to set up temporary headquarters at MACV until the wreckage at the embassy was cleared. All the windows were gone, doors and partitions had been blown out, desks were overturned. I thought fixing it up would take at least a week. I could not have been more astonished when hundreds of people, working through the night under the direction of Jack Herfurt, our administrative chief, readied the building for business by eight o'clock the next morning. By noon, everyone who was not confined to a hospital bed had shown up for work, some bloody and disfigured but determined to carry on. I have never been prouder of my American colleagues abroad.

After returning to the building I immediately arranged to visit the hospital ward where most of the injured Vietnamese had been taken and to visit the families of our Vietnamese employees who had been killed. The following day I attended the formal funeral ceremonies for the police who had died in our defense and gave, in accordance with Vietnamese custom, monetary tokens of appreciation to their families.

The embassy bombing, coming only two weeks after the start of Operation Rolling Thunder, added to the Washington pressures for further United States troop deployments. President Johnson said: "Outrages like this will only reinforce the determination of the American people and government to strengthen their assistance and support for the people and government of Vietnam." Prime Minister Quat told me it permitted him to take much more vigorous measures in support of the war. The Saigon police therefore entirely blocked off the street in front of the embassy, but it still took more than a year before the Congress would appropriate the modest amount required to build a new embassy and several more years before it was finished.

There was one amusing footnote to this tragedy: A Marine guard manning the front desk that morning told me afterwards that the British Ambassador, a rather "old school" type, had arrived punctually for his noon appointment with me. The carnage and chaos around him spoke eloquently of what had occurred only an hour before, but he became very upset when he learned I was visiting the hospital. Surely, he kept insisting to the guard, I would return to keep my appointment; after all, I had not phoned to cancel! Only with difficulty did the guard persuade him that waiting would be futile. The next time I saw him his arched eyebrows implicitly condemned me for my dreadful breach of proper manners.

The departure of General Khanh, the appointment of Prime Minister Quat, and the start of regular American bombing more or less simultaneously in February had encouraged us to think that finally we had come up with the winning combination for Vietnam. The generals, surfeited with coups and intrigues, seemed to have recognized that their political ineptitude had hurt the country. On May 6 they dissolved the Armed Forces Council. Quat set a date for provincial and municipal elections and started holding regular sessions with the Mission Council on pacification, the economy, and military security. We could sense the growth of self-assurance and effectiveness in the Saigon government.

It was too good to last. By the beginning of June the Suu-Quat government had fallen, a victim of petty political maneuvering and the near-senile obduracy of Chief of State Pham Kac Suu. We in the embassy unwittingly contributed to the debacle. Advising another government, especially a young one, is always tricky, and the fall of Suu and Quat was not the first or last time that our zeal to do good in Vietnam backfired.

Quat was a typical Tonkinese, energetic and activist, while Suu, nearing eighty, was almost a living caricature of the slow, easy-going Cochinchinese. He gave the impression of being vague and unfocused, a condition no doubt exacerbated by his many years as a French political prisoner. As Chief of State, Suu was supposed to preside but not govern; that is, to act as a ceremonial figurehead while Quat ran the government. Quat paid less and less attention to Suu as he became more immersed in running the country, a neglect that Suu found irksome.

Both Quat and the embassy knew that his Cabinet ministers of Economy and Interior were incompetent. We urged him to remove these ciphers, particularly the Economy minister who was key to our economic development and currency stabilization programs. Quat said he needed more time, but finally he moved to fire them, at least partly in response to our advice.

Legally, the figurehead Suu had to sign the necessary decree, and he seized on this technicality to derail the Tonkinese Quat. Suu refused the formality of approving the two new ministers until the former ones resigned, which they refused to do. Neither we nor the military could budge him. We asked Quat what we could do to help. He said it would take time and to let him handle it.

In the meantime, Ambassador Taylor had to attend important meetings in Washington on June 9, 10, and 11 to discuss increasing aid to the South Vietnamese government. Quat had a clear legal and practical right to choose his own cabinet, but as his stalemate with Suu festered, various political groups smelled blood and began to line up behind whichever man they found more congenial. The crisis dragged on.

At one in the morning on June 11, my bedside emergency phone rang. It was Prime Minister Quat, who asked that I come to his office immediately. As I dressed I had my Marine guard rouse my driver, my Saigon police guard, and Mel Manfull, the Embassy Political Counselor who lived nearby. Together we rushed over to the Prime Minister's office, which was on the second floor of one of the old French government buildings. All was dark, except for his office, as we climbed the steps. I knocked and entered to find him sitting in his usual leather lounge chair with Air Marshal Ky and Deputy Prime Minister Thieu sitting to his right on the couch. The three of them looked tired and subdued. No one else was present.

Quat opened without preliminaries. He said his crisis with Suu could not be resolved by constitutional means. He had concluded there was no alternative but to dissolve the civilian government by a military coup. The coup, which would obviate the constitutional deadlock between him and Suu, would also remove

Suu from power, as well as himself. Ky and Thieu had agreed to this scheme, Quat continued, and would shortly take office themselves, Thieu as Chief of State and Ky as Prime Minister. Looking somewhat abashed, Thieu and Ky confirmed the deal.

A mutually agreed-upon coup—a diplomatic first! I thought I had seen just about every permutation of coup conceivable in the past year, but this was a new twist. I immediately spoke of the tragedy this approach would represent to the objective of a stable government we all sought, and requested that they take time to explore other alternatives. Quat said they had already considered all the alternatives. Having made their decision, he emphasized, it was vital to move quickly, before dawn, so that troublemakers like Trich Tri Quang had no time to foment discord for their own purposes.

I could see his point, but my mind was still searching for other ways out and I stalled for time. I asked to speak to Quat privately, which I did in the little lavatory near his office. Quat assured me that this solution represented his considered judgment of what was best for Vietnam and that Ky and Thieu were not pressuring him. We returned to his office. All I could do was wish luck to them and to Vietnam. I returned to the embassy through the darkened streets, where I placed my phone call and wrote my telegram to Washington.

Since Ky was the sixth Prime Minister in the seventeen months since the assassination of Diem, I could not then forsee that this might turn out to be a favorable development. However, the Ky-Thieu coup marked the start of the relative stability we had so earnestly labored for. Ky, energetic and well-meaning but also somewhat of an unguided missile, was eventually eased out, but Thieu, who replaced him in open elections, evolved into an astute politician who presided until the final destruction of his government by North Vietnamese troops ten years later.

As the bombing war gathered momentum, the Strategic Air Command (SAC) had briefed us on what could be accomplished by heavy B-52 bombers using large conventional bombs on identified Vietcong jungle base areas. They stressed the accuracy they could achieve even from very high altitudes, thus assuring surprise. Although I had long since learned to be skeptical of most Air Force claims, I became convinced we should give it a try in an area free from any civilian population and went along with approving a raid. I went out with General Westmoreland in a light plane to observe the results. We circled a mile or two from the designated target area (a little close, I thought), scanning the sky for the big bombers that were coming some 1500 miles from Guam. But we could not see anything. Suddenly, however, the target area erupted in a torrent of explosions marching across the jungle. It was an awesome sight, and it was hard to imagine how anyone on the surface could have survived, but patrols later sent into the area on foot found few signs of enemy casualties.

However, SAC had demonstrated that its claims for accuracy were not exaggerated, and raids like this were used throughout the war whenever what seemed to be suitable targets could be identified. The difficulty was figuring out what suitable targets were, and whether the bombers really did help more than hurt in the political battle for the minds of the Vietnamese. A B-52 was very efficient in delivering bombs, but figuring out where the enemy was and distinguishing him from non-involved civilians was the central problem of the war.

In the first part of July, the President announced that Cabot Lodge would return to Saigon, replacing Max Taylor, and it was agreed that I would also leave after a period of overlap with Lodge. My successor, Bill Porter, was our extremely able Ambassador to Algeria.

Before Max left, Secretary McNamara, Cabot Lodge, JCS Chairman Wheeler, and others again visited Saigon. During their visit there was extended discussion about whether to deploy additional American combat forces. As usual Max and I took a "go slow" attitude while Westy saw the military situation as urgent, with the only available answer being the deployment of more troops. The President moved quickly after McNamara's return and surprised us all by announcing on July 28, just two days before Max left, that he had authorized raising the American strength from 75,000 to 125,000 "almost immediately."

Lodge arrived in a few weeks followed by my successor, Bill Porter, so that I was able to leave for Washington on September 15. Lodge's style of operating was entirely different from that of Taylor, and though I liked him as a person, it was clear that neither of us could fit comfortably with the other. So while I hated to leave a job that was so far from finished, I did not feel it would be useful to stay. I returned directly to Washington to await confirmation by the Senate to resume my former job as Deputy Under Secretary, which in the interim had been filled on an acting basis by Llewellyn (Tommy) Thompson.

I still believe that our purposes in Vietnam were basically sound. I recognize that the origins of our involvement there, in the aftermath of French colonialism, were not entirely glorious. But whatever distaste one may have for French colonialism, the French and American phases of the Vietnam war should not be equated. By the mid-1950s Vietnam had become a different war. We were not colonialists as the French had been. Mao's victory in China and the unprovoked communist aggression of the Korean War had etched the battle lines between the communist bloc and the West more deeply. By 1960 Ho Chi Minh was running a determined insurgency. He had become intimately beholden to Moscow and Peking, so that his victory would have been their victory and our defeat, a dangerous invitation to further communist expansion in Southeast Asia and elsewhere. In South Vietnam, genuine non-communist nationalists were striving to make a go of running a relatively decent government under remarkably difficult conditions. Abandoning the south—deserting an ally for whose creation we were largely responsible—would have been morally and politically wrong. The South Vietnamese themselves clearly preferred their own government, no matter how ineffective, to accepting Hanoi's crushing embrace. Even today, almost a decade after Hanoi's victory, independent journalists report that the south is being ruled more like an occupied enemy than a reunited brother.

It is important to remember that through all of the changes of administration in Washington, from Truman through Nixon, the American goal was not to make war against North Vietnam or to seek its surrender. The consistent goal was simply to persuade the North Vietnamese regime to stop what it was doing in South Vietnam. It was a limited objective, and every administration kept it so. There were those who argued that we should have shifted our objective to the defeat and surrender of North Vietnam and that if we had done so, we could have achieved "victory." Whatever the arguments might have been for such a course, it never appealed to those whose memories of Korea and MacArthur's "March to the Yalu" were still fresh.

Our hope was to raise the cost to the north of doing what it was doing in the south so high that it would cease and desist— at least for a time. This was the logic behind the tendency of LBJ and his advisors increasingly to turn to direct military intervention. It was something that could be done by ourselves without the difficulties and frustrations of filtering programs through Saigon's political jungle. However, our instruments and will proved to be unequal to the task.

Nevertheless, when I left Saigon I had confidence because of the significant progress I had seen in the south during my tour. Despite the frequent changes of government, none had been hostile to the United States or had sought accommodation with the north. In those fourteen months, the Vietnamese armed forces had increased by 25 percent to 520,000, the National Police had doubled to 42,000, and desertion rates were dropping. Thirty-six nations were contributing support to the south compared to ten when I arrived, and Australia, Thailand, and Korea had sent combat forces. "Miracle rice," land reform, improved education and health care, and other accomplishments were really improving quality of life, advances for which we and the Vietnamese were entitled to take real pride.

Even though Vietcong activity proved extremely disruptive to the economy, we figured the growing American military presence, for all its hazards, would permit the country to get on its feet. Saigon under Quat and Ky was especially interested in improving provincial and local government, where the essential battle for the people's loyalty would be fought. Inflation had been kept under control despite American aid nearing $400 million annually. The United States Mission itself was smoother-running, more unanimous in its major recommendations and better plugged into the South Vietnamese government at all levels.

My own major preoccupation in Saigon, having to struggle to keep some sort of national government afloat and under steam, concerned me. But Greece saw five changes of government during the first two years of American aid after World War II; France had six changes of government under the first two years of the Marshall Plan. I could not diagnose Saigon's maladies as necessarily terminal.

When I returned to Washington again to take up my Deputy Under Secretary position in November 1965 (for eleven months, until I left to become Ambassador to Japan), I spoke like this in Washington and in numerous addresses that I gave throughout the country and in Canada.

Of course, as everyone knows, the optimism about Vietnam I shared with other American policymakers in 1965 did not prove to be well-founded. Later I will trace subsequent developments in Vietnam as I saw them from Washington and offer some opinions about why events there turned out so badly for the fine Vietnamese people and for the United States.

·CHAPTER TWELVE·

Ambassador to Japan

I HAD KNOWN PRESIDENT JOHNSON TO BE A MAN OF HIS word, but I had my doubts about whether he would keep the promise he made to Pat at the Indonesian Embassy the day he asked me to go to Saigon—that she would "get her ambition" and return to Tokyo as the wife of the American Ambassador. Our present Ambassador to Japan, Ed Reischauer, was showing no inclination to resign when I returned from Saigon, and the Deputy Undersecretary position kept me busy, useful, and entirely content. The President never mentioned the incident with Pat to me or revealed in any way the plans he had for me, if any.

So when Ed indicated at the beginning of 1966 that he intended to resign mid-year, I was interested but not expectant. But LBJ kept his promise. Even in the face of press speculation that beat him to it, the President swallowed his inclination to show the pundits wrong and nominated me as Ambassador to Japan on July 25.

I cannot deny that the prospect of returning as Ambassador to the country where I had started in the Foreign Service thirty years before as the lowest of the low gave me a lot of emotional satisfaction. And aside from my background, I thought Tokyo presented one of the most absorbing and challenging jobs in American diplomacy. Only fifteen years after the Occupation Japan was emerging as a major world power, and many aspects of the relations between our countries needed bringing up to date. Especially important was military security, where trouble was brewing and about which the Japanese were extremely sensitive.

It took me three months to get to Tokyo, about par for the course. In late August the Senate held hearings (dominated by

Senator Fulbright's questions about Vietnam policy) and confirmed my nomination, but Rusk was reluctant to let me go until the new team on the seventh floor was firmly ensconced. Nick Katzenbach, the former Assistant Attorney General, replaced George Ball as Under Secretary, Gene Rostow filled the long-vacant job as Under Secretary for Political Affairs, and Foy Kohler, our Ambassador in Moscow and a career FSO, arrived to take my job. Not until mid-October was I free to leave Foggy Bottom.

I arrived in Tokyo on October 29, after some vacation and conversations with our Commander in Chief Pacific (CINCPAC), Admiral Felt, in Honolulu. I had been through Tokyo periodically since leaving Yokohama in 1949, but this was my first chance to reacquaint myself seriously with Japan. It was a vastly different country from the shocked and devasted nation I had known two decades before, dominated by MacArthur's SCAP, busily trying to absorb liberalism and "Democracy" into its institutions. Remarkable economic growth, which was running in excess of ten percent a year, had boosted its GNP in 1966 to the world's third largest. Evidence of its effects abounded. Tokyo had been transformed into a throbbing metropolis, full of neon signs, traffic jams, and other reflections of "progress." It had become a hub of Asian commerce, and hordes of business travelers now came to the city, as did delegations of scholars and other luminaries attending international conferences. Occupation-instituted land reform had allowed farmers to share in the prosperity; modern homes, TV antennas, and powered farm equipment had replaced the grinding poverty I had once known in the countryside. The Japanese people were proud of their rapid accomplishments and carried themselves more confidently and assertively than I had seen since before the war. This was also true of their politicians and Foreign Office officials.

The embassy compound was the first one purpose-built by the State Department, completed in 1931 after the 1923 earthquake demolished our previous building. Dubbed "Hoover's Folly" at the time because it was considered so extravagant, it boasted apartments and other facilities for the thirty Americans who then worked there in addition to the chancery and the Ambassador's residence. By 1966 the apartments had long since been converted into offices. Skyscrapers encircled us, and in fact most of the staff (who now numbered about 400) worked in a six-story annex one block north. The compound was still well-maintained, however, and wonderfully convenient. I sometimes used to think that the

Emperor and I were the only people living in central Tokyo who could walk to work in the morning.

I had a tough act to follow in Tokyo. Ed Reischauer, Ambassador for five and one-half years, had been a professor of Japanese history at Harvard (where he had now returned) and had a Japanese wife. Affable, glamorous in the style of the New Frontier, closely tied to Kennedy and fluent in Japanese, he traveled around the country, appeared on television constantly, and won real admiration and affection from the whole Japanese people. The catch phrase was that he had "restored the broken dialogue" between America and Japan that had faltered during the tenure of his predecessor, Douglas MacArthur II. MacArthur had maintained a very narrow range of contacts among the Japanese leadership, ignored the Japanese Socialist Party and other opposition groups, and appeared startled and isolated when anti-American riots swept the country protesting the 1960 Security Treaty between Japan and the United States.

While those who really run Japan—the leaders of the ruling Liberal Democratic Party (LDP), high-ranking bureaucrats, and business executives—are basically quite conservative, the "opinion leaders"—newspaper reporters, university professors, and intellectuals generally—come from a tradition strongly influenced by the Marxist leanings of the intellectuals who survived persecution and imprisonment during the war, and whom the Occupation placed in positions of authority after the purges of conservative militarists. Ed performed brilliantly with the intellectuals, broadened embassy contacts to politicians of every stripe, and consequently was able to project a very positive image of the United States to a wide audience of Japanese. He moved relations between our countries from an ugly confrontation to genuine mutual regard.

On this solid foundation, a great deal remained to be built. Relations between our two countries were still at an immature and unequal stage, not befitting the great nation Japan had become. I arrived in Tokyo intending to devote my energies to two main areas of United States-Japan relations that required, as I saw it, realignment to correspond with changed national and international circumstances: economics and security.

Japan's economic miracle was causing some growing pains in our trade and investment relations. After the war the United States acknowledged that Japan needed protection against foreign competition to get its economy going, but in the mid-1960s the trade balance was beginning to swing in Japan's direction as its manufactured goods, especially electronics, began to make big inroads in the wide-open American market.

Both countries' trade policies were supposed to be governed by the General Agreement on Tariffs and Trade (GATT), negotiated in 1954, under which member countries were supposed to eliminate progressively all barriers to free trade. Japan took full advantage in promoting its excellent products in the United States. But it refused to play this game fairly. Tokyo imposed restrictive quotas on the imports of some 120 products on top of the quotas permitted under GATT. Many of these restrictions affected exactly the high-technology manufactured goods that were most profitable for us to trade. In effect, Japan was treating us something like an underdeveloped country, purchasing agricultural products in return for its manufactured goods. American products that did penetrate Japanese customs found the domestic market very difficult to crack, with the Japanese shunning all foreign goods out of a deeply ingrained patriotic chauvinism.

I recognized that the United States Government could hardly dictate the buying patterns of Japanese consumers, and that the cohesive and xenophobic nature of Japanese society would defy repeated assaults from even the most determined American sales managers. (The president of a highly regarded research institute in economics, who had been very unusual by Japanese standards in switching to it from a job elsewhere at age thirty-five, once told me: "The Japanese are not only closed to outsiders but to each other. It was two years before I was trusted here.") But I believed Japan was going to have to grant equal access to its own market. Otherwise, protectionist pressures in America would mount until they forced legislation through Congress. I was worried that that might unleash a spiraling escalation of protectionist measures all over the world like we had seen in the 1930s, bringing a recession or depression in its wake. Japan was so dependent on trade for its survival, having virtually no indigenous natural resources, that chain reaction protectionism would cripple it faster and more severely than any other developed country. I believed this might promote political polarization into extreme left and right, a very unhealthy situation both for us and for Japan.

The Japanese Foreign Office, as well as the executives of big companies such as Mitsuibishi and Sony that could compete in the world market, perceived the importance of maintaining momentum for free trade, but Japan also had many small and medium-sized firms (and farms) that were inefficient, feared American competition, and had enough political clout in the LDP to carry the argument for protectionism. In that respect the Japanese firms were much like our own steel industry.

Another economic wrangle concerned Japanese restrictions on the flow of American capital into Japan. Japan was extremely leery of letting the United States, which it pictured as an overwhelmingly powerful financial colossus, invest directly in Japanese companies or open up branch plants of American firms. Since the Meiji restoration, the relationship between business and government in Japan had been entirely different from the antagonism we have grown accustomed to in the United States. Tokyo gave companies firm and regular guidance based on its conception of the country's overall national interest, and they paid close heed. To make sure Japan could survive in the world market, government guidance consistently stressed self-reliance. Part of Japan's resistance to absorbing American capital stemmed from a fear that American firms, no matter how earnestly they tried to be good corporate citizens, would not respond to government signals in the way that is second nature for Japanese, but would refer important decisions to American boardrooms beyond the reach of the Ministry for International Trade and Industry. Also, the Japanese have an extremely group-oriented social structure, and business, like other spheres of Japanese life, has strict rituals and behavior patterns that all who wish group approval must follow. Americans could not possibly become Japanese or enter these cohesive groups. Thus, the Japanese were concerned that allowing Americans a greater local role would disrupt the harmony of business relationships.

While I understood Japanese sensitivities, I felt principle was entirely on our side. The United States Government permitted Japanese to invest in our country, so we could justly expect reciprocal treatment. And I intended to point out to Japanese executives that many countries in Southeast Asia, where Japan was busily establishing factories and investing heavily, must fear it as exactly the same sort of economic colossus that Japan feared in America. On both trade and investment, however, I intended to fight for liberalization privately at first, because I doubted I would get anywhere if I appeared to be pressuring or threatening the Japanese government. Like every other government, Japan's had to be able to present its policies as something that served its own people. My job was to convince it that liberalization really did serve Japan's long-term interests.

Our security relations presented a much more subtle, difficult, and engrossing problem. I spent the bulk of my time and effort attempting to recast them. The basic source of difficulty was that the United States had been ultimately responsible for Japan's defense since the Occupation, under the 1952 and 1960 Security Treaties. Japan maintained its own small "self-defense forces" (Article IX of the MacArthur-imposed Constitution "renounced war as a sovereign right of the nation" and prohibited the Japanese government from possessing armed forces in the conventional sense), but the United States supplied Japan's "nuclear umbrella" and a range of conventional deterrents to aggression, including large naval and air bases. These bases caused a certain amount of inconvenience. Japan's reliance on American protection necessarily denied it complete autonomy in world affairs, though it simultaneously permitted the country the great luxuries of minute defense spending and few international responsibilities. Senior LDP members wanted American protection to continue while reducing its irritations. But the Socialists, the main opposition party, wanted to complete the pacifist vision of Article IX and advocated "unarmed neutrality"—eviction of all American forces on the assumption that no one would then disturb the country's tranquility.

Reischauer had not devoted much attention to security issues. He had not been comfortable with them and, more important, the Japanese government had not wanted to discuss them, since public opinion was still easily aroused by the "militarist" implications of any attempt to bolster the country's security. But it had become time to address this very basic question of the kind of role a mature Japan should play in world affairs. It was a question on which I had a good deal of background and some firm opinions, but it was something that had to be raised very discreetly, to avoid engaging the government's hypersensitivity to charges of warmongering.

I intended to keep a lower profile than Ed had anyway; that was my personal style, and with Ed's success the need for a highly visible ambassador had passed. It was time to move on to more "standard" diplomacy between professional diplomats, in itself a symbol of the increasingly equal relationship I hoped to build. With a low profile and my reputation for being close to Secretary Rusk and President Johnson (often mentioned in the

Japanese press), I felt I could gain the confidence of the bureaucrats, top executives, and Diet members who really ran the country and try to advance their collective thinking on security
questions. After laying this groundwork, the debate could be widened to the public at large.

I even tried to sell the press on the virtues of this approach
at my first news conference on November 9. Explaining that I
was a believer in "quiet diplomacy," I said that "To the degree
that we diplomats can resolve questions without their becoming
public issues we are successful; to the degree that we make headlines, you can say that we are not successful. When matters become the subject of public controversy, positions tend to become
frozen and the settlement of the questions becomes more difficult." This policy, with its implication that I could not be counted
on as the source of hot news stories, did not exactly make me a
darling of the press, though I believe it held their respect. In any
case, it did allow me to get things done.

Three security problems, separate but requiring a common
approach from the United States, needed the most attention. First
was America's continuing administrative control (dating from the
Occupation) of the Bonin and Ryukyu Islands. The Bonins are a
tiny chain about 650 miles south of Tokyo, of which the best
known is Iwo Jima, site of the ferocious World War II battle. Our
Coast Guard maintained some small but important Long Range
Navigation (LORAN) facilities there that helped our submarines
in the Pacific and other ships to sail accurately. The Bonins were
otherwise not important to our military posture in the Pacific.
The Ryukyus were much more significant. Among them is the
major island of Okinawa, with nearly a million inhabitants. The
Ryukyus and Bonins were still recognized as Japanese territory,
but the 1951 Japanese Peace Treaty gave the United States government "administrative rights" over them indefinitely. We had
been in no hurry to return these rights to Tokyo because on
Okinawa we had some of our largest naval and air bases in the
Far East.

Retaining administrative control over Okinawa and the
Bonins had been the price the Joint Chiefs of Staff extracted for
going along with the Japanese Peace Treaty. Because we controlled Okinawa we could use our bases for storing nuclear weapons and mounting operations outside Japan (for example, air
strikes over Korea or Vietnam). These were rights denied to our
bases in Japan proper, under the 1960 Security Treaty, without
"prior consultation" with the Japanese government. The Penta-

gon did not want to give up these very useful rights, the likely price of having Tokyo regain control.

But our presence on Okinawa was becoming anachronistic. American military governors were directing the affairs of a million non-Americans with varying degrees of sophistication, assisted since 1961 by a civilian civil administrator. The Japanese had never shown much concern for the welfare of Okinawa when Tokyo controlled it before the war; in fact, the Okinawans had been quite brutally discriminated against because the Ryukyus had been an independent kingdom entirely separate from Japan until the expansionist phase of the Meiji restoration, and its inhabitants spoke a dialect different from mainland Japanese. Nevertheless, since the 1950s Japanese politicians (some in the ruling LDP, but mostly the socialists and other opposition members) had suddenly rediscovered their close ties of affection and history with the Ryukyuans and made great anti-American hay of our continuing presence. The local population had been cooperative with the American military for the most part, even in the face of some fairly inept high commissioners. But recently there had been protest demonstrations, and anti-American sentiment was clearly rising. I saw this myself in a trip I took to Okinawa several months after I arrived in Japan, when members of the left-wing opposition were boycotting the Ryukyuan legislature to dramatize their differences with the more pro-American majority party.

The Okinawan police force was small and not terribly efficient; its only backup was American troops. If the opposition were ever able to foment a demonstration that got so out of hand that American soldiers had to fire on Okinawan civilians, the outrage would be enormous. We could not afford that. With two major airfields for F-4s and B-52s, hundreds of acres of Army storage and maintenance facilities, a full Marine Division with all its equipment, and extensive training grounds, Okinawa was a crucial ingredient in our Asian deterrent against Soviet, Chinese, and especially North Korean aggression. I was convinced it was time to return responsibility to Japan for the Ryukyus and the Bonins. They were a vestige of the war that might easily provoke an ugly incident that could unravel the patient work of two decades and force us out of our bases in Japan as well as on Okinawa.

To return administrative rights and responsibilities for the Ryukus to Tokyo took five years of very demanding "quiet diplomacy," as much within the United States Government as with the Japanese. Even the negotiations about the Bonins, which were comparatively straightforward, took two years. I will return to this story later, and I raise it here only because it ties into the second major security issue on my Tokyo agenda: the future of American bases on the Japanese home islands, and America's defense role in East Asia generally.

The 1952 Security Treaty, signed the same day the Peace Treaty came into force, pledged the United States to defend Japan in case of need and permitted the United States to retain bases in the country. The Korean War was then raging only 100 miles away across the Sea of Japan, and Japan's fledgling Self-Defense Forces were quite inadequate because of Article IX. Thus our military responsibilities in Japan were sizeable, and our military facilities were correspondingly large. In 1952 we had 2,824 bases and facilities, ranging from airfields and ammunition dumps to chapels and golf courses, covering some 1300 square kilometers. The Security Treaty gave us the right to use them as we saw fit without consulting the Japanese government beforehand, even if we wanted to mount operations against another country from them.

Many Japanese worried that this unlimited freedom for American forces might attract an attack—perhaps from Russia, seeking to neutralize the bases, or from North Korea or China bombing airfields in Japan from which we were mounting operations—and thus left the fundamental decision of whether Japan would be at war or peace to Washington. Another Occupation-era provision that rankled many Japanese (and worried American officials) permitted American troops to put down large-scale internal disturbances in Japan if requested by the Japanese government.

We had agreed in 1958 to a Japanese request to place our security arrangements on a more equal footing. Negotiations resulted in a Treaty of Mutual Cooperation and Security, signed on January 19, 1960, which governed defense relations during the whole time when I was Ambassador. Like our security treaties with other countries, it pledged us to come to Japan's defense if it were attacked. It also required us to "consult" with the Japanese government if we intended to mount combat operations outside Japan from our home island bases or introduce significantly different types of weapons (meaning nuclear) into them. The internal security provisions of the 1952 pact were scrapped.

In every important respect the 1960 treaty had enhanced Japan's control over its own affairs, but socialists and other opponents of the LDP and its conservative Prime Minister, Nobosuke Kishi, wanted the country to pursue "unarmed neutrality" and favored dissolving defense ties with the United States altogether. Unfortunately for us, the debate over this treaty provided a catalyst that crystallized long-standing differences between right and left in Japan.

Prime Minister Kishi had less appeal than the first post-Occupation Prime Minister, Shigeru Yoshida. During the 1950s, LDP governments had slightly diluted some SCAP policies in education, police, and local government. The Self-Defense Forces were expanded even in the face of Article IX. Though these conservative moves were minor compared to the changes the Occupation had wrought in Japanese society, the opposition considered them symbolically important and claimed they indicated that the government had embarked on a regressive path. Because the socialists and communists could not win a majority in the Diet they were effectively frozen out of power and turned to street demonstrations and occasional violence to force change on the government. At the time Kishi presented the Security Treaty to the Diet for ratification, the opposition was boycotting it, and because he was under the gun to get it through the Diet before the scheduled visit of President Eisenhower, he arranged for it to be debated at a special brief night session. This violated the consensus-building process the Japanese consider absolutely vital to important national decisions, and public dismay at Kishi's use of the LDP's "mechanical majority" to ratify the treaty was great. Into the streets of Tokyo thronged union members, students, housewives, and others, as many as 100,000 at a time; a small proportion of the demonstrators rioted in front of the Diet and the Prime Minister's residence. Eisenhower had to cancel his visit.

As soon as the treaty became law, Kishi was forced to resign. His successor Ikeda was more conciliatory to the opposition, politics quieted down, and Reischauer repaired the damage to America's public image; but it was painfully clear that no more explosive issue existed in Japanese politics than security relations with the United States. The 1960 treaty was in force irrevocably until 1970, after which it would continue indefinitely unless one of the parties renounced it after giving a year's notice. I expected any moves to revise or scrub the Treaty would take shape during my tenure in Tokyo.

In practice, the treaty had been working satisfactorily for the United States, and I believe for Japan as well. We had no need to mount operations directly from our bases there, but as the Vietnam War heated up they provided essential storage dumps, staging facilities, and hospitals. Yokusuka was the home port of the Seventh Fleet, nuclear submarines called at Sasebo, and our air bases were on the main transit line to Vietnam. We were able to do everything with our bases our government could reasonably want.

The growing Japanese Self-Defense Forces (SDP) took over many functions previously performed by our troops and absorbed American facilities as we cut our troop strength and diminished their visibility. Excellent cooperation at the working level grew up between the SDF and the commanders of United States Forces Japan (USFJ). A higher-level committee, composed of the American Ambassador, CINCPAC, and the Japanese Foreign Minister, was established in 1960 to review broader questions of security, but the high level of its participants meant that it met infrequently. Japan bought most of its military hardware from the United States and began to manufacture American-designed aircraft and other high-technology defense equipment under license from American companies. By the mid-1960s the SDF amounted to about 240,000 soldiers, a 200-ship navy and an air force of 900 advanced planes. By contrast, American military personnel numbered about 15,000 and were devoted entirely to logistics and support functions. Our only ground troops in the area were on Okinawa. We believed that Japan had achieved the capability of taking the major role in its own immediate and direct conventional defense, under our nuclear umbrella.

But serious difficulties still flowed from the presence of American bases on Japanese soil, at a level much more fundamental than whether American and Japanese soldiers could cooperate efficiently from day to day. The Japanese had lost the habit of thinking responsibly about their own defense. They are by nature an insular and self-centered people, and in the mid-1960s they perceived no real military threat to themselves. In the short run, this may have been true enough. The Japanese could not envision a conventional Soviet attack except in the context of a much larger (presumably nuclear) war in which the United States' umbrella would be fully raised. Though China was developing atomic bombs, the Japanese doubted China would use them against Japan, and could not perceive any Chinese conventional threat for at least a generation. They believed that renewed North Korean aggression would pose real dangers for Japan, but they hoped that containing it could be managed from bases elsewhere. So in sum the Japanese tended to consider our bases, both on the home islands and on Okinawa, as something of a nuisance, a humiliation, and a lightning rod that might involve them in hostilities not of their own choosing, a source of small daily irritations and of large strategic risk. Though they fully expected us to take the lead in figuring out how best to protect Japan, they seemed to take for granted that the best thing for Japan was to bargain us down on our base rights as far as we could be made to go.

Japan's attitude, I thought, was immature, contrary to its own long-term interest and certainly contrary to continued healthy relations with the United States. The Japanese government was in fact quite pleased that we were fighting communism in South Vietnam, and knew that our Okinawan and Japanese bases were essential to deterring renewed North Korean aggression, a prospect that alarmed both the socialists and the LDP. In public, however, both parties acted as if Vietnam and Korea were irrelevant and our bases did nothing beneficial for Japan. Anything that went wrong in Asia was blamed on us; so was anything that Japanese public opinion found objectionable about our military presence. The Japanese were trying to have their cake and eat it too, taking the benefits of American military protection without acknowledging they really wanted it or assuming any concomitant responsibilities.

I believed it was time for Japan to come to its own conclusions about the role it wanted to play, and wanted us to play, in the security of East Asia, and take responsibility for them. I was confident that Japan and the United States, possessing compatible economic and political systems, also shared the same basic interests in Asia: peace and stability, free trade, deterring aggression from Moscow, Peking, Hanoi, and Pyongyang. But whatever the Japanese concluded, I wanted them to conclude it. That was an essential element in being a self-respecting country that could enter international negotiations as the equal of other participants.

And in the long run, having the Japanese make up their own minds would serve American interests. Our bases would be useless unless Japan fully supported our having and using them. It was impossible to think of any war in Asia that we would wish to fight if our most important ally and trading partner in the region opposed it. If we were going to maintain any effective American military presence in Japan the Japanese had to want it, freely and openly, out of a conviction that it served Japan's interest.

My major task in the security field, then, was to make sure that our government took a long view of our military needs in Japan and Asia generally and to encourage Japan's government to do the same, confident that both sides would mesh if they did. At the same time, I wanted to reduce the irritations our bases caused the people living around them as much as possible. The pressure building over Okinawa was actually a blessing in disguise in this respect. It provided a carrot to make both sides take just the long-term view required. If the island reverted to full Japanese control and became covered by the 1960 Security Treaty, Japan itself would have to defend it and consult with us about whatever operations we wished to mount from our bases there. That would require it to accept more responsibility for regional security, not less as pro-reversion Japanese often assumed.

The third item on the security agenda I brought to Tokyo had less profound implications than Okinawa or getting Japan to take more responsibility for its national security, but I still considered it a main responsibility. Japan was vital to our effort in Vietnam. It provided ports, repair and rebuild facilities, supply dumps, stopover points for aircraft, and hospitals for badly wounded soldiers. Japanese labor did the great bulk of this work, for which we spent several billion dollars each year. In public both the socialists and the LDP had little good to say about our role in Vietnam, but in private the government supported us strongly, and in fact much of the opposition did also. I felt it was my duty to promote Japanese understanding and support of our involvement, both for its own sake and because it would encourage Japan to think more precisely about the kind of Southeast Asia it wished to see.

The United States Mission in Tokyo was a tremendously complex organization, reflecting the depth and complexity of the relationships between Japan and the United States. Besides the Department of State, twenty-two other United States Government departments and agencies were represented, each with its special interest and contacts with Japanese counterparts. The Treasury Department had close ties with the Japanese Finance Ministry and the Bank of Japan, the Atomic Energy Commission with the Japanese nuclear power agencies, United States Forces Japan with the Self-Defense Agency and the Foreign Ministry, the Federal Aviation Administration looked after aircraft inspection and the assignment of international air routes, and so on. About 400 Americans worked in the Mission, 150 for the State Department and 250 for the other arms of the government. Unlike our European posts, where many of these working-level relationships were carried on through multilateral organizations such as NATO and the EEC, in Tokyo the Mission handled all of them. Through periodic staff meetings and individual contact, I tried to give each Mission component a sense of how it contributed to our overall task.

Most of the day-to-day administration was handled by the Deputy Chief of Mission. It is not unusual for a new ambassador to select a new DCM, because the two operate as a team and must be able to get along. The existing DCM in Tokyo was my good friend John Emmerson. We were too close to work well together as chief and deputy; besides, John had worked for Reischauer for five strenuous years and was overdue for rotation. (I was hoping very much that he would get a Chief of Mission slot himself, but the completely unjustified McCarthy-era cloud that still pursued him frustrated the appointment.) To replace John I tapped David Osborne as DCM. He had previously been Deputy Assistant Secretary for Cultural Affairs and had worked for me during my talks with Wang Ping-nan in Geneva. A superb linguist, he spoke French, Italian, Indonesian, Chinese, and Japanese fluently; so well, in fact, that he could give a speech in Japanese or Chinese and have the audience rolling in the aisles with puns and other plays on words.

We established a very pleasant and effective relationship. Dave handled the Mission's internal administration and probably signed 80 percent of the telegrams to Washington. I gave him the same guidelines Dean Rusk had given me during the Korean War: handle anything and everything you feel comfortable with and pass on the rest. Topics he knew I was particularly interested in, especially security, he automatically let me handle first. A project in which he took particular interest was establishing a set of numerical formulas for allocating the staff and resources of the Mission according to the priority of the various jobs that needed doing. Working with the LDP, press relations, promoting trade and scores of other functions were all ranked in importance according to complex formulas he worked out; then he compared the existing staff levels in each area with its priority to see where additions and deletions were needed. I was never too sure where he was going with this or whether it served much purpose, but I decided to humor my intellectual deputy and let him go ahead. Ultimately, he tied his formulas into a neat package covering the whole Mission, to which he got the various section chiefs to agree. They (and I) thought this was a purely theoretical exercise, but in early 1968 the President ordered a large reduction in overseas government personnel. Dave had charts, diagrams, and graphs showing exactly where we could absorb the cuts most easily; and no one could complain about unfairness because everyone had already concurred in his formulas. I was thus spared a long wrangle with every Mission component trying to protect its bureaucratic turf.

Another person I brought to Tokyo was Jim Morley, Director of the East Asia Institute at Columbia University, whose reputation among Japanese intellectuals was excellent. I knew I could not personally keep up Reischauer's relations with intellectuals, both because of who I was and because my job required that I work the other side of the fence. But I did not want the Mission to lose the gains he had made. So Jim came as my personal assistant to be my eyes and ears with the artistic and academic communities. He performed this job superbly. He quickly established a broad range of contacts and made recommendations about individuals I should meet and talk to. We normally did this at his house after work, where I would come as his guest to have an informal and free-ranging bull session with a small group of influential or unusually interesting academics. The United States Information Service and our Cultural Section had general responsibility for promoting contacts like this, but as my personal emissary Jim was able to underscore my own interest in this area.

Because of the high emphasis I was going to place on security issues, I wanted to make sure the lines of communication between the embassy and USFJ were wide open and busy, which had not previously been the case. Once a month, therefore, I arranged to eat lunch with the USFJ commander, General McKee, who also commanded the Fifth Air Force, as well as with his Chief of Staff, Admiral Wilkinson, and the United States Army and Navy commanders. After a long informal discussion of our mutual problems we usually ended with a game of golf. I found Admiral Wilkinson, who handled the routine liaison work with the Japanese Foreign Office and Self-Defense Agency as chairman of the United States-Japan Security Committee, to be especially effective. He was a former nuclear submarine commander who had fallen into Rickover's bad graces, and though he had never before encountered diplomacy of any sort he turned out to be an absolutely first class diplomat who was a real help to me.

Another American military post with which a firm alliance was necessary was the US military command on Okinawa, known in bureaucratic parlance as the High Commissioner of the Ryukyus or HICOMRY. Under Reischauer relations between HICOMRY and the Embassy had become frayed. The High Commissioner, General Caraway, who served from February 1961 until August 1964, was an able fighting officer and very conscientious, but his attitude towards the Okinawans was extremely paternalistic, and he kept the limited self-government we had established for the Ryukyus tightly reined. He was convinced that we should hold on to all administrative rights indefinitely and thus interpreted any indication of Japanese interest in regaining the islands as a threat to our security. He would not even allow Japanese onto the Ryukyus without a special visa.

At the beginning of the Kennedy Administration, I and some other people in Washington who wanted to soften the more objectionable aspects of direct United States military rule arranged for a civilian to serve as HICOMRY's deputy for civilian administration. (The second of these Civil Administrators was my brother-in-law, Gerry Warner.) This dilution of military prerogatives did not please General Caraway; his successor, General Watson, who served from August 1964 until October 1966, was more receptive but still desired strongly to retain administrative rights indefinitely.

For the local inhabitants, life under American military rule became a peculiar kind of limbo. Neither Americans nor Japanese, they had no passport except for a slip of paper from HICOMRY. At first the island had no industry except supporting the bases that took up so much of the island's flat area that insufficient farmland was left to feed the population. Congress had to appropriate funds for supporting the Okinawans, which it found increasingly irritating, but to inhibit pro-reversion sentiment we refused offers of aid from Japan. Towards the end of the 1950s the islanders had established a small oil refinery and a brewery, and the economy began to diversify. But the gap between Okinawa and Japan grew larger as Japan's economy skyrocketed, and the Okinawans worried about what would happen after reversion when home islanders would have the right to invest and buy as they saw fit.

Luckily for me and the Okinawans, a new High Commissioner, General Finn Unger, was appointed just as I was named Ambassador to Japan. I saw him on October 3, before we both departed Washington, and had a good long talk to establish a modus vivendi. I started out by saying that I expected him to be my problem and me to be his problem; to reduce our mutual problems to a minimum, I proposed that we agree to sort out our differences between us whenever possible without gumming up the works by independently appealing to our departments in Washington for intervention. He agreed. In fact we worked so closely that we never once had to refer a split to Washington for resolution. We visited each other often, and we checked every policy recommendation on Okinawa with each other before sending them back.

I was very blunt about pointing out the problems Finn would face in controlling an increasingly restive and politically organized population unless the United States Government moved towards reversion. I also expressed my conviction that he would have no base to command if we lost the consent of the Okinawans or the Japanese government to our continued presence, regardless of our rights on paper. My whole approach with him, and with the American government generally, was that we had to devise a solution to Okinawa that would allow us to maintain real and enduring military effectiveness. I never urged reversion in terms of making Japan happy. Finn was quick and politically sensitive and needed very little convincing about the need to contemplate reversion seriously.

In general, I believe that an ambassador creates the most favorable impression by acting naturally, but the unusual reputation of my predecessor required that I consider the public image I wanted to project quite carefully. Before I arrived in Tokyo Japanese commentators were generally pleased that an "old pro" was coming with long experience in the Department and Asia. The obverse of this "old pro" image, however, was the concern that I was a pretty tough customer sent to make Tokyo toe Washington's line. I wanted to make sure the Japanese knew from the outset that I was accessible and interested in viewpoints other than those of the Foreign Office. But because I believed "quiet diplomacy" would help create more normal and mature relations, I cut back on television appearances, press conferences, and other splashy events.

Instead I concentrated on giving speeches to groups of influential people on subjects that, while deliberately uncontroversial in the headline-making sense, were designed to make the Japanese raise their sights to broader world developments they seldom considered: the food and population problems of developing countries, the impact of science and technology on social patterns, and urban planning and the quality of life. The country had a long tradition of insularity that had to alter if it was to play a more constructive and autonomous role in world politics. Though newspapers and the intelligentsia talked a great deal about the need to broaden the country's horizons, I found that this had not penetrated too far into the national consciousness. Even the aid program to Southeast Asia, managed by the comparatively cosmopolitan Foreign Office, focused very heavily on expanding Japan's trade rather than on the more fundamental needs of developing countries.

I also set out on a campaign of visits to all forty-three prefectures, though I was called back to Washington before I had finished. I started with all the cities where we had consulates and cultural centers, including Kobe, Osaka, Kyoto, the Nagoya area, Fukuoka and Nagasaki, Sapporo on Hokkaido, and my old stomping ground of Yokohama. My normal practice was to meet with as many small groups as possible, leaving the exact program to the local consul and cultural center. I believed strongly that consular staff should serve as extensions of the Embassy's political section, keeping in touch with local leaders and reporting on developments, and not just stamp visas in passports.

Preparations for these jaunts were quite elaborate. I could not turn over for another half-hour's snooze in the morning of a "travel day." I started early, meeting for at least half an hour with groups of labor leaders, politicians, university professors, Chamber of Commerce members, students, religious leaders and others, ten or twelve at a time. I normally started the sessions, talking as frankly as I could about whatever aspect of United States-Japan relations was likely to interest the particular group most. They responded quickly, so that we were able to get some lively and useful conversations going. Before the war this would not have been possible. "Normal" Japanese would have shrunk from debating or questioning high-ranking officials, domestic or foreign.

Normally the Chamber of Commerce would host a lunch and the prefectural governor would hold a dinner, after which I would give a speech to the local Japan-American society. I also made a point of meeting with editors and reporters from the local papers. Japanese local papers are not as important as their American counterparts because they are overshadowed on national and world news by the big national papers that are promptly delivered throughout the country. But the local journalists appreciated the chance for a background briefing, and I found they began to report American news more evenhandedly. As I told my first press conference, "A dialogue means a two-way exchange. I hope and expect to do at least as much listening as talking." That was the rule I tried to follow on these trips, and I think the Japanese appreciated being listened to.

On all these trips I used an interpreter, Sen Nishiyama, the most utterly bilingual person I have ever known. American-born of Japanese parents, he came to Japan before the war during which he lost his United States citizenship. (Thus, for classified conversations I used an excellent American interpreter, Jim Wickel.) Sen could whisper what was being said in my ear so that I could respond without having to pause for translation, which conferred the great benefit of a normally-paced conversation. My own Japanese, never that fluent to begin with and rusty with twenty-five years' disuse, was adequate for getting the gist of most conversations, but I never sought to use it except socially. Each day before starting work I took thirty minutes' intensive instruction in my office, starting from lesson one, day one, and reviewing the whole language. One of the things that surprised me most was how much new vocabulary had entered Japanese (and English) since the Second World War. Terms like ICBM, atomic bomb, space station, transistor, United Nations, NATO, World Bank, developing countries, and many others, standard parts of diplomatic vocabulary in the 1960s, were actually neologisms whose Japanese equivalents I had never learned.

In some countries not being able to speak the language fluently is a great disadvantage, and from the standpoint of effective international relations American education devotes far too little attention to teaching other tongues. But Japan, if anything, is even more inward-looking on this score than we are. During my visits around Japan, the professor of English from the local university would often be produced, and he seldom could manage more than a few halting words before he scurried off. The Japanese government said it was very eager to have people learn English to make them more internationally-minded and better promoters of Japanese products abroad, so I worked out an arrangement with Washington that would permit sending several hundred American teachers to Japanese middle and high schools to assist in teaching English. The Japanese Minister of Education turned me down flat. He said he appreciated the offer and understood the value of having native speakers teach the language, but the Japanese teachers would lose too much face. The career Vice Minister of Education made a speech while I was in Tokyo advising students to study foreign languages but not learn them too well, because their souls were embodied in their knowledge of Japanese. Even now the children of Japanese diplomats and businesspeople who become fluent abroad find that they are not accepted as "Japanese" when they return even if their Japanese is fluent, and some resort to pretending clumsiness in the foreign language to regain their standing as "real Japanese."

In Tokyo I pursued the theme of my trips around the country, to listen as well as talk. I worked very hard with the national newspapers, which are large, powerful, and profitable. Their correspondents organize themselves into very tight "clubs" according to the beat they cover; a highly developed sense of group identity actually makes it a breach of propriety for one Japanese correspondent to scoop his or her rivals. I sought out both the editors and publishers, who tend to support the LDP, and the more pro-Opposition reporters, whose copy the editors do not closely control. First I called on all the principal news executives and invited them to the Embassy, and in addition to fairly regular but deliberately unprovocative press conferences, I invited certain journalists whom I came to know, especially editorial writers and foreign news reporters, to the residence for drinks and background talks. No American Ambassador had ever done this before, so it flattered them. They respected that what I said was off the record, so I felt free to be frank, and the questions and answers were lively.

These reporters were not unsophisticated, uncritical, or toadies in any sense, but over the long haul I found my efforts bore fruit in less suspicion towards the United States over Okinawa, more sympathy if not enthusiasm for our purposes in Vietnam, and a greater willingness to examine constructively in print the role Japan and the United States could play as partners in maintaining the security of the Pacific. I repeatedly and sincerely stressed that "Japan has to make its own decisions in these matters," as I told my first press conference. So anything I could contribute to getting the newspapers to raise these fundamental security questions for public discussion was worth the effort.

In my initial contacts with the Japanese government I also stressed my desire to listen. I wanted to reinforce that I really did want Japan to take a more equal and self-determining role in its relations with the United States instead of waiting for us to take the lead. I paid courtesy calls on all the Cabinet ministers and invited them to meals at the residence within the first few months. I asked them many questions about Japan's own domestic politics, wishing to supplement what I already knew and the views of the Embassy's political section with how the main actors themselves perceived what they were doing.

Since the Occupation Japan had been ruled by the Liberal Democratic Party (known as the LDP or "Jiminto"), actually a center-right party closely tied to business interests. Throughout my tour as Ambassador its leader (and thus Prime Minister) was Eisaku Sato. He continued the basically moderate course the LDP had successfully followed since the 1960 Security Treaty riots, trying to defuse the confrontation in the Diet and the country between LDP and Opposition while remaining in power. The LDP was a coalition of factions formally centered around individual senior politicians. A Diet member would be known as part of the Ohira or Sato faction, and the Premier was selected by a series of complicated deals among them that he then repaid by allotting Cabinet posts in the proper order.

The Cabinet is normally reshuffled annually to account for shifts in the relative strength of the factions and to give each one its "turn," but because the senior ministers (in charge of foreign affairs, finance, and international trade and industry in that order) are the most powerful figures in the government save the Prime Minister, they tend to be replaced less often. Unfortunately, one can never be sure whether a minister's actions reflect the desires of the Prime Minister and Cabinet or a private campaign to catapult himself to the top job. The Foreign Minister, Takeo Miki, posed special difficulties because he was determined to replace Sato and could not always be counted on to represent Sato's attitude on United States-Japanese relations faithfully.

This seemingly unstable system works because the government is really run by its career civil servants, who draft all legislation and control the bulk of what the Minister and Parliamentary Vice-Minister (the only political appointees in each department) can see and do. The top civil servants form an extremely competent and cohesive elite, emerging predominantly from the law graduates of Tokyo University. Many ultimately switch into the Diet and become ministers themselves, giving the top layer of government an unusually deep administrative background. The key official in each department ministry is the career Vice-Minister, whose tenure can be as long as three years. In the Foreign Office that was Takeso Shimoda and then Nobuhiko Ushiba.

Another key ingredient in counteracting the high degree of divisiveness built into this Cabinet system is the emphasis Japanese culture places on consensus. The Prime Minister never makes an instant decision in the manner of an American President. Being the chairman of a board of near-equals, he must consult with them before embarking on a new course. Similarly, ministers must check with their senior officials before committing their departments to a shift in policy. This attention to consensus makes the decision-making process slower than in the American executive branch, something LBJ could never really grasp. He expected that Sato could make his government jump the way LBJ did with Washington. But once a decision is made it sticks.

When I arrived in Tokyo, Prime Minister Sato had been in power for two years, but had not yet faced a general election, having replaced Ikeda as LDP leader shortly after the 1963 election. The Left-wing Opposition parties were boycotting the Diet, trying to embarrass the LDP over recent corruption scandals and deprive the government of its legitimacy. They were preparing a strong anti-government stance from which to contest the next election, expected imminently. In 1960 the left had split over the Security Treaty into two main parties, the Socialists and the Democratic Socialists, with the Democratic Socialists being more moderate and less hostile to ties with the United States. Within the Socialists, the radical wing gained the upper hand in 1965, arguing that the party had to offer a clear ideological alternative to the LDP if it were going to gain adherents. It was they who arranged for the Diet boycott. This leftward shift generated much internal strife, however, reinforcing the voters' recurrent conviction that the party lacked leaders with the stature and ability to govern. A Japanese Communist Party also fielded candidates but was an insignificant electoral force, garnering about 5 percent of the popular vote in Diet elections compared with about 50 percent for the LDP, 25–30 percent for the Socialists, seven percent for the Democratic Socialists, and a sprinkling for independents.

Despite the disarray on the left, I did not detect any complacency among leading LDP figures about the party's future. The more thoughtful, recognizing the unusual degree of responsibility conferred on them by twenty years' continuous government, could understand the desirability of having a "loyal opposition" on the British model, accustomed to alternating periods in power, but the Socialists were led by doctrinaire theoretical Marxists and did not have the basic electoral appeal to become one. LDP leaders also saw that Japan had weak local governments, a relatively submissive judiciary, and a small group of "opinion leaders" centralized in Tokyo, all of which seemed to leave the country with few built-in institutional checks and balances against a resurgence of the extremism, latent in Japanese national character, should the balmy economic climate evaporate or other problems beset the country.

Everyone believed that the LDP would face a difficult next election. While publicly dismissive about allegations of corruption, LDP leaders knew that the party's close ties with big business (which contributed massive sums to election war chests) combined with the insulation bred by uninterrupted power did create opportunities for bribery, and that their electoral image was suffering accordingly. A new party, the Komeito or Clean Government Party, had started in 1964 as the electoral arm of the powerful Soka Gakkai religious movement, a curious amalgam of high-pressure evangelism, Buddism, and Dale Carnegie that had gained several million dedicated and heavily-tithed adherents, especially among newcomers to the big cities. The Komeito's platform called for ending corruption and inflation, improving living conditions for the mass of people (which had not kept pace with the country's economic success) and international peace. It presented a fresh alternative to the stagnant LDP-Socialist conflict, and had done well in local and Upper House elections. Commentators expected it to bloody the LDP, perhaps even threaten its majority, when it fielded candidates for the House of Representatives in the upcoming general election.

Of course the Embassy took no public position on Japanese political developments except insofar as they affected relations with the United States. The positions we did take we publicized circumspectly, preferring private conversations and background talks to pronouncements that sounded as if we were trying to dictate Japanese policy. Our contacts with the LDP were more extensive than with the Opposition parties, since it was the party of government and espoused policies more in line with our conception of United States-Japan relations than those of the Socialists or Communists. Nevertheless, I made sure the Political Section talked to Opposition figures frequently and seriously, and I kept in close touch with Opposition leaders myself, particularly the Komeito, which was groping for a foreign policy, and the Democratic Socialists, which many commentators predicted would grow into an effective alternative to the LDP. Even though the ideas of the Opposition leaders differed from mine in varying degrees on what the United States should be doing in Japan and Asia, I wanted them to know we were not automatically hostile just because they were in the Opposition. I also suspected that the gulf that now separated us from the Socialists might diminish if we talked over our differences frankly and regularly.

Since it often took delicate judgment to discriminate between Foreign Minister Miki speaking for Prime Minister Sato and Miki seeking to advance himself, it was important that I keep in close direct contact with Sato, and he desired to do the same with me. Ruggedly handsome and large for a Japanese, he had a master politician's easy, friendly manner, and I respected and enjoyed working with him. Because of the reporters and photographers who constantly surrounded the Prime Minister, however, meeting him without raising unwelcome press attention and speculation was virtually impossible. Therefore, I normally maintained contact with Sato through a senior Japanese Foreign Service Officer Teruo Kosui who acted as his private secretary. Kosui and I made considerable use of the telephone and when we needed to exchange written material, he could call on me at the Embassy or I could send a junior embassy officer to see him without attracting attention.

One way of circumventing Sato's press gauntlet was to escort the endless stream of official Washington visitors, both congressional and Executive, who wished to call on him. I have always found it strange that many American officials feel that foreign Prime Ministers, even in the case of great countries like Japan, are under some sort of obligation to receive them, even though they would be shocked if a foreign visitor of comparable rank insisted on meeting the President. However, Sato understood this situation and was always generous and gracious in receiving them. Some, of course, were useful and important for him to see. In any event, I frequently took advantage of these visits to have a quick private word with the Prime Minister, or he with me. Another pipeline to Sato was the Vice Minister for Foreign Affairs, Nobuhiko Ushiba, who had been close to Sato for many years and saw him regularly.

Sato, like many senior Japanese officials, was a graduate of Tokyo University law school. He began his career as a railroad official in 1924 and rose to Vice Minister of the Ministry of Transportation, the senior career official, during the Second World War. He was brought into politics by Japan's first post-war Prime Minister, Shigeru Yoshida, who deftly but autocratically steered the country through Occupation and Peace Treaty negotiations into independence between 1946 and 1954. Briefly discredited because of a campaign contribution scandal in 1953, Sato resumed his upward climb in 1958, and when Hayato Ikeda resigned in 1964 because of health, Sato was elected President of the LDP and thus Prime Minister with virtually no opposition. He remained Prime Minister until 1972, longer than anyone in postwar Japanese history.

Sato was firmly convinced of the importance of bolstering Japan's ties with the United States. This exposed him to some domestic criticism. But his desire to liquidate the last remnants of the war by obtaining reversion of the Bonins and Ryukyus did not have solely domestic roots. Certainly the LDP's appeal relative to the socialists and communists would increase among the voters if he managed to achieve reversion, but Sato basically shared my view that inequality between Japan and the United States was the biggest obstacle to our becoming closer allies. Blessed with an acute sense of what his electorate would accept at a given moment, he cultivated a conservative image while he gently but firmly steered Japan towards a fundamentally new policy of contructive participation in world affairs.

The appearance of caution Sato projected was dictated not only by his personal instinct and Japanese political custom, but also by the lesson of his older brother, Nobusuke Kishi.(According to a frequent Japanese practice, Sato changed his family name to that of his wife when he married.) Kishi was the Prime Minister who used his "mechanical majority" to ratify the 1960 Security Treaty, causing popular outrage, riots, and the embarrassing forced cancellation of President Eisenhower's visit. Sato never forgot this miscalculation and was careful to build a consensus within the LDP's many factions and within the electorate before making any new departures.

As I settled down to work, Okinawa was the biggest single job I faced. What the United States would do with our bases and administrative rights there was the question I heard most often and most emotionally from every Japanese group, from the Cabinet down. Prime Minister Sato was due to visit Washington in November 1967, and two months before then, Foreign Minister Miki was scheduled to attend the annual meeting of American and Japanese Cabinet ministers. These two events, especially the November summit, imposed a welcome pressure on negotiations, both within the American and Japanese governments and between them; not that we felt we had to give Sato something tangible on Okinawa whatever the cost, but it gave us a specific target date to shoot for.

The first requirement was to establish a regular mechanism for discussing Okinawa and other security subjects with the Japanese government. All security questions between the United States and Japan were handled on their side by the Foreign Office. Even the nuts and bolts work of how we ran our bases and paid the Japanese working on them was handled by USFJ on our side but the Foreign Office on their side, bypassing the SDA entirely. So shortly after my arrival I spoke to Vice Foreign Minister Shi-

moda about creating a small, private group to begin frank, informal and substantive discussions on the whole range of security
issues we both faced, including the Bonins, Okinawa, and American bases on the home islands. Shimoda was interested but understandably skittish about the storm of criticism that news of
such a group could generate. He feared that the Opposition and
newspapers would charge that the government was plotting military action with the United States without parliamentary consent,
which would violate Article IX.

The 1960 Security Treaty had already established the high-
level Security Consultative Committee, but its members necessarily spoke formally on behalf of their governments, with no real
opportunity for badly needed exploratory exchanges. To help defuse potential criticism of this new body for discussing security,
I proposed that we call it a subcommittee of the already-existing
Consultative Committee. I continued to press the idea with Sato,
Miki, and Shimoda, and in May 1967 we had our first meeting,
at the official home of the Foreign Minister in a Tokyo suburb.
It was a large, well-wooded compound to which Subcommittee
members traveled in separate unmarked cars to foil inquisitive
reporters. On their side the Sub-committee comprised the Vice
Foreign Minister (Shimoda had just become Ambassador to Washington and been replaced by Nobuhiko Ushiba), the Deputy Director of the Self-Defense Agency, and their top uniformed
officer; I chaired the American contingent, which included representatives from CINCPAC in Hawaii and John McNaughton,
Assistant Secretary of Defense for International Security Affairs.
It was a good all-day session, where we talked informally and
deeply for the first time about the military importance of Okinawa, the implications of communist China's nuclear capability,
the possibility of establishing an anti-ballistic missile defense system for Japan, and other issues.

The whole purpose of the committee was first to permit a
regular dialogue, so that the Japanese could begin to understand
our activities on Okinawa and Japan in depth and how they contributed to the overall security of the Far East. Soon I hoped it
would expand into an instrument for discussing what the Japanese
themselves thought necessary for their security and what they
wanted the United States to contribute to it.

The basic procedural difficulty we encountered on the Subcommittee was that the Japanese government was simply not
organized to deal with broad security issues. There were no reg-

ular committees in the Foreign Office or between the Foreign Office and the SDA, no reservoir of academic expertise, no habit of thinking this way. One Foreign Office official told me: "We are so ignorant that we don't even know what questions to ask." Another procedural problem was that Japanese law made no provision for preserving Japan's military secrets, because according to Article IX it was not supposed to have any. Japanese law did permit the government to protect American military secrets, but that did not cover everything the subcommittee considered. So Japanese staff work on some of the subjects we discussed was necessarily restricted. The subcommittee, which still meets regularly, has definitely contributed to the uncontroversial acceptance, now present among virtually all sectors of Japanese political opinion, that the American and Japanese governments have legitimate business consulting on security.

With the framework of consultation established, it was time to make progress on substance. Soon after arriving in October 1966 I requested Sato and Miki to put forth the Japanese government's basic position on Okinawa so we could start talking in earnest. This took time. They knew they wanted the island back, but they also had to resolve a fundamental question before settling on a bargaining strategy for obtaining that basic objective: If administrative rights over the Ryukyus reverted to Tokyo, should the United States retain its present rights to mount operations from the bases there without consulting the Japanese government? The Security Treaty prohibited such activities on the home island bases unless the government was first consulted. The question of freedom of use was especially sensitive while the Vietnam War continued, because Congress was not likely to approve any arrangement that undercut our forces there. And before Japan could decide what it wanted to do with Okinawa it had to formulate a larger view of the country's security needs. There were some more mundane but no less thorny problems raised by reversion: what financial arrangements should be made to convert the island's economy from dollars to yen and to compensate the United States for the public utilities and other civilian facilities built at United States expense that would be taken over by Japan?

The Japanese government was extremely reluctant to show its hand on these issues. It would not even advance an initial bargaining position because it had not gone through the difficult exercise of defining precisely what it wanted and did not want from reversion. But it could hardly stall indefinitely if it wanted

Okinawa back, so it tried the familiar gambit of reversing the procedure, asking us to state our minimum needs on Okinawa without indicating anything of its own minimum needs.

Foreign Minister Miki and I first discussed Okinawa in earnest on July 15, 1967, at a secret meeting held at the Hotel New Otani to avoid reporters. I was accompanied by the Counselor of the Political Section, Lewis Purnell, and my Special Assistant and interpreter, Jim Wickel; Miki brought along Ushiba and the two top people in the Foreign Ministry's North American Affairs bureau, Fumihiko Togo and Sumio Edamura. Miki had asked for the meeting, he said, to request that I forward to Washington an Aide-Memoir the Japanese government had delivered to the Embassy already. It proposed two general steps: a joint United States-Japan effort to produce a formula that would permit a proper military role for the bases after reversion and agreement on interim measures to reduce the disparities between Okinawa and Japan in preparation for reversion. Miki said that the time for reversion had come and that our bases on Okinawa and their status now constituted the main question between our countries. The core of this question, he said was "what are the requirements the United States would need as a minimum to provide defense capabilities for Japan and the area?"

I countered this view politely but firmly. I told him that the question was not what the minimum requirements of the United States Government were, but what Japan wanted in this area. In viewing East Asia in long-range terms, I said, the United States could not carry out a unilateral policy. The only policy that we could and would carry out was one that Japan supported, not one in which she merely acquiesced. Japan was the strongest and most powerful nation in this area and had to make up its own mind about what it wished to see in this part of the world, I stressed. Diplomacy could reveal what interests the two countries had in common, once each nation decided what its *own* interests were. First, Japan had to reach a decision on the military posture it wanted the United States to maintain in Japan and in the rest of Asia, and then we might find where we fit together on Okinawa.

From the American point of view, I told Miki, the basic issue raised by reversion was Okinawa's future effectiveness as a deterrent to aggression. Not just our nuclear weapons but our conventional forces on the island deterred China and North Korea from trying some aggressive maneuver that might otherwise tempt them. If our freedom of action on Okinawa was reduced, this deterrent would be also. Thus Japan had to decide what level of deterrent it thought best, strictly from its own interests. We could evacuate Okinawa entirely if we had to, I said, but at a cost to our deterrent capacity. And given Japan's stability and the harmony of views between our two countries on most security issues, no alternative base site in the region was as good.

We could also agree to put conventional operations from the Okinawan bases under the same restrictions that governed our bases on the Japanese home islands, I said, with any action mounted directly against non-Japanese territory to require prior consultation with the Japanese government. But what if China were then to conduct a massive conventional invasion of Thailand or Laos? The Japanese government might then have to decide whether to permit the United States to mount air attacks on Chinese supply routes. It would have to take responsibility for whatever decision it made before its Asian neighbors. Thus reversion could easily increase, not decrease, the Japanese government's immersion in world politics and its vulnerability to attacks from the Opposition.

In my own mind I was hoping we could eventually conclude some arrangement permitting us freedom of action to use our Okinawan forces to defend Taiwan and Korea without prior consultation. But at this point with Miki I simply wanted to set the wheels of the Japanese government turning on the general question of the bases' conventional role after reversion.

As for nuclear weapons, many Japanese commentators had speculated that the United States would easily concede our right to store nuclear weapons on Okinawa because they believed development of the Polaris submarine meant that land-based nuclear weapons were no longer essential. Miki raised this point, and I said: "Yes, we can do anything, but what is the effect?" Unleashing a Polaris attack was a drastic step that might easily entrain a spiralling series of responses and counter-responses that a smaller response with tactical nuclear weapons might not. A graduated deterrent was the most effective deterrent because it permitted us to respond at a level corresponding to the aggression. So Okinawa's nuclear weapons still had strategic importance.

Miki said several times more that Japan did not underestimate the importance of American forces in the Far East in all their variety, but even so the basic question was what were United States minimum requirements. I consequently repeated my conviction that "the broader aspects are more important. It is not the minimum the United States can get along with, but rather what is the maximum which is desirable to both of us." The issue of Okinawa was well and truly joined.

To keep the ball rolling, I said I would report back to Washington and see what its views were; we also tentatively arranged another Security Subcommittee meeting for the beginning of August that would permit Miki and me to meet again after it and before he departed for the Washington Cabinet-level conference in September.

At this July 15 meeting Miki also questioned me on American plans for the Bonins, in line with a proposal in the Japanese government's Aide-Memoir for their early return. It was only "common sense to recognize a difference" between them and Okinawa, he said, noting that his government had not received any explanation from the United States about their military significance. Privately, I quite agreed with him that the Bonins had minimal security value, but now was not the time to concede that point. First I had to prepare the soil at USFJ, CINCPAC, and in Washington to accept gracefully the idea of returning the islands, which would take some work. Whatever arrangements we established for the Bonins would set a very firm precedent for Okinawa, so we had to take care over the fine print, especially on getting compensation for facilities taken over by the Japanese government and guaranteeing the future economic rights of the islanders whose welfare we now formally represented. By maintaining a tough facade on the Bonins we might induce some concessions from Japan that would be valuable on Okinawa. And the timing was very tricky. If we hastened the return of the Bonins, pressure from the Japanese public and government in favor of Okinawa's reversion might increase rather than decrease, thus diminishing our room to maneuver.

By themselves, the Bonins boated very little to warrant so much interest. A collection of tiny outcroppings in the Pacific midway between Japan and the Marianas, their name is a derivative of the Japanese term "Bu-nin," literally "empty of men." The largest, Chichijima (meaning "Father Island,") is less than ten miles square; other "major" links in the chain include Ha-

---

*For a very interesting description of the Bonins' past, see Timothy Head and Gavan Daws, "The Bonins–Isles of Contention," *American Heritage,* February, 1968.

hajima (Mother Island) and Iwo Jima, the largest in a cluster of volcanic islands considerably south of Chichijima and Hahajima.

The Bonins were claimed successively by Britain, America and Japan, but the most enduring claim to ownership was established by five deckhands (including two Americans eager for an easier life) who settled on Chichijima with Hawaiian laborers and "wives," of whom each had several, in 1830. The soil was good, but whatever harmony could be established amidst the settlers' incessant feuds was broken by frequent visits from whaling ships, whose crews stole whatever they could get their hands on. In 1853 Commodore Perry's Black Fleet, en route to Japan, called at Chichijima and appointed Nathaniel Savory, one of the original settlers, resident United States agent. Perry also bought a plot of Savory's land as a future coaling station for the Navy's Pacific fleet, a move well ahead of its time. But Meiji Japan, waking from isolation, decided to preempt Perry's foresight. In 1862 a Japanese expedition convinced Savory and the other islanders to accept Japanese sovereignty; later that year a group of Japanese settlers arrived to substantiate the claim. The two communities did not mix. In 1876 Japan formally annexed the islands, where a growing number of Japanese settlers earned a living by supplying visiting whaling ships and hunting the abundant population of seals and turtles.

As Japanese militarism gathered strength in the 1920s and 1930s, the Bonins took on strategic importance. All non-Japanese except the descendants of the original settlers were excluded. Finally the civilian population was evacuated to Tokyo and Yokohama in 1944, including the American-surnamed settlers, who were assigned Japanese names and expected to be the Emperor's loyal subjects.

The Japanese made Chichijima into a major supply base and island fortress. But Allied planners in charge of the "island-hopping" campaign across the Pacific focused their attention on Iwo Jima, which was less fortified and more suitable for constructing an airfield that could accept disabled bombers returning from raids on Japan. American forces invaded the island February 19, 1945. The small, ugly splotch of lava became a scene of carnage, with 7,000 Americans and an estimated 120,000 Japanese dead before we took it on March 26. The 6th Marine Division established a memorial atop Iwo Jima's Mount Suribachi, which had the distinction of being the only place in the world besides the United States Capitol where the American flag flew twenty-four hours a day.

Shortly after I became Consul in Yokohama in 1945, a group
of the American-surnamed Bonin islanders approached me requesting their return to Chichijima. They claimed to be American
citizens; given names like Washington and Savory, and the record
of persecution they had suffered in Japan during the war, I understood why they thought so. However, most of them were third-
generation Boninites who had intermarried with Japanese, spoke
English poorly if at all, and had very tenuous ties with the United
States. Nevertheless, the group was small and its desire was
straightforward. I discussed their case with SCAP and, in October
1946, arranged for the return of about 130 American-surnamed
islanders to Chichijima.

Under the indulgent eye of the United States Navy, which
established a small base on Chichijima, the settlers returned to
an easy life. They lived in Navy Quonset huts and ate Navy food,
their children attended the Admiral Arthur W. Radford School,
they went to Navy hospitals on Guam, and paid no taxes. Nevertheless, they married mostly Japanese from the home island, and
no one really knew what their citizenship was. The islanders'
numbers had increased to about 250 by the time I became Ambassador, and one of the problems we now faced was protecting
the inhabitants' future under Japanese rule, which would probably
be more spartan than the United States Navy's and would certainly not educate their children in English. Former Japanese
settlers evacuated during the war would also be free to return
after reversion, as many wanted to, meaning more competition
for the resources available. Sentiment among the islanders
seemed to favor some sort of American citizenship, but this the
Japanese government would doubtless reject.

The islanders' future status was a comparatively small problem, however, easily solved if the major obstacle to full Japanese
sovereignty was swept away: Navy resistance. After my July 15
meeting with Miki, I started communicating with Washington
frequently to start the wheels turning. The Navy's basic position
was that we should not give up anything anywhere that might
someday possibly be useful. If we were to lose Japan, Okinawa,
Taiwan, and the Philippines, the Navy argued, the Bonins would
be an important reserve. I thought this was nonsense. If we were
driven from the rest of the Pacific, we certainly could not hold
the Bonins or mount a worthwhile counteroffensive from this
insignificant cluster of rocks. My position had the advantage of
being logical, and it gained headway. The Navy was making very

little use of the islands anyway, so its arguments seemed a little pale. Our total contingent there numbered about sixty-five.

The final sticking point with the military was the future of Iwo Jima. The famous picture of the Marines planting the American flag atop Mount Suribachi, and the dreadful toll the invasion exacted, made the island an important symbol to many Americans, not just the military. Its potential return to Japanese control might spark an emotional outcry that could jeopardize the whole Bonin settlement. My initial suggestion to Washington was that we ask the Japanese government to designate the whole island of Iwo Jima as a military base under the 1960 Security Treaty, which would permit us to retain effective control of the Mount Suribachi memorial and its twenty-four hour flag.

After the July 15 meeting with Miki on Okinawa and the Bonins, both governments went into high gear preparing for the September joint meeting of Japanese and American Cabinet ministers at which Miki would meet Rusk, as a prelude to the crucial November summit between Sato and LBJ. Neither government seriously doubted that reversion would eventually be accomplished, but the crucial questions were how fast and under what conditions. Public opinion in Japan, led by the Opposition parties, was moving towards something of a national consensus on Okinawa that was unfavorable to American interests. It favored immediate reversion under an agreement that would permit the bases to continue, but without nuclear weapons and under considerable restrictions as to how and when their conventional forces could be employed. There were some indications that summer of 1967 that even the orthodox Marxist Japan Socialist Party was moving towards that view.

Sato's own detailed views on Okinawan reversion were by no means explicit, but he wanted the bases to continue in an effective form, and this trend in public opinion disturbed him. He tried to moderate rising public emotionalism about Okinawa, dampening expectations of the island's early return and stressing the serious security considerations raised by reversion. He recognized that the Japanese people had no experience in forming judgments on security matters and needed time to come to terms with the strategic realities from which Article IX and the American base structure had shielded them since the Occupation. He needed to buy that time, during which this larger strategic picture could be explained to the public and could penetrate its attitudes, and to succeed in this approach he needed American cooperation.

This was in our interest as well, for if he appeared to be making no progress whatever in getting Okinawa back, his government might well be replaced by a more radical one, with more intransigent attitudes on the whole range of questions between the United States and Japan.

Within the Ryukyus themselves, and at Japanese government urging, we had been making occasional concessions to make the pressure for reversion manageable. After heavy agitation from Okinawan fishermen, we permitted them to replace the American flag flown over their vessels with a new one that incorporated the Japanese rising sun. Japanese economic assistance to the islands had been permitted to the tune of $28 million, double that of the United States. We had also allowed Japan Air Lines to start an inter-island air service.

In preparation for the Miki-Rusk and Sato-LBJ meetings, the embassy devised some additional interim measures that we might institute to reduce disparities between life on Okinawa and Japan proper while calming pressures for immediate reversion. These measures included permitting direct popular election of the Ryukyuan government's Chief Executive, and creating a trilateral United States-Japan-Ryukyuan committee to advise the High Commissioner on ways of smoothing the transition between American and Japanese administration. But we did not want to unveil these proposals just yet.

Miki came to Washington in September with instructions from Sato to scout out our irreducible minimum requirements on Okinawa while revealing as little as possible of the Japanese position. Sato wanted to retain maximum flexibility in his discussions with President Johnson; his advisors also wanted to make sure that the ambitious Miki did not try to steal Sato's thunder by committing Japan to an Okinawan settlement prematurely. Since we could always make concessions at the Sato summit if we wanted to, our strategy with Miki, worked out in meetings I had with Rusk and Defense Secretary McNamara, was to take a very hard line emphasizing the importance of the Okinawan bases to our mutual security and indicating no willingness whatever to concede our present rights to store nuclear weapons or use the bases freely.

Secretary McNamara told me that he was entirely prepared to turn over Okinawa to Japanese administration, but there was no possibility of abandoning our bases there. The real issue was whether we would accept the same restrictions on them that governed our bases on Japan proper under the 1960 Security

Treaty; namely, giving up our right to store nuclear weapons and engage in combat operations against other areas of the Far East without "prior consultation." McNamara argued that since we would never again fight a war in Asia without Japanese support, "homeland-level" restrictions on the Okinawan bases would not seriously compromise our interests. I thought this approach had merit, but more time and study was required before it became our bottom line position. We agreed that for the time being the Japanese should not know that we were even thinking of conceding these things. Although we might not now want to store nuclear weapons on the island or mount operations elsewhere without prior consultation, the right to do so in a crisis might be worth retaining. In any event, nuclear weapons storage and freedom of use were good bargaining chips that we did not want to give away prematurely. So when Miki met McNamara, the Defense Secretary took a very firm stance on the necessity of our retaining freedom of use and nuclear weapons storage rights on Okinawa.

Secretary Rusk took an equally hard line when he invited Miki to lunch and a long, private meeting on Saturday, September 16, which I attended. Miki emphasized how crucial an agreement on Okinawa was to the survival of the Sato government. Rusk countered by saying that there were two levels on which Okinawan reversion could be discussed: the requirements of Japanese popular opinion, and the deepest security needs and commitments of our two countries. The United States had pledged 100 million lives in the first hour of war to protect Japan, he said. With the war in Vietnam continuing and a newly nuclear China in the throes of a chaotic cultural revolution, the American people would have great difficulty understanding any effort by Japan to deny us the facilities we needed to protect Japan. We had no desire to administer Okinawa permanently. We understood the special importance the Sato government placed on reversion and Japan's nuclear sensitivities. But American soldiers could not be made mercenaries for Japan, Rusk stressed; if we had a common purpose, then Japan had to contribute to accomplishing it. In any event, Rusk said we were afraid that the upcoming 1968 presidential elections would prevent the United States from giving any firm commitments on the Ryukyus until 1969 at the earliest.

To soften the blow of this uncompromising presentation, Rusk offered a crucial palliative useful to both sides: we would help the Sato government buy time on reversion with the Opposition and the Okinawans themselves. One such measure would

be the creation of the United States-Japan-Ryukyus commission
to devise ways of reducing social and economic differences between Okinawa and Japan. Rusk also said the United States could
indicate in the communique following the upcoming Sato-LBJ
meeting that the United States agreed to reversion in principle
and would implement it once Japan and the United States had
concluded terms that would not interfere with the bases' security
role. He also led Miki to understand that the Bonins would pose
no insuperable problems for us, as long as Japan did not use their
return to lever us on Okinawa, and agreed to an acceptable formula for Iwo Jima.

    In fact, it was the Bonins on which the most substantial
progress was made during Miki's visit to Washington, though he
was unaware of it at the time. I had several private meetings with
members of the Joint Chiefs, as well as with McNamara and Rusk,
and attended a full National Security Council Meeting with the
President. The Navy was still advancing its view that the Bonins
would be crucial in case we were driven from the rest of the Far
East, but the rest of the Joint Chiefs and the civilian officials at
Defense, including Secretary McNamara, saw State's position, and
I left Washington fairly certain that we would be able to announce
the return of the Bonins during Sato's visit in November.

    The other Japanese ministers present in Washington spent
their three days discussing economic issues with their American
counterparts, both one-on-one and in plenary sessions that Secretary Rusk and I attended. We pressed them to liberalize trade
and especially investment policies, suggested that they penetrate
European markets as well as ours, and encouraged them to contribute more to economic development in Southeast Asia. Since
we bore a disproportionate share of the cost of maintaining military security in Asia, we thought Japan could contribute to our
common purpose in a way that suited its basic pacifism by helping
the struggling countries around China toward stability and prosperity. We especially wanted Tokyo to match our initial contribution of $200 million to the new Asian Development Bank's $1
billion capitalization, instead of the $100 million it had already
pledged. The Bonin and Ryukyu negotiations gave us some leverage in this area.

    The Japanese ministers, for their part, complained about
"buy American" sentiment in Congress and gave no encouragement to our requests. Japan was facing a spate of balance-of-
payment deficits of its own as its growing economy sucked in
imports, and the population was demanding that the government

spend more on providing a better quality of life, especially in the crowded and smoggy cities. Thus the Japanese ministers were skittish about taking on major regional economic responsibilities for Southeast Asia. Both sides' positions on these economic issues were pretty much boilerplate, but the informal talks between counterparts allowed for some very frank dialogue that gave each side an excellent feel for the problems of the other.

En route back to Tokyo I stopped in Honolulu to brief Admiral Felt about our sessions with Miki and the progress of Washington's thinking on Okinawa and the Bonins. Back in Japan, I met several times with Miki and Sato to prepare for the summit. We invoked a normal if odd-seeming diplomatic technique, focusing on hammering out the exact language of the joint communiqué to be issued at the end of the summit. I expressed the possibility that the Bonins could be returned at the summit, but made no promises. I said the President would have to decide himself, and the terms of return might include designating all of Iwo Jima as a military base under the Security Treaty. Miki argued that this would negate everything that Washington would gain from returning the islands. He also pressed repeatedly for communiqué language that would indicate that reversion of the Ryukyus would occur at the "earliest possible date," but on this subject I was adamant. I said we would consider a phrasing that would signal that reversion was in process and that we would institute the interim measures to reduce economic and social differences between the Ryukyus and Japan. But specifying a date or asserting that Japanese control would occur "as soon as possible" would put heavy pressure on both countries to reach an agreement faster than either could manage.

As the date of departure for the summit neared, Miki grew increasingly restive. He was understandably disturbed that we might not return Iwo Jima with the rest of the Bonins, and that we refused to give him a specific date for Okinawa's return that he (and Sato) could parade before the electorate. He became so pessimistic about what the summit could accomplish, in fact, that he began to seek some way of avoiding attending it. Several times he said to me: "You know, I wonder whether it is really necessary for me to go?" I gave him no encouragement in this direction whatever, believing that divisions between him and the Prime Minister worked contrary to our interests. Unfortunately, the Prime Minister's constant besiegement by reporters and photographers made it impossible for me to have a long talk with him before he left for Washington, so I was not able to make sure how faithfully Miki had been representing his boss in our bargaining sessions.

When I left Tokyo for Washington on November 8 for a week's consultations before the Prime Minister's party arrived, the issues that had to be settled within our own government were the future status of Iwo Jima and the exact wording of the communique about how fast and under what conditions we would return the Ryukus to Japanese administration. Agreement had been reached within the Executive branch, however, that the Bonins' return could be announced. I was naturally startled, therefore, to discover on the evening of my arrival in Washington that no one had yet raised the subject with the key members of the House and Senate Armed Services Committees. I was requested to do this the next day. I thought this should have been the responsibility of our people in Washington, but I had no choice but to agree. So I spent the next day going from office to office in the Capitol with Paul Warnke, the Assistant Secretary of Defense for International Security Affairs, explaining our plan for returning the Bonins.

I was very surprised to find that the legislators were quite sympathetic. They displayed none of the "we must keep all our bases forever" mentality evident in the Navy. Nevertheless, I was careful to avoid arousing their opposition by promising that whatever final agreement we reached with, the Japanese would permit us to keep our flag flying over our Iwo Jima memorial. At the time I assumed that the memorial was identical to the large and impressive bronze statue that sits in the Arlington National Cemetary, commemorating the famous picture of the Marines raising the flag atop Mount Suribachi.

Work in Washington on the communique's wording about returning Okinawa was thrown into something of an uproar when Kei Wakazumi, a Professor of International Relations at Kyoto University, and a Sato confidant, arrived several days before Sato as the Prime Minister's personal secret emissary to propose a new formula to Walt Rostow, the President's National Security Advisor. He suggested that the President and Prime Minister agree to say that "within a few years" a date would be set for Okinawa's reversion to Japan. This had the advantage of not tying us to any firm date for reversion while indicating a firm intention to do so. Miki had never mentioned wording like this to me, nor had Sato. I realized that Sato did not entirely trust Miki and wanted to make sure that he, not Miki, controlled the terms Japan offered in the negotiations.

I took a presidential plane to Seattle on Sunday, November 12, meeting the Prime Minister and his party (including the reluctant Miki) that evening and returning with them to Washington the next day. I had a discreet word with Sato's chief aide to arrange a private conversation with Sato on the plane. I knew this would not please the Foreign Minister, but a frank discussion about Professor Wakazumi's formula outside the earshot of Miki, who knew nothing about it, was necessary. After takeoff Sato and I wandered up to one of the small conference areas with my interpreter Jim Wickel and talked for most of the flight. Sato tried to convince me that a wording that said a date would be set for the return of Okinawa "within a few years" would satisfy the requirements of both countries. I explained my own feelings, that the important question to settle was not the time of reversion but the conditions under which it would be a wise move for both governments. Japan could not instantly expand its defense perimeter to cover the Ryukyus; there were significant disparities between the living standards of the local population and the Japanese on the home islands; the war in Vietnam continued, making reversion ticklish for both countries; and the political consensus in Japan would not now permit the United States to store nuclear weapons there or mount operations directly against areas outside Japan without prior consultation, which were still part of our bargaining demands. No one could now set a date by which these impediments would vanish, so it would serve neither government to raise public expectations by agreeing to reversion by some artificial deadline. Nevertheless, I told Sato that the President would have to make the final decision.

At his first meeting with LBJ on November 14, with only interpreters present, Sato put forth his "within a few years" formula. Sato's entourage (who were apparently still unaware of the Prime Minister's initiative) talked with the American side in the Cabinet Room while we waited for them to finish, and afterwards I was due to return to the State Department. But after we saw the Prime Minister off from the White House, LBJ grabbed my arm and brought me to his office for a long discussion of the Prime Minister's proposal. The President was very concerned about Congressional reaction should he commit the United States to return Okinawa within a definite period, and he asked me to sound out Senator Richard Russell of Georgia, the powerhouse chairman of the Armed Services Committee. I reported the President's views to Rusk and Bill Bundy, Assistant Secretary for Far Eastern Affairs, and Rusk called Russell, who stoutly opposed anything that would set a time limit for reversion. That evening there was a dinner during which McNamara, Sato, Senator Russell, and several others including myself discussed this language, but again Russell displayed no inclination to compromise.

We finally reached a settlement the next morning during a meeting between Sato, Rusk, and other officials at Blair House. Sato said he recognized that reversion raised both political and security problems for both countries, but expressed a belief that the effectiveness of our bases would be strengthened by reversion because "Japan would be forced to live up to its security responsibilities by this action." This was exactly the outlook I had been trying to advance with the Japanese government, and I was glad to hear Sato enunciate it. We moved quickly to examine the wording of the communique, and the American side proposed a version that Sato examined privately with his officials for twenty minutes before returning to say that he was very pleased with it. The operative section read:

> The Prime Minister emphasized the strong desire of the Government and people of Japan for the return of administrative rights over the Ryukyu Islands to Japan and expressed his belief that an adequate solution should promptly be sought on the basis of mutual understanding and trust between the Governments and peoples of the two countries. He further emphasized that an agreement should be reached between the two Governments within a few years on a date satisfactory to them for the reversion of these islands. The President stated that he fully understands the desire of the Japanese people for the reversion of these islands. At the same time, the President and the Prime Minister recognized that the United States military bases on these islands continue to play a vital role in assuring the security of Japan and other free nations in the Far East.

> As a result of their discussion, the President and the Prime Minister agreed that the two Governments should keep under joint and continuous review the status of the Ryukyu Islands, guided by the aim of returning administrative rights over these islands to Japan and in the light of these discussions.

By having the President "fully understand" Sato's desire to set a date for reversion within a few years, the communique signalled that reversion was a serious issue between the two governments and satisfied Sato's domestic political requirement, without committing the United States to a specific date for reversion that might compromise our mutual security. This was underscored by the sentence about "joint and continuous review." The communique also announced the creation of the tripartite Advisory Committee to the High Commissioner of the Ryukyus to recommend ways of "removing the remaining economic and social barriers" between Okinawa and Japan. We had resisted substantial Japanese pressure to make this a political body that could hear complaints from Okinawans about American rule, a forum that pro-reversion forces would have used to stir up discontent. On the Bonins, the communique committed our governments to "enter immediately into consultations regarding the specific arrangements for accomplishing the early restoration of these islands to Japan without detriment to the security of the area." Here was something tangible for Sato to show the Japanese electorate.

Next we went to the White House for the final meeting between Sato and Johnson, before which Rusk and I had a few words with the President to explain the agreement we had reached with Sato on the communiqué. The President, however, did not commit himself to approving it. He and Sato then met in the Oval Office for an hour and a half, considerably longer than expected, afterwards joining the two delegations in the Cabinet Room. Rusk had already left for another appointment, so I sat in his chair next to the President, with Sato leading the Japanese officials on the other side of the table. LBJ said that the two of them had considered the language on the Bonins and Okinawa at length, but he just could not see his way to accepting it. I was crushed. All our work had at length gone for naught. My mind really began to race to see if there was something we could patch up to salvage the summit and avoid the public confrontation between the two countries that this impasse would necessarily ignite.

Absolute silence gripped the room for thirty seconds while the shock of the President's announcement sank in. Then, without once looking at me, he said to the Prime Minister: "I think my Ambassador to Japan just had a heart attack, and I think we had better relieve his mind." He and Sato had actually reached complete agreement on the communique, and he was just pulling my leg in a way that was typical of his humor. Everyone had a very good laugh at my expense. This incident showed that Sato and LBJ had hit it off well enough personally to permit a little joshing. And after I recovered, I took it as a sign of the President's confidence in me as well. In fact he had approved all of my recommendations. The process of returning Okinawa to Japan under conditions favorable to our mutual security had passed its first major hurdle.

The President also announced to the group that the Prime Minister had promised to increase Japanese aid to Indonesia, a favorite LBJ cause at the time. This caused some consternation among the Japanese officials who had no idea this was in the wind. Later I learned from Jim Wickel, who had interpreted for the two leaders, that the President had twisted Sato's arm very hard indeed on this subject. With his forceful and earthy style, quite the opposite of Sato's serene authority and subtlety, the President had managed to wring out what he interpreted as some sort of commitment from Sato, though Sato, I know, did not really intend to give any commitment. When LBJ announced the "agreement" in front of the other officials, Sato said nothing; but when I was later called upon to raise it with him in Tokyo, he always winced, and never did deliver all that LBJ thought had been promised.

Wickel also told me that the President had given Sato a high-pressure sales job on providing educational television for South Vietnam. LBJ had recently visited American Samoa, where he had become very enthusiastic over an excellent televised curriculum that could reach isolated villages, compensate for the lack of skilled teachers, and knit the people together politically and culturally. He thought Japan could establish a similar system for Vietnam without violating its pacifist principles. Sato had agreed to examine this, and back in Tokyo I had some extensive talks with Japan Broadcasting Company president Maeda and Sony president Morita, both of whom got their organizations working very hard on the subject. Plans were well advanced when the Tet Offensive of 1968 knocked the wind out of both countries' interest in esoteric ways of helping build up South Vietnam strength.

Prime Minister Sato, assured at the summit that the United States could not relent on its right to store nuclear weapons on Okinawa as part of a reversion deal, returned to Japan determined to overcome the country's nuclear allergy and build a national consensus that would permit him to accept this difference between American bases on Okinawa and Japan proper. He raised this issue with the deftness and careful timing for which he was famous, but public reaction was nevertheless strongly negative. With United States B-52s using Kadena Field on Okinawa for bombing missions over Vietnam starting in February 1968, the question of freedom of use after reversion also raised emotions on both sides. We established the Advisory Committee to the High Commissioner (to which we named the most knowledgeable and able economic officer I could find, Lawrence Vass, the Embassy's Economic Counselor) and took other steps to let people know that reversion was in the works, but the political climate was not receptive to a quick fix on the Ryukyus.

The Japanese government itself realized this; when I asked Foreign Office officials what they would have done if the communique had called for the Ryukyus' immediate return, they threw up their hands in horror. I told Miki and Sato that we stood ready to begin the "joint and continuous review" at any time, but that I did not see much to review until the Japanese government could offer conditions under which Okinawa would remain an effective base. Nevertheless, we understood the government's political need to appear to progress toward reversion, and I offered our help in buying time for resolution of these serious public questions about security as long as the Japanese government did not try to place all the blame for delay on the United States.

In any event, the Summit communiqué charged the two governments to focus first on the Bonins. On my way back to Tokyo from Washington, I stopped in Hawaii to brief Admiral McCain, the new CINCPAC, and to have his staff draw up the materials the Self-Defense Agency would need to ready itself to take responsibility for protecting the islands. In my first meeting with Foreign Minister Miki after the summit, on November 29, he suggested that the two governments reach an agreement on the Bonins by mid-February so it could be submitted to the Diet in March. That gave us much work to do: deciding what would happen to American facilities (including the important LORAN stations), finding some employment for the locals after the Navy installation was removed, and most importantly, setting a procedure for replacing the dollars used on the islands with yen in a way that would not let Japan garner a balance of payments windfall in the process. This was more significant as a precedent for Okinawa than as an act in itself, though both governments maintained the fiction that the Bonins and Okinawa were entirely separate questions.

Detailed negotiations began on December 28, when we offered to turn over all administrative rights and all military facilities besides the Coast Guard LORAN stations. We also suggested that the Japanese government purchase all supplies and moveable equipment at 40 percent of market value (which would amount to about $800,000) to offset the balance of payments windfall from converting from dollars to yen. Successive drafts of an agreement went back and forth between us and the Foreign Office, and we nailed down these economic problems without excessive difficulty. Iwo Jima, however, proved more troublesome.

At our November 29 meeting, I told Miki that I had committed myself with the Armed Services Committees to retaining our memorial atop Mount Suribachi, including its twenty-four-hour flag and statue. This clearly did not please him, since he had not previously known about the statue. He said somewhat sarcastically that he hoped it was not a large one, "like those of Stalin in Eastern Europe." In January, 1968 I decided to visit the Bonins myself to get a better feel for what I was negotiating about, including the Iwo Jima memorial. With me went Vice Minister Ushiba and North American Affairs Director-General Togo, the man in charge of the Foreign Office's day-to-day work on the Bonins.

The only way to get to Chichijima, where the population lived, was to fly first to Iwo and switch to a lumbering, underpowered amphibian plane that plummeted into Chichijima harbor after skimming the island's mountains, actually submerging to above the windows in the process. Bad weather meant we needed two tries to get to Chichi. So Ushiba, Togo, and I had ample opportunity to survey Iwo and its memorial. Atop Mount Suribachi, with its twenty-four-hour Stars and Stripes, there was no grand statue á la Arlington but only a small bronze bas-relief, erected not by the Marine Corps itself but by the First Marine Division. The official Marine Corps memorial was down on the flats, on the site of the now-vacant and overgrown Marine cemetery. First-hand observation put quite a different complexion on this problem, but I still had to deliver the promised twenty-four-hour flag to the Congress.

The rest of Iwo Jima was a ghastly place, a desolate black lump of lava still amply scarred from artillery. The airstrip was built on the only sizeable flat stretch of ground, which happened to be volcanically active, venting steam and gases through the runway. Chichijima had a Shangri-la atmosphere in utter contrast to Iwo. The climate and scenery were beautiful and the islanders, cossetted by the Navy, were entirely content.

After these trips, Miki mounted a determined campaign against our retaining the twenty-four-hour flag and the Marine access necessary to look after it. On February 10, Togo came to tell me that Miki believed that continuing the flag would require a government-to-government agreement and Diet ratification, with all the resulting political controversy. Japan could not appear to be relinquishing control of its territory to the United States. We were asked if the United States could not replace the flag with a bronze one or do something else to mitigate the problem? I replied that we would do anything we could to make the solution politically palatable in Japan, but we could not relent on the flag, which was an integral part of the memorial. Although replacing the flag with a bronze one had obvious merit in the long run, I said my commitment to Congress precluded any dilution of our right to fly the flag as we saw fit. I did not believe this presented any insoluble problem to the Japanese government. If Japan went through with its announced intention of creating a memorial park of its own on Iwo, it could invite us to maintain our memorial there, too, and fly its flag alongside ours.

Nevertheless, Ushiba asked to see me on Saturday, February 16, to say that the Japanese government could not acquiesce in having an American flag crown its newly regained island. He complained that I had never mentioned the flag specifically in earlier discussions. I replied that the flag was such an integral part of the memorial that there was never any question of excluding it. I had gained congressional assent to returning the Bonins as part of a package that included the Iwo Jima memorial, and to back out on it now would open doors that might best be left shut. Since the Japanese were making such a big issue of this flag, however, I reluctantly agreed to look into the possibility of eventually replacing it with a bronze one.

On the following Monday I called General "Brute" Krulak, Marine Commandar in the Pacific, whom I had known from the Counterinsurgency Special Group and who was ultimately responsible for the memorial. I described the flak we had been getting from the Japanese government; he immediately saw the problem and said that from the standpoint of maintenance alone, bronze would be much preferable to cloth, which the high winds of Iwo treated roughly. He told me he would immediately order that a bronze replacement be cast. That was enough to satisfy the Japanese government, and with Krulak on my side, I knew there would be no grumbling from the Marines to Congress that we had sold out. In fact, the new flag was in place before the island's official reversion in June, but within a week the Coast Guard station reported that it had blown down. So the Marines had to start over again to produce a stronger flag.

Though the substantive issues were settled by March, stitching up the final agreement took quite a bit longer. For this delay Foreign Minister Miki was responsible. He was very quick and personally agreeable, but he had trouble making up his mind, or perhaps he estimated that the return of the Bonins would redound more to the political benefit of Sato than to his own. Whatever the reason, he just would not commit his government reliably. I sent what I thought was a finished package to Washington in March for the NSC and President to approve, which they did. But then Miki insisted on changing some clauses, and after some fairly lengthy negotiations I had to resubmit everything to Washington.

Miki's attitude was also extremely grudging. Instead of welcoming our decision to return this territory to Japan, he behaved churlishly and acted as if he were doing us a favor. Instead of using this evidence of our good will to dispel public pressure for Okinawa's immediate reversion as he had promised, he tried to exacerbate that pressure. His public letter thanking me for my help in completing the agreement even included a laundry list of complaints against the United States clearly calculated to make him look like a more resolute defender of Japan's interests than was Prime Minister Sato. Not even Miki's own officials could understand why his behavior had been so ungracious, and I was so irritated by it that I mentioned my displeasure to Sato. I think my complaint may have been responsible for the large public celebration held in Tokyo shortly after the agreement went into effect on June 27, 1968.

Okinawa became a secondary issue in 1968. The Bonins had first priority until their June return; a presidential election was upcoming in the United States; and in the face of a left-wing campaign against all defense ties with the United States, the Japanese government had not been able to build a national consensus on security questions that would permit an agreement satisfactory to American interests. Okinawa's future continued to surface in discussions with Japanese politicians and officials, of course, but mostly I just asked Socratic questions. Real progress did not resume until Nixon's election and Sato's reelection in November. Meanwhile, there was no lack of things to do in other areas, such as economics and space.

From my work in Washington on the United States Space Council, I was very conscious that Japan had the national pride and technological capacity to embark on its own program of rocket and satellite development. We had offered several times in general terms to cooperate with Japan, but never spelled out what we meant. At the end of 1967, when the Japanese government started reviewing its whole rocket and satellite program, I worked with Washington to develop a specific proposal for cooperating with the Japanese space effort that we could present before Tokyo's plans became firmly set.

I felt that Japan was likely to have a space program regardless of what we did or did not do. Under those circumstances, I felt it made no sense for Japan to "reinvent the wheel" on space. We had already spent many billions of dollars overcoming hurdles that Japan would also encounter. Both countries would profit if we licensed our space technology to Japan on a commercial basis: Japan in R&D time and expense, the United States in sales and balance of payments. Since space launchers always presented the possibility of conversion to military rockets, I also felt we would be much smarter to be in bed with Japan from the outset rather than have it develop a new rocket of which we would be ignorant.

On January 17, 1968, therefore, I saw Prime Minister Sato to deliver a proposal for virtually complete cooperation between the United States and Japan on launchers and satellites. It went far beyond what we had offered any other country, and it had required much arm-twisting to extract it from Washington, especially the Defense Department, which took a very dim view of any other country possessing rockets. In it we offered United States launch facilities for Japanese-made satellites. Our only conditions were that Japan use the technology or equipment obtained from us for peaceful purposes except as both countries agreed, that both countries approve any transfer of technology derived from this cooperation to third countries, and that any Japanese domestic communications satellite be compatible with INTELSAT, to preclude Japan from starting an international stampede to develop mutually incompatible "national" satellites when just a few international ones would do the job cheaper and better.

Sato did not respond immediately to this offer because he was not familiar with the details of Japan's space effort, but he appreciated our taking the initiative. The ministries concerned met to discuss this offer and ultimately accepted it. It took several years before contracts were signed, but Japan bought licenses for some non-military aspects of our launcher technology that it refined and applied itself in an extensive scientific satellite program. The American companies involved have received handsome fees, and I believe this experiment in technology sharing has worked out well if not spectacularly.

Economic matters were more urgent. On December 31, 1967, I received a flash message from Washington. President Johnson was going to announce the next day a tough, comprehensive program to curb the United States' mounting balance of payments deficit. Our trade account was in the black, but external American investment in other countries, foreign aid, and foreign military spending (increasing because of Vietnam) meant that the total dollars we were spending abroad considerably outweighed what we were taking in foreign currencies. As Japan's exports to the Unites States were increasing much faster than our exports to Japan, the net deficit we had been running with Japan since 1965 was especially significant.

Between 1953 and 1964 Japan managed to grow at a 10 percent annual rate and increase its foreign exchange reserves by $1 billion while importing $3.5 billion more than it sold abroad. This had been possible because during that period Japan received $5.5 billion from the United States in military and similar expenditures and borrowed over $3 billion from American banks, contributing significantly to our balance of payments difficulties. LBJ's remedy included hiking our income tax to reduce American demand for imports, restricting capital transfers and credit to most foreign countries including Japan, curbing American tourism abroad, and getting our allies to share more of the cost of our common defense.

The Prime Minister had to be informed immediately. Moreover, a mission led by Under Secretary for Political Affairs Eugene Rostow was arriving in Tokyo on January 2 to explain this program in detail to Sato and other senior ministers. Characteristically, LBJ was aiming to grab world attention by a flurry of fast action.

Unfortunately, the President and his advisors did not understand that the New Year's holidays are the most sacred in the Japanese calendar, during which no one should be bothered. Biting the bullet, however, I called Sato and he very affably agreed to see me that night, New Year's Eve, at his private country house in Kamakura. I arrived there at 10 P.M. with my interpreter Jim Wickel, bringing with me a letter from the President briefly explaining the new program.

Very generously, Sato said he thought this program would be effective and expressed deep appreciation because it included Japan among the few countries to which further (though diminished) capital exports would be permitted. Sato took my announcement that Rostow was en route with his customary equanimity. He telephoned Economic Planning Agency Director Miyazawa and Finance Minister Mizuta at this late hour, informing them that they would be required for meetings on January 3 and 4 respectively without giving them many details or any chance to say no. Rostow handled his mission very well and the Japanese basically supported our measures. Nevertheless, I thought it was somewhat cavalier of us to expect them to receive a high-level delegation in thirty-six hours, especially when we would seldom extend similar courtesies on such short notice. It was a very busy New Year's weekend, courtesy of LBJ.

Economic issues continued as a leitmotif throughout the year. The finance ministers of our two countries met in Honolulu in the spring, again to work on the balance of payments question. I repeatedly advanced our position within the Japanese government that Japan should assist developing countries in Southeast Asia more generously and increase its expenditures on our common defense. We had some success; Japan did match our initial $200 million contribution to the Asian Development Bank, as LBJ had requested of Sato.

More central to our relations was the question of trade and investment liberalization. Japanese exports to the United States continued to rise much more briskly than American exports to Japan (35 percent versus 10 percent in 1968), resulting in a $1 billion trade deficit with Japan alone for the United States. We redoubled efforts to induce Japan to remove its many quotas restricting the import of products that American firms wanted to sell. We pressed especially hard on agricultural products, where Japanese prices were about double ours because the government maintained a lavish subsidy program to achieve greater food self-sufficiency and keep farmers in the LDP column. Special trade negotiating teams came to Tokyo, and we threatened to register a formal complaint against Japanese practices with the General Agreement on Tariffs and Trade (GATT) organization.

In May, Japan joined fifteen other GATT members in speeding up tariff reductions called for by the Kennedy Round of negotiations while permitting the United States to maintain our tariff levels, thus helping our balance of payments. But this step did not affect many other non-tariff barriers Japan had constructed to protect domestic industry. I and other Americans expressed our disappointment bluntly to the leadership, but the Japanese were tough and had to be pushed or cajoled every step of the way.

Rostow's New Year's economic mission hardly had time to pack its bags before the next crisis of the year was upon us: the visit of the nuclear-powered aircraft carrier *Enterprise*, our biggest and fastest, to the Japanese port of Sasebo on the southern coast of Kyushu. For several years the Navy had been bringing in nuclear powered submarines and conventionally powered carriers to Sasebo and Yokusuka, our two naval bases in Japan, though subs carrying nuclear-tipped strategic missiles like the *Polaris* had stayed out of the country. Japanese left-wingers had protested only the first visits of these nuclear-powered subs and had not objected to the conventionally powered surface vessels, but now the Navy wanted to establish its ability to bring in nuclear powered surface vessels as well.

I discussed this issue at length with the Japanese government and puzzled over it myself, finally recommending that we permit the *Enterprise* to call in Japan en route from the United States to its deployment off the coast of Vietnam in January 1968. The Japanese government agreed. As the date for the visit approached I gave them every opportunity to change their minds, but they did not. I distinctly sensed that Prime Minister Sato wanted the *Enterprise* to call in Japanese waters, perhaps to help overcome the nuclear allergy of his people and thus make them more amenable to accepting the storage of nuclear weapons on Okinawa after reversion. Mayor Tsuji of Sasebo, a feisty and energetic man who got along well with our Navy, lobbied hard to let his city have the honor of this great ship's visit, and we were happy to oblige.

The visit was scheduled for January 12, but a storm delayed the carrier's progress for several days. Meanwhile, the Opposition in the Diet had been launching strident and successful attacks on the government for allowing the *Enterprise* to call. The precise logic behind its argument was difficult to follow. Japan had thirteen nuclear power plants on its territory and was building a nuclear-powered commercial ship of its own. Our nuclear-powered submarines and our largest conventionally-powered carriers had been calling at Japanese ports regularly. So why get worked up over the *Enterprise*, which differed from a conventional American carrier only in that it generated steam with uranium instead of oil? The Japanese government maintained that the presence of conventional American carriers in Japanese ports did not violate its policy of keeping nuclear weapons out of the country. The opposition argued that while this assurance might be credible for other American ships, it was not for the *Enterprise*, the very symbol of American nuclear might. The United States has a very rigid worldwide policy of neither confirming nor denying the presence of nuclear weapons on naval vessels, and of course we maintained this policy with respect to the *Enterprise*. In response to questions from the Japanese government, we have always said that visits by our naval vessels do not violate the Security Treaty.

Nevertheless, a radical student group called the "Zengakuren" started planning large demonstrations to coincide with the carrier's visit. The Democratic Socialist Party and the Komeito, which both supported the Security Treaty in principle, also planned demonstrations because they feared that the *Enterprise* carried nuclear weapons, a fear shared by the anti-Treaty Socialists and Communists. A real storm was beginning to brew— not at all the "quiet diplomacy" I prefer. But Sato did not waver, and the Navy took my advice and did not back down.

The protest demonstration, or "demo," as the Japanese call it, is a social institution unique to Japan. Certainly during my tour and to some extent even still, protest marches are ubiquitous and frequent, involving everyone from radicals set on severing United States-Japan security ties to housewives angry at increases in the price of rice. The most violent demonstrators when I was there were the radical students known as Zengakuren, thousands of whom regularly battled the police, sometimes for hours, often not far from the embassy in downtown Tokyo. But the Japanese riot police squad, a separate organization within the regular police, was superbly trained and equipped. It had huge slab-sided buses that could be parked in a line to form a completely impenetrable barrier and small mobile command posts with telescoping platforms, so that the officers in charge could be raised to see the whole picture and radio commands to the forces on the ground. Neither side ever used guns; the most lethal weapons employed were wooden staves and an occasional rock, but the police and students had helmets and shields that protected them effectively from the worst blows. Neither side tried to hurt the other gratuitously; only a certain level of violence was acceptable. Even when Zengakuren protesters en route to a clash with police over United States-Japan relations passed by the plate-glass frontage of the United States Information Agency Cultural Center, as they often did, no one ever broke a window. Perhaps this typically Japanese acceptance of social constraints, present even in violent radicals, explains why big companies like Mitsubishi were always eager to recruit radical leaders because of their demonstrated executive talents, and why the radical leaders were often happy to accept.

The police were extremely attentive to the Embassy's security; a riot squad was always on call just up the street, and a dozen or so Japanese guards were stationed around our compound at all times in addition to our own Marine guards. So well protected were we that I never worried in the slightest about our safety. Because a deranged person had tried to stab Ambassador Reischauer, the Japanese police also provided me with personal bodyguards when I left the embassy. They would always scout my route ahead of time and lead me directly to the door of wherever I was going, a great contribution to my punctuality and efficiency in a city as difficult to navigate as Tokyo. Even when I played golf they accompanied me, keeping discreetly out of sight. Once when I was returning to my hotel in Nagasaki during an anti-American demonstration, a protester managed to break through the police cordon and get in my path, whereupon my bodyguard, with a judo motion so instant and effortless I hardly saw it, sent this hapless fellow sailing through the air back into the crowd.

On January 12, with the *Enterprise* still delayed at sea, Miki pressed me to state directly that nuclear weapons were not aboard so he could transmit it to the demonstrators gathering in Sasebo and defuse the opposition in the Diet, but I could do nothing more than state that we were abiding by the Security Treaty. I pointed out that another American carrier, the *Ticonderoga,* had docked in Yokusuka two days ago, and no one had paid any attention. It was exactly the same kind of ship as the *Enterprise,* with the same armaments and planes, except that it made its steam with oil rather than uranium. I suggested that Miki make this point to relieve the demonstrators' nuclear anxieties, and told him that Captain Lee intended to stress it at his press conference upon arrival.

Eager to get the maximum mileage out of the visit to impress the Japanese with the scope, complexity, efficiency, and expense of the American armed forces on which their security depended, I arranged a tour of the ship on January 19, the day before it docked, for Diet members, Foreign Office officials, and journalists. We flew out for a carrier deck landing, quite a startling experience in itself for the uninitiated. Admiral Epes and Captain Lee briefed our Japanese guests and we spent a good day observing operations. The ship is so huge and majestic that it is difficult not to be impressed. The Diet members and officials said they found their tour very instructive; the journalists spent most of their time nosing around for nuclear weapons, which needless to say they did not find.

On shore, however, Sasebo was contending with tens of thousands of protesters that were pouring in from all over Japan on buses and trains, some chartered by the Zengakuren. The largest demonstration drew 50,000 people into the streets, though there were many smaller ones, some violent. Government officials noted with concern that many "ordinary citizens," not just activists, had taken part. Since the Zengakuren had announced that Sasebo was merely a dress rehearsal for a campaign against the Security Treaty that would peak when the Treaty came open for abrogation in 1970, both the Japanese government and the Embassy were disturbed. Following the advice of the Sasebo police, shore leave parties from the *Enterprise* stayed on the base. The radicals apparently harbored no personal animosity towards Americans, however; no Americans were injured despite all the violence between demonstrators and police.

Prime Minister Sato took a hard public line defending the vessel's call, belittling socialist claims in the Diet that it carried nuclear weapons. Privately he expressed no remorse about permitting the visit, but he let me know, with that precisely targeted indirection at which he was a master, that he recognized the visit had set back his campaign for greater "defense consciousness" among Japanese. On January 17 he told me he thought much of the Sasebo protesters' virulence might stem from opposition to the Vietnam War, a subtle signal to make sure I understood that his government was incurring political losses from the *Enterprise* visit and from its support of security ties with the United States generally. (I responded in kind, saying I thought the protesters opposed his government in any event.) Ever conscious of the need to build consensus on defense policy, he made a small bow to the anti-nuclear forces on January 30 by implying in the Diet that no American submarine carrying strategic nuclear missiles (like the *Polaris*) would be permitted to call in Japan. This represented no serious blow to American interests as we had no plans for such visits. Mayor Tsuji asked me to keep controversial vessels of all kinds out of Sasebo for a while, for while he still thought the Navy was great, his city had suffered a real pounding and needed some quiet recuperation time. In fact, the dispute over the *Enterprise* was quickly overshadowed by another incident involving an American ship.

On January 23, the day the *Enterprise* left Sasebo, an American electronic intelligence gathering ship named *Pueblo*, operating in international waters off the coast of North Korea, was seized by North Korean ships and taken into port in a carefully planned operation. Several of its eighty-three crew members were killed and the rest, commanded by Lloyd M. Bucher, were imprisoned. When General McKee, USFJ commander who was also commander of our Air Force in both Korea and Japan, first received distress messages from the *Pueblo* it was already too late. He had no tactical aircraft in Korea capable of carrying out a rescue mission. He called me immediately to report the seizure and to say he had been talking to the Joint Chiefs in Washington, and I told him to go ahead and use American planes based in Japan if he needed them. I said I would take care of whatever political flak was generated by not consulting the Japanese government first. He decided to deploy some fighters from Okinawa, but they arrived in Korea too late to intercept the *Pueblo* en route to Wonsan harbor.

I followed up with Sato later, asking what his reaction would have been if planes from American bases in Japan had been used to rescue the *Pueblo*. He confirmed my instinct that Japan would not have objected to rescuing the ship in international waters with Japanese-based planes even though prior consultation had not been sought. He repeated this assurance in the Diet. A retaliatory raid later against North Korean targets would have been a different matter, one I never raised with him.

There was some loose talk by Admiral Johnson, naval commander in Japan, that the Japanese government had blocked us from intercepting the *Pueblo* on its way into port. This was completely false. We simply did not have the aircraft we needed in the right place to respond to this completely unprovoked, unexpected, and illegal seizure. A sister ship to the *Pueblo*, the *Banner*, had been operating in these waters for many years, and Soviet ships collecting electronic intelligence routinely stationed themselves three miles off the Japanese and American coasts without incident, as they had every right to do under international law. All the *Pueblo* did was listen to radio broadcasts well beyond North Korea's claimed twelve-mile limit. With its total weaponry of two machine guns, it threatened no one, and there was no reason to expect its seizure.

Since the Korean War, the Japanese had feared that hotheads on the other side of the Sea of Japan might manage to drag them into a regional conflict. North Korea was going through a particularly aggressive period in 1968; the week before the *Pueblo* seizure a party of thirty heavily armed North Korean guerrillas had infiltrated the south on a mission to assassinate the country's president. The Soviet Ambassador, in what was probably no coincidence, had also delivered a provocative note to the Japanese Foreign Office that week trying to capitalize on Japanese fears about the *Enterprise* and the "lightning rod" effect of American bases, saying that they made Japan a partner of "American aggression" in Southeast Asia.

Reaction in Japan to the *Pueblo* incident was highly alarmed, but split into two camps roughly corresponding to the political divisions between the LDP and the Opposition. The Opposition parties cited it as a perfect example of the liability of having American bases on Japanese territory. They did not believe, or said they did not believe, our evidence that the *Pueblo* was operating in international waters, evidence that included intelligence from North Korean radio broadcasts showing that the North Koreans themselves knew it was in international waters when they seized it. With a conflict between North Korea and South Korea and/or the United States very possible, raising the potential of a larger regional war, the Socialists worried that Japan might be dragged into fighting from which it would prefer to remain aloof. When the *Enterprise* was diverted to waters off Korea as part of a general strengthening of American forces in the area, the Opposition heatedly accused us of failing to consult with the government about mounting operations against other countries from the Sasebo base.

The government and its supporters also found the *Pueblo* incident highly unsettling, but took from it the lesson that the Soviet Union and its ally in Pyongyang were dangerous provocateurs, and that American bases, inconvenient as they might be, provided the only security against similar encroachments on Japan. In a way, the ship's capture and the high-handed and brutal way its crew were treated had the unexpected side benefit of providing that sense of threat the Japanese needed to consider their security arrangements realistically. The Soviet invasion of Czechoslovakia seven months later decisively reinforced this trend in public opinion, decreasing the intensity of the Opposition's attacks on the Security Treaty.

Washington, of course, expended tremendous diplomatic effort over the next eleven months trying to get the crew back, mostly through the United Nations. I kept Miki and Sato closely informed, but after an initial Japanese proposal that a commission composed of Japan, the USSR, and a third country meet to decide the facts of the incident and secure the crew's release went nowhere with Moscow, Tokyo was not central to the developments. Like the fifty-two American Embassy hostages in Iran twelve years later, Bucher's crew could not be rescued by any feasible military operation. Unless we were going to let them rot or be executed, we had to make some sort of deal with their terrorist captors. It went against my grain somewhat, but I agreed with the solution Washington finally had to adopt, which was to apologize to North Korea in order to get the crew back, then repudiating the apology.

The first American nuclear-powered ship to call in Japan after the *Enterprise* was the conventionally-armed attack submarine *Swordfish*. It docked in Sasebo in May. The Japanese Science and Technology Agency (STA), as was customary, monitored the air and water around the vessel to warrant that no radiation was leaking out to harm the inhabitants of the city (located in Nagasaki prefecture and thus unusually prone to "nuclear allergy"). On this particular visit, no radiation was detected at 50 or 150 meters from the *Swordfish*, but at 100 meters, the Japanese technicians got brief, minute readings at three points, which news media unfavorable to the Security Treaty portrayed as a gigantic threat to health caused by the *Swordfish*. Prime Minister Sato was sharply questioned in the Diet about the alleged radiation leakage and was requested by my old friend Mayor Tsuji as well as the Opposition to prohibit all further visits of nuclear-powered ships unless the *Swordfish* could be conclusively absolved.

I went over the data with experts from the Navy and the Embassy, who said that the pattern of radioactivity detected by the STA was completely inconsistent with any sort of discharge from the *Swordfish*. In fact, they thought the cause of these brief and unrepeated readings may have been the radioactivity from a luminous watchdial passing too close to the detector. The difficulty was that there was no way to prove conclusively that the *Swordfish* did not cause the abnormal readings; though several other plausible explanations existed for this transient phenomenon, the best one being the watchdial, there was no way to turn the clock back and find the precise one. The Japanese STA scientists had not determined a cause; it was the newspapers who blamed the submarine. But no matter how many further tests found no abnormalities, the submarine could still be blamed for the first one. It was actually a "non-problem," and trying to solve it was like trying to grab air.

Admiral Sharp, the CINCPAC, was in Tokyo for a meeting of the full-dress Security Consultative Committee on May 13, and after that meeting he went with General McKee and me to see Sato about the alleged radioactivity. I told the Prime Minister that after a very thorough review of the subject, we could all say "absolutely and categorically" that the *Swordfish* was not responsible. I offered to call Washington immediately to ask that some experts be sent to Tokyo to cooperate with STA scientists in deciphering the data. Sato welcomed this offer, saying confidentially that the staff and resources of the STA were inadequate to the job. He wished to supplement the STA's budget to provide for a full-time monitoring unit in Sasebo similar to the one in Yokusuka, but in the meantime a joint study would suffice if he could also state an assurance from the United States Navy that no "damage" would result from the port call. We could not promise that *no* damage would occur under any circumstances, but we did say he could tell the Diet that we assured him categorically that the *Swordfish* did not cause the radioactivity readings.

When I talked to Admiral Rickover in Washington immediately after leaving the Prime Minister's residence, he was not unduly concerned. He knew that the sub could not have caused the problem and was not inclined to treat the newspaper sensationalism seriously. I told him bluntly that he had better respond seriously or none of his nuclear-powered ships would call in Japan again. In fact, that prospect did not bother him either, because the subs were designed to cruise submerged for long periods and he was perfectly willing to have the crew take its rest and recreation elsewhere if the Japanese objected. However, other Navy officers in Washington saw what a dangerous precedent and propaganda soft spot we would create by letting the allegation of leakage go uncorrected. They prevailed on Rickover to send out his chief assistant, Bill Wegner, who went over the STA data with some other American and Japanese scientists. Again they found no evidence of leakage from the *Swordfish;* but neither could they "prove" what had caused the abnormality, which left the problem dangling.

Round-the-clock monitoring of the sub, quickly instituted by the STA after the press storm erupted, was showing no further abnormalities, so if the first reading had been radiation from the sub, that was its totality. Unfortunately, the tininess of the first reading did not make it any less of a problem, because despite the fact that everything is radioactive to some degree, and we voluntarily receive doses considerably higher than normal from riding in airplanes or getting X-rayed, purists will contend that any additional radiation is theoretically harmful. Hostile Diet questions and editorials continued, completely impervious to our responses; the issue almost had a life of its own. I spent all my time every day for weeks on this subject, and finally visited Sasebo, talked to Mayor Tsuji, and held a large press conference. Another eighteen months passed before a nuclear powered sub was able to call in Japan, and by this time the STA had set up a revamped and adequate full-time monitoring staff in Sasebo. The Opposition wanted us to allow Japanese scientists aboard the sub to inspect its reactor, but this was a bad precedent and carried obvious security risks, so we refused. When I looked back on this incident, I decided that it was one time when I should have ignored my own advice on "quiet diplomacy" and tried something dramatic at the outset, like taking a swim in the slimy waters of Sasebo harbor.

Because I believed in what we were trying to do in Vietnam and considered it my duty to protect continued access to the bases and support facilities in Japan that were crucial to our war effort, I worked hard to promote Japanese understanding and support for our activities there. In general, the Japanese government took what I considered a responsible though limited role on Vietnam: supporting our involvement publicly, not bowing to the constant pressure from the left-wing press and Opposition, and probing peace prospects through quiet diplomacy. Vice Minister Shimoda told me when I first arrived in Tokyo that, since Vietnam was a limited war that would end in a negotiated settlement, the Japanese government thought it would be helpful to the United States if Japan kept a little distance away from the dispute. Fortunately or unfortunately, Shimoda said, Japan was not in a position to offer military help; that gave it a special ability to take advantage of whatever openings for diplomatic resolution presented themselves. We encouraged Japan to contribute more to South Vietnam's economic development, which it did to a limited extent, and some Japanese businesses saw attractive markets in the country. I regularly brought Saigon embassy officials, General Westmoreland, and other knowledgeable Americans to Tokyo, so Sato, Miki, and their officials could understand our efforts and ask questions about both the progress and the problems.

Of course, the Opposition parties predominantly opposed America's fighting in Vietnam and attacked the government, particularly Prime Minister Sato, for supporting us. In general, I think most Japanese were fairly relieved that the United States was willing to take on the dirty work of fighting communism in Southeast Asia, but among the young and the left wing particularly, the war raised the temperature of an anti-Americanism that the irritations of our bases and memories of the War and Occupation had i.stilled.

I never tried to paint an overly rosy picture of the time and sacrifice our mission in Vietnam would entail. I saw no prospect for a quick, simple resolution, and I told the Japanese government so, believing that "fair weather" support would not be reliable. But I did see grounds for guarded but genuine optimism. Steady progress was occurring on the military, economic, and pacification fronts. Despite Vietcong efforts to disrupt the September, 1967 presidential election, voting was conducted in areas containing 75 percent of the population, with a 15 percent increase in voter participation over the previous National Assembly elections. The Saigon government was not exactly popular, but the Vietcong were even less so. Where we could provide the population with physical security, their participation in self-development efforts and politics increased enormously. By 1968, we had effectively pushed the bulk of the Vietcong into sanctuaries or fragmented them into very small units, and the burden of the fighting was falling on North Vietnamese regulars.

President Johnson was strenuously trying to contact Hanoi to arrange negotiations, but our many lines were ignored, except to string us along quite skillfully. The Japanese government tried to act as intermediary several times, as did many other governments, but was cold-shouldered by Hanoi. Then came the Tet Offensive of February, 1968, which, though actually a great military victory for American and South Vietnamese troops (an estimated 40,000 enemy troops were killed compared to 4000 Americans and 5000 South Vietnamese), became a great political triumph for Hanoi because of inaccurate American reporting at the time. In the aftermath, President Johnson decided to announce a partial bombing halt on March 31 to draw the other side to the bargaining table. LBJ also stunned everyone by declaring he would not run for reelection.

Nowhere was the shock of the President's speech felt more deeply than in Japan. With a liberal assist from the American press, the Japanese universally saw it as a major reversal of policy and a declaration that we were seeking to get out of Vietnam instantly regardless of the consequences. This had profoundly unsettling implications for Japan-United States security relations. LBJ's declaration of non-candidacy was interpreted, in purely Japanese terms, as a resignation to admit a mistake in policy. The Opposition and most of the left-wing newspapers thereupon called on Prime Minister Sato to resign because he had so closely identified himself with United States policy in Vietnam, including the bombing, and with LBJ personally. It was obvious that Sato had not been notified of this "reversal," much less consulted, and LBJ's action pulled the rug out from under him. "Sato should admit his own mistakes with the same courage as the President and retire from the Prime Ministership," one newspaper advised. I know the President had good reason to keep his speech secret until delivery, but people in Washington often do not realize how profoundly their actions can jolt the political standing of important allies abroad.

Explaining this speech was more difficult than anything else I had to do in Tokyo. With nothing in the way of guidance except the text and my own feel for the situation in Washington, I was convinced that the Japanese were seriously misinterpreting it. The bombing halt was a dramatic and magnanimous gesture to spur the communists to negotiate, but our basic objective of a free and independent South Vietnam remained constant. I spent hours and hours talking with Sato, Miki, Opposition leaders, reporters and many others to help them see it our way, including five hours with the Prime Minister on a Sunday evening. Sato initially considered sending a special envoy to Washington to express his government's concern that we were abandoning Vietnam and Asia and to find out our plans at the source. I had the Department ask the President to send a special letter of reassurance to Sato, which he did and it convinced Sato that the special envoy was unnecessary.

While much of the anti-Sato sentiment expressed after Johnson's speech was genuine, it was also being exaggerated by his political rivals, both on the Left and within his own party. His term as President of the LDP (and thus Prime Minister) was going to expire in the fall, and the LBJ speech gave his rivals (notably Miki and Takeo Fukuda) an excellent opportunity to encroach on his support. Upper House elections were going to be held in July, contributing to Sato's troubles. The only way to quiet this unheaval was for Washington to maintain a constant policy on Vietnam, which I was sure would happen, but unfortunately this would not become clear to Japan for a while.

One fascinating consequence of the Japanese assumption that we were abandoning Vietnam was the discovery that a wide spectrum of Japanese, even those who had criticized the war quite vehemently, really wanted us to stay and fight. The general attitude was: "Well, we've criticized you on Vietnam and we wish you would end the war and go home. But we didn't want or expect you to take our advice seriously; we expected you to resist communism near us regardless of what we said." The Japanese image of the United States as a permanent Asian policeman ready to fight for our allies at any cost was considerably shaken up, and while this produced no radical shift in Japanese attitudes, it did make them realize that we could not always be taken for granted. That was precisely the realization I was most determined to promote. If the Japanese wanted us to remain here, it was important that they communicate this message to the American people and take political responsibility for it themselves.

Another fear arising in Tokyo from LBJ's speech was that the United States would move suddenly towards an accommodation with China, again leaving the Japanese government out on a limb. The Japanese felt a special cultural and racial affinity for China, and were restraining their desires for closer ties largely on our account.

After March 31 voices were heard calling on the government to cast off its "subservience" to Washington on China policy and move out more boldly on its own. I worked very hard counteracting this misreading of Washington as well. China was in the throes of an extremely xenophobic Cultural Revolution; no matter how much any Administration in Washington might wish to reverse our China policy, it would not matter as long as Peking, in Dean Rusk's words, "kept hanging up the telephone." In any event, I knew of no move in Washington towards detente with Peking and I could not conceive that we would take such a radical step without including our most important Asian ally. In fact, President Nixon was to do just that in 1971, devastating for no reason the trust that had built up between the State Department and the Japanese Foreign Office.

The turmoil LBJ's speech unleashed in Tokyo in fact died away relatively quickly. Our ability to establish peace talks in Paris, combined with our obvious determination to persevere towards a durable and just settlement in Paris and on the field, allayed Japanese fears that American desertion was imminent. Japanese officials, Diet members, and journalists also began to take a more responsible role in promoting peace in Vietnam. Instead of telling us simply to "make peace," they started thinking seriously about exactly what sort of peace would best serve Japanese interests—another step towards international self-reliance. The partial bombing halt also calmed some of the anti-Americanism in the Opposition.

But all over the world, 1968 was a tough year for America's image. The war, the increasing social divisions and violence in our cities, the assassinations of Martin Luther King in April and Robert Kennedy in June, the campus protests and the chaos at the Democratic National Convention all contributed to making the United States seem less worthy of respect. In Japan three local events hurt our image: the crash of an American fighter from Itazuke Air Base into a building on the campus of Kyushu University (no one was injured), the reopening of the American Army Hospital at Camp Oji in the heart of Tokyo to treat Vietnam casualties, and the presence at Kadena Air Base in Okinawa of B-52s that were used for bombing missions over Vietnam.

No one likes living near an airfield, and after the crash at Kyushu University the Opposition predictably blamed the government's "laxity" in providing safety. In a move more political than realistic, the government proposed that the giant base be relocated to a less populous area.

The Oji Hospital dispute was tied into a series of demonstrations mounted by the Zengakuren against the construction of a new international airport at Narita. In February and March there were many demonstrations; on March 28, aiming specifically at the Camp Oji Hospital, the Zengakuren battled 2,000 policemen for ten hours, with 110 injured and 169 arrested. The socialist governor of Tokyo, Minobe, also seized on the hospital as an issue, claiming that its germs would infect the children at nearby schools and that helicopters ferrying patients to Oji might crash into the surrounding residential district. In fact, the helicopter approach to the hospital did not come within two blocks horizontally or a thousand feet vertically of the areas Minobe was concerned about, but he would not accept my invitation to fly into the hospital to see for himself, or to tour it.

In February pressure from Okinawans to remove the B-52s stationed there was intense. The Okinawan Legislature passed resolutions against it and the Japanese government, sensitive to the need to appear Okinawa's powerful big brother, formally expressed its concern February 12. Discontent was especially severe after the March 31 partial bombing halt. General Unger and I saw considerable value in relocating the planes because elections for the island's Chief Executive were approaching; the left-wing parties that claimed to want the bases out altogether were using this issue effectively against the more moderate Liberal Democratic Party that had been in power for many years. All in all, between the *Enterprise,* the *Pueblo,* the *Swordfish,* LBJ's speech, the Itazuke crash, Oji Hospital, and B-52s on Okinawa, the first half of 1968 was something of a low point during my tour in the number of highly visible and contentious issues between Japan and the United States.

However, the rest of the year improved, aided by the reversion of the Bonins, announced in May, and our December proposal for a comprehensive reduction in the number and size of our bases. But most responsible was Sato, whose campaign on behalf of LDP candidates for the July 7 House of Councillors election stressed the importance of close ties between Japan and the United States. Sato had once told me that Japanese who simply rejoiced in the country's material prosperity without appreciating its unique freedom from heavy military expenditure were "cripples bragging about their own prosperity which really depended on others" and were not "real Japanese." Nor, he said, were those who did not fully appreciate the importance of continued friendly relations with and reliance on the United States. He banked on his intuition about the electorate's basic political alignment and won. The LDP maintained its majority despite losing two seats; the Socialists lost eight, and the Komeito and the DSP both gained four. Commentators widely considered the results a vindication of Sato's pro-United States stance.

It was in the wake of Sato's success that I decided to make a major speech on United States-Japan relations, one which I wrote very carefully without staff help. I thought the time was ripe for Japan to consider not just what it suffered because of our close economic and security ties, but what it gained and what the United States lost. I delivered it August 10 to a Jaycee political seminar in Tokyo, and in it I frankly discussed, for the first time with a public audience, the perception of most Americans that Japan was profiting considerably more from our relations than we were. I started with our economic ties. I did not want to "complain" about Japan's booming exports to the United States, I said, "for it is also in our interest to see a prosperous and growing Japan." But Japan's restrictive quotas, relatively minute defense expenditures, and balance of payments surplus were well-known facts in America that were bound to influence our future relationship. My basic message was that Japan had to give us reciprocal treatment if it wanted liberal trade terms from us.

Now that Japan was the world's third greatest economic power, I said, "our countries can better deal with each other on the self-respecting basis of true equality rather than on 'he basis of inequalities where the weaker is seeking special cons.deration from the stronger . . . Thus I feel we can better arrive at agreements and understandings solidly based on that mutual common interest that must be the foundation of all constructive relations between nations." Japanese commentators frequently spoke of "countermeasures" that Japan should take against various American policies, as if our countries were enemies; I said I thought Japan should appreciate that success in international relations, in economic affairs, and in other areas, did not always mean advancing one's own interests at the expense of another, but rather seeking to find areas where interests overlapped and then expanding them.

I drove home the same point in relation to our security arrangements. The presence of American bases in Japan, I said, did not serve American interests exclusively but contributed significantly to the "sure fact" that "from the time this security relationship was initiated up to the present Japan has lived in complete peace from outside attack at minimum cost to itself and while enjoying the highest rate of economic progress of any country in history." In the same period, the United States had spent many billions of dollars and thousands of lives resisting communist aggression in Asia and elsewhere. We had hardly been infallible in executing this basically sound policy of mutual security, I said; "I would not deny that with the wisdom of hindsight we could have at times done better." But it was crucial for the Japanese to understand why our bases, with all their irritations, served Japan's interest. "They are here to help deter a war in which Japan might be involved, and to help Japan fight that war if deterrence fails. Seen from that perspective, which is the correct perspective, the U.S. and Japanese community of interest can be clearly grasped." My basic theme was that the United States should not be taken for granted.

This speech made quite a stir in Japan, which I had hoped it would. The press gave it wide coverage and the Cabinet and Prime Minister discussed it. I had aired these sentiments to government officials many times before, but I wanted to wait until I was well established in the country before taking this somewhat provocative case to the public. Foreign Minister Miki and I had quite a little debate about the speech ten days later at a secret meeting at the Hotel New Otani, where we reviewed the general state of United States-Japanese relations for several hours. "No Japanese feels that the United States would defend Japan no matter what," he told me with some feeling. "The Japanese people are not aware that it is only the Americans who are making sacrifices, and do not feel that they are the only ones gaining benefits." I backed off from directly contradicting him, believing I had already made my point, and Miki did close this part of our discussion by saying that the Japanese government had to take responsibility for convincing its people that its economic and defense ties with the United States served Japan's own interests, not ours. He believed that was the only way to assure continued healthy relations; I could not have agreed more. The Soviet invasion of Czechoslovakia two weeks later very eloquently reinforced to Japan the value of the Security Treaty. The Foreign Office started getting out pamphlets and speakers to explain to Japanese audiences why the country's present arrangements with the United States were good for Japan.

In addition to trying to address the climate of public opinion from which Japanese government security policy took its cue, I also continued working closely with government officials to ask the questions and provide the information that would help Japan formulate its own coherent ideas about what defense posture and international strategy it would pursue. A significant development in the summer of 1968 was the LDP's decision not to renounce or try to revise the Security Treaty when that became possible in 1970. That meant it would continue in force, and that the Opposition would not have any specific event, like a Diet vote, around which to build a protest.

Meetings of the Security Subcommittee took place in January, June, and September. The June meeting was held in Washington, mainly to give the Japanese members a chance to meet a wide range of people in Defense and State. I also arranged a trip for Ushiba, Defense Agency Vice-Minister Obata, and some of their staff to Cape Kennedy, where they observed both civilian and military aspects of our space effort, including preparations for the next Apollo moon shot. A Polaris submarine was in port at the Cape, and because the Commander of Submarines in the Atlantic was an old friend of mine, I was able to arrange a tour, which they found very interesting. They also visited Strategic Air Command headquarters in Omaha.

I used this visit in Washington to meet extensively with the Joint Chiefs, Deputy Secretary of Defense Paul Nitze, Secretaries Rusk and McNamara, Walt Rostow, and the President about the future of our base structure in Japan. The demonstrations over Camp Oji and Itazuke Air Base were only the visible signs of a generally low-grade but widespread discontent among Japanese at all the prime real estate our bases occupied. In 1968 our base system numbered 149 facilities, from huge airbases to oil tanks to chapels, covering 366 square kilometers. That was one-twentieth of its 1952 size, but it still managed to retain some frills, like golf courses, and such highly obtrusive items as large numbers of American-style bungalows with lawns for military personnel in Yokohama. To the Japanese, crammed onto a tiny island, the American style of land use was profligate. Worse was that many of our airfields built in the countryside during the Occupation had been encircled by urban sprawl. Not unlike Okinawa, I believed we would be much smarter to prepare a plan for rationalizing this base structure ourselves and present it as a package to the Japanese government, rather than have tensions mount piecemeal until some ugly breaking point was reached.

Before I went to Washington in June I held long consultations with General McKee and Admiral McCain, making sure they concurred in my approach before I took the case to higher authority. In Washington, State, Defense, and the White House agreed that we should cut the visibility of our bases to the minimum consistent with military effectiveness. I arranged to have instructions sent to me and McCain to review this subject and make recommendations for reductions. These arrived in Tokyo shortly after I returned, having briefed McCain en route about my sessions in Washington. Because McCain was on my side and I had made sure that these instructions to recommend reductions came jointly from State and Defense, I felt that the politically most difficult part of this process was over.

Admiral McCain and I submitted our joint report on base reductions to Washington on September 26, 1968. Two weeks previously we had shown a preliminary version to Japanese Foreign Office and Defense Agency representatives at a Security Subcommittee meeting. (This was the first such meeting we announced publicly, but the storm of press complaints about "warmongering" the Foreign Office had feared did not materialize.) After initial surprise, the Foreign Office and Sato were very pleased at the number and size of the bases we were willing to turn over to the SDA. But the SDA itself was somewhat aghast. It objected on the grounds that we were giving them "too much." It did not have money in its budget to cover the cost of absorbing what we wanted to hand over. I had no patience with this attitude, because the SDA had regularly leaked stories to the press that the United States was always rejecting its requests for facilities. For too long they had been putting the monkey on our backs, and if it discomfited the SDA somewhat to get what it had been loudly wishing for I was not going to shed copious tears. Nevertheless, the SDA kept stalling.

Fumihiko Togo, Director-General of the Foreign Office's North American Affairs Bureau, worked with the SDA but could not budge them, so finally I had to see Ushiba and put our dissatisfaction to him quite bluntly. He recognized immediately the embarrassment the Japanese government would suffer if we made public that it was refusing to accept our base reductions, and he was finally able to extract a more cooperative attitude from the SDA.

The package McCain and I suggested to Washington was diluted slightly compared to our original plan in order to lessen the SDA's qualms. Washington approved, and we formally announced our plan at a meeting of the full Security Consultative Committee on December 23. We released thirty-two facilities entirely and indicated willingness to relocate twenty-one others, which in total comprised more than a third of our existing bases and half of the land area used. Included were sixteen of the twenty-four facilities the Japanese had specifically requested we examine. We also announced that a new set of procedures was being instituted at all our airfields to make them less annoying, including special flight patterns, a reduction in night flights, and most importantly, a significant curtailment in operations from Itazuke. After outlining this package before the Committee, I said: "I am convinced that neither of us wants or can long endure a base structure that does not have the solid support of both of us. It is my hope that the actions taken today will help produce a structure that warrants such support." We were able to let the press know discreetly that the SDA had blocked us from divesting ourselves of even more. In any event we had gotten ourselves in the very satisfactory position of being well in front of the Japanese government on a very contentious issue.

Another issue, however, was not moving forward so satisfactorily. The Sato-LBJ Communiqué from the 1967 summit said our two governments would take the subject of Ryukyuan reversion under "joint and continuous review" with an eye towards setting a date for it "within a few years." Miki and I and our staffs held only one "joint and continuous review" meeting, in May 1968, after the details had been settled for returning the Bonins. The Japanese government had no specific proposal to make because it had not fixed its bargaining position, which Sato likened to a "blank sheet of paper." Exploratory talks continued, however, in private meetings with Miki and Sato and in sessions of the

Security Subcommittee. We talked at length in these forums, mainly about the specific contributions the Okinawan bases made to a credible deterrent in the Far East, both conventional and nuclear. Other topics included the effect of the Vietnam War on the timing of reversion, the work of the tripartite Advisory Committee that was busily recommending ways to bring Okinawan life up to Japanese standards, and political developments on the Ryukyus themselves. Especially significant in this area were the November, 1968 elections for Chief Executive of the Ryukyus, which saw the anti-bases Opposition leader, Yara, beat the LDP candidate, another indication that the political costs could continue to mount unless reversion took place in the near future. These conversations with Japanese officials did not resolve anything conclusively, but did reveal that blocking reversion were two familiar issues of substance and one of tactics: nuclear weapons storage, freedom of use of bases for conventional operations, and how the timing would be handled.

Sato had staked his political life on accomplishing reversion, so his government considered action in this area its highest priority. Miki pressed me to agree that within the next year we would set a date for reversion. I still objected to setting a date before settling the important issues. Neither the United States nor Japan could afford to have reversion take place on an arbitrary day if the other side had not relented on some essential point. Miki's officials agreed with me.

On the disputes of substance, as 1968 progressed, I came to believe that the United States could ultimately accept "homeland-level" restrictions on freedom of use and nuclear weapons storage for the Okinawa bases—playing these cards carefully, of course, to make sure the Japanese did not get them without doing what they should do in return. Our government had not fixed its position on whether Okinawa had to have nuclear weapons to deter China and North Korea, but the preponderant opinion, shared by Rusk, McNamara, other high-ranking civilians in Defense, and me, was that we could do without them. We already possessed a sufficient nuclear deterrent in South Korea. And if international tensions began to mount to such a degree that returning nuclear weapons to Okinawa became necessary, the Security Treaty would allow us to do that as long as we consulted with the Japanese government. Moving the weapons themselves would not take much time.

Freedom of use was a stickier problem. Obviously the bases would be more versatile if we did not have to consult the Japanese government about how we used them. But in the long run, I thought this freedom might be counterproductive. Japan would have to take more responsibility in regional politics if its security depended on its own decisions about how those Okinawan bases could be used. Increasing Japan's sense of international responsibility was an important goal of American policy. I also believed that the United States was very unlikely ever again to fight in Asia without Japan's full support. Thus, under almost any circumstances, we ourselves would wish to consult with the Japanese government before deploying forces from Okinawa. And I also understand Japan's basic view that the third-ranking economic power in the world could not delegate to the United States the fundamental question of whether it would be at war or peace. If the Pentagon and Washington generally could accept homeland-level restrictions on freedom of use, I thought the nuclear weapons problem would fall into place. And with those security problems disposed of, the economic and other aspects of the reversion agreement could be worked out relatively quickly.

In December 1968, Sato removed Miki as Foreign Minister after Miki ran against Sato for LDP President (and thus Prime Minister) on November 27 and lost 249-107. The chief plank in Miki's platform was that he would demand the United States withdraw nuclear weapons from Okinawa, to which Sato responded by saying that while he was determined to regain Japan's complete independence (including the Soviet-occupied Kuriles in the north as well as the Ryukyus), no conditions could be set before reversion negotiations formally began. Needless to say, I was glad Sato won. And given my relationship with Miki, which was never bad but never really cordial, I was glad Sato replaced him as Foreign Minister with Kiichi Aichi.

Aichi and I took an immediate liking to each other, and because I knew he was very close to Sato and would reliably transmit the Prime Minister's views to me and vice versa, we were able to quickly shuck off diplomatic fencing and talk frankly. At our first private meeting on December 11, he said his fundamental purpose as Foreign Minister was to improve relations with the United States, which he hoped to accomplish by "enlightening" the public about the importance to Japan of Japan-United States ties. Without such enlightenment, he said, anti-American sentiment would increase and manifest itself overtly, further straining our bonds. Ushiba and Togo had obviously briefed Aichi well on what would create a favorable first impression on me, and he succeeded.

My response was a friendly but forthright variation on the theme of my August speech to the Jaycees. The United States felt it was being taken for granted, I said, and if this trend continued we would ultimately decide to pack up and go. If Japan wanted us to stay, for its own reasons and not as a favor to us, it should make that clear.

About Okinawa itself, Aichi said he wanted to resume the joint and continuous review process. That made sense for both countries now that Sato had been reelected as LDP president and a change of administrations in Washington was bringing Richard Nixon to power. I said my tentative plan, if I were kept on as Ambassador, was to lay the necessary private and discreet groundwork for reversion within the next few months. During January I wanted to get Sato's and Aichi's frank views on the ingredients of an acceptable reversion agreement. I would go to Washington in mid-February to explore the thinking of the new Administration, then return to Japan to see if the outlines of a path between the two governments' positions was visible. In the meantime, I said, it was vital to avoid press leaks that would stir up the Armed Services Committees of the Congress prematurely, force the Administration to deny the leaks, and thus limit both sides' maneuvering room.

With my timetable in mind, Aichi called me to his official residence on the morning of December 28 to set forth some preliminary views on Okinawa that I could take back to Washington. We went round and round on the familiar question of setting a date for reversion before we had agreed on all the conditions, which Sato and Aichi clearly preferred because they expected a general election within the next year, before Japanese popular opinion could be "enlightened" fully about the Okinawa bases' significance to the defense of Japan and the region. Though I could not speak for the new administration, I said I doubted any American President could maintain congressional support if he approved a formula for reversion before the conditions were established. Nor could I see how the Sato government would profit from automatic reversion on an arbitrary date. Japanese public opinion overwhelmingly favored "homeland-level" restrictions on nuclear weapons and freedom of use as a condition of reversion. If the United States was not willing to concede these points by reversion day, I asked, could Sato accept the consequences? Nevertheless, Aichi said Sato wanted to set a firm date for reversion at his next Washington summit in November, 1969. If Sato wanted that, I said, then we should try to agree on the conditions by then.

At another meeting with Aichi on January 9, 1969, we had a significant breakthrough on Okinawa, the first since I had come to Tokyo. The Foreign Minister said that over the New Year's holidays he had organized his thoughts, talked to Sato, and probed opinion within the LDP on Okinawa. Sato still wanted to come to an understanding about the timing of reversion at his summit with Nixon in November. Reversion itself might take place around 1972. As for conditions, Aichi continued, Japanese opinion would have trouble accepting anything but "homeland-level." But if the United States could not accept homeland-level restrictions immediately and insisted on an agreement permitting our Okinawan forces, for an interim period, to store nuclear weapons or have freedom of use without prior consultation, then it was especially important for the strength of Sato's government to reach a reversion agreement quickly. So Aichi proposed a new formula: that the bases' present freedoms continue through reversion, to be phased out gradually when both governments agreed that the homeland-level restrictions could be applied without jeopardy to regional security. This was an entirely new approach, which I told Aichi we would consider carefully. I was very encouraged. It showed the Japanese were finally devoting serious thought to defining their own security interests. I thought this formula might serve as a good basis for agreement.

One of the reasons Aichi worked so hard to devise a new formula he could discuss with me personally early in the new year was that he had heard the same press rumors I had, namely that President-elect Nixon was going to appoint me to a senior job in the new Administration. Some of the stories said I was being considered for Secretary of State, others for Under Secretary. I also received letters from friends in Washington advising me that Mr. Nixon had high regard for me. This mystified me somewhat because I had known him only slightly. He had come through Saigon while I was there and visited Tokyo in 1967 working as a lawyer for Pepsi-Cola, and I had invited him to a lunch and had a long talk with him, as I would have done with any distinguished visiting American. I found we had very compatible views about Asia, but that was about the extent of our contact. I heard nothing directly from the President-elect or his staff, so I took a very relaxed attitude about all the gossip. I was very happy in my job and eager to see Okinawa through reversion and the Security Treaty through 1970. I had no special desire to return to the seven-day weeks and fourteen-hour days of Washington.

·CHAPTER THIRTEEN·

Undersecretary for
Political Affairs

ON FRIDAY, DECEMBER 27, SECRETARY RUSK SENT ME A
personal message asking me to return to Washington immediately. I went right back, and after a ten-minute chat, Dean asked
me to go see the new Secretary of State-designate, William Rogers,
who was working on transition problems in a small conference
suite on the first floor. Rogers saw me immediately. After some
preliminaries he asked if I would be willing to become Undersecretary for Political Affairs. I told him that my honest reaction
was negative, that I hoped to stay in Tokyo, where I felt I could
do the most good. Besides, the job he was offering me had only
been filled sporadically through the years. In contrast to my old
job as Deputy Undersecretary it had always had very vague responsibilities and had tended to be something of a "fifth wheel"
in the operations of the Department. Although it would be nice
to have the Undersecretary title, I said, the job would not interest
me unless it carried all the functions I had performed as Deputy
Undersecretary for supervising the Assistant Secretaries and handling relations with Defense and the intelligence community.
Even if I could perform those tasks, however, I reiterated that if
I were given free choice I would remain in Japan. We agreed
that we would both sleep on it and talk again the next day.

During that second conversation Rogers told me that he
wanted to establish the Undersecretary for Political Affairs as the
equivalent of the Permanent Undersecretary in the British system, the entirely apolitical senior career official who stayed on
as Cabinets and Ministers came and went. He said he did not
foresee any difficulty transferring to it the Deputy Undersecre-

tary's functions and abolishing that job. He said that the President very much wanted me in Washington and hoped I would take the job. Under those circumstances, I replied, I had no choice and would do it willingly and to the best of my ability. Rogers said that the President himself would announce the appointment in a few days from his transition headquarters at the Hotel Pierre in New York. Elliot Richardson, then Attorney General of Massachusetts and a colleague of Rogers when Rogers had been Eisenhower's Attorney General, was to become Undersecretary.

As I walked out of Rogers' office, my fate sealed, one of the first people I saw was John Getz, who had worked with me in Thailand and had since worked extensively on European affairs and NATO. Aware of my lacunae on those areas, I asked him impulsively what he was presently doing. He said he was still working on politico-military affairs in the European Bureau. I told him he should go right back and tell his boss, Assistant Secretary John Leedy, that he was now working for me. I had to go to New York in three days and then directly to Japan to wrap things up there. I would have to be back in Washington before January 20, landing at a run and ready to go. John was enthusiastic and we drew up a checklist of everything he would have to do in my absence. It was a long list.

One of the first things I had to do was send a message to Pat telling her she was going to have to leave the Tokyo Embassy residence she loved and move for the fifteenth time in our career, with me going ahead as usual and leaving her behind to pick up the pieces. I also informed the Embassy of the tight schedule of farewell visits they should set up so I could observe all the proprieties while getting out of Tokyo within seven days.

The night of January 5, I accompanied Rogers to New York and stayed in his apartment. The next morning we entered the frantic confusion of the President-elect's headquarters, where I met Elliot Richardson for the first time. Then we went in to see Nixon. He asked that I return to Washington via Saigon and sound out Ellsworth Bunker about whether he wanted to stay on as Ambassador. I said I certainly welcomed the opportunity to reacquaint myself somewhat with Saigon, but this would necessarily delay my starting work for a few days. This was agreeable to the President. Then Nixon graciously introduced us and Dick Pederson, who was to become Counselor of the Department, to the press.

Before we left the Pierre we saw Henry Kissinger, newly appointed as the President's National Security Advisor, for about fifteen minutes. That was long enough for me to see that some rough roads lay ahead. Henry outlined his thoughts for wiping out the SIG-IRG interdepartmental system General Taylor and I had developed in 1966 that gave State broad responsibility for directing the interdepartmental work of the government in foreign affairs. Henry intended to establish a system centered on the National Security Council staff with himself as head. I had only two minutes to expostulate with Henry. As I was going down the elevator to get a cab to the airport, I tried to brief Rogers and Richardson on the important bureaucratic theology involved in SIG-IRG as far as State was concerned—an area with which, of course, they were entirely unfamiliar. I brooded about this on my flight back, and as soon as I arrived in Tokyo I sent a long back channel message to Richardson trying to explicate the issues involved and urging that he and the Secretary mount the ramparts before January 20 against the Kissinger/NSC takeover of State's interdepartmental functions.

In Tokyo I entered a flurry of meetings with the Embassy staff, American military commanders, newspaper editors, and the American business community; dinners with the Foreign Minister and the Minister of International Trade and Industry; a full-scale press conference in the ballroom of the Okura Hotel; and a formal reception for all Cabinet members, Chiefs of Mission in Tokyo, and members of the Japanese and American business communities. Pat and I also had a delightful afternoon tea with the Emperor and Empress. I frequently dispensed with the interpreter and his formal court language in favor of my fractured plain Japanese, and the Emperor did the same with his English. The result was that for the first time I saw him smile and laugh. I felt that my tour in Japan had truly been a success.

I departed Tokyo on the cold morning of January 15 in a small Air Force passenger jet. By the time we reached Okinawa the low fever I had started with had climbed, and I was feeling groggy. General Unger took me to the dispensary, where they gave me some pills that mildly revived my spirits and enabled me to have an excellent talk with him on what we foresaw for Okinawa. Then I left for Clark Field in the Philippines, and when the pills wore off it was clear that I had a heavy case of the flu. With some more pills I left for Saigon, where I was really looking forward to the embassy car at planeside and a quick trip into bed at Ambassador Bunker's residence. Eager to get me down on the ground as fast as possible, however, the crew blew some of our tires landing and it took another half hour before I could disembark. Bunker took me directly to the same house Max Taylor and I had occupied in 1964, and the same houseboys took care of putting me to bed in my old bedroom. I already felt better. The arrival of my son Stephen, who was serving in the embassy, cheered me further. An Army doctor confirmed my fear that I was really ill and would not be able to move for some days.

It took a week before I was able to navigate again, somewhat shaky of leg, but I was able to get out for some talks with President Thieu, Vice President Ky, and some other Vietnamese officials. I also had a long lunch with our commanding general, Creighton Abrams, talked to the embassy staff, and especially to my son Stephen. Stephen was reporting on developments in North Vietnam—following Hanoi's radio, examining interrogations of NVN prisoners and defectors, and by talking with friendly embassies whose countries were also represented in Hanoi. Bunker and I also had ample opportunity for conversation.

Thieu seemed an entirely different man from the Corps commander I remembered sitting in Prime Minister Quat's office in the wee hours of June 11, 1965, suddenly thrust by mutually-agreed coup into the job of Chief of State. His self-confidence and political abilities had obviously grown enormously. He talked and acted liked a real leader and seemed in command of himself and his government. Ky, on the other hand, was still the same flamboyant "fly-boy." General Abrams also impressed me. I remembered him from State-JCS meetings when I was Deputy Undersecretary, where as Army Vice Chief of Staff he would sit in the back row impassively puffing his cigar. All the accounts I had received in Tokyo rated him very highly, and to me he seemed to have the best grasp of the complex and subtle politico-military environment he faced of any senior officer I had known.

I reluctantly agreed to meet with Vietnamese and foreign press at the airport as I left for Washington. I spoke with deliberate blandness, expressing pleasure at seeing old friends like Thieu, Ky, and Prime Minister Huong, my encouragement at the progress South Vietnam was making militarily and politically, and my hope that the Paris peace talks would succeed. Then I was asked whether I intended to recommend to the new administration that we change our "commitment" to Vietnam. I knew that a waffle on this answer would produce adverse effects in Saigon and contradict my own convictions in any event. So I said: "I would not make recommendations for changes in the American commitment." When I arrived in Washington, I was told that Senator Fulbright, having read my comments in the *Washington Post*, said that he intended to have a "Johnson Day" when the Foreign Relations Committee held its hearings on my nomination.

I started work January 23, and although my office was larger than my last one in Washington, everything else, thanks to John Getz, was in place. I felt as if I had come home. I knew the Department and its people, its strengths and weaknesses, how the machinery worked and how to get things done. I felt I could work effectively for the President, as soon as he made clear what he wanted done.

Richardson, Rogers, and I met promptly that morning to get acquainted, and Rogers had us to lunch, at which we discussed how to divide up our work. We met again that evening before going home. We continued this pattern of conferences in the morning and evening and an occasional lunch with other departmental officers, schedules permitting. I quickly took a great liking to both men and was satisfied we would be entirely compatible. Richardson turned out to be more interested in administration than I had expected, and I cheerfully deferred to his desire to chair the Board of the Foreign Service, which I had somewhat envisaged for myself.

My first conversation with Rogers and Richardson revealed that Henry Kissinger had already ensconced himself in the lordly position he had outlined at the Hotel Pierre, getting the President's signature on the necessary Presidential order within hours after the inauguration. I could see problems ahead, particularly for State. But I could also see the logic of this new system, which people besides Henry advocated. If a President wanted to be personally active in foreign affairs, a system that allowed him to reach down deep into the decision-making process, before State, Defense, and other agencies had concerted their positions and presented an impervious joint recommendation, was obviously more suited to him than SIG-IRG. I know that Andy Goodpaster, former aide to President Eisenhower, had strongly recommended to Nixon that he shape policy before the bureaucracy left him with only a few options that he might not like. Nevertheless, my experience had convinced me that the interplay of personalities determines policy more than organization charts. As it turned out, the formal structures and personalities so reinforced each other that the result, I felt, was a President who took less advantage of the State Department's capabilities than any President since Roosevelt during World War II.

From the start it was obvious that Kissinger was extremely insecure and had an obsession, which persisted throughout his

White House years, that the State Department and Foreign Service were determined to undermine him. Perhaps this was a defensive mental posture he assumed to make it easier to emasculate the Department in just the way he blamed the Department for trying to do to him. In any event, he reinforced Nixon's longstanding paranoia that the Foreign Service consisted solely of Democrats who despised Republicans, and him in particular. Apparently Nixon had not always been warmly received in our embassies when he traveled abroad as a private citizen, and he did not forget it. His virulent distrust of the Department did not seem to be mitigated by the fact that its new Secretary was his early political supporter and friend. The President and Kissinger never lost an opportunity to humilitate and degrade Bill Rogers, both publicly and privately. Bill is a first-class human being who was slow to take offense and tried his best to avoid and deflect the confrontations that the White House continually forced on him. I respected him for his forbearance, but its result was to leave the field to Henry. Without Rogers to take the lead, I could only go so far in opposing Henry.

Before officially assuming my job I had to endure not one but two grueling sessions before the Fulbright Committee on January 28 and 29. He made sure to hold them in the large Foreign Relations hearing room, where he sat in magisterial solemnity on the impressive raised dais of which senators are so fond; I sat at the enormous witness table quite alone, bathed in the full panoply of floodlights and TV lenses, feeling rather like a criminal defendant, which I am sure was not far from Fulbright's intention. I have never felt more alone or under more unfriendly pressure. As the first State Department nominee with any kind of history in foreign affairs, I became Fulbright's vehicle for getting at the administration on Vietnam. Besides that, he wanted to land a few blows on me personally. Having no knowledge whatever of what the administration intended to do on Vietnam, I had to answer everything based on my own knowledge and convictions. Believing as I did that we should continue to help South Vietnam resist communist domination, my answers did not satisfy the Senator. He voted against my confirmation—the only such vote cast against me in the seven times the Foreign Relations Committee was called upon to confirm me for a senior position.

My calendar for these years records that this job carried the same pressured pace and variety of problems I had grown accustomed to in Washington. I had a meeting on a new subject about every thirty minutes, and between the meetings, phone calls, memos, and telegrams, I put in twelve or fourteen hours a day six days a week. From the outset I sought to use the enormous breadth of knowledge, experience, and wisdom of which the State Department is the repository instead of building up a large personal staff, which is the tendency of most newcomers. Between me and John Getz there was virtually no subject on which we could not pick up the phone and get hold of an in-house expert or at least someone to tell us where the knowledge could be found. I felt the Department served me and the government well, and that being called on directly by someone on the seventh floor was good for staff morale.

Another technique I used to boost my efficiency was to have one of my long-time and trusted secretaries, Elinor Murphy or Martha Watts, monitor all my phone calls automatically and take notes, except for those with the President or Secretary. This was not eavesdropping but a vital part of operating effectively. They were so familiar with my work that I could hang up the phone and turn immediately to something else, secure in the knowledge that they would convey (usually through John Getz) any commitments I had made for information, letters, or decisions to the people who needed to know. The alternative was for me to take the time to repeat it myself, subject to the vicissitudes of a fallible memory. Their brief records I considered part of my official files. It seemed no different from having someone take notes during a conversation in my office, but since Watergate this practice has come into disrepute, and the buttons on secretaries' telephones allowing them to listen in without being heard have been disconnected.

I always assumed that any senior official I was talking to had a secretary monitoring; in fact, I hoped they had. I tried to persuade Rogers to do this but never succeeded, and consequently I felt information that should have been conveyed and things that should have been done fell through the cracks. One of my hardest jobs through the years was finding out what the Secretary had been up to in areas that concerned me.

As for more nefarious eavesdropping, I always assumed that someone was trying to listen in, whether from a hostile government or our own. Early in the administration I was at the White House when the President called Rogers and myself in to show us some material gleaned from a wiretap on a foreign correspondent from a friendly country that indicated that Bill Sullivan, a

top-notch Foreign Service Officer then working on   ...amese
affairs, had been talking to Averell Harriman, for whom he had
once worked. I thought Sullivan's contacts were quite innocent,
commendable in fact, but from then on I assumed that my phone,
too, might be a target. Henry Kissinger told me that he thought
his phone was being tapped by the government. Because I had
served four years behind the Iron Curtain, security was an automatic reflex, and I never said anything on the phone that I
cared about anyone overhearing. Nor did I ever take home any
classified document for evening work or carry one to a meeting
in another building without having someone accompany me. It
was my observation, however, that the more senior the officials
the more careless they were likely to be in speaking over open
phone lines and the more reluctant they were to use the secure
phones with which they were all provided.

Ambassadorial appointments occupied much of any new
administration's attention, and as the only career officer on the
seventh floor, I had a fair amount of input into the decisions about
who from the career service became ambassador. For political
appointees, the White House, Elliot Richardson and I set up an
orderly screening system. Peter Flanigan in the White House had
operational responsibility for putting their names before us, responsible to Commerce Secretary Maurice Stans, who was Nixon's
chief fund-raiser and liaison with the business community. Besides
Walter Annenberg, whose appointment to London was automatic,
Flanigan sent the candidates to see Elliot and me. We separately
interviewed them to get some sense of their background, character, and potential ability. Sometimes they had specific countries
in mind, other times not. Many had family wealth, others had
made fortunes in business, but they all coveted that title of Ambassador.

We did not have to accept all of them, but we certainly
could not reject them en masse either, since the President clearly
wanted them. Besides, many distinguished ambassadors have
been political—Ellsworth Bunker, David Bruce, and Averell Harriman, to name a few. However, what surprised me about many
of this crop was, frankly, how dense they were, even though they
might have made tremendous fortunes in business. Several candidates came in clutching photo albums showing wives, houses,
horses, stables, servants, gardens, and tasteful interior decoration
all evidently designed to show that the candidate knew how to
live right and would be a credit to the United States abroad. Of
course, these types wanted a nice post where they could entertain

properly. Their conversation about foreign policy was generally not as interesting as their photography.

Elliot and I would get together afterwards and see if we shared conclusions. If we agreed that they "passed," we would discuss what posts they might do best at and negotiate our preferences with Peter Flanigan. When we thought things were just about settled, Maury Stans would call and insist that the White House have four more ambassadors. Some of the political appointees turned out to be quite effective; others did not interest themselves much in the embassy, letting their deputies do the work while they stuck to entertaining; and others regularly gummed up everything they touched.

In general, I had stepped back into the many of the responsibilities I had handled from 1961 to 1966: overseeing relations between State and the Pentagon; serving on the interagency group overseeing intelligence (called the 40 Committee instead of the Special Group); and being the seventh floor agent on science, space, and other technical fields. I also became the resident Japan expert. However, I soon found that most of these responsibilities tended to be rather hollow shells of their former selves. Nixon and Kissinger systematically froze out the State Department from real influence on the subjects they considered most vital: ending the Vietnam War, detente, relations with Peking, SALT, and later, the Middle East. It was not a heroic time for the Department.

Under Kennedy and Johnson the Department had more or less been at the center of things, and I had been able to make some constructive and lasting changes in the way American foreign policy was formulated and implemented. But under Nixon my mission became chiefly defensive, trying to shield the Department from the pummelling that rained down upon it from the President and Kissinger. As the senior officer with a lasting commitment to the Department and the Foreign Service, I felt very deeply about wanting to protect it, and more importantly to see it make the contribution to foreign policy I knew it could and wanted to. But I did not have the necessary political clout, and I was not inclined to use my elbows too vigorously. I felt I could best accomplish my purposes by working from within rather than by creating antagonisms that would leave me on the outside.

While Kissinger certainly enjoyed putting the boot in State whenever possible, I never doubted that Nixon was ultimately behind him. I always considered it my duty as a Foreign Service Officer to serve the President as he chose to be served, and if he chose to ignore the Department that was his right. So I was always torn between my duty to the President and my loyalty to an institution that I knew would serve him well if only he let it. And whatever they may have thought about the institution I represented, the President and Kissinger always seemed to respect my experience and judgment as someone who could "get things done." I was part of the Washington Special Actions Group (WSAG), the crisis coordinating board that Kissinger established and chaired; I served on the 40 Committee; and I think I was generally accepted as the pipeline between the NSC staff at the center of things and the accumulated knowledge of the State Department they needed. I never leaked anything, never told stories against Kissinger, never complained in any way that would embarrass the White House. In fact, I held information from WSAG very tightly so that it would not leak, which did not make me popular in the Department. I did not pretend to play in the league of world superstar to which Kissinger aspired, but for the skills I did offer I believe I was respected and, compared to many others in the Department, decently treated. Even so, it is not a period I look back on with excessive fondness.

There were subjects in which Kissinger was not particularly interested, and some of those he left for the Department to handle. One, by and large, was Japan. Kissinger was fascinated by the Chinese, especially the urbane and sophisticated Chou En-lai. By contrast the Japanese always seemed prosaic, obtuse, unworthy of his sustained attention. As Henry once complained: "Every time the Japanese ambassador has me to lunch he serves Wiener schnitzel." I was fortunate that one of my major interests was one of Henry's major blind spots. I had a fairly free hand in some other areas that I will describe, but they were not numerous.

Relations with the military continued to concern me, but early in the administration I reluctantly agreed that what had been my small politico-military affairs staff, which had grown into a large entity of its own, be broken off to become a Bureau in its own right. I remained its chief broker on the seventh floor and in interdepartmental disputes. At least once a month I continued the State-JCS meetings I established as Deputy Undersecretary, seeing the Chiefs for the kind of informal "hair-down" session they seldom engage in. I often brought an ambassador who was back in Washington from some particularly critical or interesting post to see them, and both sides seemed to enjoy the exchange. As time went on, however, the WSAG that Henry established to do joint politico-military contingency planning and crisis management took more and more time, and I ended up dealing more with the JCS Chairman when we saw each other at the various White House committees on which we both sat, rather than with the whole group. The first chairman was Earle (Bus) Wheeler, who served for three terms (six years), longer than anyone in history. He was an officer of broad background and experience with whom I found it easy to work. His successor was Admiral Thomas Moorer, who to my mind had the most difficult job any JCS Chairman ever faced. It was the period of on-again, off-again bombing of North Vietnam, the "secret" bombing of Cambodia, the mining of Haiphong, sporadic peace negotiations with Hanoi, the withdrawal of our troops and a rising public and congressional tide against Vietnam, in particular, and the military, in general. He had to deal with an unpredictable President, a dictatorial Kissinger, and an elusive Defense Secretary Laird. He had to support his commanders in the field while trying to mollify the Congress and State Department. I always admired how he kept all these balls in the air with rarely a slip.

One of my staunchest partners in the Pentagon previously had been Paul Nitze, Assistant Secretary for International Security Affairs. He and I had settled a great many problems between us. ISA had since fallen on hard times, however, and its then chief, Warren Nutter, had none of Paul's flair for making decisions and getting things done. I therefore had to take up an unusually heavy volume of business between State and Defense with the Deputy Secretary of Defense, David Packard, former president of Hewlett-Packard, the giant electronics firm that he and Hewlett had started in a garage while students at Stanford. Except possibly for McNamara, he was the most successful case I ever observed of an executive from big business making the switch to government. Dave was a big man, physically and mentally, calm and unflappable and with a tremendous capacity for absorbing facts. He never took doctrinaire Pentagon positions and was always prepared to resolve thorny issues with common sense and patience. Though many of the issues on which we collaborated were insignificant and should have been settled at lower levels, such as minor export licensing matters, I found Dave a real pleasure to work with.

Apart from Vietnam, I dealt with Dave on a host of subjects—the negotiations with Japan on Okinawa, Soviet moves in Cuba, Libya's decision to expel us from our important air base at Wheelus, the Spanish base negotiations, the Canadian grab for what had been high seas, the Iraqi attack on Jordan, the Indian-

Pakistani war, and innumerable operational items arising from elsewhere in Southeast Asia stemming from the war in Vietnam. In addition to phone calls, we saw each other almost daily as fellow members of the same NSC Committees: WSAG, 40 Committee, DPRC, and the Vice President's Outer Space Committee. Sometimes we were not sure until we sat down what committee was meeting, since Kissinger would usually be at the head of the table when he eventually arrived, late and out of breath. There were, of course, also the NSC meetings at which Dave and I would be representing or backing up our principals.

As far as Vietnam itself was concerned, my own role was only peripheral and sporadic as incidents occurred or operations were planned that required the use of the facilities and expertise of the Department. The same is true of negotiations with Peking. I will recount some of these, but am in no position to give a full account of everything that happened. Although I was peripherally involved to some extent with the SALT negotiations, Elliot Richardson sat for the State Department on Henry's Verification Panel for that subject, and, in any event, the most important decisions were made in conversations between Henry and Soviet Ambassador Dobrynin, without State even being informed.

Yet in spite of all this, there was plenty to do.

On April 14, 1969, North Korean planes shot down an unarmed electronic intelligence-gathering EC-121 plane operating in international airspace far from Korean territory. The plane and all its crew were lost. This incident was extremely similar to the *Pueblo*, only more provocative and cruel. It was the first major crisis of the Nixon Administration, and it caught the White House unprepared. Kissinger responded by creating and chairing the Washington Special Actions Group (WSAG), a crisis-management and contingency planning body that met regularly thereafter. It included Deputy Defense Secretary David Packard, the JCS Chairman (first Earle Wheeler and then Thomas Moorer), CIA Director Helms, and me.

Nixon was furious about the EC-121, but though Henry said he was determined to retaliate, in fact he gave the impression of dragging his feet. To mean anything retaliation must be quick, but the subject was so startling and the mechanisms so new that we spent several days in almost desultory discussion of alternatives. The JCS proposed that we destroy the airfields from which the offending North Korean planes had been launched, and in principle this suggestion met with fairly wide approval. However, this faded when I pointed out that when their radar picked up our planes coming in for the attack, the North Koreans might easily conclude that we had launched a general attack and consequently put into motion all their well-prepared plans for attacking the south. That would unleash a much larger war, for which we were not prepared. We could not devise any way to communicate with Kim Il-sung as the raid was occurring, to let him know it was "only retaliatory" and would soon be over, so the air strike was dropped. We considered capturing a North Korean vessel at sea, but dropped that when we discovered that North Korea had no ships at sea. In the end nothing was done, but the administration took an important lesson that we should have contingency plans ready for a wide range of potential emergencies.

I had been a strong exponent of joint politico-military planning since my period as Deputy Undersecretary, especially after the Cuban Missile Crisis. The Joint Chiefs had always resisted on the ground that there was such a thing as a "pure" military plan that had to be stringently preserved from the rest of the government no matter how politically unrealistic it might seem. I admitted, however, that State had all too few people capable of engaging constructively in such planning, and that the military had some justification for worrying about security leaks. As time went on and WSAG became increasingly active in real and potential crises, I attempted to relieve Pentagon (and White House) fears about leaks from State by selecting a single officer in whose discretion and capabilities I had full confidence and installing him for the duration of the incident in an office adjacent to mine. He used only my secretaries for the necessary work, consulted others in State only with my specific authorization in each case, and worked full-time with his designated counterparts on the NSC and JCS. The officer I came to select regularly for this purpose was Thomas Pickering, then Deputy Director of Politico-Military Affairs and since ambassador at a number of posts and an assistant secretary. Keeping WSAG close to my chest (of course, I kept the Secretary fully informed) did not endear me to the rest of the Department, but it was the only way to moderate Kissinger's tirades about real and imagined leaks and make sure State preserved any influence at all on WSAG.

One troublesome aspect of WSAG was that where its chairman went, there went WSAG (as well as numerous other committees); its chairman always went where the President went; and the President often went to San Clemente, California. That required me and the rest of WSAG to join Kissinger in California often, sometimes several times a month. It was exhausting, but I did not mind the waste of time and money this effort to show activity at San Clemente required as much as I would have normally, because my mother and three of my children were living near Los Angeles at the time.

WSAG prepared some contingency plans that were very useful exercises for all the members on various possible situations such as a renewed attack by North Korea on the south (the attacks on the *Pueblo* and the EC-121 had ominous overtones), hostilities between China and the Soviets, a Chinese "shoot-down" at sea of one of our patrol planes, a Libyan attack on one of our aircraft in the Mediterranean, and a blockade of West Berlin. These plans still sit, I fear, sealed in their envelopes in safes at the Pentagon's National Military Command Center, the White House Situation Room, and the CIA and State Operations Centers, their existence long forgotten. If planning is to be useful, it must be continuous and must engage those who will actually be making the decisions.

The government, as I have described, had no mechanism for funding various projects abroad that were not "official" but that still performed worthy functions in the interest of the United States—organizations such as Radio Free Europe (RFE), Radio Liberty (RL), the Asia Foundation, the International Commission of Free Trade Unions, some student organizations, and moderate publications of various sorts. Though none of these groups performed any covert intelligence work and some had private sources for part of their funds, the government monies for them were channeled secretly through the CIA. That CIA was the source of the funds was naturally kept confidential, though the appropriate committee chairmen in the Congress were kept informed. The 40 Committee kept close watch over their budgets and activities.

In the late 1960s a series of exposés came out revealing the CIA connections of these groups, and many in Congress joined the political bandwagon against such "nefarious" activities. We still considered their work very much in the national interest, however, and did not want them suddenly to collapse as all their government funding disappeared. The Johnson Administration sought other ways to provide them with government funds, and this work continued under Nixon when I was on the 40 Committee. Figuring out a budgetary home for these "CIA Orphans" required considerable work, especially with the Office of Management and Budget and the appropriate Hill committees. I testified frequently before the Senate Foreign Relations Committee and its perpetually hostile Chairman Fulbright in favor of a government-funded foundation to support RFE and RL. As a result, Congress agreed to establish the Board for International Broadcasting to oversee and act as a funding channel for those radio activities.

The excellent work of the Asia Foundation in book distribution, specialized educational exchange, and development assistance had received a good deal of government assistance through CIA, and a lot of work over many years had been necessary to keep it alive. Foreign countries raised hardly a murmur when its CIA connection was revealed; even such staunch neutrals as Afghanistan, Indonesia, India, and Cambodia's Prince Sihanouk expressed the hope that the Foundation's work would continue. They had assumed it received government funds all along; the department through which the money was supplied made no difference to them. I squeezed a little out of AID and the Department's Cultural Bureau, and combined with the redoubled fund-raising efforts of the Board of Trustees, the organization managed to find enough sustenance to stay alive. It is still being forced to try to continue as best it can this hand to mouth existence.

Few subjects gave more aggravation per square foot or consumed more of my time as Undersecretary than the little island of Malta that lies off the tip of Italy in the Mediterranean. All I knew about it when I took the job was that it had successfully held out as a British possession through World War II despite fearful bombing raids and heavy losses to the ships that kept it supplied. At the height of the war it was the key that kept the Mediterranean from becoming a German lake. It gained independence from Britain in 1964. With less than half the population and about twice the area of the District of Columbia, only its location gave it importance.

The President, returning from a trip to southern Europe early in 1971, asked Rogers, Laird, Tom Moorer, and me to listen to his report. He had visited Naples, where our ambassadors in the area and the commander of the Sixth Fleet had briefed him. Nixon had been particularly impressed by reports that Dom Mintoff, a left-leaning "neutralist," was likely to be elected Prime Minister of Malta, this "unsinkable aircraft carrier" in the Mediterranean, and would then proceed to expel Britain from the naval and air facilities it had retained on the island. He turned to me and said: "Alex, I want you to see that this doesn't happen. Also make sure the ambassador is changed."

As the President feared, after his election Mintoff's demands on the British began to escalate. The British themselves did not care much about retaining their military facilities on the island and were not inclined to pay Mintoff what he asked for. Because the facilities were assigned to NATO, however, we campaigned in NATO to raise some money, added some of our own, and enlisted Italy to seek moderation from Mintoff. In the meantime, the Soviet Union and Colonel Quadaffi of Libya were making bids for the facilities. Mintoff, erratic but very shrewd, always brought the crisis to a head just at Christmas, so that my 1971 and 1972 holidays were largely spent in the office on the phone trying to avert Britain's expulsion. The British thought Mintoff was bluffing and I agreed. I wanted to call the bluff, but the President did not want to take any chances, so we had to keep scraping up more money. By the beginning of 1972 I was able to tell the President that a career FSO in whom I had much confidence was going to be recommended to him as ambassador. He was John Getz, my Special Assistant, whom I sacrificed to the cause. As of this writing, the British have left Malta and Mintoff is still Prime Minister.

Ending the Vietnam War, of course, was a major preoccupation of the Nixon administration, which had come to Washington making it clear it wanted to end the American involvement but not clear at all about how that would be accomplished. A delicate course had to be charted among the requirements of popular and congressional opinion, the needs of our military forces, our long commitment to South Vietnam and its own desire to survive, and our reputation as a world power who supported our allies and kept our word. The secret negotiations Kissinger conducted with Le Duc Tho to establish the conditions of the "decent interval" largely bypassed me and the State Department, but because I served on WSAG, I participated in many of the stormy decisions along the route to complete American withdrawal—supporting Lao forces against the North Vietnamese advance in March 1970, the "Cambodian incursion" in April–May 1970, the mining of Haiphong just before the May 1972 Brezhnev summit, and our efforts to supply Saigon with sufficient equipment to fight on its own as we moved toward an armistice.

In June 1969, Nixon announced his decision to withdraw

some American forces, which surprised me. It was a decision in which I did not participate. I had opposed deploying our combat troops there in 1965, but having done so I thought taking them out would not convince Hanoi to be less belligerent. I know Rogers believed this would check the rising domestic pressures for total withdrawal. I feared that this was wrong; "feeding the crocodiles" would only whet their appetite. In August, Kissinger began his series of secret meetings with the North Vietnamese, about which I was not told anything. I would have had little to contribute in any case, because decisions were being made on domestic political grounds rather than the actual situation in Vietnam.

My personal involvement in Southeast Asia picked up in March 1970, however, when North Vietnamese troops, dropping all pretense of being native Pathet Lao rebels, mounted a serious offensive in Laos, the "back door" to Vietnam with which I had much familiarity. The North Vietnamese attacked in force and drove General Vang Pao's Meo guerrilla force out of the Plain of Jars back to its main base at Long Tieng, which seemed to be North Vietnam's objective. In the 40 Committee we debated whether to support Vang Pao in defending the base or encourage him to evacuate it and withdraw toward the Mekong lowlands. I was doubtful it could be defended, but Lao Prime Minister Souvanna Phouma and Thai Prime Minister Thanom were extremely anxious to make the effort. However, we worked out a program for deploying some Thai volunteers to reinforce Long Tieng. Despite my doubts the operation turned out to be successful.

Another back door to Vietnam was Cambodia. In March 1970, Sirik Matak (whom I had known when he was ambassador to Tokyo) and General Lon Nol mounted a successful coup against the government of Prince Sihanouk, who was away on a trip to Moscow. With more courage than judgment, Lon Nol and Matak set out to expel the approximately 40,000 North Vietnamese troops then in Cambodia. This development, in principle at least, encouraged us, but we were quite sure that the Cambodian forces were not equal to the task. We worried that they would bite off more than they could chew and then appeal for help from American forces. After Lon Nol's troops managed to close the port of Sihanoukville as a North Vietnamese supply point, the North Vietnamese did attack and Lon Nol appealed for our intervention. In WSAG we strained to find ways to help that would not involve all of Cambodia in hostilities that we feared would lead to Lon Nol's overthrow and a communist takeover of the whole country, and which would they could have put to good effect against Vietnam. We arranged to supply communist weapons captured in Vietnam to Lon Nol's forces, but it was not enough.

In WSAG we first worked at various programs for harassing North Vietnamese troops in Cambodian border areas, using air attacks and raids by South Vietnamese forces. For all practical purposes these border areas were under North Vietnamese occupation with no Cambodian inhabitants remaining. Their purpose was to support communist forces operating in South Vietnam, so actions against them were clearly in self-defense. I never had reservations about them. Neither Sihanouk nor Lon Nol ever objected as long as we did not face them with an issue of principle by publicly declaring they could not keep the North Vietnamese out of their territory. Despite our efforts, the North Vietnamese Army continued to augment its strength in Cambodia.

Our daily intelligence briefings always had a map displaying the location of "COSVN" (Central Office for South Vietnam, the Vietcong command center) which shifted around on the Cambodian side of the border. Although briefers stressed that it was not another Pentagon, the circle drawn on the map gave the impression of its being a large and important nerve center. In fact, it was no more than a dozen men with a few handcranked radios that could be easily carried or replaced. Nevertheless, unable to shake themselves of the American concept of a military headquarters and its key role, many in the Pentagon, White House, and even State were attracted to the idea of a lightning raid against COSVN by a well-equipped American force, which they thought would have devastating results for the NVA. More realistic thinking stressed the value of destroying the large supply caches in these sanctuary areas, and of relieving the NVA's pressure on Lon Nol.

We debated the pros and cons of an American assault against the communists' Cambodian sanctuaries in the WSAG during March and April. Nixon, Kissinger, Rogers, and Laird were doing the same. Rogers told me he opposed it primarily because he was concerned that American opinion would interpret it as widening the war, though in fact it was the NVA that had widened the war. Bill also had some skepticism that I shared about the military's claims about what they could achieve. But the decision was unequivocally the President's. Feeling beleaguered by domestic criticism, he hyped himself up by seeing the movie "Patton" three times in a week and announced the Cambodian incursion on national television the evening of April 30, with an emotional speech he wrote largely himself. Instead of describing the operation properly and soberly as a logical continuation of our efforts to get at the North Vietnamese Army wherever it was located, he presented it as a dramatic and courageous move and almost taunted his opponents to challenge him. It produced exactly the kind of over-reaction among domestic critics of the war he needed to prevent. Reason fled from both sides.

My responsibility had been to prepare the political scenario for briefing our allies and handling the UN and the North Atlantic Council in Brussels, as well as getting out the many telegrams and messages required to our embassies. After listening to the speech with Rogers at the Department, I went home and went to bed. At about two in the morning, an insistent telephone woke me from a deep sleep, and I groggily picked up the receiver. The caller's voice blasted out: "This is the President. I want you to make sure all those sons of bitches are fired first thing in the morning!" I had no idea what he was talking about, but it was definitely the President and I woke up fast. In the course of a twenty-minute tirade full of abuse and expletives, I gathered that the news tickers had reported that a group of Foreign Service Officers had signed a letter opposing the Cambodian action. My categorical instructions were to fire them by 8 A.M. I told him I would investigate, but since I was not sure what had happened I carefully avoided making any promises. Nixon was holding me, as the senior Foreign Service Officer, personally responsible instead of complaining to Rogers. According to press reports Nixon subsequently wandered around town all night, appearing at dawn on the steps of the Lincoln Memorial to deliver a homily to a few tourists present at that hour.

Early in the morning I called Rogers, who suggested I talk to Haldeman as soon as I pieced together the facts, which I was able to do by mid-morning. About fifty junior FSOs, none of whom had served in Southeast Asia, having heard rumors of the impending incursion, had addressed a protest letter to the Secretary. They were perfectly entitled to do this, as long as it remained private. But they naively xeroxed multiple copies to maximize the number of signatures, and inevitably copies reached the press. I did not want to see these officers fired, and I told Haldeman that I thought doing so would only fuel public distress about the incursion. He agreed, but would not substitute for me in telling that to the President. So Rogers and I went to see Nixon, who was still consumed with anger, and we managed to talk him out of immediately firing the lot. Instead he wanted all of their names by that evening.

I had no enthusiasm for this idea either, because I was sure the officers' careers would be ruined if the White House political mafia found out who they were. However, Secretary Rogers agreed to take my list, which he would lock in his own safe. At the same time I promised the President that I would keep an eye on all of them to make sure none were promoted or posted in Southeast Asia. Then I had a meeting with those I could identify as having signed the letter, not a happy occasion for any of us. Though I obviously disagreed with the content of the protest, I did not criticize them for that but only for their naiveté in thinking that a sensitive letter in multiple copies would stay private. I stressed the loyalty that we all owed the President, unless we chose to resign, and the harm they had done the Foreign Service in his eyes and those of the country. I did not reveal the President's initial reaction to their letter or what I had done to save their jobs. Emotions ran high, and some were bitter that I appeared to be taking the President's side.

Of course, having a "political" list of fifty officers who could not be promoted or posted to Southeast Asia was anathema of our personnel system and my own idea of the way the Service should work, but it was better than having them all fired. As it turned out, I never had to intervene to halt their promotions, and after Nixon left office their careers resumed their normal pace. I worked out a complex arrangement with Ellsworth Bunker to have some of them go to Southeast Asia. But Nixon never forgot. For a year afterwards he regularly asked me for written and oral reports on what was happening to them. I always answered, "We've got it all under control."

Between the self-defeating way Nixon handled the public relations and the self-imposed 30-kilometer limit on our Cambodian advance, the operation backfired badly. The congressional and public outcry was so severe that the administration was forced into announcing a premature date for terminating the operation. Even though the will-o'-the-wisp COSVN continued to operate just ahead of our forces, we did capture or destroy large quantities of military supplies and equipment before the NVA could withdraw them behind the 30-kilometer line. The North Vietnamese refused to give battle except at times and places of their own choosing, so their casualties were light and their gains were substantial.

The public turmoil and panic in Congress resulted in the Cooper-Church Amendment, prohibiting the United States from using military aid or troops to assist Cambodia. Beleaguered Lon Nol could not even have any American advisors. The McGovern-Hatfield Amendment, which called for the cutoff of all Defense Department spending in all Indochina, only lost by a narrow margin after a huge lobbying effort by the Administration. Hanoi could only conclude that persistence would ultimately exhaust the United States into quitting, just as it had with the French in 1954. In the public negotiations in Paris and in Henry's secret talks they stood pat on all their positions. Morale in South Vietnam consequently plummeted. Nixon compounded his difficulties by implying that we were withdrawing completely from Cambodia when, in fact, we were continuing to provide tactical air support and supplies for Cambodian forces. When this surfaced, as was inevitable, the credibility of his policy suffered badly.

Unfortunately for me, this period coincided with Elliot Richardson's departure in June 1970 to become Secretary of HEW. We had worked well together, and he had great skill in repairing the damage caused by some of Kissinger's more outrageous outbursts against Rogers and the Department. His absence meant that I got placed in the nutcracker more often, which added to the burdens of an already stressful job. Elliot's replacement was John Irwin, a prominent New York lawyer who had been the Assistant Secretary in defense for International Security Affairs (ISA) during the Eisenhower Administration. "Jack" Irwin was an equally fine person, but he never immersed himself in the turbulent seas between the White House and the Department with Elliot's enthusiasm.

The key to Nixon's strategy was building up South Vietnamese forces so they could survive in our absence, a process known as "Vietnamization." For this to have worked, we should have started it in the early 1960s instead of relying on American heft to compensate for every advance and South Vietnamese shortcoming. Building an army takes time, and time was now against us. So was the nature of the war, to which American doctrine and equipment had still not adapted. A conventional mechanized war on the plains of north central Europe had nothing to do with the resisting twenty-five-year veterans in the art of jungle fighting. The bankruptcy of hasty Vietnamization became painfully evident in February 1971, when a South Vietnamese force sought to interdict the Ho Chi Minh Trail by penetrating Laos from the northern part of South Vietnam. Previous congressional action denied this force American advisors or American ground controllers for American air support. The action was ill-conceived from the start. It required an unproven group of soldiers to strike at an objective that the enemy would defend stoutly in a region where it had superior logistics. I argued against the operation in the WSAG and Rogers argued against it with the President, but Nixon and Thieu ordered it, with the result I feared. The South Vietnamese forces were forced to withdraw with heavy losses after penetrating only a few miles, far short of their objective of Tchepone in Laos.

I visited Saigon in November 1971, as well as Phnom Penh, Vientiane, Bangkok, Tokyo, and Taipei. South Vietnam had made obvious progress, but I felt great anxiety about its future, which grew more uncertain with every act of Congress. Thieu had continued to mature politically and had a grip on events. At a dinner Ambassador Bunker hosted, attended by a large number of politicians representing divergent factions, I was struck by how completely they accepted the existing framework and wanted to work together within it. That was a vast change from 1964–65. I felt that the south could hold out, that Vietnamization had a chance, if we could only supply them military equipment and maintain air support after our ground troops left. But I was not able to be optimistic because many in the United States seemed determined to throw away all we and the South Vietnamese had been able to accomplish after long struggle. I had to give the same message to Lon Nol, who seemed to be faring about as usual despite North Vietnamese troops being a few miles from the end of Phnom Penh's runway. It disappointed me to have to say that Congress had tied our hands so that we could not help him no matter how well he did.

On February 4, 1972, I suffered a fairly severe heart attack that put me out of circulation until April. When I returned to work (minus three packs of cigarettes daily), South Vietnamese forces were no longer faring well against a strong North Vietnamese offensive. I resumed my usual duties including WSAG, where Vietnam was regularly discussed. So I was surprised and disappointed to learn from my television at home on Sunday evening, April 15, that the United States resumed bombing Hanoi and Haiphong. Not only were Nixon and Kissinger shooting from the hip, they were not bothering to consult or even inform the agencies in the government directly concerned. In spite of the supreme indignity of learning about it the same way I had, Secretary Rogers handled himself magnificently when he had to defend the decision before the Senate Foreign Relations Committee on Monday morning. We worried and the press speculated that Brezhnev would cancel Nixon's scheduled May 22 visit to Moscow, but the President's reading turned out to be correct. Peking and Moscow both reacted mildly. The bombing reinforced Nixon's "tough guy" image and possibly helped morale in the south, but had no effect on the fighting there.

A cryptic phone call awoke me at 6:45 A.M. on Sunday, May 7. It was Secretary Rogers in Bonn, on a trip to touch base with our allies before the Moscow summit. Jack Irwin was out of town and I was Acting Secretary. Rogers said he was immediately returning home and he hoped the statement he had just given the press would not be misinterpreted. He knew the keynote was supposed to be "low profile," but it was difficult to cancel his appointments in the various capitals and return to Washington without creating something of a stir. While I was still puzzling over what this was all about, I had a call that Henry Kissinger wanted to see me at 9:30 A.M.

He started by saying the President had been very unhappy about how much publicity Rogers' statement had received (the 8 A.M. radio news had carried a brief item about the sudden cancellation of the Secretary's trip). I pointed out it was hardly possible to hide such a thing, or to prevent speculation about it. Henry then proceeded to brief me on a plan for an immediate mining of Haiphong harbor, coupled with a heavy bombing campaign against overland traffic from China into North Vietnam. The object was to starve the North Vietnamese forces in the south of materiel. This idea had been around a long time. My first reaction was to tell him that whatever adverse political effects the mining might have, I very much doubted the Air Force's claims about what they could do to interdict overland supplies from China. In Korea and so far in Vietnam we had seen repeated examples of the impossibility of choking off supply lines with bombing. But even if the Air Force did achieve what it promised, I said, that would not affect the course of the current battle in the South, which depended on supplies long since stockpiled. Mining the harbor, which was full of Soviet and other non-Vietnamese ships, would also generate a storm of charges in the UN and elsewhere that we were violating international law. The prospect of having the summit cancelled also weighed heavily on me.

Henry said he agreed with me. He felt the chances of losing the summit were 95 to 5, while the President only rated it at 50 to 50. He said he had been trying to persuade the President against the mining, which he claimed was the brainchild of John Connally and John Mitchell, but to no avail. He said we would have to rely on Secretary Rogers to sway the President's mind at the NSC meeting scheduled for Monday morning. Laird could not do it because "he was always on every side of every problem." In case the President went ahead with the plan, however, he asked me to get lawyers from State and Defense working out a legal justification for the action, and for me to draft a scenario for all the other international political steps that we would have to take. I said I would have something ready to consider at the WSAG meeting scheduled for that evening, to which Henry agreed I could bring Bill Sullivan who had continued to work on Vietnamese matters.

I met Rogers at Andrews Air Force Base late that afternoon and briefed him on what I knew. He said he doubted that Kissinger really opposed the mining. After the WSAG meeting that evening, however, when I sensed that JCS Chairman Moorer had no great enthusiasm for the scheme, I talked privately to Henry again, and he confirmed that he opposed it. He acted depressed about the way the President was heading. He asked me whether I had told Rogers about our earlier conversation and asked me to relay that he hoped Rogers would speak up against the mining at the NSC meeting. Henry said he did not intend to himself because he did not want to oppose the President in an open meeting.

Rogers' hunch that Henry was only pretending to oppose the plan turned out to be right. Kissinger's memoir recounts in great detail, and I presume more or less correctly, how he had concluded that mining Haiphong was the right route and obtained Connally's support on Thursday, May 4; persuaded the President the same day; and had Moorer start the military planning. He also describes how he fought off doubts among his staff and opposition from Laird and CIA Director Helms. I can only speculate, of course, about why Henry misled me so blatantly during two extended conversations. Given his addiction to Machiavellian intrigue, perhaps he was trying to discredit Rogers further with the President by setting him up to attack a decision the President had already made. There were few things the President dreaded more than open confrontation. Rogers, however, eluded the trap. Kissinger's account of the NSC meeting states: "Rogers was ambiguous."

The NSC meeting was obviously a charade to front for the decision already made. In the meantime, with the help of Bill

Sullivan and John Stevenson, State's Legal Advisor, I prepared all the necessary messages to countries around the world announcing and providing a justification for the mining. This act differed fundamentally in character from anything we had done previously in Vietnam, since blockading a port with mines threatened the interests and safety of ships of all other nations. Done in the absence of a formal declaration of war, an act like this was at best in the twilight zone of international law. An essential part of these messages was the minimum time before the mines activated, so that vessels of other countries could leave Haiphong without risk of being sunk.

Shortly after lunch on May 8, Rogers was told that Nixon had approved the plan, and an hour later Kissinger called a WSAG meeting to review the military and political scenarios. All of the messages I had prepared for foreign chiefs of state, the UN Security Council, and individual countries, as well as the President's speech announcing the move, were based on my understanding from the WSAG meeting that the mines would not activate themselves for seventy-two hours after sowing. I stressed the importance of accuracy on this point, for we did not want to have ships being blown up in the period we described as safe. Tom Moorer had his aide call the Navy to get this point absolutely confirmed, but he returned with the answer that seventy-two hours "was only an average"; some would arm themselves before and some after. This, of course, produced consternation. After some more checking, fifty-eight hours turned out to be the best estimate of the minimum safe period. We set about changing all the messages that were already being processed.

The President's speech was sober, avoiding the supercharged histrionics of the Cambodia speech. Even so, public and congressional reaction was predictably outraged. Henry phoned me the morning following the speech with his customary tirade against the Department for leaks revealing the inside story of how the government made the decision, but in fact the Department held together very well. At a meeting of senior employees the Secretary gave the rationale for the mining and effectively appealed for support for the President. Although Henry denied to me that he had even seen the correspondent whose story had contained the most revealing details, I learned for a fact that they had had lunch together just before the story appeared. Henry, like most geniuses, has spectacular talents but corresponding faults. He was amazingly successful juggling a profusion of balls while pirouetting atop a highwire. When some of the balls dropped, however, it was obvious that devotion to truth was not always his guiding principle. Perhaps someone who achieves so much may be exempted from normal moral standards, but in the long run, I feel that the confidence of other countries, their belief that we mean what we say, is the only sound basis for foreign policy.

As I expected, the entire blockade and air campaign never had the slightest effect on the NVA offensive in the south. By August 21, when I discussed with Henry the Paris-Saigon-Tokyo trip from which he had just returned, the north was using heavy ammunition, rockets, and mortars at the greatest rate of the entire war. No shortage of supplies was evident. They were receiving shipments from China by truck, by coastal steamers unloading on the beaches, and by "lighters" that took goods from larger ships into docks at ports besides Haiphong. Air power, particularly the high-speed jets we were using, just could not do the job required. The President's hunch about the Soviets turned out to be right; however, they contented themselves with a mild protest and carried on with the summit. What incentive the mining may have provided for the north to be more forthcoming in Paris I cannot say. However, it certainly did not produce any quick agreement.

In October 1972 it appeared that Hanoi might be willing to move towards some sort of agreement, perhaps because they thought that Nixon would win the election and would have the greatest incentive to make concessions beforehand. At Henry's request, with Bill Sullivan, Walt Cutler from Sullivan's staff, and George Carver from the CIA, I worked out a proposal for a cease-fire in place, including supervisory machinery, that Henry could table if appropriate. During the Korean Armistice negotiations and the 1954 Geneva Conference on Indochina, the United States always resisted a cease-fire in place, which is extremely difficult to guard against violations. But there we had a position on the battlefield that permitted us to hold out for better terms. We could not obtain on paper for Vietnam what we had not been able to win in battle. So the task was to make the best of an inherently bad situation.

Despite the drawbacks of an in-place cease-fire, we thought that what we had drawn up might have some chance of working, because the South Vietnamese Army had succeeded in obtaining control of most of the countryside. With the election near, however, I feared that the President and Henry were becoming so anxious to get an agreement that it was beginning to influence their judgment. But Al Haig, who was Henry's principal assistant and deputy, shared the desire of Bill Sullivan and me to do all that could be done to tighten up the inevitable loopholes, and he was very skilled in dealing with Henry. As it turned out, some of what we had drawn up survived into the final agreement, only to be promptly ignored by the north.

Henry returned to Paris October 8, and by October 12 it looked as if a settlement might be imminent. We thus undertook a major effort to increase South Vietnam's supply of equipment in anticipation of a moratorium on further increases when the agreement came into effect. My role in this became to persuade our Ambassadors in some of the countries to which we had supplied F-5 fighter aircraft to relinquish them to Vietnam immediately, in exchange for replacements eventually to be supplied by us. Taiwan, Iran, and Korea were the prime candidates. Chiang Ching-kuo, the Taiwan leader, was very forthcoming, as was the Shah of Iran. Korea dragged its feet, and in Japan, peace protesters for a time blocked the road leading from our main Army depot to prevent the departure of tanks we were seeking to ship to South Vietnam. However, the Japanese government handled the situation very effectively.

Having worked out a deal with the north, Henry went to Saigon on October 19, and on October 26 he made his "peace is at hand" press conference statement. However, the "chemistry" between Thieu and Henry was not good. Thieu flatly refused to accept some of the points already agreed to, and Henry was finally forced into the position of agreeing to reopen negotiations with the north. It was a good demonstration of our propensity often to pay more attention to our enemies than to our friends. However, the north showed little disposition to agree to what was required to obtain Thieu's acquiescence. It was only after the "Christmas bombing" of the north and Al Haig's skillful twisting of Thieu's arm, as well as the President's assurances that we would react to violations of the agreement by the north, that the agreement was finally initialled on January 23. Poignantly, Lyndon Johnson had died the previous day.

Of course, in a series of actions Congress promptly vitiated any threat that we would react against the north in the event they violated the agreement, thus removing whatever incentive they had for its observance. This, together with Congress's message to the south that they could not expect any more military supplies from us no matter how well they did, inevitably and surely set the stage for the debacle of 1975 that "liberated" the south from the best government it had had, then turned it over tó the tender mercies of the north. The hapless people of Cambodia were also turned over to the knives of Pol Pot's executioners.

Just before Christmas 1972, when I was about to leave the Department to head our SALT delegation, Vietnam presented me with one final task to perform. I was out playing golf the Saturday afternoon before a Monday Christmas when I received a call from our Operations Center. The news tickers were reporting that Swedish Prime Minister Olof Palme had made a statement comparing the United States in Vietnam to the Nazis in Germany. The President and Kissinger were in Key Biscayne and the Secretary was in the Bahamas, so as Acting Secretary I had to take on this unpleasant situation. Outraged, I asked the Op Center to get the Swedish Ambassador, my long-time good friend Hubert de Besche, down to the Department immediately. I would be waiting for him.

I told de Besche that I found the statement attributed to Palme entirely unacceptable. In my recollection such an offensively hostile remark was unprecedented for the head of a government that professed neutrality and desired to maintain diplomatic relations with us. I told him that the Chargé of our Stockholm Embassy, who happened to be in the United States, would not return for the time being, and though we had given *agrément* for de Besche's successor to replace him in January, I did not feel that it would be useful for him to come. I regretted having to be so harsh with an ambassador I liked so well personally, especially during his last week in Washington; but the fact that I had, coupled with my Swedish ancestry, which was well-known to the Swedish government, gave my words extra force.

I called Key Biscayne to report what I had done and heard promptly that the President was very pleased with my actions. On Sunday de Besche called me to say that Palme had been misquoted, but he did not disavow the basic sentiment or apologize for the misunderstanding.

A message from our embassy in Stockholm reported that the Swedish foreign office was extremely distressed at the severity of our response, which was just the reaction I was seeking. I felt it was high time they did a little worrying about keeping up their side of our relations. Throughout the war I had found the Swedes, and especially Palme, very difficult to understand. They always seemed to go out of their way to attribute to the North Vietnamese, who were far removed from Sweden's concerns and knowledge, the highest possible motives, and to us the worst.

Another issue that remained to be resolved was the future of Okinawa, the biggest potential problem in Japanese-American relations. Despite my responsibilities on the 40 Committee and WSAG, this problem was my own top priority when I returned to the seventh floor in 1969. I felt it was important to maintain the momentum established when I was Ambassador to Tokyo by the Johnson-Sato communiqué of November 1967 and subsequent measures. In that communiqué the United States had modified its long-standing rigid view that our military rule over Okinawa could not be changed until the "security situation in the Far East permitted"; henceforth, the island's status was to be kept under "joint and continuous review" by the two governments. The United States-Japan-Okinawa Advisory Committee, established by the communiqué to recommend measures that would minimize the dislocation of reversion, had been proceeding steadily with its work. A new administration provided an opportunity for further progress.

From my conversation with Nixon when he visited Tokyo in 1967, I was satisfied that his instinct about reversion would be favorable as long as he thought it was politically feasible. So timing was important—time for our military to accustom itself to the idea, and time for the Japanese to think through their own security needs fully enough to agree to the concessions that would enable us to maintain security in the Far East without the liberties we had previously enjoyed on Okinawa.

The basket of basic issues remained the same. Under American administration we were able to store nuclear weapons on Okinawa and deploy our forces from our bases there without consulting the Japanese government. This was not true of our bases on Japan proper, which came under the 1960 Security Treaty and had considerable value, particularly in deterring aggression from China or North Korea. But the Japanese felt deeply that Okinawa, including the bases, should return to their administration, and Prime Minister Sato had staked his political future on being able to arrange it. A small militant minority was able to organize demonstrations against American rule on the island and in Japan with mounting intensity, and while these militants were not too worrisome at present, I never wanted to see them bring about a situation in which American troops had to fire on demonstrating Okinawans to prevent them from entering an important base facility.

Reversion was obviously the right thing to do for the larger interests of our two countries. Any "freedoms" we had on paper would be entirely theoretical in the face of a hostile population. The question was how best to do it so that our bases on Okinawa would retain maximum effectiveness, so that Japanese public and government would be prompted to review their entire relationship with us and realize how much our bases on Okinawa and Japan contributed to their security, and so that the whole process would foster mutual regard and good relations instead of confrontation. The only approach that appeared possible was to bring Okinawa under the 1960 Security Treaty the same as the rest of Japan, but both sides had to resolve to what extent the United States could and should retain "free use" and nuclear storage rights after reversion.

In the flurry of activity Kissinger generated in the bureaucracy following the inauguration, one study examined our relations with Japan. Dick Sneider, still Country Director, ably represented the Department and assured that the final report contained language from which we could move toward reversion. I also talked to Kissinger and Rogers myself, and when my old friend Marshall Green became Assistant Secretary for East Asian and Pacific Affairs, I was quite sure my flanks were guarded. The next step was to get Defense moving along the same path. Secretary Laird did not seem to have much personal interest in the subject, so I worked with Dave Packard, who took his usual cooperative attitude. I also resumed my private talks with JCS Chairman Wheeler and the other concerned Chiefs, having already made sure that their subordinates in the field, Admiral McCain at CINCPAC and General Lampert, the new High Commissioner of the Ryukyus, would basically support the line I took.

Admiral McCain visited Washington in March and once more I had a thorough talk with him. On April 11 I had a long meeting with the Chiefs where I reviewed the entire range of political and military questions involved. While they did not disagree about the necessity of reversion and seemed to recognize that this would impose some new constraints on our freedom of use and nuclear storage rights, Wheeler nevertheless reiterated that they wanted to retain full freedom of use. I countered that it was an illusion to think we would have any freedom of action whatever, on Japan or Okinawa, if the local population was hostile to us no matter what "fine print" was included in our agreements.

Foreign Minister Aichi was due in Washington at the end of May for the stated purpose of discussing Okinawa. Armin Meyer, formerly Ambassador to Iran, was about to depart as Ambassador to Japan. The time to move the government to some decisions was clearly at hand. Just before Aichi arrived the NSC staff prepared and the President signed a "Decision Memorandum" that stated he was prepared to agree to Okinawa's reversion to Japanese control by 1972 if a satisfactory understanding could be worked out in 1969 on the essential elements the agreement would contain, and if detailed negotiations could be finished by 1972. If everything else could be settled satisfactorily, the document said the President would be willing to concede about withdrawing our nuclear weapons. This was consistent with the conversation I had with Secretary McNamara in 1967, when he said that automatic storage rights on Okinawa were not essential to our military capabilities.

If Okinawa came under the provisions of the Security Treaty we could always reintroduce nuclear weapons there in times of crisis with the Japanese government's agreement. Because the negotiations were going to be long and complex, however, I thought it essential to reserve this decision for the President to make in the final stages. But even at this stage in the administration, security was such that a story appeared in *The New York Times* two days later reporting that we were willing to withdraw our nuclear weapons. The only way to counter it was to state the fact that the President had not yet made a decision.

Aichi arrived for his four-day visit, proclaiming 1969 as the "year of Okinawa." He was a pleasure to work with: honest, straightforward, a close confidant and ally of Sato who obviously spoke for the Prime Minister and government. The point we stressed to him was that the United States needed the capacity to defend Japan and East Asia both in reality and appearance, and that the terms of Okinawa's reversion could not detract from this. Aichi understood our point of view and also recognized Japan's interest in an effective American military presence in East Asia. He also wanted reversion as quickly as possible, however, and stressed that Sato hoped to visit Washington no later than November and then announce a date for reversion. Rogers and Aichi agreed to establish a joint United States-Japanese working group in Tokyo to see whether sufficient agreement could be reached by November to permit announcing a date. I suggested that the Working Group employ my favorite negotiating tactic, focusing on the communiqué to be issued at the end of the Nixon-Sato Summit, and this was also agreed on. Aichi and Ambassador Meyer were to be the principal negotiators. Dick Sneider, steeped for many years in United States-Japan relations at State and the NSC, went to Tokyo as Meyer's assistant for the talks.

Meyer and Sneider proved to be an excellent team. An interdepartmental working group in Washington chaired by Marshall Green with representatives from Defense, Treasury, and the Bureau of the Budget handled the many technical questions arising out of Tokyo, so I was able to decrease my day-to-day involvement. Some issues still came up, however, that required me to pick up the phone to Packard, Secretary of the Treasury David Kennedy, or his assistant Tony Jurich, or JCS Chairman Wheeler, or his successor Tom Moorer.

Although the details would have to be worked out later, the financial issues turned out to be particularly complex and difficult. We thought the Japanese should compensate us for the extensive public works we would leave behind on Okinawa, most of which served the civilian population as well as our bases. We also thought Japan should absorb the cost of relocating our military units and facilities in order to make room for the Japanese units that would be deployed for the immediate defense of the islands. Most importantly, given our balance of payments problems, we did not want the Japanese government to end up with a balance of payments windfall as it paid out yen in return for the dollars the island's economy now used. At the same time, however, we realized that Japan could not appear to be "buying back" Okinawa.

The military negotiations centered on whether we would retain free use of the bases after reversion as the JCS desired. Secretary Rogers termed it the "reality and appearance" question: would potential aggressors in the area believe that American forces on Okinawa had sufficient freedom to retaliate against attacks, particularly those against South Korea and Taiwan, to deter such attacks? If deterrence failed, would they actually have such freedom to retaliate? We recognized that Japan could not possibly agree to any conditions that would permit us to involve its territory and people in a war without its approval. But we also wanted the Japanese to recognize that there was no purpose in our maintaining forces on Okinawa if Japan paralyzed them in time of emergency. Whatever formula we developed had to respect Japanese sovereignty and closely follow the "prior consultation" clause in the 1960 Security Treaty, which neither side wished to amend. Threading a path through this delicate area required considerable ingenuity.

The summit imposed pressure on Japan to make progress, and deliberately we did nothing to relieve it. In September Aichi returned to Washington, as did Meyer and Sneider, to see if some way might be found to break the logjam before Sato's upcoming visit. Two late-starting issues had arisen, on top of the financial and military questions: what would happen to the sizeable Voice of America transmitters on the island (which Japan wanted removed and we insisted on maintaining); and what would happen to American business enterprises after reversion. The existing regulations governing their operations differed considerably from what they would face when Japanese law came into force. Neither side showed much inclination to give, and our meetings were somber. The only event that picked up Aichi's spirits was his chip shot into the cup for a birdie on the seventh hole at Burning Tree during the golf game Secretary Rogers hosted for him.

Even so, we were making sufficient progress to alarm the JCS. They urged that the whole process be dragged out longer, as if five years from our initial moves in 1967 to the expected finish in 1972 was not long enough. No one else in Washington supported them. Procrastinating on Okinawa would likely bring down the Sato government, unleash virulent anti-American sentiment in Japan and call into question the continuance of the Security Treaty after 1970. As I told the JCS, it was not possible to maintain the status quo on Okinawa eternally; events in Okinawa and Japan were already changing it. The question was whether it would change in a way that favored or harmed our interests. At the same time, I too wanted to bargain hard to make sure we secured satisfactory terms, both before the summit and in the detailed negotiations leading up to 1972.

As the summit approached, work intensified in both capitals. Ambassador Shimoda had frequent private meetings with me to find acceptable formulas for free use and nuclear weapons. In good Japanese fashion Sato dispatched a "secret" emissary to Kissinger to act as a "nakadachi" or "go-between" with the President. The Japanese knew this would appeal both to Kissinger's love of the conspiratorial and Nixon's dread of face-to-face confrontation. Fortunately, Henry told me about it, just as Walt Rostow had told me about a similar gambit by Sato before his summit with President Johnson. Between us we worked out replies that reinforced what I was telling Shimoda and Meyer was telling Aichi.

By October the JCS had reconciled itself to the inevitability of reversion and the consequent need to remove nuclear weapons from Okinawa. So our bargaining with the Japanese focused on granting us maximum freedom of use consistent with Japanese sovereignty—the core subject on which I had concentrated ever since my first discussion with Foreign Minister Miki at the Hotel

New Otani in July 1967. We did not want to force free use conditions on Japan that it would resent and seek to vitiate in practice. We made clear that whatever formula they agreed to had to flow from their own conviction that an effective American military presence in East Asia was vital to their security.

Working in both Washington and Tokyo we finally agreed on a tolerable arrangement. Finding a way to express that arrangement was crucial to agreeing on it. The formula came in two stages. First was the joint communiqué between the two countries, in which we both agreed that Okinawa, after reversion, would come under the Security Treaty the same as any other part of Japan. That meant no nuclear weapons, and no direct operations against targets outside of Japan, without prior consultation with the Japanese government. The second stage was a speech to be given by Sato at the time of his Washington visit, asserting that the Japanese government would in practice respond favorably to American requests to use bases in both Japan and Okinawa in the event of communist aggression against Korea or Taiwan.

In the two weeks before Sato's arrival on November 17 there was the usual flurry of crises, big and small, and the phones between Washington and Tokyo received heavy use. Though Okinawa was the most important issue, several other problems had to be moved along if the summit was to succeed. One of the most politically charged concerned Japanese textile imports to the United States, which will be treated in detail later in this chapter. It was an extremely volatile situation, exacerbated by clumsy handling on both sides, and I worried constantly that it might suddenly ignite in a way that would jeopardize the rest of the summit. Another worry concerned the Joint Chiefs, who, in the concern over leaks to the Congress, had not been told about the President's decision to concede eventually on nuclear weapons storage. However, the Pentagon and the Armed Services Committees on the Hill might kick up a real storm if we sprung this on them without warning. I was also concerned about my own reputation with the Pentagon, especially Packard and the JCS. But Henry said he would take care of it; he would tell Wheeler to "pipe down" and Laird to "keep quiet." Whatever he said to them, they never raised any fuss.

Another worry was induced by a call from the President shortly before Sato arrived. To pep me up, or to have someone to blame if things went wrong, Nixon reported that he had just told a prominent White House visitor that I was "handling everything" on Japan. I was just in the process of signing the briefing memorandum for the President, and told him that I felt everything was in hand.

Sato first met with Nixon on November 19. Afterwards and again on November 20, Armin Meyer, Dick Sneider, and I had long sessions with Foreign Minister Aichi, Vice Minister Togo, and Ambassador Shimoda to work out the last details on the final Nixon-Sato meeting, the text of the communiqué, and the delivery of the Prime Minister's speech before the National Press Club on November 21.

The communiqué, the centerpiece of our long negotiations, contained a statement by the Japanese government, very forward-looking at the time, recognizing that its security was directly linked to our ability to carry out defense obligations to other countries in the Far East, for which we needed our Japanese bases. Japan stated flatly for the first time that it recognized the security of South Korea was "essential" to its own. Sato's speech at the Press Club elaborated on that statement. If the United States should ever need to use its Japanese bases to meet an armed attack on Korea, Sato said, the Japanese government "would decide its position positively and promptly." As for Taiwan, the communiqué said that its security was "a most important factor" in Japan's security, and that Japan would take a positive attitude toward letting us use our bases if Taiwan was attacked. The United States never confirms nor denies the location of its nuclear weapons, but the communiqué implied that following reversion the United States would not store nuclear weapons on Okinawa without the Japanese government's agreement. Finally, both sides said they planned to continue the Security Treaty indefinitely. All in all, it was a very satisfactory package.

I gave an extensive background briefing to the press at the White House after the communiqué was issued on November 21. I told them that while this two-stage package of a communiqué and a speech was unusual, it was more appropriate that the Prime Minister make certain statements on his own rather than in a joint declaration with the President. Nevertheless, what he intended to say in his speech (which had been the subject of long negotiation) had influenced the language we were prepared to accept in the communiqué. I also explained that while the communiqué envisioned reversion by 1972, the technical negotiations would be long and complex and I did not expect them to be finished until well into 1971. Within two days the entire text of my background briefing appeared in the newspaper of the Japanese Socialist Party. But I had given careful thought to what I said and was not required to explain or withdraw a single word despite the sensitive nature of the subjects discussed.

Both sides felt we had witnessed an historic moment in Japanese-American relations. I told the press that it was the most important development since the 1951 Peace Treaty, and as President Nixon said, it turned a page in our relations from the postwar era to a new era. In the process of returning Okinawa to Japanese administration, a move potentially divisive to United States-Japanese relations and harmful to our defense capabilities in the Far East, we had actually enhanced our relations and the security of both countries. Japan was more of an equal partner than it had ever been, aware of the responsibilities attendant to its strategic position as well as the benefits. Japan was going to regain Okinawa, and we had Japan on record about the conditions under which it would approve our taking action from our Japanese bases to maintain regional security. Together our two countries had shown that diplomacy does not always require one party to lose for the other's gain.

The agreement embodied in the November 1969 communiqué carried the important proviso that it was "subject to the conclusion of specific arrangements with necessary legislative support." This required eighteen months of intensive work, primarily centered in Tokyo with our Ambassador Armin Meyer and Foreign Minister Aichi, with a task force chaired by Richard Sneider on the Embassy side and with Vice Minister Fumihiko Togo and North American Bureau Chief Bunroku Yoshino on the Japanese side. On Okinawa itself preparations were handled by a Preparatory Commission chaired by the United States High Commissioner, General James Lampert, with the support of our last Civil Administrator, Robert Fearey, and on the Japanese side Jiro Takase, a Special Ambassador.

However, reaching agreement in 1969 enabled Prime Minister Sato and his party to win an election overwhelmingly in early 1970 and to prevent opposition parties from bringing about a situation in which they could try to abrogate the 1960 Security Treaty, which was subject to renunciation for the first time in 1970.

The detailed negotiations to implement the agreement on Okinawa were virtually without precedent. I do not know of any case in which an area with over one million people and a sophisticated economy has peacefully been transferred in an orderly manner from one sovereignty to another. It involved virtually every aspect of civilian life—banking, currency, customs, public utilities, police, courts, laws, prisoners, schools, civil aviation, public lands, postal service, the Voice of America broadcast facilities—and, on the military side, what American facilities would be turned over to the Japanese Self-Defense Forces to enable them to carry out their responsibilities and which would be retained by the American forces.

All of this required detailed negotiations with virtually every ministry of the Japanese Government, which, like ministries everywhere, were vigilant in guarding what they felt were their interests, as were many departments and agencies on the American side. On our side the financial settlement was worked out so that a considerable portion of the funds received from Japan could be used to fund a United States-Japan Friendship Commission, which was established by the Congress to promote cultural exchange between the two countries.

This complex document as finally approved was simultaneously signed on June 17, 1971, by Secretary of State Rogers in Washington and Foreign Minister Aichi in Tokyo in a unique and historic two-way television hook-up, so that they and the other participants could see and talk with each other. Because of the time difference this took place early in the morning in Washington and late in the evening in Tokyo. Thus the ceremony not only marked a new phase in United States-Japan relations, but also a new step in applying modern technology to diplomacy.

With strong and effective support from Bill Fulbright and Mike Mansfield in the Foreign Relations Committee, which along with the Armed Services Committee had been kept fully informed throughout the negotiations, the Senate gave its approval to ratification by an 84 to 6 vote on November 10, 1971. In spite of opposition efforts to block action, the Japanese Diet gave its approval shortly thereafter, ratifications were exchanged on March 15, and at midnight on May 14, 1972, the United States High Commissioner, James Lampert, formally departed from Okinawa. His assignment for the past two years had been an unusual one for a United States Army Officer, and the grace, understanding, and dignity with which he carried it out reflected high credit on him and the United States.

Although the major question of Okinawa was handled to the mutual satisfaction of both Japan and the United States and became a positive factor in their relations, the relatively minor issue of limiting Japanese exports of wool and man-made textiles to the United States was, through gross mismanagement on both sides, to bedevil relations between the two countries for more than two years.

To begin with, the issue was overwhelmingly more political than economic in both countries. However, instead of handling the matter as a political issue, both governments permitted themselves to become pliant tools of the confrontation tactics of their industries. The American side bears much of the blame for this, but the Japanese all too readily fell into the pattern.

The story starts with a promise candidate Nixon made, while pursuing his "Southern Strategy" during the campaign, to "do something" about the presumed damage the southern textile industry was suffering from Japanese competition in wool and man-made textiles. (Cotton textiles had already been covered for some time by a multinational agreement.) It was politically important that Nixon be able to show some results prior to the next election in 1972.

Stanley Nehmer, the textile expert in the Commerce Department, persuaded the new Secretary of Commerce, Maurice Stans, that the way to handle the matter was to keep the "softies" in the State Department and the Special Trade Representative's White House office out of the subject, and that he, Stans, together with Nehmer, should go out to Japan, "lay down the law" to the Japanese, and in good World War II fashion, demand their immediate and "unconditional surrender" on the issue. While Nehmer was technically very competent in the area of textiles, he was already notorious throughout much of the world for his ability to insult those with whom he was "negotiating." He was also well known for his inability to look beyond whatever the textile industry demanded.

The outcome of Stans' trip was inevitable. Far from achieving any settlement, he was simply successful in incurring the resentment and hostility of the Japanese industry and bureaucracy. This increased the difficulty for Prime Minister Sato in bringing them along on a settlement that would help satisfy Nixon's requirements.

There ensued almost two more years of secret emissaries, both Japanese and American, carrying proposals and counter proposals. This period featured the Chairman of the House Ways and Means Committee negotiating an agreement of his own with the Japanese; Sato changing his MITI minister in a desperate and unsuccessful effect to handle his own bureaucracy; the American industry refusing to consider anything less than 105 percent of their original demands; Americans threatening to invoke our

"Trading with the Enemy Act" of 1917 to obtain unilateral quotas against Japanese textiles; the stunning shock in July of Nixon's announced plan to visit Peking without any advance warning to Japan; and the Japanese industry refusing to go even a little way in meeting Sato's and Nixon's political requirements until former Secretary of the Treasury, David Kennedy, with the help of his assistant Tony Jurich, bludgeoned Japan into an agreement in October 1971 by playing agreements with Hong Kong, Taiwan, and Korea off against them. In fact, a whole book has been written on this period.*

Throughout the negotiations the American industry flatly refused Japanese requests for data to justify the claim of "injury" as defined by the General Agreement on Tariffs and Trade, to which both Japan and the United States were parties.

My role during this period was intermittent and primarily involved the "secret" emissary that Sato used for communication with the President through Henry Kissinger.

Prior to Sato's arrival in November 1969, this emissary was used to inform the President that although Sato did not want any specific reference in their communiqué to textiles in order to avoid charges he had "traded textiles for Okinawa," he would move to achieve what Nixon wanted in negotiations at Geneva being carried on in the GATT framework. At the time of his visit this was again indirectly reaffirmed to the President, and Sato gave him to understand that in order to carry this out I should take a hard line on the subject with Ambassador Shimoda, so that this could be circulated through the Japanese bureaucracy. Shimoda would take a hard line back with me, but in due course their position at Geneva would be modified. This sounded reasonable to me, since I knew that Shimoda was close to Sato.

Therefore, immediately after the visit I called in Shimoda for a private talk, to play my part in this charade. He promised carefully to report my remarks, and in a few days he came back with virtually a flat rejection from the Ministry of International Trade and Industry (MITI). This seemed to be within the scenario that Sato desired to have us play for the benefit of his bureaucracy, so I gave him an equally hard line in reply. However, when December passed and by January there were no signs of any movement in Geneva, I decided something was wrong, and that Shimoda and I were probably not playing from the same sheet

---

The Textile Wrangle, I. M. Destler, Haruhiro Fukui and Hideo Sato, Cornell University Press.

of music. Knowing him as well as I did, and having complete confidence in him, I outlined the plan that Sato had passed on to the President. When he professed complete ignorance of the whole thing, I urged him to be sure to bring the situation to Sato's attention in some way. Henry suggested the same to Sato's "secret" emissary, but this produced no results. It was obvious that Sato was in the embarrassing position of not being able to deliver his MITI minister and the Japanese textile industry.

When in the summer of 1970 Sato replaced his MITI minister with Kiichi Miyazawa, whom I knew well, and asked for a meeting with Stans in June, our hopes were again raised that there might be some movement. Stans invited me to sit in on the meetings, but the only movement was a regression in the Japanese position. I confirmed this in a private meeting with Miyazawa.

Then in the fall of 1970, when Sato came to the United States for the United Nations anniversary meeting, he sent ahead a new emissary to Kissinger with the message that he was now really determined to settle the textile issue once and for all. He repeated this in person to the President and to Henry, but again nothing happened.

I could understand his inability to deliver on his first promise to Nixon, but I was never able to understand why he made this second commitment without being sure he could deliver. I always wanted to ask him this after he left office, but unhappily he passed away before there was an opportunity for me to do so. I have asked the question of many Japanese familiar with the negotiations, but have never received an informed answer. I did not and do not now question Sato's sincerity. The fact of the matter was that the political problem he faced was probably even more intense than that faced by Nixon.

As Phil Trezise, our Assistant Secretary for Economic Affairs in State, used to insist to me, the stupidity of the positions of the industries on both sides and the non-substance of the problem was illustrated by the fact that after so much "blood had flowed," the Japanese never even filled most of the quotas provided under the agreement Kennedy eventually negotiated.

In addition to these politically contentious disputes over textile imports, other aspects of economic relations with Japan were strained in the early 1970s. Both countries tended to be several steps behind in aligning their policies to a fast-changing reality, and both seemed to be letting themselves be pushed around by specialized interest groups while the many other diverse economic interests remained unheard. Starting at the end of 1969 I sought to put together a free-standing private advisory council to the government on United States-Japanese economic relations—one that could take the broadest possible perspective on the subject, and on a private level deal with Japanese counterpart organizations. No existing body, I thought, could perform this task. The United States Chamber of Commerce was too narrow in its membership and interests, excluding the growing sector of our agricultural exports, and other business councils interested in Japan were too specialized by commodity or region.

My efforts switched on several buzz saws, especially the Chamber of Commerce, the Department of Commerce, and the Department of Agriculture, who all felt their oxen were being gored. State was unfairly moving in on "their turf." I sidestepped this complaint by labelling the council I sought to establish as advisory to the Joint United States-Japan Cabinet Committee on Trade and Economic Affairs, which the Secretary of State chaired on the American side. After many meetings inside and outside the government, the Advisory Council was formally established on April 8, 1971. Najeeb Halaby, President of PanAm; David Rockefeller; Carl Gerstacker; and George McGhee, President of the Business Council for International Understanding, all strongly backed the group, and its other members included the heads of all major American companies having interest in United States-Japanese economic relations.

A Japanese counterpart group was established under the leadership of Fuji Bank President Iwasa, and an active exchange greatly contributed to the quality of discussion at the Cabinet Committee meetings that fall. In recent years the Cabinet Committee has tended to become moribund, but the two Advisory Councils continue to be active and productive.

As Kissinger's relationship with Nixon grew more confident and his ascendancy in the foreign policy area more established, his scorn for the Department of State became more obvious. From the start Nixon and Kissinger had excluded Secretary Rogers from most conversations with foreign visitors and had relied on foreign interpreters rather than use any from State. Every embassy in Washington got the message that matters of importance had to go through Kissinger. The Soviet Ambassador was given free and immediate access to the White House at all times, and if he chanced to have a conversation with Secretary Rogers, Kissinger let him know that Rogers did not necessarily represent the President's views and should be ignored. Henry sought to humiliate

Rogers further by having subordinates on the NSC staff call him with what they said were instructions from the President. Rogers put a quick stop to this, but then Henry found ways of passing messages through Elliot Richardson, me, or someone else in the Department.

Jacob Beam, our Ambassador in Moscow, was rendered entirely impotent by being kept ignorant of Henry's dealings with the Kremlin. Henry plotted with the Soviets so that neither Rogers nor Beam knew about his trip to Moscow in April 1972. Beam did not even know that Kissinger was in Moscow. No more diabolical plot to discredit the President's Ambassador or his Secretary of State could have been conceived.

Henry's passion for secrecy, combined with his contempt for the Department and disdain for the Japanese, threw a devastating wrench into our relations with Japan on the question of China. Few thoughts aroused more trepidation in the Japanese government over the years than the possibility that the United States would suddenly reverse its policy toward Peking, leaving Tokyo, which had loyally kept Peking at arm's length despite many reasons not to, red-facedly bobbing in our wake. Asakai, one of the first Japanese Ambassadors to Washington and a very competent diplomat, once said he had had a dream that we abruptly switched policy toward Peking without even informing Japan, and this scenario became known in the Japanese Foreign Office as the "Asakai Nightmare." Given the extraordinarily strong relations of trust and confidence that we had carefully built up with the Foreign Office, however, I and everyone else involved in American policy toward Asia scoffed at the nightmare and assured them that such a thing would be impossible. They accepted our assurances at face value.

Late in the evening of July 14, 1971, I received a call from Al Haig at San Clemente. My presence there was desired immediately, though he gave no hint of the reason and asked me to say nothing to Rogers, who was already there with the President. A White House plane would be waiting for me at Andrews in a few hours. I was intrigued, but I was not unaccustomed to such cryptic instructions, so I calmly dressed and got ready to catch the plane. Within the hour, however, Al called again and said the signals had been switched; now I should take a flight leaving the following afternoon.

When I arrived at the El Toro base near San Clemente the following afternoon, I was told I would have to take a car to San Clemente because all the helicopters were tied up taking the

President and a large party into Los Angeles. Winston Lord, one of Henry's principal assistants, was at the motel near the Western White House when I arrived. He told me that the President would shortly announce the startling news that he was going to visit Peking. My first thought was the Asakai Nightmare. I asked what steps had been taken to notify Japan and other countries who were vitally concerned. Winston told me that Secretary Rogers (left behind, as usual, by the President) was at his house telephoning as many ambassadors in Washington as he could reach, which of course was difficult since it was after working hours there. I immediately took a car to join him, and as I walked in the door I discovered that Japanese Ambassador Ushiba was on the phone frantically trying to reach me. Covering the mouthpiece, I learned from Rogers that he had reached Ushiba about twenty minutes before I arrived and had given him the bare news that the President had gone to Los Angeles to announce on television that Kissinger had just returned from a secret trip to Peking, where the President himself would soon visit.

I knew nothing more, and there was nothing to be gained by trying to stall Ushiba. He and I had a very good relationship developed through many battles fought together, over the Bonins, Okinawa, military bases, textiles—literally every issue that had confronted the two countries during the last four eventful years. His first words to me were: "Alex, the Asakai nightmare has happened." I had to agree with him, but talking as fast as I could to forestall questions I could not answer, I tried to cite all the reasons I could think of on the spur of the moment why Tokyo should not be too surprised or take it too hard. I must say I did not sound very convincing even to myself. The damage had been done. After this "Nixon shokku" as the Japanese called it, there has never again been the same trust and confidence between our two governments.

How easy it would have been to avoid. I later learned that the initial plan, and the reason for Haig's first phone call, was to send me directly to Japan to inform Prime Minister Sato on behalf of the President. That would have enabled Sato to perserve his carefully acquired posture of having a special relationship with Washington, something that was valuable to both countries. Instead he had to confess that, on a subject of such great importance to Japan, he only learned of the "nightmare" in the middle of the night, via a phone call from his Ambassador, just as Nixon's statement was being carried on the wires. Kissinger told me that

Nixon's phobia about leaks caused him to cancel my trip to Sato, though I am entirely confident that Sato would never have leaked a development of this kind.

I am afraid that the scintillating Kissinger mind let itself get mesmerized by the charm and urbane intelligence of the cosmopolitan Chou En-lai. Kissinger, and later Nixon, understandably found Chou (and Mao) fascinating, but the resulting policy was lopsided. America, including supposedly hardheaded business executives, embarked on a period of rapturous enchantment with China and all things Chinese, a recurrent phenomenon in our history. Japan, for the foreseeable future our most important ally in Asia by far, was shoved rather obviously to the back burner— another example of taking our friends for granted. Instead of our playing "the China card" against the Soviet Union, what really happened was that China very adroitly played the "American card." I had ample opportunity to view the President's visit to Peking in February 1972 from the hospital bed where I was re-cuperating from my heart attack. His public relations people had flown a satellite ground station to Peking to make sure every second received maximum coverage at home. One would have thought Nixon had landed on Mars rather than the very solid earth of North China.

I could not help but think, watching those pictures of Nixon sitting on the edge of his chair while Mao reclined royally, that the Chinese must have felt triumphant. For years they had la-bored without result to arrange a meeting between our respective foreign ministers. Now the President himself had journeyed to their capital, learning that he was to be granted the "privilege" of seeing Mao only after he arrived. For centuries kings and am-bassadors from outlying "barbarian" states, as the Chinese called them, had come to Peking to pay obeisance and deliver tribute to the imperial throne of the Middle Kingdom. The similarity in symbolism of Nixon's trip, which represented such a dramatic reversal in our policy, was not lost on the Chinese or those familiar with the history of China's relations with other states. Nor did we improve our performance with time. Ford's and Carter's Cabinet members all made their requisite pilgrimage to Peking, with very little in the way of reciprocation. It was not lost on Japan that Tokyo was a very incidental stop on this pilgrimage, usually just to refuel. I agree wholeheartedly that the time had come to nor-malize relations with China and that Nixon and Kissinger deserve great credit for doing so. But the way they did it unnecessarily damaged our ties with Japan and weakened our hand in the hard bargaining that has followed to put our relations with China on a sound footing.

In November 1971, not long after the Asakai nightmare became reality, I made a trip to Asia that included a stop in Japan. Conversation with Sato and Foreign Office Officials naturally centered on the future of American relations with Peking, since they did not want to get caught behind us again. I told them not to expect a rush of progress just because Washington and Peking had started communicating. We had had diplomatic relations with Moscow for more than three decades, but our problems had hardly been resolved. Our defense arrangements in Europe, especially NATO, had played an important role in the context of our relations with the Soviet Union, and I told Sato I expected we would be equally attentive to our allies and defense capabilities in Asia as our relationship with China progressed. They had nothing to gain by making concessions to Peking without getting something substantial in return, I told them; and I also said that Peking would not respect us if we lightly abandoned our relations with Taiwan. I blamed Washington's failure to consult with Tokyo about the Nixon journey on our experience with sensitive material leaking via Japan, but given our own record on leaks I must say I had a hard time putting conviction into these excuses.

Having accomplished what he proclaimed was his highest ambition—securing the return of Okinawa to Japanese administration—Prime Minister Sato resigned in 1972 after eight years in office. His Okinawa reversion and his approach to foreign policy generally had been conducive to good relations between our two countries and had strengthened his Liberal Democratic Party's hold on the Diet, which was much to our interest. Sato's successor, Kakuei Tanaka, was not even a university graduate, let alone from Tokyo University. He had come up through business and party channels rather than through the bureaucracy and was thus quite out of the mainstream of postwar LDP Prime Ministers, but he had great political skill and personal charisma in Japanese terms. President Nixon, in a very adroit move that offset some of the negative effects of his handling of China, invited Tanaka to meet with him in Hawaii.

I was asked to participate in the summit, so I flew to San Clemente on Tuesday, August 29, to work with Kissinger on the preparations. We did not face any particularly divisive issues. White House Special Trade Representative Bill Eberle had just completed a meeting in Tokyo on our continuing wrangle over imports and exports. Okinawa had also been settled. So there was a chance for the two leaders really to get acquainted, which was the kind of meeting Nixon liked best. That was a great relief to me. Henry said that the President wanted me to take "full charge," a remark I took with the normal grain of salt, but it turned out largely to be true.

We departed for Hawaii the next morning on Air Force One, with the President's normal entourage and Secretary Rogers, Assistant Secretary Green, and myself. Being weary from the trip to San Clemente and the midnight oil burned the previous evening, I took off my shoes and curled up for a little nap. Soon Bob Haldeman shook me awake and said that the President wanted to meet with me, Kissinger, Rogers, and Green, so I padded into his state room. One of my favorite presidential photos shows me sitting opposite Nixon in my stocking feet, with Kissinger, Rogers, and Green sitting on the couch alongside. We had a very relaxed discussion about Japan for several hours, during which I did most of the talking.

Arriving in Honolulu late in the afternoon, we immediately helicoptered to a reception that Clare Booth Luce was giving for the President. I had never encountered Honolulu so hot and humid, and standing in the garden without any breeze I became quite faint, which was not good after my recent heart attack. Dr. Lukash, the President's doctor, saw what was happening, laid me down on a couch, and gave me a pill. That revived me sufficiently to rejoin the President's chopper for the fifty-mile ride to the Kuilima Hotel, where the meetings were to take place. After thirty minutes for a shower and change of clothes, we choppered out to Hickam Field to meet Tanaka's plane and then back again to the Kuilima, where I fell into bed.

Henry Kissinger's idea of someone else being in "full charge" is a very elastic one, and consequently the summit did not get off to a smooth start. As was customary for Nixon, he wanted to start with a private meeting with the Prime Minister, with Kissinger the only other person present. Tanaka did not like this idea at all. He had little experience in foreign affairs, and he emphasized that Foreign Minister Ohira was very much his full partner in setting foreign policy. Moreover, the Japanese Cabinet tends to decide by consensus, not by diktat from the Prime Minister. The compromise worked out was that Ambassador Ushiba could accompany Tanaka to his meeting with Nixon and Kissinger. While they talked for an hour and a half, Rogers, Green, and I made small talk with Ohira and several others in the Japanese entourage. The dinner turned out to be more convivial and relaxed.

The next morning began with another round of separate meetings, and during the course of them I left with Bob Ingersoll, our new Ambassador in Tokyo, to brief the press. It encouraged me that Henry, as he had during other Japanese summits, left me to handle the press. I felt the briefing went well and that the resulting stories were satisfactory to both sides. After we returned to Washington, however, Henry called to report that the President was furious with Tanaka because of a story by *New York Times* correspondent Richard Halloran ascribing some adverse thoughts about the Security Treaty to Tanaka. When Henry read me the item out of the White House press summary, it seemed to me that Halloran had probably gone a little farther than Tanaka had intended. But more importantly, those who prepared the White House summary had as usual slanted this news about the State Department so that it would irritate the President.

I had taken advantage of the summit to transact a little foreign policy of my own, in a private talk with Foreign Minister Ohira. A reduction in the number of our aircraft carriers was then underway, and I agreed strongly with Admiral Zumwalt, Chief of Naval Operations, that we should obtain agreements to "home port" a few of the remaining carriers abroad. That would permit the crews to bring their families along and see them during routine maintenance layovers, and would also increase the amount of time the ships could be on station, instead of having to steam all the way back to the United States. Greece and Japan were good candidates, but I had not been able to arouse any enthusiasm in the geographic bureaus for taking up the cudgels. For various reasons, including their internal political developments, Greece was dropped, but Japan still seemed to me a natural. The Japanese specialists in the Department had visions of another *Enterprise*-style explosion of demonstrations, problems in housing the dependent families near the base, and other drawbacks. I decided that the only way to tackle the problem was to do it myself with Ohira, who could understand our problem and be willing to find a practical answer. I took it up with him at Kuilima. He was receptive, the Embassy worked out the detailed agreement, and the carrier *Midway* still has Yokosuka as its home port with scarcely a whimper from anyone.

Another problem of long acquaintance that presented itself

when I returned to the Department in 1969 was the recurrent controversy about the arrangements governing our airbases in Spain. Even the same actors were involved as when I had last worked on it in 1963: the Pentagon, the Spanish government, and Senator Fulbright.

When the medium-range B-47 became the backbone of our nuclear deterrent force in the early 1950s, we had to find bases not vulnerable to Soviet attack from which the planes could reach Soviet territory. Spain was a good candidate, and in 1953 we entered into an agreement with the Franco government permitting us to build bases in exchange for some military equipment for the Spanish armed forces. The agreement contained no security or defense commitment to Spain, so the Eisenhower Administration obtained the concurrence of Senate leaders, including those of the Foreign Relations Committee, to employ a simple Executive Agreement rather than a treaty requiring Senate approval. Over the years the Congress regularly approved the appropriations necessary to send the military equipment to Spain provided for in the Executive Agreement.

In 1963, the Agreement expired. We sought to renew it without change; Spain, excluded from NATO because Western Europe objected to Franco's dictatorship, sought a full-fledged mutual security treaty with the United States. The B-47s were disappearing from our inventory, but the bases, in which we had invested several hundred million dollars, had become places to station the tanker aircraft that refueled B-52s, training areas for tactical aircraft stationed in northern Europe, and transit points for aircraft en route from America to southern Europe and the Middle East. We had also secured Madrid's agreement to use a Spanish port to support our new Polaris submarines, which enabled them to remain on station longer than would be possible if they had to return to the United States for servicing. In 1963, as Deputy Undersecretary responsible for politico-military affairs, it fell to me to negotiate renewal of our Spanish base arrangements with Spanish Ambassador Antonio Gairigues while satisfying the Foreign Relations Committee that the administration was not cozying up to Franco.

I knew that a mutual security treaty with Spain was not only undesirable but hopeless to get through Congress. Our 1953 arrangements had worked well, and we had a strong interest in keeping them unchanged, so I concentrated on getting a simple ten-year extension. The Spanish government, however, stressed that it was not willing to continue as a "second-class partner" providing "a piece of real estate for rent." Their position was entirely understandable, and I was convinced we had to make at least a ritual bow toward it. So I then worked out a formula with Secretary Rusk and Gairigues that included a "Joint Declaration," signed by Rusk and the Spanish Foreign Minister, and established a "Joint Consultative Committee on Defense Matters" in Madrid headed by our ambassador and the Spanish Foreign Minister, with senior military commanders as their deputies. The Joint Declaration was carefully worded to give the appearance of close military collaboration without a great deal of substance. It said: "A threat to either country and to the joint facilities that each provides for the common defense would be a matter of common concern to both countries, and each country would take such action as it may consider appropriate within the framework of its constitutional processes." To get Spain's agreement to this wording we had to convince them that the Senate would not permit us to go any further; to get the Foreign Relations Committee's agreement we had to convince them that the language merely stated a truism and did not have the force of a treaty. Senator Fulbright was skeptical but most of the other members agreed. When Foreign Minister Castiella came to Washington in September 1963, he and Rusk signed the Declaration and a five-year renewal of the 1953 bases agreement.

It expired while I was Ambassador in Tokyo. Spain requested new negotiations but no progress was made, so both sides agreed to renew the terms for two years, until September 1970 to provide time to bargain.

And so I entered the picture again. Within two weeks of my return to Washington in 1969, Spanish Ambassador Marquis Merry del Val met with me to ask that we begin work on negotiating a new agreement. Over the next eighteen months I had more than thirty meetings with Merry del Val and his successor, Jaime Arguelles, five formal meetings with the Senate Foreign Relations Committee, and innumerable conferences with Rogers and others in State and Defense. Advising me through all of it was George Landau, an extraordinarily able and experienced Foreign Service Officer who was then Country Director for Spanish and Portugese Affairs, and Charles Brower from the Legal Advisor's staff, a lawyer who could always find ways of doing what was needed instead of pleading it was impossible. The staff people at Defense and the JCS, as well as Dave Packard, were always

virtually every bureau in the State Department, and I quickly found myself being asked to resolve them. When I was briefed on the fantastic number of questions and conflicting American interests involved, I saw readily that we had to work out a concerted national position on how the seas should be used. So I established and chaired what was called the Committee on International Policy in the Marine Environment (CIPME), on which seventeen separate departments and agencies were represented. Resolutions were being proposed in the United Nations. The Senate Foreign Relations Committee was taking a very active interest in the subject, and CIPME had to move fast. On one of the many occasions that I testified before the Foreign Relations Committee on law of the seas, in June 1969, Senator Claiborne Pell made an observation with which I heartily agreed. He said he had been "fascinated by the number of different views and the intensity with which they had been expressed. The issue as a whole is sort of like the proverbial iceberg." That iceberg covers 70 percent of the earth's surface.

The first crisis in this area came with Canada. The discovery of oil in northern Alaska revived Canada's interest in vastly extending its territorial waters, an idea first advanced in the 1960s. As Deputy Undersecretary, I made several trips to Ottawa to dissuade them from the course they were contemplating, which was basically to draw "closing lines" across the mouths of large bays to put them under Canadian jurisdiction. We worried that this might lead other countries to do the same, shutting off large areas previously considered the high seas to international fishing and navigation. At that time we largely succeeded in convincing the Canadians to postpone action. But with oil presumably present in abundance in the Canadian Arctic, Canada also wanted to declare all waters around its numerous islands in the north as inland waters subject solely to its control. Concerned as well that we would want to ship Alaskan oil through those waters and along the Canadian coast, Ottawa also proposed to declare a large "pollution zone" on the high seas through which no tanker could pass without subjecting itself to Canadian inspection and control.

On face the proposals were not outrageous, but we were extremely concerned that they would create a precedent enabling other countries to close off massive areas of the oceans to air and sea traffic, including military vessels. The Canadian "archipelago thesis" was particularly threatening to navigation in and around Indonesia and the Philippines. I was startled when my good friend Marcel Cadieux, the Canadian Ambassador, came to tell me on

March 16, 1970, that he had been instructed to inform me that his government was proceeding immediately to introduce the legislation necessary to implement these plans and saw no reason to discuss it further. I suggested to President Nixon that he immediately telephone Prime Minister Trudeau to ask him to postpone legislative action until we talked again. This the President did, and I journeyed to Ottawa on March 20 with a delegation drawn from Defense, Navy, Coast Guard, and the Departments of Transportation and Interior, along with some legal experts. We devoted an entire day to thrashing out the issues with External Affairs Minister Sharp and his delegation, and while they did not amend any of their positions they did, in fact, postpone action for the time being.

Law of the sea disputes began to take a disproportionate amount of my time, and since they were obviously going to require sustained attention, I finally persuaded the Department's excellent Legal Advisor, John Stevenson, to take over the chair of CIPME and act as the government's focal point on these issues. That eventually led him to head our delegation to the 154-nation Law of the Sea Conference in Geneva. Elliot Richardson succeeded him in 1977 and worked on it full-time until he resigned in February 1981.

Meanwhile, the space program was also raising some issues that required attention. After the success of the first Apollo moon landing in 1969, the program confronted "where to go next." Manned flight enthusiasts naturally looked to Mars. I had resumed my membership on the National Aeronautics and Space Council, and while we heard many fascinating proposals for sending men to Mars and, more importantly, bringing them back, none seemed economically feasible. With the existing rocket technology the astronauts' journey would take several years and many tens of billions of dollars. Despite the enthusiasm of our Chairman, Vice President Agnew, and the inherent fascination of the idea, the project never went anywhere.

More "down to earth" ideas presented themselves instead. An explosion in the practical uses of satellites for communications, weather forecasting, earth and ocean resource surveys, navigation, and reconnaissance, inspired interest in finding a cheaper way of launching them. This led me into two very important international negotiations. The first was trying to persuade European countries, who were investing large sums trying to develop space launchers that duplicated ours, to give up that wasteful effort and join with us in a "post-Apollo" international space transportation program. The second was to persuade at least all of the countries outside the Soviet bloc to join in a worldwide satellite communications network that could interconnect and serve everyone, rather than a hodgepodge of uncoordinated national and regional systems. The bedrock technical fact was that just three satellites could cover the entire globe.

In the years after Apollo, our planners conceived of the Space Shuttle as the best way to put all the technologies and lessons learned during Apollo to practical use. A reusable craft able to haul large payloads into orbit and repair or fetch devices already there would show vast economies, the planners believed, over "throw-away" boosters that were destroyed with first use. The negotiations to involve Europe in developing the shuttle had two levels, technical and political. NASA carried out the technical discussions, but first the political framework had to be established.

Persuading the Europeans to give up their own launcher programs and join us in a cooperative enterprise obviously required that we share some of our technology and information with them. The prospect, however, raised the hackles of the ultra-nationalists in the White House (like John Erlichman) and elsewhere in the government, who felt we had nothing to learn from abroad and should seek to build a "titanium curtain" around our present superior knowledge. Always a strong proponent of the benefits (and inevitability) of technological transfer, I argued strongly for sharing with Europe, and so did the rest of State, as well as NASA. It took some time to overcome the resistance within the government to opening negotiations with Europe at all, but authorization to start talks finally came from the White House.

The group with whom we negotiated was the European Space Conference, a consortium of eight European nations chaired by Theo LeFevre, a Belgian with whom I spent many hours in vigorous debate. The advantage to the Europeans of cooperating with us was the saving of hundreds of millions of dollars to discover things we already knew. In return, we offered to launch all the satellites they developed, except for communications satellites that would directly compete with the single world-wide system we were encouraging. All the European countries could see the logic of a single international communications system except France, which wanted its own satellite for broadcasting directly to the Canadian province of Quebec and all the Francophone countries of Africa. So France held out for the European launcher that would not be subject to any American control. The French position did not arouse much enthusiasm among its neighbors, let alone Canada. But Germany was then trying hard to improve relations with France, and England, having generated enough friction with Paris over Concorde, was loath to cause any more. It took several years before France's objections were overcome and the European Space Conference agreed to join in our post-Apollo program by building the space laboratory that was a part of our shuttle launch program.

To my mind, one of the most important and least appreciated negotiations of recent years was the one that established a permanent framework allowing all countries to share in the management and benefits of communications satellites. The tremendous economies and technical advantages of using satellites to relay communications, as opposed to cable or ground-based radio, became apparent at the dawn of the Space Age. In 1964, twelve countries led by the United States signed an interim agreement establishing the International Telecommunications Satellite Organization, or INTELSAT. Congress chartered an American corporation, some of whose directors were appointed by the President, called the Communications Satellite Corporation (COMSAT), which received powers from INTELSAT to manage the building, launching, and operation of the satellites. By 1969 COMSAT had established a global system of four satellites, and much of the world had watched men walk on the moon "live by satellite." The demand for the high-quality telephone circuits that satellites could provide was rapidly outgrowing the system's capacity as many countries rushed to build the relatively simple ground receiving stations.

It was obvious that the twelve-nation Interim Agreement had become obsolete. The rapidly increasing number of client countries wanted more control over operations, especially in setting rates. They were not content to have an American company, no matter how competent or well-intentioned, have complete authority over what had become a world network. To replace the Interim Agreement with a permanent and more equitable one, a seventy-nation conference opened in Washington in February 1969 chaired by Leonard Marks, previously director of USIA. Enormous financial, technical, and political complexities were immediately apparent to all. The Conference established a small Preparatory Committee to draw up recommendations for when the full Conference reconvened, which it did in February 1970, chaired by Abbot Washburn. However, the Preparatory Committee had not been able to hammer out a consensus. Instead it submitted a badly split report to the Conference, presaging stormy sessions ahead.

Because COMSAT had its own interest in the negotiations

separate from that of the United States Government, we had separate delegations at the Conference. COMSAT's basic objective was to preserve its monopoly as the owner and operator of international communications satellites with minimum interference from anyone else. Large investments and even larger potential profits gave it a powerful incentive.

The United States, on the other hand, sought to create an international system that other countries would have an incentive to join. We did not want to stimulate the growth of needless competing systems, and we therefore exerted pressure on COMSAT to be reasonable in meeting the objectives of the many nations attending. Those objectives boiled down to: an effective voice in managing the system, especially setting rates; a share of its profits; and a chance to bid on the necessary equipment, including the satellites themselves. So it turned out to be a very complex negotiation. Within the United States Government the Federal Communications Commission and the White House Office of Telecommunications Policy took divergent views. The COMSAT Board of Directors took a very tough line against any dilution of their present privileges and had strong backing from their congressional guardians, especially Senator Pastore of Rhode Island. And on the other side were some seventy countries with widely varying interests and technological capabilities.

Bridging these many gaps was not easy, but Abbott did a superb job, calling on me only in times of crisis to meet with foreign representatives, singly or in groups. I also maintained contact with COMSAT President Joe Charyk, whom I had known well since the Kennedy Administration, when his role as Under Secretary of the Air Force put us in regular contact over sensitive and esoteric reconaissance questions. Joe was disposed to be cooperative and practical, but he had to look over his shoulder at a tough Board of Directors.

The Conference finally reached an agreement providing that INTELSAT's membership include any country willing to invest a certain amount in its operations. The membership would elect a Director General, who would contract with COMSAT to run the satellites under his direction. Profits would be shared proportionally to investment and mechanisms were established to give the smaller countries an adequate voice in INTELSAT's policies.

The COMSAT Board was reluctant to agree to this dilution of its previously untrammeled authority. Even when it came to the crunch, with the signing ceremony scheduled for the next day, May 21, 1971, the COMSAT Board dragged its feet in giving Charyk authority to sign. Clearly, some sort of pressure was needed.

It so happened that I was attending the White House reception for the diplomatic corps that evening, and by chance I had an opportunity to tell the President about the work of the Conference. I told him I felt that the signing ceremony would be a truly historic occasion, even though the press had not covered the Conference extensively because the issues and negotiations were intricate. On impulse I suggested that he might like to attend if that were possible, and equally impulsively he said he would.

I told Secretary Rogers, who was at the reception, and left as fast as I could to phone Joe Charyk. I told him he could pass the word to his Board that the President was going to attend the signing ceremony. The Secretary of State would sign for the United States; I said I hoped he would be there to sign for COM-SAT. He said he would see what he could do, but could not promise anything.

I heard nothing from Joe the next morning, and went early to the conference hall. Those in charge assured me that all the documents were in place for COMSAT's signature, but still there was no word. Just before the President arrived, however, a smiling Joe Charyk got out of his car, ready to sign. With a great sigh of relief I heartily shook his hand.

The new INTELSAT organization has worked extremely well. Headquartered in Washington, by 1980 it had 102 member countries. It consisted of twelve satellites in synchronous orbit furnishing more than 16,000 circuits through 180 ground stations in 111 countries, with a possibility of 750 earth-station-to-earth-station pathways. And this is just a beginning. For those who despair of international organizations ever operating successfully, here is an example of one that works and does good work. It was exciting to have a small part in attending at its delivery.

It is perhaps a good note on which to close this brief summary of another four years of the "seventh floor," this time as Undersecretary for Political Affairs.

·CHAPTER FOURTEEN·

SALT

===================== ⟋ =====================

FEBRUARY 2, 1973, MARKED THE BEGINNING OF MY LAST AND MOST frustrating job in the Foreign Service. On that day I was sworn in as Ambassador-at-Large and designated Chief of the United States Delegation to the Strategic Arms Limitation Talks (SALT) [now known as Strategic Arms Reduction Talks (START)] with the Soviet Union. I continued in this position until I resigned at the beginning of the Carter Administration four years later.

I came to the job partly as a result of Nixon's strange behavior following his 1972 election victory. The morning after his overwhelming triumph, Nixon summoned his Cabinet to the White House. All of them sat around the table expecting to be greeted with thanks by an exultant President. A grim-faced Nixon strode in the room, however, and without even sitting down curtly demanded that all of them immediately submit their resignations. He turned on his heel and stalked out. Bob Haldeman, trailing behind, stuck his head through the door as he left and said to the shocked Cabinet that he hoped they understood that the President meant what he said. Nixon had done the same thing with his White House staff, who had been straining for a year to get him reelected.

After telling me of the meeting, Bill Rogers said that he had confirmed that the President's demand included me. Though I was shocked at the way it was done, the news was not entirely unwelcome. I had had just about enough of the strain of being caught in the nutcracker, between the President and Kissinger on one side and Bill Rogers and the State Department on the other. Later both Rogers and Henry Kissinger (who was exempted from the purge) told me that the President wanted me to know I could "have any other job I wanted." I had long ago learned to discount such statements from the President, and in fact after Tokyo and Under Secretary there were few jobs that interested me. But knowing that Dave Kennedy had been something less than a success in the North Atlantic Council (the parent body of NATO) and that our representative on the NAC had never been a career officer, I said I would like to give it a try. First refusal had already been given to Don Rumsfeld, however, and when he accepted, that was that. My real desire was for Saigon. I thought that Ellsworth Bunker was doing a superb job, but I was very interested in the post in the event that he left. I told both Rogers and Kissinger that I was not trying to be quixotic and probably knew the difficulties better than anyone, but based on my previous experience and established relationships with most of the Vietnamese leaders, I wanted to try to hold the country together in spite of our inability to obtain a satisfactory agreement from Hanoi. Everyone, including Dean Rusk, thought I was crazy and told me so. I finally had to agree that in view of my heart attack of less than a year ago, it would not be prudent for me to return to the stressful maelstrom of Saigon. In spite of what subsequently happened there, I still regret that it was not possible.

On Monday, December 11, Bill Rogers surprised me by asking whether I would be interested in taking on the SALT negotiations. I thought about it overnight. The next day I told him that while I still preferred Saigon, if the President really wanted me for the job I would do it, as long as certain ground rules were established. The present chief of our delegation to SALT, Gerard Smith, had also been Director of the Arms Control and Disarmament Agency (ACDA) at the same time. I was only willing to take on SALT if the ACDA job went to someone else. I had no animus against ACDA, but having to wear two hats had limited Gerry's effectiveness both in Washington and in bargaining with the Soviets. ACDA was charged by law with formulating arms limitation policies. In carrying out this responsibility it had to work with other concerned agencies, including Defense, State, the JCS, and the NSC staff. I believed it was important for arms control to have a strong advocate in bureaucratic battles, which meant a full-time director in Washington. Nor was being SALT negotiator necessarily compatible with heading ACDA. The SALT Delegation is bound by instructions issued by the President and worked out through interdepartmental debate in which ACDA is only one part. The rest of Washington, especially the Pentagon, tends to view ACDA as "soft." Though Gerry Smith had been scrupulously fair in performing both jobs, other people, including the Soviets, were not always sure from which viewpoint he was speaking. I had always felt combining the two jobs was a mistake, and under no circumstances did I want my authority as the President's negotiator dissipated by departmental responsibilities in Washington. My desire to head SALT by itself as Ambassador-at-Large was acceptable to Rogers, Kissinger, and the President.

The other ground rule I wanted established was that Kissinger keep me informed about all his "back-channel" negotiations with Ambassador Dobrynin and others. Most of the substantive developments in SALT I had been worked out privately in Washington, via Kissinger, and he had been content to leave the SALT Delegation ignorant of these crucial developments while the Soviet side knew all about them. I refused to be subjected to such indignities and told Kissinger I wanted to be kept informed at least as much as my Soviet counterpart. He gave me this assurance and, to the best of my knowledge, kept it throughout my tenure. With these conditions successfully negotiated, I was happy and eager to take on the job. I knew of no subject more important to the United States and the world than limiting nuclear weapons.

The United States Delegation to SALT consists of a Chief, which was me, and representatives from Defense, the JCS, State, and ACDA, plus a "public" member. This variety of voices is quite unusual. My first job was to put together my delegation, which was easier said than done.

Because of our long relationship and my respect for the man, I very much desired to retain Paul Nitze as the Defense Department member. He was extremely well-versed in the subtleties of arms control and would also be valuable as our "institutional memory" from SALT I. The political side of the White House, including the President himself, objected because Paul was a well-known Democrat. With Kissinger's intercession I finally obtained the President's grudging acquiescence. Having served as Director of Dean Acheson's Policy Planning Staff as Assistant Secretary of Defense for International Security Affairs, and as Secretary of the Navy and then Deputy Secretary of Defense under Kennedy and Johnson, Paul was uniquely qualified.

A replacement for Roy Allison as the JCS representative proved even more difficult, though I was less directly involved there than in Paul's case. Admiral Thomas Moorer, who was then Chairman of the JCS, and Secretary of Defense Elliot Richardson recommended an officer whom I did not know well but who was acceptable, and they forwarded his nomination to the White House. But Senator Henry "Scoop" Jackson insisted on another officer, Lieutenant General Edward Rowny, who was then serving as Vice Chairman of the NATO Military Committee. He could not be readily replaced there, but the White House was not willing to take on Jackson over this issue, especially after he remained adamant in spite of a personal visit from Tom Moorer. Thus, Ed Rowny, to whom I had no objection, was snatched away from NATO and assigned to the delegation.

The White House wanted Phil Farley, then Acting Director ACDA, to be the ACDA representative. Although Phil was a longtime colleague from State for whom I had great respect, I argued that it was much more important for ACDA and me that he be in Washington where my instructions were being written. In this I prevailed, and instead I was assigned Sidney Graybeal, a very able officer with a wealth of background in SALT. As the State Department member I was fortunate to obtain Boris Klosson, a Russian-speaking FSO who had long served as Deputy Chief of Mission and often Chargé of our Moscow Embassy. Harold Brown, whom I had known well as Secretary of the Air Force and who had since become President of the California Institute of Technology in Pasadena, agreed to continue as the delation's "at large" or "public" member, which was very valuable. His experience and imagination were consistently helpful, as they would be later to the Carter Administration, in which he served as Secretary of Defense. I was also pleased that Dick Helms, then CIA Director, agreed to retain Howard Stoertz as my intelligence advisor, though he was not a formal delegate.

While trying to get the delegation together, I was also fully briefing myself on SALT and doing all I could to push for instructions that would enable us to get off on the right foot when we met with the Soviets. I was not entirely a stranger to SALT from my previous job, so the former task was not too difficult, but the latter task—getting meaningful instructions or at least some sense of where we wanted to go—proved impossible.

Arms control is a subject of long history and dense complexity. The strategic nuclear weapons discussed in SALT (those designed to strike deep within the enemy's territory, as distinct from tactical weapons designed for local battlefield use) have many variations. New ones are constantly emerging from the fertile minds of weapons designers. Thus the target for arms controllers is always moving, if only for technological reasons. But even if the weapons remained the same the task would be daunting. Soviet and American armed forces have different missions to begin with, and the weapons designed to accomplish these missions have different capabilities, so that merely subtracting an equal number of a certain type of weapon from each nation's arsenal does not necessarily produce equivalent reductions in military strength.

The Strategic Arms Limitation Talks with the Soviet Union are about first limiting and then reducing the numbers and destructiveness of these weapons so that neither side gains unilateral advantage in the process. Like currents flowing in the atmosphere, the negotiations have different planes, each identifiably different, having their own pace and direction but not separated by rigid boundaries. The first and highest plane concerns the broadest and longest-term questions in Soviet-American relations. What is the overall balance and trend of political, economic, and military strength between the two sides? How durable and resilient are our respective alliance systems? To what extent does either perceive China a likely ally of the other? To what extent can the Soviet Union really accept "peaceful coexistence" with powers it perceives to be basically hostile? Is "essential equivalence" in the strategic capability at a lower aggregate level of arms the goal of both sides, or is SALT just a temporary gambit for gaining advantage in the arms race? What numbers and types of forces and weapons, including nuclear, are really essential for national security? During the SALT I and II negotiations, questions at this highest level were resolved by the President with the input of his chief advisers when a unilateral determination was required, by the President and Brezhnev when both sides needed to agree. In the case of Nixon and Ford, Kissinger was by far the most significant advisor, but others also had influence.

The second plane of considerations affecting SALT is shorter term politics, domestic and international. This includes such factors as the personal commitment of the President to arms control; the views of the various agencies, legislators and constituencies concerned with SALT and their clout with the President and Congress at any one time; fluctuations in public opinion about SALT and about how "tough" we should be with the Soviets; negotiating constraints and incentives created by elections; international behavior in other sensitive areas, like the Soviet invasion of Afghanistan or Congress' refusal to grant the USSR most favored nation trading status; and the perceptions on each side of the other's military strength and belligerent intentions. While I was SALT negotiator, if matters on this level properly concerned both sides we sometimes discussed them at Geneva, but they were more typically handled between Kissinger and Soviet Ambassador Dobrynin, with both of them obviously taking their instructions from higher authority.

The third level was what we negotiated at Geneva. It would be misleading to describe it as "technical," for though we concentrated our attention on the actual weapons systems, their power is so awesome that any change in them has enormous military and political consequence. Our basic task was to find agreement with the Soviets, taking the utmost care, on proposals for limiting and reducing strategic arms that, given the initial differences in the weapons portfolios of the two sides, were militarily sound, verifiable, and not destabilizing to the strategic balance. Not only did we have to possess strategic forces that were fully the Soviets' equal at the end of any negotiation, they had to be perceived that way by other countries as well.

I am not a Soviet expert, and I did not really concern myself with the larger climate of Soviet-American relations affecting SALT. I was content to let the President and his advisors in Washington handle the first plane and most of the second. I did, however, have certain views about the extent to which SALT should be linked with more transitory ups and downs in the way our countries got along.

When I took the SALT job one of the key words in our international lexicon was "detente," by which the President and Kissinger meant the relaxation of tensions between us and the Soviets. I always tried to avoid using the term because there were vast differences in how it was interpreted, not only among Americans but also between Americans and Russians. Statements by Soviet officials to their own people on what they meant by detente left no doubt that they intended the struggle with us to continue, though perhaps through less provocative means. No long-term alignment of interests was envisioned.

In my view the desirability of SALT, then and now, in no way rests upon one's opinion about detente. SALT stands on its own as being in the hardheaded self-interest of our two countries, precisely *because* we are basically antagonistic. In most ways strategic nuclear weapons do not cause the hostile relationship between us, but are rather a symptom of more fundamental discord. However, each country has a real self-interest in avoiding suicide,

ABM networks protecting their own missile fields and major cities, it was reasoned, great sums would be expended with nil or even negative net contribution to security because any side that felt it could defend itself successfully against a nuclear attack might be more aggressive, and in the meantime would provoke the other to develop weapons capable of ABM penetration. (In fact, the original reason for MIRVs was to penetrate ABM defenses with a blitz of warheads; it is a textbook argument for ongoing arms limitation that the MIRV genie could not be put back in the bottle even after ABMs were emasculated.) The ABM Treaty allowed the United States and the USSR to build only two ABM sites, one guarding the national capital and one a field of ICBM silos. (In 1974 the treaty was amended so as to permit only one site for each side.) Both sides were making themselves deliberately vulnerable to the other's nuclear forces as a contribution to mutual deterrence.

The other component of SALT I was known as the Interim Agreement, which, unlike the ABM Treaty, was to operate for five years only. It froze the number of launchers on each side for ICBMs and SLBMs. Each side could also introduce a limited number of new SLBMs if those replaced older ICBMs or SLBMs one-for-one. Though the Interim Agreement did not itself mention how many launchers each side possessed ("launchers" being chosen rather than "missiles" or some other measurement because silos in the ground and firing tubes on submarines are easy to verify), the United States at that time had 1710 launchers, 1054 for ICBMs and 656 for SLBMs. The Soviet Union's total was 2347: 1607 for ICBMs and 740 for SLBMs. Even though the Interim Agreement permitted them to have 637 more launchers than us, it was a balanced agreement for three main reasons: we also had 450 heavy bombers compared to the Soviet Union's 155; we had a considerable lead in MIRV technology that gave us a vast advantage in the number of warheads that compensated for the Russians' superiority in launchers; and we had no programs restricted by the ceilings, while they did.

Another provision of this SALT I Interim Agreement dealt with so-called modern large ballistic missiles (MLBMs), also known as heavy missiles. Both sides were restricted to their existing levels, which for the Soviet Union meant about 300 and for us meant none. We possessed 54 large missiles known as Titans, which were single-warhead liquid fuel rockets, but these were not modern since we had not deployed any since the early 1960s. We had opted instead for smaller, highly accurate and efficient solid fuel

ICBMs known as Minutemen and saw no need for a new generation of larger missiles. That is why we had no qualms about accepting the five-year ban in SALT I on enlarging any Minuteman silos to accommodate MLBMs. But the Soviets did have about 300 of an MLBM known as the SS-9, which carried a single warhead. This was not especially worrisome in the short run, since it was less accurate than our Minutemen. However, a larger missile can carry more warheads, so there was concern that after the Soviets developed MIRV technology, the MIRVed version of the SS-9 would be an especially devastating weapon for which we would have no counterpart.

I have always found that negotiations work best when you know at the beginning what you want at the end, so my first priority after versing myself in the details of SALT I was to get a sense for where the Administration wanted to go on SALT II. But this was impossible. Washington was in complete disarray about its objectives for the next round. This was not surprising, since I came to the job only a few months after the Interim Agreement had been signed, and no common view of it could be forged among State, ACDA, the JCS, CIA, and the civilian officials in the Pentagon, nor in fact within those agencies themselves. During SALT I the government had been brought into agreement quite often by the President or Kissinger arranging terms with the Soviets privately and then springing them on everyone, including the SALT delegation, as accomplished fact. In early 1973, however, neither Kissinger nor President Nixon had a highly developed vision of SALT II either. What surprised me was how long this vision took to develop—two years, in fact. The SALT Delegation and I did lots of discussing, drafting, exploring, presenting to the Soviets and presenting to Washington, but we did not get down to the hard business of drafting a treaty until Brezhnev and Ford cleared the decks with some important conceptual breakthroughs at their Vladivostok summit in November 1974. My work at Geneva, then, divides clearly into two phases: pre- and post-Vladivostok.

In the first phase, the only thing Washington could agree to as I sought negotiating instructions early in 1973 was the need for "essential equivalence" in the strategic balance under the terms of the permanent SALT II agreement that would follow the 1972 Interim Agreement. Senator Jackson had approved SALT I, but he also sponsored a resolution at the same time, easily passed by Congress, directing that future strategic arms agreements not permit the disparities in weapons numbers—about

2500 for their side, including ICBMs, SLBMs, and heavy bombers, versus about 2200 for us—enshrined in the Interim Agreement. Jackson wanted "equal aggregates" of ICBMs, SLBMs, and heavy bombers. Henry Kissinger thought that too confining, and his response was the attractively elusive concept of "essential equivalence." He thought we might be better off if, for instance, we used a willingness to settle for a lesser aggregate to get them to limit their MIRV or heavy missile programs. This concept was known as "offsetting asymmetries"—they would have more of some things and we would have more of others, but in total we would achieve "essential equivalence."

The problem with an elastic term is that it attracts as many definitions as beholders. The Joint Chiefs, for instance, supported by Jackson, had a very straightforward approach to essential equivalence: permitting an aggregate of 2500 on each side. That would stop the Soviets at their present level and allow us to build up to it. Ease of verification was this proposal's only virtue. A 2500 ceiling would not be arms limitation but arms expansion, and in any event we had no desire or plan to increase our own arsenal, for which appropriations would certainly not be voted even if the Pentagon proposed it.

ACDA and other agencies more interested in actual reductions proposed limits on the number of MIRVs, on maximum throw weight, and on total arsenal megatonnage they considered compatible with essential equivalence. It was clear that restricting MIRVs would have to be done soon if at all, before the Soviet programs to develop and deploy them gained too much momentum to stop. But the Pentagon strongly resisted any approach that would inhibit our deploying more MIRVs, where they wanted to exploit our technological lead to the hilt. That this lead would have to evaporate someday did not seem to concern them. In any event, though we went round and round and had two NSC meetings with the President on SALT before I left for my first stint as Chief of the United States Delegation in Geneva, I did not take with me any clear instructions. I was merely to propose essential equivalence in general terms and "probe" the Soviet side for its own views while the Washington machinery ground on. Though I did not know it at the time, this was to be the pattern for the next eighteen months.

I arrived in Geneva aboard an Air Force transport the evening of Saturday, March 10, 1973, with the members of the delegation, some wives including Pat, and staff members including Elinor Murphy, my indispensable secretary. After almost four years of commuting between Prague and Geneva in the 1950s for the Indochina and Korean Conferences and then for my talks with Wang Ping-nan, it was almost like returning home. The city changes only slowly, and its spectacular mountains and lake, never. Geneva's stolid Swiss burghers have seen generations of kings, presidents and ambassadors come and go, and pursue their own lives with little regard to the international currents swirling around them. Thus our arrival was greeted calmly, and there was only a small group of officials and press to listen to my innocuous statement. We were then whisked off in a convoy of cars to the Hotel des Bergues.

Early Sunday morning I went to our crowded offices in the old buildings of the United States Mission to the European Office of the United Nations and met with my delegation to discuss our plans, thin though they were.

On Monday morning, being the "new boy on the block" I called on Vladimir Semenov at the Soviet Mission to become acquainted with the man with whom I was to have hundreds of conversations over thousands of hours during the next four years. Semenov was a true SALT veteran, having opened the SALT I negotiations with Gerard Smith in Helsinki in 1969 that led up to Interim Agreement and the ABM Treaty. The only member of my delegation with comparable experience was Paul Nitze. Luckily, my interpreter, William Krimer, the dean of all American interpreters with a photographic memory and sharp ear for nuance, had also worked for my predecessor for many years.

Semenov was a stocky man of medium height with a pale round "moon face" typical of Slavs. He welcomed me effusively, and we exchanged pleasantries and expressed our respective desires for success in our important task. He was a bit unhappy with Geneva as a locus for our talks as compared with Helsinki and Vienna, which had been the alternating sites for SALT I, and he noted in passing that the Swiss were not providing motorcycle escorts and champagne after each session, as had been the case in Finland and Austria. Although each of us was well read on the other's biography, we nevertheless exchanged some reminiscences—I of Molotov and Kuznetzov during the 1954 Geneva Conference, and he of General Clay and Bob Murphy while stationed in Berlin as "political adviser" at the end of the war. Since he spoke some German and no English and I spoke some French and no Russian, we had to communicate through interpreters. But I do not find this a disadvantage in serious and delicate conversation; rather, it provides time to think and select words carefully. Bill Krimer also kept extensive notes, so I had no trouble accurately recording important conversations.

In this first meeting we agreed to continue the practice of alternately meeting at each other's offices. He accepted my suggestion that we discontinue "plenary" meetings, at which all the members of the two delegations including staff were present (about twenty-five on each side), and confine ourselves to "restricted" meetings, normally twice a week, which only the five or six principal members of each delegation would attend, together with a "note taker." In this way I hoped I could encourage him to some informal exchange across the table instead of just reading statements to each other. We also agreed that following each meeting we would continue the practice of adjourning for refreshments to give the two of us and our subordinates the chance to talk with counterparts privately. He was more reluctant about accepting my suggestion that the "refreshments" be confined to coffee or tea rather than the more stimulating beverages the Finnish and Austrian hosts had made available. This immediately earned me the name of "Mr. Dry" in the Soviet delegation. (It is not that I do not enjoy a libation on appropriate occasions, but eleven o'clock in the morning during meetings on one of the world's most serious subjects did not seem to me an appropriate occasion.) We also established that we could, of course, meet privately at any time at either's initiative.

The first meeting of our delegations was the next day, Tuesday. We each made a formal opening statement, and then I was introduced to Semenov's idea of a private conversation over refreshments. He pulled out of his pocket a sheaf of typewritten notes to which his interpreter had a corresponding set. Reading, he started out by saying how nice it was to have this opportunity for an informal conversation, how he hoped we could promptly complete our work, etc. When I responded, he would look down through his sheets and read back what he felt fit most closely. He continued this practice through our four years of discussions, even resorting to it on social occasions like lunches and dinners until I was often ready to climb the wall. It was precisely this practice that Foreign Minister David had used in meetings with me in Prague. It impressed on me like nothing else the state of fear in which communist officials exist, especially those like Semenov who had come up during Stalin's period. In the 1930s Semenov had been a junior Commissar overseeing the collectivization of agriculture in the Ukraine, in which hundreds of thousands died. After the East German uprising in 1953, when Semenov was serving in Berlin, secret police chief Beria almost executed him; reputedly his life was saved only because he was absent from Berlin when the message came to return to Moscow immediately. Semenov's deputy took his place on the plane and in receiving Beria's bullet.

While death was no longer the normal penalty for a mistake, dismissal and disgrace were, especially if it could be charged that a civilian functionary had somehow disclosed military secrets in the highly sensitive area that was the subject of our conversations. In my formal statements and private talks with Semenov I often referred to our data on the numbers and characteristics of Soviet weapons. Usually this information had long since been published in the United States. But as they had in SALT I, the generals on his delegation would let my general know that they wished I would not talk so freely to Semenov about such matters because "we do not tell our civilians such things."

That the Soviet delegation was strongly influenced by its generals and controlled tightly from Moscow was demonstrated repeatedly. Several times Semenov could not give me answers on routine matters, such as agreeing to a recess, without checking with his delegation. In Moscow SALT was apparently handled entirely through Party and Defense channels. Semenov received his instructions from a subcommittee of the Party's Central Committee, which in turn took its cue from Brezhnev, the General Secretary. Even Foreign Minister Gromyko was not able to speak knowledgeably about SALT with Kissinger, because Moscow's SALT channels bypassed the Foreign Office entirely. Only when he became a member of the Party's Central Committee was Gromyko brought into the picture. It is quite difficult for us to imagine this degree of secrecy, but I do think that Semenov learned things about Soviet weapons from our presentations in Geneva that his own government had not told him.

Within the American delegation I established some new ground rules. It used to be that each delegation member would have a separate staff, who tended to get isolated from each other. We established a joint staff by consolidating them, and the delegation's staff work was done by all and overseen by my staff aide. This gave some cohesiveness and continuity to our operations. Another change on which I insisted was to have all cables to Washington go across my desk. I did not mind if delegation members communicated with their home agencies, but I wanted to make sure they would not try to go behind my back and get something changed that we as a delegation had recommended. They were free to express dissent, but I wanted it in the same message I sent. Nor did I want to fight Washington's battles in Geneva by having to repel suggestions for changes in my instructions made by one agency or another via their delegation representative. The Chiefs frequently tried to end-run the President and Kissinger by asking me to do something different from what my instructions stated. I always told them I was interested in their views and would be glad to comply as long as they could clear it in Washington. I was the President's representative and was responsible only to him for instructions; the delegation was responsible to me for carrying them out. And our job was negotiating, not framing basic policy. I tried to avoid having the delegation becoming a mini-Washington.

Nor did I want to become a fifth wheel by concentrating my energies on shaping the interagency debate at home about what an ideal agreement would constitute. I was willing to offer advice about what I considered negotiable, but only very sparingly did I suggest what I thought would be "best" in some abstract sense. That was for them to decide.

The delegation met virtually every day, whether or not we were actively negotiating with the Soviets. If we had a new proposal to present, all the delegation members would be briefed on what to say to their counterparts during the "informal" refreshments period, and we would jointly discuss the formal statement I was to make on behalf of the delegation. If Semenov made a statement, we would meet afterwards to discuss our interpretations and to draft a reporting telegram back to Washington. If controversy were to arise, it would be over what our next step should be, but this was usually resolvable. Then we would appoint someone to draft my statement for the next meeting consistent with what we had agreed. We did not ask Washington for new instructions after every meeting. I preferred to have broad guidelines and proceed as I thought best consistent with them. The delegation worked extremely hard despite long periods of underemployment while our superiors worked out the larger strategy, and though we did not always agree, we functioned effectively as a team.

In our first few months we put forward the general principles on which we were willing to conclude a SALT II agreement and listened to the Soviets' ideas. Of course, I insisted that essential equivalence on our central systems (ICBMs, SLBMs, and heavy bombers) be the basic approach, more particularly an equal aggregate for both sides of 2350 with separate ceilings for land-based ICBMs and ICBM throw weight. (The JCS would not agree to any lower aggregate, even though we had no plans for increasing from 2200.) In the context of such an equal aggregates agreement, I said we would be willing to consider a ban on intercontinental cruise missiles. (Cruise missiles are small jet powered, drone-like devices that can hug the ground and use advanced radar to home in on their targets with uncanny accuracy. They thus differ from ballistic missiles, which are rocket-powered, have inertial guidance, and reach their targets in a characteristic arching trajectory.) We would also consider a ban on strategic ballistic missiles on surface ships, air-to-surface missiles with a maximum range greater than 3000 kilometers, and ballistic missile launchers located on the seabed. We proposed no SLBM restrictions.

The Soviet position was very extreme. They proposed simply extending SALT I into a permanent agreement and expanding its provisions to cover American heavy bombers and "forward based systems," or FBS. FBS was a major Soviet focus. They contended that we had many missiles and aircraft not based on American territory (stationed on carriers, in Europe, in Korea, and elsewhere) that could inflict nuclear damage on Soviet territory. They said that all these had to be accounted for in assessing the strategic balance and proposed, therefore, that we withdraw to United States territory all aircraft based on land or sea capable of delivering weapons on the Soviet Union, as well as close our submarine bases in Britain and Spain. None of their medium-range nuclear missiles aimed at Europe and Japan, their thousand medium-range bombers or their own carrier aircraft would, of course, be in any way restricted. They proposed that we remove nuclear weapons from our heavy bombers and that both sides not undertake "major new programs." When asked what American programs they had in mind, they said the Trident submarine, the B-1 bomber, the MIRVing of Minuteman and others, without citing any of their own. I felt their own medium- and intermediate- range missiles contributed as much to their arsenal as our FBS did to ours, and after taking a strong line refuting their reasoning on FBS, I refused to discuss it any further. Clearly, there was little in the Soviet position that pointed toward a quick meeting of minds. I was not too concerned, however, because Brezhnev was scheduled to visit Washington in the summer and Semenov was under pressure from his superiors to make progress, which I wanted to turn to our advantage.

One responsibility of my job that I took very seriously was briefing the ambassadors on the North Atlantic Council, the parent body of NATO, about the progress of SALT. I did so immediately following our first meeting with the Soviet delegation and about monthly for the duration of the talks. I was quite free in discussing what we had already done but more reticent about revealing future tactics, out of concern for the security of all the foreign offices to which my words would be reported. The NAC was quite content with whatever approach we wanted to take on central systems as long as we promised not to touch our European FBS. The Europeans wanted our intermediate-range ballistic missiles and medium bombers on their territory to protect them. As long as I emphasized we had no intention of withdrawing our FBS or even debating the subject, they would nod and smile appreciatively. The Soviets were also suggesting "non-circumvention" language, meaning we would not try to get around restrictions on our central systems by furnishing delivery systems to our allies. The NAC showed recurrent concern that such a provision might inhibit their access to conventional weapons. I was also able to reassure them about this, but in terms so general that not every member was satisfied.

Despite the vagueness of my original instructions, no revisions were forthcoming out of Washington as the second round began. This lack of direction, especially the unresolved dispute with the Chiefs over whether we aimed to reduce, expand, or keep at 2200 our aggregate of central systems as we sought essential equivalence with the Soviets, limited how far we could go. I sent private messages to JCS Chairman Moorer and Admiral Zumwalt, Chief of Naval Operations, encouraging them to think through their views on SALT thoroughly, but this was not enough. In mid-April, I returned with the delegation to Washington to seek new instructions. I had to make a sudden detour to California, however, to be with my mother in the last few days before her death, which came peacefully on Good Friday 1973, after ninety-one years of an amazingly full life. She always reminded me of Oliver Wendell Holmes' one-hoss shay "that was built in such a logical way it ran a hundred years to the day." We had always been close, and I missed her very much indeed. After the cremation and simple burial next to my father's grave in Glendale, I left within the hour to return to the struggle in Washington.

We had three extremely acrimonious meetings of the Verification Panel, the interagency group responsible for SALT chaired by Kissinger and consisting of the Deputy Secretary of Defense, the Under Secretary of State, the JCS Chairman, and the directors of ACDA and CIA. Deputy Defense Secretary Clements, who impressed me as a remarkably unprofound thinker on these matters, played the heavy, knocking down all proposals that would restrict our freedom to expand. Bill Porter, who had taken my place as Under Secretary for Political Affairs, took an equally extreme position on the other side, arguing for an unconditional ban on all MIRVs. No consensus at all emerged about the direction I should take. I returned to Geneva on May 2 with no new instructions.

The following day I received word from Kissinger that he was going to Moscow and wanted to see me before he got there. We met in Copenhagen the morning of May 4 and spent about two hours in his plane while it was being serviced. Having been unable to prod Washington into any movement, Henry was hoping to manage an end-run by reaching some accord with the Soviets. We discussed several alternatives, but I told him I did not expect the Soviets to stop insisting on their FBS proposals so soon. When I met Henry in London May 10 on his way home, that assessment turned out to have been correct. The Interim Agreement, combined with the nature of our existing missile forces and programs, conferred potential advantages on the Soviets they were loath to give up. They had more launchers and throw weight. Though neither side could increase its number of launchers any further, by "qualitative" improvements to their missiles (like MIRVing), the Soviets could still greatly upgrade their strategic capacity. Convincing the Soviets of the value of qualitative restrictions was not easy.

After seeing Henry in London, I briefed the NAC in Brussels, then returned to Geneva to find a surprisingly ambitious new instruction from Washington calling for a freeze on the MIRVing of ICBMs. We wanted to restrict their MIRVing now, before we faced the prospect of thousands of additional Soviet warheads atop their larger throw-weight arsenal. Even if our 7000 warheads were adequate to destroy the Soviet Union several times over, it was feared the Soviets might be tempted by a superiority in warheads to launch a first strike that would try to knock out all our missiles and bombers so we could not retaliate. Further, the political repercussions of such a disparity would be severe.

Given the Pentagon's fondness for the "we have them and they don't" line of argument, I wondered how they had been induced to acquiesce in the ICBM/MIRV freeze. I was also sure it would go no place with the Soviets, followers of the "they have it and we don't" school, even though this proposal would still concede their superiority in throw weight. Our intelligence was picking up evidence that they were just about to test a whole new family of ICBMs, some of which undoubtedly would be MIRVed. Now would hardly be their chosen time for a MIRV freeze. Even so, there were good arguments to be made for it, and I welcomed the opportunity to engage the Soviets in a concrete and substantive debate.

This played itself out fairly fast. The next morning I saw Semenov at ten to alert him to this development, then at eleven I made the formal proposal at the regular Friday meeting of our delegations. We went back and forth for a few weeks. I emphasized that we looked on MIRVs as a counterweight to their advantage in throw weight, and would be less interested in maintaining a MIRV asymmetry in our favor to the degree they restricted their throw weight. But once I explained our proposals thoroughly, I thought it best not to search for new ways of presenting them, which could result in confusion and leave us negotiating with ourselves. It became clear that Semenov was not going to receive any instructions permitting him to respond until after Brezhnev completed his visit to Washington, so I pressed for a recess to last that long. Semenov agreed, and we set the adjournment for June 12.

I had wanted, before this recess, to table a comprehensive draft agreement embodying our individual proposals, which I thought would put us in an excellent bargaining position. At Paul Nitze's suggestion I brought in Ralph Earle, a very able Philadelphia lawyer who had had experience in the Pentagon, to work with us on such an agreement. I was very pleased with what we produced and hoped to present it at the end of May. I therefore sent it back to Washington for clearance, with Earle following in person to explain its rationale to any who had questions.

Weeks passed and no clearance arrived. Defense and the Chiefs were trying to end-run my instructions calling for a MIRV freeze by not approving treaty language that stipulated such a freeze. The fact was that the Chiefs did not want any SALT agreement that was negotiable. Kissinger was in Paris trying to negotiate an end to the Vietnam War, and Nixon was beginning to throw up the barricades against a mounting barrage of Watergate complaints. Without the White House actively knocking heads, the government's position on SALT disintegrated into interagency squabbling. I became quite bitter about the Pentagon's entirely negative attitude, but had no way of exercising decisive leverage.

A series of articles on SALT I, written by John Newhouse, was published during May and were later expanded into the book

Cold Dawn. His information was extremely detailed, and he obviously had full access to the most sensitive records. He revealed things that even delegation members did not know. The only possible source for the leaks was Henry Kissinger. Newhouse told Paul Nitze that he had received his materials from the White House and that he had even listened to tape recordings of Verification Panel meetings (which I, for one, had not been aware were being taped).

I sent Henry a tongue-in-cheek telegram, saying I was sure he would be as appalled as I was about such detailed leaks, which certainly jeopardized our ability to work with the Soviets. What could I say to the Soviets?

Henry replied that he had seen Newhouse only briefly and had not given him documents nor authorized the staff to do so. He maintained this position consistently despite its considerable improbability. I did not believe him, and I think Henry and I understood each other on this. It was this sort of reflexive deceptiveness that made the whole administration seem unworthy to the public, and very difficult to work for.

Before the delegations recessed at Geneva I received a request from Henry to comment on the communiqué the Soviets proposed we issue about SALT at the end of the Washington summit in late June. It was typical Soviet language, extreme and transparently self-serving. I argued that if any communiqué was issued it should advance the negotiations somehow, and suggested my own draft. This the Soviets rejected. After more exchanges we ended up with the most innocuous sort of text, calling on negotiators to work something out that could be signed in 1974. I was sure that Henry was not consulting Secretary Rogers or anyone else in the Department about any of this, but I knew that if I attempted to do so I would cut off the tenuous but useful relationship I had established with Henry on SALT.

That Henry was indeed hypersensitive about involving the Department became clear to me as soon as I returned from Geneva. Bill Rogers briefed me about an agreement Brezhnev and Nixon were intending to sign on "The Prevention of Nuclear War," which, as was typical, Rogers had been told about only in passing. What he related of it immediately set off alarms in my head because it sounded like the agreement the Soviets had been trying to get us to sign for years binding us to "no first use" of nuclear weapons in war. That, of course, would undermine our entire NATO strategy, which preserved the option of using tactical nuclear weapons on European battlefields if NATO defenses were in danger of being overwhelmed by Warsaw Pact conventional forces. When I saw Henry at the briefing sessions for the press and Congress on the SALT communiqué, he was furious that Rogers had had the temerity to ask him about this "prevention of nuclear war" document. (It actually turned out to concern procedures for consultation during crises that might escalate to nuclear war.) Henry launched into a long tirade about how the "Seventh Floor" (his euphemism for Rogers) repeatedly tried to sabotage everything he and the President were trying to do. I talked for seven or eight minutes to the congressional leaders about recent developments in Geneva, but to the press Henry, as usual, did all the talking.

I found the deference with which Brezhnev was treated during the summit quite repellent and did not seek to become directly involved. No friendly chief of state ever received such lavish hospitality. Several streets were blocked off to traffic; in addition to the usual White House dinner there was a cruise on the President's yacht, meetings at Camp David, a ride with the President on his plane to San Clemente, a trip to Hollywood to see the movie stars, etc. I suppose there was a certain kind of fascination for Nixon in the power of his opponent and in the power they both wielded in sum. I was and am thoroughly in favor of doing what we can to improve our relations with the Soviet Union, but I felt that this extravagant behavior toward a Brezhnev, who remained a ruthless thug for all his endurance at the top, would neither moderate his conduct nor reassure our allies, many of whom we regularly treated cavalierly during their visits to Washington. I cannot recall that anything of substance to emerged from the Brezhnev summit. On SALT, a high-priority issue for both countries, nothing happened of moment. Kissinger told me that the only progress was that Brezhnev said he would go into it personally and make a counter-proposal initially through Ambassador Dobrynin to Kissinger.

Nevertheless, to keep up the pressure I asked Dobrynin to tell Semenov, as I had told him before leaving Geneva, that I was prepared to meet with him immediately. Dobrynin repeated what Semenov had told me, that August is an important vacation month for Soviets. I repeated I was ready and awaited his proposal for a definite date.

With little happening on SALT, I took a slow trip by car to California with Patricia. It was even slower than anticipated because we had to pause several weeks in Durango, Colorado, for Patricia to have her gall bladder removed. My daughter, Judith, came from Los Angeles with her three sons to help care for her mother during her convalescence, giving me an opportunity to arrange with a wrangler and hunting guide to take my three grandsons on a trip along the spine of the Rockies out of Silverton. It was a great experience for all of us.

It was while driving through Kingman, Arizona, after having renewed our journey, that I heard on the car radio the President's announcement that Henry Kissinger was replacing Bill Rogers as Secretary of State. While this was inevitable, in fact longer in coming than I expected, I nevertheless felt real sadness. I have never known anyone that I liked or respected more than Bill Rogers and his very capable wife, Adele. They both worked hard at their jobs and did much to gain friends and respect for the United States. But Bill was too much of a gentleman to cope with the White House mafia from the President down, and no match for Kissinger in bureaucratic infighting. I had tried my best to support him and maintain relations between him and Kissinger, but to little avail. I immediately sent him a message saying how sad I was to see him leave. I also sent a message to Kissinger wishing him well and telling him I was sure that the Foreign Service would do everything it could to support him.

While we were visiting our children in Santa Monica, Henry called and asked that I come down to see him at San Clemente. Sitting on the terrace to his little office overlooking the sea, we had a long talk about the organization and personnel of the State Department. Looking ahead through the end of Nixon's term in 1977, I said I felt the primary problems in foreign as well as domestic affairs were going to be finance, trade and energy, not defense-related issues like liquidating the Vietnam War. I felt neither the State Department nor the White House was well organized to handle them. As far as his own relations with the Department and Foreign Service were concerned, I said I thought the main difficulty was going to be Henry himself. Given his propensity for playing things close to his chest, he might not give the Department and Foreign Service a sufficient sense of participation to really enlist them. If he could, I was sure that in spite of the past he could depend on their loyal and full support. He said all the right things in response. I told him I had great respect for the office of Secretary of State, and that as far as I was concerned, the day he was sworn in he would to me no longer be "Henry" but rather "Mr. Secretary." I suggested that he encourage this change in everyone. I wanted to do everything I could to make Henry's appointment work. The only thing I worried about was his propensity to shade the truth when he considered it expedient.

When I returned to Washington, I received word from Semenov that he would be prepared to resume negotiations on September 24. I also had myself fully briefed on all recent developments, including some in the Soviet Union that were very disturbing but not surprising. After Brezhnev's visit in June, the Soviets started conducting a very intensive testing program for a whole new family of four types of ICBMs, three of which were being tested with MIRVs. We had trouble assessing their motives, but of course this largely overtook the MIRV freeze proposal I had made in May. Since it was up to the Soviets to reply to our May proposals, however, I did not seek new instructions, but proposed to wait for their promised counter-proposal.

Before I left for Geneva, I had a series of meetings on the Hill with Senators Jackson, Muskie and Case and Congressman Zablocki of the House Foreign Affairs Committee. There was no criticism of any of the positions we had taken. I strongly endorsed the section in the President's State of the Union Message that said we could not expect people to negotiate for what they could get free, meaning I supported a strong defense establishment to convince the Soviets that we were prepared to do what is necessary to maintain equality with them. I said the Soviets would never be willing to cut back strategic arms unless they were persuaded this was true.

I had some more inconclusive sessions with the Chiefs, particularly Admiral Zumwalt, who seemed to have the greatest capacity for taking a broad view on SALT. I stressed and stressed again that the JCS should be taking a positive view toward arms limitation, proposing their own ideas in light of what they considered the best long-term security interests of the United States, instead of dragging their feet on everyone else's proposals. Sometimes it seemed to me that there was more community of interest between the Soviet and American military on SALT—both wanting unlimited freedom to buy new hardware—than within the various agencies of the American government.

Back in Geneva, I next met with Semenov on Tuesday, September 25. He had to stall for time since he obviously had no instructions. On October 9, however, he caught me by surprise when he tabled a draft treaty of which he had just informed me at a private meeting the previous evening.

The draft was a typical Soviet ploy, so extreme and one-sided that at first glance we could see it contained nothing from which we could negotiate. It was a common Soviet tactic to take maximum positions, but if this was Brezhnev's counterproposal it certainly did not advance things in any way from where we had started in March. The Soviets wanted to maintain the advantage in ICBM and SLBM launchers conferred in the Interim Agreement, and for us to reduce the nuclear weapons on our bombers and to withdraw all our FBS, including all carrier aircraft that were capable of carrying nuclear weapons.

I was so outraged at the unconstructive and propagandistic positions taken in the draft that I told Semenov there was just nothing in it from which we could begin negotiations and, therefore, I would not even attempt to comment on it. He tried hard to get me to talk about it, but I completely frustrated him by refusing to say anything further. When it came my turn to speak at our formal meeting, I simply stated I had nothing to say.

In our private conversation he asked me why I did not table a draft of my own if I felt so exercised about his. In fact that was exactly what I wanted to do and had wanted to do since May, though of course I could not tell him that. I had the delegation renew work on our draft treaty that would contain in concrete language all of the general propositions we had advanced so far. The draft we developed, while taking forward positions to give us negotiating room, was nevertheless balanced and reasonable. I sent the text back by telegram on October 24 and at the same time sent Ralph Earle to Washington to explain it. I also sent private messages to JCS Chairman Moorer, Jim Schlesinger (who had replaced Elliot Richardson as Secretary of Defense), and General Brent Scowcroft, who had taken over running the NSC staff on a daily basis from Kissinger. Boris Klosson also telephoned State. The purport of these messages was to ask them all to defer judgment until they had a full explanation from Earle, because the draft was a complex structure with many interrelationships between the various sections that would not be apparent from a hasty reading.

The response was very discouraging. Even before Earle could see the Chiefs, General Rowny had word from the Chiefs' Joint Staff that the draft was entirely too "soft" even if the Soviets signed it as it stood. Under no circumstances were they going to recommend that the JCS accept it, even as a negotiating document. This was par for the Joint Staff and thus not too surprising to me, but disappointing nevertheless. William Hyland, Henry's Soviet expert on the NSC, also treated Earle pretty roughly. I asked Washington for authority to propose a recess because it was clearly necessary to go back with the delegation to discuss the draft and make whatever modifications would be required to obtain clearance. Then I hoped to come back and table it before the usual Christmas recess so we could get down to serious bargaining when we resumed in January. That way during the first half of 1974 we might be able to reduce the issues sufficiently in number and complexity to permit the top-level political decisions in both governments necessary to conclude an agreement.

Watergate and the Middle East October War intervened to frustrate all my finely laid plans. I returned to Washington in mid-November. As far as the government was concerned, SALT had come to a complete halt.

Before my departure Semenov had Patricia and me to one of his usual four-hour lunches. It seemed, somehow, typical of Soviet dealings with the West, even of their nuclear weapons— crude, overwhelming, trying to make up in heft what was lacking in sophistication and subtlety. Semenov was an experienced diplomat and considered himself rather a refined intellectual, but we had six courses, five wines, a complete overabundance of everything. Perhaps he was trying to show that Russia was a rich country too. Madame Semonova, his second wife, was much younger than he and had quite an unproletarian taste for European high fashion, for which she frequently shopped in Brussels. He told me beforehand that he had about two hours' worth of things to discuss with me after lunch, but we did not finish eating until after four o'clock and this was too late to start talking. So I had to see him again two days later. His main message was a plea for a counterproposal to his draft treaty, but he also indicated somewhat obliquely that the Soviets would agree to our position on equal aggregates if we would agree to theirs on FBS. It wasn't much, but it was a sign they might be ready to negotiate seriously.

At home during Christmas 1973, I resumed my discussions with Admiral Zumwalt on the attitude the JCS took toward SALT, reiterating my concern that the JCS as an institution took such a defensive attitude toward arms limitation that their views tended to be ignored. I urged that the JCS find some way to approach SALT from a positive point of view, putting forward some considered ideas about what kind of strategic balance we should seek between our two countries for the 1980s instead of just trying to shoot down everyone else's ideas. That was probably their most important responsibility as the country's highest-ranking uniformed officers. But as Zumwalt said to me, "You know, we Chiefs don't even talk about SALT among ourselves. All we do is look at staff papers." He suggested that I meet privately with the Chiefs. I agreed on condition that there would be no deputies in the back row taking notes, ready to spread stories if someone was not "tough enough," so we could have a real hair-down session.

On January 7, 1974, we had this meeting, with only Secretary of Defense Schlesinger and the Secretary to the JCS present, along with the Chiefs themselves. We had an excellent two-hour meeting, very ably chaired by Moorer, of a kind that was unprecedented in my experience, but it did not produce much in the way of lasting results. The institution of the JCS is structured to deal only with papers prepared by their Joint Staff, whose colonels seek to outdo each other in being "tough." With their own deputies and staff sitting behind them at every meeting, the pressure is on the individual Chiefs to do the same. This results in their taking not only extreme but sometimes absurd positions. The Chiefs seem to never sit down over lunch and chew things out for themselves. The system makes them prisoners of their subordinates. New ideas can be forced on them only by the President or an unusually strong Defense Secretary.

As soon as I had arrived in Washington I had set to work trying to hammer out the consensus needed on our draft treaty. Kissinger had been having the NSC and the various departmental staffs crank out his famous "options," putting bits and pieces of the strategic equation together in different combinations to see if anything turned out to be particularly interesting. But these were mostly make work projects, and at a long Verification Panel meeting on November 23 we paid no attention to them.

The week before that meeting I worked out a proposal containing the principles I thought should be embodied in a SALT II treaty and wrote it up as an instruction to me. I gave it to Henry, telling him I had shown it to no one else and suggested that, if it conformed to what he and the President thought best, I thought it stood a reasonable chance of gaining approval within the government and with the Soviets in Geneva. Its basic concept was very simple: both sides would reduce over ten years to an aggregate of 2000 central systems, meaning ICBMs, SLBMs, and heavy bombers. We would also seek essential equivalence in throw weight of MIRVed missiles and total throw weight, factoring bombers at about one-half of their actual carrying capacity to compensate for their slowness compared to missiles. Reaching this 2000 target would require the Soviets to reduce their large missiles, the SS-9s and its new MIRVed version, the SS-18. We, in turn, would reduce our bombers, one bomber for every Soviet ICBM. I thought we would have to forego building the Trident submarine to keep under 2000 central systems. Trident was extremely costly, put a lot of missiles (24) in one container, and did not add that much to our security compared to equipping our existing Poseidon subs with the new Trident-generation missile.

There were several weeks of interruptions while Henry performed his Middle East shuttle diplomacy, but his final response was that the Pentagon would never possibly approve my suggestion.

On January 10, I attended an NSC meeting with the President that was truly impressive. In spite of Watergate, Nixon was in superb form, obviously determined to demonstrate his capacity as a statesman. On SALT Nixon gave Defense and the Chiefs a firm message that they could not expect any large increases in appropriations for strategic weapons. While we should play on Soviet uncertainty about our intentions in this area as a bargaining lever, he said, in reality we should not plan on major new programs. He told me to play to the hilt his well-known anti-communist history and unpredictability to persuade Semenov that a SALT agreement would be valuable. I had no problem doing that and told the President so. Unfortunately, the President did not approve any specific course of action for the next round of negotiations in Geneva. Nixon also ranged widely and philosophically over many world problems, including his concern that "a bunch of thugs" would come to power after Brezhnev and his questions about the leadership succession in China and the future of Sino-Soviet relations. Gerald Ford, newly appointed Vice President, attended but did not say much.

After this NSC meeting the Verification Panel met several times to forge the draft agreement I wanted to take back to Geneva. The big question was whether to pursue a separate agreement on MIRVs, which Nixon could sign at his June summit in Moscow, or to hold out for a comprehensive accord, which would obviously take longer to negotiate. I argued strongly for a comprehensive agreement, though I knew MIRVs were time-sensitive, because I felt deeply that comprehensive agreements were SALT's raison d'etre, and that the likelihood of a separate MIRV agreement was small. The Verification Panel agreed—the Pentagon wanted as much delay as possible—but the bureaucracy was typically fragmented over what a comprehensive draft treaty should contain. The Pentagon contended there was no way to include bombers in the aggregate because there was no accurate way to rate their strategic contribution compared to missiles. Once again a text eluded us, and once again Henry sent me back to Geneva to face Semenov armed only with statements of general principles. He was scheduled to visit Moscow in March and thought some breakthrough might materialize then.

Before I returned to Geneva, Henry and I also had some long private talks. He said he thought the Soviets felt very bruised over their lack of a role in arranging the Middle East settlement and the little they had to show for detente generally. He did not want me to press Semenov too hard now, thinking that it might take time before Brezhnev could build up enough strength to overrule his generals and conclude a SALT treaty. He also told me that Nixon, despite his growing Watergate difficulties, felt no special pressure to obtain a strategic arms agreement by the time of his summit, and that Brezhnev might well be feeling more pressure in this area than Nixon.

The delegation returned to Geneva in mid-February, our instructions due to meet us there after Henry had obtained the necessary clearances. Again the JCS Joint Staff objected to a few minor points, and again we had to meet the Soviets for a few sessions without instructions. When we did get them, they contained ambiguities and even contradictions revealing hasty drafting—this after three months in Washington. Even so, we could carry them out. Before Henry's trip to Moscow, I made a few presentations to Semenov about controlling MIRVs by restricting throw weight and suggested an initial aggregate of 2350 central systems dropping over five years.

Originally, Henry had wanted me to accompany him to Moscow, but at the last minute Brezhnev asked that I not come because he did not want to have Semenov there too. Henry described his meetings with Brezhnev after his return, but there was no progress. Since I had nothing useful to do in Geneva, I requested permission from Washington for a recess so we could return home to get agreement around town on what to do next. This was granted, and we came home in mid-April.

An issue on which the delegation had been working hard during this fallow period was how a MIRV agreement could be verified. From the air one missile silo looks like another, and the nosecones themselves need not reveal anything about the payload underneath. We found there was no sure way to verify an agreement in which some missiles of a given type would be MIRVed and others would not. It became clear that this issue would require a lot more work before any agreement could be signed.

Concerned that Nixon would reach an improvident SALT agreement to rescue his sinking reputation, Paul Nitze resigned from the delegation on June 14, to my great regret. I understood his desire to dissociate himself from an administration that was appearing more unsavory each day, but I did not share his worry that Nixon would make a rash SALT agreement and told him so before he resigned. It seemed to me the domestic political dynamics pointed in just the opposite direction, since a "soft" agreement would certainly alienate the conservatives in the Senate to whom Nixon would have to turn to avoid impeachment. Nevertheless, Paul resigned and I missed him greatly. We did not always agree, but he was innovative and thoughtful and I always welcomed his counsel.

To replace Nitze I was fortunate to obtain Dr. Michael May, Associate Director of the Lawrence Livermore Laboratories. Though he lacked Paul's broad background, Mike was very conscientiously interested in finding a way to limit nuclear weapons. Coming from the Livermore Laboratories, which helped design these weapons, he was excellently poised to talk on a level with the scientist on the Soviet Delegation, Academician Shchukin, who had helped develop the Soviet weapons. Mike had to resign in 1976 because of family responsibilities, but again I was fortunate in that Defense selected W. J. (Jack) Howard, Executive Vice President of the Sandia Corporation, as Mike's replacement. Jack was also very knowledgeable about the design of nuclear weapons, so he was both helpful in the delegation and effective with Shchukin. I also persuaded General Rowny and the JCS to release Colonel Norman Clyne to become my personal assistant and Executive Secretary of the Delegation. Norm was the most knowledgeable and able military officer in the SALT field I ever met and was extremely helpful in the final months of 1976, when we were seeking to complete the draft of the treaty. He stayed on with my successors, eventually resigned from the Army, and became Executive Secretary of ACDA.

The most important personnel problem affecting SALT in mid-1974, however, was Nixon's slow and agonizing political demise. Washington was preoccupied with the spectacle of his fall, and SALT went nowhere at all. We worked out within the government a minor protocol to the ABM Treaty that Nixon and Brezhnev could sign at their June summit, under which both parties would agree not to build the second ABM site they were entitled to. There were some NSC meetings at which we discussed the elements of a more comprehensive agreement including

MIRVs, throw weight, and the other important issues, but as usual no consensus emerged. I was growing very impatient and frustrated, not being used to underemployment and not seeing any prospect of progress. Pat and I took another vacation.

I did not think the Soviets would settle with us until they had fully caught up on MIRVs, and that would take some time yet; we had moved from having three times as many warheads as the Soviets in 1972 to four times as many in 1974. With the 1976 election approaching, I also thought the Soviets might be inclined to wait to see if a new President might give them easier terms. Kissinger agreed about the difficulty of working with a wounded President, but when I saw him during my last visit to San Clemente on July 27, he said he felt the Soviets were inclined to reach an agreement before the elections. We talked about starting up at Geneva again in September. Henry also poured into my ear his unhappiness at the way his Department colleagues had handled the recent crisis in Cyprus. I sounded my usual theme about the importance of his keeping information flowing downward.

The greatest obstacle to achieving a unified position within the government on SALT was removed on August 9, when Nixon finally resigned. President Ford took hold of his new job in a very impressive way. Within days he had received all of the foreign Ambassadors in Washington and sent individual messages to foreign governments. (Kissinger initiated much of it but Ford had to do the work.) He also called all presidential appointees to the White House, asked for our help and talked individually to us. Although he did not have Nixon's brittle brilliance, he was a solid citizen who reassured the country and knew the government thoroughly.

Ford got down to work quickly on SALT, with which he had some familiarity from his period as Vice President. Henry got him to agree that I should ask to start again with Semenov in the middle of September, though this required intensive work to settle a position in Washington from which I could negotiate. As the deadline approached, Henry suggested that I ask for a further postponement, but I resisted. More delay would simply permit the bureaucracy to procrastinate. On the other hand, I did not want to return to Geneva to tread water aimlessly. For the first time I gave real thought to resigning and retiring from the Foreign Service.

Prodded by my scheduled departure on September 16 to meet the September 17 date Semenov and I had agreed upon, an NSC meeting was held Friday afternoon, September 13. In addition to the President there were Henry Kissinger and Bob Ingersoll, Deputy Secretary, from State, Jim Schlesinger and Bill Clements from Defense, the new JCS Chairman George Brown, Bill Colby from CIA, Fred Ikle from ACDA, and me. For over two hours there was an excellent discussion of contending points of view from which nothing resembling a consensus emerged. Defense and the JCS as usual laid tremendous stress on the Soviets' large program for modernizing and MIRVing their missiles. Logic would have seemed to dictate that anything we could achieve to put a ceiling on these Soviet programs would be to our advantage, but typically the military concluded that we should make proposals that were even less likely to obtain Soviet agreement. The JCS, and to a lesser extent Defense, were torn between trying to put meaningful restraints on the Soviets and leaving ample room to expand our programs. They always overstated the Soviets' strengths and our weaknesses, which may have been natural enough, given their responsibilities, but which was not helpful.

As usual, Fred Ikle spun finely drawn analyses that quickly lost most people's attention, including the President's, and did not reveal just where he stood. Henry and I urged trying somehow to cap MIRVed ICBMs on both sides, but were put off by Colby's emphasis on the difficulty of verifying any such limitation.

The President said he wanted everyone to understand he felt strongly that we should seek a SALT agreement. He remarked pointedly that he was not prepared to approve positions that would appear to prevent one. At the same time, he did not want an accord simply for the sake of having one. The only thing on which everyone agreed was that with Semenov I should show "open-mindedness and flexibility" and a willingness to take new approaches without walking back on anything we had said in the past. I pointed out that this was going to be quite a trick and that I would need everyone's tolerance, because I could not please everyone. Henry replied that I had ample experience in balancing on a tightrope. Henry was scheduled to visit Moscow in October, and the plan was to hold two more NSC meetings before then to firm up our position so Henry could take it with him. Then I would follow up on it at Geneva.

At the end of the meeting Henry asked me to give him a draft he could show the President of what I felt my interim instructions should be. Not unexpectedly, both Schlesinger and the JCS objected to my very anodyne draft, and again I spent the first week at Geneva without instructions.

When they did arrive, however, my instructions were surprisingly good. Ford and Kissinger had clearly knocked some heads. Beforehand I had reluctantly begun to conclude that the only agreement we were likely to get was one that restrained future programs only, not existing ones. But these new instructions enabled me to put forward at Geneva some constructive propositions about existing programs, which were formalized in the more comprehensive agreement reached by Ford and Brezhnev at Vladivostok in November and subsequently embodied in the SALT II treaty itself. They called for both sides to reduce their aggregates gradually until reaching equality until 1985. In determining the total throw weight of each side, I said the United States would be willing to take account of our larger number of bombers, which was a considerable ·concession to the Soviets' view. (In fact, if heavy bombers were factored into total throw weight at 50 percent of their payload, the total missile and bomber throw weight of both sides was "essentially equivalent," for whatever meaning that figure may have had.) I also said we were willing to discuss limiting not only present MIRVs but future ones, which we thought might interest them since we had a lead in the technology.

Semenov clearly had no new instructions. He kept insisting that we include FBS in the negotiations, implying that they were not going to agree to equal aggregates in central systems unless we withdrew our nuclear-capable fighter bombers from Europe and Korea and pulled out our Sixth and Seventh Fleet aircraft carriers from the Mediterranean and Pacific. He also insisted that "allowance be made" for British and French nuclear missile submarines as well as China's nuclear capabilities. He rejected my plea to "agree to disagree" about FBS and go on to the propositions I had put forward.

In the middle of October I made a quick trip to Washington for one of the promised NSC meetings, stopping en route for a few hours to brief the North Atlantic Council in Brussels. The NSC meeting, on October 18, was very discouraging. Defense and the JCS were strenuously retrogressing from the limited propositions I had been authorized to put forward at Geneva. The JCS reverted to their hoary favorite that all we needed was an agreement on equal aggregates of central systems, though overall numbers are one of the least meaningful measures of capability. Schlesinger put forward an extreme and unrealistic proposal for limiting Soviet throw weight that would have required them to abandon the programs they had under way and completely res-

tructure their forces. State put forward a more reasonable proposition for offsetting asymmetries in the two forces that would
have permitted the Soviets a larger aggregate in return for a
larger number of MIRVed warheads to us. But this drew considerable fire.

During a brief talk before I returned to Geneva, I found
Henry quite depressed about the future of SALT, a feeling I
shared. I could not help him much with Washington, but on the
Soviets I reiterated my belief that they were so strongly attached
to their FBS position that they would not abandon it until we
made a strong counterattack, which I thought could and should
be done.

There seemed little point in my going to Moscow with him,
but he said he would send one of his staff to Geneva to report to
me on the meetings, which were to lay the groundwork for the
Ford-Brezhnev meeting November 23 and 24 at Vladivostok. The
report did not sound too encouraging, so I obtained Semenov's
agreement to a recess and returned to Washington in early November with the delegation to await the results of Vladivostok.

To my great and pleasant surprise, the Vladivostok communiqué and the long private message Henry sent Schlesinger,
George Brown, and me sounded very promising. Brezhnev
agreed to drop discussion of their position on FBS, a big breakthrough I had not expected. He also agreed to the principle of
equal aggregates at a level of 2400, which meant they would have
to destroy some missile launchers while we would not. He also
agreed to a separate MIRV ceiling of 1320 that was lower than
our intelligence people estimated they had the capacity to go;
even so, we were much closer to the limit than they were and
to a position that went a long way in resolving our difficulties
with counting their MIRVed missiles. We also agreed to stop seeking separate restrictions on the Soviets' heavy missiles, but the
MIRV limit somewhat compensated for this. Ford had pulled off
a major accomplishment, and instead of resigning, as I had been
contemplating, I looked forward enthusiastically to the big job of
translating this agreement in principle into specific treaty language.

When the President and Kissinger returned, we started this
task. With the bureaucracy bound by the summit accords, this
went much more smoothly than I had grown to expect. Nevertheless, three issues requiring more work were revealed in a series
of Verification Panel meetings in December 1974 and January

1975. First, there was a genuine and important ambiguity about whether the ban agreed between Brezhnev and Ford on "air to surface missiles" with ranges beyond 600 kilometers included air to surface cruise missiles as well as air to surface ballistic missiles. The Soviets insisted that it included both, while we maintained it excluded air-launched cruise missiles (ALCM). In the hasty and pressure-filled discussions and drafting that make summits both productive and dangerous, I had the impression that neither side realized the other's interpretation.

Bill Clements suddenly developed an enthusiasm for long-range ALCMs, in which neither Navy nor the Air Force had previously show much interest. It was true that their ground-hugging radar, accuracy, and maneuverability gave them significant strategic potential, but they were still in their infancy. Why let another nuclear genie out of the bottle—for the remarkably lame reason, as Clements put it, that "we have a five-year lead in the technology"—when our purpose was to keep them in? Long-range cruise missiles became a major issue within our government and between us and the Soviets. Henry's efforts through Ambassador Dobrynin to have them interpret the Vladivostok agreement as we did were not successful.

Another issue that emerged immediately was whether a new Soviet bomber code-named "Backfire" would be counted as a heavy bomber in adding up their central systems aggregate. There was no question that its principal mission was as a medium bomber designed for use at sea and against Europe and China, but it was supersonic and considerably more worrisome than the model it replaced. Our intelligence people estimated that if it flew out of a base in the extreme north of the Soviet Union and followed a theoretical flight profile at high altitude and modest speed to maximize its range, it could bomb a portion of the eastern United States and still have fifteen or twenty minutes to land in Cuba. With refueling it could be a formidable weapon, but the difficulty was that the same could be said of several of our medium bombers and fighter-bombers which we resolutely refused to discuss as intercontinental weapons.

Henry said Backfire had not come up during the Vladivostok discussions, and in a background press conference following the summit he declared it was not counted as a heavy bomber in the figuring of the Soviet aggregate. In all the official public statements of the Secretary of Defense and Chairman of the Joint Chiefs over the years, the accepted figure for Soviet heavy bombers was 140; no one disagreed that Backfire was a medium peripheral bomber. Its inclusion in the heavy bomber category had never really been discussed in the government before Vladivostok, and that we might seek such a definition clearly surprised the Soviets. When the JCS asked Kissinger whether he would object to my raising it at Geneva, however, he said I might as well give it a try to "see what we could get out of it." He certainly did not expect me to get anywhere because counting it as a heavy bomber would require the Soviets to make an unanticipated further reduction in their central systems. Secretary Schlesinger also told me before I returned to Geneva that he did not expect me to get very far but to "see what I could do." During the debates on SALT II during the Ford and Carter Administrations, die-hard opponents of all strategic arms limitation eagerly seized on the Backfire, building it up far beyond what it deserved, because they knew it was non-negotiable to the Soviets and would block the Treaty.

Because of the difficulties of verifying with certainty whether an ICBM is MIRVed or not, the third thorny issue to arise from Vladivostok was how exactly to spell out a position on counting MIRVed land-based missiles. The easiest provision to verify—counting any launcher capable of holding a MIRVed ICBM as holding one—would operate against us, because our Minuteman silos could all hold the MIRVed Minuteman II version though half of them did not. We needed a formula that would be airtight applied to the Soviets, but would not penalize us. A somewhat less pressing issue was what to do about mobile land based ICBMs, which were less vulnerable to attack than fixed missiles but consequently destabilizing. In SALT I we had taken a very rigid position against any mobile missiles, but in the meantime it appeared that the Soviets were developing them.

Before I returned to Geneva I sought to prepare and clear the draft text of a treaty based on Vladivostok from which we could have the Soviets negotiate, rather than face one drawn up by them. I did not succeed, however, and unfortunately, at our very first meeting, on February 1, 1975, Semenov tabled with a flourish a full draft treaty. Contrary to Henry's hope that we would confine our negotiations to the issues set out at Vladivostok without the introduction of "extraneous elements," Semenov's draft took extreme positions incorporating every past Soviet contention and some new ones too: limiting our Trident submarines, making FBS an automatic part of future SALT negotiations, and others. As usual, I was in the position of having no instructions whatever for the first ten days. When they did come they still prohibited me from tabling any draft of my own and said I should "exchange views" on the general principles to be incorporated in a treaty. Whatever merit that may have as a negotiating tactic (and usually I think it has little), it had no merit whatever in dealing with Semenov. By nature he was ill equipped for such explorations, and it was clear that his instructions confined him to very narrow limits, which his KGB and military officers guarded closely. My instructions, however, did permit me to draw up a draft to submit to Washington for approval. In fact, I already had the delegation working on it, and I now stepped this up.

On February 24, I took advantage of a trip to Brussels to have lunch with Al Haig, who had just become Supreme Allied Commander Europe. I had known him since he was a captain in the Eighth Army in Yokohama at the end of the war. As Kissinger's military assistant on the NSC, he had been a calm and orderly rock of Gibraltar in the stormy seas surrounding Henry. During the trials of Watergate, particularly those last few days when Nixon was becoming desperate for a way out of his corner, Haig was clearly the voice of sanity who prevented the President from taking rash actions. The country owes much to Al. From his White House experience he was thoroughly familiar with SALT, and it was good to talk to him. I knew he went to SHAPE with several strikes against him. He had only been a colonel at the beginning of Nixon's term, he replaced the popular Andy Goodpaster faster than Goodpaster wanted to leave, and his role during Watergate was not widely known. However, his good sense and easy manner quickly overcame his initial difficulties, and it was already clear that he would become one of the outstanding officers among many outstanding officers to hold that complex position, which calls for political as well as military skill.

In the meantime Tom Graham, whom I had been fortunate to obtain as legal advisor, took to Washington the draft treaty the delegation had worked out. To my intense surprise, agreement was prompt. The only major change involved MIRV verification. A much tougher position than we had expectation of obtaining was inserted to demonstrate to Senator Jackson how tough we were. It provided for counting as MIRVed all missiles of any type tested with MIRVs or any launchers constructed to handle them. Nevertheless, I was able to table our draft on March 5. At the same time I managed to get Semenov's agreement to set up three working groups—a drafting group, headed on our side by Boris Klosson and Ralph Earle; a verification group, headed by Harold Brown (or Michael May when Brown was absent from Geneva);

and a definitions group, headed by General Ed Rowny, the JCS representative. So equipped, we settled down to intensive work.

After both sides had ample opportunity to explain their respective positions in plenary and working group sessions, I persuaded Semenov with some difficulty to work from a Joint Draft Text (JDT) that incorporated the positions of both sides. In our version the Soviet terms were put after ours in brackets, and in the Soviet version ours followed theirs. The focus of negotiations became the removal of brackets to get agreement on a common text. Thus, every word in the final test was subject to prolonged negotiation and struggle, not just between the two delegations but between the delegations and their respective governments.

When seeking to establish the three working groups I had particular difficulty obtaining Semenov's assent to a definitions group, his attitude being that "everyone knew" what an ICBM was, what a MIRV was, what bombers should be counted as heavy, and so on. As it turned out, the definitions article of the Treaty, Article II, turned out to be the key one, on which the greater part of the negotiations and controversy focused. Its eight paragraphs and thirty-five agreed amplifying statements involved such crucial issues as whether the Backfire was to be counted as a heavy bomber, when a launcher of ballistic missiles was to be counted as a launcher of MIRVed missiles, what was to be included or not included in the cruise missile limitations, how to measure throw weight, and others. The sessions between Rowny and his counterpart, General Trusov, quickly moved from technicalities to questions of the greatest substantive importance. Progress was not aided by Rowny's theory of how to bargain with the Soviets, which was to state and restate our position without making any concession until the Soviets agreed to it. In relatively short order the Soviet definitions group refused even to talk to Rowny. To get around this impasse, Semenov accepted my suggestion that the drafting group be assigned the job of working out the definitions.

Framing the definitions was especially tortuous, because even when there were not substantive differences, the vocabulary in this highly technical field had grown up separately in both countries. It was not just a matter of literal translation from one language to the other, but of finding words that would express a concept accurately in both. As a small example, we used the word "bus" to mean the device that carried the separate warheads of a MIRVed missile into space and released them individually toward their targets. The Russian word for the device was not "bus," so a literal translation from one language to the other would be imprecise and meaningless. The result was that it took sixty-nine words in the final treaty to express the concept accurately and completely. Almost every word presented such problems.

The struggle over the definitions article also exemplified what was from the start the entirely different approaches of the two sides. As in most negotiations, the Soviets preferred broad and sweeping language that could be left open to whatever subsequent interpretation they desired to make. With our legal tradition and past experience of Soviet adherence to international agreements, we wanted a meticulously drafted document leaving as little as possible to interpretation. SALT I had shown that the Soviets would go right up to the edge in observing the literal language of a carefully drafted agreement, but would not step over. Any loopholes or ambiguities, however, would quickly be penetrated. I needed no encouragement to do all that was humanly possible to be sure the text of the treaty was tightly drafted. During the ratification hearings, while there were differences over substance, I know of no case where anyone was able to point to an inaccuracy or ambiguity in the text. And whatever may be the future of SALT, the struggle we went through over the definitions and some other articles provides an agreed "glossary" of terms in both languages that need not be negotiated again.

Though the two delegations made considerable progress in removing those brackets, we became hung up on MIRV verification, cruise missiles, Backfire, defining a heavy missile, mobile ICBMs, and a few less important issues. I returned with the delegation to Washington at the start of May to see what the government could work out. Kissinger saw Foreign Minister Gromyko in the middle of the month of Vienna. Gromyko paralleled Semenov's line exactly, but in their private sessions Henry told him that there would be no SALT agreement unless we had something satisfactory on MIRVs. He said that if the Soviets wanted to ban airborne ICBMs they would have to consider limits on their land-based mobile ICBMs. He also said that if we were going to agree to limit cruise missiles, the point at which they would be counted as "strategic," and thus included in the aggregate, would have to be much larger than the 600 kilometers established for airborne ballistic missiles at Vladivostok—about 3000 kilometers. But the exact range was negotiable.

The Soviets had proposed a ban on long-range cruise missiles (LRCM) whether launched from land, air, or sea. The more

I thought about this issue the more I felt that accepting something along the lines of the Soviet proposal would be in our interest. Proceeding with LRCMs would open up an entirely new area of strategic competition that in the end would not necessarily benefit us, despite Bill Clements' obsession with what he said was our five-year technological lead. (What the situation would be after five years he refused to consider.) I agreed that cruise missiles launched from aircraft could undoubtedly penetrate Soviet territory. But given their slow speed, I did not think the Soviets would have great difficulty upgrading their massive air defense system to shoot them down. Sea and land launched cruise missiles would suffer the same drawback. So I thought the proponents of long-range cruise missiles greatly overstated their strategic importance.

And I also felt they overlooked how formidable a tactical weapon LRCMs armed with conventional warheads would be if used against us. Once the problem of target acquisition had been solved, the Soviets could quite easily choke off our supply lines to Europe and Japan—vital to our war-fighting strategy—simply by standing off at great range and firing LRCMs at any ship that moved on the Atlantic or Pacific. The Soviets, who could largely rely on their own internal lines of communication, were much less vulnerable to conventionally armed LRCMs. And once cruise missiles were deployed, verifying their location, let alone their range, would be virtually insurmountable because they are small, easy to hide, and relatively cheap to manufacture. Cruise missiles are certainly "sweet" in a technical sense, and I could see some merit in relatively short-range ones as bomber penetration aids. But long-range ones were about as destabilizing and unwise a weapon as I could imagine. My arguments did not go far with the Chiefs or Clements.

While I was back in Washington, President Ford asked me to represent him at the state funeral for former Prime Minister Sato in Tokyo. Though I was only in Japan for two days, June 16 and 17, I was pleased to be able to pay my last respects to Sato, whom I greatly respected and had always liked. The day following the funeral I called on my old sparring partner Takeo Miki, who was now Prime Minister, and on Deputy Prime Minister Fukuda, Finance Minister Ohira, and former Ambassadors to Washington Shimoda, Ushiba and Takeuchi, all of whom I had known well. Before leaving the following morning I called on Mrs. Sato to pay obeisance before the household shrine for her husband. This trip, though brief, was an excellent opportunity to renew my acquaintance with Japan. In the following year I paid two more short visits, once to brief its government on SALT (in which they were very interested but not well informed) and the second time to represent the State Department at the dedication of the new (and to me hideous) Chancery building, for which the lovely old one had been demolished.

I made preparations to return to Geneva to resume negotiations at the end of June, though Washington had not made up its mind about MIRV verification, Backfire, or cruise missiles. The day before the delegation was due to leave, the Soviet Embassy called to ask for a week's postponement. When we resumed on July 2, I could not see that the postponement had produced anything, because Semenov simply restated all of his old positions. In light of Kissinger's proposals to Gromyko in Vienna, however, I felt it was Semenov's responsibility to respond, and told him so. Kissinger was due in Geneva on July 10 to meet with Gromyko on a range of issues including SALT, so in the meantime I made some general statements about MIRV verification, the need to count cruise missiles in a category separate from the central systems aggregate, and the importance of a definition that would clearly distinguish between light and heavy ICBMs because of their different capabilities. The day before Kissinger arrived, Semenov proposed that we whittle away at peripheral issues, leaving major ones to be settled between Brezhnev and Ford at the summit later that month, where they would both sign the Helsinki Accords.

Unfortunately, Kissinger's talks with Gromyko were inconclusive, and the Ford-Brezhnev conversations turned out to be extremely confused and without specific result. All the sticky issues remained. Our talks in Geneva had no agenda to follow. That meant reaching agreement by the end of the year would be problematic, and once the election year began in the United States I knew that the President would be skittish about injecting into his reelection prospects a complex strategic arms treaty that an opponent could easily misconstrue. Time was running out if we were to get a treaty before 1977.

I tried to do what I could by working with Semenov on some of the peripheral issues like information exchange on our respective weapons systems, advance notification of acts that would change the systems and other such matters. I was unable to make any progress despite a series of three- and four-hour private meetings with him in August and September. He was a frustrating and exhausting opponent. When I would back him into a corner, he would start reciting sayings from the Bible, Kant,

Goethe, or old Russian proverbs, which as far as I could see had no pertinence to the subject and were simply diversions to avoid giving an answer. When I would try to force him back to the point he would get angry, and then I would get angry, though we both maintained the proprieties.

Another of his favorite devices was to read a long statement that contained nothing new during a plenary meeting and then ask me in our private meeting to study it carefully because it contained some "nuances." I would reply that I was "just a boy from Kansas," and no matter how much I studied the statement I could not find the nuances of which he spoke. Could he not just point to those portions of his statement that contained the nuances? He invariably replied that I just had not studied it carefully enough, at which point I would mentally climb the wall but bite my tongue.

He retained his absolute phobia about opening himself to any charge that he had given away a "military secret." It was amusing that throughout all of SALT I and up to the very end of SALT II—ten years of talking—no Soviet ever referred to any of their weapon systems by their Soviet names; it was always the airplane "that you call the Backfire," the missile "that you call the SS-18" and so on. Only at the final stages of the negotiations, during the Carter Administration, did they give what they said were their names for the weapons mentioned in the Treaty. When we sought clarification about the Backfire's characteristics to see whether it should be classed as medium or heavy, they would always say, "We have told you that it is not a heavy bomber. It is a medium bomber, period. There can be no further discussion of the subject." Even President Ford received that answer from Brezhnev at Helsinki.

With his own delegation Semenov exercised little authority. Even on minor matters such as dates of meetings he always had to refer to his delegation—probably first of all to the generals on the delegation. One time he and I settled privately a minor dispute over how to insert a troublesome point into the JDT. Later he was very embarrassed to have to say his delegation had refused to approve what he had done. I remonstrated vigorously at this way of doing business. He went back to his delegation, and I won the point.

There were some rare occasions, after lunch or finishing our business in a private meeting, when I felt I could wax more philosophical with him. One of my themes at these times was how absurd it was that the two of us had to sit and argue about these beasts of weapons poised to destroy each other within thirty minutes. We had never had a war with each other; we had no territorial disputes. We were both great continental countries with no inherent geopolitical reason to warrant destroying each other. But still there was an underlying problem, in addition to the tensions created by the weapons themselves. I told Semenov I thought this underlying problem was that the Soviets had not matured sufficiently to be willing to "live and let live." They were in the stage of many Christians in the middle of this millenium, and later some Moslems, who felt their sole possession of the only true faith conferred a divine right to impose it by force on non-believers. I said it had taken a long time and many deaths and wars before we in the West had learned to tolerate diversity, but the lesson had been learned. We did not talk of "detente" or "co-existence" with Canada, Brazil, or the United Kingdom. We could live side by side in the same world. Driven by their doctrine, however, the Soviets were still where the Christians and Moslems were hundreds of years ago, seeking to impose their system on others in one way or another. When they matured sufficiently to tolerate differences among people and governments, I said to Semenov, the problem of these weapons would fall into place. Until then, important though our task was, we were dealing with symptoms.

I never could get him to challenge my argument. He would only respond: "Give us time. Some of us in the Soviet Union feel differently."

I returned to Washington in September to participate as the bureaucracy attempted once more to settle the remaining tough issues: Backfire, cruise missiles, MIRV verification, and mobile ICBMs. Backfire and cruise missiles in particular had become politically charged. If we appeared to be "conceding" on Backfire, the conservatives on the Hill might well oppose the treaty. Similarly, if we did not manage to choke off cruise missiles, the liberals might oppose it for opening up a whole new arena of strategic competition. Remembering how blithely Backfire had entered discussions at Geneva—Kissinger telling me to "see what I could get" without expecting anything—I regretted that what was essentially a bargaining chip had been transmuted, by deft Pentagon political maneuvering, into a major obstacle to concluding and ratifying SALT II. We had suggested at Geneva a number of ways the Soviets could mollify us on Backfire, such as not basing them where they could reach the United States without refueling and not providing them with a refueling fleet, but they had not budged, nor were they likely to. Still, the President was under great pressure to come up with something.

When I arrived September 12, I found Washington in the greatest disarray on SALT I had ever encountered. Schlesinger was mad at Kissinger, the Chiefs were mad at Schlesinger, and the key people on the Hill were distrustful of everyone in the Administration. On September 17 there was an NSC meeting, but I did not expect much to come of it because the Pentagon had previously been insisting that the Soviets wanted an agreement so badly they would agree to include Backfire in the 2400 aggregate. As it turned out, Schlesinger proposed a new approach to the NSC. It would permit the Soviets 300 or so Backfires if we could have the same number of bombers equipped with nuclear medium-range cruise missiles (600 km to 2500 km) in return. There were some complex formulas factoring ships with cruise missiles and our F-111s into the Backfire-cruise missile equation. Nuclear cruise missiles over 2500 km would be banned, but conventional cruise missiles of any range would not be covered. In addition, the Soviets would have to agree not to talk about FBS ever again. Schlesinger also wanted to keep our options open for deploying mobile ICBMs. He had worked this out with Fred Ikle at ACDA, and it was such an involved package that those at the meeting did not clearly grasp it. The JCS had not heard anything about it. We broke up in characteristic confusion, leaving the President with no concrete proposal before him on which he could make a decision.

Moreover, when Kissinger presented a version of Schlesinger's plan to Gromyko the following Monday, Schlesinger got angry because he thought Kissinger had left out important aspects. The whole debate was getting curiouser and curiouser. Nevertheless, it was some improvement that Schlesinger had climbed down from his rigid insistence that the Soviets accede completely to our position on Backfire. I returned to Geneva September 23, largely to mark time and gnaw away at the peripheral issues.

We did make some progress on those. The delegations agreed to language prohibiting, "rapid reload" on ICBM launchers, as well as strategic systems on the ocean floor or in orbit. Mutually acceptable definitions of ICBM, heavy bomber, MIRV, and other terms were worked out. The Schlesinger-Ikle proposal of trading Backfires for nuclear cruise missiles was flatly refused. Even if they had assented, it could not easily have been verified, because there is no obvious way to distinguish between conventional and nuclear-armed cruise missiles.

The Ford "Halloween Massacre" intervened, when Defense Secretary Schlesinger was replaced with Don Rumsfeld, CIA Director Colby with George Bush, Henry Kissinger's original job as National Security Advisor (but not as Secretary of State) with Brent Scowcroft, and Nelson Rockefeller announced he would not run for Vice President. The President's political stock seemed to be sinking, especially with the Republican right wing that would be important for ratification. Schlesinger's absence would also hurt SALT with the conservatives. I became quite discouraged about the possibility of accomplishing anything else of value until the elections. I thought the best thing for SALT might be to put it in hibernation, to protect it from partisan attack.

I made another trip home, leaving Geneva November 21, expecting to find Washington immobilized. Instead everyone was in high spirits and eager to find a common position so we could move forward. The delegations formally recessed in December, and I spent several months in Washington. Don Rumsfeld, the new Secretary of Defense, and JCS Chairman George Brown showed considerably more willingness to come up with a position on Backfire and cruise missiles that the Soviets could accept. But actually deciding on such a position proved a different matter, and there was no real progress until January, when a consensus began to form around "Option Three," which called for a separate limit on Backfire outside the 2400 aggregate and another separate limit for cruise missiles.

But then the favorable trends broke down. The other members of the JCS undercut their chairman and reverted to their spoiling position insisting that the Backfire count against the 2400 aggregate. A flurry of meetings among the President, Kissinger, Rumsfeld, and the Chiefs in various combinations, including some NSC meetings that I attended, failed to clarify things before Kissinger had to leave for Moscow on January 20. I said at the end of the final NSC meeting that I was certainly glad I was not Henry, because I had no idea what had been authorized.

The state of confusion was exemplified by an incident during Henry's trip, when he cabled back for additional instructions on a point involving long range cruise missiles on ships. Previously, great emphasis had been placed on the Navy's eagerness to pursue these weapons. But during the meeting that considered Henry's telegram, Admiral Holloway, the Chief of Naval Operations, said (to everyone's consternation including the President's) that the

Navy had no cruise missile program for surface ships and was not contemplating one. He also dashed the common assumption that cruise missiles developed for submarine torpedo tubes could be used in surface vessel torpedo tubes, which turned out to be much smaller. Nor, at that meeting, were we really clear about what Henry or the Soviets had said in Moscow.

One interesting development in this period was that Henry Kissinger asked me if I wanted to head the United States Liaison Office in Peking. It would have been interesting to be there, but I was sure there would not be much of a job to do, since Henry conducted relations with the Chinese himself in Washington. Also, I would not be able to observe much or have much in the way of meaningful contacts with Chinese officials as, at that time along with the rest of the Diplomatic Corps, our Liaison Office in Beijing was kept in rigid isolation. Also, Pat's health was poor. So I said I would stick with SALT.

Henry settled one item during his trip to Moscow: how to define a heavy missile. We agreed to their proposition to allow silo enlargement by 32 percent in return for their agreeing to the more meaningful concept of judging missile size by either throw weight or launch weight, whichever resulted in the larger figure for missile size. More important were the new Soviet proposals. They offered to permit air-launched cruise missiles on our bombers of 2500 km range, up from their previous figure of 600 km. They continued to hold out for the 600-km figure on land and sea launched cruise missiles. And if we agreed to their cruise missile provisions, they would agree to reduce the aggregate for both sides, to 2300 or even lower. This was quite a surprise. Less surprising was that the Soviets showed no interest in Kissinger's proposal that they count all Backfires manufactured after October 1977 against their aggregate in return for our agreeing to count all bombers with ALCMs against our 1320 MIRV limit.

I returned to Geneva before Washington had time to work out its response to the Soviets' interesting proposals, but I heard that Defense and the Chiefs still intended to oppose any solution that did not include Backfire in the aggregate. I considered this a big mistake. Backfire was more a political issue than a security one. I felt strongly enough about this to send a message to the President on February 6.

I told him that while I did not want to complicate his life, I felt it was my duty to let him know my views. From the beginning of SALT II, I said, we had three major objectives: to have equal aggregates without compensating the Soviets for FBS, to establish limits on ICBMs that took account of throw weight, and to reduce aggregates. All were now attainable, and would constitute a useful and defensible agreement. The Soviets had agreed to a 2500-km range for ALCMs, as much as our bombers could use for penetration aids. The exact range to which sea- and land-launched cruise missiles should be held required investigation, I said, but I thought the basic principle of the Soviet 600-km proposal had merit. Cruise missiles had value as tactical weapons, not strategic, on it was in our interest to keep them that way. I also told the President I thought we could move to an aggregate of about 2200.

But the Chiefs and the Defense Department maintained their intransigence on Backfire, and Fred Ikle threw a real wrench into the works by arguing that cruise missile ranges were not verifiable, which is only partially true. So Kissinger found himself the only advocate in Washington of the view we shared—that an agreement now was possible and valuable—an isolation brought about by playing his cards so close that the rest of Washington had grown to resent and suspect him. The President did not feel he could risk breaking his bureaucracy open, with Reagan and Senator Jackson looming on the Right, so a dusty reply went back to the Soviets. Any chance of reaching agreement before the election evaporated.

At Geneva it was back to whittling away at the peripheral issues. Even here, however, the Chiefs and Defense requested insignificant but annoying language changes in some of our definitions solely to throw sand in the gears of progress. Sometimes they even changed their minds and insisted I reopen discussions after I had obtained agreement with the Soviets in accordance with my instructions. I found this very frustrating and had considerable sympathy with Semenov's annoyance.

Feeling their oats in the anti-SALT political climate, the Defense Department hard-liners descended to remarkably childish depths of petty harassment. In May, Washington instructed me to ask for a recess, and I put in the usual request for an Air Force plane to transport the delegation and its sizable collection of secret files back to Washington. There is no commercial service between the two cities (one must fly Geneva-Zurich, Zurich-New York, New York-Washington) and the cost to the government of hiring a commercial charter was greater than flying its own plane. But my request for an Air Force plane was rejected without explanation. I telephoned Clements to find out why, and he curtly told me that a plane could not be made available, even if the delegation paid Defense the cost of flying it, unless it was in the "national interest" and commercial transport was not available. He knew perfectly well that there was no commercial service between Geneva and Washington, and I expressed astonishment that he felt, after seven years of talks, that SALT was not now in the "national interest." I was so mad I appealed to the White House, and they persuaded Clements to relent for that one trip. But it was quite clear that he was out to do whatever he could to sabotage SALT, even to this puerile level of bureaucratic guerrilla war. Many anti-SALT leaks also emerged from his office. Everyone on the delegation, frustrated with the pace of work and the obstacles Washington continuously threw up to block agreement, was considering resigning.

Henry, Semenov and I agreed that we would resume at Geneva in early June for a brisk "summer session" that would terminate July 30, shortly before the start of the Democratic Convention. Having made some progress in Washington unsticking the remaining problems in the definitions article, Semenov and I wrapped up quite a few points. A good example of the difficulties we faced in this period was the teapot tempest over how the Soviets' smaller missiles would be described—"light," as had previously been done, or "non-heavy," as the Pentagon desired. For many months we sought Soviet acceptance of "non-heavy," with no result. Finally, I was authorized to go ahead with "light," and after waiting a day I traded this for some much more important concessions from Semenov, including the text of the definition itself, our throw weight definition, and a ceiling on the number of heavy missiles they were permitted. As soon as I returned to my office from this conversation, however, I received a phone call from Bill Hyland, the NSC SALT staffer, asking me to delay implementing my instructions because Pentagon officials were saying that Secretary of Defense Rumsfeld, then in Africa, would appeal "light" vs. "non-heavy" to the President as soon as he returned. I was glad to be able to reply that I had already agreed to "light" and to explain what I had obtained in exchange.

Following the Presidential nominating conventions we resumed in Geneva, trying to clear the decks of all remaining problems except Backfire and cruise missiles. We worked out with the Soviets a provision for verifying MIRVs that was very satisfactory. All missiles of any missile type flight-tested with a MIRV would be counted as MIRVed. On October 29, we finally tied up all the remaining loose ends with the Soviets into one package and got their approval. General Rowny, the JCS representative, suddenly sought to add some more conditions. The rest of the delegation and I strongly opposed him and we had some very vigorous words at our meeting. Finally I pulled rank and overruled his objection. He put his dissent on the delegation's message to Washington, but my decision stuck.

I had been hoping the President would see his way to putting aside cruise missiles and Backfire to the next round of SALT and signing the agreement as it stood to consolidate the gains made in three years of tough bargaining. But obviously he did not feel it politically possible before the election, nor his responsibility to do so afterwards. When Carter was elected, we simply had to wait for him to take office and bring himself up to speed. Except for a few small but useful additions, the treaty Carter submitted to the Senate in 1979 was essentially identical to the one he inherited three years previously.

After a slow drive to California over Christmas, I called on the prospective Secretary of State, Cyrus Vance, and Secretary of Defense, Harold Brown, who had been a member of my delegation in Geneva. I told them I would be happy to finish up the negotiations, having come so far, but being far past normal retirement age I would cheerfully resign if they had other plans. Vance asked me to wait until they saw who the new ACDA Director would be. Paul Warnke had been offered the job, but he desired to be Chief of the Delegation as well. I had great respect for Warnke, but I told Vance they would be making the same mistake that had been made with Gerry Smith if they agreed to combine the two jobs. Vance said it was not decided and asked me to stand by until after the inauguration. When it was decided to let Warnke head the delegation as well as ACDA, I set the wheels in motion to retire at the end of February.

In the meantime I was invited to attend the new Administration's first meeting on SALT and was given my old seat in the White House Situation Room. The new President joined us, and I was impressed with the very knowledgeably way he spoke on the subject for about forty minutes without notes. I was slightly concerned that he had what I considered some pretty "way out" ideas, extending to the goal of eliminating all nuclear weapons, but I recognized that he was still in the phase of tossing around ideas before deciding. After calling on Vance and Brown, Carter asked for my general views on the best way to make progress with the Soviets. I had not been prepared to speak, but said that in my experience the Soviets were tough, persistent negotiators, and though I agreed with Vance that they probably wanted an agreement, we had to keep reinforcing to them the fact that the costs to them of not having a SALT agreement exceeded those of having one. I said we could only do this if they recognized that we had the technological and economic base to "smother" them in a real strategic arms race, even though it would be extremely costly and make doubtful military sense. He thanked me, but I did not have the feeling he was very impressed with what I said.

On the last day in February, Secretary Vance gave a very large retirement party for me on the eighth floor of the Department, said some very extravagant things, and gave me the highest State Department decoration to add to my Rockefeller Public Service Award and the President's Award for Distinguished Federal Civilian Service. Dean Rusk called me from Atlanta expressing his regret that he could not be there but passing on his thought: "Alex, you know when it happens, you're going to feel a sense of real exhilaration."

I must say he was right, except I knew my life was going to change when my driver, Caraway, drove Pat and me home after the party. When he said goodnight and shut the car door after me, I realized that for the first time in twenty-five years I was going to be without a car and driver.

After retiring I kept generally informed on SALT, and at Paul Warnke's invitation visited the delegation for several days early in 1978. However, I was not consulted by the Carter Administration nor did I seek to intrude. I was very happy that I was not the negotiator when the Administration, virtually ignoring everything that had gone before including the Vladivostok understanding, put forward an entirely new concept for an agreement in March 1977. Not only was it new, but much of it was made available to the press even before it was transmitted to the Soviets. It was clearly not the way to do business with them, and when the Administration had to give it up, as was inevitable, its negotiating effectiveness with the Soviets and its domestic image both suffered.

After the treaty was concluded in June 1979, very much along the lines where we had left it in December 1976, the White House began to orchestrate a campaign for its ratification that was nothing less than infantile. Anne Wexler, a White House political operative, was put in charge, and she handled it as some kind of primary election campaign. I got on her mailing list and was inundated with paper and suggestions that it would be nice if I would walk the streets in favor of the treaty. This I refused to do because I was put off by the way the treaty was being presented as almost a "second coming." It was no such thing. It was only a modest step forward on a long road, and I felt the Administration's overstatement was so heavy that it was prejudicing ratification rather than promoting it. On one occasion, a large heterogeneous group (including Jesse Jackson, Coretta King, some New York bankers, General Goodpaster, Jack McCloy, and me) were invited to the East Room of the White House. Secretary Vance and Zbigniew Brezenski gave straightforward explanations of the treaty which, however, anyone not informed about SALT would have found complex. Then the President himself appeared and launched into what can only be described as a revivalist fire-and-brimstone picture of the horrors that awaited us if the treaty were not ratified, but not a word about its merits. At the end the President paused as if he expected at least some to get up and walk the sawdust trail to the altar, or at least stand and shout, "Hallelujah, we are with you!" There was dead silence. Finally Jack McCloy, that veteran of many a battle with the Soviets and the Congress, stood and said respectfully that it was his experience that when the Senate faced a really serious issue, they wanted and expected that the administration would treat it as such. If it did, they would respond. The implication of Jack's remarks was unmistakable. The President said "thank you" and walked out of the room.

I avoided invitations to testify on behalf of the treaty in the Senate, until one day my old associate from the Kennedy days, Lloyd Cutler, called to say that he had joined the White House to help in the ratification process and wanted me to testify. The news that he was taking over delighted me. He wanted me to summarize the negotiations up to the time I had retired to demonstrate that the treaty was in fact largely complete by the time Carter came into office. I was delighted to do so, but I wished that Carter had recognized the fact when he became President, rather than trying to walk up the hill with the Soviets only to have to walk back down again.

In my testimony on July 16, 1979, before the Senate Foreign Relations Committee, I summarized the negotiations for the four years that I was Chief of the United States Delegation. In doing so I repeated the statement of Ralph Earle, who had become Chief of the Delegation, that at least 80 percent of the treaty had been completed by the time we recessed in November 1976. I pointed out that the two issues outstanding at the time, Backfire and cruise missiles, were still outstanding, having been put over by Carter to a protocol that ran out in 1981. I did, however, note that the Carter Administration had been able to make one important improvement, which was to obtain a limit of ten warheads on the large MIRVed Soviet missile, the SS-18. Since it clearly had the throw weight to carry more, this limit reduced its effectiveness as a first strike weapon against our own ICBMs.

I closed my presentation to the Committee with the following statement:

> Criticisms can readily be made of what has or has not been accomplished by three administrations in this very complicated field. The ideal would be an agreement so comprehensive, so perfectly balanced, and so well anticipating the future that we would never again have to concern ourselves with the ominous shadows that these beasts of nuclear weapons cast over our lives. However, we must deal with the world as it is, not as we would wish it to be.
>
> In my own view, SALT has nothing to do with what one's view may be with respect to detente, co-existence, or any other such terms. It has nothing to do with whether one likes the Soviets or does not like the Soviets, or whether one trusts the Soviets or does not trust them. I accept the statement of the Soviet leaders that they intend to remain our implacable foes, if not physically then, as they say, ideologically. However, this should not prevent us from recognizing what is an obvious common interest in doing what can be done by agreement to reduce the danger of mutual suicide by the limitation of the strategic forces of the two sides in a way that will contribute to stability in time of crisis.
>
> I feel that the SALT dialogue at all levels—Chiefs of State, Foreign Ministers and Delegations, as well as Congressional and private debate—has been useful, even though it has not by any means led to a full meeting of minds, even among ourselves. This is understandable as, apart from differing philosophies among ourselves, we are dealing with a fast-moving and evolving technology which no agreement is going to freeze. However, as specific points of common interest emerge during the dialogue, we should seek to negotiate agreement on those points without judging the outcome against the impossible standard of such a comprehensive and definitive agreement that all of the problems for all time to come would be resolved. Rather each agreement should be judged as whether it is a constructive and useful step forward.

I said I thought the treaty met that test and favored its ratification.

A short time later I met a member of the staff of a Senator who opposed ratification. He had been given the task of feeding the Senator questions that could be used to attack my testimony, but, he said, "you handled it in such a straightforward and low-key manner that we could not find any place to lay a finger on you." I am still convinced that if the administration had handled it the same way, it could have obtained ratification at that time without great difficulty.

Only after ratification had to be postponed in the face of likely defeat did the treaty's opponents wake to its merits. Then they realized that only the treaty prevented the Soviets from utilizing their throw weight advantage to saturate our poorly conceived "race track" for mobile ICBMs with a profusion of MIRVs; that only the treaty prevented the Soviets from concealing whatever new developments they undertook in strategic weapons; that nothing in the treaty would prevent us from carrying out any of the strategic programs we had in mind for the period it would have been in force. But by then we had a new President, one less convinced than Carter of the value of SALT.

Most people do not recognize that every advance in weapons technology since World War II has left the United States less secure than before. In 1939, insulated by two big oceans, our physical survival as a nation would have been extremely difficult for any enemy to jeopardize. But each successive "advance"—long-range bombers, atomic bombs, hydrogen bombs, ICBMs, SLBMs, MIRVs, cruise missiles—has made it possible for the Soviet Union, should it so choose, to kill 50 or 100 million people, shred our social fabric, obliterate for generations any life worth living—all in thirty minutes. So far the balance of terror has worked, but it may not always. SALT is one of the most complex subjects in the world and it is easy to get caught up in its technicalities. But these weapons are beasts. Building more of them serves no rational purpose on either side. Reducing them, gradually enough to preserve stability, as fast as we can determine how to do it, is the only route of sanity.

It is ironic that after making the alleged disaster of SALT II treaty, a major plank in its campaign, in the fall of 1983 the Reagan Administration embraced the treaty by stating it would observe its provisions if the Soviets did so. Thus START is substantially back to where SALT was when Ford completed his meeting with Brezhnev at Vladivostok in November 1974.

1980 *Harper's*: "The country will never be able to understand the world, or its challenges, unless it stops thinking of foreign policies, or wars, as crusades in which the godly or the revolutionary go forth to do battle with the unrighteous or the reactionary; and unless it stops instinctively assuming that those doing battle with the forces of darkness or reaction must (by definition) be legions from the forces of light or progress, or vice versa. Indeed we may not survive the last two decades of this strife-ridden and now thermonuclear century unless we stop confusing foreign policy with theology, thus inadvertently increasing the risk of thermonuclear Armageddon."

Our legislation on economic and military cooperation with other countries over the years has now become so encrusted with the pet strictures, conditions, and demands of so many members of the Congress responding to this or that ethnic or ideological group that governments are often inclined to say "thanks very much, but we will try to get along without you." The executive is also not without this fault. It is all too easy for Washington to instruct an Ambassador to lecture foreign leaders on the importance of being something other than what they are. As the occasional recipient of such messages, I never found that course of action productive. I sometimes had to resort to the principle that Ambassadors are paid to know when to ignore or shade their instructions.

In 1971 I wrote:

> I cannot understand the argument that we should reduce our military strength as a contribution to the national search for peace. In my experience military strength is not an alternative to a national search for peace. It is an essential element of it. In the world as it is—and is likely to be for the indefinite future—military strength and diplomacy are fingers of the same hand. A national commitment to the search for peace not backed up by military strength would not be a policy at all. It would be a pious expression of hope, devoid either of credibility or effect.

Unhappily, nothing has yet happened to cause me to change that view. In spite of the internal difficulties within its Empire and its economic failures, the Soviet Union continues to demonstrate an ability to extract from its population a higher proportion of their production for military purposes than any other country. The exponential result of relatively small but steady growth over a long period has now produced a truly formidable force, both in quantity and quality. By contrast, our expenditures have fluctuated violently. For many years Soviet forces were employed exclusively to maintain control in that nation's restive satellites, but the invasion of Afghanistan gave pause to those who assumed this would continue. The United States and Russia have never gone to war; we have no territorial disputes and few purely bilateral ones. But Soviet leaders continue to espouse vigorously the eventual universal triumph of their brand of communism and their duty to promote it by all means available. We cannot ignore the threat this represents to us and those who share our belief in the doctrine of "live and let live" for the human race.

The purpose of military force is not to fight but to accomplish our national aims while deterring a fight. The Cuban missile crisis of 1962 was an excellent demonstration of how diplomacy and military capabilities were orchestrated by a President to achieve important national security objectives without resort to violence. Without deft diplomacy, our military strength would not have been sufficient. But without strength and the evident will to use it if necessary, the most brilliant diplomacy could not have met that challenge to our security.

We could do a much better job of integrating political objectives with military capabilities than we have done. We should provide a continuing and secure organizational arrangement between the Department of Defense and the military services on the one hand and the Department of State and Foreign Service on the other, to use the best expertise on both sides in long-term planning of our force structure and short-term contingency planning. In addition to the all-too-often knee-jerk reactions to each other by State and Defense, we are burdened by the bitter fragmentation of what should be a national military establishment into four jealously individualistic services. Present technology and political complexities absolutely require that military policy be framed in the national interest. But interservice rivalries are becoming, if anything, more virulent.

The Rube Goldberg command structure of the new multibillion-dollar Rapid Deployment Force—the product of no logic except that each service was determined to get some of the funds and publicity—is only the most painful of recent examples. Logrolling between the services and their congressional guardians in an era of booming costs and technology has resulted in colossal waste and loss of effectiveness. And the battles for bureaucratic turf do not stop outside the Joint Chiefs of Staff. After many years of working with the JCS and observing its strengths and weaknesses, I think the time has come for a major overhaul of that institution. In spite of the competence and dedication of most of the individual Chiefs, the responsibility each one (except for the chairman) has for the bureaucratic battles of his service makes it impossible to assure that our political leaders receive the pertinent and objective advice that the JCS in its collegial role is supposed to provide. On almost every military and politico-military issue where I dealt with the Chiefs, from Cuba, Vietnam, Jordan, and SALT, the jockeying among them to see which service would end up with the biggest piece of the action and the most command positions seriously intruded into the quality of the advice they gave their superiors.

Nor is the staff on which the Chiefs rely geared to taking the broad view that is really their highest responsibility. The Joint Staff to the JCS is composed of officers drawn from the various services, who return to those services after a brief tour. It is natural that they guard zealously the narrow interests of the services on which their future depend. Nor are the military services set up to seek out officers with political gifts and systematically expose them to problems of increasing sophistication. As Dean Acheson said, the result of the interservice rivalries on the JCS and its inadequate staff is that the system only produces oracular utterances instead of real military advice. And because the Chiefs primarily react to papers prepared by their staff or by others in Washington, they end up resembling, as Acheson also observed, the little old lady who could not say what she thought until she heard what she said.

Many competent and energetic individuals have served on the JCS, and several distinguished chairmen have risen above the system. But that does not change the fact that the system itself is seriously flawed and entirely unsuited to coping with our dangerous age.

I believe we now need two distinct types of senior officers. First, we need those who are supremely competent in their service and specialty. These must continue to be the backbone of our military strength. However, we also need those who can look at the whole gamut of national military and politico-military issues without being encumbered by the baggage of service loyalties and promotion channels. I think these officers should constitute a separate corps entirely removed from any specific service, perhaps starting at the rank of major or colonel. The sole function of this group would be to provide perform staff work for a single

Chief of Staff of the Armed Services, who would alone have responsibility for military advice to the President, the Secretary of Defense, and other members of the NSC.

This corps could find its members among officers who have served on combined commands and in other services, who have participated in exchanges with State or CIA, or who have gone through the higher educational systems of the government, such as the War Colleges or the State Department Senior Seminar. Once officers entered this corps their promotion would be decided internally, not by their former service. The present Chiefs would be relieved of their collegial responsibilities as JCS members to devote full time to running their services. They would, of course, keep in close touch with each other directly and through joint meetings chaired by the Chief of Staff of the Armed Services. Individually they should, of course, have direct access to the General Staff in order to present their views on matters being considered by him.

Besides this new structure for directing our regular forces, another and separate structure is required for assisting countries facing less-than-overt attack from surrogates of the Soviet Union. I refer to what we used to call "counterinsurgency" or "internal defense" the problems posed by such countries as Laos in the 1960s and El Salvador more recently. In Vietnam, counterinsurgency doctrine was never really applied systematically during the crucial early following years, and what little we did introduce was then smothered by the deployment of American regular forces in quantity. In Laos, however, the CIA carried out internal defense work with great success until swamped by the loss of South Vietnam and Cambodia. Good internal defense requires the use of some military skills, but the organization, training, equipment, and supplies required to do it well are seldom to be found within the Pentagon. There is no inherent reason that counterinsurgency work must be performed by the CIA, although it has demonstrated its competence in this area in the past. (I hope that competence was not lost during the purges forced on that organization in the 1970s.) Perhaps the function could be performed with an entirely separate structure attached to the Defense Department operating under the direction of the NSC.

The basic challenge of an internal defense program, the reason the United States has done it so badly in the past, is its requirement that the political and military sectors be closely harmonized at the tactical as well as the strategic level. We harmonize political goals and military capabilities badly enough at the national strategic level, as my thoughts about the JCS and the need for closer State-Defense integration testify. At the tactical level we do not do it at all. We frequently faced the problem in Vietnam, for example, of what a squad leader should do when his men were tied down and taking casualties from Vietcong fire coming from an inhabited village. He could try to have the squad deal with it by itself, crawling along slowly and directing careful individual shots at carefully selected targets positively identified as Vietcong. That meant low civilian casualties in pursuit of the overall political objective of "winning the hearts and minds of the people," but high casualties in the squad. Or he could call in artillery or air support to destroy the village along with the Vietcong. That would save his men but erode popular support for our side. The decision was never easy, but our problem was that we provided no political framework in which commanders could decide; either way, the decision was highly political.

In Vietnam we finally achieved a high level of coordination between our civilian and military assets under the COORDS organization, in which a civilian (first Bob Komer and then Bill Colby) became in effect a deputy commander in all but large-scale combat operations. It went a long way toward liquidating the effectiveness of Vietcong guerrillas in the south; in 1975 a Soviet-made tank spearheading a large North Vietnamese conventional force, not a barefoot boy in black pajamas, broke down the gates to Saigon's Presidential Palace. But I fear that our desire to wash our hands of traumatic memories has made us forget many of the lessons learned in Vietnam after so much struggle and sacrifice. I also fear the Army has not incorporated into its doctrine some of the most obvious lessons from Vietnam: the suicidal error of expecting "ticket-punching" officers, there for eighteen months, to direct a war against natives fighting for a lifetime; the tremendous waste and ineffectiveness of over-sophisticated, expensive, and hard-to-maintain equipment; the need to develop an effective land blockade; and, most importantly, the importance of recognizing that an enemy who makes victory an absolute priority regardless of the time and cost will be very hard for us to beat in a country remote from our immediate interests.

Important as it is, however, military power at best is not the answer to the fundamental question as to whether the rapidly exploding population on this little planet is going to find a way to survive in harmony and with a reasonable quality of life. It seems certain that economic considerations will dominate foreign policy at least to the end of this millennium. Technology is rushing us into the future at a rate that neither our understanding nor our institutions, including our diplomatic ones, seem able to comprehend or cope with. And even though there has been modest economic development in much of the underdeveloped world, the gap between rich and poor, or as it is often called, "north and south," is growing at a disturbing rate.

These two phenomena—rates of growth and their distribution—present the world with two serious dilemmas: First, how can the many governments of the world concert their separate decisions on resource use that, taken together, will determine whether the human race will prosper or perish, either from starvation or from suffocation in its own garbage? Second, how can the job be done without denying to either the developed or underdeveloped nations the resources and rates of growth on which their prosperity and stability depends?

I do not pretend to have the answers to these questions, but I am certain that they require much more thoughtful consideration by us and the rest of the world than they have thus far been given.

I would not want these final paragraphs to be interpreted as meaning that I am pessimistic about our future. In spite of the somber picture I have painted, we are, nevertheless, still the strongest and most productive country on this globe. Our ability to note and seek to correct our shortcomings is our strength. We as a people want to continue to play a constructive role in the world, one that is commensurate with our potentialities. The leadership must come from within each of us.

· I N D E X ·

Index

Index

Index

Index